N. Bamford

Essence of
Leadership

■ GLOBAL MANAGER SERIES ■

Essence of Leadership

Andrew Kakabadse
and
Nada Kakabadse

INTERNATIONAL THOMSON BUSINESS PRESS
I(T)P ® **An International Thomson Publishing Company**

London • Bonn • Johannesburg • Madrid • Melbourne • Mexico City • New York • Paris
Singapore • Tokyo • Toronto • Albany, NY • Belmont, CA • Cincinnati, OH • Detroit, MI

Essence of Leadership

Copyright © 1999 Andrew Kakabadse and Nada Kakabadse

First published by International Thomson Business Press

 A division of International Thomson Publishing Inc.
The ITP logo is a trademark under licence

British Library Cataloguing-in-Publication Data
A catalogue record for this book is available from the British Library

First edition 1999

Typeset by LaserScript Limited, Mitcham, Surrey
Printed in the UK by TJ International, Padstow, Cornwall

ISBN 1–86152–368–8

International Thomson Business Press
Berkshire House
168–173 High Holborn
London WC1V 7AA
UK

http://www.itbp.com

Dedication

It is with deep love and heartfelt appreciation that we dedicate this work to our parents, George and Elfrieda Kakabadse and Mila Lisa and Dmitar Korac, as our way of saying thank you for your loving support and wise counsel over these many years. We hope that your presence and influence, which will remain in us always, is captured in this book.

Contents

Acknowledgements

Our gratitude and thanks to our colleagues and associates of Cranfield for their encouraging comments and views on the various drafts of this book.

Particular thanks to Pauline Thomas, Dorothy Rogers, Jane Tyrell and Hilary Bishop for their patience, good humour and endeavour in typing draft after draft. Thanks also to Mairi Bryce for her sharp eye, attention to detail and literary application in her editing of this book. From your comments, you are now more expert than us in this area of strategic leadership.

About the authors

Andrew Kakabadse
Bsc, MA, PhD, AAPSW, CPsychol, FBPS, FIAM, FRSA, MBPS

Andrew Kakabadse is currently Professor of International Management Development, Chairman of the Human Resources Network and Director of the Cranfield Centre for International Management Development, Cranfield University, Bedford, England.

He previously worked in the Health and Social Services field, and from there undertook various consultancy assignments concerned with local government re-organization and on large capital projects in developing countries. He is currently consultant to numerous organizations including banks, motor manufacturers, high tech companies, oil companies, police and other public sector organizations, and numerous multi-national corporations. He has consulted and lectured in the UK, Europe, USA, South East Asia, the Gulf States and Australia.

His current areas of interest focus on improving the performance of top executives and top executive teams, excellence in consultancy practice, and the politics of decision-making.

He has published 18 books, 12 monographs and 104 articles, including the best-selling books *Politics of Management, Working in Organisations*, and *The Wealth Creators*. He has recently edited, along with Frédéric Nortier and Nello-Bernard Abramovici, *Success in Sight: Visioning* published by International Thomson Business Press (1998). He holds positions on the boards of a number of companies and is external examiner to several universities. He is the joint editor of the *Journal of Management Development*, is the previous editor of the *Journal of Managerial Psychology* and associate editor of the *Leadership and Organisation Development Journal*. He has also been advisor to a Channel 4 television business series.

Nada Kakabadse
Bsc, MPA, PhD, Grad Dip Management Services

Nada Kakabadse is currently Senior Research Fellow in the Information Systems Department at the Cranfield School of Management, Cranfield University, Bedford, England. Together with the management development research team, she has undertaken a comprehensive study of leadership at senior civil service level, Federal Government of Australia.

Previously, she was employed as a Senior Information Technology Officer with the Australian Public Service's Department of Employment, Education and Training. In the role of Innovation Manager, Nada led a research and development team that attracted a multi-million dollar budget which affected the work of 16,500 employees and their 300,000 service providers.

Her other activities in government have included liaison across various agencies and chairing and participating in a number of committees, as well as coaching others in improving job performance.

Her work with the international organization, Alfa-Leval, and with the Canadian Federal Government, Department of External Affairs and Trade, provided her with the opportunity to work within a variety of cultures in Europe, the Middle East, Canada and North Africa.

Her research interests include: the strategic use of information systems; management best practice; organizational design; strategic decision support systems; and vulnerability. She has published two books, a monograph and numerous articles.

Introduction

Overview of leadership

As so many in history have discovered, people love their leaders. They equally love to hate them. More often than not, they love, hate, and love again the very same person, all in surprisingly short periods of time. Hence, the search for what makes great leaders has been pursued with a zealous enthusiasm by philosophers, historians, anthropologists, politicians and latterly by writers and researchers of management and organizational disciplines.

Ancient writers, such as Confucius, Aristotle, Socrates and Plato emphasized the importance of leadership as a prime shaper of societies. It was Socrates who proclaimed the power and impact of leadership, but soon discovered the topic to be a double-edged sword. As a spiritual and intellectual leader of Greek society, Socrates was charged with impiety and the corruption of the youth of Athens. At his trial in 399 BC, Socrates, in his defence, presented himself as one who had accomplished humility and hence such charges held no weight. Unfortunately, his version of humility and wisdom was not shared by his fellow Athenians and rather than renounce his beliefs, he took the hemlock that painfully facilitated his passage to the life beyond.

From the ancient philosophers to Hobbes and Nietzsche, to current scholars, finding out what makes the visionary hero, the super human, the great man or woman, tick, has become an obsession. Through assumption, predisposition or just painstaking research, the search has been on to identify those elements that lead to super-human drive, a sharp eye, a decisive mind, all of which put together generate in an individual a force that makes for an extraordinary impact. The hope is that once these attributes are isolated, they can in turn be replicated and through training or other means be inculcated in others. Historically, it has been assumed that transformational leaders make the big strides that break out of existing constraints, help or force others to rethink the shape of their lives, and enthuse, cajole, or drag them forward into a brave new world.

Then something happened: the twentieth century! The twentieth century has witnessed one transformation unprecedented in history – the emergence of the large structured work organization. With the divorce of ownership from capital, and capital now seen as a resource for investment, which in turn requires managing not only by managers, but also by bankers, politicians, trade unions (trade unions worldwide invest and control especially through pension funds) and by civil servants, the point has been reached where the vast majority of us are now employees, irrespective of our status and immediate responsibilities. Hence, whether chairman, chief executive, operative, or secretary, all are primarily employees. Despite the fact that chairmen and chief executives may own shares in the company, the vast majority still do not own the company. What, however, the secretary, chief executive and chairman share, is that each in his/her own way, influences the development of the company, to a greater or lesser extent.

It has been the introduction of the medium to large-sized work organization, requiring responsiveness to market, community or even political needs, that a uniquely different impact has been made on leadership. Leadership now, unlike the supposed, individualistic leadership of the past, is influenced by the impact of the immediate and surrounding context. Context refers to circumstances, specifically the prevailing circumstances in different organizations, even the varying and different circumstances within the same organization. The contention put forward is that organizational context(s) provides the parameters within which current leadership is contained.

An effective leader in business, the civil service, central and local government, health and other personal services, is one who does not necessarily keep breaking the mould and taking big strides forward. Effectiveness of leadership is determined by being able to recognize the appropriateness of actions relevant to the circumstances of the situation. Hence, a leader who is seen to be good in one organization, may not fare too well in the next. Why? Because circumstances may be different and the man or woman may not have been able to adjust.

In today's world, any analysis of leadership requires exploration of what makes the leader function, but equally required is an examination of the culture and context of an organization, and also of followership. The great political contributors and leaders – of whom Margaret Thatcher immediately comes to mind – have paid particular attention to that fact, as the history of Thatcher's relationship with the miners shows. Not until she felt she had the necessary support from her followers, did she press ahead with her reforms of the mining industry.

Unless the requirements of colleagues, subordinates and the overall mood of teams, departments or even whole organizations, are taken into account, any leadership effort may be ineffective, or even counter-productive, if followers have not given their 'tacit' permission for their leaders to act. Add to that simple insight the modern-day phenomenon of the speed of information transmission, the increasingly indistinct boundaries between home and work (how many people have computers and faxes at both home and in the office in order to conduct their work?), the growth of multi-national and multi-cultural organizations, the fact that key client accounts can be enhanced or damaged by junior subordinates irrespective of the behaviour of the boss, the fact that millions of dollars, pounds, Deutschmarks' worth of business can transfer along with the 27-year-old pension fund manager, sales manager or equities dealer, to his/her next job irrespective of his/her contract, indicates that contextualism in today's work organizations is a phenomenon of paramount importance.

History has searched to understand the make up of the great leader. This century has firmly said that no matter who you are, you had better also take into account what others around you think and feel, or else!

Categorizing leadership

The elements not only of what makes for greatness, but also of how one manages one's immediate circumstances, in order to be a better leader, form the basis of this book. The fundamental argument put forward is that the capability to lead must be coupled with the practical skills that leaders need to have to manage their day-to-day affairs, which range from administration to working through and with people the tactical demands which require immediate response. In order to build up a picture, the views of some of today's great thinkers on leadership are captured below.

■ Leadership is a distinct kind of work. According to the challenges provided by any situation, a combination of forces throws up a demand for a leader of particular qualities who can remedy or change the situation.
■ Leadership does not necessarily mean status, authority or the holding of office. Leadership may be exerted by people who may or may not be in a position of authority. The great fourteenth-century Scottish hero, William Wallace, reputedly of low birth, is said to have inspired, directed and driven Robert the Bruce eventually to defeat the English at Bannockburn. Historical evidence suggests that had the phenomenon of William Wallace not occurred, Robert the Bruce would not have had the will to confront the English in open battle, and could well even have sided with them.
■ Leadership is not always necessary. Not everything that happens in an organization is the result of good leadership. Steady success can be achieved equally by good management.
■ Leadership is a special form of power, and as such, is a way of commanding and focusing resources to achieve a particular vision,

change or goal. On this basis, any leadership influence that allows people to achieve and to remobilize resources, whether through exciting or coercing individuals, is still the exercise of power, despite the fact that it is felt as positive and motivating.

■ Leadership involves broad capability, in that knowledge of products/services, use of functional skills, and familiarity with the organization's markets, namely facts, have to be combined with experience of markets and competitor behaviour, for example, and a drive and will to improve the status quo. Hence, leadership requires people who are pragmatists as well as thinkers; those who have risen through the ranks as smart, insatiably tireless workers as well as those who have reached top positions because of their intellectual superiority.

■ Effective leaders require to have developed a high level of people skills. Such leaders need to display an appreciation of their own talents and flaws, enhance the former and eliminate, or at least compensate for, the latter. From such insights, effective leaders may then understand and work with others in a manner which genuinely brings out the best in them.

■ An effective leader should possess well-attuned conceptual skills, so that the he/she can see opportunities where others cannot, and can capitalize on current trends in order to turn them into future advantage.

■ Effective leaders must artfully have evolved good judgement, which is a dynamic mixture of attention to detail, conceptualization and intuition. But these three attributes do not sit comfortably together. Intuitive people can become easily bored. Detail-oriented people can learn to dislike, or even despise, intuitive people, because they generate discomfort by being too quick and too clever. Yet such are the characteristics that are required in order that leaders can sensibly use judgement in order to see and understand what is happening and thereby respond decisively and intelligently to the circumstances.

■ Leadership requires the development of key aspects of character, namely a balance of ambition, ability and conscience, so that the individual can see what is an ethical and appropriate avenue forward, do the 'right thing', and equally accept full responsibility for his/her actions and for those of the organization.

■ Effective leaders need to be politically astute, not simply seek power, but know how to use it in situations that are not easy to address and that provide obstacles and pitfalls to leaders.

This list of attributes of effective leaders and sound leadership is heavily tainted with managing opposites. How can one be ethical and political at the same time? How can one be sensitive to people, and yet drive through change? As already questioned, how can one be attentive to detail, and yet quick to grasp and pursue half-formed possibilities? The answer is, because leadership involves constantly addressing contrasts, contradictions and paradoxes.

Transformational and transactional leadership

The greatest paradox of all is that between leading and managing, pushing for great change and yet keeping the organization ticking over. The point emphasized in this book is that both are required in today's world. Following this line of argument, two words capture the uneasy fit between leading and managing, namely 'transformational' and 'transactional'.

Leaders that transform the status quo create a vision for the future, then invest considerably in sharing that vision. Through sharing their vision, they clarify the present, show how the past has influenced the present, and propose a view of the future. Successful transformative leaders then powerfully project their vision, gain support for that vision, are consistent, persistent and focused in order to maintain momentum and empower others to take responsibility and become part of that movement. Such people display energy and yet can listen, so that they can monitor performance and learn from their errors. The world famous American writer, Warren Bennis, argues that all of these factors stimulate a transformative power, because leaders of such fortitude can turn intention into reality and equally sustain that momentum. According to Bennis, the transformational power of the leader is to so penetrate the soul and psyche of others, that there is raised in others a level of awareness that reawakens people to strive for even greater ends.

It was the researcher J. M. Burns who provided the counterweight argument to leadership. In his reformulation, Burns coined the phrase 'transactional leadership', namely the skill and ability required to handle the more mundane, operational, day-to-day transactions of daily life. Managing the detail of budgets, periodically reviewing and following through on projects and initiatives, keeping meetings to their time limits, ensuring the agenda is adhered to, and conducting appraisals of subordinates, are but a few examples of transactional management. Table I.1 highlights certain of the more obvious differences between transformational and transactional leadership, the point being that effective leaders need to manage efficiently some of the routine tasks, not only in order to maintain their credibility and effectiveness, but also to keep the organization on track.

The lead partner (who wished to remain anonymous) of a world famous consultancy organization, in addressing his colleagues about the virtues of conducting thorough appraisals of their subordinates said:

> If you think that I look forward to that part of the year when it's time to do appraisals, let me relieve you of such a misconception. Appraisals

Table I.1   Distinguishing transformational from transactional leadership

Attributes	Transformational	Transactional
Approach	Innovative (creates opportunity, imagines new areas to explore)	Balance of operations
Interaction	Personal in their orientation to group members	Role-bounded
Focus	Focus on vision, values, expectations and context	Focus on control, production and results
Influence	Within and outside the construct of structure and their immediate jurisdiction	Within the designated group
Motivates through	Volitional activity (emotion, offering suggestions)	Formal authority mechanisms
Use	Influence (power)	Control
Values	Co-operation, unity, equality, justice and fairness in addition to efficiency and effectiveness	Co-ordination, efficiency and effectiveness
Communicate	Indirectly and directly, give overlapping and ambiguous assignment	Directly giving clear direction, solitary assignment
Represents	Direction in history	Process
Oriented towards	Ends	Means
Is	Philosopher	Technologist
Has	Transforming impact	Transactional impact
Role	Discretionary	Prescribed
Main tasks	Defines and communicates goals, motivates	Implements goals, referees, coaches
Thinking time-frame	Futuristic (tomorrow and the day after)	Current (yesterday's output and today's problems)
Thinking context	Global	Local
Main direction	Renewal	Maintenance

are no fun, but are vital for our people and our business because it is the only formal mechanism for reviewing and improving everyone's performance. Yes, I am sensitive to people, but I also apply attention to detail and discipline. When you are doing your twentieth appraisal that week, you sure need to be disciplined.

These comments were made at a time when the senior partners of the firm were displaying the enviable skills of managing their clients, but simultaneously neglecting their own staff. Hence, the firm was winning orders, but the partners were losing control of key client contracts because they had not won the loyalty of their staff. Costs were rising, as a result, and the turnover of staff and consultants had reached damaging proportions. That company had got itself into a position of needing to improve internal management as well as to continue winning clients through expert and flamboyant leadership.

Context is the intervening variable between the two forms of leadership. Transactional leadership refers to the interactions between individuals and groups in the performance of their job, but within particular contexts. Context, or the situation in which the individual, team, department or function in the organization finds itself, is a potent influence affecting the interaction between people and the quality of administration that binds the organization together. The power of context is substantial, for context helps form the attitudes and perspectives individuals hold about life, work, people and the organiza- tion so that attempts at transformational change can be resisted, hindered and even undermined. Whereas transactional leadership is driven by context, transformational leadership restructures contexts, by removing the old and replacing it with the new.

Pathway through leadership

On the basis that effective leadership in structured work and social organizations means that management and leadership are intertwined, a pathway through leadership is provided in order to clarify and position appropriately the myriad of terms that abound in the organizational and strategic literature (Figure I.1).[1]

Two key issues of transformational leadership thinking are highlighted, namely are individuals 'born to lead', or does a person adopt an, 'I did it myself', philosophy? The assumption behind the born to lead school of thought is that the favoured few display inherent, possibly genetically determined, but certainly deep-rooted, characteristics of greatness. The search is to find those traits of personality, those elements of character that are fundamentally universal, which promote understanding of the men and women of history, and which can be promulgated to grow the path breaking leaders of the future. Such was the pre-conception of the great German philosopher, Frederick Nietzsche, whose search for the attributes of the Ubermensch (Superman) added to the belief that the only block to greatness was the fact that those unique transformational abilities had, as yet, not been comprehensively uncovered.

The alternative philosophy is developmental in nature, which is encompassed in the 'born in poverty', but 'made it good' story. The

Figure 1.1 Pathway through leadership

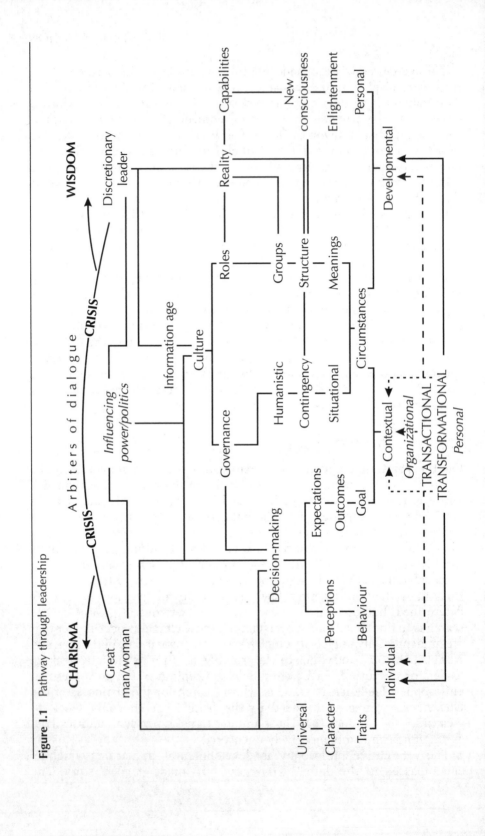

developmental perspective of transformational leadership highlights the ways that people can truly stretch themselves to reach a state of enlightenment which, if sufficiently well practised, will evolve in the person a new and higher level of consciousness. Having attained profoundness of insight leading to greater wisdom, the leader utilizes his/her newly found knowledge to enhance his/her capability to negotiate a new reality among those he/she wishes to influence within and outside the organization. While the search for the characteristics of a great leader engenders the belief that there exist great men and women with special qualities, the underlying philosophy of the developmental school is that the maturing of leaders takes place through the exercise of choice. Within developmentally driven concepts of leadership, leaders are viewed as requiring to exercise discretion, for they occupy roles and find themselves in circumstances where they have to make sense of what is happening around them, in order to provide the steer and steel desired by their followers. The route of development pursued by the individual is of crucial consideration, for that route determines the learning gained, which in turn sharply determines the quality of discretion exercised. Similar to the 'born to lead' school, the developmental philosophy of 'stretch yourself' is equally historically, deeply rooted. Socrates, Plato and Aristotle, Taoism and Buddhism all strongly proclaim the need for becoming 'in touch', with the inner self, that inner self being the source of humility which opens the individual to the benefits of reflection. As Socrates claims, an unexamined life is not worth living.[2] Thus developmental leadership, as an exercise of humility, leaves nothing untouched, and is an exercise in the willingness to aspire to wisdom.

Ironically, the two camps of transformational leadership thinking have a deep-rooted opposition to each other. Certain accomplished individuals see themselves as naturally rising through the *mêlées* of life, providing order and direction, and desire that they be recognized for their greatness. Their view is that the unique nature of charisma distinguishes them from others. In contrast, those who attain commanding heights as a result of their endeavours, but not birth, feel that everyone should be given a chance and that anyone can be successful, should they so desire. In addition to choice, crisis can also unexpectedly throw up new people to take charge, turn those who have stagnated into exciting 'movers' and 'shakers', to provide new values, new standards, and drive the organization into a new age. The charismatic great leader equally is viewed as driving people and events forward to an exciting new era. Identifying with one camp, by definition, negates membership of the other. It is no surprise to witness that those who relate more to the one school, are distrusted by and distasteful to the other. The developmental transformational school has been labelled as 'soft, wishy-washy' and that of the 'San Francisco flower people', doing odd things just to understand the meaning of life. The individual trait school is viewed at one extreme as 'psychobabble', and at the other as 'silver spooned', providing an excuse to create elites for the privileged, and furthermore, to inhibit others from joining these privileged circles. The divide between the two schools of thought is so great because charisma promotes ego, while the other cherishes humility. Ego and humility are the ultimate enemies in the philosophical divide of who is to take charge to mould the nature of the human race.

In exploring the nature of transactional leadership, two fundamental issues require attention: goal-directed behaviour, and the nature of context within the organization (particular teams, departments, units or divisions) where such behaviour takes place. Clearly set goals provide people and the organization with immediate direction and purpose. The degree to which the goals pursued clearly relate to expected outcomes, determines whether people and organizations achieve these goals and even relate to the goals set.

In addition, people's expectations are strongly influenced by the circumstances prevalent within the organization. The manner in which the structure of the organization influences views, is matched by the strength of group opinion, which in turn is influenced by the degree to which rational, and even seemingly irrational, forces influence the staff and their local leadership. The degree to which the leadership is then responsive to the varying situations in the organization, shapes their capacity to be alert to the various contingencies they may then encounter.

So far, the stroll through leadership concepts has highlighted a clear delineation between the transformational and transactional dichotomy. However, the leadership landscape is more complex. Topics such as corporate governance and culture of organization, which obviously are topics of significance for leaders, do not easily fit into any one camp. Culture of organization is seen as a meeting point of different strands of thinking, which primarily cover considerations of context as well as the capability of individuals to nurture and develop particular cultures suited to their desires and aspirations.

Further, the topics of power and politics hold transformational and transactional implications. Power and politics in organizations are viewed as both the processes and levers that leaders need to utilize in order to influence the outcomes they desire, bearing in mind the reality of the context within their particular organization. Power and politics are viewed as higher order transactional leadership skills, which bridge the divide between the great men and women of history and the self-reliant, self-developed discretionary leader. Both forms of transformational leadership have to overcome complexities and may well resort to approaches of power/politics as their way of influencing agendas in their favour. It is equally assumed that the practice of power and politics requires subtlety and craft. The ability to apply basics effectively, such as setting goals, needs to be supplemented, in the effective management and leading of the expectations of others, the making of decisions, the influencing of cultures and people's views, by mastery of power and politics. Ineptness at power and politics is all too readily, and probably damagingly, apparent. Political skill, well applied, may not add to the popularity of the individual, but certainly makes them a person who can substantially shift agendas. Bill Rogers, now Lord Rogers, who together with Shirley Williams, David Owen and Roy Jenkins, as the original 'gang of four', formed the now defunct Social Democrats, described the former Conservative Foreign Secretary, Malcolm Rifkind, who lost his seat in the May 1997 UK general election, as a 'tricky customer'. The comment made was one of admiration for the subtlety of debate and the ability to work the House of Commons procedures, as exhibited by Secretary Rifkind. The point made by Bill Rogers is that transformational leaders equally need to apply themselves to the appropriate usage of transactional skills, before total accomplishment of leadership can be attained. The capability to apply oneself to transformational and transactional challenges, produces two ultimate leaders, those who display charisma, and those who have evolved a comforting wisdom. Rarely do people exhibit both. Where one sits in transformational leadership, self-made or born to be great, is probably a reflection of one's own philosophy. However, the point being made is that irrespective of where one resides, no leader will govern effectively without being well able to manage details and life's daily transactions.

The balance each leader determines between transactional and transformational, and whether one's self view is driven by the belief of innate 'greatness', or the insights that wisdom provides, makes each leader unique. That uniqueness determines the contribution of the individual to the greatest challenge of all, how to pursue dialogue in circumstances where different parties adopt contrasting and seemingly irreconcilable positions. The ultimate challenge is that of arbiters of dialogue, viewing pathways through different positions to see if workable ways forward can be realized. Whether through wisdom or charisma, finding pathways through the use of dialogue to reach settlement or resolution, is the ultimate hallmark of leadership.

Structure of the book

The book consists of 11 chapters following this introduction. The book is also sub-divided into two parts. Part One explores the transactional side of leadership, while Part Two examines the nature of transformational thinking.

Part One of the book, concentrating on the transactional, management skills side of leadership, begins at Chapter 1, with an analysis of roles, relationships and organizational form. An overview of the contribution of the founding 'fathers' and 'mothers' of management theory, highlights an ongoing juxtaposition within managerial thinking, and that is the need for order and a well-balanced structural design, along with the requirements of flexibility, in order to enhance relationship building and co-operation in order to provide service to customers and communities. The point made in the chapter, is that with market stability, the attraction of neat organizational configuration became the dominant mode of thinking for the middle thirty years of the twentieth century. However, with the onset of ever mounting pressures, demands for success, the requirements for service and a reduction of lead times, the luxury of well-established organizational form and design has disappeared. Instead, the transactional skill of constantly stitching together 'best as you can' solutions has become the norm, with no particular sign that current conditions will revert to the more established ways of 'neatness of design'. In effect, fragmentation and dissonance are the norm, so the question posed is, what are leaders going to do about it? In discussing the transactional skills required to fight fragmentation, the chapter, by implication, highlights an additional point, that to be even transactionally competent, requires high energy and commitment.

If organizational boundaries are continually splitting and being restitched, due to market pressures, mergers, takeovers, or due to a belief in the need to change frequently to combat all or some of these, what then happens to the shared values and beliefs people hold, commonly called culture? Chapter 2, in attempting to appreciate the nature of organizational culture today, starts with a few old favourites, such as Roger Harrison's fourfold cultural typology, and the ethnic cultural distinctions of Geert Hofstede. However, the analysis of their contributions is balanced by the results of the Cranfield studies, which strongly emphasize that an untidy mix of cultures exists in any organization and in any country, which, inconveniently, does not neatly fit into traditional organizational boundaries or country borders. So what to do? It is at this point that the concept of context is introduced. A culture, whether organizational or national, is identified as being made up of many contexts, namely realities that differ by degree, do not necessarily merge, but still emerge as an organizational or national whole. In order to 'know your way through culture', it is necessary to become familiar with the nature of multiple contexts, and the recommendations of how to know your way, support that theme.

The debates in Chapters 1, and 2 throw up one key conclusion, namely that differences rather than similarities, diversity rather than unity, epitomize organizations. How then should leaders handle circumstances of adversative difference? There are two ways, is the answer – through the use of power, the topic of Chapter 3, and through political manoeuvre and influence, the focus of Chapter 4.

Power in terms of 'A having power over B so that B does what A wants', is the theme explored in Chapter 3. Particular focus is given to identifying and discussing the levers of power that are available to leaders. However, in order to emphasize the point that particular understanding of contexts is crucial in order to be transactionally effective, analysis proceeds with how the key power levers might be applied in the diverse, international cultures identified and discussed in Chapter 2. The purpose in so doing, is to promote the notion of contextual sensitivity in order to assist leaders to be that much more transactionally effective.

The theme of 'work your way through' sharply contrasting diversities is continued by examining what needs to be done when direct power is dysfunctional to apply. The proposition is, that if power 'don't work, have a go at politics!' Politics is identified as a more indirect form of influence, whereby the only real lever is the individual and his/her ability to influence through dialogue, and through his/her presence. The essence of politics is captured in the phrase, 'nudging meanings', namely moving understandings between people forward, either overtly or covertly, through appreciating the mindsets of others, and not only their strengths, but also their areas of vulnerability which may require as much protection as discussion. The aim of politics is to bring people 'on side'. Having appreciated the mindset of 'relevant others', Chapter 4 concludes by identifying the steps to enhancing personal influence within tense transactional circumstances.

Part Two of the book highlights the transformational side to leadership. Although history and popular perceptions today have glamourized the transformational aspect of leadership, the point to remember, so aptly made in Part One (Chapter 1) and in Part Two (Chapter 8) is that the transactional side of work dominates a leader's time, with estimates of 75–80 per cent being utilized transactionally. The continuous rebalancing of the transactional and transformational makes for good leaders, despite the attractive pull of displaying the glamorous transformational aspects.

In order to provide a balanced view, the two sides of transformational leadership – the 'born to be great' and the 'did it myself' – are explored. Chapter 5 examines in depth the nature of born to be great, and establishes that early life-influencing experiences are the likely source of the grandiose assumptions and extravagant behaviour of this school of thought. Initially utilizing Freudian analysis, then continuing with the work of Alexander Lowen and bioenergetics, and finally examining the intricate natures of charisma and narcissism, the picture that emerges is one illustrating that, what was done to each one of us in infancy, has a deeply profound impact in later life, which for those searching for supremacy conveniently adds to the belief of, 'born unique and great'. Perhaps one or two are! – but certainly the greater majority are assumed to be the product of their earlier years.

The question of what happens to leaders, their progress through life and their development after being moulded from an early age, is addressed in Chapter 6, whereby the alternative assumption of 'achieved it myself' is equally put under the spotlight. The chapter provides an exploration of the impact of the forces of socialization, namely demographics. Of all of the views and attitudes, the length of time in the job, and the length of time in the organization (tenure), and the balance of accountabilities and responsibilities in one's role are high-lighted, by the Cranfield studies, as crucial to the forming of profound leadership philosophies. Age is also considered as influential. However, overlaying the three primary forces of tenure, accountability and age, is development. Those older employees, with lengthy experience of their job and the organization, who have had to learn to live with their mistakes, and have exposed themselves or been exposed to varying experiences, whether on or off-the-job, which have matured and developed them, have emerged as leaders with wisdom, deeply impactful on their colleagues, subordinates and the organization. The message emanating from Chapter 6, is that, no matter how strong were early childhood experiences, and no matter how forceful are current circum-stances, adopting a position of standing back and reflecting on one's circumstances, with a view to not accepting the status quo, is crucial to maintaining the independence of mind required by high performing leaders.

The theme of high-level leadership performance is continued in the next five chapters. Women leaders are given special attention (Chapter 7) in order to ascertain how these latecomers to the field of structured work employment, are faring. All the indications are that blockages, prejudice and 'ceilings' of a glass or concrete nature, exist for those able women ready and hungry for responsibility. The path of 'getting there' does seem to be strewn with obstacles, whether intended or unintended. However, the story of 'got there', is not so clear cut. Certainly, one strong perspective to emerge from research and current writings, is that women are as much prejudiced against on their way up the ladder, as they are once they have reached the pinnacle. However, the Cranfield studies offer a counter view. Yes, numerous hurdles do exist on the way up, but once there, the picture is somewhat different. Through the results of studies and case examples of successful women in government, politics, business and social welfare, clearly concluded is the perspective that there are as many differences among women leaders, as there are between men and women. The pattern of good and bad choices and good and bad decisions, is replicated across the sexes. On the basis that drawing a distinction between men and women at work is less helpful than exposure to managing diversity, the chapter concludes that eradicating discrimination through codes of conduct and the promotion of diversity training, is the more fruitful pathway to pursue on behalf of the development of women. In so doing, how to address the needs of minorities, a category into which men may, in certain circumstances, fall, is given consideration.

The Marxian dialectic of counterbalancing equal and opposite forces – in the conclusion of Chapter 7 – also becomes the theme of Chapter 8. Best practice transformational leadership, termed the seven sides to great leaders, is the theme of this chapter. The seven sides, namely the seven areas of best practice, weave in and out of transactional activities and transformational contributions. Visioning, dialogue, team activity, maturity, wisdom, discipline, communication and cabinet responsibility, are examined in detail, as are the steps to adopt towards effective transactional implementation. Case examples, highlighting the practice experiences of well-known leaders, and data gathered through the Cranfield studies, provides the support to the arguments presented.

A particular point made at the beginning of Chapter 8, is that leaders are exposed to a 'goldfish bowl' experience. Their 'ins' and 'outs' are under constant scrutiny, their every move is examined, and their daily existence provides for a continuous spectacle for interested voyeurs. Their 'open to comment' existence, coupled with the balancing of paradoxical pressures, leaves each one wary of and vulnerable to the debilitating impact of the erosion of emotional stamina, known as 'burn out', the topic of Chapter 9. The phenomenon of burn out, namely finding difficulty in doing what one previously did well, is an experience from which all can suffer, but especially those whose role exposes them to the storms of life. Why those people occupying 'big time jobs', where discretionary choice is broad, can fall prey to the destructive impact of 'emotional sapping', is explored. How then, either as the victim of burn out, or as the boss of the individual who is at the mercy of performance deterioration, should each individual react in order to improve the situation, is discussed in considerable detail. Just as Chapter 7, concludes by examining best practice for men and women, to improve the lot of women and other minorities, and Chapter 8 discusses best practice transactional and transformational leadership, so Chapter 9 also pursues the theme of best practice, as much on how to enhance the positives, as on how to minimize the negatives.

The perspective adopted in Chapter 10 is that if all best practices were adopted, each leader would then face the ultimate challenge – his/her conscience. The theme of Part Two, is work through paradoxes, find pathways through contradictions, steer a tight line, cut through and get great things done, and yet be sensitive and caring and responsive to both the traumas and trivialities that affect others. The more accomplished the leader, the more, when under extreme circumstances, is he/she likely to face the immortal Socratic question of, 'What ought I to do?' The chapter explores the ethical dilemmas leaders inevitably have to face. The history, philosophy and nature of ethics is explored. The two sharply contrasting schools of deontology and utilitarianism are discussed from the perspective of how leaders are likely to react under ethically compromising circumstances. Through such analysis, four ethical paradoxes emerge, as well as the routes to take to find ways through such taxing contrasts. However, the inevitable question still remains, what ought one to do? This is a question that is ever present, irrespective of being found in circumstances of ethical dilemma or not. Hence, in order to introduce change, or sponsor improvement, the conscience, and the ethical position adopted by leaders are as important an issue to appreciate as are the steps to promoting change. Best practice is brought together at this point by combining the ethical pathways to pursue with the meaning of ethics to the individual. The message is, if you adopt a philosophical position that is alien to yourself, even the simplest of changes could feel impossible to attain. When all is said and done, the emerging wisdom is, 'Be true to yourself!'

Having examined best practice from a multitude of angles, the remaining and outstanding question is left for Chapter 11 to address, namely, what pathways should leaders, prospective leaders, and their organization consider pursuing in order to promote a higher order leadership capability? The inevitable answer of promote both on and off-the-job development highlights one fact, that development for leaders is not about 'learning facts', but about releasing the insights that already exist within people. This point is strongly emphasized in Chapter 8, where it is shown that discomfort in relationships can lead to paralysing inhibition. Grown men and women can exhibit similar dysfunctionality as a 10-year-old child, who, at the receiving end of a severe scolding, is unable to think effectively, to speak, or move. Adults can find themselves just as helpless, knowing what is wrong, but unable to do anything about their situation. Hence, the theme of Chapter 11 is about the releasing of potential through mechanisms which unlock the fixed positions in which individuals can find themselves, through a level of dialogue not previously experienced, and which opens in individuals, potential which they may not otherwise have realized. The studies conducted through the International Management Development Centre at Cranfield have produced trends which highlight not only the manner in which discretionary leadership can be nurtured and developed, but also the application of such learning to the drafting of instruments (questionnaires) which help people understand their capability in the area of visioning, the ways of attaining greater buy into the vision being pursued, and how to promote a higher quality of dialogue. The Cranfield studies have spawned programmes equally for the development of top managers in post, and for those exhibiting the potential for high office. The approaches to the growth and development of leaders outlined in Chapter 11, are the sum of the Cranfield experiences for the enhancement of discretionary leadership.

Driving philosophy

The philosophy adopted in this book is in line with the, 'I strove hard and achieved it alone' school of thinking. The insights, experiences and research work are the result of the endeavours of numerous Cranfield teams, including that of the International Management Development Centre. The work of Mel Scott, Keith Patching, Liz Bridge, Martin Clarke and others at the Management Development Unit (MDU) has been extremely influential in identifying how to structure appropriate programmed training for high flyers and prospective leaders.

In the book, the counterbalance of 'born to lead' has not just been offered for the sake of balance of equity, but because the bioenergetics concepts are a central platform for the development of leaders in the work of the Praxis group. The ultimate irony is that the contribution of Jacquie Drake, the Director of Praxis, and that of other Praxis members such as Sandy Cotter, Andy Logan and Ido Van der Heyden, is to take concepts which highlight the impact of character forming forces and utilize these to help leaders adapt and change their personal perspective, so as to be able maturely to accept ever greater responsibility.

In a similar developmental vein, Susan Vinnicombe and her team, examining issues of women in management, have provided lessons on how the best can be drawn out of women, to realize their full potential.

The work of Gerry Johnson and Cliff Bowman, world renowned in the areas of culture and strategy, and who captured the phrase, 'zone of uncomfortable debate', is conceptually intertwined with the philosophy and studies of the International Management Development Centre. In turn, the focus of the Centre has been to explore 'discretionary leadership', the exercise of choice in order to formulate ways to drive the organization forward and to take the people in the organization enthusiastically in the direction being pursued. The position adopted is that dialogue and choice are the two sides of the same coin, entitled leadership in practice.

The studies by the Centre have taken many twists and turns, and the key contributors to these studies are outlined below. Together with Charles Margerison, a comparative analysis of the behaviour and activities of UK and USA CEOs was personally undertaken. Further, Siobhan Alderson contributed to an examination of ethics and the ethical behaviour of top managers. Lola Okazaki-Ward, has made a crucial contribution to an in-depth exploration of the capabilities and philosophies of Japanese top managers. Zhong Ming Wang of Hangzhou University, the People's Republic of China, undertook an interesting exploration of leadership in Chinese state-run and joint venture enterprises. Paul Dainty helped pioneer the mental mapping of senior managers. Originally by Adrian Nelson, but latterly and principally by Andrew Myers, to whom we owe a great deal, the psychometrizing of questionnaires to high standards of reliability and validity, has been achieved. Jenny Simpson and Tim Scott of the British Association of Medical Managers (BAMM), jointly worked with Andrew Kakabadse and Andrew Myers to examine leadership practice in health service organizations. Professor Leo Murray, Director of the Cranfield School of Management, has been a constant source of support in all we have done, echoing the message of development in his question, 'What can I do to help?' Peter Shergold and Dennis Ives provided for us the opportunity to work with the Australian Federal government. Finally, based on the assumption that all can and do improve if there is the will to do so, we the authors, in pulling together all of this work, have focused on addressing the question, 'How can we help leaders perform more effectively?'

The message is, attention to development pays extraordinary dividends.

Notes

1   Figure I.1 is adopted from Figure 2.1, ch. 2, *Leadership of Government: Study of the Australian Public Service,* by Andrew Korac-Kakabadse and Nada Korac-Kakabadse (1998).
2   Quote from Plato (1956:36).

Further reading

For further information on the different perceptions of leadership, read:

■ Selznick (1957), who emphasizes the difference between critical as opposed to routine decisions, who equates leadership with statesmanship and not with position in organization and who recognizes that leadership is dispensable, in that not everything that is done in an institution can be called leadership.
■ Burns (1978), who sees leadership as a special form of power, the ultimate purpose being to achieve aims and objectives and in so doing, introduces a vital distinction between managing the more immediate operational concerns (transactional) and engaging followers to pursue an alternative vision of the world (transformational).
■ Tucker (1981) who equates leadership with politics.
■ Bennis (1984), whose studies indicate that leaders fulfil a number of contrasting functions, and in order to do so, are required to practise five key qualities, namely technical competence, people skills, conceptual skills, judgement and character. Bennis also introduced the notion that leadership is paradoxical, in that certain activities are contradictory to each other, but nevertheless, need to be simultaneously pursued.

For further information on the philosophers, read Aristole (1986), Plato (1956), Nietzsche (1969), and for Taoism and Buddhism and how Eastern philosophies are being applied in the West, read Ross (1980), Mair (1990) and Hesse (1985).

PART ONE

Essence of transactional leadership: managing

CHAPTER 1

Managing Daily Realities: Goals, roles and relationships

Case analysis

Francois's just being negative

The senior managers of the European hardware division of a European-owned international information technology company had gathered for a two-day meeting to discuss their half-year operating results. Their situation was not too good. The Italian team had not achieved its results and equally had overspent on its cost budget. Similarly, the Scandinavian team had fallen considerably short of its half-year revenue target, but had at least kept its costs under control.

The German/Swiss team had been well on target until just a month before the two-day meeting, when a key contract with a government agency collapsed, much to the surprise of everyone in Germany and at the corporate Centre. Not only was the German team not going to hit its half-year targets, but also it was fairly evident that the year's target contribution was not going to be met. The Germans faced another particular problem; they were spending in large amounts in order to recruit good people. The German team was in the middle of attempting to grow market share. For Hans Wegler, General Manager, Central European Region, the question was, could he continue with his plans for expanding the sales force, or would he have little choice but to introduce redundancies in the newly formed teams in his region and thereby undermine what he had already achieved?

The Eastern European region was dramatically off target. The sales and revenue targets set were likely to be under-achieved by 80 per cent. A F900 million franc, end-of-year sales forecast was, at best, likely to realize F200–250 million francs. Francois Gilbert, the Eastern European GM, strongly suspected that even this was unrealistic. The Polish Treasury bid was unlikely to be commissioned that year, if ever. The machinations of dealing with Eastern European governments had tested even the most experienced of general managers. Francois knew he was being 'stretched to the maximum', even with his impressive general management record in Eastern Europe and SE Asia.

The only two regions meeting their targets and likely to maintain their current level of performance, were the UK and Italy. Both general managers had initiated substantial programmes of reform, involving restructuring, downsizing and the building-up of new business areas. Both concentrated heavily on a strategy of promoting services and total solutions for their clients, well supported by highly motivated and well-trained sales and support teams.

After the usual introductions, each of the general managers gave a report of the performance of their region, and their expectations for the third and fourth quarters of the year. The presentations continued all morning and into half of the afternoon of the first day. The group debated how better to focus on key client accounts, how better to support each other with those clients who criss-crossed their regional boundaries, and how they as individuals, and as a group, could improve their utilization of the headquarters function and the Group Directors. Although, in the opinion of most of the group, their debates and discussions were not inspiring, at least progress had been made in trying to address some of these issues.

The one who made least comment was Francois Gilbert. He said little at dinner that evening, and when he did contribute, he seemed particularly critical. Early into the proceedings the next day, Francois's frustrations came to the surface.

> Just look at what we have achieved, here, together – little! We informed each other yesterday about issues we already knew. There was no need for such detail, other than to depress us even more. We then discussed the situation and concluded what? We need to co-operate more on European key accounts, use our directors more and *voila*, things get better. Why do we not say what is on our minds – the way we are handling key accounts and the way we are treated by our directors are the reasons for our problems!

The Company's European President, a Frenchman, said nothing. The Italian GM asked Francois to elucidate.

> We all know that at least my targets are impossible to achieve. They have not been set by me. Paris dictated what I should do. You, Hans [the German GM], have experienced terrible frustrations with Paris. Only two weeks ago, the dinner with Treasury Ministers was cancelled because two of our Headquarters directors could not turn up because of other pressing commitments. What did the politicians do? They took offence and said they, too, were called urgently away.

Francois was interrupted. 'You know the Group President had a meeting with the Interior Minister in Paris. It was important that I attended. There was no choice,' commented the European President. Francois continued:

> There is always a better reason! Always! What we are being asked to do is impossible. These are not our numbers. Most of us cannot achieve these targets. When we need support, more often than not, it is not available. Whatever is promised at the beginning of the year, is unlikely to be kept just six months later, let alone at the end of the year.

The European President responded:

> You know there are difficulties. We have to work together. Margins, as you all know, are dropping in our business. Things change – we have to be flexible to cope with the changes that occur. No-one here is unrealistic enough to expect that life can proceed smoothly. There is just no point in being negative. We all face the same problems.

Francois said little after that. The meeting continued and certain resolutions and changes to the budgets were agreed. The group dispersed, but Hans Wegler and the Italian and English GMs remained behind to finish their coffee.

'Wasn't Francois negative!' exclaimed the Italian GM.

'Well, he was accurate about me and the government contract', commented Hans.

'I was very shocked when Pierre Rodin [European President] rang and said he could not make the dinner. The real problem is that having convinced the Mayor of Hamburg to host a dinner – and he was the one who never trusted our company – he is now having a great time telling his political friends to have nothing to do with us. Rodin told me, last night, that this is my problem. I should sort it out!'

The Englishman said:

> Francois is right. Most of these problems are not of our doing. What is the point in all of us having clear goals when we know they are unrealistic. We cannot manage to do what we ourselves want because we are being asked to make money so that redundancies in France do not take place. Then there is all that interference. What's more, the way Francois is going, he is likely to lose his job.

It was no surprise that two weeks later, the general managers were informed that Francois Gilbert had resigned.

Stephen Covey *et al.*, in their best-selling book *First Things First* (1994) talk about the power of goals. Covey and his colleagues recognize the need for focus, and the need to place to one side, irrelevant and unnecessary experiences that could sidetrack managers from the pursuit of their goals. In helping to keep people on track, the authors introduce an alternative dimension to pursuing goals and that is, be realistic. Setting goals is one part of the equation, achieving them is the other. Achieving goals requires appreciating the nature of the current circumstances prevalent in the organization, and externally in the marketplace, and then setting targets with which people can identify. If goals are to be consistently achieved, people have to recognize their value, feel that they are realistic, and identify with their pursuit and achievement.

Francois, in the above case, obviously did not! His assessment was that of a headquarters that interfered with the work and decisions of its managers, did not listen to their views, and set them priorities that most felt were impossible to attain. It is little wonder that the organization had a history of poor achievement.

Managing the direction that others have to take, requires clear goals and the creation of an environment where people identify with the goals they are set, and desire to pursue their stated aims. In effect, setting clear and unambiguous goals, and effectively communicating so that staff and managers can identify with their goals, are two sides of the same coin. Hence, the leadership challenge of providing direction needs to be coupled with the people management skills of motivating, co-ordinating, co-operating and interfacing. In exploring the leadership challenge of how to manage the daily realities of keeping people focused and motivated, attention is initially given to an overview of the history that has influenced thinking on goal-setting, motivating and the managerial, namely transactional, component of leadership. Following the examination of the 'founding fathers and mothers' concepts of goals, purpose, co-operation and the need to manage direction, attention is given as to how managing goal-setting, managing organization structures, establishing purpose and co-ordination, have been addressed post Second World War. The middle thirty to forty years of the twentieth century are viewed as the 'era of the ideal', wherein theorists and practitioners believed that the setting of clear goals, the configuring of unambiguous structures, and working towards the making of 'rational decisions' would alleviate the problems of discontinuity and demotivation. However, experience and research have clearly shown this not to be the case, that fragmentation of the organization and splits of loyalties are today's reality. A number of reasons are identified as to why splits and dissension exist and will continue to be commonplace experiences in organizations. The chapter concludes by discussing best practice management that leaders should pursue in focusing people to achieve goals, and in enhancing team and organizational relationships.

Historical overview

Founding Fathers (and Mothers)

Henri Fayol (1841–1925)

The Frenchman, Henri Fayol, was a mining engineer who spent a large part of his life with the French mining and metallurgical enterprise, Commentary-Fourchamboult-Decazeville, within which, in his latter years, he was appointed managing director. Although he published specialist works in the field of mining engineering, Fayol, in his seventies, wrote the 'Administration Industrielle et Generale – Prevoyance Organisation, Commandment, Co-ordination, Controlé' (Fayol, 1916). His fame rests on this one publication.

Fayol categorized the activities undertaken by an industrial enterprise and then identified the managerial route to ensuring the survival and prosperity of that enterprise. The activities of an enterprise he categorized as the:[1]

- technical activities (production, manufacture, adaptation of products, minerals or resources)
- commercial activities (buying, selling, economic transactions)
- financial activities (money supply, liquidity, making optimum use of capital)
- security activities (protection of property, resources and people)
- accounting activities (managing the balance sheet, costs, statements)
- managerial activities (planning, organizing, command, co-ordination, control).

Fayol's premise is that these six activities are, in part or whole, and to varying degrees, present in most key managerial jobs in organizations. Equally, he makes the point that such managerial activities are required to be exercised by those who hold roles where command over people and resources is required. In emphasizing the managerial component of enterprise activities, Fayol was one of the first to specify the managerial tasks of leaders. He identified management as being composed of five elements:

1 *Forecasting and planning*, a core activity, which provides the means for better securing the future of the organization. Planning not only involves making use of information in order to forecast, but equally to integrate the sub-objectives of each part of the organization, by building sufficient flexibility into the plan to cope with external market changes. Fayol held the view that the disruptive impact of change could be minimized by accurate forecasting.
2 *Organizing the enterprise* to achieve its tasks by paying attention to drafting appropriate structures and focusing resources and people to fulfil

the goals of the plan, he argued, are central concepts. Structure is viewed as fundamental to organizing, as plans need to be accurately prepared and then appropriately discharged. The implementation of plans is undertaken through unity of command, which involves clear definitions of responsibilities and rules, and precision in decision making.

3 *Commanding* involves the manager attaining the best possible performance from staff and subordinates. Some of the ways identified by Fayol are, leadership through example, through having a detailed undertaking of the business, through in-depth knowledge of the employees in the organization, and through being comfortably in touch (in effect, communicating) with the staff and managers below,

4 *Co-ordination*, refers to the process of bringing and binding together those 'not-so-easy'-to-harmonize activities in the organization. Fayol argued that providing clear direction and consistency to the work of departments needed to be coupled with the co-ordination of inter-departmental activities. Not to do so would allow departments to splinter from the parent organization, by departments pushing for their own goals. Fayol's recommendation was that information should be exchanged freely, and management across the organization should meet regularly.

5 *Control*, is that aspect of organizational functioning which checks that the other four elements are performing as ascribed. Fayol used terms like 'conformity' and 'command' to describe the need to control the various parts of the organization to achieve the goals that had been set.

Based on his own experience, Fayol outlined fourteen principles that he believed were necessary to consider in applying the above five elements of management. These included division of work, managing ambiguity, discipline, unity of command, unity of direction, subordination of interests to the greater whole, remuneration, centralization/decentralization of structure, order, equity, maintenance of tenure of employees, clear structural configuration of the organization, the encouragement of initiative and, interestingly, 'esprit de corps'. Establishing an 'esprit de corps', namely a shared and values driven identity among staff and management, was considered an intangible, but vital aspect of organizational management. Through a meaningful 'esprit de corps', individuals would be encouraged to co-ordinate, use each other's efforts and abilities, thereby reducing the likelihood that divisions and suspicions would disrupt work effort and the harmony between people.

Fayol's work is fundamental, as he provides a twofold contribution. First, his coverage of managerial activities being broad, yet comprehensive, ranging from predicting, structuring, command and co-operation, has withstood critical analysis and has influenced many managers for more than 80 years. Second, he is the earliest known writer to have promoted a clear theoretical analysis of twentieth-century management.

Chester I. Barnard (1886–1961)

Similar to Fayol, Barnard was a practical man, having held the positions of President of the New Jersey Bell Telephone Company and State Director of the New Jersey Relief Administration, and having founded and managed the United Service Organisation Inc. during the Second World War.

Barnard's fundamental thesis, first published in 1938 and entitled *The Function of the Executive*, rests on the premise that co-operation and communication are the vital proponents to achieving purpose in an organization. Co-operation is crucial, as individuals have only limited influence and powers due to restrictions of circumstances, situation or constraints within the person him/herself. Therefore, in order to attain ever higher levels of accomplishment, and further to reduce the impact of limitations, 'co-operative social action'[2] is posited by Barnard as the desired way forward. With co-operation being his central theme, Barnard equally gave attention to the processes of interaction in groups. Effective interaction involves clarity of purpose, so that people can recognize why persistence is necessary in co-operating to achieve goals, and also to further the desire on the part of individuals who wish to co-operate. Barnard termed the formal organization a 'system of consciously co-ordinated activities',[3] or, 'forces of two or more persons'.[4] In using such terms, Barnard assumed universal application of his thesis, namely that his form of organization could be applied to an industrial or commercial enterprise, to a church, a military unit, or to the family. The willingness to co-operate and equally to contribute, Barnard recognized as requiring the 'surrender of the control of personal conduct'. Barnard also felt that the commitment to contribute varies according to how people feel about their situation, their rewards, and their views of the people with whom they interact. Hence, willingness to co-operate is dependent not only on the purpose of the organization, or the clarity of the goals of the organization, but also on people's satisfaction and dissatisfaction with their circumstances. In effect, Barnard introduced personal and subjective elements to concepts of organizational design.

Having coupled personal nature with organizational concepts as necessary considerations to the internal workings of any enterprise, Barnard offered his view as to how these two elements could be knitted together in his analysis of the functions of executive leadership. First, all those who hold a managerial position are leaders and for leadership to work effectively, leaders need to identify with two key aspects of a complex organization, their home unit and the broader executive, which goes above and beyond the person's immediate working parameters. Thereby, managers who strongly identify with their team or department, equally need to relate effectively with the management to whom they report. The same principle applies to more senior managers, who may be directors of operating businesses, in that they may relate well to their subordinate or colleague managers in their division, but equally they need to relate positively to the headquarters, and contribute to the process of ironing out any inconsistencies between the two organizational units. Having highlighted that differences of agenda exist in complex organizations, and that effort is required by the organization's management to reduce inconsistencies in order to mould the enterprise into an organic whole, Barnard evaluated the nature of executive work.

On the premise that not all the work undertaken by the executive is executive work (a fundamental tenet of this book is that not all of the work carried out by leaders is leadership work), executive work is recognized as that of managing the organization in three ways,[5]

■ enhancing organizational communication
■ getting the best out of people
■ formulation of purpose and objectives.

Communication is identified as consisting of two elements. The first is that of identifying the structure of the organization and people's position in that structure. Hence, attention to well-drafted organization charts, job descriptions and dotted line (co-operative) relationships, is crucial to the effective running of an organization. The second involves the daily tasks and activities of communication within the organization. Communication, in this sense, is viewed as running meetings, delivering presentations, and generally day-to-day interacting with lower level management and staff. It was Barnard who introduced the concept of the 'informal' organization, and maintained that the formal aspects of executive work, other than routine decisions and emergencies, were largely unnecessary, if sensitive and appropriate informal ways of operating have been nurtured within the enterprise.

Hence, getting the best out of people involves two aspects; helping to engender co-operative relationships with people and, from a base of positive relationships, eliciting their services on behalf of the organization. Such a process would be achieved by paying attention to issues of morale and by initiating schemes of incentives, effective management and supervision, and training.

The formulation of the purpose of the organization refers to the allocation of responsibility so as to mobilize the organization through clear accountabilities, a task which distinctly lies within the executive. The executive (i.e. the senior managers), in turn, need to inform and communicate to lower level staff and management the purpose and vision of the organization, because without their co-operation, pursuing such a purpose would be obviated.

Whereas Fayol identified the different activities of management that leaders would need to practise, Barnard's contribution was that of specifying the tasks of the senior management of an enterprise, and extending the debate as to the linkage between authority in role and the need for co-operation between people. Barnard emphasized that paying constant attention to the motivation of people is essential in order to grow and maintain a cohesive organic whole.

Mary Parker Follett (1868–1933)

The American, independent writer, Mary Parker Follett, had a broader spectrum of interests, as her adeptness of prose covered philosophy, history and political science, as well as business administration.

Follett argued that the management challenges facing leaders in the private sector were parallel to those of the public sector. In addressing two primary issues, the desired activities that employees should undertake, and the extent to which science should be applied in controlling and monitoring their work, Follett, with Barnard, was one of the first to recognize the importance of the use of psychology in the workplace. She proposed that the leadership of the organization, in attempting to direct the work of others, needed to appreciate the nature and dynamics of groups, and to utilize such insights to promote a unity of purpose and experience among groups' members.

Based on this assumption, she offered four fundamental principles of organization,[6]

- *Direct co-ordination*, emphasizing the need for the leaders and managers in the organization to be in direct contact with the staff, irrespective of the leaders' managers' position in the organization. By so proclaiming, Follett emphasized that 'horizontal' communication is as important an issue to address as vertical lines of authority and control.
- *Early co-ordination*, highlighting that people in the organization should be involved in the process of formulating and applying policy, strategy and operational activities, and not just be informed afterwards. Follett emphasized the benefits of increased motivation and morale of staff through participation.
- *Reciprocal co-ordination*, meaning that for co-ordination to work, the quality of interrelationship between key individuals in the organization should be given particular attention, so as to enhance the process and improve the willingness to discuss and to enter into dialogue.
- *Continuous co-ordination*, emphasizing that the making of decisions is likely to be inadequate unless supported by a process of trying to knit people in the organization together to co-ordinate their activities, and for them to co-operate towards that accomplishment. In her view, an executive decision is simply one small part of the whole process of deciding and accomplishing.

It was Follett's view that promoting mechanisms for continuous integration is an element of striving towards a common purpose. In attempting to achieve what Follett termed 'integrative unity', differences between individuals and between groups would need to be brought into the open and talked through. Her assumption was that such airing was possible because managers and leaders made decisions based on an objective assessment of the situation, and not on personal desires. On the basis of openness, clarity and objectivity of decision making, and consistency of implementation, staff and lower level management in the organization would identify with the demands of the situation, know what was required of them to contribute, and be prepared to accept the responsibility to pursue what they needed to do, to the best of their ability. The fundamental premise of Mary Parker Follett's ideas, were that individuals do not readily take orders from each other, but recognize what orders should be 'taken' within defined circumstances.

Mary Parker Follett was one of the first writers in the management leadership crucible to examine partnership deeply. Her experience of philosophy and political science led her down the track of wondering how to promote a democratic society in the workplace. She particularly stood out in her time as the individual who challenged the then established concepts of authority, leadership and power, by introducing the view of working with people, rather than utilizing power to dominate, or exercising authority over people. She promoted the notion of joint responsibility. In essence, Follett's ideas questioned whether the leadership of an organization was concentrated at the top, or whether, in fact, multiple leadership at different levels in an organization was a reality that needed to be acknowledged.

Era of the ideal (1940s–1970s)

The middle thirty or so years of the twentieth century can be described as the era of a belief in the existence of the ideal organization. The search for, and application of the ideal organization notion was based on the following principles:

Clear purpose/clear goals

The assumption that clarity of intent (purpose) and focus on targets (goals) are prime levers for enterprise success, spurred a wave of thinking and publications in the areas of planning and management by objectives (MBO). Both private and public sector organizations so welcomed the clarity concept, that, as a result, a new breed of executive emerged – the corporate planner. In large organizations, such as oil companies, and especially in local and central government, planners became the fashionable strategic support to line management. The value of corporate planners was seen as identifying and promoting clarity of objectives and improving the speed and precision of communication, and the two in combination were considered to be sufficient to improve morale and motivation in the organization. As long as staff and lower management knew what the organization was trying to do, what they were tasked to do and how that fitted into the greater picture, and were also quickly informed of changes, challenges of morale, motivation and leadership were assumed to have been addressed. Clear thinking and unambiguous communication would lessen the need for flamboyant leadership; this was the notion of the day. Such considerations did not apply only to the strategic and operational work of organizations, but also to the training and development of managers. During this era, numerous texts and exercises emerged in the area of training by objectives, as well as management by objectives.

Clear structures

Clarity of purpose and direction were viewed as needing to be accompanied by clarity of role relationships in the organization. Not only did such thinking extend the basis of corporate planning to corporate restructuring, but further sparked a new era of management thinkers and consultants. Particularly influential was Lyndall F. Urwick, the principal founder of the international consulting group, Urwick Orr. Urwick seems to have been particularly influenced by Fayol, as his thesis rested on the assumption that the logical configuration of the organization provided for efficiency and improved morale. The more complex the organization, the more the need for clear lines of authority and accountability, with each role being allocated distinct duties, defined in writing. With greater specialization, each individual should be required to perform only a limited number of well-defined functions. For a manager to be able to discharge the duties required effectively, spans of control should equally be limited, with the recommendation that these should not exceed six subordinates, except where work is shared across departments and teams in the organization. Urwick was firmly convinced that leadership and management were intertwined, as the administrative elements of the leadership role, such as controlling, selecting and co-ordinating, are of primary consideration and by implication involve substantial usage of transactional skills.

Although prescriptive in nature, the concept of ideal forms of organization sparked new thinking on how to structure enterprises effectively.

Drawn from the original work of Sir Geoffrey Vickers, but considerably developed by Professor John Child of the Aston group, four alternative models of role hierarchy emerged as the ideal organizational forms, namely:[7]

1 functional structures
2 product/services structures
3 divisional structures
4 matrix structures.

Functional structures are those normally adopted for organizations that are of small to medium size, or that require simplicity of configuration in order to achieve their goals.

Functionally structured organizations, group activities into departments, led by a departmental head, each department clearly knowing its contribution towards the overall mission of the organization. The co-ordination of these activities is through an overall director (managing director), often supported by an executive committee on board.

Product/services structures attend to the needs of those organizations focused in the promotion/manufacture of particular services or product lines. Managers are appointed to address product or service responsibilities, having to consider the short and long-term requirements of their areas of responsibility in relation to external demands.

Each key, but separate, product/services section is treated as a mini organization, within a much larger whole. Within a product/services structure, roles may well be duplicated across the organization, but each section has, at least, flexibility to respond quickly to its own requirements. Central support services would be limited to providing specialist support to the line, ranging from legal, planning or personnel services.

Divisional structures promote the creation of distinctly separate and virtually autonomous units, each providing separate product lines or services to its own market. Divisionalization occurs largely as a response to size. The organization has grown and each sub-unit requires its own directors and its own board, to pursue its business to best advantage. Also in this category fall group-structured organizations, whereby central headquarters is a separate legal entity, but holds the shares of legally separate business organizations underneath, each with its own company name, but which reports to its shareholder (the centre) by virtue of the central shareholding dominance. Hence, the centre is both owner and manager of the Group. Within the Group, each division, or subsidiary, may have its own structural form, as well as a distinct, day-to-day way of operating

Matrix structures arose from the requirement to co-ordinate the activities of different companies to satisfy the demands of space exploration in the USA in the 1960s. The bringing together of large numbers of specialists, line management and support staff, on temporary projects, spurred the recognition that drawing clear lines of authority and accountability would not be sufficient, as the requirement was for more closely knit teams to co-operate in a much more flexible, trusting and open environment. Although serving two senior managers, who may be pursuing different objectives and holding different personal values and styles, may cause dilemmas and ambiguities, it was important to relate positively and respond to contrasting demands, as the marketplace, in terms of government, required a quality of product or service that no one unit or organization alone could afford to deliver.

Clear decision focus

The assumption made during the '40s–70s' period was that clearly thinking through options, making decisions that would be optimal within a given set of circumstances, and then implementing the decision made in a disciplined manner, are interwoven processes. Critical logic will win the day.

Influential proponents of such thinking were Victor Vroom, originally of Yale University, and Philip Yetton. Vroom and Yetton considered that managers modified their style and behaviour according to the requirements of given situations. Through an examination of varying circumstances, three primary decision styles were identified that managers repeatedly utilized, namely authoritative, consultative and participative.

- *Authoritative.* The manager singularly addresses the issues at hand, solves the problems, or makes decisions on his/her own, according to the information available.
- *Consultative.* The manager shares addressing the issues at hand with the subordinate group, and then makes a decision, which may or may not reflect the subordinate group's standpoint.
- *Participative.* The manager shares addressing the issues at hand with the subordinate group and jointly they generate alternatives, evaluate these options and thereby work towards reaching an agreement on the way forward.

The underlying assumption made by Vroom and Yetton is that managers make decisions in an orderly and rational manner, which they captured in their decision tree model. According to Vroom and Yetton, managers weigh up all the factors, through assessing the quality of the information they have available to them, assessing the degree of acceptance of the decision by subordinates, and evaluating the degree of commitment of subordinates to implement the decision. Hence, if it is preferable and acceptable that the manager make a decision on his/her own, it should be so. If, however, the manager requires further information, and if people's involvement is necessary for decision acceptance and effective implementation, then the manager should adopt a more consultative or participative approach.

Dependence on clarity

The underlying philosophy in management and leadership thinking of the middle thirty years of the twentieth century, has been clarity. Clarity as to which decision required what information and whose involvement, was the order of the day so that a quality solution might emerge. Such clarity, devoid of presumption would, by implication, be experienced as a motivating stimulus by managers and subordinates alike, as all would recognize and share a common rationale to explain and understand what was happening in a given situation. On this basis, promoting clarity leads to a shared common sense, in which everyone instinctively knows his/ her role and contribution.

The principle of clarity strongly influenced thinking in both business and government circles throughout this period. The central and local government, and health service reforms of the late 1960s and 1970s in the UK, were dominated by philosophies of clarity. Attention was given to specifying clearly, and in detail, reporting relationships, highlighting the different models of organization best suited to provide for, or to deliver specific products or services, and to providing detailed descriptions of jobs and roles. The work of the Brunel Institute of Organisation and Social Studies (BIOSS) at Brunel University, an influential consultative body to government, highlighted specificity and prescription. Max Weber's work was used as the conceptual foundation from which, initially, academicians such as the Aston group at Aston University, and eventually practitioners, especially in the USA and UK, drew inspiration for their work and contributions. Scant attention was given to the influence of context and personal impact. Context was viewed from the perspective of organizational environment or culture, a subject in its infancy and in the domain of theoretician academics. The subject had not yet reached practitioners. Personal style was firmly entrenched in the authoritative/participative arena. The taboo subject of the time was, 'playing politics'. The human performance assessment levers, such as appraisal, were used more for maintaining prescription: Have you achieved your objectives? If yes, how can you do better? If not, why not? However, the era of clarity and the innocence that accompanies simplicity soon came to an abrupt end.

Fragmentation – today's reality

Undoubtedly, in this century, and even in the last, a preoccupation in management and leadership literature has been the question, 'What do managers do?' Today's emerging picture is one of fragmentation. One study of top managers showed that any senior manager has the opportunity of devoting eight minutes to him/herself, once every two weeks. This and other studies indicate that senior managers are likely to spend only between seven and twelve minutes on any one task, without being interrupted or distracted. Trying to provide direction and yet complete relatively simple tasks, can be an experience fraught with frustrations. A statement frequently heard from managers is, 'I try to get to work early, before everyone else, so that I can get some real work done!'

The implication is that once everyone else arrives at work, the frustration starts and no 'real' contribution can then be made by the manager. Why is today's managerial experience expressed as one of distraction and diversion from the pursuit of an established direction and defined goals? We give the reasons below.

Fragmented nature of roles

Professor Henry Mintzberg's original observations, made in the 1970s, present a different picture to the orderly precepts of Fayol, or even of Vroom and Yetton. Mintzberg describes ten contrasting role-related behaviours which managers adopt. The ten behaviour categories are subdivided and outlined under the three headings of interpersonal role, informational role and decisional role.

The *interpersonal role* comprises three aspects: figurehead, leader and liaison. The figurehead aspect is the symbolic part of the role, whereby the leader represents the organization, or area for which he/she is accountable. External networking, building up of image, and the PR aspects, according to Mintzberg, can involve 12 per cent of a CEO's time. The leader aspect involves the use of formal authority, direction and goal-setting, and the motivating of staff and management to pursue and achieve those goals. The liaison, or more internal networking side of a senior manager's job, involves the nurture of relationships and the process of building up trust, so that a sense of community emerges within the organization. Through establishing a positive set of relationships, business activity is presumed to be enhanced.

The *informational role* involves handling and processing written and verbal information, which Mintzberg estimates can eat up to 40 per cent of a senior manager's time. The collating, ordering and recording of information into a coherent format, Mintzberg terms the monitoring role. The communication of information involves its dissemination, and its presentation to interested stakeholders, which is identified as fulfilling the spokesman function.

The *decisional* aspect of a senior manager's job involves assessing and improving the quality of information needed to take quality decisions, the actual making of the decisions, and the process of implementing the decision in the workplace. Overall, the manager needs to take into account the tasks at hand, the quality of work of others in the organization, the way the organization is structured, the attitudes and perspectives of the people involved, the time needed for the decision-taking and implementation process, the continuous changes taking place, and the need to adjust to the predominant forces driving circumstances, all of which impact on the decisions made. Mintzberg concludes that in order for senior managers to apply themselves effectively to the overall decisional process, they need to perform effectively four roles, those of entrepreneur, disturbance handler, resource allocator and negotiator.

Through behaving as an entrepreneur, the manager becomes sensitive to actual or potential changes in the external environment, and attempts to prepare the organization and its staff and management to be responsive to such changes. In modifying objectives, restructuring the activities of individuals and/or teams, in setting up new project teams, introducing and ensuring the application of performance measures, and in assisting individuals' growth and development, the disturbance-handler role comes into play. In effect, the manager is responding to pressures and unexpected events. Disturbance-handler role behaviour arises from needing to respond to short-term demands and breakdowns in understanding and communication, in order to re-focus people to achieve their targets.

Becoming excellent at responding to short-term crises could be detrimental to planning and taking a longer-term view. Hence, the need to apply the resource allocator role, namely entering into dialogue over how people and other resources are to be distributed and allocated, across the organization. In so doing, the manager is considering the various demands of the different parts of the organization, and is entering into negotiation with internal and external stakeholders, in order to emerge with a workable agenda.

Mintzberg's analysis of the senior manager's role highlights the nature of the contradictory demands made on leaders. The assumption is that competence in certain aspects of the role, but not in others, is likely to undermine overall performance. Mintzberg's conclusion is that the fragmented nature of the demands on a senior manager, requires the development and application of multiple skills.

Rosemary Stewart adopted a similar approach, but from a broader perspective, namely that of examining the environment surrounding the role of the senior manager, and including analysing the role itself. Her view is that managers shape and design their jobs, tasks and activities according to the demands and constraints they experience, which impact powerfully on the resulting choices they make.

Demands refer to particular requirements, such as the accountabilities in the role that need to be actioned, the performance requirements that need to be met, the expectations of colleagues, subordinates, bosses and external stakeholders that need to be nurtured, and the credibility that needs to be won, in order to pursue and achieve one's targets. The nature and level of demands may be unequal. A powerful boss, an angry customer, or supplier may require such attention from the senior manager as possibly to be to the detriment of others. Unequal demands, in fact, are one constraint the manager has to manage. Constraints refer to the limitations which restrict the freedom of choice and manoeuvre of the manager.

As a result of balancing the demands and constraints, the manager makes choices, in order to determine a way through current circumstances. The greater the demands and constraints, the more limited are the choices that the manager is likely to be able to make. The fewer the demands and/or constraints, the greater the opportunity for choice, which can be capitalized upon through the individual defining his/her direction and designing his/her role.

Both Mintzberg and Stewart emphasize the continually changing balance of demands made on senior managers. Each individual will need to decide how to respond to the varying demands made on them according to how they both view and experience the impact of various interested stakeholders. Inevitably, different senior managers respond in different ways, and in so doing possibly promote the view that senior management members are incohesive and inconsistent in their handling of challenges. As a result, the level of trust of staff and lower level management, in their leaders, may be eroded. Equally, senior management's response to particular challenges becomes unpredictable, as each senior manager may be seen to respond differently to each challenge. The lack of predictability may, in turn, induce substantially different responses from subordinates, as they might predict differently their bosses' reactions, should innovative practices and new ideas not work out.

Fragmenting impact of information technology

The information revolution of the 1990s is epic in scale, and although now well documented, its true impact is yet to be understood. Fundamentally, the application of information systems (IS), has and will continue to influence dramatically the pattern of interfacing and authority relations within the organization. New IS creates possibilities that will benefit business and communities through providing multiple points of access to common databases. The freedom to respond quickly to challenges, by those in localized work stations, is increased, as they have available immediate, comprehensive and relevant data. However, in practice IS is, and is likely to continue to be, used to increase the power of the centre, through centralizing ongoing surveillance over performance, while decentralizing certain task-related activities.

Equally, IS has vastly improved communication links in the organization through e-mail or bulletin-board-type infrastructures, and has also made possible the bringing together of vested interests that until recently have had little to do with each other. The combined effects of improved IS communication (through increased flows of relevant information), electronic brokerage (the connection of many different buyers and suppliers instantaneously, through a central database electronic market), and the enhanced possibility of integrating various units in the organization and inter-organizational processes, has had a profound impact on the way organizations function.

The greatest visible effect is the impact of IS on organizational structures. The generation of different channels based on an analysis of varying information requirements has put lower level management more in touch with the CEO or other members of the top team. The in-between levels of management may be bypassed and informed, or bypassed and uninformed, in the communication between lower levels and senior levels in the organization. Keith Todd, the newly appointed Group CEO of ICL computers, jokes of the occasion (January 1997) when having e-mailed all staff in the corporation at Christmas time, wishing them and their families warmth and best wishes for the festive season, he then read the response from a lower level of manager in New Zealand, of, 'that's fine, but who are you?'

Just as information can be transmitted freely throughout the organization, so too IS knowledge can be used to weave new patterns of dependency. By possessing crucial information at a critical time, by having exclusive access to key data, or by possessing the ability to synthesize discordant channels of information at a particular point, individuals in various positions in the hierarchy can increase their influence in the organization. For example, a statistician involved in compiling data on a major survey of customer behaviour can potentially drive the agenda both in terms of emerging issues to be debated, and the time frames by which the project will require completion.

Just as information has become more freely accessible, so have organizational boundaries become blurred. Differentiation by level, function and status, has become less clear, as access to particular data sources provides individuals with greater choice and opportunity to act upon different challenges. In effect, IS has potentially provided those in the organizational hierarchy with greater choice to behave in a transformational manner. Add to that the demanning that has occurred directly and indirectly through IS, the result is that younger people are entering into roles which provide greater scope than previously was the case. Inevitably, loyalties are determined by a number of uncomfortably fitting, but nevertheless, interrelated factors. Staff and managers may feel a loyalty to particular colleagues with whom they interact, to particular customers, to client accounts, to suppliers, to their local office, to the professional organization and, or, to their employing corporation. With so many pulls and pushes in any one context, loyalty to the boss, loyalty to the team, loyalty to the department, or to the whole organization, cannot be relied upon.

Further, IS is likely to have one additional unintended consequence, and that is, people are more likely to meet, but informally. The present state of IS technology transmits explicit information. Explicit information allows clearly documented statements and reasonably well-defined arguments to be communicated openly in order to help those at the receiving end appreciate the point being made. However, people also communicate through tacit information. Tacit information, by nature, is undocumented, spoken, understood and assumed, between people who have worked together for periods of time. Widely shared tacit information is the foundation of context and culture. The experience of living and working together, forming personal bondings, and using that understanding to improve confidence in each other and enhance relationships and work effectiveness, is the essence of tacit information. Effective use of tacit information provides the basis for trust. Explicit information conveys facts, data and opinion, but in itself does not provide a bonding between people.

As stated, the greater the transmission of explicit data through advancements in IS, the more traditional and assumed boundaries are blurred or broken down. With the continual distortion of boundaries, the basis of trust is undermined. Thus people more need trust to maintain effective transactions, and especially believe in their managers in transformational circumstances. When a person makes a commitment at a meeting, those others present need to trust that the individual will honour that commitment. In transformational circumstances, negotiating a sufficient level of agreement on what views, values and attitudes people should hold, is crucial to effective change. On this basis, how can leaders trust the present or predict the future sentiments and values of their staff, with the ever greater transmission of explicit information? The different views and perspectives that people are likely to adopt in any given situation, will increase, possibly to dysfunctional proportions. Hence, people will need to meet face-to-face in order to understand each other better, and to negotiate acceptable ways forward.

Tacit information can be effectively generated only through face to face encounters, where people can 'size each other up' and form relationships which they would consider meaningful. Not even video conferencing can replicate the intimacy of context necessary for tacit interchanges. Depending on the nature of the issues which are being negotiated, and the context in which people find themselves, different perspectives, resolutions and agreements are likely to be reached, adding to the multiple identities that exist in the organization. More meetings to 'sort things out', are likely to become a way of life. However, in circumstances of poorly shared tacit information, the likelihood is that more meetings will 'sort out' more differences, adding to the discordant experience of life in organizations.

Fragmenting impact of networks

Different interest groups in the organization are likely to form themselves into networks of people who recognize the benefit of mutual exchange. The members of the network may be individuals who do or do not share similar organizational goals, may or may not be of the same status, and may or may not share similar expectations, but at least they share an interest in exchanging views, information and, without fear, talking more candidly, People who share similar professional interests, or are exposed to similar experiences, may form more tightly structured interest groups. However, not all networks are stable. Networks are constantly being reconstructed and altered as a result of the actions of particular members. The shaping and reshaping process may not be cohesive, as individuals are constrained by organizational position and other external loyalties, and hence may act in their own interests and not necessarily in those of all of the network members.

Networks, in themselves, are not intended to compete with the formal structure of the organization. However, as networks are as much an entity as an exchange process (the stimulus to promote new views, ideas and share information is high), the emerging 'wisdom' from the network may well be the undermining of the shared views and ideals of the organization, thereby promoting a situation of split loyalties, confusion and a damaging of morale. People see the sense of the ideas and views emanating from the network and become dispirited by the rhetoric they hear from their leaders in their own organization. The very presence of networks may generate the unintended consequence of sapping the emotional energy and the will to identify with the organization, as what emerges from the network may make more sense, and being a member of the network, more attractive, than listening to, and belonging to, the formal organization.

Discordant balance between accountabilities and responsibilities

Accountabilities and responsibilities are role-related concerns. Account-abilities refer to assessing individuals on the results of their endeavours; in effect, an output concept. Responsibilities relate to the pursuit of an activity or initiative. Individuals are held responsible for something, for example, promoting a sales campaign, introducing a training programme, updating IS/IT (information technology) in the organization, or rethinking the marketing strategy of the company. However, being held responsible does not automatically mean being held accountable. Being held accountable means that a person is judged on the results of an activity – do targets and objectives reach the desired standard within the specified time frames? Organizational 'heaven' is being held responsible for certain pursuits, but not accountable. Life is fun because of the opportunity to be involved in new initiatives and interesting projects, experimenting with different approaches, and attempting to introduce new thinking and ways of behaving in the organization, without being held to account for the results. Organizational 'hell' is being held accountable, but with no responsibilities. An individual is being judged on the quality of results of certain initiatives and ventures, without necessarily having any control over the day-to-day activities of the project and/or, the project members.

With downsizing, delayering and the overall flattening of organizations, numerous roles have emerged as ill-balanced in terms of accountabilities and responsibilities. Teams which span organizational boundaries; virtual teams, namely groups which attract a mix of people and skills to a group, all of whom have different backgrounds and may rarely meet; self-managed teams and larger teams, which have grown in size due to delayering, are all prone to generating roles where there exists an imbalance between accountabilities and responsibilities, which in turn, encourages dysfunctional behaviours and attitudes.

Although the team leader may be accountable for the results of the team, it may be difficult to exert control over the team members. The team may have members from different parts of the organization, each of whom has different reporting relationships, and different accountabilities and responsibilities according to their functional role. Further, certain of the team's activities may be outsourced, so that some of the team members hold consultant status, again making it difficult to share accountabilities more proportionately. If, in addition, rules are not clearly specified, and organizational boundaries are 'fuzzy', due to the interweaving nature of straight and dotted line relationships, one person could be accountable for the output of ten or more people, each of whom has clearly allocated responsibilities, but with the boss being unable to control their activities. The team leader is totally reliant on personal influence and the effective use of tacit information to build trust and a shared identity within the group.

Where the relationships are positive and trust has been established, the experience of working as a team can be exhilarating, and the output of the team, positively astounding. Where a strong bedrock of relationships and of trust are not established, as much for personal and/or organizational demographic reasons, the experience of team-working can be destructive, and the output of the group disappointing. Overall, an imbalance between accountabilities and responsibilities has two effects, that of increasing the levels of immaturity and that of promoting cynicism.

Those who hold numerous responsibilities, but few, or no, accountabilities, naturally feel free to explore different approaches and make suggestions for improvement. However, their activities and comments may soon take on an air of unreality. Individual team members may offer views on how to improve, which make sense from their perspective, but are impractical from the team leader's viewpoint. A team leader who accepts the views of others in order to maintain a positive relationship with them, may be appraised as incompetent by his/her own boss when held to account. Team members who offer suggestions which the team leader feels unable to accept because of their unworkability, may feel offended and lose trust in their team leader. Continuing to live in an environment where few are held accountable, but many are held responsible, has the danger of generating immature behaviours and emotions, in that people are not required to face up to the 'true' value of their endeavours. All can offer 'great ideas' and suggestions, if they are not required to think through the applicability of their inspired contributions. What is worse, is that some members can be upset when their suggestions are declined. Under such circumstances, petulance within the team can become an aspect of team working.

The team leader, in turn, recognizing his/her own isolation, the level of immaturity among the team members, and also the reality of what will and will not work, may resort to more political/covert behaviours, in order to exert his/her influence over the team. Understandings and deals may be struck outside team meetings, as the supposed only way to keep people focused and on track. However, such behaviour is exhausting, promotes dissension, and can leave the team leader cynical towards colleagues, team members and the organization. Over-reliance on personal influence at the expense of balanced accountabilities and responsibilities in roles, may be effective in the short term, but is likely to promote greater division and feelings of fragmentation in the organization over the long term.

Diversity of agendas

The HR director of a well-known multi-national company approached the Cranfield management development team, requesting assistance to improve the standing, image and credibility of one of the company's more important and influential divisional directors.

> John [the divisional director] is not able to pull his team around him. If this continues, not only may he lose his job, but we could also have a business disaster around our necks. This is the time when we desperately need greater focus on sales.

One of the present authors (AK, in the capacity of consultant), agreed to see John, and found a pleasant, open, relaxed individual, who freely admitted the nature of the challenges he faced. He was also very clear about his personal future prospects, and showed great concern for his colleagues. It was difficult to imagine why this individual was facing problems with anyone.

We then began to discuss the cross-relationships at senior levels. Certain of his subordinates equally reported to the corporate centre functional directors. Further, John's drive to introduce change, although following the brief given to him by the Group CEO, was putting him in a conflict position with certain other corporate centre directors at his level. Overheads needed to be cut and it was generally recognized that certain support services needed to be repositioned within the divisions. Some of the cutting back on overheads needed to be undertaken in John's organization. It was apparent that certain members of John's team felt greater loyalty to their corporate centre functional directors, than to John, even though he was their line manager. John was aware that he was becoming known as a maverick, a non-team player, in an organization of interwoven relationships and compromises. Further investigation highlighted that a number of the corporate centre functional directors were deliberately manipulating the sentiments of the functional managers in John's team.

John's circumstances are a common experience when multiple reporting relationships and a negative culture are the norm. The original matrix thinking was of organizations where straight-line reporting relationships would be complemented by dotted-line, co-operative relationships. Today's reality has managers in circumstances where dotted-line and straight-line relationships are confused, and where managers are reporting to three or four superiors. Even if that is not the case, and the formal relationship is a dotted-line one, that is, not a straight-line boss/subordinate relationship, but one in which bosses are predisposed to influence and promote dialogue, a subordinate may feel obliged to behave or be browbeaten into behaving, as if he/she is reporting to four bosses. It is highly unlikely that 'the four bosses' would be pursuing complementary agendas, or even fully co-operating with each other, thereby placing the subordinate in a considerably difficult position, at times forcing the individual to ascribe loyalty more to one superior than another. Even then the situation does not stabilize. Within a short period of time, as much due to short-term pressures and developments particular to that organization, loyalties may shift. The outcome is diminished trust, greater fragmentation, less certainty.

Hence, diversities of agendas can occur because of:

■ the incompatible nature of certain conflicting reporting relationships as already highlighted above
■ rapid changes which lead to quickly actioned, but poorly thought through, internal restructuring. With such a development, the likelihood of internal friction increases. Senior management may ascribe the fault to particular individuals who are seen as deliberately not co-operating. However, because senior management have not thought through their situation, they may not recognize that split

loyalties and damaged relationships are due to a poorly conceived structure, or even to the behaviour of the senior managers themselves
- repeated rapid changes, which leave not only staff and management, but also senior management, mesmerized and demotivated. No-one in the organization really cares about the logic of the latest change. Instead, people attempt to continue working as before, even though reporting relationships may have changed, in the belief that the latest change will not be long lasting – 'keep your head down and the latest changes will go away' – is an often-heard comment
- a senior management being more interested in turf and territory than sales and success. Instead of appropriately restructuring the organization, too many damaging compromises are reached in order to accommodate the whims and wishes of senior, influential managers, with the end result being that a confusing pattern of reporting relationships emerge. The organization has been 'cosmetically tampered with', so that certain senior managers are able to boast that their organization is intact, whereas additional cuts are needed in order to attain greater clarity of focus
- the business of the organization itself being naturally complicated. Managing a complex organization may involve continuous interaction between the lines of manufacture, business streams organized for enhancing market penetration, local sales organization, and the involvement of central functions, such as marketing, to promote global or regional brands, which may not easily fit with the pattern of local sales, or the finance function to control spending and costs, all leading to conflicting priorities
- insensitive, independent, egoistic senior managers, who talk 'co-operation', but behave 'control and territory'.

Mixing together some or all of the above ingredients adds to the feelings of organizational fragmentation.

Demotivating impact of merit pay and performance

A considerable degree of evidence is emerging, showing that in today's more flattened, downsized and devolved structures, satisfactorily assessing pay and performance is problematic. In fact, introducing merit pay and performance has ended up demotivating people more than enthralling them, for the two following reasons.

1 Pay does not compensate for a lack of career path. The lack of a clear career structure in downsized organizations has meant that pay is the key mechanism of providing what is felt to be fair reward for employees. However, pay has been shown not only to be incapable of providing the same degree of motivational stimulation as the

expectation of pursuing a structured career, but also it cannot accommodate the need for development that career structures can. Pay is simply a reflection of the value of work undertaken. Pay cannot satisfy the developmental needs of people at work. In fact, pay does not prevent boredom, which can result if individuals are over-exposed to repeating the same behaviours, irrespective of financial reward. The British actor, Michael Crawford, who made the *Phantom of the Opera* an outstanding success on New York's Broadway, simply refused further lavish financial rewards to keep him in the show. He needed a change, and new challenge and increasing his financial rewards was no compensation.

2 Assessing merit pay is not easy, as today's more downsized, customer-responsive organizations require co-operation and team work. Unless roles are particularly clearly structured so as to be able to assess individual performance, adequately assessing a person's contribution to overall performance is difficult to demonstrate clearly. Adapting group/team-related bonuses can be as much a problem as a value. Differences in effort and contribution in a team are unlikely to be fully captured in a team bonus system. In fact, greater tension and rivalry may emerge between individuals in the same team, as they may feel aggrieved that they are being rewarded with the same amount as someone who genuinely may not have contributed to an equal degree. Team-based merit pay really only works effectively with high-performing, well-developed and accomplished teams, where the levels of trust and respect among the team members are high.

Eye off the ball

With the advent of downsized and flattened organizations, senior managers are finding it difficult continuously to pay attention to daily detail. Where managers are being held accountable for an increased number of direct reports, the need to be informed of developments within each subordinate's area of responsibility, increases. However, as much due to rapid changes, the need to pay attention to particularly demanding challenges, and the need to address morale issues, the senior manager's attention may be diverted from application to organizational detail, to focus on only particular issues.

Further, it is not unusual for a senior manager to attempt to improve sales by more focused targeting, improving relationship marketing, and motivating teams to sell. Such a period can be even more exciting, through people being given 'permission' to spend. Staff and managers spend more to make more. The discipline for cost management becomes subdued. Senior management, through concentrating on enhancing revenues may be unaware of the spending that is taking place, leaving them with the unwelcome task, at some point in the future, of re-introducing a discipline for expenditure, while the rest of the organiza-tion is geared to enhancing revenues. Not only may the people in the organization become demotivated, and resist such a discipline, but also the organization may have incurred damaging debt, through over-investment and unnecessary acquisitions. The situation will eventually require further restructuring. Naturally, people's loyalties waver, as they recall the 'good old days' of motivation, drive and achieving ever-increasing revenues.

Throwing in a wobbly

The arguments for fragmentation occurring have so far concentrated on more rational reasons. Life is rarely that clear or logical. The motivations driving individuals may be many-fold, and although any single reason for action may make sense to one individual, others can be left puzzled. Hence, the seemingly irrational nature of any one individual's actions may confuse others. People do not understand why an individual may have undertaken a certain action, because they do not share the same rationale. On this basis, any one person can use confusion to his/her advantage, or behave in an 'illogical way', simply as a way of displaying a grievance. Confusion is generated by 'throwing in a wobbly', that is to say by making a comment, or undertaking an action, that will leave others uncertain and even insecure. Manipulating circumstances where others 'wobble', could also be done for reasons of personal satisfaction. A grievance from the past is 'repaid' by doing something that will make others feel insecure. If too many wobblies are thrown in, people can come to despise their place of work – 'You should be where I work: people are just nasty!'

Way things are done here

An organization with a history and tradition, and especially one with a track record of past success, may resist change, even though change may be necessary for the survival of the enterprise. Organizations with an envious history are likely to have evolved ways of working with which its staff and management readily identify. Especially if the organization has evolved a distinct capability and attracted professionally qualified, high-performing people, the internal culture may be so strong as to be particularly resistant to change, for good reason. Such a culture and way of working was obviously beneficial in the past, and a reality check may show that to change too quickly, or even at all, may damage the fabric of the organization as it currently exists. Further, due to a shared ethos, people in the organization trust each other. The powerful controls that exist are at the 'understand level'. People know what is required of them;

they police themselves; they deal with 'misdemeanours' and even more serious 'felonies', at the local level.

As locality, 'the way things are done here', is a strong sentiment, when change occurs, people naturally explore how change will affect them, rather than fully appreciating why change may be necessary at the broader, organizational level. If change introduces unwelcome practice at the local level, people will resist – 'it is not the way things are done here'. Such exclamations are likely to be followed by a list of reasons, often historically based, as to how the existing ways of working have led to past and present success. Continued pressure to change is likely to drive people to resist even more, to the point where people take pride in rejecting change. A once proud culture is reduced to a continued state of negativity. As a result, management may feel they have no choice but to continue down their road of change, which induces yet another response, that of people leaving. To lose well-qualified and highly experienced people, especially in service organizations, may result in having only a 'shell' of a company. Staff and middle-level management are very quickly likely to become aware of top management's quandary and soon learn a new skill, that of "never buying in" – they [top management], will soon give up – look how we dealt with the last changes they tried!'

Best practice management

In effectively managing roles and relationships in order to knit together an organization of inherent diversities to pursue a meaningful direction, the following areas of best practice are highlighted.

Achieving a transactional and transformational balance

The emerging evidence from the Cranfield studies strongly suggests that daily attention needs to be given to the transactional component of leadership. The 'rough and ready' guide to emerge is that 80 per cent of a leader's time needs to be given to attending to transactional activities, while maintaining a transformational outlook (see Chapter 8 for further support of this argument, 'power of detail'). Circumstances, personalities, context and culture, all require that a number of ill-fitting demands are constantly being re-balanced. Hence, it is likely that a satisfactory balance is never attained, but always worked towards. Ken Cusack, the MD of Sorbus UK, a previously independent computer maintenance company (now Sorbus ICL), adopted a transactional strategy in order to turn his organization into a successful sales-oriented company. Every manager and engineer in the organization underwent sales training, so that all, including those who did not interface with customers, would adopt a sales philosophy, in terms of pursuing every possible opportunity. The emphasis was on attention to detail, through trying to turn all potential, chargeable jobs into contracts, paying particular attention to improving service, reducing complaints from customers, establishing internal competitive league tables which highlighted key indicators in the areas of sales, quality and productivity, and having all in the organization involved in setting and improving sales and quality targets. The initiatives worked, in that Sorbus was achieving an annual compound growth of over 30 per cent at a time of recession. Although transformational in nature, the Cusack strategy was 90 per cent or more, transactional. Particularly close attention to detail, even to the point of how many times the telephone rang, became part of the culture of the organization. An overview of the Sorbus success story highlights a substantial focus on transactional leadership. Stephen Covey's view that attention to detail means power, is borne out in the case of Sorbus, UK.

Know the people

Knowledge of the individuals in an organization, knowledge of what motivates them, and knowledge of the key opinion makers and their objectives and desires, are crucial aspects of information for leaders to possess. In constructing a pattern of desired roles and relationships, will the key opinion makers in the organization adhere to the reasons for re-structuring? Will people wish to listen to arguments concerning the broader picture, or will arguments naturally revert to 'what affects me?'

Whether the debate for clarifying and justifying the current or new purpose and direction remains at the level of broader enquiry, or deteriorates into local defensiveness, it is highly likely that all the parties involved understand the arguments being presented. Equally likely is that those who do not wish to accept a restructuring of their department or organization, are likely to be knowledgeable about the arguments for and against, and even acknowledge the reason and sense behind introducing change. A leader managing a restructuring may be seduced into thinking that because others understand the key issues in the debate, that means they accept the need for change leading to a reconfiguration of roles and will co-operate. That may not be the case! What people understand, and what they consequently do, may not coincide, for reasons of context. The experience of their context may drive people's attitudes and actions in a contrary direction to the prevailing wisdom.

Hence, the advice for leaders is, be realistic. A thorough understanding of the different contexts in the organization, with an appreciation of the more powerful individuals, allows the leader to introduce and pursue change more realistically. For further insights into how to manage contexts and personalities, see Chapters 2, 3 and 4.

Support the people

Change brings about disruption, which in turn can engender negativity and demotivation in people. A particularly effective way to re-energize staff and managers is for the boss to show an interest in, and to spend time with them. People need time with their senior manager to explore how best to adjust, question and re-examine why roles and structures have changed. Most of all, the time given to individuals and teams by senior managers confirms that management are truly behind the reconfiguration that has taken place. Through spending time together and paying attention to learning, trust is established between staff and middle-level managers and the leaders of the organization. The interest and sincerity of senior management, crucial elements to trust building, are exhibited through making oneself available to staff and management during critical periods. (For further analysis of how attention to detail helps build trust, see Chapter 8, especially the section, 'Passion for results'.)

Build winning teams

Knowing the merits and desires, the drawbacks and strong points of key individuals surrounding a leader, provides the advantage of setting the basis for creating high performing teams. Appreciating how the personalities blend together needs, also, to be coupled with identifying clear goals for the team.

Clarity of goals provides for successful accomplishment, even though the task at hand may be challenging, even daunting. Clarity and focus motivate. People know where they are going. Add to that, effectiveness of communication, and people will then know why they are asked to pursue certain targets. Ambiguity of goals shrouds purpose and can give rise to misinterpretation, which if unheeded, may generate animosity and team disintegration.

Ambiguity over daily tasks need not, however, induce demotivation. Once people know where they are going and why, needing to rethink how to accomplish tasks may prove to be a stimulating challenge. If relationships among the team members are positive, then the supportive nature of their context turns the most demanding task-oriented challenges into stimulating learning experiences. However, even if relationships are strained, ambiguity at a task level is still manageable, if goals and team purpose are clear.

A friend, who in a previous career was a professional soccer player, recalled a tale of two of Liverpool Football Club's (UK) most exciting strikers, Kevin Keegan and John Toshack. The two used to tear opposition defences apart, seemingly playing with such understanding and being unselfish in their use of the ball, that most people assumed them to be the best of friends. 'Not so', was the friend's declaration. Apparently, the two disliked each other. The atmosphere in the dressing-room was sometimes overwhelmingly tense due to the sharp words the two exchanged off-the-field. 'But the two were real professionals,' explained our friend, 'Nothing got in the way of scoring goals.'

The Keegan/Toshack story highlights that clarity of purpose and trust of the professionalism of others to find ways to overcome daily hindrances and ambiguities, can overcome personal tensions. It is preferable, of course, if people can 'get on'.

In addition to ensuring the clarity of focus and goals, a current trend is that of empowering groups through creating self-managed teams. The concept, is not new; for self-regulatory teams were introduced into English coal mines in the 1950s, popularized through the Volvo initiatives in Scandinavia in the 1960s and 1970s, were to be found in the USA, particularly in the Gaines Dog Food Plant, Kansas, and in the worker/management collaboratively driven organizations in Yugoslavia and Spain in the 1960s and 1970s. Through the more recent influence of Japanese-inspired quality circles, the topic has reached world prominence.

Self-managed teams refer to more formal and 'permanent' organizational units that typically consist of four or five or more members working together on an ongoing, day-to-day basis, but running their own affairs. Empowerment fundamentally requires team members to execute similar levels of responsibility and accountability as those ascribed to their former supervisors. Empowered teams may be tasked to deliver an entire product or service, with little or no supervision. In order to achieve such levels of performance, team members, in self-managed teams, need to gather and synthesize information, act on it, and take collective responsibility for their actions. To be able to carry out the tasks required of them, they need to display a variety of skills, which can be as much learnt on-the-job, through rotating tasks.

However, any group of people needs time to develop into an effectively performing team. Being given too much responsibility, too quickly, without sufficient time to grow into the job, can be damaging. At the start, a collection of individuals need to learn how to work together, to make decisions, to resolve conflicts, and to delegate roles. The members of the team need to feel sufficiently comfortable with their surroundings, so as to learn from mistakes. In effect, people are becoming more accustomed not only to accepting responsibility, but also to being held accountable for the results of their endeavours. Facing up to challenges and being honest about where the 'buck stops', is crucial to the future of an effectively performing self-managed unit. Such experiences enhance the maturing necessary for working towards greater team effort, which usually induces enthusiasm and excitement among its members. With proper guidance and support, a team can move on to being self-managed, whereby team members encourage one another, share information, work together to overcome obstacles, and are proficient in exploration and debate, essential precursors to quality decision-making. For a self-managed team to function effectively, all members of the team need to undergo the same stretching experience.

As the team psychologically grows, so too must staff and managers in the organization respect the new circumstances. Senior management, and in particular the CEO, need to display their trust in these more capably managed units. An improved quality of dialogue may need to evolve, not only top-down, but also laterally. As the impact of these new units is likely to reverberate powerfully throughout the enterprise, the whole organization will be required to understand how the company defines empowerment. In order to do so, empowerment needs to be identified as an integral element of mission and strategy. The questions to ask are: What is the organization's mission? How does the mission relate to overall business strategy? And, in turn, how does that relate to the goals of the team? And within that context, what is the true meaning of empowerment? In order for team members to accept accountability and responsibility, they need to have a clear understanding of what the organization expects of them. Sincerely applied empowerment redistributes responsibility and accountability for debate, decisions and actions throughout the organization. The act of introducing empowerment generates new values. For empowerment to really work, top management, in particular, must be committed to the organization's new values. Regardless of the quality or quantity of training, and on-the-job development, self-managed teams cannot be effective without the support of senior management.

The advantages of effectively functioning self-management teams are that team members are motivated to push for even higher levels of performance, while at the same time having the maturity to 'police' themselves, reduce costs, and keep on target. There are, however, certain downsides that need consideration. If the leadership of the organization has not defined desired boundaries, a 'blank cheque' mentality can arise. People are given the feeling that they can do as they please. The situation is one of promoting responsibility without any accompanying accountability, resulting in considerably irresponsible behaviour. Within such an environment, if someone wants something, he/she tries to get it. If such members are refused, they assume their manager is negative, is not in keeping with the times, and hence, someone who should be encouraged to leave.

Not fitting in and being seen as outside the current vogue, give rise to a further disadvantage of self-managed teams, and that is the nastiness of political correctness. Political correctness can encourage aggressive and defensive behaviour in managers and employees alike. People who do not fit can be pressurized to leave. Further, the moment that sensitive and embarrassing problems arise, senior management may become defensive or adopt unduly upbeat social behaviour, in order to project the right image and to deflect the conversation away from the topic that is perceived as threatening. Although by so doing individuals are protecting themselves, they would rarely acknowledge that this is the case. In the name of being positive, individuals will imply that they are protecting the group, the department, or their organization. In the meantime, conflicts are ignored, damaging and poor practice continues and morale and motivation slip.

An additional negative outcome of poorly empowered teams is groupthink, when unreal, even dangerous decisions, are made by people blind to the consequences of their actions, because of the lack of sharp debate in the group. Harvard University Professor Chris Argyris's study of 6000 people suggests that gender, ethnicity, identity, education, wealth, power and experience are no shield against defensive behaviour. He argues that, 'all over the world, in every kind of business and organization, and in every kind of crisis and dilemma, when defensiveness arises, people are in danger of leaving their own behaviour unexamined and of avoiding any objective test of their assumptions and conclusions'.[8]

In organizations ambitious for the promotion of self-managed teams, but living within a context of role diversity and fragmentation, leadership which combines clear boundary management, supported by a bedrock of positive behaviours and ethics, provides the inspiration for positive team-work.

Repeat the message

For the purposes of clarity and affirmation, as a leader, repeat the message. Spell out the shape and nature of the organization. Spell out what is required of individuals in terms of basic and added value contributions. Spell out what is required from people in order to make the existing, or new structure, work. Then repeat the message and if necessary repeat it once more and if still required, yet again. Repeating the message provides for clarity. Others in the organization have an opportunity to question, rethink and equally recognize possible problem areas which require further clarification. As people learn iteratively, people need time to comprehend, digest and recognize how to adapt their thinking and behaviour to new circumstances, especially if the parameters surrounding their jobs have changed.

As repeating the message clarifies and, in so doing allows for the opportunity of further learning on the job, the process equally affirms the interest of senior management in day-to-day progress. It becomes clear that senior management are firmly behind their statements and are in no mood to be diverted from actioning these, or to enter into energy-sapping compromises. Repeating the message emphasizes clarity of direction and strength of purpose.

Cut through

Once all has been said and discussed, action is required. If resistance is being experienced, it is important that senior management cut through diversions, and focus on making the desired role structure and relationship interactions pursue management's desired pathway.

Cutting through involves two processes, follow-through and cutting through opposition. Follow-through is the application of discipline to ensure that new or existing projects and initiatives are suitably tracked, and problems and issues arising, resolved, before the situation becomes too dramatic. Hence, negotiating with colleagues and subordinates concerning what and how to follow through, can be a substantially motivating experience for staff and middle management. The interest of senior management in wishing to be kept informed of how others are performing is obvious. Effective follow-through can naturally enthuse people to work to improve performance from one meeting to the next.

Cutting through opposition and diversion, is a different process. Cutting through is more directive and less participative. When everything has been said, agreed and re-agreed, yet still the necessary courses of action are not being pursued, then do just what is required, and demand the same of others. Under positive circumstances, effective debate and discussion are likely to lead to clarity and commitment from others to pursue what senior management desire. However, debate and discussion can be turned into a time-wasting, energy-sapping experience of ensuring that whatever senior management wish to do, does not become a reality. Under such circumstances, there is little point in further dialogue, as the two parties are on different wavelengths, and the words between them hold little or no meaning. Hence, cut through! – get others to do what is needed of them, irrespective of how they feel or what they say.

Cutting through may be necessary, but it must also be skilfully applied. Cutting through undermines the giving of feedback, not just in the immediate circumstances, but also in the future. Subordinates may be unwilling to offer further views because they feel senior management are not interested, or are even irritated, and punitive in their response to feedback. Subordinates fear that giving feedback may end up with 'shooting the messenger'. In turn, senior management may feel the feedback they are receiving is irrelevant, or even meant to sidetrack them from the pursuit of the 'real issues'. That may well be true, but it can leave an unpleasant atmosphere in the organization. Cutting through has the advantage of speed of results, but also the drawback of leaving behind a demotivated and anxious organization. The recommendation is that cutting through, if used, should be used sparingly.

Key points summary

- A fundamental aspect of leadership is the paying of detailed attention to the management of daily affairs, particularly in the area of goal setting.
- Effectively pursuing direction involves, in addition to clarity of goals, paying attention to morale and the quality of co-operation within teams and groups and among various sections of the organization, in order to ensure that people keep on track, share responsibilities and support each other in achieving targets.

Historical overview

- In examining goal-setting, goal-attaining and effective co-operation and interrelationships, a historical overview of the area is undertaken through an examination of the works of key writers of management and leadership, and of those concepts that have been powerfully influential.
- Henri Fayol's contribution identifies the five primary managerial tasks of leaders, namely, forecasting and planning, organizing the enterprise, commanding, co-ordinating and controlling. His thesis is that attention to all five tasks would ensure that the enterprise achieved its goals.
- Chester Barnard's premise emphasizes that positive co-operation and effective communication are fundamental to the continued functioning of an organization. Having established what he considered as the crucial organizational parameters, Barnard specified the key functions of the executive, required to maintain and enhance the organization, as the maintenance of organization communication, the securing of essential services from individuals, and the formulation of purpose and objectives.
- Mary Parker Follett's thesis highlights the vital need for the continuous integration of people, if the organization is to achieve its targets successfully. In drawing attention to the people component of leadership, she offers four fundamental principles of good organization: co-ordination by direct contact; co-ordination in the early stages; co-ordination as a reciprocal process; and co-ordination as a continuous process. In attaining 'integrative unity', openness of dialogue between individuals would be achieved, which Follett considers a vital component.
- The early pioneers of management and leadership thinking were succeeded by the structuralist theorists, whose view was that through clarity of logic, and with agreeing to a single rationale, the ideal organization could be created. The elements of the ideal organization are, a clear purpose and goals, clarity of structural configuration and

pursuing an optional path in decision-taking and decision-making, bearing in mind the nature of the decision to be reached and the environment in which decisions have to be taken and applied.

Fragmentation

■ Latterly, research and experience emphasize fragmentation and devisiveness as prevalent in organizations.

■ Fragmentation is considered to occur because of the multiple challenges leaders have to address. Managerial work is identified as consisting of numerous, at times, ill-fitting activities, requiring substantial interpretation as to which task or activity to pursue, thus opening the possibility of different course of action to be pursued. The impact of IT communications allows individuals to bypass organizational levels in order to access those people they desire to contact. Also, networks can have a divisive impact, as people's loyalties may be challenged. Further, distortion can take place, as certain roles may be poorly balanced in terms of accountabilities and responsibilities, which can arise through re-structuring, through the introduction of poorly conceived empowerment programmes, and through attempts to motivate staff and more junior managers by increasing their responsibilities without attending to their accountabilities, thereby, for any one or more of these reasons, leaving senior management exposed to possible immature and petulant behaviour. Fragmentation can also occur because of people pursuing diverse and wide-ranging agendas in the organization. Another reason for dissonance is that resulting from poorly designed merit pay systems. In addition, dissension in an organization can occur through people deliberately being negative and damaging, and through the impact of a 'strong' culture resisting change. Under such pressures, leaders may react in different ways as they apply different skills and approaches to different challenges, thus emphasizing the turbulent nature of organizations. With so much pressure and challenge, leaders can be so stretched that they find it difficult to pay full attention to the daily management of routine and detail, and hence, their control of day-to-day activities is eroded.

Best practice

Best practice management for leaders is considered to involve:

■ balancing the transactional and transformational elements of the leader's role, bearing in mind the need to be attentive to detail, and also the contrasting need for flexibility to adjust constantly to new challenges, changing circumstances and the influence of internal and external stakeholders,

■ appreciating the overall nature of the organization, and the needs of individuals and groups within the enterprise, so as to be more informed as to how to respond appropriately to different challenges

■ supporting staff and management through difficult periods,

■ building strong, professional, externally focused team identities, where individuals are sufficiently mature not only to accept responsibility, but to be held to account for their performance and results, and to work with the ambiguity of co-operating and interfacing with people who may not hold similar objectives, but whose involvement is required in order to meet objectives successfully,

■ if necessary, repeating the same message, in order to clearly establish the path to pursue, and the need for co-operation and discipline,

■ not being side-tracked into addressing less important issues, but having the personal drive to cut through resistance, if all other best practice measures are considered to be ineffective.

Notes

1 Adapted from Pugh *et al.* (1973).
2 Quote from Pugh *et al.* (1973:66).
3 Ibid.
4 Ibid.
5 Adapted from Pugh *et al.* (1973:69).
6 Ibid., p.103.
7 Adapted from Kakabadse *et al.* (1987).
8 Argyris (1994:81).

Further reading

For a historical perspective, Henri Fayol (1916) can be read in the original or in the translated version by Catherine Storrs (1949); see also Chester Barnard (1938; 1948) and Mary Parker Follett (1920; 1924). For further reading on the founders of management thinking and theory, Pugh, *et al.* (1973), and Pugh and Hickson (1993) provide a thorough grounding.

Particularly prominent in the area of organization structures are L. F. Urwick (1947) and Wilfred Brown (1960). In addition, see Sir Geoffrey Vickers (1983), whose contribution was to identify and popularize the four structural configurations of functional, product/services, divisional and matrix. For a more structured view of decision-making/taking, read Vroom and Yetton (1973). Interesting work examining the 'dark' side of empowerment and self-managed work groups is that by Argyris (1994).

For more information on the disruptive experience of managing in today's organization, read Henry Mintzberg (1973) and Rosemary Stewart

(1982). Further works of interest include Carlson (1951) and Semler (1993).

For further information on self-managed teams, read Barry (1991), and for a historical view of self-managed teams, read Trist *et al.* (1963). For self-managed teams popularized in Scandinavia, see Bolweg (1976), the self-managed teams concept applied in the USA, see Ketchum (1992) and in Japan, see Sundstrom *et al.* (1990).

Covey *et al.* (1994) cover goal-setting and the character of stakeholders.

For additional information on how information systems (IS) and information technology (IT) impact on leadership and the organization, see Huber (1990) for an examination of the decentralization/centralization argument, Korac-Boisvert (1993) for an examination of the broader issues concerning the impact of IT on organization structure, Korac-Kakabadse and Korac-Kakabadse (1997) for the manner in which leadership behaviour influences IT applications and Boettinger (1989) for an examination of the blurring of role boundaries.

For an examination of how networks are of fundamental influence to the running of an organization, see White (1992), and for the manner in which relationships are formed, crucial for the continuance of the network, see Burt (1990).

CHAPTER 2

Knowing Your Way Through Culture

Case analysis

Cultural tales

A chemical view of foreigners

Prior to the merger of Glaxo and the Wellcome Foundation, which made the new company (Glaxo Wellcome) one of the world's leading drug companies, employing over 54,000 people and spending over £1 billion on R&D, an interview was held with James Cochrane, who then held the position of Director of European Operations, Wellcome plc.

A. My role is dealing with all operations of Wellcome in Europe, and that involves the making of drugs, the clinical trial of drugs and the selling of drugs.

Q. Could you give me some sort of view as to the total budget size . . . that you are describing?

A. We've got annual European sales of the order of £700 million. We've got 5000 people overall, with manufacturing in four countries, and we've got operations and subsidiaries in virtually every country, including some of the Eastern European countries. Essentially, we have a representation everywhere in all the sophisticated countries in the world and also we've got agreements in the unsophisticated countries in the world . . .

Q. How does the business operate culturally?

A. We provide brands to a variety of customers, but our business has been changing quite dramatically over the last few years. Our principal customers used to be doctors. Doctors made the decision as to what they were going to prescribe . . . Today, we are now talking about a whole range of customers, with doctors probably the most important customers. For others of our customers, like government, we are not promoting brands, we are promoting healthcare concepts, value for money, outcomes and cost benefits . . . Ten, fifteen years ago, doctors wrote a prescription and the pharmacist gave to the patient what the doctor had written on the prescription. The wholesaler was merely the chain in the middle. He ordered from us, the manufacturers, and supplied it to the pharmacists, and governments paid the bill. That has now dramatically changed. Governments are now telling doctors what they can and cannot prescribe; patients are now refusing to take the medicines the doctors have prescribed them . . . You walk into a pharmacy with a prescription which says a particular product and the chemist is then changing it, under various regulations, to something different from what the doctor has written. So the chemist is a customer, a stakeholder . . .

The questions then proceeded to explore how Wellcome was structured to meet the challenge of the changing customer profile, and how management responded to the prospect of having to run the company somewhat differently to the manner in which it had previously been led.

Q. In your meetings, how would you describe the manner in which the key interfaces are handled?

A. I treat . . . the cultures differently. I treat an Italian operation in a different way to that of a French one. The culture of medicine in Italy is different to that of France. You can see that what is acceptable in Italy is not acceptable in France. So I think there are two sorts of levels that I would respond to your question on interfacing, on an individual basis – dealing with an Italian problem, I would try and have an Italian solution; I would respect and try and understand what works in Italy, what matters in Italy, to the Italian government, to Italian doctors and Italian distribution chains, which is different to what happens in other countries – then at the European level, I would have informal groups and task forces. We would have regular meetings of these groups to exchange European strategies and European concepts, but I would never impose on an individual country, a concept that I felt was not going to work in that country.

The conversation continued to explore best practice and the sharing of best practice in the corporation.

Q. Are there reasons why there may be resistance to best practice?

A. A Belgian will never love a Frenchman. A Frenchman will never love a Belgian . . . it's a natural characteristic, so what I try and do . . . is to ensure that we have enough team-building type meetings, which are not all business related, where you will talk through the

European strategy, and then have dinner afterwards. I find these enormously valuable, because a lot of mutual trust and respect comes from these sorts of meetings . . . The Belgian finds that the Frenchman is not as bad as he thought he was, but it does take time. You have to build it up, and you cannot do it overnight . . . To try and create that openness . . . can only be built over time . . . It is important to understand that the practice of medicine is so different in different countries, and unless you take that into account, you won't understand the business. For example, in France, for a woman to undergo a hysterectomy is seen as virtually immoral, whereas in other countries, hysterectomies are seen as fairly normal procedures. In the USA, constant diagnosis is important, but that would not be the way that doctors in Spain and Portugal would go about their particular business. So in distribution channels, little things like, there are no hysterectomies conducted in France unless it is absolutely essential, must be taken into account.

Best of the British mandarins

Interview with Sir Terry Burns, Permanent Secretary to the Treasury, Her Majesty's Government, Great Britain.

A. . . . there is really quite a substantial, 'upstairs–downstairs' climate within the organization and quite a lot of resentment as you come down it, with people who feel they are not highly valued by the people they are working for; they are not consulted; they are not told about what is happening; their advice is not sought about how to do the job, and they think they would do the job better if they had the opportunity to make a contribution . . . It is a very old organization. It does things in a particular way and changes relatively slowly . . . at a time when we are looking to bring about substantial change. We are having a fundamental expenditure review. All of that is very unsettling and it brings out, not surprisingly, some of these fears.

Q. . . . For those . . . who are managing the Treasury, have they been more responsible for some of these demotivating incentives, or has it really been out of your control?

A. Well, they vary. Market testing, which is an aspect of government policy which affects substantial groups of people, is an issue as you work down the organization. It is enormously threatening to the people concerned . . . To a large extent, that is something outside our control. The issues to do with the reputation of the Treasury, the barrage of criticism I spoke about, is a very difficult issue. It involves complex relationships, particularly about who is responsible for what. What has been within our control is that we decided about two years ago, to look at the Treasury and ask ourselves whether it was correctly structured for the job it had to do . . . Since then, we have been engaged in the process of trying to identify ways in which it should change . . . The Fundamental Expenditure Review is also something that is part of government policy, something that we have to do alongside other departments, but we have chosen to use it to reinforce the process of change . . . We are engaged in three substantial issues . . . We are trying to identify the job we should be doing, how we should be doing it, the types of relationships we have with other departments, and how to avoid doing low value work . . . The second issue is trying to make it a better place to work. We have a lot of very old-fashioned command and control systems for personnel management . . . The third is trying to improve our relations with the outside world. Up to now, the Treasury has been isolated. It works through other organizations all the time and it has tended to leave it to other organizations to handle the interface with the outside world . . . Historically, the Treasury has been an under-managed organization. It is composed of a large number of units of people who are dealing with various clients in the outside world . . . The whole pattern of the Treasury has been one of getting people in, and doing the policy job with the resources being controlled centrally. In a sense, they are rather like SAS units who see that they have a clear job to do and they have got to get on and do it, but they don't want to be fussed about where the money comes from, or the concerns of their staff. They look to the centre of the department to do all that. They do not see their job really as a management job . . . This explains the feeling which you get, as you go down the organization, of a lack of caring and lack of concern for them as people . . . So we have the structure to try and put more of this work out to a number of directors . . . and try to get the management of the policy groups to spend more of their time doing what people think are managerial tasks.

Q. Is this sort of extension of responsibility at the 'understood' level or is it at a written level?

A. We have been trying to develop a view of what the responsibilities of the directors are, but so far we have not yet got below that into assessment procedures . . . The big challenge is whether this really will be a significant feature in terms of people's pay and promotional prospects. People are quite cynical. Often they will say, 'you say this is the behaviour you want to see, but when it comes to the crunch, the people who get promoted are still the people who are best able to help ministers out of a difficult corner, rather than those people who are going to run, or motivate teams of people' . . . we are not the only people who have this . . . the law, the accountancy business, the consultancy business . . . The challenge is how you manage professionals, and the weight that is given to the professional aspect of their work, and the weight that is given to their management skills . . . I think there is a lot more we can do to learn from the experiences of the past. Typically, Treasury people take on challenges, almost impossible tasks, and by one means or another actually manage to produce something. They will move quickly from one subject to the next, at extraordinarily short notice . . . they are very clever and quick – quick to see where problems are emerging, and quick to see where the weaknesses are . . . But the process of learning from these experiences are not institutionalized . . . So you have a lot of people giving you lots of stories about how it could all be done better, and almost a prediction of how the same kinds of problems will emerge again in other circumstances. Often it seems like a system without feedback. It does not generate the signal for the individual to take action, to help avoid the problem from happening next time.

Two different top directors, who face different challenges, talking about two different organizations. However, central to the theme of their conversations is culture of organization. James Cochrane identifies three themes of culture, ethnic culture (Belgian, French, Italian), the culture of medicine as practised in different countries, and the culture of the European organization of the Wellcome Foundation. His thesis of first understand the culture of medicine as practised in each country, then focus the organization and its management to discuss and address the business cultural issues of each country, places the topic of ethnic culture third in rank order of challenges to overcome. His view of the Belgian and Frenchman, eventually understanding each other, and working better together if they openly talk and share ideas and experience, places ethnic culture in the category of the easiest pressure point to change.

In contrast, Terry Burns identifies two themes, old Treasury culture/ new Treasury culture, and professional and managerial ways of working. In order to progress from the old to the new culture, the Treasury must change from being solely a professionally driven, values organization, to one which will inculcate managerial values into its *esprit de corps*. Although for both organizations different attributes of culture are described – which over time need to evolve and change and which in turn will generate new pressures and diversities – both men emphasize one point, the power, influence and dominance of culture. Having to contend with such an all-pervading influence, it is important to ask, just what is culture?

Through people living and working together, certain attributes, such as behaviour, feelings, attitudes and views of life, become shared. These shared attributes are the foundation of the culture of an organization. In turn the culture within which people live, work and interact, in itself becomes a powerful determinant of the attitudes, values, views of individuals, their ability to distinguish appropriate from inappropriate ways of behaving, and the people to become close to and the people from whom to shy away. Culture refers to the place where people sit (or stand) to do their work; the place where an individual will hang up his/her coat; the place where people spend considerable time, and in turn are developed or inhibited by the experience. The more individuals pursue particular ways of doing, thinking and feeling, the more strengthened is the identity of the culture. As the fundamentals of transactional leadership are to 'make the workplace work better', it is a prerequisite to direct time and attention to one aspect of best practice, namely, get to 'know your place intimately and then shape it to what you want'. In effect, the argument is double-sided. The more the culture influences individuals, the more individuals can shape and determine their culture.

The themes pursued in this chapter are twofold. First, an analysis of the different interpretations of culture is undertaken, namely those forces that shape and mould an organization, or nation state. Second, from a broad overview of culture, attention is then given to examining ways of influencing processes and events in cultures. From the wider examination of organizational identity, to a 'what does one do?' analysis to improve elements of the organization, the essence of transactional leadership is specified – appreciate the broader parameters, but then know how to manage and interact effectively within particular circumstances.

Analysing culture

Culture can be viewed as the sum of the shared values and beliefs people in the organization hold, the shared assumptions they have made and will continue to make, the shared philosophies and ideologies with which they identify, and which they pursue. In fact, culture is all those aspects of living and working together which emerge from interacting in particular contexts, which in turn become the overall norms to which people relate and which bind them together as a community. *Norms* are a key dimension to consider in analysing culture. Norms may be positive in inclination, in that people in the organization feel comfortable about speaking openly, feel secure in being more adventurous to pursue new approaches to problem-solving, and be innovative in their thinking and actions which challenges the status quo, but equally moves the organization forward. Equally, certain cultures can be the result of an accumulation of accepted ways of doing things (norms) which are inhibitory, whereby few in the organization feel comfortable enough to challenge their bosses and colleagues for fear of being seen as difficult or 'trouble makers', and hence are less likely to be innovative for fear of punitive retaliation if seen to make mistakes. An analysis of culture identifies the parameters and boundaries which highlight the acceptable and unacceptable behaviours and attitudes desired by the majority community within the organization or nation state.

Cultural norms, however, are not static. People's attitudes and expectations change over time, making *orientation to change* a second dimension of culture. The experiences that mould and re-mould people's perspectives towards change, include:

■ *the founder of the organization*, and the powerful impact the founder makes in terms of emphasizing very particular attributes, such as distinct skills, level of energy, drive, commitment and loyalty from staff, and the focus and determination to succeed, as is the case with the founder of Dell computers. A strong leader provides the dream which gives the organization a distinctive clarity and a strong sense of purpose, and which is reinforced through particular patterns of socialization – working together, getting to know each other, supporting each other – all of which are clear signals of each person's commitment to that community.

■ *the period following the succession of the founder* that can be extremely disruptive to the organization, as the quest for re-defining old values, establishing new values and preserving the 'best of the past' are processes pursued concurrently. Such was the case of Wilf McGuinness, the unfortunate manager of Manchester United soccer club, who following the legendary Matt Busby, lead the club into decline and to his abrupt departure. It took a succession of managers to 'get rid' of some of the old players and staff, who supposedly, were holding the club back from its pursuit of the glory trail. Few organizations comfortably find their way through these pressures. Internal strife and split loyalties are likely to emerge. In the worst of cases, candidates for senior roles may be judged by the degree to which they strongly proclaim the traditional (i.e. the founder's) values, and the strength of support they have negotiated among their following.

■ *diversification, in terms of new products or services*, which promotes excitement, challenge and a new focus. Apart from the motivational stimulus that new product development engenders, it is equally likely that new views and attitudes will emerge, as the organization recruits people of a different skill base, to pursue a new purpose. Another aspect of diversification is that of geographic expansion, which can provide equal challenge and stimulus, and the emergence of new cultures of a more regional nature, in addition to those which may take less heed of the centre. Geographic diversification is likely to nurture a norm of 'challenge head office'. The question that may be asked in the region is, 'what are we really getting in return for paying head office costs?' – 'do we need to be part of this organization, or are we just the unfortunate casualties of the shackles of history?' Geographic expansion goes hand in hand with challenging the source of authority, the centre of the organization.

- *proceeding towards globalization*, which can grow a strong, singular company culture, into a diverse, broadened, international culture. Due to the need for not only standardization of products, but also sophisticated branding of products, the pursuit of globalization can generate a comprehensive set of norms across regions and lines of business which are far stronger than the influence of the original local brand or ethnic culture. Coca-Cola and McDonald's are examples of two, strong, single-brand-driven businesses that exhibit substantial similarities across their various international locations. In contrast, where globalization does not provide for an overarching unity of culture, tension exists between the global product organizations and local or regional product companies. Local brand managers may choose, or be driven by, the preferences of their regional centre, as to which products should be given greater attention at any one point in time. The international drinks company, International Distillers and Vintners (IDV), have global brands such as Smirnoff Vodka and Bailey's Irish Cream as part of their portfolio of products, but which are accompanied by numerous regional and local brands, such as Kenya Gold. The pull/push nature of the debate as to which brands should really be given preference, may make the relationship between the Centre and local marketing/brand companies tense and difficult to manage, the point emphasized by James Cochrane in the case analysis at the beginning of this chapter.

- *acquisitions and mergers* that drive the parent organization to integrate the new culture, namely the staff and management who are likely to hold substantially different attitudes and views on current issues and future direction, with its own staff and management, who may resistantly hold onto their own views and protect their own culture. To not integrate is tantamount to losing the newly acquired investment. Poor integration is likely to result in people leaving which, especially for a service organization, could be disastrous, as the current stock of staff and managers are the lifeblood of the organization. However, to try to integrate too quickly would mean losing the highly capable people from the parent organization, upon whom effective integration may depend. The situation could deteriorate to one of unworkable tension. Such were the challenges facing the UK brewing company, Bass, in their acquisition of the worldwide franchise for the hotel group, Holiday Inns. However, under the able leadership of Sir Ian Prosser, not only were their problems minimized, but further, Bass has become an impressive international business organization.

■ *the impact of restructuring*, which often results in re-engineering and downsizing, and which can be experienced as turmoil, accompanied by loss of organizational identity, and the discarding of certain established processes. By implication, the new systems introduced will generate norms, values and ways of working which people may find inhibiting and unwelcome. In order to enforce the new ways, a period of 'political correctness' may be necessary, during which, how people speak and behave will be formally and informally judged according to newly established criteria. Despite the undesired nature of such changes, at least an opportunity exists to revitalize the organization and its surviving staff and management.

■ *the introduction of new technology* which can result in communications improving, so that internal and external stakeholders' requests can be dealt with more speedily. As a result, a number of staff and management are likely to be required to upgrade their skills in order to learn to work the new IT. Individuals who resist re-learning or find re-learning too difficult, may leave the organization. Equally, certain process-oriented administrative jobs will no longer be required, adding to change being experienced as turmoil.

■ *becoming old*, 'dining out' on previous glories and by so doing, constraining innovation, which is an experience many organizations face, as much due to the maturing of markets, as through attempts to create an internal stability, which unfortunately results in stagnation. In order to break out of this mould, an extreme version of re-engineering may be introduced, whereby most of the senior management are removed, a new management is put in place, and coercive persuasion becomes the underlying, prime lever for the change of culture.

Hence, cultural progression can be incremental, whereby through step-wise change, essential values and practices are preserved, or in terms of dramatic change, which is likely to involve turmoil and a substantial number of key people being replaced.

A third dimension of culture is that, despite all else, certain norms can become so deep-seated that they occupy a position, and these the American professor, Ralph Kilman, calls *hidden assumptions*. Essentially, hidden assumptions are the fundamental and deeply held ways of thinking, feeling and doing which instinctively drive people in the organization to react to circumstances and challenges without, at times, explicitly knowing why they have so reacted. Hidden assumptions, in a cultural sense, are those shared instincts operating below a level of immediate consciousness, which people in the organization may experience as their 'normality'. Hidden assumptions can be so deeply rooted that such instincts survive change.

The sum of the norms, passions and identities that drive culture, has a distinct impact on people's perceptions of *time*. Perception of time, the fourth dimension of culture, is likely to influence decision-making, decision implementation, and the quality of completion of projects, ventures and activities. A statement sometimes heard is, 'in this organization we are fast and efficient – we get things done quickly'. Certain shared norms drive people to respect speed, namely 'quick-time'. In contrast, other shared norms, irrespective of what is said, drive people to hold different assumptions about time, whereby 'slow time' is valued. With slow time, people confer, check out, take their time and, even deliberately, do not increase their speed. Quick-time cultures are less likely to respect conferring and sharing. Quick-time cultures value entrepreneurial ways of working, with staff and management challenging decisions if the direction provided is not suited to the external market or community environment. The irony is that people in both quick and slow-time cultures value achieve results, but may strongly assert that effectiveness of results can be achieved only by their way.

The fifth dimension of culture is *homogeneity*, or the lack of it. Certain cultures are tight-knit, whereas others are more individualistic, exhibiting less sharing of attitudes and norms. The lack of homogeneity may be due to the fact that the forces that shape attitudes and values in one locality, may be different in other parts of the organization. These differences could be the result of external pressures. Different markets require different products or standards of service from the organization. Hence, different outlets in the organization become accustomed to providing different standards of service and attention to external stakeholders. Further, different regions may value different behaviours and manners of interaction. The Greeks can be considered friendly and outgoing, and judge others by similar standards. However, New Yorkers, who are popularly seen as expressive, assertive and quick, may bear little similarity to other Americans on the eastern seaboard. Hence, in order to relate, senior managers need to consider how to adjust their approach to suit the local temperament. An additional and third powerful driver of levels of homogeneity in any one organization is budgets. The constraints or freedom provided by budgets can generate multiple identities in an organization. Providing tight financial control requires people who are focused, disciplined and value 'driving things through' in order to manage the organization. In contrast, leading an enterprise which is financially decentralized, and budgeting is more 'bottom up',

requires flexibility, co-operation and understanding from its management. Even then, the influence of budgets may not be consistent across
the organization, varying by region, lines of business and/or by the
revenue and cost targets set by the centre.

Certain organizations take pride in proclaiming their individualistic
nature, as it displays flexibility and an enviable capability to integrate
differing identities, which together shape a powerful, successful,
forward-thinking organization. Other organizations would consider
displaying multiple values and attitudes as a sign of damaging weakness.
Whatever split identities may exist in an organization, it is important for
the management of the organization to ensure that the external world
sees a united front, a shared sense of purpose, and a total commitment to
the betterment of the enterprise.

Analysing organizations according to the five dimensions of norms,
orientation to change, hidden assumptions, time, and homogeneity, can
produce a picture of those organizations which resist change, some
which experience turbulence, others which require their members to
display loyalty and unity actively, and still others which may simply
require their employees to be efficient in their work.

Certain practitioners and researchers have concentrated on drawing
together different strands of cultures common to particular organizations
or nations, and have emerged with a single-culture concept. Others adopt
the view that multiple cultures exist in any organization or nation, and
offer a relativist view of culture. In attempting to understand culture
better, the five dimensions of culture will be applied to the single-culture
concept and to the relativist, multi-cultural concept. In the subsequent
tables in this chapter, the five dimensions of culture will be analysed in
the following order, norms (termed visibly shared), orientation to change,
hidden assumptions (termed deeply rooted), attitude to time and
homogeneous/individualistic.

Single-culture concept

The single-culture concept has been applied at both the level of
organization as typified by the Treasury example (traditional and
professional), and the level of nation. The works of two key writers are
highlighted, those of Roger Harrison and of Geert Hofstede.

Culture at the level of organization

An immense array of books and articles has been produced on the theme
of culture. The vast majority of texts, discuss the themes of values and
attitudes, offering guidance on ways of analysing culture, but without
specifying particular categories of culture. One writer, Roger Harrison
has offered a categorization of different cultural forms at the level of

organization, namely power, role, task and person cultures. Harrison, although offering his ideas in the 1970s, has not only stood the test of time, but has inspired others, such as Charles Handy in his *Gods of Management*, to develop these ideas further. Harrison specified how different cultural identities display varying shared values, which in their own different way are said to be deep-rooted, and to promote different attitudes towards ways of working, ways of relating, time and speed for accomplishment.[1]

Power culture

Decisive, upfront and strong leadership is the hallmark of a power culture (see Table 2.1) A central power figure or a small group controls, directs and manipulates activity within the organization. The power figures are usually accompanied by functional specialists who provide professional advice and information to promote further the image of the, 'all-powerful'. A power culture provides excitement and exhilaration for the small minority in positions of influence. For the rest, working in such an organization has been described as ranging from 'exciting', 'to threatening and inhibiting'.

In conversation with certain managers, Lord Hanson, formerly of Hanson Industries, was described as a dominant figure, leading a power culture organization. One of his senior managers indicated that when Hanson came into the office, everyone awaited his edict, and only the foolhardy, or those bored with their careers, would contradict the statements of the 'great man'. The industrial barons of the nineteenth century in the UK and USA, similarly, would fit the image of dominant men driving forward their organizations.

A power-culture-oriented organization functions mainly by subordinates anticipating the wishes, decisions and attitudes of those at the top. In practice, those at middle and lower levels react quickly to rumour, and use the grapevine as the main source of information.

Although regulations may be formally stipulated, in practice few rules and procedures are adhered to, as bureaucracy is viewed as more of a hindrance than a help. In-fighting at the top of the organization can be intense, and a number of casualties may result, at both the top and lower down the organization. In a power culture, decisions are largely the outcome of a political struggle.

Such a culture can be summarized by words such as 'competitive' and 'challenging'. The leaders in the fray have to be seen as strong, proud and able to accept ever-increasing responsibility. Persons who perform well in power cultures are those who value dominance, money and status. Personal influence and status are utilized to charm others, so as to add to the powerful person's list of contacts. To this end, considerable time and effort are invested in creating and maintaining access to useful people,

Table 2.1 Harrison's cultural typology

Dimensions	Power	Role	Task	Person
Visibly shared	■ Strength ■ Charisma ■ Show no weakness	■ Identify with existing structures, systems and roles ■ Hierarchical relationship ■ Defined procedures	■ Display skill ■ Willingness for flexibility ■ Loyalty to project	■ Work and live together ■ Joint decision-making/taking ■ Abide by community standards
Orientation to change	■ Risk taking ■ Mistakes are punished ■ Success at all costs	■ Resist change ■ Incremental ■ Experienced as traumatic	■ High willingness to change ■ Driven by challenge	■ By agreement of community ■ Openness of dialogue over change
Deeply rooted	■ Decisive leadership ■ Be uncompromising ■ Be vengeful ■ Rules and regulations are for others	■ Role related authority ■ Maintain systems ■ Initiatives can be damaging	■ Loyalty to competent colleagues ■ Status determined by knowledge/skills ■ Rewards for performance	■ Help each other ■ Warm, supportive environment ■ Acceptance by community
Attitude to time	■ Quick time ■ Speedy in order to dominate ■ Individual drives agenda	■ Slow time ■ Work within set targets/parameters ■ Protocol-driven	■ Quick time ■ Ignore protocols ■ No compromise of standards ■ Results-driven	■ Slow time ■ Slowest member may determine pace ■ Participation-driven
Homogeneous/individualistic	■ Highly individualistic ■ Self aggrandisement ■ Outward displays of unity ■ Chaotic organization ■ Covert interactions ■ Personal success at all costs	■ Centralist/homogeneous ■ Behaviour driven by structural configuration ■ No outward confrontation ■ Organization greater than individual	■ Individualistic ■ Disband project groups on completion ■ Confrontation ■ Task greater than individual	■ Homogeneous ■ Suppress cultural conflict and confrontation ■ Community greater than individual

and to valuable information. In so doing, dominant power holders are able to predict and influence future events, thereby extending their dominance of situations.

Consequently, a power culture is one where personal success, displays of flamboyance, constant change and risk-taking are virtually common, everyday experiences. A dominant and successful leader in a power culture, is likely to be considered a source of inspiration.

Despite the self-centred nature of the dominant power-culture figures, in order to prevent the organization from fragmenting, extraordinary displays of unity may be displayed by them for the benefit of the external world. Maintaining such a charade is unlikely to disturb the conscience of the power-culture-oriented executive. In fact, projecting a convincingly charming public face is seen as a desired skill. It would not be uncommon for two or more power-driven leaders, in deep rivalry with each other, to agree on how to display an acceptable public front, while freely admitting to each other their mutual disdain.

Role culture

A role culture is one where functions, job specialization, procedures and rules are seen to predominate (see Table 2.1). Consequently, far greater attention is given to job descriptions, the definition of authority relationships, procedures for communication, rules for the settlement of disputes, and to an urgency to establish suitable cross-over points in order to identify who has the authority to arbitrate and make the final decision.

In a role culture, the formal definition of tasks and roles is considered to be of paramount importance. Role-culture thinking makes it marginally less important that an individual be considered as competent or not so competent, but more that he or she is capable of working within the parameters of a particular role. Performance beyond the requirement of the role is not necessary.

Personal displays of power are considered inappropriate. The application of power within a role culture is synonymous with the rightful issuing of rules and procedures, and the appropriate allocation of work. Such an organization is synonymous with the sociologist Max Weber's ideal bureaucratic form. The predominance of rules and procedures as a form of communication, the allocation of work to roles rather than to individuals, and the need to support and preserve the hierarchy, are the principal features of Weber's rational-legal model.

A role-cultured organization can operate effectively only in a stable environment. The banks and insurance companies of the 1960s to the 1980s in the UK, operating in stable, controllable environments, made it a virtue to 'go by the book', and hence displayed the rigidities and lack of customer responsiveness typical of a role culture. The dramatic changes experienced by these organizations, due to chip and fibre-optics technology, have fundamentally altered their ways of working. The redundancies introduced by the banks are by no means over, as the debate rages as to whether the retail arm of banks should be drastically restructured and cut back. The core of the argument for banks is the question, are they in the business of lending and transacting money, or selling information, or both? Which way will the markets go? Will people still wish to avail themselves of the services within the traditional banks? In response, so far the banks have considerably reduced the number of process/administrative jobs. However, how far banks will move towards restructuring retail banking and concentrate on the investment side of their business, will become clear over the next few years. Certainly, all would agree that role-driven formality can no longer dominate business development.

Task culture

Task cultures attract persons whose preference is towards solving new, challenging and interesting problems. Groups of skilled experts gather to focus on a common task or problem, whether it be an organizational problem, or one of a technical nature (see Table 2.1). Credibility and respect are based on the level of a person's expertise rather than on position or personal power.

The philosophy of task-cultured organizations is to work in teams. Differences of individual objectives, status and style are quickly sacrificed for the continued life of the team. Staff and management may quickly identify with the objectives of particular units, but equally may have difficulty in respecting the overall objectives of their employing organization. The reported opposition of doctors to the newly formed National Health Service Trusts in the UK, on the grounds of infringement of clinical freedom, highlights loyalty to professional practice. What is particularly irksome for clinicians, is that Trusts are structured to respond quickly to community needs, including focusing and directing doctors to fulfil particular duties, but not necessarily in return, responding to the requests of the medics. The emerging dominant influence of Trusts adds fuel to the potential tension between the organization and the professional.

A major advantage of a task culture is its adaptability. Project teams and task-force groupings are relatively quickly formed to pursue challenges and can be equally speedily disbanded upon solution of the problem. Establishing formal roles has little meaning, as judgement is based on expertise, control over one's work, easy working relationships and mutual respect. Hence, the task culture and the role culture are at opposite ends of the spectrum to each other. The former is sensitive and flexible, while the latter is inflexible, driven by procedures and clear accountabilities for control purposes.

Control is not easy to practise in task cultured enterprises, especially in terms of economic stringency. Allocation of resources to one area could mean a cut for another field of activity. From a positively-oriented task culture, where high personal expectations and performance standards are the norm, under tighter conditions, morale in work groups can easily begin to decline. Dissipation may emerge as individuals begin to pursue their own objectives, or leave the organization. Management, in order to control the situation may introduce additional rules, procedures and regulations and in so doing, damage the spirit of innovation, certainly a challenge that has taxed Sir Terry Burns, as Permanent Secretary to the Treasury.

The task culture, championed by the behavioural scientists in the 1960s and 1970s, is now, in theory, a norm in today's society. The 'be quick, be flexible, be responsive' philosophy is a necessity in the downsized, more laterally-oriented organizations, currently in vogue.

Person-driven culture

Person-oriented-culture organizations exist for the benefit of those in the organization, and not primarily to achieve particular short, medium or longer-term business objectives. The prime purpose of person-oriented cultures is to promote and provide service to the members of its own community. People-centred cultures are a way of being; an identity that reflects the pace of development and maturity of the members of a particular group or community. In essence, the community is the organization.

Organizational structures, rules, procedures and roles are there to provide for the needs of individual members (see Table 2.1). The formal aspects of the organization are prone to substantial change according to the wishes and requirements of individuals in the community. Of the four cultures, this is the one that offers a higher order of moral values. Examples of such organizations would be voluntary taskforces, commune-type environments, religious orders, service organizations, all driven by a particular philosophy that provides assistance and friendship to people in need.

Order in such organizations functions effectively only by mutual consent. Each person has to have established with other group members, a deeper and meaningful understanding concerning the values upholding the community, and the mode of behaviour towards each other. Under such circumstances, eviction is difficult. People who identify with the values of a person-driven culture hold great loyalty to each other and to the client community groups with whom they work. Person-oriented-culture individuals will place high emphasis on personal warmth, support and consideration towards others.

Nation singular culture concept

In addition to analyses of culture at the level of organization, considerable research has been pursued to discover and appreciate cultural influence at the country level. Specifically, the analyses conducted have focused on staff and managers, with the intent to discover how national culture impacts on the attitudes, views, norms and meanings that people in the organization hold. Attention is given to two international researchers, Geert Hofstede and Fons Trompennaars.

Grandad of international cultures

The world-renowned Geert Hofstede conducted a massive survey across 40 countries, producing a total of over 116,000 questionnaire returns from managers, and concluded that country cultures differ according to four key dimensions, Power Distance, Uncertainty Avoidance, Individualism and Masculinity (see Table 2.2).

Different societies play down or accentuate status differences between haves and have-nots, men and women, bosses and subordinates. The concept of *power distance* applies to those societies where the differences between boss and subordinates are accentuated, in that those more powerful than others exercise that power to maintain distance. By one party maintaining distance between him/herself and others, he/she can equally maintain control over others, concerning the manner and allocation of responsibilities and accountabilities to roles and individuals. The boss maintains control by favouring some persons and not others, irrespective of the rights and wrongs of the situation. Hofstede maintains that the values upholding differences between people are inculcated from childhood and hence are so deep-rooted that wherever a person from a particular culture is located, his/her need for low or high power distance will strongly influence his/her organizational and managerial orientation.

Uncertainty avoidance measures how people face up to, confront, or shy away from uncertainties in their personal and working life. In combating and responding to uncertainties, people develop particular beliefs and rituals to reduce the fear, stress and damaging emotions of facing what they would perceive as an unpredictable future. Therefore, creating rules, practising particular rituals, using particular techniques, such as planning, and the use of expert opinion, are highlighted by Hofstede as the means by which individuals, nations, and organizations reduce the negative experience of uncertainty.

Alternatively, other societies have socialized their people to cope better with uncertainties. The 'tomorrow will look after itself' or 'take one day at a time' syndrome, epitomizes a lifestyle in which people naturally take more risks, but do not dramatize their circumstances.

Table 2.2 Hofstede's ethnicity typology of culture

Dimensions	Power distance	Uncertainty avoidance	Individualism/collectivism		Masculinity/femininity
Visibly shared	■ Singular exercise of power ■ Strength ■ Charisma	■ Display rituals ■ Learn rituals from youth ■ Fearful of the future	■ Do own thing ■ Reject inhibitions to personal space	■ Group centred ■ Acceptance by community	■ Be dominant ■ Be assertive ■ Macho
Orientation to change	■ Driven by the leader ■ Driven by personal agendas	■ Incremental ■ Change provides anxiety ■ Driven by precedence	■ Incremental or revolutionary ■ Individual determines pace	■ According to views of community ■ Incremental	■ Man sets the agenda ■ Be strong to make tough decisions ■ Done for instrumental reasons
Deep rooted	■ Maintain distance ■ Inequality ■ Some born better than others	■ Share beliefs to reduce uncertainty ■ Adherence to ideology ■ Compliance	■ Confidence for decision-making ■ Uproot if necessary	■ Community values ■ Authority not questioned	■ Sharp division between sexes ■ Men are tough/women gentle ■ Men need freedom
Attitude to time	■ Quick time ■ Determined by power leader	■ Slow time ■ Rituals preserve the past	■ Quick time ■ Individual determines timetable	■ Slow time ■ Live the history ■ Community ties preserved	■ Quick time ■ Achievement driven
Homogeneous/individualistic	■ Individualistic ■ Context determined by single power figures	■ Homogeneous ■ Rituals bind community	■ Individualistic ■ Self-interest ■ Loose ties	■ Homogeneous ■ Care for others	■ Individualistic ■ Man is boss

Ironically, those societies which are more relaxed about the future and its uncertainties, are equally more relaxed about work, and also more tolerant towards people who hold different values and opinions. Their 'live and let live' predisposition highlights their not feeling threatened by anything new or unusual.

The *individualism/collectivism* concept is a measure of how people prefer to live. Some are more group-oriented. These people gain a deep satisfaction from living and interacting with others in a community environment. Others prefer their freedom, their slice of space. Their need is to be free, to go their own way whenever they please; to make up their minds and change them again without having to refer to anybody. The more individualistic the person, the less he/she needs approval, and for some, to the point where they resent asking for, or even being given, approval. Those societies that are more group/community-oriented, tend not to question authority, especially the pronouncements of the elder members of society. Age is revered and respected, as the elders of the society preserve the historical rituals, symbols and customs which bind the community. Through the elders, societal ties are maintained.

Masculinity/femininity, refers to one of the historically greatest debates of all, the differences between the sexes. Certain of the stereotypic gender-driven norms, for example, that men are more assertive; women are more nurturing; men want greater freedom; women want more friends; men want further advancement; women want more social working hours, are either emphasized or played down in particular societies. These contrasts are the differences that arise from being socialized in particular ways from an early age, so that the expectations of what men and women should think and feel about themselves and about each other, are deeply ingrained by the time people accept the responsibilities of adulthood. The only real fundamental difference is the biological configuration that allows women to conceive, and men to impregnate. Therefore, in examining the concept of masculinity, Hofstede explores particular processes of socialization, whereby any one society would influence the way the nation, business and social organizations are led, decisions made and goals achieved.

In emerging with these four cultural elements, Hofstede also took account of a number of demographic influences, such as GNP wealth, economic growth, population size, population growth, population density, in fact, nine demographic indicators that were presumed to influence people's patterns of behaviour, rituals, thoughts, attitudes, norms, symbols and feelings which would determine the nature of one society from another. The results were a categorization of nations. The British, Americans, Canadians, Australians, Irish and Swedes emerged as having low needs for uncertainty avoidance, and also not requiring their managers to be distant from their subordinates. The Japanese, French, Italians, Spanish, Greeks, Belgians, Mexicans and Brazilians displayed the exact opposite characteristics, namely those of high uncertainty avoidance and the preservation of power distance. Similarly, the more masculine, risk-taker cultures were identified in the Anglo-Saxon cluster, plus in certain Asian countries such as India and the Philippines. The less risk-taking, and more the 'talk it over'-centred nations were identified as Taiwan, Thailand, Iran, France, Spain, Israel, Turkey, Greece and Brazil.

The implications to draw from Geert Hofstede's findings are twofold. In conducting business in another country, or hiring staff in that country, and acquiring or running an organization in that country, particular attention needs to be paid to local traditions, symbols, values and culture, for the influence of these is likely to be dominant in determining people's attitudes and behaviour in the workplace. Further, people socialized in a particular country take the values of that country with them to whichever country they go to live. On this basis, a Greek will behave as a Greek, even though he/she may live in Australia, Germany or the USA.

Equally, the single-culture perspective emphasizes that strong linkages exist between national cultures and organizational cultures. Other researchers, including Fons Trompenaars, the managing director of the Centre for International Business Studies, Amsterdam, Holland, have travelled down the same road of enquiry and have confirmed that national culture is *a*, if not *the*, most powerful force determining business cultures. Trompenaars' research produced four separate corporate cultures, family culture (strong internal bonding), Eiffel Tower culture (analytical, efficient and power distant), guided missile culture (project-centred, cross-disciplinary and professional) and incubator culture (shared, creative and process-driven). Similar to Hofstede's findings, countries were identified as being of one or other of the cultures, with USA, Canada and the UK epitomizing the guided-missile culture, whereas the family culture is typified by the French, Indians, Spanish and Japanese. Trompenaars' analysis, similar to Hofstede's, falls into the single culture concept.

Relativist view of cultures

Cultural relativists, who are in the minority, seriously question the assumptions behind the single culture concept. From a 'commonsense' perspective, namely from life's experience, do British managers behave much the same as each other? The question similarly applies to Americans, French, Germans, Danes, in fact to all managers in all the nations of the world. The view of the relativists is that any one of us can meet someone from another country and lo and behold, we are on the same wavelength, possibly sharing more similarities with that person than with others from our own country. Relativists argue that multiple cultures exist in any one organization or nation state, and that in fact, such boundaries are an artificial distinction and do not capture what is really happening 'on the ground'.

What these questions raise is the nature and influence of demographics, that is, the underlying forces which determine the nature and shape of our lives at a personal, organizational and national level. Ethnicity is just one demographic. Other demographics include organization size, age of managers, structure of organization, industry sector, clarity of communication etc.: the list of possible demographics is a long one (see Chapter 6 for a discussion of demographics). Although Geert Hofstede used national demographics such as GNP, his substantial and impressive original study was conducted only among IBM employees worldwide, while he himself was employed by IBM (he termed his research site, Hermes). The question concerning Hofstede's research is whether his study truly differentiated national cultures from the corporate culture of IBM, or whether all he captured was the 'bureaucratic' nature of the corporation, and the ability/inability of IBM top management to control its local offices. It is well worth bearing in mind that one of the accusations thrown at IBM, was that it had been unwieldy for a considerable period of time, and had been unable to be flexible and responsive to new challenges. Hence, there exists the possibility that what Hofstede was analysing was an organization resistant to change, with each of its country offices, doing its own thing. Trompenaars seems to have utilized only one demographic, ethnicity, in terms of nation state, in his differentiation of international cultures. Not surprisingly, if the search is to identify differences between countries, and not differences of organization culture within countries, as well as between countries, it is all too easy to conclude that national culture is a dominant influence in determining the culture of organizations in that country.

In contrast, most cultural relativists analyse cultures by identifying varying dimensions by which to view cultures, leaving the reader to reach his/her own conclusions as to the final shape and appearance of cultural forms. Two studies that fall into the relativist camp, and which were conducted at Cranfield School of Management, do emerge with distinct typographies, but do not fit into a single culture framework!

Social services study

Adopting the Harrison four-cultural typology, a study conducted by Andrew Kakabadse, in the Manchester region (UK), of 12 social service (social work) departments strongly highlights that culture mix is determined more by organization level and type of work, than by geographic dispersion, leadership style, personal influence or any other factors. Therefore, being located near to, or away from the central office is less important than what sort of work an individual undertakes, and his/her position and status in the hierarchy (see Table 2.3).

The social workers emphasize pride in the quality of their work, and in supporting their team, especially during difficult and demanding periods. However, many of the social workers interviewed complained of a lack of information about projects or other programmes in the organization, and of a general feeling of not knowing what was happening, serving to generate feelings of animosity towards management. Hence, although team identity is high, poor relationships are reported to exist between those at the lower end of the organization who are concerned with professional service delivery but who argue that they have little autonomy, and those in middle-level management. In contrast, senior social workers/middle-level managers are identified as spending a large proportion of their time ensuring that social workers strive towards achieving their goals, for they in turn have to face the demands of the next level of management. A great deal of time is spent by senior social workers in attending group meetings, and discussing issues pertinent to the organization's hierarchy. The amount of time spent discussing casework issues was identified as not as high when compared with that

Table 2.3 Cultural characteristics in 12 SSDs

Social workers	Supervisors/managers	Directors
Positive experiences	*Positive experiences*	*Positive experiences*
■ Team identity	■ Identity with hierarchy	■ Good facilitation of inter-personal relations
■ Emphasis on quality of work	■ Hierarchic career development	■ Effectively managing grievances
■ Supporting the team in emergencies	■ Positive management attitude to complex organizational relationships	■ Allocation of resources and people towards strategic ends
Negative experiences	*Negative experiences*	*Negative experiences*
■ Poor relationships between superiors and subordinates	■ Criticized by social workers	■ Liaison with other departments and organization is poor
■ Low emphasis on challenge and responsibility	■ Little support for organization and system from levels below	■ Joint planning is poor
■ Low job autonomy		■ Administering policies is poor
■ Low questioning of authority		■ Driving through change is difficult
		■ Obtaining greater commitment from other chief officers is difficult

Note: SSDs = social service departments
Source: Adapted from Kakabadse (1982)

spent by social workers. Two conflicting sets of norms are identified as being in operation.

It seems, therefore, that the two contrasting norms cultures 'meet' at the supervisory level. Those undertaking supervisory activity (senior social workers, team leaders) occupy the *first order gatekeeper* line, for the service they provide is reconciling the demands of two contrasting sets of norms (Figure 2.1).[2] Task norms, concerning client welfare, have to be reconciled with organization norms such as maintaining the necessary processes of administration.

The responses of only some of the senior social workers indicated that the demands of both cultures seemed to be within their control. Facilitating relationships within teams, and acquiring resources for the team (aspects of a task culture) are seen in an equally positive light with personal career development and the more organizational demands of supervision and administrative process (role culture). Yet an expressed fear was that their role could potentially be undermined. Although some senior social workers indicated that they were able to manage conflicting demands, others stated that they experienced ever greater strain in reconciling, for them, the seemingly almost irreconcilable.

For the senior management group, the common link between the positive responses, such as the facilitation of interpersonal relationships, managing grievances, and the negative responses of liaising, joint planning, administering policies, coping with change and obtaining greater commitment from the top, is that these activities involve facilitating a broad range of relationships with an array of individuals and groups. Working towards obtaining and allocating resources, controlling and influencing the activities of others is symptomatic of persons whose primary objective is strategic development from a position of power. In fact, the third cultural level to be identified in social service organizations, is that of power culture.

Figure 2.1 shows the two levels of gatekeepers. The *first order* level is the boundary between the task culture and role culture. The *second order* gatekeepers, are likely to be represented by the assistant directors, because of their responsibility to liaise between the various units within the SSD, and between the department and other organizations. Their work in terms of liaison, planning and delegation is to maintain an acceptable balance between the SSDs and other interested bodies. The second order gatekeepers operate at the boundary between the role culture and the power culture.

However, such cultural spread is unlikely to be maintained with the introduction of change. In circumstances of downsizing, the strength of the role culture is likely to be undermined. The drive for flexibility, responsiveness and entrepreneurship may be appreciated by the task culture part of the organization. In addition, the emphasis on task professionalism and client care, coupled with the demands made by

Figure 2.1 Three culture organization

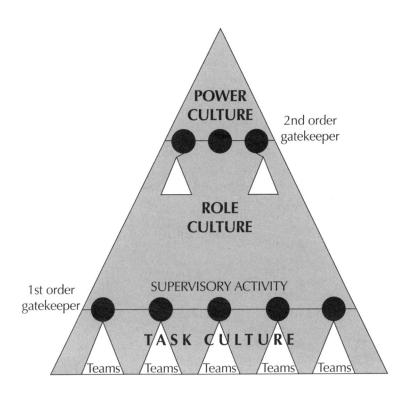

Source: Adapted from Kakabadse (1982)

senior management in the power culture for the attainment of results, is likely to undermine the middle-level management, who would be tasked with meeting targets, managing task culture teams, controlling costs, and ensuring some degree of adherence to rules and procedures.

Such has been the case, especially in investment banks. In an international, competitive and de-regulated financial services market, where revenue, profit, marketplace performance, brand image and continuous attention to costs are the norm, middle-level managers and general managers are caught 'between a rock and a hard place' (Figure 2.2). Above them are the individually dominant, power-culture-oriented directors, driving the bank forward and where necessary cutting out levels of management. Although the organization is more

Figure 2.2   Cultural impact of downsizing

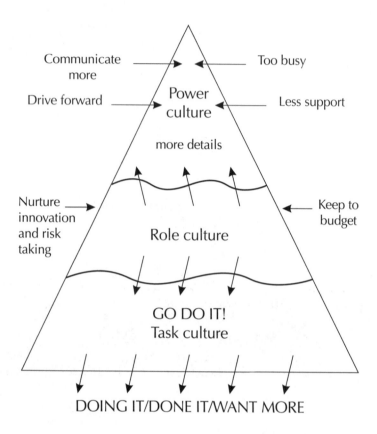

flexible and cost effective, the senior directorate now have less support to call upon, as the numbers of middle-level managers have been reduced. Hence, in driving the business forward, senior management are faced with more detail to attend to, a greater need to communicate with staff and management, and less support to call upon. The paradox for leaders is that, when faced with an overwhelming number of day-to-day demands, they attend less to their people communication/ management responsibilities, when the need for communication is paramount.

The management underneath, reduced in numbers, but tasked to ensure the successful implementation of policy, achieve their ends by attention to detail, strict control of budgets, while being pushed to nurture freedom of manoeuvre and entrepreneurial flair among their professional dealers, market makers and financiers, as long as no mistakes are made!

Needing little encouragement, the career-mobile and market-driven investment bankers take risks. In circumstances where revenue and profitability predominate over control and co-ordination, in effect, where a role-culture management is emasculated, the end result is the Nick Leeson syndrome! The book written by Judith Rawnsley, outlines the secretive nature of Leeson's actions, but highlights that there existed a considerable level of awareness of his actions within Barings Bank. Nick Leeson is simply a symptom of a now public, uncomfortable and deep paradox pervading investment banks and so many other organizations, that of diminished control, risk taking coupled with a requirement that no mistakes or embarrassment emerge. Damaging the role culture aspect of organizations is only just beginning to show its hidden costs.

Global organization cultures

The management development research team at Cranfield School of Management has only recently completed an intensive worldwide study of the attitudes, behaviours and values of chairmen, chief executives, managing directors, directors and general managers; in effect, 5500 top managers from 12 countries namely, the UK, Ireland, France, Germany, Sweden, Spain, Austria, Finland, Japan, China, Hong Kong, USA (different aspects of the study are reported in Chapter 8). In keeping with Hofstede's approach, demographics were used in order to ascertain the prime determinants of culture, but the demographics were of an organizational, not national nature. The age of top management, the size of the organization, the quality of communication of corporate directives and objectives, the structure of the organization, differences of view as to the future direction of the organization, ethnicity and level in organization, were the demographics applied to differentiate possible cultural differences. Four markedly different 'boardroom' cultures emerged, termed *consultative, divisive, developmental* and *cohesive*, each with its own philosophy and approach to leadership. These differences of leadership philosophy and style bore no significant relationship to ethnicity (see Table 2.8). The combination of demographics used identify such contrasting cultures of organization, crossing ethnic and organizational boundaries, as to place this study very much in the relativist camp.

Consultative culture

A consultative culture is typically driven by 45–55-year-old top management, in more medium-sized organizations, where senior, middle and lower-level management concern is for operating business objectives and corporate directives to be clearly communicated throughout the organization. Equally, senior management highlight that few differences exist between them in terms of the vision, mission and the future shape and direction the organization should pursue. Where differences do arise, they are openly discussed and a consensus decision is reached (see Table 2.4).

A consultative culture is a caring culture, epitomized by an open management style, in which respect for others and being respected, are integral to working in the organization. The style of management is supportive, in which debate and discussion are crucial to the nurture and growth of trusting relationships. People are sensitive to the feelings of others because the ultimate aim is to hold the community together. In

Table 2.4   Consultative culture

Dimensions	Attitudes/actions
Visibly shared	Caring towards others
	Open management style
	Easy to talk to
	Talk to others from different functions
	Never demand, suggest
Orientation to change	Incremental
	Proceed together
	Disciplined
	Effective at follow-through
	Kept informed of progress
	Keep others informed of progress
Deep rooted	Respect for people
	Sensitive to feelings of others
	Value others
	Feel valued
	Develop others
	Right and wrong ways to treat people
	People make organization tick
Attitude to time	Not too fast/not too slow
	At the pace of the group
	Balance issues according to circumstances
	Mature overview
Homogeneous/individualistic	Tolerance towards others
	Homogeneous
	Hold community together
	People encouraged to talk through their problems
	Criticism not taken personally
	Commitment given to the people in the organization

Notes: Demographics:
Age of top management – 45–55
Size of organization – medium sized, but with some larger organizations
Objectives clearly communicated – yes
Corporate directives clearly communicated – yes
Difference of views on direction of company – slight differences, but aim towards total consensus
Structure of organization – varied.

fact, the people in the organization, rather than the organization itself, are more valued. Change is not resisted, but is allowed to proceed at the pace of the group, even at the pace of the slowest member, if necessary. However, the care displayed towards each other is coupled with a discipline to work and be effective at administration and communication. The discipline applied to following through on projects and other initiatives to ensure that the work will be completed on time and to the required standards, is coupled with a clear intent to keep others informed of progress. Work effectiveness, an emphasis on continuous communication with and attention to people, are intertwined in the daily life of a consultative cultured organization. The people-care side of consultative cultures highlights certain parallels between that of Harrison's person culture.

However, a consultative-cultured organization is epitomized by having a leadership who are contextually sensitive, by judging what style and line to take in different circumstances. The leadership emphasizes being disciplined, and yet encourages freedom of speech. The difference between the managers of Harrison's person-centred culture and the senior managers in a consultative culture, is that the latter need to be capable of balancing a number of juxtapositions. The reason for the attention to balance is to ensure that the organization remains homogeneous, and that the community is held together.

Divisive culture

A divisive culture is one in which there exists a broad spread of age of management, in organizations that are medium to large-sized and of varying structural configuration. Senior, middle and junior-level management emphasize that operating business objectives and corporate directives are not clearly communicated (see Table 2.5). Equally, top management are seen as, and admit to being, split on issues of vision, mission and the future direction and shape of the company. In addition, no strong sense of cabinet responsibility exists, so whatever decisions are agreed upon, they become distorted upon implementation.

Living in such a culture is more a matter of survival than anything else. The divisive nature of the top management pervades the organization. Individuals pursue their own courses of action with little or no referral to anyone else. The organization may be dominated by ever-changing cliques, adding to the feeling of instability that staff and middle management may experience. Friction, arguments, rows and shows of strength predominate. People display their emotions and, if necessary, vent their anger and frustration on each other. Handling assertive, aggressive and dominating people, is the skill to develop, if a person is to survive and progress in such an organization. Where managers do display loyalty, support and concern, it is towards their team or department.

Table 2.5   Divisive culture

Dimensions	Activities/actions
Visibly shared	Check with no-one, just do
	Do things my way
	Bully others
	Meetings changed at the 'Drop of a hat'
	Be tough
Orientation to change	Driven by individuals
	Dislike interference
	Chaotic
	Divisive
	Concerned only with own part of organization
	Poor co-ordination
	Encourage team to discuss issues
	Task-driven
Deep rooted	Enjoy challenge
	Know who will/will not fit
	Handle friction
	Promote self
	Communicate with others of similar background
	Blame others
	Customer is king
Attitude to time	Quick time
	Meet targets/goals
	No time for co-ordination/co-operation
Homogeneous/individualistic	Individualistic
	No corporate loyalty
	Loyalty to self/own team/unit
	Rely on systems to bind organization

Note: Demographics:
Age of top management – complete spread (30–65)
Size of organization – medium to large sized
Objectives clearly communicated – no
Corporate directives clearly communicated – no
Different views on direction of company – yes – no discussion – no cabinet responsibility
Structure of organization – varied.

Within units or departments, subordinates are encouraged to air their views and, in turn, are supported by powerful bosses in their progress through the organization.

The individualistic nature of the leaders of the organization incurs communication and co-ordination nightmares. Mistakes, and miscommunication are relatively normal experiences across the divisive organization. Change in the organization is driven by individuals pushing forward their own agenda, often with little heed to the impact of such initiatives on the overall organization. The speed of change is likely to be fast, goal-driven and probably passionately championed. With an ever-greater number of change champions promoting their own desires, and with a number of new projects being pursued simultaneously, most people in the organization are left with the feeling that chaos is normal. Even the champions of change, pushing forward their own pet projects, complain that too much change and lack of co-ordination are damaging for the organization.

The over-concern of each individual with only his/her part of the organization encourages loyalty to self, or towards only the person's immediate team. If conflicts of interest arise, senior managers in the organization are likely actively to discourage loyalty to the corporation.

Despite the internal tensions, one value is shared, namely attention to customers. The customer is placed on a pedestal. Most individuals in the organization would attempt to provide a high level of service to their customers. Ironically, and in turn, the customer would experience both a high and poor quality level of service, poor due to ineffective internal co-ordination, and high because of a willingness to please. The ultimate irony is that such a culture displays an advantage in terms of the performance in the marketplace.

The Cranfield research team introduced a number of organizational performance measures, namely customer perceptions of the effectiveness of service, the impact of poor or high quality interfacing, quality of relationships with suppliers and other stakeholders, and the capability of the organization to sustain competitive advantage. The consultative cultured organization, no matter how supportive it is viewed internally, made little difference to external performance ratings. The consultative cultured enterprise is seen as neither good nor bad, just bland! The divisive organization, despite all the internal tensions, principally harms itself externally as a result of poor internal co-ordination and communication. Otherwise the energy and commitment displayed to customers, the drive displayed at the individual level to succeed, is highly valued by clients and other stakeholders.

Developmental culture

A developmental organization has a vibrant young senior management aged between 25–40 years, is small to medium-sized, and nurtures a culture of a highly motivated management dedicated to success (see Table 2.6) In development culture-driven organizations, operating business objectives and corporate directives are clearly communicated. The structure of the organization varies in form and shape from one organization to the next. Although senior management do admit that differences of view are held by the leaders of the organization concerning the vision, mission and future shape of the company, leading to intense and assertive debate, they equally state that all relevant issues are brought out into the open, and once discussion has taken place and

Table 2.6   Developmental culture

Dimensions	Attitudes/actions
Visibly shared	Work with the team
	Be successful
	Pursue all initiatives
	Communicate across the organization
	Ask for forgiveness, not permission
Orientation to change	Change-driven
	Flexible
	Results-oriented
	Disciplined
	Value co-ordination and co-operation
	Positive experience of change in the past
	Systems and controls are supportive
	Organization-wide perspective
Deep rooted	Be stretched/stretch others
	Committed to organization
	Be positive
	Make the best out of each opportunity
	All problems are challenges
	All challenges are opportunities
	Help others understand my part of the business
Attitude to time	Quick time
	Results-oriented
	Make time for interfacing
Homogeneous/individualistic	Cohesive
	Success binds organization
	All pull together to achieve
	Communication is as important as success
	Burn-out is a serious concern

Notes: Demographics:
Age of top management – 25–40 years
Size of organization – medium to large sized
Objectives clearly communicated – yes
Corporate directives clearly communicated – yes
Differing views on direction of company – yes, but discussion is followed by disciplined cabinet responsibility
Structure of organization – varied.

decisions reached, cabinet responsibility pervades. No matter where an individual stands on an issue, top management pull together when 'making things happen'. The discipline of cabinet responsibility is a prime difference between the developmental and the divisive organization.

Energy, drive to achieve, and teamwork are the three pillars upholding developmental cultured organizations. The message is, pursue every opportunity, be positive and bring all necessary expertise together to address the challenges posed by the marketplace. Hence, attention to internal communication and co-ordination is respected and practised. Time is made for meetings and for interfacing across the organization. Equal discipline is applied in terms of attention to detail, and the supervision and follow-through of projects and initiatives that are under way. The discipline applied to daily, routine work, and the abundance of energy and drive in the organization, are likely to sponsor numerous, but co-ordinated initiatives, simultaneously.

Favourite phrases are likely to be, 'all problems are challenges; all challenges are opportunities', demonstrating an energetic way of life which makes the steady state and change almost impossible to distinguish. The high results orientation and flexibility of response, are likely to make change an everyday experience. An additional reason as to why staff and management have little fear of change, is that their forward-looking attitude will have sponsored positive experiences of change from the past.

An important characteristic of a developmental organization, is that speed of achievement and the discipline applied to the efficient completion of activities are accompanied by a supportive view of systems and administration. Organizational controls are likely to be seen as helpful, providing parameters and guidelines, especially on matters of quality, standards, and financial stringency.

As far as organization performance indicators are concerned, strongly positive correlations emerge across all the business measures, especially in the area of change-management capability. External stakeholders respect the professionalism of the staff and management, and indicate they are proud to be identified with a successful enterprise.

The great danger facing the developmental organization is that although success leads to success, no one is able to shift the vehicle out of top gear, and out of the fast lane. As a result, such a culture can induce extreme burn out in its staff and management, without their even being conscious of what is happening, until it is too late.

Cohesive culture

A cohesive cultured organization is one in which top management are older (45–65 years) and respected. The majority of cohesive cultured organizations are large sized (see Table 2.7). Most people in the organization would agree that operating business objectives and corporate directives are clearly communicated. Senior management admit that differences of view between them are held, concerning matters of vision, mission, shape and direction of the company, but that all key issues are discussed and resolved, mostly behind closed doors. Whatever decisions are reached, the stand-together nature of cabinet responsibility accurately reflects the attitude of top management in the organization. The strong displays of discipline and togetherness, which

Table 2.7   Cohesive culture

Dimensions	Attitudes/actions
Visibly shared	Be team player
	Listen
	Accept feedback
	Check out before acting
	Display calm
	Ask for permission not forgiveness
	Treat others with respect
Orientation to change	Incremental
	Co-ordination across organization drives pace of change
	Stop/start feeling to change
	Getting details right, more important than speed of change
	Planned
	Aim is long-term impact
	Incompatible with short-term efficiency
Deep rooted	Committed to organization
	Never do things own way
	Right and wrong way to do things
	Identify with mission of organization
	Respect more important than sentiment
	Disciplined
Attitude to time	Slow time
	Driven by project speed
	Get details right
	Driven by long-term view
	Great discomfort if rushed
Homogeneous/individualistic	Homogeneous
	Trust in organization
	Paternalistic
	Speed of change can be damaging
	High trust in leadership

Notes: Demographics:
Age of top management – 45–65 years
Size of organization – large
Objectives clearly communicated – yes
Corporate directives clearly communicated – yes
Different views on direction of company – yes – discussed – implemented through strong cabinet responsibility
Structure of organization – varied

at all costs are adhered to, give an impression of little internal disagreement. However, disagreements, even deep tensions, do exist, but are discreetly dealt with in seclusion.

The drive for success is coupled with a strong commitment to the organization, more so than to its its staff and management. Tradition is a strong enforcer of attitudes and accepted ways of behaving in a cohesive organization. Tradition is maintained through being respectful towards others, and making the time to listen to the views of others. In many ways, respect is considered more important than sentiment. Through displaying respect for others and for the organization, through listening and accepting criticism, people feel themselves to be an integral part of the organization and readily identify with its mission and purpose.

People are open to change and accepting of new ways, as long as the organization can digest the changes and disruption is kept under control. Staff and management will accept strain, but not dissection, in order to accommodate change. Hence, the pace of change is slow, incremental in nature, and in reality more driven by the speed of co-ordination in bringing forward all parts of the organization jointly, than by external events and forces. Getting details right is more important than the speed of change. The attitude towards change is one of taking a long-term view. Senior management strongly attempt to control the change process by allowing planned change to drive the organization, at times at the expense of short-term efficiency and expediency. To outsiders, the organization can seem to be exceptionally slow to adjust. Management at times prefer to hold back progress, in order to reflect on, or re-examine issues as they arise. By implication, the cohesive cultured organization adopts a stop-start practice to change. Both staff and management are likely to feel uncomfortable if rushed to change, or to complete a programme of activity, faster than the agreed plan.

Despite the paternalistic nature of the cohesive organization, the discipline displayed towards tasks and co-ordination, the attention to detail, attention to customers, and the development and application of meaningful longer-term strategy, highlight the positive nature of such an enterprise. The respect shown towards others supports positive relationships within the organization, and especially enhances the trust in senior management's capability to lead. Long-standing suppliers and customers are treated with the same respect as long-standing employees. Few are likely to describe the organization as caring, but they are likely to consider themselves to be valued.

Global culture spread

Unlike the Geert Hofstede and Fons Trompenaars' results, in no country in the Cranfield survey is there displayed a clear link between organizational culture and ethnic/national culture. As Table 2.8 highlights, the picture to emerge is one of diversity. The British and Spanish display the broadest spread across the four boardroom cultures, followed by the Irish, Swedes, Americans, Austrians and Germans. The French and Japanese do not show any representation of the supportive culture category, but both display a substantial number of cohesive cultured

Table 2.8   Spread of boardroom cultures (%)

| Country | Styles of leadership | | | |
	Supportive	Divisive	Developmental	Cohesive
UK	34	23	17	26
Ireland	23	22	41	14
France	3	28	29	43
Germany	11	2	51	35
Sweden	36	12	20	32
Spain	27	25	27	21
Austria	53	7	25	15
Finland	4	2	41	53
Japan	0	38	2	60
China	7	46	9	38
Hong Kong	6	13	53	28
USA	20	9	36	35

organizations. Surprisingly, the Japanese and Chinese score highest of all the countries in the survey, in the divisive culture category. This result, especially as far as the Japanese are concerned, challenges a commonly held stereotypical image of the integrated and personally non-aggressive nature of Japanese enterprises as 38 per cent of Japanese businesses emerge from the study as being considered as strife oriented, led by a management that is divisive in nature. In contrast, the Austrians are heavily weighted towards working in supportive-cultured organizations, whereas the Germans, Finns, expatriate and Chinese enterprises in Hong Kong display a strong affiliation to developmental and cohesive business cultures. In contrast, mainland Chinese enterprises display a low score in organizations that have evolved a developmental culture.

Why is there no obvious link between national ethnic and business enterprise cultures?

First, it should not be assumed that so-called national cultures fall into clearly defined parameters which uniformly impact on the inhabitants of a country. In contrast, national cultures can be described as a loose set of influences, varying considerably for reasons of regionalism and organizational demographics, in terms of impact on a country's inhabitants. The obvious regional differences within any one country support the view of ethnic diversity within a nation state.

Further, each organization has its own history and is at different stages of economic and social development, thereby, impacting on its staff and management in considerably varying ways. Not to be underestimated is the fact that the leadership of an organization can make a substantial difference in terms of the growth, prosperity, demise, and internal values and culture of the enterprise, irrespective of the business's position in the economic cycle. In fact, leadership influence, from the Cranfield survey, is identified as the distinguishing feature between a thriving and forward-looking organization and a discontented, vulnerable one. Despite the influence of the size of an organization, or even the age of senior management, the telling difference is that between a senior management which promotes flexibility to market demands and changes, effective internal communication, and the capability to resolve differences and apply discipline and consistency to moving forward, and one that does not. Irrespective of other forces, good leadership makes all the difference!

Fragmentation – a cultural reality

The theme of fragmentation is continued from Chapter 1, in that the evidence emerging from the Cranfield studies is that organizations are considerably diverse. No neat set of parameters exists comfortably to package an organization structurally, culturally, or in terms of leadership philosophy and impact. Instead, a spread of attitudes, drives, influences, symbols and contrasting norms exist at both the organizational and national level (typified by the Social Services study and the Cranfield global study), promoting a picture of fragmentation. Nevertheless, leaders still have to manage their businesses. Different parts of the organization have been found to, or have been targetted to, pursue their own objectives, but these still need to be co-ordinated to meet the broader corporate objectives. Of course, leading the whole organization forward requires transformational capabilities. However, maintaining a balance between the elements of a diverse and culturally rich organiza-tion, attending to detail, and achieving shorter-term goals and objectives, require substantial transactional skills and sensitivity, a point empha-sized by James Cochrane of the former Wellcome Foundation, who views dining as a mechanism for discussing ethnic and business differences.

Influencing contexts

The way forward is through focusing on context. Context refers to locality, office or workplace, whereas culture is a broader concept encompassing attitudes, values and behaviours on an organizational or countrywide basis. Drawing together differing contexts is the way to balance the contrasting elements of culture present in any organization, and from thereon to focus the enterprise towards the achievement of its goals. The skills for influencing a spread of contexts are identified as, accurately reading contexts, gaining respect and utilizing the strengths of subordinates.

Accurately reading contexts

In order to influence people and circumstances, an ability to 'read contexts' is necessary in order to form a view as to what is happening and why, and from that, ascertain appropriate ways forward. Reading contexts accurately requires interpreting intent and behaviour. What individuals and groups intend, may or may not be observed in their behaviour. The greater the divergence between intent and behaviour, the more covert are the interactions between people. The more people display their intentions in their behaviour, the more overt are their interactions, and the more what they say can be trusted in terms of what they will do. The covert nature of interactions is examined in the two following chapters, on 'power' and on 'politics'.

Overt-oriented interactions have been given the greatest attention, in the literature, under the theme of situational leadership. Two of the more well-known writers on situational leadership, Paul Hersey and Ken Blanchard, identified two dimensions as being central to effective leadership, those behaviours required to accomplish tasks effectively, and those necessary for the nurturing of relationships.

Task-oriented behaviour refers to leaders organizing and defining the roles of their subordinates, and explaining the activities each has to accomplish. In essence, the leader is establishing a well-defined, structured way of working.

Relationship behaviour highlights the extent to which leaders maintain and enhance personal relationships between themselves and their subordinates, and between the subordinates themselves, by being supportive, accessible, listening-oriented, and by making the time to help the members of their team. Relationship behaviour opens up two-way communication through encouragement, openness and recognition.

On the basis that there can be no common style of leadership, as according to task demands or relationship requirements in given situations, different approaches are required. Hersey and Blanchard identified a four-style leadership model, dependent on whether the need for task-related behaviour is high or low, and/or whether the need for relationship-related behaviour is high or low.

The key as to which style to choose is strongly influenced by the levels of maturity of the followers, namely the ability and willingness of people to accept responsibility for directing their own behaviour. Subordinates who are willing to take on responsibility, who are confident and highly committed, can be described as mature. Those who back away from responsibility, who lack confidence and ability, and who display low levels of commitment, are described as immature. Hence, a more authoritative, telling style, is ideally required for subordinates with low maturity levels, who need direction, whereas subordinates with higher levels of maturity, need less attention and supervision, and hence a style of delegating would be more appropriate. The Hersey/Blanchard contribution is in the emphasis that the skill of transactional leadership is in matching style with the needs of subordinates.

To misread or mismatch a style according to subordinate needs, can cause friction, a lack of respect and ultimately, a lack of trust. For example, a sincere attempt to delegate can be seen as abdication by a group that needs greater focus and attention from its boss. Conversely, too much attention from the boss can be viewed as oppressive. A more mature team needs its boss to be available for consultation and discussion, rather than setting down clear parameters to their work activity.

Gaining respect

Hersey and Blanchard point out that directing, leading and interacting with others crucially depends on the levels of respect that the parties involved have for each other. According to Frank Scott-Lennon, the Irish consultant, respect is an intangible but powerful emotion one person has for another, which strongly determines the levels of trust and willingness to communicate and co-operate, necessary for leadership to be applied effectively. Frank Scott-Lennon's research highlights three elements to leaders gaining and winning respect, honesty of intent, grassroots accessibility, and consistency of behaviour, with one additional consideration, the discipline to display commitment.

If intent is perceived as honest and visible, people will forgive certain indiscretions or inappropriate behaviours. However, intent, due to its impressionistic nature, is difficult to quantify at any one moment in time. Respect for someone who has positive intentions is as much the response to an impression one gains over time, as it is to reality. Despite its intangible nature, the following consideration can assist in more clearly communicating intent.

First, there is little point in continually trying to display positive intentions if these are not the sentiments held. Over time, the real intentions of any individual do show despite what the person says. Why? Because it is simply too strenuous, over long periods of time, to project an image contrary to the way one feels. People hear slips of the tongue. Decisions are made, but not acted upon. Further, staff and middle management see a general unwillingness to pursue a course of action that the leader has previously indicated he/she would champion. What in fact most people see, over time, is a lack of commitment.

The situation is intensified by the encounters the members of the senior management team have with each other, formally or informally, on a one-to-one, or group basis. Each team member depends on the others to be focused, to manage and control costs, to meet targets and to co-ordinate their activities with their colleagues. The failure to function effectively in one or more of these areas, quickly shows. Others can see the problem: is the underperforming director too stretched, or does the person not appreciate the extent of the challenges he/she faces, or is the individual not sufficiently skilled to cope, or is the person not committed to what they are saying? Intense encounters promote intense scrutiny; colleagues can see the individual's true level of commitment. Under such scrutiny, each individual does need to believe in what he/she is doing, because if not, others immediately around are very quickly likely to become aware of the lack of conviction, and react accordingly.

Second, intent is strengthened by displays of commitment, namely a discipline to pursue a particular course of action. Discipline such as this is not feigned, but exhibited on a daily basis. People witness commitment as the individual goes about his/her work. It is that natural display that convinces others of a leader's intent. People do live out their beliefs and, over time, most people cannot hide their convictions, or lack of them.

Third, despite the scrutiny under which each of the team members is likely to place the other, intent is still impressionistic. The closer the relationship, the more quickly and the more accurate is the impression formed. The more distant the relationship, the more inaccurate the view that is formed. What, however, is clear, is that a view will be formed. Hence, part of positively presenting intent is to recognize that impressions must be managed according to the needs, requirements and developments within the context at the time. The forces that shape opinions in any one situation vary and, therefore, being sensitive to what is contextually relevant is important in positively managing transactions which promote positive intent.

Fourth, being contextually responsive requires having access to grass-root opinion. A well-identified and important requirement of leadership is to 'walk the talk', that is, be close to people, get down to everyone else's level, and be seen not to be in an ivory tower. There is nothing new in the recommendation to be close and accessible to those lower down the organization. So why is it still a concern? Because it is so difficult to achieve. Many leaders in today's organizations find it difficult to get close to staff and middle management's experiences and sentiments, partly because of the demands made on top management's time. As shown earlier in this chapter, with downsizing, senior managers are more stretched, needing more support but often being offered less from a decimated middle-level administration and management. Attending important meetings, dealing with financial details crucial to leading the organization, and nurturing external stakeholders, are vital responsibilities of leaders. Not doing so would lead to the accusation of 'having taken your eye off the ball'! However, certain leaders use the excuse of 'pressure of time' to avoid exposing themselves to middle management comment and questions. Despite the fact that it is painfully obvious to all that the leader is being defensive, he/she just does not change. Hence, the recommendation that senior managers should more 'walk the talk' more, is simply futile. The recommendation that should be made to the leader is, 'look at your job and see what needs prioritizing'.

Of the many myths surrounding different leaders, one in particular concerns Fergal Quinn, the Irish entrepreneur, who has grown a highly successful supermarket chain, Super Quinns. The story goes that Fergal felt that he and his management team were out of touch with the sentiments and experiences of staff in the stores. Super Quinns was an already successful business in the Republic of Ireland with a need to capitalize on that success by maintaining and enhancing quality. Fergal Quinn, therefore, required that he and his team go into the stores and serve. For a period of a few months, the Super Quinns boss and top team ran the organization by mobile telephones, worked in the warehouses, served customers in different sections, in different stores, and apart from deeply appreciating the demanding experience of being customer-responsive on a continuous daily basis, they also learned another interesting fact, their customers were mainly women accompanied by children. The Super Quinns management team learned that shopping, for mothers with bored and irritable youngsters is a stressful and frustrating experience. To improve the lot of the mums in Super Quinns stores, Fergal Quinn spent money. At each of the checkout counters, Quinn stationed people other than the cashier. The first person took the shopping out of the trolley/basket and placed the goods on the conveyor belt. The second 'cashed up the items', and the third packed the shopping neatly into carrier bags and placed these back into the trolley, and offered to help the customer pack the goods into their car. If the mother seemed particularly harassed, certain stores had available a pool of cars so that one of the store's employees could take the shopping to the customer's home, in order to relieve the strain on the mother. This story does make the point that being close to the grass roots requires deliberate action. Time has to be purposely set aside, in order to be closer to the different parts of the organization. Inevitably, only periodically can leaders make the time to be close to the sentiments of staff and management. In between times, leaders may be seen as 'out of touch' and, consequently, so accused, simply because they are not seen to be around. It takes sensitivity to and knowledge of particular contexts to appreciate the feedback of being told that one is not sufficiently often around, and that one needs to be seen more.

A danger to observe is that intent is undermined if a leader is viewed as inconsistent. Inconsistency refers to 'saying one thing but doing another'. A certain degree of inconsistency is a normal experience in anyone's life. To be absolutely consistent makes a person inflexible and difficult to relate to. Therefore, consistency or otherwise is a matter of degree. However, on important issues, whatever is said or promised, must be implemented. A damaging message to convey is, 'I will make the time to find out what is wrong, commit myself to improving the situation', and then nothing happens. Hence, maintaining consistency on key tasks and on crucial matters of concern is vital. The research at the Cranfield Management Development Centre clearly shows that effectiveness of communication is more down to how people behave than to what they say. What one does, speaks a thousand words.

Harnessing the strengths of subordinates

Only after one has gained the respect of colleagues and subordinates can progress be made to capture and mould the strengths of subordinates. Frank Scott-Lennon's research clearly shows why. People need to trust that their leader is able to pursue a particular course of action, for as they are members of the same team and will, by nature, be implicated, few wish to be involved in failure experiences. Further, if staff in the organization witness damaging tension, contradictions and splits of opinion on even minor issues at senior levels, how can they trust that the individual senior manager, who is attempting to harness their energy to achieve better performance, will deliver on the commitments he/she has made? Hence, being respected is pre-requisite to making good use of the strengths of subordinates.

Harnessing the energy of subordinates is primarily a process of promoting upward feedback. Upward feedback is a matter of capturing opinion across the organization, so as to inform senior management of the views, attitudes and opinions of middle and lower-level management and staff in the organization. Common practice is to conduct attitude, management style and opinion surveys, internally, and customer complaint and satisfaction surveys, externally. Equally, opinion can be fed upwards through the use of workshops and seminars, whereby, particular senior managers will attend events, listen, and participate in discussions with their staff concerning how improvements can be achieved.

Similarly, opinions about particular individuals can be channelled through an upward feedback route. For a period, senior managers in the Information Division of a world famous aerospace company conducted appraisals, on the basis that they would first interview the subordinates of any one manager, make no judgement on the views expressed, but then lay out the material in front of the manager concerned, and conduct the appraisal with those views in mind. An additional development to upward feedback-based appraisal is 360 degree feedback, namely feedback to a manager, but from all sorts of interested parties. 'Three-sixty' degree feedback is becoming increasingly popular and is considered a powerful medium for the development of managers.

However, whichever approach is utilized, feedback as a development tool needs to be treated with care. Feedback concerning broader views is likely to generate interest from the rest of the organization. People become disappointed if nothing happens. If information is gathered, how it is then used, especially in particular contexts, requires sensitive management. A European bank, that wished to remain anonymous conducted a number of customer surveys to discover that improvements in service to customers were needed. They introduced a number of customer service initiatives, which considerably improved customer care. However, they equally tightened up on costs, requiring their line managers to control expenditure substantially. The bank has, as standard practice, conducted annual surveys examining customer satisfaction, and other internal attitudinal surveys. Those carried out recently have highlighted certain customer complaints, such as customers feeling that bank staff are trying to sell them additional services or products which they, the customers, do not want, but also that qualified and experienced staff are not present to assist them. The staff, in turn, complain that they are being asked to sell more, do not have the support of more experienced staff (they having left the bank), and that the opportunities for career progression are now considerably curtailed due to cutbacks. The local branch manager complains that he/she is being targeted to sell more, in a climate of cost constraint, and is in danger of being judged as unhelpful and unpopular by customers and staff because the policing and cost control elements of their role have increased. The results of the surveys have been published in the bank as a series of league tables. The danger is that the feedback could be used in a manner that detracts from rather than enhances the performance of branches and branch managers, as a considerable number of managers feel that there is little they can do to change their circumstances. They are being asked to motivate staff to sell more and at the same time, strictly control costs by not replacing people once jobs become vacant. This bank is a professionally and capably-led organization that has made great strides in Ireland, the UK, and the USA. Despite their obvious competence, the value of survey feedback data may need to be re-thought by the bank.

Sensitivity, equally, needs to be applied to the manner in which individual-based upward feedback is utilized. To be at the receiving end of 360 degree feedback does require considerable resilience to wish to continue to listen, and the maturity to be able to harness the feedback offered. 'Three-sixty' degree feedback is likely to be experienced as inconsistent, for each person offering feedback will have his/her own particular reasons for his/her comments, the sum of which are unlikely to fit well together. To not feeling unduly hurt, but to make use of the information, is no easy matter.

A feature story in the business section of the Sunday Times (22 September 1996), outlined British Airways' (BA) intent to reduce distribution and operating costs, and improve service to passengers. The Chief Executive of BA, Bob Ayling, clearly spelt out the necessity for such action despite BA's current strong performance. What Bob Ayling did not state was how he positioned his senior team and the rest of the organization to the point where they, as an enterprise, could publicly make such statements. As part of the process of change, a programme of leadership development was commissioned, initially, for the top 200 managers of BA, and since then has been cascaded further down the organization. The aim of the programme was to improve the leadership and communication skills of senior management, as one means of helping them address the challenges they faced. Bob Ayling and his top team, like all others, attended the programme. On the first evening of the programme, each of the managers received 360 degree feedback. To make the point that the leadership programme was an integral part of improving BA, the first to receive his 360 degree feedback in front of his top team, was Bob Ayling. His example made the point – 'we are all in the same boat; we all need to improve; we all listen, then act, and I am no different to anyone else'. With that sincere display, the reluctance to enter into 360 degree feedback was dramatically reduced. 'The World's Favourite Airline', slogan of BA, is not lightly made, and hidden behind those words is an enviable quality of management and leadership.

Two-sided leadership

Although the ideal is to match the needs of individuals, particular contexts and overall cultures with appropriate transactional leadership practices, all too often experience indicates that mismatches frequently occur. One reason could be that the manager over-relies on a single style, and has become inflexible and insensitive. Another may be that subordinates have become comfortable, or too strongly identify with their current context to even conceive of changing. Possibly, a third reason is that attempts to improve present circumstances could be viewed as an attack on the organization. Through resistance, bad management and poor timing, respect and trust can diminish and resentment increase. Senior management can find themselves marooned in a sea of negativity. As Chapter 1 outlines, improvements can be introduced through restructuring roles and formal relationships, and through team-building. In addition, this chapter emphasizes that through an in-depth understanding of cultures, making progress by changing particular elements of the culture (context) is an equally effective tool of transactional leadership. However, if life is particularly troublesome, and leaders need to find alternative ways through dark and damaging contexts, they need to turn to other aspects of transactional leadership, the use of power and of politics, the topics of the next two chapters. The two sides of transactional leadership, the overt and covert, will then have been addressed.

Key point summary

■ Culture refers to a broader location, a country, an organization, a town, in effect a place which shapes and moulds the views, attitudes, philosophy and perspectives a person adopts and develops in helping him/her to make sense of his/her surroundings and effectively to interact and contribute.

■ Five dimensions of culture are identified which strongly shape people's views and attitudes, namely, norms (visibly shared ways of thinking, feeling and acting), orientation of people to change, hidden assumptions (norms that are so deeply held that they operate below the immediate level of consciousness in the person), orientation to time (the speed at which issues/tasks are addressed), and homogeneity (holding community-based values) or individualism (individually determined attitudes and norms). These five dimensions are applied to the subsequent analyses of culture in the chapter.

Single-culture concept

■ The single-culture concept refers to a single, dominant, cultural force determining the nature of an organization or even a nation.

■ The singular organizational-culture concept championed by Roger Harrison, identified four organizational cultural norms, power, role, task and person-oriented cultures.

■ A power culture is one where a key power figure, or small group, controls, directs and manipulates the activities and direction of the organization as he/she/it desires.

■ A role culture is one where role boundaries, procedures and rules, drive the shape and nature of the organization, so that managers rely more on definitions of relationships, procedures for communication, and rules for the negotiation and settlement of disputes, than on their leadership capabilities to work towards appropriate solutions.

■ A task culture is one where preference is given to expertise, people's skills and qualifications, and flexible structures to address challenges. Credibility is gained through exhibiting expert performance, rather than through practical and personal power.

■ A person-oriented culture is one where the organization meets the needs of the people within the enterprise, by exploring ways to provide service to the members of its own community.

■ The single culture analysis has also been applied to examining nation states, particularly championed by the European Professor, Geert Hofstede.

■ Hofstede concludes that country cultures differ according to the degree of power distance, uncertainty avoidance, individualism, and masculinity that is exhibited.

- Power distance denotes the degree to which particular societies accentuate status differences between elements of their society, leading to those more powerful persons exercising their power to maintain their distance.
- Uncertainty avoidance examines whether and how people face up to, confront or feel inhibited by, uncertainties in their personal and working lives. Those who experience uncertainty as negative, create rules and rituals to reduce the experience of negativity.
- Individualism, contrasted by collectivism, explores the degree to which certain societies uphold the values of individuality, as opposed to those who are more group-oriented, whereby people gain satisfaction from living and interacting with others in a community environment.
- Masculinity refers to those societies that revere gender-based stereotypic norms, which highlight maleness, or conversely, femininity.
- Nation states are characterized according to the above four dimensions with, for example, the British Canadians and Americans emerging as exhibiting a low need for uncertainty avoidance, and the French, Italians, Mexicans and Belgians displaying the opposite characteristic.

Relativist view of cultures

- The relativist view of cultures challenges the single culture concept as too simplistic, in that any one organization or nation encompasses a multitude of cultures within its parameters and borders.
- The social services study conducted by Andrew Kakabadse, highlights that three of the Harrison typologies, namely power, role and task cultures, co-exist within the same organization.
- The global top manager survey, conducted at Cranfield School of Management, identified four international business cultures, namely the consultative, divisive, developmental and cohesive cultures. These cultures of organization are spread, in varying proportions, across an array of countries.
- A consultative culture is one where respect for others, an open management style, the nurture and growth of trusting relationships, are integral to working in the organization.
- A divisive culture is an individualistic driven culture, whereby power-oriented people pursue their desires, at times with little reference to anyone else. Being seen to be strong, winning at all costs and driving one's own goals, is the valued way of operating.
- Divisive cultured organizations are burdened by communication and co-ordination problems due to top management's low need to co-operate.

- A developmental culture is promoted by a positively minded, younger top management, whose members place quality of operational and strategic performance as a prime strength of the organization. The developmentally driven organization is epitomized by an open but assertive management style, that values success, discipline and cabinet responsibility.
- A cohesive-cultured organization is one in which staff and management are commited to the continued growth and prosperity of the organization, in preference to their own. Respect for the traditions of the organization and for its elders, are the hallmark of a cohesive organization. The paternalistic nature of the organization supports the practice of protecting all who work for the organization.

Influencing contexts

- Organizations, as well as nations, hold multiple identities and in order to influence and mould such diversity, influencing various elements of the culture (contexts) realistically allows leaders to impact fully on their organization on a day-to-day basis. Three strategies for influencing contexts are identified; accurately reading contexts, gaining respect and harnessing the strengths of subordinates.
- Accurately reading contexts requires realistically interpreting the intents and behaviours of others, so as to judge how to influence people within particular circumstances.
- Gaining the respect of others requires leaders to be honest and display the honesty of their own intentions, to negotiate their accessibility to the 'grass roots' of their organization, their display of consistency of behaviour and to convey a commitment to pursue their stated aims. The trust subordinates have in their leaders is considered to increase substantially once they witness top management exhibiting the above stated best practices.
- Having gained the trust of subordinates, leaders can then harness the drive, energy and motivation of their staff and lower-level management to adapt and change the culture of the organization. It is crucial, however, to be 'in touch with subordinate views', which can be achieved by meeting and being with people who can accurately provide 'grass roots opinion', by the use of internal surveys, upward appraisal, direct upward feedback and 360 degree feedback.

Notes

1 The four cultures are adapted from Kakabadse (1982).
2 Adapted from Kakabadse (1982).

Further reading

For further explanation of the different interpretations of culture, read:

- Deal and Kennedy (1982), who pursue the theme that 'strong' cultures are instrumental in forming effective organizations.
- Kilman, Saxton and Serpa (1986), who consider that the nature of culture depends on the stage of evolution of the organization.
- Korac-Boisvert and Kouzmin (1994), on the negative aspects of culture, (cultural dark side), which lead to, dysfunctional behaviour.
- Harrison (1972), and Handy (1978) on how the various dimensions of culture interrelate.
- Rawnsley (1996) and Doherty (1995) on the inadequacy of transactional leadership in circumstances of downsizing, or when certain sections of the organization become out of control of the centre.
- Hofstede (1980) and Trompenaars (1993), on how the globalization of work environments adds an additional dimension to the cultural diversity of organizations.
- Servaes (1989) and Bhagat *et al.* (1990), on how communication styles and particular local elements of culture epitomize the nature of particular nations.
- Kakabadse *et al.* (1995) and Kakabadse (1982) on the fragmented nature of cultures at an organizational and at an international level.
- Scott-Lennon (1996) and Hersey and Blanchard (1988) on how to overcome communication gaps that exist between the levels of management.

CHAPTER 3

Working Through Differences – Power

Case analysis

The government report

One of the recently completed studies by the International Management Development Centre team at the Cranfield School of Management, is that of a leadership capabilities analysis of senior civil servants of the Australian Commonwealth (federal) government (see Chapter 6). The report, submitted to the appropriate Federal Commissioner, has subsequently been well received by the civil servant population. The report was also sent to the Prime Minister's office where it received attention from the Minister for Labour, who holds direct responsibility for the Civil Service.

'He [the Minister for Labour] is going to be reading this report to hit the Labour party with. All the problem areas identified in the report, according to him, were allowed to occur in the last administration. We've been asked to prepare a brief along these lines,' commented one of the senior civil servants that we (the authors), were talking to.

'Well this is how politicians work to get their own way. Using power is an everyday thing for them', added another in the group.

As the brief was being prepared, we continued to discuss how the report could be implemented. It became clear that the different interests of the various departments and of senior civil servants would make implementing the recommendations of the report challenging.

'Do you think the various departments will support the actions we think the Minister will pursue?', we questioned.

No response was forthcoming, but an uncomfortable silence descended.

'No, not really,' came the reply.

'It's just that we're inclined not to talk too openly about how matters tend to be addressed or resolved between us', said one of the civil servants.

'You mean you don't talk about power plays inside the organization, but you quite openly talk about the use of power by politicians, why?' was our question.

'Well politicians are all about power, aren't they?'

'Well, what are you about? A federal civil service is probably akin to a highly complex multi-national in the private sector. Your interests range from managing money [Treasury], to IT [information technology], to education, to health, to housing, to publishing, to security, to foreign affairs, and many more interests. How do the civil servants at the top of these silos sort out their affairs? By just sitting there, talking, smiling at each other and hey presto, problems solved?' we queried.

The response followed these lines:

'Well it's not easy. Departmental heads have not formally met, at all, for something like five years. The Ministers in the last administration told them not to meet with each other. They [the departmental heads] were considered to be a threat to Ministers. We're not used to talking to each other.'

'Well, departmental issues, overlaps of responsibility, things that you needed to do together, someone must have been trying to sort things out somehow', we suggested.

'One or two tried, but that's something we tend not to talk about. I tell you, it's more than my job's worth!'

We were given a 'job's worth' response (it's more than my job is worth), but from that individual's point of view, it was understandable. The civil servant concerned was anxious, uncomfortable and wished to withdraw from the conversation. The person seemed genuinely concerned that to pursue this theme, or to be identified and quoted out of context, would damage his/her career prospects.

However, the Australian civil servants do have precedence on their side. Power has not traditionally been a topic of organizational psychology or administrative leadership. Power has been the interest of warriors and kings. Alexander the Great was a champion at fighting, riding, swimming and thinking. Ironically, he shared power with his soldiers; he consulted them before battle and before embarking on campaigns. The Duke of Wellington, and Montgomery, although immortalized, fall more into the category of anti-heroes. Wellington was a 'cold fish', but proficient, abrupt, dispassionate as a writer, quite willing to use power to achieve his own ends. Montgomery was disliked by his own troops as a self-publicist, seen to do little for them, but a great deal for the desert campaign. As far as military and political leaders are concerned, open analysis of them, their strategies, their personalities, and even their personal and sexual behaviour, has been an accepted practice.

In contrast, the topics of power and politics in organizations have been everyone's nasty little secret, until about 30 years ago. Out of the writings on community power and politics emerged analysis of the use of power in organizations. By so doing, a new dimension to thinking about motivation and leadership emerged, namely, that of recognizing the degree to which organizations are full of contradictions, with people pulling in different directions; some exercising their leadership responsibilities honourably, others not so; some acting quite independently, while others tow the line; some changing their minds, irrespective of what was agreed, while others stick to their commitments, come what may.

Hence, standardizing procedures, clearly establishing roles and working relationships, are not sufficient. The range of conflicting interests in the organization requires additional approaches to role and procedural clarity and a willingness to co-operate, so that a settlement of issues and improvements to performance can be achieved. In order to handle challenges in the organization, leaders will at some point resort to using power as a way of resolving difficulties. The problem until recently has been that people have found power, as a leadership tool, difficult to talk about, in the mistaken belief that power is inherently immoral, and as the civil servant in the case study admitted, 'that [power] is something that we should not display'.

Still today, people have a problem talking about the power acts in their organization, although most can and do talk about the use of power in other people's organizations. The fact is that power is a key dimension of transactional leadership, and requires examination in order that leaders can positively and effectively utilize power. The emphasis on 'transactional' is highlighted, as power in organizations is about 'getting things done' when blockages and irritants are in the way, rather than promoting major transformational change. For this reason, attention is given to understanding power, and to exploring the different levers of power, how they can be utilized, especially in an international context, and to considering how to apply power effectively to induce change. Throughout this chapter, the underlying message is this: understand how to use power, talk about power and, if necessary, use power.

Understanding power

Power can be viewed from the following standpoints:[1]

■ as a base from which to act,
■ as driven by individuals, but its exercise can be made to look as if an organization or team is driving the necessary power plays,
■ if effectively applied, power can lead to personal and organizational success,

- the application of power can be exciting, an aphrodisiac-type of experience, according to Henry Kissinger, and hence can feel transformational but, in reality, is very much transactional,
- subtlety is required to apply power effectively,
- power, ineffectively or hurtfully applied, can be turned into a 'black art'.

Power involves the potential to use particular resources, in order to achieve particular ends, which are referred to in this chapter as power levers. Hence, power provides a base from which to act. Individuals may use their authority, their contacts, their money to influence others, all in order to achieve their particular goals. Using power, however, does not guarantee success. Power has to be used in a manner appropriate to the context in which it is being applied. Sensitivity towards the attitudes and feelings of others in a given situation, as well as to the values and traditions of the broader organization, is crucial in effectively applying power. Each context, and in the broader term, each organization, is likely to have evolved accepted ways which influence what is and what is not, legitimate behaviour. It is quite feasible for people in one part of the organization to hold views concerning the legitimate use of power which contrast sharply with the views and behaviours of others in different parts of the organization. The fact that context strongly determines the effectiveness of the application of power, places power firmly in the transactional camp of leadership. However, the exercise of power can feel transformational. Henry Kissinger's boast that power is an aphrodisiac, highlights the degree to which people can be deceived into thinking that they are making great things happen, when, in fact, they may just end up, 're-arranging the deckchairs on the *Titanic*'. Power interlinked with vision is transformational. Power on its own is transactional, but with a 'feel good' factor. Hence, power has its limitations and no more so than when crudely applied. Power requires subtlety of thought and application, it becomes a bullying and crude tactic, which will eventually be resisted. Power, therefore, when well applied, can not only lead to success, but can also help bring about certain meaningful change. However, ineffectually or spitefully used, the exercise of power can be regarded as sinister, which may end up damaging all parties involved, including the person who is utilizing it inappropriately.

Conditions for power use

Power is likened to a springboard from which to act. Hence, it is important to consider the conditions that influence the why, when, and where to act. Four conditions are identified:[2]

1. *Resources* Wielding power involves the use of resources. The resources can be under the control of an individual or organizationally based.

Someone who has the authority to recommend the promotion or demotion of any one person, would classify such power as an organizational resource, and could exercise that power, as an employee of the organization. In contrast, personal resource power can range from wealth, intelligence, and knowledge to physical appearance. Whichever resource power is utilized, the use of that power allows an individual to influence the thinking, behaviour and attitudes of others.

2 *Dependency* The capability to influence others through the use of resources is achieved only if those being influenced need, or are attracted to the resources in question. Needing a particular resource is likely to make a person dependent on the resource wielder. For example, it is not uncommon for banks to influence senior management appointments in client organizations. As consultant to a well-known investment bank in the City of London, I (Andrew) and was invited to attend a dinner at which the senior managers of the investment bank were hosting the top management team of a company that was about to float its shares in the market. The bank was the agent in the flotation. The evening passed smoothly and amicably. After dinner, informal talks were held between the hosts and the company managers, and for a period of time, the bank's Director of Corporate Finance, the MD of the bank, and the CEO of the client company were in deep conversation. I noticed that the CEO of the client company did not appear to be comfortable. Apparently, the Director of Corporate Finance and the MD both of the bank clearly indicated to the CEO that if they were to approve and invest their money in the flotation, they would insist on a change of Finance Director in the client company. They did not consider the client's Finance Director to be sufficiently capable to meet the challenge. Despite the fact that the company was the client and the CEO had personally appointed the Finance Director, the individual was fired. The CEO depended more on the resources of the bank, than he did on his Finance Director.

3 *Alternative sources of resources* and their availability also influence the ability of individuals to utilize power sources. If an individual can call on others who can provide alternative resources or channels of influence, the individual's dependency on his/her original source is reduced.

4 *Contextual acceptance* The discussion so far, in terms of the use of power resources, has been confined to those who wield resources and those who need resources. However, there exist interested and influential onlookers. These stakeholders may or may not like the manner in which power is wielded, even though they may not be directly involved in any transaction. They may be offended if they witness behaviour which they consider inappropriate. Hence, an

additional consideration is the tacit permission of those who are 'generally around'. If these significant others disapprove of what is happening, nothing is likely to arise immediately, but a body of opinion against the power wielder is likely to grow, marginalizing, over time, the individual and his/her influence. Basically, the message will be – 'don't do business with this guy!'

Power levers

The use of power reflects what an individual desires to achieve, determined and influenced by the individual's context and his/her ability to access certain levers of power in order to assist such people to achieve their goals. Numerous analyses of power strategies and power levers have been offered by writers on organizations and social communities. Two of the most prominent have been the US researchers, French and Raven, whose power-levers analysis has dominated thinking in this area. However, theirs, as with most others' analyses of using power, is on a general basis, in that they identify the power levers potentially available to all people, in all organizations. The analysis undertaken in this chapter is one of identifying and discussing the power levers likely to be utilized by the leaders of an organization. Seven power levers for leaders are identified, namely, role power, personal impact power, reverence power, numbers game power, context power, access power and experience power.

Role power

Role power is the power assigned to an individual as a consequence of occupying a particular role in the organization. In the literature, such power is equally termed 'legitimate' power. The distinction being drawn in this chapter is that a leader can make role power legitimate if the role holder has people believe in the legitimacy of his/her actions, irrespective of how power is being used. Research and observation indicate that role power is continuously used in both legitimate and non-legitimate ways, according to how the role holder sees fit. From a leadership point of view, what people in different contexts accept, in reality, determines legitimacy and success. There exists a wide range of potential power resources associated with a senior manager's role, namely, title, authority, rewards, control of resources (technology, finance, people), power of dismissal, power to promote/demote or reward, power to change the structure of the organization, power to reconfigure other people's roles or even the whole organization, power to frighten and threaten, and the power to act as arbiter of decisions made, revised and implemented.

Role power stems from the use of authority. Authority is ascribed to various roles according to the desired level of influence that role should have in the organizational hierarchy. By clearly differentiating one role from another, it is possible to attribute various levels of authority and control to particular roles. A director of finance may be assigned particular duties and authorities in both obtaining financial information from line management, and in influencing line management as to how they should use and present financial information. Hence, having access to line managers' accounts, requiring that meetings be held, and equally, requiring that work be revised if it is not of the desired standard, are authorities written into a job description.

Legitimacy is exercised by three factors, clarity of role boundaries, the recognition that the role is part of a much larger structure configured to achieve particular ends, which has its own purpose and the backing that the individual receives from his/her boss. Of the three factors, the boss's backing is by far the most influential in terms of guaranteeing the legitimate use of power. Roles that are not too well defined, and structures that are not too well thought through, do not, in themselves, undermine the legitimacy of power. An individual can legitimately use power to influence and improve his/her circumstances by gaining the support of his/her boss. In contrast, the person who is facing problems with his/her own boss, or critical suppliers, or customers, may find him/herself under considerable pressure, even though roles and structures are well defined. Resources promised may be unavailable, or in short supply, simply due to changes in the purchase behaviour of bulk customers, for example. It needs only one or two key accounts to terminate their orders, to create panic in any organization. Despite these difficulties, an individual can help him/herself through the legitimate use of power in four ways:

1 The effective use of information, which may concern technical, product, financial or human resource issues. The greater the amount of information the individual can attain, the more aware is he/she of developments in the organization. In this way, potential difficulties may be foreseen and acted upon. Further, attracting appropriate information allows the individual the freedom to choose which information should be released and when. Hence, the legitimate power of that role is emphasized.
2 Negotiating access to other people, or various networks, inside and external to, the organization, provides for support, and adds to the sense of legitimacy in the use of power. Irrespective of whether the person's role allows for any access to other networks, negotiating entry to personal and professional networks or groups can positively add to the perception others hold of the role, in terms of legitimacy.
3 The setting of priorities, which is part of a manager's job, adds to the perception of legitimacy. Organizing other people's work within a

consistent theme and direction, is a potential way of influencing others in the situation. Establishing priorities for subordinates' work, so that the success of one particular activity is emphasized, is one way of exhibiting the senior manager's competence. Equally, it is a reasonably good way of turning people's attention away from areas of less than adequate performance.

4 Getting closer to the boss to try to understand his/her pressures and challenges, in order to judge more appropriately when to call upon the boss's support. Strengthening the relationship with the boss, understanding how to gain the support of the boss and respecting the nature of the demands faced by people who hold positions of authority, assist in understanding how to win the support of the boss to legitimize the use of power. Once the dynamics of a situation are appreciated, and the degree of freedom of manoeuvre that anyone with authority in their role can realistically call upon, then acting as a guarantor of a subordinate's actions is more likely. A boss is likely to respect anyone who 'realistically' calls upon his/her support. Then the boss is unlikely to lose face, and the chances of successfully managing a situation are increased. As respect and trust grow, a boss is more likely and willing to support his/her subordinate in the future.

An alternative to the legitimate use of power, is the adoption of methods that are more punishment and coercion oriented. The successful application of punishment power depends on others realizing that the manager can, or will, punish. There is a significant difference between threatening to use coercion and actually being able to use it. A frustration for managers in certain larger organizations, especially if driven by local employment laws, is that they may not be allowed to fire or transfer people. Under such circumstances, power is gained from the threat of firing rather than from its actual use. However, if others recognize that it is only a threat, the power base is likely to collapse.

The effect of punishment as a power lever also depends on how others have observed the use of such power in the past. The individual may hold the authority and, as a person, may be comfortable in applying coercion. A history of application will strongly influence the response of others. If a boss threatens retribution for not meeting deadlines, and it is known that he/she can apply punitive measures but in the majority of cases has not, then that boss's capacity to influence is substantially diminished. Credibility through consistency of application is all important.

A third alternative exercise of role power is through the use of reward. Reward power is used to both influence others, and to create dependency on the power wielder. For reward power to be utilized successfully, a person must have access to the rewards desired by others. The rewards can take the form of tangible resources, money, or a bigger and better office; or non-material resources such as status. The most obvious material reward, money, can be viewed as a motivator, or simply as a basic commodity. Either way, a manager who can utilize money as a reward, holds substantial power to influence the performance of employees. Resource-based power increases, if he/she is required to hire and fire.

In public sector organizations, which operated more on fixed pay-scales and established conditions of employment, individual tendering for contracts, and procedures for hiring and firing reduced the power of their managers. When government organizations in the UK, New Zealand, Australia and the USA experienced a change of status to an agency structure, reward power became a dominant lever of influence. More contracts are now individually negotiated, in terms of pay, conditions of employment and compensation, and length of tenure.

Non-material rewards, such as status and privilege, can also be powerful levers of influence, especially in organizations which are not required to be driven by being market responsive. It was a common experience in both the UK and the USA in the 1980s, to witness status and privilege being offered as a reward in banks. High status people had their own exclusive lifts and dining rooms. The rest of the staff were herded into the remaining space available. People could observe and perhaps desire the status of others every morning, lunchtime and evening. Structuring organizations to be far more market-sensitive has cut out the worst of such practices, and has gone some way to substituting status and privilege with money. If the opportunity is available, people are now more likely to negotiate for tangible rewards, recognizing that their length of appointment may be limited.

The success in using reward power, depends on the degree to which rewards are desired. What one person considers 'exclusive', may well be commonplace for others. Further, even rewards that are desired may be given in a way which is disliked. Organizations that are predominantly paternalistic in nature could be held in contempt by their employees, if they believe that rewards are offered to those who are subservient. The senior management of such organizations may find it difficult to understand why substantial rewards are at times only grudgingly accepted.

The exercise of rewarding through role power needs to be handled extremely carefully. No one likes feeling manipulated. Inappropriate use of rewards, even desired rewards, can substantially damage the respect that one individual has for another.

Personal impact power

Personal impact power[3] depends on one individual presenting them-selves as attractive to others. Terms such as charismatic, popular, having panache, exhibiting flair, are used to describe someone with personal power. Equally, physical attributes such as height, size, weight and strength, would be considered to be aspects of personal power. Rather than through using role, rewards, coercion or knowledge, the person influences others by being charming, attractive and, overall, projecting a 'nice-to-be-with' image. Having stimulated rapport and sympathy, the individual can then use the relationship to focus the feelings and behaviours of others to their own advantage. Very simply, others want to be in the presence of, or gain the favour of, or simply be liked by, the charismatic person. They will offer that person what he/she wants in order to be allowed near to him/her.

Successful application of personal impact power depends on two factors: first, that others are attracted to the individual as a person, which is not always the case. It is a common experience to see senior executives whose style has worked well with one department, division or group, but not with another. Second, being personally influential depends a great deal on physical presence. It is difficult to feel the charm of a person through e-mails, or the minutes of meetings, or even through radio, book or television, although the latter two media are substantially used to project the desired personality of the individual. Personal influence is best exercised in meeting people.

An attractive image is projected by the individual, his/her actions and by context and circumstances. A common criticism of John Major, the former Prime Minister of Britain, is that as a person he lacked charisma, especially when compared with his predecessor, Margaret Thatcher. The combative instinct of Thatcher, the power of her comments at the despatch box in the House of Commons, and her ability to rebuff Neil Kinnock, the opposition leader of the day, added to her powerful image. Major's image is of a person unable or unwilling to project such strength of character. How did his spin doctors combat the situation? They projected the image of the ordinary 'man': 'I'm just like you, your John Doe citizen, even though I'm the Prime Minister of Britain.' Despite stringent efforts, his image became tarnished, not so much by the stories of sleaze that have surrounded the Conservative Party, but much more by Major's seeming inability to confront the problems faced by his party, the situation being made worse by his ordinary, dowdy image. The reality was that Major had the slimmest of majorities in the House of Commons and anyone, including Margaret Thatcher, in his situation would have been stretched to the maximum, between appeasement and being assertive. Unfortunately, his inability to change his image made him look incapable, rather than highlight the delicate nature of his situation prior to the UK's general election of 1997.

Relying solely on personal power in order to influence successfully is unwise, as any one person proficient at influencing one situation may be perceived as ineffective in another context. The successful application of power often requires additional power levers to that of personal power alone.

Reverence power

Intertwined with personal impact power, is reverence power, namely how powerful is the image of the individual in the minds of others. Being revered makes for a 'hell of a wallop', as the mystique of the individual may reverberate far more strongly than actuality merits. Reverence can be manufactured through cleverly stage-managed personal impact. The, 'I am one of you' Ronald Regan image or, 'I am not definitely not one of you, as I am so superior' perspective of De Gaulle, are equally powerful messages to promote and each in their own context is significantly influential. At the extreme end of the manipulative scale lie Stalin or Saddam Hussein, who both controlled and control the media and news channels, pervading their presence in people's daily existence. On reflection people may well say 'how could I have been so fooled?' but at the time, the reverence displayed was awesome. In conversation with elderly Russians, who lived through the Stalinist pre- and post-Second World War period, astounding is the revelation concerning the power of Stalin in the people's psyche. For so many, Stalin held an immortal presence – people believed and trusted him – and equally for so many, the betrayal they felt on discovery of his true intentions, actions and dark identity, was as profound.

Contrastingly, others do not seek favour, but due to their diligence, devotion, good works or powerful example, are so admired that, eventually, favour turns into god-like reverence. For those falling in the category of 'do not seek favour', when granted acclaim, embarrassment and even anxiety, are commonplace reactions. The embarrassment response is understandable, for it epitomizes a natural humility of 'I am not worth it. Others are better than me.' However, the anxiety response should be expected for it holds slightly darker connotations. As people are built up, they can as easily be knocked down. Images are so easily tarnished either through accident or design. Images are equally a magnet, for reverence promotes curiosity but does not guarantee compliance. As reverence can promote adoration, it can equally attract a jealous distaste – 'Who the hell does he/she think they are! Let's teach this smart arse a thing or two.' Reverence, for those who desire it and for those on whom it is bestowed, is akin to riding a bucking bronco, the adulation is overwhelming, the ride breathtaking, but only few make it back to the corral, still astride.

Numbers game power

One often-utilized power lever by senior managers is numbers power.

A managing director, formerly employed as a senior manager under Lord Weinstock, the previous boss of the GEC corporation, recalled how Weinstock ran GEC.

> He [Weinstock] had no problem with ringing you up at 6.30 pm – on a
> Sunday evening, just when you were about to cut the family roast, and
> tell you – 'I'm just going through some of your figures, and they do not
> tie up; please, could you ring me back and give me the answer in 2
> hours' – and you'd have to leave the table, rush into the office, find the
> figures, ring him and give him your response. God help you if you were
> a minute later than the time he gave you. I have seen hardened
> businessmen reduced to tears in front of Weinstock. Numbers and
> absolute fear, that's how he ran the corporation. Ruthless, unscrupu-
> lous, and for what – cash mountains? – absolutely no investment in
> the people or the company. Everyone was drained for the sake of a bank
> account! (undisclosed interviewee)

According to the interviewee, Weinstock would not allow expenditure
on costs, unless they were tied to a contract, even when that included
more mundane, day-to-day items. For example, if a manager or scientist
needed a new desk, he/she could not purchase the item unless it was part
of a contract, and for which the client paid. A visit to the Marconi site in
Portsmouth provided the evidence that the interviewee's statement was
accurate. Highly qualified scientists, men and women, in certain offices,
were sharing two or three to a desk (witnessed in 1994), of the flip-up
desk variety that school children used thirty years ago, although then
each child had his/her own desk.

The impact Weinstock made on this man was so considerable, that the
individual, many years later, is still so anxious that he does not wish to
be identified, through fear for his former boss. He has continued to recall,
on numerous occasions, Weinstock's use of numbers game power.

For senior managers, numbers are a prime lever of performance
assessment and control. Attention to how effectively each department,
unit, division, or total corporation is operating, crucially requires focus
on income and expenditure detail. One of the criticisms of Sir Phil
Harris, the retail carpet king, was that in the latter days of his Harris
Queensway empire, he took 'his eye off the ball' – he did not observe how
the corporation was proceeding, through detailed analysis of its day-to-
day financial performance.

Although numbers are an obvious lever of control, they can be utilized
in three different ways, through fear, as information, and as a mechanism
for enhancing performance.

A considerable number of people, even at senior levels in an
organization, are fearful of numbers. Facing a page full of numbers can
(for some) have a numbing effect. People know they should be able to
read numbers, but find they are looking at a 'jumble'. Being competent at
reading numbers is akin to mastering a new language. Some people are
more gifted at languages, while others have to work harder to acquire
that skill. Many individuals are influenced by who their 'tutor' is and if

their experience of that role model is unsatisfactory, then their inhibition with numbers increases.

Apart from the fact that people experience 'numbers dyslexia', the fear factor can be accentuated by the manner in which numbers are utilized. Catching people 'off guard', through questions or requests for further information, and by giving people no chance to prepare, can generate considerable anxiety. Especially for busy managers of operating businesses, who have to be responsive to issues of financial performance, marketing issues, IT challenges and people relationship concerns, they are more likely to be unprepared than someone who makes it his/her full time job to study financial returns.

An additional way of raising the fear factor is to change parameters. The criteria under which a person is financially assessed, can be changed, leaving individuals fearful that they cannot accurately predict what questions are going to be asked and why. One common way of switching criteria, is for part of the financial year to emphasize sales/revenue returns, and then concentrate on expenditure and costs, without giving adequate preparation time to others, to reconsider what numbers to present in support of their case.

Because numbers are potentially anxiety provoking to a considerable number of people, and also due to the fact that numbers have a feel of 'objectivity' about them, whereas in reality, the criteria needed to assess figures are highly subjective, the easiest and potentially most powerful way to use numbers is through fear. Ironically fear, in itself, can be a motivator for the short term. In the longer term, fear drastically inhibits initiatives being pursued. A person who encourages fear through adopting numbers game power can become unassailable. Others do not know what they are to be asked, when, and what would be the consequences should their response be inappropriate. Generating fear through numbers game power can maintain leaders in post for considerable lengths of time.

Alternatively, numbers game power can be used for effectively communicating information by providing others in the organization with facts, figures, trends and projections through numbers, helping to keep people informed, and also highlighting that the leadership are keen to communicate with their staff and management. The decision to make is which numbers should be made generally available, and what key messages does senior management wish to project?

By focusing on numbers to communicate particular messages, an additional benefit emerges, that of encouraging people to become more enterprising. By taking certain aspects of the organization's financial performance, sales and/or costs in a particular product line or within a particular region, senior management can help focus others' attention to address specified challenges. Numbers provide the benchmark 'this is how well/badly we have done'. The challenge then is whether the situation can be improved. By so challenging, numbers are used as a mechanism for line management to participate in decision-making. Through emphasizing performance to date, people are asked to participate in the process of rethinking current practice, and to identify new ways to improve future performance. However, for numbers to be utilized to encourage others to offer innovative ideas and enterprising actions, requires a commitment to mentoring and on-the-job development. Subordinates are likely to need their manager to talk them through the implications of the numbers, so that individuals can relate figures to context. Interestingly, a considerable number of those managers surveyed worldwide through the Cranfield Management Development Centre, stated that they learn more about finance and accounts from their boss spending time with them to analyse and discuss the company's budgets, than from attending business school programmes. With such investment required to use numbers to motivate rather than control, it is not surprising that many leaders use numbers to generate fear more than to promote confidence. Promoting fear, or supporting openness and entrepreneurship, is driven by the level of confidence of the senior manager, the time they wish to make available for dialogue with their subordinates, and by his/her philosophy of leadership. It is unfortunate that a considerable number of leaders knowingly prefer to adopt the fear factor in promoting their power through the numbers game.

Context power

Using power to advantage by being contextually responsive, involves combining intellect (technical, functional and analytical skills) with an ability to understand and read contexts. Such capability requires a level of robustness not to be unduly influenced by immediate circumstances, so that sufficient mental and emotional space can be created within the person to interpret accurately the motives and behaviours of others. The stand back, but not stand apart, stance, needs the person to control his/her inner uncertainties when experiencing the ambiguity of trying to understand what is happening around them, without yet having grasped the full picture. So many managers under ideal, non-threatening conditions can appraise other people and situations with a reasonable degree of accuracy. Accomplishing the same while being a participant in a dynamic situation, is considerably more demanding. The challenge is to avoid making snap judgements, or attempting to control uncertainty by reducing tasks and activities to manageable parameters, until the individual is fully aware of what is happening in the situation. As indicated in Chapter 2, by keeping a more open mind, the leader is likely to display his/her interest in, and sensitivity to, appreciating the unique nature of each context, and thereby have a better opportunity to massage and renegotiate relationships. The leader is respected for attempting to understand the nature of particular circumstances before acting, especially in organizations which have supportive and long-standing traditions, or which have evolved a service-oriented philosophy. In these 'softer'-cultured environments, people operate by more tacit than explicit criteria. They know each other, they understand each other, and respect each other. Gaining credibility or attempting to introduce change in tacit-driven cultures, initially requires becoming part of that culture in order then to renegotiate the way 'things are done'. The combination of intellect and social flexibility is a distinct asset in helping leaders to form judgements accurately in circumstances of uncertainty, while at the same time winning the trust of others.

Access power

Top managers, through their role, have the opportunity for access to various groups and individuals within and external to the organization. One potential usage of access power is to grow and nurture networks. Another is to use the authority and status of one's office to gain access to another influential person, which through normal channels would have been impossible.

Growing a network involves access on a personal, professional and social basis to different people inside and outside the organization. The greater the number of people to whom one has access, the greater one's power through one's connections. Making contacts at conferences, at dinner parties, exchanging business cards, and following up on casual meetings, are all part of enhancing a person's network of contacts. The contacts made may be useful immediately, or may be called upon at a later date.

Particularly important to enhancing access power is to nurture relationships with 'gatekeepers'. Gatekeepers are individuals who, metaphorically, open doors, so that access to important people may be achieved. Gatekeepers facilitate introductions to influential others through their contacts, or through their access to particular networks. Gatekeepers, in turn, may facilitate relationships to others, who in turn can facilitate further access. Nurturing a network of gatekeepers can prove to be a valuable exercise, as such connections can potentially provide unlimited access to key people. Political party lobbyists act as gatekeepers. They have learnt that they can solicit support from being able to 'introduce' the right people to each other.

A current vogue in the management literature is the emphasis on networking. A manager wishing to determine the views within the organization would be encouraged to nurture a network of contacts. A manager made redundant, starting again as a consultant, would also be encouraged to grow a network that can provide access to fee-paying clients. A powerful concept in marketing is relationship marketing, whereby relationships are used to interest people in purchasing products or services. Further, and despite laws concerning confidentiality and privileged information, some organizations sell lists of named individuals to other organizations to facilitate sales activities. Power through connections, in today's world, is big business in its own right.

An alternative is to use the power of one's office to gain audience with other key parties. The chairman and/or CEO of an organization may use the influence of their positions and that of the organization, to gain access to government ministers, in order to discuss privately a sensitive issue that may be affecting their company. Equally, access can be gained to particular members of the press and the media in order to present an organization's viewpoint on key issues.

Very particular roles may provide for privileged access. The CEO of a company may have access to a select network of other CEOs. Privileged access such as this provides the opportunity to offer, and be the recipient of, 'self-disclosure' information. Self-disclosure information is that information of a personal and private nature that is freely offered by one individual to another on the basis of trust, and through showing membership of an inner circle. Two or more individuals who know each other and have accepted unspoken ways of interacting within that inner grouping, feel sufficiently confident to discuss matters of a confidential nature that could be otherwise damaging or embarrassing if they became public knowledge. Trust, in such circumstances, is not based only on personal confidence in each other, but also through each being a member of a privileged inner circle, whereby people have accepted the tacit rules of that group.

Experience power

Experience power is dependent on an individual having spent time in an organization, function, role, or industry, or a combination of the aforementioned. The individual, more than likely, will have some sort of expertise of a functional or professional kind, but through having spent substantial periods of time within a particular context, will have gained insights into how to apply their expertise, and how to address issues effectively, within that situation.

According to the nature of each context, being seen as credible and as effective, will vary. A combination of numerous demographic factors will be responsible for forging varying realities. For example, a new function in a newly established company may value entrepreneurial drive and hence effectiveness of performance could be interpreted as making meetings short, attending to customers (to the point of neglecting internal administration) and displaying high drive and devotion to the organization. Alternatively, in a more traditional industry, or in a company with a powerful and seductive history, where precedence and tradition count, management's view of effectiveness of performance could be interwoven with displays of respect for protocol. Having lived in the organization, having become acquainted with the key opinion drivers in the industry, and having witnessed what different companies in the same or other industries truly value, provide the individual with a road map to navigate his/her way through contrasting cultures. Experience is held to be synonymous with the concept of the road map, namely the guide on how to steer ways through different people and organizations, while enhancing one's own credibility and concurrently being viewed as effective.

Organizations value highly and will pay considerable salaries to people who are seen as competent and experienced. Such individuals have learnt, over time, to read and react to circumstances in ways that are considered as appropriate. A professionally competent and experienced senior manager is likely to display confidence in his/her own actions, as opposed to displaying hesitation, a symptom of lack of sureness about a particular situation. Most people appreciate interacting with a person who displays confidence. No-one can ever be sure as to which path to take in circumstances of social and business diversity. Taking a lead from someone who is credible, performs effectively and displays confidence, is a satisfying and comforting experience. Such comfort may not be forthcoming if the leader is an expert credible person, but one who does not display the experience and insight to survive in a challenging situation. When people are under pressure, they want someone who can show them the way forward, but does not necessarily have the best brains!

Tried and tested experience, displays of confidence, coupled with functional knowledge or relevant subject area expertise, can make a top manager unassailable. Experience power is the most impactful of the six levers. A person can alter substantially the mindset of bosses, colleagues, subordinates and other interested stakeholders, through the sole application of experience power.

Application of power levers: a global view

As already highlighted in the last chapter, multiple cultures exist in any one organization, whereby ethnicity is no strong differentiator of cultural or contextual ways. The values, attitudes, behaviours and mannerisms of the staff and management of an organization can vary by site, by department, by function, due to the impact of external pressures, the orientation and personalities of local senior management, geographic location, the positive or negative feelings one part of the organization holds towards another part, and/or the position adopted by corporate headquarters towards the operating businesses.

There exist as many differences between the members of one race of people, as there are differences between American, English, Japanese,

French and German people. What induces success in one place, may not work in another.

On this basis, a sensitive application of power levers in different contexts is as important as knowledge of the power levers themselves. Hence, an analysis of power lever application within the global cultures identified in Chapter 2, namely on how effectively to adopt the power levers in a consultative, divisive, development or cohesive culture, is examined.

Powering in consultative cultures

The effective application of the power levers in consultative cultures requires taking into account the feelings and views of individuals and of the community before acting (see Table 3.1). A community might not tolerate someone powering their way through.

The use of power to offer rewards will vary according to the person and circumstances, but is always likely to centre on one theme and that is,

Table 3.1   Consultative cultures: use of power levers

Type of power	Description
Role power	Dependent on the guidelines set by the community; issues addressed through dialogue; sensitivity to feelings of others; reward is membership of community and acceptance by community; punishment would be subtle and covert; criticized for not portraying values of community; ultimate punishment is to have membership of community withdrawn.
Personal impact power	Sharing, caring and listening; generating a warm and supportive environment; mentoring, counselling and support.
Reverence power	Respectful towards others' values and ways of life; actively show no desire to control.
Numbers game power	Share interpretation of numbers implications; gather data jointly; use numbers to inform of current circumstances; cautious in presenting bad news.
Context power	Cautious not to offend; high capability to read tacit communication; form views but declare only when appropriate; become expert at communicating through tacit means; gain credibility/standing in the community before using tacit knowledge to negotiate.
Access power	Make external contacts available to other members of community; help others to make appropriate linkages; share information; if necessary give up ownership of sources of information.
Experience power	Offer advice, do not assert; inform without being seen to know more; display wisdom/expertise with humility; influence guidelines set by community.

acceptance by, or membership to, the community. A powerful reward is access to the community. People are allowed access to meetings to discuss issues with members of the community. Certain academic departments, for example, may reward people whom they call upon to undertake work on the department's behalf by offering them visiting scholar status. The individuals offered the title of Visiting Fellow or Visiting Professor, may or may not be academics, but they are respected and valued by the academic community. No financial reward is offered. The status of the visiting title is reward in itself. However, the greatest reward of all is to be offered membership of the community, in recognition of having the necessary qualities that the community values. The ceremony that accompanies being accepted, signifies the importance of such an event.

For those within the community, praise from the other members of the community is often considered sufficient reward. Recognition of being seen to have done a good job is superseded by praise for having contributed significantly to the development of the community. The greatest reward of all is to be recognized as an individual who represents the community and hence is seen as a fundamental pillar of that society. It is unlikely that anyone is formally voted to such a position of honour. Through discussion among the 'elders' of the community, such recognition is tacitly bestowed. In effect, in being given the reward that shows that the person epitomizes the fundamentals of the community, they have been voted into the inner circle. The person is now likely to be seen as a first among equals; in fact, as an elder.

Open use of coercion, punishment and/or pressure is unlikely to be tolerated. If pressure needs to be brought to bear on any individual or group, it would be subtly applied, and covert in action. Suggestions would be made to the erring individual that he/she should change his/her ways. Others in the organization would be asked to 'talk sense' to the person who is seen to be a problem. Coercion would be applied in the form of pointed discussion and counselling. If the softer approaches do not produce a change of behaviour, open criticism may be made, more in the form of the person not portraying the values of the community, and possibly damaging the image of the community in the eyes of its members or the outside world. Under extreme circumstances, the person who is seen to be at fault may have their membership of the community withdrawn.

In a consultative culture, it is difficult to distinguish between organizational role and personal impact power. To influence others depends on an individual's capacity to nurture a warm and supportive environment within which people feel comfortable to discuss and raise issues. The more comfortable the other members of the community feel, the more accepted certain behaviours and practices become. Effective use of personal power provides a platform for the legitimate application of role through the delicate use of sensitivity, according to the needs of the situation at the time. For a consultative culture, the purpose of which is to provide for the individuals in the organization rather than the individuals provide for the organization, effectively applied role and personal power are, in reality, gaining influence through mentoring. The potential for influence is enhanced if deep respect is shown to the values and ways of others in the organization. Understanding, coupled with a desire for involvement, but not control, builds a platform of trust, so much the foundation of consultative cultures.

Similar to role, personal impact and reverence power, the use of experience is dependent on the tacit guidelines that are established by the community. For expertise and experience to be respected, they need to be channelled so as to be of benefit to the community. Expertise can be seen as threatening, and even the best of advice can be rejected if it is seen as damaging the fabric of the community. In order to reduce the perceived levels of threat, the use of expertise and the offering of advice may need to be tested out in more private meetings with certain senior managers, to ascertain their acceptance. The skill is not to assert, but to inform others without being seen to know more than they know. The display of expertise and experience needs to be coupled with sobering humility. The effective application of expertise and experience is through educating others and, if necessary, relinquishing the ownership of that knowledge base by transferring key insights to other highly respected members of the community.

As with experience power, the appropriate use of contacts and information is through sharing. Sharing before being asked to share is a route to being trusted more. If the community feels it appropriate, an individual may need to transfer ownership of his/her sources of information, so that other colleagues can benefit. Further, the value of information in itself is limited, unless guidance is provided in terms of how information should be interpreted. Particular sensitivity would need to be applied when interpreting information that is perceived as negative and critical. People would need to be guided gently through the feedback they receive. Having access to the sources of information as well as to the information itself is important, in case it is necessary to protect the organization from bad news.

The appropriate usage of the power levers is through sharing and being non-threatening. For example the Senior Vice President for Corporate Communications of the Swedish company, Khabi Pharmacia, Rune Borg, described his organization as one in which, 'we involve people very much ... we involve the unions together with the production people from different levels and work in a group to try and get consensus'.

Pharmacia is no small business. At the time of Rune Borg's interview, Pharmacia employed over 20,000 staff worldwide, with a turnover of billions of Kroner, represented through marketing companies in 34

countries, and whose products are sold in over 100 countries. In Pharmacia, the way people are treated is a vital consideration. Establishing an open communications approach to management is a prerequisite. A similar philosophy is applied externally, in order that the organization should promote its values and beliefs, and that others can benefit from such linkages. Such thinking is not idealism, for as Rune Borg highlights, Pharmacia's 100 per cent acquisition of the Italian company Elbermont will account for 40 per cent of Pharmacia's turnover. Making the right linkages in the newly acquired organization, sharing insight and views among Pharmacia's managers so as to facilitate a sincere and better culture of open communication management in Elbermont, is a necessity. Should Elbermont underperform, Pharmacia could be in substantial difficulty. With Pharmacia, performing and underperforming are intrinsically tied together with the culture of the organization. Consultative practice and doing business go hand in hand.

The effective use of experience power in the step-by-step development of Elbermont, is likely to be crucial. Developing a map of the organization which will guide managers through the varying contexts of the enterprise, while maintaining credibility with internal stakeholders, will be a necessary way forward for Pharmacia leaders. It would be of paramount importance for Pharmacia managers to take the time to understand the various parts of Elbermont. In so doing, Pharmacia management would highlight their interest and caring. They would wish people in Elbermont to know that they were wanted. The aim would be to nurture a culture in Elbermont that is not only acceptable to Pharmacia, but is also approved of by the Italians. In a consultative organization, the more accomplished are its leaders in the use of tacit knowledge, the more credible they become in the eyes of their community. Pharmacia's likely aim would be to become accomplished at interacting with Elbermont on their tacit wavelength. Whether that is what Elbermont desires, remains to be seen.

Powering in divisive cultures

Few would publicly admit that they work for, and uphold the values of, divisive cultures, but it is surprising how many organizations have evolved ways of working that are fundamentally unpleasant, but are still successful as organizations.

A divisive culture primarily depends on the dexterous use of reward, coercion and personal impact power (see Table 3.2). The prime aim within such an organization is to win, but in the sense of personal rather than organizational gain. Such behaviour would be justified on the grounds that entrepreneurship and energy attain success at an organizational level. In reality, people promote themselves and their own causes. Win, even at the expense of others, is justified. Reverence is demanded

Table 3.2   Divisive cultures: use of power levers

Type of power	Description
Role power	Proclaim virtue of rules, systems and regulations; apply systems and regulations to others but not to self; punishment/coercion; browbeat; get one's own way; use charm and fear; punish mistakes, minor errors, and anyone who could be a threat; win if necessary at the expenses of other(s); use negative reward – if I cannot win, no-one else can.
Personal impact power	Displays of personal strength; uncompromising; displays of charisma; manipulate others; support only those on same side.
Reverence power	Demanded and must be displayed; a smokescreen to hide behind; just for show.
Numbers game power	Numbers mean little; numbers used to support predetermined arguments; truth and logic not valued; concrete information – facts, figures, trends, projections hold little meaning; decisions based on personalities, not data.
Context power	Used for survival; to prevent oneself from being manipulated; to enhance manipulation of others; courage is required to say 'no' to manipulation; courage is required to leave; counter productive if insights are too penetrating.
Access power	Emphasis on establishing wide range of connections, internally and externally; generate exclusive club; membership of club open to trusted protégés and to outsiders who could be useful; use outsiders to put pressure on insiders.
Experience power	Use/manipulate expertise of others; even display false level of expertise; manipulate information and expert databases.

and has to be portrayed. For divisive culture leaders, reverence does such wonders for the ego.

Winning would be achieved by results, external success, and through displays of personal strength. Being uncompromising in negotiations, and manipulating others would be coupled with displays of personal charisma, especially through spectacular, or even evangelical, presentations.

An additional display of personal strength would be to punish anyone else who displays just such a strength. Further, punishing mistakes and errors, even minor ones, takes place to act as a deterrent, communicating the misfortune that could befall anyone who challenges a power figure in the organization. Charm, fear, browbeating, demotion, isolation and other tactics of the 'black art' of power, are utilized liberally in divisive cultures.

In order to hide the rule-by-fear climate, senior management proclaim the virtues of discipline, co-operation and working according to the rules, systems and regulations. The formal aspects of role power would be placed on a pedestal. Senior management would display adherence to the system, but with no intent to follow through. Their hypocrisy would be visible to the rest of the organization, which inevitably undermines senior management's credibility. By implication, senior management would need to adopt even more coercive measures in order for them to maintain control and achieve their ends.

An equally powerful smokescreen, is an alternative use of reverence power. Often applied, just-for-show, reverence power, displays a non-threatening presence and hence will minimize attracting unwelcome attention. This way people can get on with what they want to do, partially covered by a blanket of safety.

Successful senior managers in a divisive culture would use the expertise and experience of others to support their particular case. Senior management would manipulate information and distort the interpretations that could be made from expert databases. Therefore, whatever the experts say, senior managers would be selective in their use of information in order to enhance their self image or that of their function or department. Any one senior manager may appear broadminded, displaying a balanced argument to indicate thoughtfulness and good reasoning, but is likely to pursue a purely personal agenda.

For those senior managers who wish to survive in a divisive culture, it is important for them to grow a network of contacts inside and outside the organization. In so doing, the temptation of the senior management would be to constitute an exclusive club, accessed by the privileged few. Control of membership of that inner circle would be in the hands of just a few of the senior managers in the organization. The exclusive inner circle would be open to the few trusted protégés of the club's members, and open to influential outsiders. Overall, the aim of the inner circle would be to protect itself and to promote its interests.

Organizations with a strong entrepreneurial culture are in danger of becoming divisive, especially if the organization attracts intelligent, energetic, verbally skilful individuals who are driven to succeed only on behalf of themselves. The ability and expertise of each person are used to gain marketplace advantage, while internal systems are viewed as inhibitory. Living in such a culture for any length of time can lead individuals to believe that sharing and trust are 'silly emotions', even though people may mouth the words of team work. University departments, with a history of dissension and poor management, could find themselves deeply embedded in a divisively-oriented environment. So too could consultancy practices, and health service organizations, where short-term goaling and a history of resistance to management controls have become a norm. Certain investment banks exhibit similar traits, where getting the deal and looking after oneself go hand in hand – 'If I cannot get what I want here, I will go somewhere else and take my clients with me.' Again, clever, well-qualified and articulate people can become almost paranoid about the actions and intentions of senior management, and see any initiatives emanating from the centre, as a threat.

Crisis rather than incremental change alters these disturbing and deeply held attitudes. Ironically, a leader skilled in the use of power levers in a divisive way, but with honourable intent, is likely to succeed in changing divisive cultures. The powerful leader would need to remove, or manipulate out of the organization, a sufficient number of the existing senior managers, so as to appoint newcomers who would hold different attitudes and values, and most of all display a loyalty to the person who hired them. With a quorum of new leaders in place, it is possible to introduce new ways of working which form the basis of a new culture.

Selfishness and personal survival characterize a divisive culture. In order to function effectively in such an organization, experience power will need to be extensively used. Who are the individuals in the organization not to upset? Who are the individuals to walk away from? How does one say 'no' without unfortunate outcomes emerging? How does one survive? With time, experience of the organization promotes greater understanding of the more powerful individuals who dominate agendas. Using experience power allows the person the emotional freedom to stand back and view the organization for what it really is! Being so disciplined has its positive outcomes. First, the individual may recognize some of the good points of the organization and thereby learn to appreciate the enterprise. Second, the individual may be able to decide more clearly whether to stay or leave. The danger with entering into a divisive culture, or staying too long in such an organization, is the loss of confidence and self-respect the individual may experience. Over-exposure to unhelpful, or even abusive ways of working, can be personally damaging. Standing back gives the person a chance to recognize that he/she is the one who is OK, and it is those who drive the organization who need help and attention. It could, however, be counter-productive to feed back one's insights, especially if those insights are too penetratingly accurate for others in the organization to accept. The individual is likely to be seen as threatening. Unless others in the organization wish to change their ways and values, the effective use of experience power is for self-survival and for personal development.

Powering in developmental cultures

The essence of a developmental culture is to focus on performance, effort and success through application, determination and ability (see Table 3.3). Reward in a developmental culture is gained through hard work and applying one's skills and being successful. Being recognized as a high quality performer is in itself seen as just reward. Equally, reward for

Table 3.3 Developmental cultures: use of power levers

Type of power	Description
Role power	Success through legitimate means, i.e. expertise, effective leadership, challenge; act, then check out; reward through results, which could be praise, recognition, money, or position; preference not to use coercion/punishment; sacked for poor performance/incompetence is ultimate sanction.
Personal impact power	Displays of success; leadership skills; charisma; for task at hand, not for self; dislike personal aggrandisement; take control only if necessary.
Reverence power	Not demanded but accepted; offered if successful or for outstanding performance; dynamic and earned.
Numbers game power	Decisions based on data, not personalities; attempt to record trends accurately; arguments driven by information, trends; accurately representing information becomes a deep-seated value; honest use of numbers promotes trust.
Context power	Valued for new insights; together with cognitive power, is highly valued; experience power may be naturally utilized, but is not recognized as such.
Access power	Always extending network of contacts; drive for greater access to new information; constant display of loyalty to organization despite access to outsiders; share contacts and new information internally.
Experience power	Acclaim strength and expertise of others; bask in glory of others; get others to share expertise; share experiences for development of others.

extraordinary effort, for high energy, for the successful attainment of goals, for effective leadership and for extraordinary contribution as a team member, could be praise, recognition, being voted as top of a league table, position, or money. For rewards to be meaningful in a developmentally cultural organization, they have to be directly linked to performance, and for them to be motivational, they need to be publicly recognized. On this basis, rewards for individual performance are easy to organize. Team, group or departmental rewards are more difficult to implement, as the direct relationship between effort and success is not clear. Hence, motivating people through group based bonuses is less likely to be effective, as individuals may feel that their efforts are worth more than the final reward they receive. Further, group based bonuses could demotivate people, as they may feel their efforts are being diluted by persons who are not contributing to the same degree. If the reason for pursuing group based rewards is to bind a team or group to a mission, or common set of values, there is little need to pursue that avenue, as the enthusiasm and positive nature of individuals drive people to identify fully with, and promote, the organization. Perhaps the greatest reward of all is the reverence offered to those who are successful, or those who display outstanding skill. Reverence power is far more dynamic in developmental cultures than in the other three cultures. People earn the right to be revered and as the criteria for effective performance and success are ever changing, reverence is potentially attributable to all, is also deeply satisfying, but an all too short lived experience.

Coercive and punishment-oriented power levers would be reluctantly applied because of their potential to demotivate the high performers. The danger with sacking people is that others are discouraged from being adventurous, as they may feel that making a mistake would be seen as incompetence. Hence, it is sufficient sanction to be told that one's performance is poor and requires improving. Receiving negative feedback is likely to hurt the individual's sense of self-worth, and as a result, the person is likely to make extra effort to improve, or to leave the organization voluntarily. In developmental cultures, it is bad enough to not be the best, but to be seen as the worst is difficult to tolerate. However, for incompetence, for consistent poor performance, or for displaying behaviours and attitudes of mind that demotivate others, the response induced is likely to be, 'leave the organization'. Once it becomes absolutely clear that all has been done to improve the performance of those less capable and nothing has improved, then sacking people is not viewed negatively, just as, unfortunate.

Further, the threat of firing is also an effective technique for dealing with managers who will not resolve differences among them. Allowing for differences of opinion can act as the grit which sharpens and stimulates debate. Not resolving differences, and allowing damaging conflicts to continue, especially between key players in the organization, can substantially distract a considerable number of people from the task at hand. Distraction not only undermines the focus and discipline necessary for maintaining sustained performance, it can equally demotivate a large number of people in the organization. The attitude is, 'we are all in the same boat; leaders, managers, experts, operatives and support staff – do not ask of others what you yourself cannot do! A developmental cultured organization requires positive leadership from the front. To witness leaders fighting each other, or not communicating, instead of focusing on the 'common enemy out there', is a cue that the organization is now on a downward path. The more able personnel may leave. The less able are likely to become demotivated. Warring differences publicly played out, are just as damaging as inconsistency of performance.

Hence, legitimacy in the organization is gauged by success. Success can be achieved through expertise or through the exciting and forceful leadership of others. What is achievable and leads to greater success, do! Then check it out! The developmental culture is a 'can-do' culture. The effective application of power levers in a can-do culture is, achieve success, but also be legitimate.

As the aim is achievement and success through legitimate means, the appropriate use of personal impact and of experience power intertwine. Individuals need to display their capabilities, which may involve risk-taking, leadership, team skills, charisma, effective communication, as well as promoting the strength and expertise of others, and if successful, basking in their reflected glory. In a developmental culture, it is not necessary to display one's own skills, as reward and acclaim are given as much to those who get the best out of others.

As striving for success requires continuous improvement in one's own performance as well as in that of others, an equal drive is exhibited for acquiring or generating new ideas and insights. Being one step ahead of the competition through innovation in products or services is import-ant, but so too is being innovative in terms of marketing, sales and segmentation. Hence, the belief is that through gaining new informa-tion, sharing that information internally, through challenging current mindsets, new insights emerge, which if harnessed, provide for competitive advantage. At all costs, data about markets, products, or people and numbers, in terms of financial performance, are preserved and reported in their raw state. It would be sacriligous to attempt to distort the reality that emerges through information. The attitude is 'let's be clear about our current circumstances, and then face all challenges head on!'

In order to support the process of gaining new insights, staff and managers in the organization are likely to be encouraged to extend and grow their external networks. Making new contacts provides for developing a broader and more insightful view of what various stakeholders are doing in the marketplace. Mixing and debating with outsiders is more likely to stimulate continuous learning than attending structured management programmes. However, individuals are likely to be reminded of their need to display and uphold their loyalty to the organization, despite the stimulation of being with interesting people.

In a developmental culture, where use of expertise and up-to-date information are so highly desired, people in the organization may not recognize the value of experience power. Hence, in order to make a significant impact, experience power, in addition to being linked with personal impact power, needs to be blended with context power. The capability to stand back, recognize the nature of trends and develop-ments, provide interpretation as to how to respond effectively, and then to provide viable ways of responding, would be deeply valued by the rest of the organization, if the case were appropriately presented. Rational discourse is so strong, that providing insight has to be coupled with expert opinion and up-to-date information, in order to be valued as credible within the context of a developmental culture.

Powering in cohesive cultures

As a cohesive culture attempts to match clarity of communication with effectiveness of co-ordination and the successful attainment of goals, the effective use of power levers requires being systematic and displaying respect toward the position and status of others in the organization (see Table 3.4).

People are rewarded for not only competent performance, but even more so for staying within the system and for maintaining positive relationships with others in the organization. A fine line exists between raising issues which require discussion and attention, and not being seen as threatening. People are rewarded for being not only successful in terms of paying attention to detail, for being disciplined, but also for being predictable. Being predictable provides the comfort of knowing that no individual is likely to disrupt his/her surroundings, which could ripple uncomfortably through the organization.

Table 3.4   Cohesive cultures: use of power levers

Type of power	Description
Role power	Keeping within defined formal relationships; exhibit contextually correct behaviour; rewards for keeping within existing parameters; rewards for nurturing positive relationships; rewards for success, but also for attention to detail and being disciplined; be predictable; raise issues but do not be threatening; punishment/coercion through loss of face; excessive use of punishment can undermine leader's position.
Personal impact power	From role status; status from age; seen as a sage; through listening.
Reverence power	Respect to elders; respect for founders; respect for system.
Numbers game power	Responsibility of lower level staff to produce data, information; responsibility of leader to interpret/contextualize data; numbers less important than guidance provided; information in itself holds little meaning; others need guidance in how to use/view information; tacit knowledge outweighs concrete information.
Context power	Need time to learn/appreciate tacit knowledge; insights gained from mentor; insights also gained through activity on task/job.
Access power	Develop and use connections to fulfil requirements of role, and for the sake of co-ordination; seen to develop connections for sake of organization and not for self; must not disrupt internal/external balance of relationships; not for personal gain or self aggrandisement; once access made, all legitimate parties should be made aware.
Experience power	Expertise less important than harmony; through informing/educating others; through not showing one is more skilful.

As with rewards, the appropriate use of role power generally depends on respecting what is constituted as legitimate. Legitimacy, in a cohesive culture, is behaviour that is in keeping within defined boundaries. How to behave within particular contexts, how to communicate and how to relate to others, would already be historically established. On this basis, personal impact power and reverence power are deeply intertwined, as so much depends on the status of the role one holds in the organization. Overall, however, in cohesive cultures, the degree of role discretion is limited, and so too is the opportunity to adopt personal impact power. But the particular manner in which even limited discretion is exercised, is crucial. Becoming influential but in a non-threatening manner, is fundamental to a cohesive culture, emphasizing the necessity of accomplishment at the use of reverence power. Being influential, non-threatening and older carries even greater credence. Age carries connotations of wisdom through years of exposure to and assimilation of, different experiences. Age and the capability to listen, distinctly portray wisdom; the sage whom all respect, but equally, in moments of difficulty, can approach for counsel and comfort. Although personal impact power can be enhanced through individual brilliance, the image of the sage is the more inspiring symbol. It should be noted that, the combination of wisdom and exceptional intellect do not sit comfortably together. In a cohesive culture, one precludes the other, for clever people are seen as unlikely to be predisposed to listen to the mundane, but nevertheless important, concerns of others. The fear is that talented people will quickly recognize pathways through problems, but are likely to exhibit impatience if others are slow to grasp the way forward. In contrast, the sage will invest time for others to benefit fully from their journey of discovery. The contradiction of time-frame and philosophy, force the two desired attributes to remain apart.

Similar to personal impact power, the effective use of experience power is through sincere dissemination of one's tacit knowledge of the organization. Experts are highly regarded in cohesive cultures as long as they know their place in that society. Displaying or using particular skills on projects or tasks is respected. On the other hand, an expert that strays beyond their task and project boundaries, is likely to be seen as threatening, for the individual may question the validity of the current role structure and by so doing upset harmony. Disrupting harmony is viewed as the greatest of crimes. Therefore, accomplishing and achieving, without showing one knows more than others, is appreciated and recognized to be in itself a skill of experience power.

Greatest respect and reverence is shown to the person who makes the time to inform and educate others to his/her own standard. Thoughtful application of experience power is necessary if the individual is embarking on the long journey of becoming a sage or wise man in the organization. The road from expert to wiseman, however, holds sexist overtones. Wisdom is symbolized by men in cohesive cultured organizations. Successful women within this value system, whatever else they may achieve and whatever bonuses they earn, are still unlikely to be seen as wise. The sex roles in cohesive cultures are sharply differentiated, as much is driven by tradition and precedence, and it is men who historically have been held as the elders.

As length of job-related tenure is extensive, people learn where the boundaries lie between each other, between departments and divisions, on specific issues, and even with change, as the process of change is incremental. Hence, coercion or punishment would be used with extreme reluctance, as that would signal that the accepted and every-day checks and balances had failed. Failure such as this would reflect on everyone and not just on the erring individual. However, within the bounds of day-to-day functioning, the most anxiety-provoking experience in a cohesive culture is loss of face. Punishment and coercion are likely to be used to threaten loss of face, and the purpose in threatening would be two-fold, to act as a deterrent to others, and to bring the sinful individual into line and gain his/her compliance. Apart from being seen as a failure by the community, an additional reason for the reluctance in using the coercive power lever, is that excessive use of coercion can upset internal harmony and hence, through loss of respect, undermine the leader's position. Above all else, the prime task of each individual is to maintain harmony, for it is believed that through harmony, success is achieved.

Numbers game power, or more broadly, the acquisition and use of information, is used according to what is legitimate in particular roles. As such, most information would be task related and hence would not be in danger of disrupting the internal balance of relationships. Information used to enhance a person's position in the organization, would be considered as inappropriate, and would likely damage the person's standing in the eyes of others. Equally, surprises are unacceptable. A person who holds relevant information would need to make time to keep all legitimate parties informed as to its content and how it is to be used.

As with the sharing of information, sharing of contacts and connections, equally applies. Access power is considered legitimately utilized if the requirements and objectives of one's role and task are fulfilled. On this basis, it is acceptable to foster internal connections, in order to improve co-ordination and co-operation. Similarly, with growing external contacts; the purpose would be to grow a network for the sake of the organization and not for personal benefit. In fact, in order for a person's activities to be legitimized, the individual may need to deliberately show that he/she is nurturing a network on behalf of the organization.

The effective application of context power is to enhance the 'ways' of the organization. The nature of the understandings people have with each other, and the customs and rituals that people entertain, are important to appreciate and observe. Standing back and taking time to learn about the organization are behaviours that are respected and expected. Little pressure would be applied to speeding up tacit learning about the organization. However, the knowledge learnt would be considered as inappropriately used if a person were to offer new and novel insights as a result of his/her learning. The purpose of context power, namely the gaining of tacit knowledge, is to know how to find one's way through the organization, ensuring that relationships are continuously well balanced. Tacit knowledge used to improve people's performance on task activities, is desired. Using tacit knowledge for providing feedback on how the organization functions, or how strategy should be developed, is valued only when offered by a person of status. No matter how valuable the insights, especially from newcomers who have the opportunity to review the organization from a fresh perspective, if a person does not hold the desired status, or is not asked to offer his/her views, not only would the feedback be rejected, but its offer would also be considered an insult. For a newcomer to offer penetrating, and by implication potentially valuable views about the organization and its strategy, would damage his/her prospects of promotion in that enterprise. Equally, the person who may have verbalized his/her thoughts, is unlikely to be informed that such behaviour was counter-productive. After all, being given the opportunity to think and learn about the organization should have led them to the conclusion that they should know when to speak, and about what. Inappropriate use of context power is likely to indicate that this person cannot be trusted with responsibility. A slow, but progressively effective use of tacit knowledge, initially on task-related matters, but over time on group and departmental issues, is likely to promote an image of a more trustworthy individual, in line for consideration for senior office.

By nature, a cohesively cultured organization is slow, attentive to detail and to relationships. Such a seemingly slow-moving organization is, however, relentless in the pursuit of its own goals. People know that their efforts and sacrifices will be appreciated. In turn, the leaders need to reflect these values in their daily actions. The wise application of power in cohesively cultured organizations is, proceed with caution and do not forget to display reverence, at least once a day!

Power to change

As highlighted, appropriate application of the power levers will vary from one organization to the next, according to the culture, history, leadership influence, impact of market forces, influence of the shareholders and stakeholders, and position in the economic cycle, that an enterprise is experiencing. The appropriate application of power levers helps leaders gain and maintain credibility in the organization. There exists another side to the effective application of power levers, and that is to alter the dynamics of contexts, namely to introduce and effectively progress change. Making power interventions work is likely to involve the addressing of the following issues (see Figure 3.1).

Recognition

Recognition of the issues that require attention in any one context needs to take place. As the change to be pursued is likely to be more of a transactional nature, only one, or a few people (the change agents) are required to pursue change purposefully. If most people identify the need for change and can broadly agree the direction change should take, there would be little need to use power as a vehicle for making change happen.

Discussion amongst the few who realize that change is necessary should highlight those areas that are deemed problematic, and how these challenges should be addressed. If too many change agents enter the situation, each pursuing his/her own path, chaos may reign for a while, until the most determined of the change agents' agendas win through.

Approaches

Having identified what needs changing and why, the individual or group will need to assess which approaches to change are required in order to address both the challenges being faced, and the needs of the context. Overt or covert use of the power levers could be equally effective, according to what is seen to be required. Whether overt, covert, or both, which power levers are considered the most appropriate to apply, is the next decision. The specific objective, at this point, is to induce particular changes of behaviour in individuals, according to context. No great changes need to be engineered, but what is done differently may involve altering certain day-to-day routine activities. Often changes to certain daily rituals and routines are powerful stepping stones to making broader changes come about. The more people are positioned to adjust their daily lives, the more they are likely to adopt new routines, thereby promoting change in a more natural way.

A review of the impact of initial change should be undertaken at this point (level 1 review), simply to examine whether or not certain old behaviours are being erased and new behaviours are being adopted. At this particular point, focus and detail are important. Proclaiming generalities will create opposition. Indicating what specifically needs to improve and why, without making judgemental comments, is likely to induce greater co-operation. The more focused are the power levers in bringing about change of specific behaviours, the more likely the level 1 review will show change and improvement.

Figure 3.1 Making power interventions work

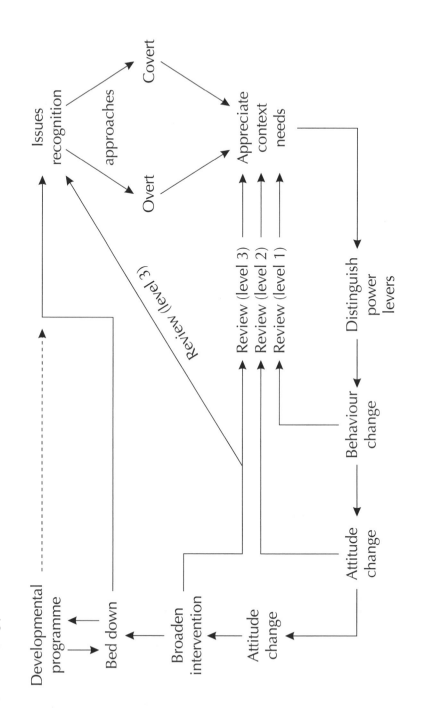

Attitude change

Depending on the conclusions drawn from the level 1 review as to which power levers to continue to apply, the focus on changing certain behaviours will begin to impact on the underlying attitudes held by people. As a result of the particular tactics used by the change agent(s), or the impact of particular project groups, focus teams, or even working parties, people are likely to question their own attitudes, as old practices are discarded and new ones adopted. By focusing on particular behaviours, old attitudes begin to be rejected. Adopting new ways, for any length of time, is likely to allow for the development of alternative views. However, the one factor that can prevent or hinder attitude change is emotional discomfort, which psychologists term as, 'dissonance'.

Dissonance is the experience of extreme discomfort, tempting the individual to withdraw from his/her situation, or to reject whatever is making him/her emotionally perturbed. Dissonance occurs when an individual cannot accommodate the different influences they are experiencing at a particular moment in time. Having one's opinions challenged, or one's work and/or behaviour criticized, can provoke dissonance. Unable to cope, the individual rejects his/her immediate experiences and reverts to old and familiar ways of working. However, if a person can live through the emotional challenge of having his/her accepted ways and attitudes questioned, he/she may adopt a new or adapted perspective towards life and work. The basis of new attitudes begins to be formed.

At this point, a second review is required, level 2 review. The level 2 review will not only provide insights as to the degree of attitude change that is taking place in the situation, but will also highlight the degree of dissonance and negativity prevailing among those involved in the change programme. To help consolidate the degree of change and to reduce the levels of dissonance, project groups and working parties should examine the structure of people's jobs and the structure and objectives of work groups and teams, in order to ascertain the degree of clarity of the tasks and activities required of people, and of the targets they have to pursue. When people know what is required, when people are given clear key performance indicators, and are being measured against those indicators, ambiguity is reduced, which in turn reduces anxiety.

In addition to restructuring people's daily work lives and introducing new rituals and daily routines, time for discussion and feedback should be allowed. The opportunity for people to exchange experiences and the manner in which they have overcome particular challenges, not only allows for a sharing of wisdom, but equally motivates individuals to continue making changes work. People will recognize that they are not alone, and will probably discover that they have been coping better than they initially considered. Apart from 'the feel good factor', people talking to each other about their change experiences provides for one further benefit, consolidation of the change process. Through talking, people not only share problems, but also successes. By concentrating on the success part of their experiences, the advantages of change can be realized. By recognizing the personal gain and the organizational advantage of change, people are likely to be personally and publicly content to continue with the process of change. Offering commitment, especially publicly, is difficult to retract. To verbalize commitment to change is to proclaim ownership of the new developments that have taken place, and a public statement, consequently, means that people cannot comfortably use the excuse that they are merely carrying out someone else's commands. They are now firmly following through, not receiving orders. No longer is there one champion of transactional change, but many.

Broaden the intervention

Should the scope and pursuit of the intervention be enlarged? Should change be cascaded through different parts of the organization? The answer to these questions requires a judgement of balance; balancing internal developments with the impact of change on key stakeholders. Having changed certain parts of the organization, new expectations will have formed amongst the organization's staff and management, as well as among external parties, such as customers, suppliers and shareholders. Broadening the intervention to address the needs of a wider group of stakeholders, whose concerns may not easily coincide, takes transactional change into the arena of transformational alteration. Level 3 review will not only require a re-assessment of the impact of the change process at a contextual level, but a fundamental re-examination of the issues that first led to the journey of change.

Bedding down

Assuming that transactional change has not tipped over into transformational restructuring, an important part of the change process is to return to normality, but a new normality. The now-famous Kurt Lewin model of unfreezing leading to refreezing, applies. Bedding down is refreezing, a post change experience, a moulding of new ways into the organization. Bedding down is refreezing, but with internalization. Internalization is the result of an individual having undergone behavioural change, attitudinal change and job-related change, having come to terms with the changes and the negative emotions emanating from change, and has emerged from that experience with re-shaped values, norms and ways of functioning. Internalization provides for a new normality, whereby the changes that are experienced become so accepted, that the person no longer sees the new ways as change.

In order to assist the internalization process, numerous companies support their staff and management by providing programmes of development. The developmental process could be more on-the-job related, highlighting the key skills and attributes required of people in order to improve their performance. Further, mentoring, counselling, workshops and seminars could be organized to allow people to question, practise and learn about how to apply the newly developed skills effectively.

Equally, off-the-job courses could be arranged, combining developmental experiences, such as feedback from psychological and management-style tests, group exercises and activities, with educational inputs such as case studies and lectures on topics of change-management, organization culture and structure, leadership and team skills and, if desired, functional skills such as marketing or information technology. Through programmed tuition on courses, individuals will be helped not only in terms of job-related performance, but equally offered frameworks to help them better understand how organizations function, the skills necessary for running organizations and the doing of good business, and why and how people experience change processes. The frameworks are designed to help people place their own experiences into perspective, and in so doing help them more fully understand what are the challenges commonly associated with change. For greater detail on the developmental pathways to pursue on behalf of managers and leaders, see Chapter 12.

As people internalize their newly found skills and ways of conducting their affairs, and consolidate their learning, their view of the issues that are important to address will have altered. Even the debates and feedback that will have taken place through the development programmes, will raise new views and concerns as to the future challenges to address. And so, the process of change continues or is resisted, according to the views people hold of their own needs, and what they desire of their newly determined context, and the challenges that need to be faced in the future.

Power is?

Whatever power is, it is not a 'black art', or 'the dark side' to management, or the 'worst side' of leadership. Power is a means of working through differences in an organization, in the recognition that not all people in an enterprise share comparable, or even compatible agendas. In such circumstances, open discussion without an examination of intents and underlying motives, leaves a leader vulnerable to the manipulation of others. Such vulnerability does not extend to just the person in charge, but to all those who report to, or are dependent on the leader. The proposition is that the working through of differences without due attention to power and its use, is tantamount to damaging neglect. On the positive side, the well-integrated combination and application of the power levers, especially in scenario changing circumstances, provides for an awesome force.

Key points summary

- The topic of power in organizations is a relatively new entrant into the field of organizational psychology and administrative studies.
- Until relatively recently, power was viewed as a difficult topic to discuss openly in the field of management studies, despite its prevalence and exposure in community and political studies.
- Power has been viewed from numerous standpoints such as, a fundamental way of behaving in organizations, as a form of personal influence, as a key factor that leads to success, the manner in which resources are used, as a means for creating dependency on the power wielder, and as an exciting experience.

Power levers

- The use of power is identified as applying seven key power levers, namely role power, personal impact power, reverence power, numbers game power, context power, access power and experience power.
- Role power emanates from holding a particular role in an organization, from which a range of potential resources can be used to influence, to the role leader's advantage, such as power of authority, power to allocate rewards, power to punish, power to control resources, power of dismissal/demotion, power to change structures, power to coerce, and power to arbitrate.
- Personal impact power involves the application of individual characteristics, such as elements of personality (extroversion), personal style (charm), or physical characteristics (attractive appearance), in order to influence others.
- Reverence power involves promoting a mystique whereby the adulation of the leader reaches almost immortal proportions and as such can substantially sway the opinions and behaviour of others.
- Numbers game power involves utilizing financial and numeric information to influence and control the activities of others. Numbers can be used to control through fear, by the asking of questions on points of detail for which the other person is unprepared, thereby generating sufficient anxiety in the individual that they will not confront their boss on other unrelated issues in case they should experience being 'caught off guard'. Numbers can also be used to

inform and thereby influence people's views, through presenting them with trends. Using numbers as information can also promote debate and participative decision-making.

■ Context power involves understanding the nature of particular circumstances, and having the credibility in particular contexts to use that understanding to influence and to re-negotiate agendas.

■ Access power involves having personal access, or having access through networks and other third parties, to key people, to either influence them, or to harness their support.

■ Experience power requires an individual to have spent time in an organization, role, or industry, in order to appreciate the manner in which decisions are made and implemented, the manner in which relationships evolve, and the manner in which issues are addressed, and then to use that tacit information to influence people and circumstances.

Applying the power levers

■ The manner in which to apply the seven power levers is discussed in relation to the four global cultures examined in Chapter 2.

■ Effectively powering in a consultative culture, involves taking into account the feelings of individuals and the community, and ensuring that the sharing of information is done in such a way that individuals feel supported and confident to enter into debate, thus proceeding to participative decision-making. Achieving consensus through helping people feel good, even over more difficult issues, is a necessary consideration in applying the power levers in consultative cultures.

■ Effectively powering in divisive cultures requires the use of personal power, reward and coercion, in order to be able to make an impressive impact in, essentially, an uncompromising organization, where displays of personal strength and charisma tend to win the day. The apt combination of personal charm with bullying tactics, can give rise to the darker aspects of power, those of manipulation and fear.

■ Effectively powering in developmental cultures requires openness and honesty in addressing key issues facing the organization. Being successful and professional can be achieved through many routes, as long as individuals do not attempt to turn situations solely to their personal advantage, as is likely to be the case in a divisive culture.

■ Effectively powering in cohesive cultures involves taking into account the cultural norms of the organization, ensuring that protocol is respected, and being respectful towards rules and the status of others in the organization. Unlike the consultative culture, in which attention to and nurture of personal relationships are crucial in establishing credibility, paying attention to formality, roles and the organizational status quo is vital in order to apply the power levers in a cohesive culture effectively. Applying oneself in a disciplined and systematic way needs to be coupled with displays of predictability and subservience. The system has to move forward at a pace which does not damage the organization.

■ Using power to introduce change into the organization requires taking into account the degree of change desired and the particular stages of change that need to be negotiated, namely, recognition of the issues that need to be addressed, the approaches to take to address those issues, managing the process of attitude change, deciding whether the intervention requires broadening, and finally working towards bedding down and having change accepted as part of an everyday normality.

Note

1 Adapted from Kakabadse *et al.* (1988).
2 ibid.
3 ibid.

Further reading

Different perspectives of power can be found as follows:

■ Seen as one of the 'last dirty little secrets' of the social sciences – Bennis (1974: 62).
■ Power has little to do with leadership, because of its antisocial connotations – Pfeffer (1992).
■ Balancing out inequalities and differences between people – Bachrach and Lawler (1986).
■ Psychological power – Machiavelli (1958).
■ Organizational power – French and Raven (1959).
■ Power-behavioural tactics – Fairholm (1993).
■ The leader recognizing that the use of power and influence is important to realizing achievements in the organization – McClelland (1975).
■ How power should be used in more indirect, people sensitive cultures – Wierzbicka (1991) as opposed to more direct, explicit cultures – Korac-Kakabadse and Korac-Kakabadse (1998).

CHAPTER 4

Working Through Differences
– Politics

Case analysis

It's just like a cult

A friend of ours, newly appointed as a director of a well-known US company, met with us for dinner, seven months after his appointment. We had hardly finished asking him how he was getting on when he blurted out, 'It's just like a bloody cult. That's what it's like where I am. It's just like a bloody cult!'

There was no need to ask what he meant, as he continued:

> There's this one strong character, the Marketing Vice President, he runs the place as if it was his own garage. He controls what happens in the organization; who is in favour, who is out of favour. Every damned idea just has to have his OK. But when you confront him, he denies all this. He then asks you why you are being so negative. Is something wrong? Is there anything he can do to help? Smart-arsed bastard. What makes it worse is that he is good at his job. He really does know his marketing.

Further discussion revealed a friend, considerably frustrated by the fact that his views, ideas and contribution were not valued, were rejected, and he did not feel respected:

> Every time I say something it's 'Oh! That's not the way we do things here', or 'Arnie, you're only saying that because you're new', or 'we recognized over the years that what you are saying just wouldn't work!' I'm going crazy! If I don't find a way through, I'll leave. The reason I haven't left so far is that I have invested so much in this move. The family's been moved, Margaret gave up her job, we've not yet sold the last house and we've sunk our capital into the new one. I want to leave, but I've got to make this job work.

Arnie continued with the tale of his problems. He ended up by saying,

> You know what it's like with that damned guy calling the shots, it's
> just like a cult. It's not just getting everyone to do what he wants,
> but he's telling them how to think, how to feel, even, damn it, how
> to dress. It's just like a cult. It's lifestyle blackmail.

Three weeks later, and by coincidence, we were invited by the
company in question, to come in and discuss how best to develop their
up-and-coming managers for senior responsibility. The CEO stated:
'We have a very particular culture here. One of the reasons why we are
successful is the great performance of the marketing function.'

'Yes, we have worked damn hard to make sure we have a successful
business. Our branding and marketing are powerful and we have
everybody inside 100 per cent bought into us being a success. If they
are successful the business is successful', added the Marketing Vice
President.

(Arnie was not present at this meeting.)

'Would your organization be described as having a strong, thrusting
culture?', it was Nada who asked.

'Yes, I reckon that's how you would describe it', responded the
Marketing VP.

'How do newcomers fit in then? If you are so successful, what
contribution do people new to the organization feel they can make?',
Nada continued.

'That is and has been a problem,' replied the Marketing VP. He
continued:

> We've worked hard to know what will make this company
> successful. We know we demotivate some new guys when we tell
> them what they have got to say won't work. Our real problem with
> new hires is to help them fit in, use that part of their contribution
> that will work and still keep our own minds open to new ideas.
> Well, I guess that's one of the reasons why we are talking to you. We
> want to make best use of our people; we want new people and new
> ideas but we don't want to lose what's good in the place!

The different positions of Arnie and the Marketing VP generated
contrasting viewpoints. Arnie's was one of being shut out and excluded;
the Marketing VP's, one of thinking to bring on board new talent, and yet
wanting to preserve and promote the best of what existed. In their own
way, both parties were well intentioned. Both wanted to do well and yet
could not bridge the contrasts between them.

Organizations are made up of differences and contrasts. What one
person feels is valuable and should be preserved, someone else may wish

to change. Over time, some may adapt their point of view, while others rigidly stick to their ideas. However, in order to live and work together, bridges need to be built between people who hold such differences of perspective. In order to promote 'bridges' in the organization effectively, account would need to be taken of the different contexts, culture and ways of doing, that exist in the organization. Attention will equally need to be given to influencing key people in the organization. These people need not only be senior managers. Influential managers running geographically distant locations need to be brought on board. Upset these managers and they may walk out, taking with them their network of clients. Other influential figures in the organization also need to be convinced of a likely course of action, or of the necessity to pull together to form a united front, after a change exercise.

Therefore, the second part (the first part being the use of power) to working through differences in the organization, is to be able to influence people in a manner that is beyond charm, being nice and, as so many business school programmes would proclaim, 'being interpersonally skilful'. Complex circumstances require that thought be given to who needs to be influenced and why, how they need to be influenced, and what these individuals share which needs to be reckoned with if both are going to 'buy into' the influence process. For the successful leader, understanding politics in organizations is as important as understanding the dynamics and volatility of share prices.

Why do politics arise? Why can politics in organizations feel energy-sapping, irrelevant and irritating, but still require attention and careful handling? What is the nature of differences that give rise to so-called political interventions, and how does one then understand and appropriately respond to political circumstances? An all-too-often reminder of inappropriate transactional leadership, is the observation of a senior manager attempting to power his/her way through active or passive opposition, ending up in a worse position than if he/she had done nothing. The impotence of the person shows, as does his/her inability to read situations effectively. His/her insensitivity to distinguish between power and politics, particularly shows. The 'bull-in-the-china-shop' leader has not distinguished the value between direct action and skilful influence, between push and cajole. The net result of such inappropriate behaviour? – someone, probably a good person, leaves, or gets pushed out! Some worthwhile initiative falters, runs out of steam and dissipates. The net result is lost opportunity and waste.

From an examination of why the need for politics, attention then turns to exploring why tensions continually arise in organizations. The point emphasized is that strain in organizations is an experience of normality; but nevertheless, it needs sensitive management, as strains and tensions can lead to a deterioration of relationships and possible punitive behaviour. From an understanding of why tension arises, analysis then focuses on how and why problems emerge within particular settings, with the emphasis being on context. It is the actions of individuals within particular contexts that require consideration. Finally, the actions that can enhance political influence are provided and discussed. The reason this chapter concentrates on analysing political circumstances rather than describing successful political behaviour, is because research and experience highlight that, instinctively, most leaders are aware of the desired political behaviour that suits the context. However, many do not behave as their instincts suggest, due to reasons of lack of confidence, anxiety, or more because of a deeper moral or philosophical disdain of politics. As the reasons for behaving (or not behaving) politically seem to be more influential in determining what people do, rather than being insightful into appropriate 'political behaviours', this chapter reflects this perspective, in the hope that being better informed will help people to act in ways that enhance their and others' quality of life.

Why politics?

Arnie did not stay long in the organization. He felt he could not make sufficient headway at the rate he felt he deserved. Arnie concluded that he failed because the politics got to him. In his view, he was out of favour, others were more in favour, and it was 'too damn difficult' to really break into the place. For him, it was like fighting a cult. Others who progressed, in this, as it turned out, highly successful enterprise, attributed their success to their abilities, drive, hard work and personal sacrifice. Arnie saw politics in a negative light, related to failure and damage, but still a powerful experience. Others never see politics, 'just themselves as successful, so what's the problem?'

As highlighted in Chapter 1, managing one's day-to-day affairs requires more than just doing a good job, especially in today's world of networking, and confusion over responsibilities and accountabilities. To continue to be successful as a leader requires skills in negotiation, skills in planning, skills in making projects work, all within particular contexts and with particular people. The effective management of activities within particular contexts, supported by particular opinion leaders, emphasizes the need for political skills. The effective application of politics is demanding, time consuming and can feel like time-wasting. Some not too fortunate, may devote considerable effort to vie for limited resources, but fail or not just quite achieve what they desired. They may accurately put their lack of accomplishment down to their being the victim of politics, seeing themselves as possibly having good ideas, but not being able to convince others, or fit with others. It is easy to see why politics is related to failure and damage, and perceived as a negative experience.

Even in the most positive of cultures, it may be necessary to apply political sensitivity. A new initiative is introduced, and most in the organization overtly indicate that they are working with the new system, but are, in fact, tampering with the initiative, ignoring it, but not declaring their discontent. The reason why people behave in this way is that they may recognize the logic of the new systems or ideas of their leaders, but dislike the impact the initiative has on their own group. They may not wish to change, but prefer to preserve their identity, professional ethics and traditions. Until their anxieties have been reduced or aired, their covert activities are likely to continue, damaging one initiative after another.

Hence, it is commonplace to experience that the actions and intentions of others can be misinterpreted, emphasizing the need to negotiate and influence in order to overcome blockages between people in the organization. Becoming more politically adept requires an understanding of the strains and differences that occur in an organization, and appreciating why different people react in different ways. Being effective at managing political interactions is no easy matter, for it is a strain to live in the middle of contrasting forces, while trying to negotiate appropriate pathways through tense relationships. Hence, discipline and personal robustness are as important to apply as are political skills.

Differentiating power from politics

As emphasized in the previous chapter, one key aspect of power is the use of direct action. A has to get B to do something whether B likes it or not. That should not be the case with politics, as the process of influence applied by A is to have B feel that he/she wish to accept A's ideas and apply them, because he/she identifies with A, and/or A's views. Hence, power can achieve change in others without their needing to feel ownership of what is being asked of them. For political influence to be successful, those being influenced need to feel some sense of ownership in terms of what is being asked of them (see Table 4.1). Power involves the use of something, a resource such as information or role authority, making power a potential to be applied or utilised in a situation. A person using political influencing skills has no tool other than him/herself. Such persons have no other lever except how well they influence people. In contrast, power can be applied in situations, and even if met with opposition, people are still likely to do, against their will, what they are being asked or pushed to do. Through political influence people act, or feel, differently, because the quality of the relationship is such that they themselves desire to pursue the new line. The aim of political influence is to change mindsets while being unable to call upon any other resource for assistance.

Table 4.1   Differentiating power from politics

Power	Politics
■ Speedy	■ Requires patience
■ Direct action	■ Influence others for them to wish to do

■ Applies to
   individuals
   groups
   organizations
	■ Applies to individuals
	■ Influence anyone
	■ Can apply with no other potential
	   leverage at hand

■ Downward influence	■ Needs to be subtle to be successful
■ Potential to do	■ Can achieve only with transfer of
■ Can be crude or subtle and still successful	ownership ■ With power is formidable
■ Can achieve impact without transfer of ownership	
■ With politics is formidable	

Power can be crudely or subtly applied, but still be successful in terms of achieving desired goals. Politics in contrast, requires delicate application. If individuals do not wish to listen or be influenced, they can simply walk away, thereby making the encounter unsuccessful. Influencing others through political behaviour requires, first and foremost, keeping their attention. Threatening, or inappropriate, comments or manner, will turn others away.

Power, can be applied equally well to individuals, groups or the total organization. Change through the use of power can be systematically applied throughout the organization, as departments and units can be either equipped with additional resources or deprived of them. Hence, the broad-range application of power levers provides for a strong downward influence approach. In contrast, politics is only concerned with influencing individuals. Politics is a process between individuals, each wanting something different out of his/her encounter with the other. The processes of winning trust and commitment, apart from requiring considerable sensitivity and personal skill, also require patience. Little or nothing can be achieved speedily.

In contrast, the effective use of power can produce quick results. Once a select and appropriate number of power levers is set in motion, events can move forward at an ever-increasing pace. People work towards particular targets because they are required to. With political influence, either party can proceed only at the speed of the other. No matter what one person may desire the other person to do, little progress will be made until both move forward. The political player needs to come to terms with the fact that there exists no resource other than him/herself.

In recognizing the contrasts between the two avenues to working through differences in an organization, should any leader combine the force of power pressure with political influence, his/her impact on the organization could be formidable.

Perspectives, contrasts and differences

How do strains and differences arise in organizations? Differences of opinion can arise over how to utilize resources. Further, certain individuals may hold a firm belief that particular values and traditions should be preserved, while others take a contrary view. Strain can arise through someone disliking or mistrusting another. These contrasts, which can become pressure points, are a reflection of the demands of varying interests, cabals, personality clashes, hidden deals and alliances, and as such reflect normality in an organization. It is normal for different people to hold different interests from each other. The question is, how can reconciliation or just settlement of different interests be reached? The first step in identifying a way forward is to appreciate why differences arise in organizations. Five reasons are highlighted to explain why tensions and differences arise, and why political skill is a fundamental aspect of transactional leadership.

Operating business versus the centre

The centre (headquarters) of a medium to large sized corporation is primarily concerned with the examination of strategic issues, identification of pathways for the corporation to take, and application of these pathways, in order to enhance the prospects of the organization surviving and prospering into the future (see Table 4.2). A great many writers have applied various terms to the process of total organization development, with words and phrases such as 'strategy', or 'grand strategy' being used. The aim of the centre is to pursue the interests of the group as a whole. The group centre directors may conceive of strategies involving further

Table 4.2 Operating business vs the centre

Operating business focus	Group centre focus
■ Improving operations	■ Policy/grand strategy
■ Improving systems	■ Re-investment
■ Improving service	■ Divestment
■ Identifying with team	■ Shareholder perceptions
■ Identifying with business	■ Stakeholder perceptions

investment in one or more of the business areas. Equally, they may wish to invest in an entirely new business area, which in turn may require divestment of existing interests.

The operating businesses of the corporation may or may not concur with group centre thinking. The concerns of the former are likely to focus on the continuous improvement of existing processes and internal systems at their business unit level (first order synergies). The issue of re-investment at operating business level might be interpreted as a possible consideration of implementing the latest technology in order to upgrade efficiency on existing product lines. Accompanying changes of processes and systems would be changes to customer service, or levels of service within the organization. The potential threat of group centre thinking is that whatever improvements are made at operating business level may not alter the fact that divestment of that business may still take place. The nature of the tension between the centre and the operating business is due to the fact that the two parts of the organization are operating from different parameters, with only some overlap. Suspicion of the group centre in the operating businesses is likely to be matched by irritation at the centre with the businesses, for not pursuing sufficiently vigorously, particular centre-sponsored strategies.

Apart from hierarchical position and differing responsibilities, both the operating businesses and the group centre have substantially different constituents to satisfy. Group centre needs to pay particular attention to share price (higher order synergies). Share price is a crucial barometer of externally perceived worth in the markets, no matter how unfair or inappropriate that perception. What the shareholders think, influences whether others will invest in the company. If the shareholders perceive the organization as unworthy of investment and release their shares, a panic can ensue – get rid of these shares and cut your losses! Trust in the company collapses, as well as trust in the organization's brands.

Shareholders are only one influential group of stakeholders with whom the centre has to be concerned. Other stakeholders exist, the press, influential local and national politicians, as well as professional pressure groups. Paying attention to their demands and desires may be just as important, as they can affect the share price and the image of the corporation. An environmental pressure group can successfully mount a campaign to have a potential pollutant removed from an organization's portfolio. The campaign not only removes the offending substance, but equally attracts the attention of a hostile press and damaging publicity, which in turn can just as easily panic shareholders.

These pressures are understood by the management of the operating businesses, but their lack of immediacy means that other factors are foremost in their mind. Operating business management are likely to want a stable workforce, and the display of a positive attitude to performance. The more stable and focused the teams, the more middle management and the staff and workforce identify with the operating business's objectives. Rumours of shareholder and stakeholder displeasure, may undermine the morale of the operating business's staff and management, but the focus on positioning products and services to the marketplace remains. Naturally, the sentiments of the top management of the operating business are likely to be more closely attuned with their own management and workforce, than with the centre. The centre could be seen as an unwelcome influence, undermining the good work of the operating business. The leadership of the businesses may see themselves facing the unwelcome task of motivating their own people due to the actions and perceived inabilities and insensitivities of the centre.

The two managements are in fact working from different platforms. Operating businesses are pursuing approaches concerned with how to make their products and services attractive to the market, how to reduce costs and how to maximize revenues. The group centre holds an interest in costs and revenues, but they are equally concerned with what business(es) the group should be in, what the priorities are of the shareholders, and what market and world trends indicate in terms of future investment patterns. The two agendas do not comfortably sit together, and are likely to require continuous dialogue in order that the two co-exist, not just because of trying to smooth over differences, but because of the more sensitive issue of where senior management loyalties really lie. The actions taken by the senior management of both sides may reflect their true loyalties. If the loyalties of the two managements do not overlap, then the pursuit and application of corporate-wide synergies and policies become an almost impossible task.

Subordinates versus bosses

An immediately noticeable difference between a boss and his/her subordinates, is role. The boss is accountable for the work of the subordinates (see Table 4.3). The subordinates have the responsibility of completing particular tasks, but not necessarily of facing the prospect of being blamed for the overall activity/project should anything go wrong. The boss will get the blame. The relationship between the two is, by nature, unbalanced, by one having control over the other, which in itself can lead to tension. In turn, that tension can be exacerbated by the role relationship being poorly structured. The boss may not be given sufficient authority in the role to be able to focus the subordinates sufficiently to pursue a particular direction. The accountabilities of the boss may be in excess of the authority given and the responsibilities to fulfil. Hence, the boss is in a vulnerable position, unduly dependent on the degree of co-operation from subordinates.

Table 4.3 Subordinate vs boss

Subordinate	Boss
■ Task	■ Authority
■ Responsibilities	■ Accountabilities
■ Respect authority	■ Sufficient authority in role
■ Part of a team	■ Manage others/drive forward
■ Get on with others	■ Motivate others
■ Increase personal earnings	■ Status/salary/conscious

In addition to the structure of the roles, the nature of the relationship between the two may not be positive. The subordinate may or may not respect authority, and may equally not respect the boss as a person. Hence, no matter how hard the boss tries to improve the relationship with certain subordinates, it may prove to be difficult, due to the attitudes held.

However, what is clear is that it is the boss's prime responsibility to initiate a positive relationship between the two. The boss has to manage others. The subordinate has to fulfil his/her job requirements, and co-operate with colleagues and the team. Crucial, therefore, are the people and team skills of those persons holding authority roles. The subordinate could be obstructive, not because of his/her lack of respect for authority, but because he/she perceives, the boss to lack social skills, functional skills or planning and administrative skills. It is difficult to nurture a positive working relationship when, in the subordinate's view, the boss is of lower calibre, but earning more money and enjoying a higher status. Due to reasons of lack of respect, tensions between the two will eventually emerge, overtly or covertly. Harsh words can be exchanged. Further, the subordinates may attempt to undermine their boss, which may eventually create a situation where they show little commitment to the organization. Sprinkle into the equation, the question of image, status and salary, and relationships could be further damaged. The boss may not wish to have 'bad news' become public, as his/her image could be tarnished, and his/her own prospects for recognition and promotion could be undermined. Hence, the boss may not wish to listen to the views of subordinates. Furthermore, why should the subordinate care to continue dialogue or offer feedback? If one of a subordinate's prime motives is to increase earnings, he/she can accomplish that as well by keeping his/her own counsel. People can get on just as well by keeping their mouths shut!

Experience shows that despite the social and other skills of bosses, the capability to pull people together to work as a team is successful on some days, but not on others. Hence, despite a positive attitude and accomplishment in the management of the superior/subordinate relationship, tensions and differences are not eradicated, simply reduced, and may equally re-emerge, for a variety of personal and organizational reasons.

Internal versus external focus

According to the jobs people hold, the team of which they are a member, or the function to which they belong, or just because of themselves as people, their focus in working life may be to pay particular attention to issues outside, or to issues inside, the organization (see Table 4.4). Not that the two perspectives are mutually exclusive; they are not. However, the orientation of the individual is likely to be stronger in one direction than the other, which in turn is likely to influence their values, their ideas and even with whom they would prefer to interact.

Internally-oriented people are conscious of how the organization functions, and their ideas and opinions are influenced by the current structures and prevailing attitudes. As their orientation is towards being watchful of how the organization operates, they are likely to be both conscious of and influenced by the opinion of others. They are equally likely to be conscious of status, which in turn may influence their opinions of others in the organization. The opinions of people of high status are more likely to be respected.

Fundamentally, people who are internally oriented need structure. They need roles with clear parameters and boundaries. Through structure, they satisfy one half of their need for belonging, sureness. Through interacting with the people with whom they work, they satisfy the other half of their need to belong, social relationships but with no surprises. They know the people with whom they work, understand these people, they may like them, they may argue and fall out with them, or even both, but overall they feel secure with them.

A person who is externally focused neither needs the same degree of security, nor desires structure. In fact, structure is likely to be seen as constraining of movement, speech and even innovation. An externally

Table 4.4   Internal focus vs external focus

Internal focus	External focus
■ Status conscious	■ Customer sensitive
■ Driven by opinion of others	■ Driven by self opinion
■ Loyal to organization	■ Loyal to self/external stakeholders
■ Balance things out	■ Need for independence
■ Need structure	■ Value professional network
■ Value internal network	■ Take broader view
■ Details driven	

driven person trusts his/her own opinion as to what actions to take and how to behave. They too can be influenced, but by outsiders, such as customers, suppliers, professionals, or by people in other organizations. Externally-oriented individuals more positively respond to customers. Substantial patience would be exhibited in listening to customers, attempting to respond to their requests, and in being viewed as positive by the customer. The same level of attention would not necessarily be shown in terms of response to internal issues. In fact, externally-oriented people could be dismissive of internal issues and tensions.

Those externally-oriented value nurture and grow their network outside the organization. Those internally-oriented take pride in knowing large numbers of people inside the organization. Externals would take a broader view on issues, whereas internals would be conscious of and attentive to, administrative details.

The differences between the two need not be problematic. In fact, the two could value each other in providing two perspectives, both of which are necessary for the effective functioning of the organization. However, what can lead to tension is the external's need for independence, and the internal's need to be accepted by his/her peer group. The lack of respect shown by externals for the processes and precedence that permeate the organization, could well offend the internally-oriented persons. Attending meetings, for those externally focused, could be considered as a waste of time and hence their attendance may be sporadic. Letting other people know of day-to-day points of administration may also be ignored. Neglect of certain protocols, even though they may be only minor, could build up to tension and poor relationships.

Revenue versus service

Those externally focused could even hold differing values as to how to operate with suppliers, clients and other stakeholders (see Table 4.5).

Table 4.5   Revenue vs service

Revenue	Service
■ Short term	■ Time eclectic
■ Control costs	■ Spend to win customers
■ Sell self/organization	■ Identify best possible solution
■ Sales oriented	■ Market driven
■ Pride in meeting budget targets	■ Pride in being valued
■ Close the sale	■ Nurture relationships
■ Use client-oriented words	■ Practise client-oriented behaviour
■ Beat the competition	■ Find ways to help client

Through being more sales oriented, the focus of the person is more short term, with the prime aim being to 'get the sale'. The individual finds the process of interacting with customers exciting, from the point of view of persuading them to buy the organization's products or services. Part of the reason for the 'buzz' is that in selling the organization's wares, the individual is also selling him/herself. Equally, excitement stems from the fact that a successful sale has been made in the face of competition. Closing the sale means much, as it denotes beating the competition.

For the individual who is more service driven, the competition is oneself, in that the challenge is to deliver the best possible solution for the client. The short-term nature of the revenue-oriented individual is contrasted by the time-eclectic quality of the service driven person – whatever time it takes to help the client. Their need is to identify the best possible solution for the customer, irrespective of its source. Although selling the company's products and services is important, it is not uppermost in the service-oriented person's mind. At the time when certain of the building societies became public limited liability companies, namely they changed from being mutually helping organizations to revenue driven and cost conscious businesses, the behaviour of some of the staff was interesting. Some, on viewing a customer's account, would try to sell them additional services offered by their newly structured, sales focused organization. Other staff at the counter would ask how satisfied the customer was with his/her account and the service provided by the building society. If the customer expressed needs which the building society could not satisfy, all too often the advice given was, 'try some other organization' (naming one), which provided a better service specifically to meet the customer's needs. Such a statement would often be followed by, 'Please don't say I said this. We've been told to sell only our building society products and not give you [the customer] the best advice.' The staff behaved as they did when the organization was a 'mutual' – they provided unbiased advice. In contrast, the newly structured building society desired the sale of only their products and services.

The service-driven person is market-oriented, and not sales focused. His/her concern is to be constantly responsive to developments in the marketplace as opposed to just clinching sales. Not that service-oriented persons are disloyal to the organization. They are not, although they could be seen as such. Their orientation being to provide the best possible solution for customers, means that they would strive to convince their organization to adapt to meet market requirements. However, if the organization resists or is slow to change, the service-oriented person may feel guilty that they are offering a 'less-than-best' solution to their customers. In extreme situations, the service-oriented person could well offer the best solution at the expense of a sale for the organization. Eventually, the individual is likely to leave the organization due to what he/she would term a lack of professionalism on the part of the employer. Such is, and has been the case, with computer hardware companies who offer total solutions to clients. Part of the solution may be to use a competitor's hardware, but the drive on the side of the organization is to use their own, much to the discomfort of the solutions-driven, customer-focused, specialists.

The motivation for the service-oriented person is in being valued for his/her professionalism, by customers. The stimulus for the revenue driven person is in meeting targets. Exceeding expectations of sales and costs targets, and being recognized in so doing, is reward in itself for the revenue driver.

However, individuals holding either perspective are likely to use client-oriented phraseology. For the revenue-oriented person, client-oriented words are what they are, just words. For the service-oriented individual, words hold little meaning unless accompanied by the systematic exhibition of client-oriented behaviour. For these individuals, such behaviour needs to be displayed inside as well as outside the organization. Colleagues, subordinates, bosses, as well as customers, would be seen as clients. For the revenue driven individual, successfully closing each transaction is his/her desired way of operating.

Empowered versus controlled

Certain enterprises have made sincere attempts to delegate responsibility down the organization, in order to develop people, by their becoming more responsive to customer and market needs (strategy of empowering). Other organizations, either deliberately or inadvertently, have not journeyed down that route. The differences in attitude that people in the two types of organization adopt over time, can have a considerable impact on individual and team performance (see Table 4.6).

In the empowered organization, staff and management are given the responsibility to strive for more stretching targets, or to be accountable for

Table 4.6 Empowered vs controlled

Empowered	Controlled
■ Give and accept responsibility	■ Narrowly focused
■ Trusted	■ Controlled
■ Freedom of choice	■ Meet specific targets
■ Grow network	■ Limited inter-relations
■ Support from boss	■ Orders from boss
■ Curtailment if unsuccessful	■ Punishment

a greater range of decisions than previously was the case. People are trusted. Mistakes and errors, if genuine empowerment is in place, would be treated more as learning experiences. The individual would still be assessed, but the prevailing attitude would be one of learning from both errors and successes, as part of a culture of continuous improvement. Errors would still incur penalties, but the emphasis would be on learning from the experience, so that a similar situation would not occur in the future.

Such attitudes are unlikely to prevail in a more control driven organization. Staff and management are likely to be narrowly focused, working within more clearly prescribed roles. The work of individuals is more likely to be scrutinized, partly for the sake of control and partly as a mechanism for reducing the number of errors. Individuals are likely to be set specific targets as opposed to working within looser targets. In the more control driven organization, the relationship with the boss is more likely to be one of being given orders and facing punishment if objectives are not met or errors occur. In the more controlling organization, rule is by fear, rather than by learning and development.

The focus on task and targets is equally likely to be accompanied by restricting the interrelationships people have with each other. Growing an internal network is unlikely to be encouraged. Getting to know others in the organization is in itself not a concern, but such activity would be seen as wasting time. The attitude from management would be, work only with those that you need to work with in order to do the job. In complete contrast, within the empowered organization, growing an internal network would be encouraged as part of the learning and development process.

Although empowering people seems more attractive than controlling them, empowerment does have its disadvantages. If an empowerment initiative turns sour, staff and management in the organization may view the allocation of additional responsibilities and activities as an infringement of their rights and their daily lives. Management could be seen to be asking people to work longer and harder, for the same pay, with more responsibility, and less time for development than before. People may rebel and refuse to accept the added responsibilities.

If problems arise in a controlling organization, greater restrictions are likely to be applied. Although the level of dissatisfaction would rise, people in the organization, already dependent on being given direction, may complain to each other, but do little else. In the empowered organization, should it be seen to infringe on individuals' rights and lives, it is likely that people will resign or openly display their negativity. An empowering organization will have taught its people self-reliance, so that when life and events are experienced as unfavourable, people are likely to examine their conscience and act accordingly.

So long as members of the two styles of organizations do not meet, tensions and concerns are unlikely to arise. However, if the two organizational styles are to be found within divisions or subsidiaries in the same group of companies, or in companies about to merge, or when one company acquires another, that is when attention needs to be given to the impact of culture on people's attitudes and behaviours. Although the potential business synergies of the two organizations could be considerable, the substantially different behaviours and attitudes of staff and management could inhibit any real co-operation between the two. Those persons empowered are likely to see the staff and management of the restrictive organization as unadventurous and impossible to work with, so why try? For those whose lives have been controlled, the empowered person comes over as arrogant, self-assured and threatening – it is seen that protocol is discarded at a whim. The differences between the two can lead to deep resentment. Ironically, to attempt to merge an empowered and a controlling organization may require transformationally 'getting rid' of certain key managers who strongly espouse their host organization's values, as well as transactionally behaving in a politically sensitive manner.

Political wavelength analysis

Normality in an organization is having to face differences of view and perspectives on various issues. People do not hold the same values. Individuals develop in different ways and aspire to different objectives. If differences and the subsequent tensions that arise are so normal, why then do people find managing differences a strain? The answer is because managing and eradicating tensions is a demanding and ongoing process and experienced as draining. Substantial effort can be invested to sort out situations, with seemingly little impact being made, or at least, that is how it can feel. It is much easier to live and work with others if all share certain basic values, such as,

- it is the manager's right to manage,
- authority should be respected,
- people should work to common objectives,
- it is the manager's right and requirement to motivate staff and teams.

From the above list, the common theme is one of shared meaning, namely people in a situation hold comparable attitudes, feelings, share common experiences, share similar drives and wants and overall, desire similar norms of behaviour. There is nothing wrong with living in a world of shared meaning. Affection, trust and deep ties grow between people if they experience satisfactory shared meaning. As a society, we tend to see individuals who have experienced little shared meaning as people who have been deprived and are missing the experiences of one of life's deep joys. However, deeply held, shared values and expectations can leave a person vulnerable if confronted by the unexpected. The person may hold a limited view of normality. When the abnormal occurs, he/she has not developed ways of coping.

Despite the attraction of shared meaning, unfortunately, people do not behave in predetermined ways. They do not desire similar ends, or pursue comparable objectives. There exists as much unshared meaning as shared meaning in work organizations, communities and families. In fact, the underlying theme of the great tales in literature, opera and the arts, is how heroes and heroines have coped or collapsed under the burden of unshared meaning. Unshared meaning is as much, if not more, a part of life, as is shared meaning.

In work organizations, managers and leaders may be unprepared for the degree of unshared meaning they are likely to encounter. Their experiences, training, status and authority in their role may lead them down the shared-meaning path. Through training, managers are greatly encouraged to take part, get involved, work with the team, pull together with the team, and achieve best fit between the person, the group and the organization. Of course, to pursue shared meaning is desired and sensible. People do need to work together; they do need to co-operate to flourish and prosper. The danger is that the assumption that exists in the notion of shared meaning can become so compulsive that the only way people can cope with their differences is through being damagingly covert, while overtly denying that problems exist.

Productive life in organizations requires competence at handling both shared and unshared meaning. Such competence is gained first by appreciating the nature of the tensions, constraints and differences in the organization. The second way is in understanding the individuals who are caught up in living in and working through those differences. The third is in developing a repertoire of skills and tactics that can be applied when called upon to smooth out and overcome differences of a demanding or damaging nature. The first has been examined through the above analysis of the five sources of tension in organizations. Now for an in-depth look at people.

Politics of the Court of King Arthur

An entertaining and bewitching film for children and adults alike, is that of tale of the *Connecticut Yankee at King Arthur's Court*. From a novel by Mark Twain, of whose work many films were made, this one of which starred Bing Crosby, a hapless Yankee (Bing) falls through a time warp and finds himself at the Court of King Arthur, trying his best to find a way through a maze of complex relationships. He meets the straightforward, honourable White Knight, Sir Lancelot, the unscrupulous, deceitful Black Knight, Sir Mordred, the fickle courtiers and the Merlin figure, elderly, wise and patient. Poor Bing finds life very difficult, juggling with these relationships!

What that delightful story and accompanying film highlight are the challenges anyone would have to face when entering a new organization and trying to both understand and work with the various people he/she encountered. Developing the competence to survive and thrive in an organization requires consideration of two dominant influences, namely, how to analyse and understand context, and how people behave in different contexts (see Figure 4.1).

As outlined in Chapter 2, there exist contexts that are clear, open and explicit. The prevailing circumstances are relatively easy to 'read' and people can see how they should behave. However, other contexts are more implicit, that is, are difficult to discern, and in which appropriate and inappropriate behaviour is unclear. People embedded in implicit contexts know each other sufficiently well to understand what to do, what to say and how to say it. Outsiders need to be guided through more complex circumstances, as they are unlikely to be given feedback if they step, or are seen to step, out of line.

Figure 4.1   Politics of the Court of King Arthur

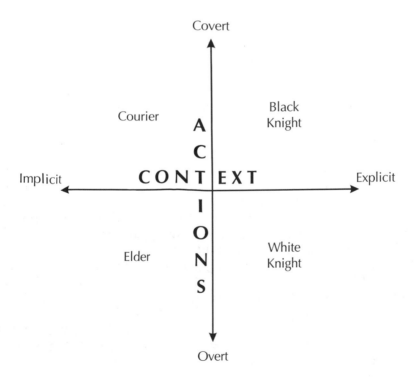

However, individuals may or may not behave according to the norms of their context. The actions people adopt can vary enormously. At one end of the continuum, people can behave in an overt manner, clearly indicating what they feel, what they desire and what they wish to do or pursue. Such a person is direct in his/her manner, and up front with his/her comments. Conversely, others may be more covert, saying one thing, meaning another; indicating they wish to pursue one line of thinking or direction, while silently intending to go in an opposite way. Whether the person means to or not, he/she is in danger of being deceitful.

The two dimensions of overt/covert actions, and explicit/implicit context, provide a framework for understanding, and then deciding how to respond to, different people in different situations. For all those 'Yankees at court', a roadmap of how to find pathways through the politics of the Court of King Arthur, is provided.

The Yankee is likely to meet the White Knight, who is most effective in explicit contexts. White Knights value and practise being overt and open with everyone. Equally, the Yankee will encounter the Black Knight, ambitious but frustrated, energetic but feels thwarted, and all too ready to put blame onto others. The Yankee will probably trip over a courtier or two, busybodying around, at the centre of gossip and attention, over-concerned to be seen to be acceptable and to fit with the rest of the organization, rather than asserting a particular perspective or viewpoint. The Yankee, however, is unlikely to bump into an Elder. Elders are likely to meet him, when they are ready. Elders understand the organization and its people, have learnt how to influence, and when to be honest and open.

Greater understanding of people within contexts is an important step in becoming politically agile, hence, below are further analyses of the people.

White Knight

The White Knight is one who offers his/her views and states his/her opinions (see Table 4.7). The 'take me as you see me' style can be off-putting to some people. The individual can be seen as overly forthright, assertive, even rude and aggressive. However, the avuncular, up-front image, is likely to hide a more caring and sensitive individual, probably deeply concerned about issues, and the quality of experiences in life that others face. Motivated by a concern for honesty, openness and justice, the White Knight openly speaks his/her mind and expects the same degree of honesty of response. The White Knight is likely to accept people and their statements at face value. The straightforward nature of the person applies to all aspects of his/her life. The White Knight is likely to keep a promise made, and expects others to do the same. The White Knight is likely to follow through on commitments made, and see an endeavour through to fruition.

Table 4.7   White Knight

Behaviour	Attitudes
■ States views	■ Accepts statements at face value
■ Offers opinions	■ Finds ambiguity irritating
■ Stands up for own rights	■ Trusts authority
■ Keeps promises	■ Expects follow through on commitments
■ Expects others to be straightforward	made
■ Does not easily read double meanings	■ Expects others to keep promises
■ Lost when subtlety prevails	■ Straightforward
■ Honest in emotions	■ Innocent in politics
■ Take me as you see me	■ Politics is negative
■ Assertive style	■ Caring and sensitive
■ Direct	■ Naive, thinks most others operate to
■ Accepts responsibility for self	similar agendas
■ Energetic and self-reliant	■ Selfish, concerned with own feelings
■ Do as I do	■ Expects other to be straightforward
	■ Stands above context

The expectation that others should be as straightforward, is the weakness of the White Knight. Even in explicit contexts, such predictability of behaviour is unlikely to be forthcoming from most. People do not live their lives according to someone else's criteria. Not emotionally comprehending this fact, leaves the White Knight irritated with ambiguity and subtlety of meaning. The individual can understand the various interpretations that could be slanted onto any one statement, but finds entering into a world of wondering, 'what did X mean by this?' or, 'what is Y intending by behaving the way they do?', time wasting and tiresome. Politics in organizations in their eyes, is negative, and hence should be eradicated. By not developing a proficiency at political interaction, the individual does not easily read double meanings even though he/she recognizes the advantages of so doing. The person is an innocent in a political arena.

The personal stamina and strength, coupled with the acceptance of responsibility for one's self and one's actions, are the attractive features of the White Knight. Yet, the up-front straightforward nature, also masks a lurking selfishness. The White Knight is naive to think that everyone else does, or should, operate as he/she do. Such naiveté is not ingrained, but emanates from a lack of attention to, or disinterest in, the daily lives of other people. The White Knight is continuously concerned about his/her own feelings – am I being honorable? Am I being just? He/she, in fact, judges others by his/her own standards and criteria. The emphasis is, 'Do as I do!' It is true that the vast majority of people do judge and relate to others by their own standards, but the question is one of degree. The White Knight can be excessive in this respect. The White Knight is not really interested in understanding why others are different. In effect, White Knights stand above the daily context. To be given the feedback that naiveté is more a result of his/her disinterest in others, is likely to be denied. White Knights genuinely believe that they do care. What they do not recognize, is how much of that is on their own terms.

Black Knight

The Black Knight, strong, influential and equally as dominant as the White Knight, is more likely to speak in code than be consistently forthright. The Black Knight will be open when it is to his/her advantage (see Table 4.8). The person is equally likely to be overt in order to give the 'right' impression, but then act in a contrary way. The 'say one thing, do another' practice is all too commonplace. There exists a number of reasons as to why a person behaves in a double-edged way.

First, to so act could be of considerable advantage in organizations that have an outward appearance of being open and explicit, but are, in reality, more devious. To survive and do well in this context requires covert actions, but overt statements. Most people in the organization would prefer to believe that they have nurtured positive values in the enterprise, but do not like to face or be confronted with the truth that the organization is not what it seems. To be overly truthful in the Black Knight organization is of no advantage. The person making statements about the organization, especially the more accurate the comments, is

Table 4.8 Black Knight

Behaviour	Attitudes
■ Speaks in code	■ Finds confrontation difficult
■ Says one thing/does another	■ Finds the organization distasteful
■ Deliberately covert	■ No opportunity to develop further
■ Unscrupulous	■ Disrespect turned into an art
■ Can appear scrupulous	■ Subordinates not valued for their
■ Over-assertive leader promotes covert behaviour	feedback
■ Response to continuously facing incompatible agendas	■ Low in trust
	■ Side-steps responsibility when necessary
■ Recognizes boss is influenced by last person, and exploits that	■ Quick to judge
■ Effective for survival in a divisive culture	■ Dislikes organization/leader but does not leave
■ Submissive, yet rebellious	■ White Knights can become Black Knights when they feel frustrated
■ Ambitious, but frustrated	■ Black Knights can become White Knights when they have broken out of their constraining circumstances
■ Energetic, but feels thwarted	
■ Blames others	

likely to face hostility and venom. Behaving as a Black Knight can be effective in a divisive culture (see Chapter 3 for a further discussion of cultures).

Second, the individual has become expert at being unscrupulous, so why change? The alternative generates more angst. The Black Knight may find confrontation problematic. He/she may find dealing with the anger of others too uncomfortable and hence resort to more underhand ways of operating, so as not to experience emotional trauma. The Black Knight has learnt that being underhand works – just don't get caught. Hence, the person can appear unscrupulous, as much because they find confrontation difficult, as they can be devoid of morality and scruples. As a result, Black Knights are despised, as they make others feel anxious and inhibited.

Third, the behaviour of the boss can induce Black Knight behaviour in others. The boss may be unduly controlling with subordinates who are capable and confident, as the boss finds them threatening. Further, the boss may be as much caught up in a 'macho' culture as others in the organization, all trying to out-do each other in terms of exhibiting his/her resilience and prowess. Equally, the boss, feeling uncomfortable, may try to keep on good terms with everyone, but unfortunately ends up being influenced by the last person he/she meets. Whatever commitments are publicly made, people have learnt that seeing the boss privately, after a meeting, produces the desired result. Either in an effort to please and be seen as a motivator, or because he/she genuinely does not wish to inhibit the development of others, the boss changes his/her viewpoint but to the point of unconstructive inconsistency.

An additional reason why the Black Knight behaves as such, is that he/she feels thwarted, because he/she feels there is no further room for promotion and development. The person may have outgrown the organization. He/she may have made a substantial contribution to the organization, but have now become stale. They are low on ideas, but still high on energy. They are ambitious, but feel held back. They have come to dislike the organization and its leaders, but will not leave. White Knights can become Black Knights when their energies are misdirected or dissipated. It is unfortunate that energetic, talented individuals find themselves in circumstances where they cannot focus their efforts toward positive ends. The more stifled they feel, the more negative and destructive they can become.

Whatever the reasons for being a Black Knight, the overall result is the same, the individual does not positively contribute. His/her frustration can set off a chain reaction of dissatisfaction in others in the organization. The Black Knight can appear submissive, and yet is rebellious. Disrespect can be turned into an art through clever sarcastic wit. Subordinates are unlikely to be valued. Similarly, feedback is unlikely to be acknowledged. In fact, offering honest feedback to a Black

Knight could further raise the level of tension between him/her and others. The Black Knight is quick to judge and blame others for activities and events that do not succeed. In so doing, the Black Knight does not easily accept responsibility for his/her own actions.

The Black Knight is potentially a positive and energetic individual, for whom life has gone wrong, or, at least, that is how he/she feels. However, the good news is that Black Knights can become, or return to being, White Knights, when they manage to break out of constraining circumstances or a negative viewpoint. Their extensive energies would then be more positively focused.

Courtiers

Courtiers are the most fickle of the courtly characters (see Table 4.9). Comfortable in operating in complex contexts, where life is one of double meanings and people are conscious of the finer points of how they address and communicate with each other, the courtier has developed a portfolio of contrasting approaches to interrelate effectively with different individuals.

Courtiers are busy, but also nosey people. They like to know what is going on in the organization, who is friends with whom and who has fallen out with whom. They feel that such information is valuable in helping them be more receptive and more aware of potential tensions and problems that exist in the organization. Courtiers are rarely taken by

Table 4.9 Courtiers

Behaviour	Attitudes
■ Slippery	■ Confrontation is frightening
■ Difficult to pinpoint	■ Jealous when others are complimented
■ Difficult to hold to account	■ Status conscious
■ Everyone's friend	■ Value privilege
■ No-one's friend	■ Look for negatives in others
■ Not to be trusted	■ Need attention
■ Too quick to praise	■ Natural networkers
■ Thrive on gossip	■ Necessary lubricants of an organization
■ Through gossip, could be malicious	■ Easy to live with
■ Use grapevine for communication	■ Outwardly friendly and charming
■ Criticize behind others' backs	
■ Deny responsibility	
■ Provide solutions for others to fail	
■ Like to know everything	
■ Like to know everyone	
■ Up-to-date on everybody else's business	
■ Cannot keep a secret	

surprise. They are the natural networkers, recognizing who is worth knowing and taking pride in being seen as important. Courtiers like to feel wanted, which is the principal reason why they busy themselves with everyone else's business.

Courtiers recognize that nurturing an ever-growing circle of inter-relationships is important in the more decentralized and influence-based organization. Furthermore, courtiers take pride in being recognized as influential gatekeepers. They are able to introduce other colleagues to influential and powerful figures. Equally, they may take pride in sidelining someone who does not fit into the organization, or is a threat to them.

In their own 'busy bee' way, courtiers are loyal to the organization, as they are deeply transactionally driven. The running around, knowing everyone whom there is to know, being known and being in tune with the latest gossip and conversations about each other, emphasize the Courtier's need for the organization. Courtiers work well within established structures, within which their transactional inclinations can be given free rein.

Loyalty to the organization, may not necessarily be matched by loyalty to people. Even more so than Black Knights, courtiers are likely to find confrontation uncomfortable to experience. Hence, their preference is to find an alternative route to address emotionally difficult and challenging circumstances. They can face issues in an obtuse manner, seemingly going round in circles and getting nowhere, but in fact providing an invaluable service of making the uncomfortable, at least addressable. However, their circumventing approach can make Courtiers difficult to pinpoint and to hold to account. Some would perceive their style as slippery. Others, as friendly and welcoming. Courtiers are everyone's friend, and yet no-one's friend.

The courtiers' transactional nature is accompanied by a deep need for attention. They thrive on being talked about. They take pleasure in being contacted and told the latest news and gossip. Courtiers have to be the 'first to know'. They use the grapevine for communication, and are able to be at the centre of attention. They even promote an air of mystique about themselves, because they have learnt one lesson, nothing gets round quicker than bad news. As such, courtiers cannot be trusted. Not only can they not keep a confidence (secrets, like bad news, go round fast), but they look for negatives in others and criticize them behind their back. A few negatives thrown into the grapevine certainly add to the Courtiers' status and standing in the community, or so they think. Upfront, they may be too quick to praise, in order to ensure that they are not criticized or accused of being negative. As they promote, as well as thrive on, gossip, their embroidered tales of others could, often, border on the malicious. If ever confronted, they would deny all responsibility for having helped to circulate unwelcome rumours. Further, whoever confronts them, would not easily be forgiven, for such an encounter would be experienced as deeply traumatic. Courtiers who run amok, could end up nurturing their own little cults, where what counts is who fits, not who is the best person for the job.

Despite the gossipy, status-conscious and attention-seeking behaviour of courtiers, they do provide two valuable services. First, they are the natural lubricants of an organization. They are the ones in the know and the ones who circulate information and news to others. They keep the organization running and, in many ways, make life fun and interesting. The courtiers are the natural mixers who enjoy social events, parties and, because of their social skills, make people feel welcome. Second, it is easier to live with them and their decisions. Uncompromising confrontation is not one of their accomplishments. Whatever is said, or whatever decisions are made, courtiers are likely to turn the uncomfortable into something that is sufficiently comfortable to live with. For courtiers, there is always a way out. Taking an uncompromising position is viewed as going down a 'dead end'.

Elders

The elders at King Arthur's Court, or any organization for that matter, promote the sage, wise man syndrome (see Table 4.10). Their understanding of the organization, how to behave in the organization and how to present arguments and issues to the best effect, are valuable insights to draw upon. Being an elder is neither age nor gender related. Young men or women, as well as older men or women can effectively fulfil the role. The role itself is one of bridging a gap. The gap is in the confusing and

Table 4.10   Elder

Behaviour	Attitudes
■ Listener	■ Merlin syndrome
■ Sensitive to context	■ Wisdom prevails, irrespective of age and gender
■ Can resist context	
■ Provides support where necessary	■ Judging but not judgemental
■ Accurate judge of character	■ Looks for positives in others
■ Does not project ego	■ Nurtures positives in others
■ Helps others reach their solutions	■ Comfortable with ambiguity
■ Rarely offers advice	■ Appears innocent
■ Politically aware	■ Strong scruples
■ Seldom confronts	■ Clear philosophy
■ Prefers to work within comfort zones	
■ Appears predictable	
■ Can be unpredictable	
■ Seems soft: is tough	

energy-draining complexities that exist in any organization, which can all too easily lead people into blind, unproductive alleys. The bridge is in the overarching insights and wisdom which can provide pathways through unaccustomed intricacies.

Elders are sensitive to people and contexts. The traditional image of 'elderly' arises from those individuals who portray well their numerous experiences, so that their understanding of life shines through. People who exhibit extensive experience are naturally expected to be older, but they need not be. Some learn exceptionally quickly. Another stereotypic view is that man is the worldly-wise traveller. Again, that is not the case. Women are as well versed in finding pathways through complex contexts, through good use of particular capabilities, such as listening, standing back, observing, nurturing, applying high standards and values, all of which have little to do with gender or ageism.

Sensitivity to context, coupled with being proficient at listening, helps the elder be resistant to the siren charms of the present context. They know what is happening but are not driven to do what all else do! Further, the elder's genuine concern to develop others with little need to be the centre of attention, establishes the basis for their wisdom. Elders tend not to judge others too quickly, but they will form a view after observation and contemplation. Elders are judging, but not judgemental. They look for the positives in others and having identified the same, concentrate on nurturing these positives. Weaknesses are not down played, but placed in perspective. Should greater emphasis be given to reducing and eradicating weaknesses from which a difference in performance or quality of experience can emerge, or on enhancing the strengths of an individual? In effect, the elder will be balancing the benefits of entering into steep or shallow learning curves, against the investment necessary to emerge successfully from a learning experience. The attitude of the elder is that nothing is, or should be wasted, including time, energy, devotion and experiences.

The ability to see ways through the changing nature of different contexts, highlights a comfort with ambiguity. As the elder does not need to project his/her own ego, maturity is displayed in helping others. Elders rarely give advice, but would devote considerable time to mentoring others in order to assist them to explore how solutions to their predicaments could be found. Elders would try to use positively challenging circumstances to help others feel stretched, and from these, learn new skills and grow in confidence and stature.

The listening, mentoring and talking through of experiences exudes an air of innocence on the part of the elder. The reality is that the person is considerably politically aware of the various agendas being pursued and the intentions, objectives and values of the key players in a scenario. Being politically aware does not necessarily mean being politically active, but it does mean being politically challenging. Elders hold strong scruples. They hold values concerning ways of behaving and relating, and equally are likely to promote their views as to the shape, size, moral identity and worth of the organization. Elders will confront issues and people. Their air of innocence, however, emerges from the fact that elders prefer to work issues through with people in a way that is reasonably comfortable for all concerned. Elders will try to help people be committed to and responsible for, their own actions. Their view is that by identifying problems and concerns and then discussing them through in a reasonably comfortable manner, the process of conversation is more likely to ensure greater ownership of the decisions each person makes.

Concern for others and an unselfish nature promotes an aura of calm around Elders, which can be mistaken for their not being fully aware of what is happening. A further false impression that Elders can generate is that they are predictable. The reality is substantially different. Elders can be considerably unpredictable in their actions, quite independently forming their own views as to the appropriate measures to take within particular situations, driven by a clearly held and well thought through philosophy. The soft external appearance, masks an inner steel, which is called upon whenever required.

Not for stereotyping

Can people switch approaches and style? How do others see individuals, as being in one box, or having a capability to stretch across all four? Providing models of different forms of human interaction assists understanding, but these should not be so used as to be constraining. People do not easily fit into simple stereotypic boxes. All of us have been at some point in time, one or more of the characters at King Arthur's Court, as a result of circumstances and other pressures. As people dip in and out of particular roles, providing ways to read others helps position a person at a point in time. From that appreciation, learning how to respond to influence effectively, or to build positive relationships, is the next challenge to address.

Being politically agile (or helping all Yankees at Court)

Awareness of contexts, and the reactions of people in various contexts, are valuable insights. Calling upon a repertoire of approaches in order to influence people across a variety of contexts, and achieving positive outcomes requires experience and skill in knowing what to do. Below, several action strategies are described, which if applied are likely to enhance a person's political agility. Proficiency in the usage of these strategies should ensure that all Yankees at Court are no longer to be marginalized.

Stakeholding analysis

Conventional wisdom would rightly indicate undertaking a stakeholder analysis in order to ascertain the spread of vested interests impacting on an organization. Stakeholders are individuals who have an interest in the organization, and are likely to pursue their interests so as to realize their investment. Stakeholders drive particular agendas through the organization. Influential stakeholders may or may not have formal authority, and may or may not be members of the organization. Stakeholders may exert influence directly, or they may exert pressure through other channels. Appreciating who are the key 'movers and shakers' in any situation does help, but such insight is not enough!

Deciding on how to deal with political interactions requires an understanding of the range of potential agendas prevalent in any situation. Drawing a map of the possible challenges and interests in an organization provides the overview necessary to recognize the different positions any stakeholder could take, currently, or in the future. In contrast, undertaking a stakeholder analysis is a more limited exercise, for it is likely to show the interests of those people operating in the present context. However, a stakeholding analysis helps to pinpoint the range of concerns, any one of which could arise at any point in time.

Once a broader and more insightful stakeholding map is drafted, then it is possible to know how to move forward with no surprises. A stakeholder analysis, no matter how cleverly configured, could still lead to surprises – one stakeholder has been successfully influenced, but leaves. All of a sudden, someone else pops up into their place. A clear understanding of the complete range of issues and their diversity, assists in more effectively moving forward.

Work to the comfort zones

Armed with an understanding of the issues, the agendas and the people involved in promoting particular viewpoints, it is possible to move forward by deciding to confront or work with, key stakeholders. Working issues through with other people requires respecting them, their behaviour, their values, their attitudes and ideas. Displaying such respect will require not unduly contradicting them to the point where they feel too uncomfortable to discuss and examine issues. In effect, working through issues with others requires working within their comfort zones. Working to the comfort zone is a transactional tactic; people feel sufficiently comfortable to continue talking about the issues they share and require to settle or resolve.

People will address the challenges they face so long as their own interests are not threatened. Once transactions with others become one sided, or are experienced as threatening, the individual is likely to switch off. People continue to trade and transact if they can maintain, at least, one of two interests: outcomes, i.e. what is in it for them; process, i.e. how the discussions are being conducted.

Working to people's comfort zones involves managing process issues and outcome concerns so that the interested parties are motivated to continue talking and interacting. However, different people require a different approaches. Handling the White Knight involves being straightforward and up front with any views or feedback that need to be given. With the Black Knight, his/her negativity would suggest not offloading all comments at once, as the person may not respond positively. With courtiers, more attention needs to be given to process than to outputs. Conscious of image, courtiers are sensitive to how others feel about them. Potentially, most issues can be discussed if the individual feels sufficiently confident that they will not lose face. Focusing on issues too quickly, without building up a relationship with the courtier, is likely to make the simplest of issues extremely difficult to address.

Working with elders requires adopting a collegiate perspective. Whatever issue is raised, the elder is likely to offer his/her views on the issue, processes of interaction and the person(s) with whom he/she is interacting. Greater attention should be given to preparing oneself for how the elder will respond, rather than how the person should be treated. Elders are robust, do not accept the status quo, but are equally unlikely to be dramatic or aggressive. They will, however, probe, explore and by implication, put the other party in the firing line. Interacting with elders in a thoughtful and mature manner is the only way to gain their respect.

Warning: a fine dividing line exists between working to the comfort zones of others and giving way to their whims, while one's own needs and issues are relegated to second place. Being effectively transactional is no easy task!

Decide about being the loyal servant

At the end of a long discussion that we the authors both held with a senior Australian Federal Government civil servant, tasked with introducing a major programme of change, the individual made a surprising comment: '. . . At the end of the day, I just do what my Minister says.' Our response was, 'Do you mean that after you have discussed the various sides of the argument, you then jointly move forward?' The reply was, 'Oh no! I just do what he says.' We had to ask, 'What if you disagree?' and he said, 'Well that's a choice you have to make. Me, I do what the Minister says, even if there is a change of Minister and a change of policy. Me? I am a loyal and faithful servant.'

Some time after the discussion, we read of a change of Minister, and a declaration by the new Minister of a change of policy that would directly affect the very same senior civil servant's department. We later discovered that this particular civil servant had survived the change of Ministers, and was recognized as having championed a highly successful government-wide programme of change. He became a celebrity, briefing the press on, 'the new ways of government'. For him, being a 'loyal and faithful servant' worked.

The case of the civil servant raises a vexing question: 'What should individuals do if they disagree with what is happening around them; swim with the stream or go against the tide?' Each person has to look to his/her own conscience and philosophy. The civil servant's view was that by working from within, one could at least achieve something positive, as opposed to agitating unproductively from outside. Thus is captured President Lyndon B. Johnson's logic in exclaiming about General Haig, 'that son-of-a-bitch is more use inside, pissing out, as opposed to being dangerous outside, pissing in'. Although Johnson's view is now conventional wisdom, the learning point is that no-one will tolerate from an insider the same degree of challenge issued by one outside. Staying in means working within existing parameters, a statement which most would recognize as commonsense, but for some, is unacceptable.

Valuing patience

In addition to the application of a considerable range of skills, transactional leadership also requires patience. Helping people become more comfortable to discuss issues, timing the raising of issues, and following through on decisions made, require committing time to a complex and energy-sapping process of dialogue and interaction. Under pressure, a leader's patience can be strained. Feeling obliged to, for example, talk through a particular concern or requirement for action with a colleague or subordinate, while simultaneously responding to numerous other demands, could well leave the senior manager feeling, 'Why can't this person just get on and do what I ask of them?' However, in flatter organizations, and in more team-oriented cultures, to not make the time for dialogue could damage the credibility of the senior manager. People need time to learn and appreciate the viewpoint of others. Exhibiting a lack of patience indicates that the leader does not wish to invest the time to help others learn. Patience, in today's more network-driven organizations, is not a virtue, but it is a basic quality as assisting others to learn to adapt their behaviour and views is becoming more fundamental to high levels of performance.

Being conscious of image

After having spent a few days working with a group of senior managers from the Royal Insurance corporation (now Royal/Sun Alliance), I

(Andrew) was invited to attend an evening dinner with the group, whose guest of honour was Richard Gamble, the Group CEO of the Royal. The occasion was to be used to announce the merger of the Royal and Sun insurance companies. That evening, Richard Gamble was fluent in speech and impressive in performance. During his talk, one of the senior directors of the Royal lent over and whispered, '. . . He's impressive, isn't he? He really does fit the image of a chief executive about to turn things around in a big way.' I had to agree. The ovation at the end of the speech not only displayed the audience's high regard for him, but equally that the senior managers of the Royal were committed to his ambitious plans. Richard Gamble was substantially instrumental in the subsequent merger of the two organizations, and on his departure late in 1997, he left behind a formidable world player in the insurance market.

The power of imagery should not be underestimated. As goods are branded, so are people. Imagery is a visual metaphor. Image is a way of symbolizing concepts, and values, but in a visible way. When the image portrayed and the words used, match, the trust that others are likely to have in the words they hear, dramatically increases. When a message is verbally delivered by someone whose image is incongruous with the words used, trust is dented. The question in people's minds is, 'How can we believe that this person will do what they say?' It is emotionally difficult to separate what is being said from the profile the speaker projects. The two are rolled into one, thus making imagery for executives as crucial a concept as branding is for products.

Trading on credits

Building up goodwill, through being seen to be helpful and supportive, works. An individual who consciously attempts to become acquainted with others, to understand their circumstances, who appreciates the nature of others' challenges, and shows that he/she is willing to integrate and work with others, builds positive and supportive relationships. The more the individual attempts to both fit in and contribute, the more others are likely to wish to relate and interact with that person. The individual is building up a bank of goodwill credits. The more co-operative the person, the greater the bank of credits. The person is soon in a powerful position to influence when it comes to redeeming his/her surplus account of credits.

Being a wolf in sheep's clothing

Being the 'nice guy' does not always work! Hence, the error that many people commit is that in acting the opposite way from the nice guy, they behave in a nasty way. Projecting an unpleasant disposition generates resistance, even passive resistance. People obstruct or just do not do what they are required to pursue. A nice guy with a touch of steel is what is required. Be a wolf in sheep's clothing, but make sure the coat is thin enough to show what is underneath. The message to others is, 'We can talk, but when a decision is reached, clear, disciplined and consistent action will take place, or else!'

Knowing when to back off

Managing daily transactions involves effectively managing relationships so that people in the organization feel comfortable in continuing to interact and contribute. The point of working through differences in an organization is not only to iron out tensions and difficulties, but also to build and maintain positive relationships. Needing to behave in a more complex and/or covert manner in order to reduce the negative impact of differences in the organization should be undertaken within a perspective of continuously being focused on building professional relationships so that challenges and issues can be addressed. On the basis that managers are faced with the paradox of building relationships and yet needing, at times, to behave in a covert manner, timing when certain issues should be brought to the table for debate, is important. The team and other individuals involved need to feel ready to enter into debate. Therefore, if the time is not right for debate, stand back and revisit those issues at a more appropriate time. Better still, back off and help people grow a level of robustness and preparedness to discuss known challenges. Backing off in order to revisit the debate, is not backing off as such! People need to feel prepared to enter into dialogue over issues which they perceive to be too sensitive to discuss. However, just backing off without any real intent to confront people, or organizational or business matters, is abdication.

A fine dividing line exists between timing and abdication. Knowing the difference between the two is a matter of honesty with oneself. It is as damaging to discuss certain topics at an inappropriate time, as it is to feel oneself that one is biding one's time, when in reality, one has backed off from confronting tensions altogether.

Just doing it and then saying it

If all the political levers have been applied, and no real progress is made in terms of discussing known concerns or eradicating the number of distracting differences in an organization, then when all else fails, just do it and then say it! If a lengthy process of discussion and negotiation is leading up a cul-de-sac, do what needs to be done, and then declare what you are doing and why, or alternatively back away completely. One of the questions every leader is likely to consider is whether or not being too sensitive to people and to context, in reality, inhibits the taking of initiative? There is no answer to that question, other than the one that each person concludes from the reading of his/her context, and his/her insight into their own preparedness to act. Therefore, when all else fails, act first and then say what you think is best.

Massaging meanings revisited

The purpose of political action is to build relationships and move discussions forward without damaging those relationships, although, if necessary, straining them is alright. The decision to work through differences by utilizing more political action strategies, highlights that a transactional way forward has been adopted. Certain leaders, however, may instinctively react adversely to such a way of thinking. Yet, there may exist few alternative choices. Tensions and differences exist in an organization possibly because of the resistant attitudes of certain people. From a customer relationship perspective, it would be unwise to replace some of these people. Moving certain people out of their jobs may end up with their taking valued clients with them. Relationship-building has to be undertaken in conjunction with sorting out pockets of tensions. The sensitivity that is desired to conduct transactions appropriately across multiple contexts is considerable and when well applied, highly effective and influential.

Key points summary

- Organizations inherently consist of differences and tensions.
- In order to address or force through change, to reach settlement, and to overcome differences and constraints, the approaches of both power and politics may need to be utilized.
- 'Power' is identified as the use of one or more resources which, voluntarily or involuntarily, requires that people do something differently to what they did before. In contrast, 'politics' is a process of influence which can be effective only if others identify with the individual and/or the manner in which he/she influences, and/or, the reasons for his/her wish to influence.

Contrasts and tensions in organizations

- Five reasons are identified as to why tensions continually arise in organizations, namely: due to differences between the operating businesses and the group centre; differences between subordinates and bosses; differences between people who are more internally as opposed to externally focused; differences between people who are more sales as opposed to service oriented; differences between organizations that have introduced empowerment as opposed to being more controlling.

■ The centre of a corporation is focused on addressing a broad, more portfolio, range of interests, which may or may not be to the advantage of any single business stream or subsidiary in the group, whereas, an operating business is primarily concerned with the timely and efficient delivery of its services or products.

■ Tensions between subordinate and boss arise due to role differences. The boss is the person held to account for subordinates' behaviour and contribution and hence, is likely to focus, restrict and discipline subordinates who, in turn, are unlikely to respond positively to such tension.

■ Tensions arise between people who are more externally than internally (organizationally) focused and vice versa, because both sides respect different stakeholders and protocols (ways of behaving).

■ Tensions arise between people who are more revenue oriented, as opposed to those who are more service driven. The 'clinch the sale and get the business' attitude of sales motivated individuals sits badly with those who primarily wish to provide the best possible service to others, irrespective of whether they win the business.

■ Tensions, to the point of incompatible differences, can arise between organizations (within the same group of companies) that have introduced a programme of empowerment and have helped people become more self-reliant, and those organizations that control and direct the activities of their staff and management, leaving them dependent on the organization.

Being politically effective

■ Political wavelength analysis involves effectively applying political skills in ways suited to particular contexts and particular people. The mythical Court of King Arthur is used as the setting in which to analyse context and apply different behaviours appropriately.

■ A number of action strategies towards improving one's political influencing capability, are identified, namely undertaking a stakeholding (not stakeholder) analysis; working to the comfort zones; being, or not being, the loyal servant; valuing and displaying patience; being conscious of the impact of image; trading on credits; being a wolf in sheep's clothing; knowing when to back off, and if all else fails just push ahead.

Further reading

Of the different interpretations of politics in organizations, particular emphasis is giving in the literature to:

■ politics being viewed as a process of negotiation (Kakabadse and Parker, 1984),

- politics being viewed as a mechanism for reconciling the interests of a divergent society, historically championed by Aristotle (1946), in his analysis of the need to attain unity in the Greek polis (city state),
- politics from a moral perspective, representing the darker side of humanity (Burke Warner, 1976),
- politics needing to be more comprehensively understood (Baddeley and James, 1987),
- politics being an off-shoot of cognition and learning theory (Bandura, 1977; Mischel, 1977; Carnevale and Stone, 1994),
- politics from the point of view of contextual sense making (Weick, 1979),
- identifying distinct political strategies (Pettigrew, 1977).

PART TWO

Essence of transformational leadership: leading

CHAPTER 5

Born To Be Great

Case analysis

Colin Sharman

A few years ago, Colin Sharman, the UK senior partner of KPMG (the worldwide consulting/auditing practice), introduced the concept of 20/20 Vision as the way forward for KPMG. This was at a conference of the key and senior partners of the firm. He was considered by most as an impressive performer. One of the senior partners sitting next to me (Andrew), said: 'He's good. He's also got what it takes to make it happen!' My instinctive response was, 'What do you mean?' To which he replied:

> Look, he's got them [the audience] in his grip. He's got credibility. He was a good accountant, an excellent consultant and as senior partner, a very effective leader of Peats [Peat Marwick]. But it's more than that. He's got them in his grip. He's strong and everyone knows he'll push 20/20 through.

Some time later, I interviewed Colin Sharman, whereupon he made some interesting comments:

> Now we are beginning to sit down and have very robust discussions about performance. One of the changes I have made in style is that until I became senior partner the operational meetings weren't really operations meetings – they were about anything but operations, about trying to fix what we were going to do. Operations now are operational review meetings largely, and each regional partner comes in and presents his region very much as you would see in any other group – it is discussed, analysed and he is subjected to a fairly thorough grilling by his colleagues, and that is now going back down in the organization. There is a way of

doing things – senior regional partners know they can't come along and say, 'Well, I'll tell you what I want to tell you.' That is no longer acceptable.'

The senior KPMG partner's assessment of Colin Sharman proved to be accurate. His instinctive view of Sharman's strength and deeper substance, was later supported by evidence of a determination to push through change, based on a belief that the organization needed to be more responsive to its clients, and in order to be so, needed to be more internally integrated. Sharman's vision of a customer-driven industry facing groups backed by support groups, was somewhat counter-cultural to the more intellectually, independently minded model of service that ran through the KPMG organization at that point in time. Irrespective of the logic of Colin Sharman's vision, a strength of presence was needed to push the reforms through to the point of acceptance. The predominant view of the day was, 'If anyone can do it, Colin Sharman can!'

Colin Sharman's intent to promote and pursue a shared vision for the enhancement of KPMG, was plainly evident among the partners and senior management of the organization. What made him stand out in that forum? One view is that he was the most senior member of the group and, by implication, needed to display greater resolve than his colleagues in defining new goals for KPMG, and convincing others that the new challenges were within everyone's grasp to attain. The point being made is that role distinguished Sharman, not the person himself.

An alternative viewpoint is that Colin Sharman displayed one or more unique features of outstanding leadership, which placed him in a position of commanding influence. Pursuing this line of thinking, had he not held the role of senior UK partner, but had been in another position still able to influence policy, his strengths would have even then shown through and he would, presumably, have still made a substantial impact on the future of the 'firm'.

This latter interpretation is the one that in this chapter explores what particular strengths within people distinguish them as leaders. Two primary concepts from philosophy, 'desire' and 'will', are considered as the crucial parameters to examine in an exploration of the inner side to leaders.[1] 'Desire' denotes reasoning, argument, thought and balanced or even imbalanced conclusion, in effect intellect, which acts as the basis of understanding giving meaning to what the leader desires. 'Will' is exemplified by inner resolve, passion, steadfast resolution, in effect, the focusing of energy to single-mindedly achieve. The able use of intellect and will are expressed through volition and action, the outward expressions of leadership. The question is what is it about the particular combination of desire, will, intellect, volition and action in any one person, that can make them appear unique? The search in this chapter for the unique characteristics of leadership goes down the line of how mind and body are developed, and how different influences combine to form in people certain particular identities crucial for leadership. In so doing, two further questions are raised, namely those relating to confidence and charisma, the former concerned with the surety that one is right, and the latter examining the capability to promote a powerful image.

In this chapter, the deeper side to leaders is explored, through an examination of, initially, Freudian concepts of personality, and also through post-Freudian thinking, especially the work of Alexander Lowen and his theory of bioenergetics. Attention is also given to defining charisma, namely, having the confidence to lead and in so doing, display the qualities of leadership. The dark side to being gifted with the qualities of leadership, is that of over-confidence in one's own ideas which leads to a pre-occupation with only one's self, commonly known as narcissism. Hence, an examination of charisma and narcissism are considered to go hand in hand.

Personality and Freud

The term 'personality' refers to the distinctive, or as some theorists prefer, the fundamental characteristics of an individual. Some imply that once these characteristics are moulded, each person's character is formed for life. Others argue that a more fluid relationship exists between these elements of character, which implies that people can adjust in their evolving relationships with others. These characteristics, or personality structure, are taken to include temperament, meaning emotions and moods, and the individual's outlook and attitudes. In understanding personality, psychologists make use of the terms 'trait' and 'type'. 'Trait' denotes a fixed, or an element of character that remains reasonably constant across different contexts. Extroversion would fall into this category. 'Type' is typified by a fixed pattern of traits which distinguish one cluster of traits from another, for example, the question 'Are you a type A or type B personality?', is one that addresses such a distinction. Trait theories date from the time of the Ancient Romans, who recorded a great variety of personality traits held to be characteristics of those barbarian peoples who lived on the borderlands of the military empire of the Caesars.

Freud postulated that each individual displays traits of character in adult life which result from particular childhood experiences. Such experiences are driven by the way a child reconciles external forces of control and constraint with their personal needs, in particular, those of their sexuality (libido). Freud considered that the body orifices of the mouth, and anus (and genitals), are primary to the understanding of human development. He postulated that interest in the orifices, and the need to satisfy desires, mould character, but in a chronological sequence from birth onwards. To the new-born child, the mouth is the primary organ of pleasure, for it is through the mouth that baby makes contact with his/her first object of desire, the mother's breast. Freud believed that during the first six to ten years of life, the 'formative' years, our experiences deeply impact on our mind, creating deep and powerful, in Jungian terms, preferences that later direct our lives. Many may not be conscious of that development, as strained or damaging experiences can lead to various kinds of repression that resurface in a disguised form at the later stages of life. The steps in the sequence of development referred to by Freud are termed as the oral phase, the anal phase, the pre-genital phases, the phallic phase and the genital phase.

Oral phase

The oral phase is the period spanning birth to approximately one year. During the oral stage, the infant becomes increasingly aware of others and attempts to form relationships with his/her primary carers. During this phase of development, the infant needs attachment, bonding and a need to feel secure. If these needs are met, a baby develops a sense of trust, and the child is enabled to grow positively, confidently facing new experiences. If the baby's needs are not gratified, trust will not be established. The baby could either become withdrawn and cry, or become needy and clingy. A school of thought in psychoanalysis considers that many successful executives have a narcissistic (self-love) character, rooted in sublimated forms of oral deprivation, which in later life, is expressed as continuous drive, rarely attained, towards the satisfaction of the individual's needs. Such individuals are likely to be aggressive, attempting to be successful and to win recognition from others; in effect, a 'me/me orientation'. The greater the deprivation in the oral phase then, supposedly, the greater the drive for the satisfaction of one's own needs, and the more successful the executive.

Anal phase

The anal phase, follows the oral phase and is characterized by gaining control over the anal sphincter muscle, which ability develops towards the end of the first year of the child's life. As the child slowly gains control over its own body, it also needs to separate emotionally from his/her primary carer, in order to develop a sense of self. The child needs to assert him/herself to gain confidence and grow emotionally. In so doing, the child can become frustrated, as he/she does not have the skill or ability to do much for him/herself. The need is to have patient primary carers (parents) to be nearby, so that the child can go to them and be comforted whenever feeling insecure or frightened. If the primary carers are overly controlling, or not available, the child can develop doubts about him/herself, prompting a deep-seated lack of confidence which can pervade all aspects of later life. In later life, such insecurity would be displayed by the talented individual who never pursued the job with great responsibility. All expect the person to 'have a go', but he/she never does, for fear of failure.

Pre-genital phase

Pre-genital sexuality, as the third stage of development, coincides with the end of the third and emerging fourth year of life. The tensions and challenges experienced by the child in this phase strongly influence later attitudes toward generosity, submissiveness, affection, optimism and indifference. The child is beginning to recognize him/herself as a 'whole person' through becoming more aware of its own sexuality. This sensitive, 'breaking out' period requires substantial support and care from his/her primary carers, in order that the infant can develop the necessary levels of self-confidence. Difficulties experienced at this stage may lead to undue dependency, later observed as a dependency emanating in the relationship between leaders and followers, where people look to others rather than to themselves to initiate action.

Phallic phase

The fourth stage, the phallic phase, more into the fourth year of life, is distinguished by a boy's interest becoming centred upon his penis, and a girl interest in her clitoris. In this period, children develop a sense of initiative and continue to discover who they are, most through imaginative play. Support from parents (or parental figures) is crucial, as children need to have all aspects of their personality validated by their primary carers. During this phase, boys experience sexual attraction towards their mothers, the well known Oedipus complex, while girls develop an attachment towards their fathers, which is the Electra complex, from the Greek tale, whereby Electra, 'connives the death of her mother, Clytemnestra, who had murdered Electra's father, Agamemnon'.[2] The phallic phase is the important time in the socialization of a child. Parents that reject the child or show disapproval of certain elements of his/her character, will leave the child confused, feeling inadequate or even worse, feeling guilty. The child may respond either by becoming wilful and determined, or by withdrawing and becoming isolationist. Such an orientation may demonstrate itself in the later years, as a leader with an aggressive, individualistic personality engaged in self-confident, exhibitionist behaviour. For such leaders, satisfaction is derived from being visible and 'a winner', and being acclaimed as such.

Genital phase

Between the ages of five to ten years, the child enters into the genital stage, and as the term denotes, becomes more aware of his/her own genitals. During this phase, children discover the extent of their personal power in the outside world, develop problem-solving skills, and become more competent in the management of themselves. They need acceptance, and praise for their efforts and achievements. However, undeserved praise is counter-productive, for it can lead to unrealistic expectations from, and of, others. A balance needs to be achieved as a child requires quiet reassurance in unpleasant experiences, to help the child keep a positive sense of self. If the parent or primary carer also competes with his/her child for attention, unduly criticizing the child, and demeaning his/her views and contribution, the child can adopt a perspective of becoming compulsively competitive, or alternatively, withdrawing from competition, feeling resentful. The child in adult life can see him/herself as a victim, feeling he/she needs to be manipulative, or even sabotaging, to protect self, or repay the world for the wrongs he/she has experienced. In adult life, the individual may find work as an outlet for their repression. This kind of sublimation often underlines the rage behind workaholism, on which so many organizations depend.

Freud believed that in the process of maturation, desires are either brought under control, or are banished to the unconscious. The unconscious thus becomes the well for repressed impulses and painful memories and traumas, which periodically erupt with dysfunctional consequences. The adult deals with these powerful emotions in a variety of ways, engaging in various defence mechanisms to keep him/herself in check. From the leadership perspective, what others may call 'born with', Freud would interpret as the irreconciliation of contrasting demands, now emerging as a form of 'pent up' energy! Whereas society may value particular characteristics of leaders, Freud would view the same phenomenon as mild or substantial pathologies. Adopting a Freudian interpretation of leadership cannot be described as an 'ego stroking' experience.

The Freudian disciples

Melanie Klein, a post-Freudian British psychoanalyst, suggests that many of the disorders that Freud attributed to human sexuality, have their origins in early patterns of socialization, which if unresolved, emerge in adulthood as defences against anxiety. In so assuming, Melanie Klein broadened Freud's concepts to include environment, and thereby added an additional dimension to personality-based concepts of leadership, namely, context. It was then Wilhelm Reich, the Austrian psychiatrist and social theorist as well as an orthodox Freudian, who took Klein's ideas further through his interest in the influence of social factors on character formulation.

Like Freud, Reich believes that during early childhood, a person, 'establishes deep habits of thinking that later can limit and distort the way one lives one's life'.[3] He holds that during the early years of development, a child's mind is forming sufficiently strongly to be able to determine whether to be or not to be, talkative, aggressive, tender, or withdrawn, and that the body reacts to these conclusions. These powerful forces and tendencies, in turn, have a profound impact on the child's musculature embodied into a pattern of physical manifestations, significant in shaping the child's body profile. He argues that the clinches, the tensions, other facial features, and movements of people, reveal their emotional state. In his systematic study of neurotic attitudes in the body, such as anxiety in the hunching of the shoulders and in veiled eyes, rage in a tight chin, disgust in a certain expression of the mouth, he concludes that these physical states are all consequences of early development. Attending to the former will have a freeing impact on the latter. Reich developed the concept of 'muscular armour' from his earlier work on 'character armour', to refer to a set of chronic defensive attitudes that a person adopts to protect him/herself against external injury, such as being hurt or rejected by other human beings, and against one's own repressed emotions, especially rage and anxiety.

Alexander Lowen and bioenergetics [4]

Reich's ideas were further developed by Alexander Lowen and John Pierrakos who, working in the USA, devised a practical model of body/mind therapy called bioenergetics. Lowen postulated that during the formative period of a child's life, there exist five separate developmental stages requiring that the individual and their needs be respected in order that a psychologically healthy individual graduates from childhood to adulthood. He terms these stages as, the right to exist, the right to nourishment, the right to be separate, the right to be autonomous, and the right to love and move with desire. When these rights and needs receive insufficient gratification, the child emerges as distressed and the body-mind responds defensively to lessen the pain.

Lowen's five body-mind types therefore, correspond to unresolved needs within each of the five phases. According to which stage of development is frustrated, different personality forms emerge. Each form is considered to display mental and physical characteristics, as a result of the person attempting to come to terms with the distress and tensions he/she feels. Lowen called such interactions 'holding patterns'. The holding patterns form key personality dimensions known as the 'hold together', 'hold on', 'hold up', 'hold in' and 'hold back'.

Each of these five holding patterns corresponds to each of the five periods of child development, which may emerge in later life as frustration or trauma, and significantly influence the leadership philosophy and approach the person adopts.

Hold-together personality

Helpless and totally dependent on his/her carers, a baby's right to exist is confirmed by a sense of warmth and welcome provided by the carers. If the child is deprived of affection, he/she develops a 'hold-together' personality, due to the need to hold him/herself together against the shattering pressure he/she experiences in the world around him/her. Denial of the right to exist, experienced by the baby as emotional distance or physical coldness, is damaging to the physical, emotional and mental development of the child. If a baby stays long in hospital, or if the primary carer is hostile, abusive or punishing, bioenergetics theory assumes that the baby turns away from contact with the world, becoming detached, distant and even unreachable, as it concludes that the world is a dangerous place. In order to stop the flow of dangerous sensations and passions, the child holds his/her breath, sucks in the belly and stiffens the musculature into tight, deep contractions.

The end result is that the hold-together personality is considered as creative, deep with integrity, but at the same time is withdrawn, unrealistic and may even become violent. He/she is committed and hard-working but in a more insular way. Hold-together personalities are genuinely anxious of contact with others and can become seriously distressed, and even paranoid, when having to deal extensively with people. In a situation of conflict and of being unable to cope, they may withdraw or take an inflexible and unreasonable stance, appearing negative and aggressive.

Hold-together executives are considered to lead from the rear. They lack spontaneity and act 'as if' they are communicating and managing, but find leading unduly demanding. In Sandy Cotter's opinion, the bioenergetics and management guru, 'they are often perceived by others as unreachable and unreadable'.[5] It is postulated that they can do exceptionally well in research and development, where creative thinking is valued and also where precision and technical excellence are required. Hold-togethers are perfectionists, and may find responding positively to the pragmatism of the 'bottom line' painful.

The appearance of a hold-together type is typified by a slight and somewhat tight body, and a clinched and square jowl. The body of the hold-together type is stiffened to inhibit the flow of breath and feelings, manifesting in chronic tension in the joints. Overall, the hold-together displays what Cotter calls a 'spaced out', look, emphasizing the withdrawn and emotionally frail perspective of these people.

Hold-on personality

Commonsense dictates that babies need care, attention, affection and an active display of responding to the child's needs in the early stages of its life. Thus, individuals who experience deprivation in that period of babyhood, emerge in adulthood as less robust, less sure of themselves, and less able to handle the world effectively, than those who have positive experiences in their first year of life. In effect, they try to 'hold on' to other people in dependent and needy relationships. Such personalities are considered as prone to alcoholism, depression or more susceptible to physical illness. The chronic deprivation of attention and love develops a personality that is substantially dependent on others for positive self-regard, but unfortunately is low in drive and energy.

The hold-on personality is sensitive, relaxed, open, low to anger, but lazy, and can be bitter. Their easy style can lighten a team of overly serious individuals. Hold-ons, because of their desire for attention, present well, network effectively, and make for powerful social facilitators. They often prefer thinking rather than doing, but can appear lazy about getting matters concluded, as they simply lack the energy to get the job done. When they do muster the necessary energy, they may have difficulty in being truthful and forthcoming, as that may be perceived as damaging relationships, the trauma of which can exhaust or even devastate them. The unfortunate side to hold-ons is that their substitute to being 'up-front' is silent resentment, making them spiteful and suspect in seeing through their responsibilities. For them, life is experienced as unfair. Their genuinely low energy-charge, perceived lack of commitment to finish tasks, and attitude that life is unkind, often prevent hold-ons from reaching senior executive positions and as managers tend to lead from the rear.

The hold-on's physical appearance is characterized by an under-developed musculature, elongated in face, limbs, neck, torso, hands, feet, with caved-in chest. Due to their poor physical development, Lowen viewed hold-ons as not containing the growth of long bones. Unkindly, their body form can attract remarks as 'weedy' and 'inadequate', adding to their distress. Their lack of aggression is displayed through a soft, pointed jaw and eyes that are relaxed and appealing, almost giving a soft, vulnerable puppy like image.

Hold-up personality

On leaving babyhood, confident and full of energy and entering into a new phase of first adolescence, the child develops a capacity to discern, and engages in a sort of negotiation with his/her carers. In many ways, the child tries to separate from its primary carers, and become his/her own person. If that right is denied, or if the child has not learned to respect the rights of others, problems are likely to occur in later life. These individuals develop a 'hold-up' personality, by holding themselves up above the rest of the world in a heroic or grandiose stance.

Adults shape the child's view of him/herself by their responses to the child's behaviour and emotional reactions. Obviously, primary carers need to encourage the toddler in his/her achievements, but at the same time the child needs to learn certain restrictions and limitations in keeping with his/her surrounding context. If the primary carer is psychologically immature and finds it difficult to set reasonable boundaries, that sets the genesis for the formation of the hold-up personality.

Hold-up individuals are considered to be highly intuitive, exhibiting a remarkable political sensitivity, a gut feel for events around them and taking 'big strides' and substantially shifting position, often to the confusion of others. They are charming, successful, strategic in outlook, but at the same time, pretending to be intellectual, domineering, scheming and ruthless. They easily sense power relations, the desires and objectives of others, using that insight to gain advancement and advantage. They seem, intuitively to know what to say and how to say it, to move issues their way. They are charismatic, are driven to be superhuman, and display a need to be in command, and be seen as such.

On the positive side, they can project the image of the soft, heroic-type leader. At the opposite end of the spectrum, they can also be hard tyrants. The gentle hold-ups are protective and would shelter their constituents from the world at large, similar to medieval knights protecting the peasants. Such practices can be frustrating for stronger personalities in the family or organization, who would consider themselves as stifled and restricted. Unfortunately, hold-ups are likely to feel that they have no equal, thus thwarting the development of talented and able colleagues. In extreme cases, hold-ups can be uncompromising and unethical with able colleagues, bosses or subordinates who are seen as competitors. Although they are attuned to the power and political interplays in the organization, hold-ups can make serious mistakes by being over-focused on their own concerns, rather than to developments in particular contexts.

The hold-up's physical appearance is characterized by an inflated chest and broad shoulders, forming an overbearing posture, with an often distinguished-looking jaw. Sometimes, the lower body and legs are relatively under-developed in comparison to the upper body. They can produce a forceful, piercing gaze, which is the hallmark of their overly aggressive image due to not having developed realistic parameters to their behaviour during their formative development.

Often displayed as larger than life, and whether they are more the soft heroic, or the hard tyrant leader, they drive themselves, often remorselessly, believing that the ends justify the means, with the ultimate end inevitably involving their personal grandiosity. 'High fliers' or charismatic executives, more fall into the mould of the hold-up personality type, operating as benign dictators or heroes, or as coercive and tyrannical, controlling through domination and humiliation.

Hold-up personalities are the classical image of leaders most frequently found at the top of organizations. In both cases of the softer and harsher 'hold up' personalities, the gifts of charisma and strategic ability are attributed to being innate and inbred.

Hold-in personality

From about the ages of two-and-a-half through to four years, the child enters the developmental phase of learning the right to autonomy. If during this stage, the child is over-disciplined, it is assumed the he/she will lack confidence when he/she enters adulthood. The person will have difficulty trying to be direct, because he/she does not wish to upset the feelings of others. Such individuals develop a 'hold-in' personality, as they learn to hold in their passions for fear that they will not be liked. The positive values of being nice and polite, so highly regarded by hold-in personalities, stems from their childhood when being good and loving usually meant not upsetting others.

Hold-in individuals are practical, responsible and reliable in whatever jobs they undertake. They display considerable energy and are able to work effectively for long hours and through a crisis. Despite their reliability, they may need a substantial push to get them going. They thrive when they have many activities running concurrently and yet still are genuinely caring about others, despite the pressure.

Hold-in individuals are paradoxical, as they are on the one hand, reliable, warm and have an endurance to sustain pressure, and on the other can be passive, submissive to authority, and on certain occasions, explosive and sometimes even violent. The hold-in's capacity to be understanding and generous towards others is his/her attractive feature. However, because they do not wish to cause emotional distress to others, they find difficulty in being assertive and straightforward. They are particularly vulnerable to confronting under-performing team members. Despite their display of considerable energy, they are risk-averse, fearing, but not openly admitting, that being adventurous ends up in failure. They value security and have an ability to implement and maintain the status quo. As leaders, they are likely to revert to transactional activities, despite their flamboyance with words. However, the paradox of displaying high levels of energy and yet subjugating those drives to transactional outcomes, leads initially to frustration, but ultimately to pent-up anger. When the anger building up in hold-ins is not released, that energy can mutate into negative moods, resentment and spite. Their experience of such feelings can be personally upsetting, as they believe that the expression of anger destroys relationships.

The hold-in body displays considerable tensions. The shoulders are curved down in an attempt to control anger from its expression. The jaw is broad, round, but not jutting. The body is strong, sturdy or broad and may carry weight. They have a relaxed chest, and eyes that are warm and friendly.

Overall, the biggest obstacle to a hold-in executive's success, is his/her lack of assertiveness. As they do not wish to upset anybody, hold-ins find it difficult to provide focused feedback, or take a fair stand on sensitive issues. For them disagreements are emotionally difficult!

Hold-back personality

Between the ages of four and six, sexual impulses arise in humans and thus initiate the right to love and move with desire, or what Freud refers to, as the Oedipal stage of development. As previously mentioned, the child experiences romantic attachments to the carer of the opposite sex. If the carer does not know how to respond to the child's initiations and how to establish clearly a safe boundary, the child may feel rejected and worse still, shamed. Ideally, the opposite sex carer should display a positive, supportive but 'safe' response to the emergent sexuality of the child. The parental figure should equally display a warm and affectionate relationship with their spouse, so that the child loses his/her competitive edge with the same-sex carer. By so doing, the same sex carer is afforded the opportunity of providing a positive role model, so that the child grows gracefully towards healthy adulthood. Frustrated individuals at this stage of development can surface their feelings in later life, in terms of hysterical and compulsive behaviours. Individuals who develop a 'hold-back' personality learn to hold back their sensitive and tender feelings, because they are guarding a 'wounded' heart.

Hold-backs are honest, fair and rational, but at the same time can be insensitive, even arrogant, rigid, inflexible and hard-driven. They are usually not imaginative or creative, but rather rational and logical and goal-oriented. Although they are implementers rather than creators, hold-back personalities do strive for excellence. Because of their over-determination to win, the hold-back can become inflexible and insensitive in their determination for success. They often lose out with people, because of their over-focus on goals. Others may see them as unapproachable, put off by their intellect and logic, and lack of display of sentiment. When hold-backs encounter failure, they need a long time to bounce back, as the firm ground on which they have stood, feels destroyed. Relationships are usually managed on a competitive basis, where little trust is exhibited. Hold-backs generally avoid evolving relationships with emotional depth. They use feelings as a defence against feelings, by exaggerating and theatrically acting out superficial feelings.

The hold-back's body is characterized by a powerful and erect energetic posture, with square shoulders and a pulled-back pelvis, displaying tension in the lower back. This type exhibits a sense of dynamism and displays considerable confidence. Their eyes show a direct, cool challenging gaze but in repose, often look sad, revealing that painful, inner wound.

Hold-back executives are determined, energetic, realistic and focused. Their need to win is enhanced by their straightforward nature and by their desire to be fair. However, they do not worry about upsetting others or about being nice or polite. They have no difficulty in saying 'no', and may display anger in an argument. When the argument is over, negative emotions and words are forgotten. However, much to their surprise, others, often, are not so forgiving and do harbour grudges, something so alien to the hold-back.

Differentiating self-confidence from self-love

Lowen postulates that when the natural 'formative needs' and the 'critical rights' of an individual are respected in the early years of development, positive developmental experiences are catalogued in the mind and as a result, the person becomes strong, able and loving, forming positive, helpful and warm relationships with others. In contrast, when natural potential is suppressed, damaged, blocked, misguided or misused by frustration or by poor upbringing, the individual will become hardened, negative and, in extreme cases, twisted.

One assumption, therefore, is that emotionally healthy individuals have little need for attention or self-projection. The Insead professor, Manfred Kets de Vries posits that only those who are emotionally tarnished need to push for acclaim. Thus a fundamental issue in leadership is raised, identifying the dividing line between self-confidence and self-love, in effect, knowing what to do and when to stop. Presumably, Kets de Vries would argue that self-confidence is exhibited by knowing when to stop, but narcissism is exhibited by the unsatisfied need for acclaim. Kets de Vries views narcissism as stretching on a continuum, where leaders can occupy a position ranging from healthy narcissism to pathological narcissism. In fact, he distinguishes between three categories, 'reactive narcissism' (pathological), 'self-deceptive narcissism' (mid of the range) and 'constructive narcissism' (healthy).

Narcissism

In his work on the personality, Freud labels an individual whose main interest is self-preservation, and the maintenance of their independence, as a narcissistic, libidinal personality. However, individuals displaying such characteristics can powerfully impress others as strong personalities, aggressive, independent, action-oriented, and are often found in leadership roles. Freud, suggested 'the leader himself needs love no one else, as he may be of masterful nature, absolutely narcissistic, self-confident and independent'.[6]

Constructive narcissists

Time magazine reports of Bill Gates, Microsoft's CEO and acclaimed as the richest man in the world, a somewhat tense relationship with his mother, one of the reasons for his subsequent visit to a psychologist.[7] A strong-minded mother, who is described as having to accept that her equally strong-minded son, today purportedly earning $30 million a day, would not do her bidding. *Time* ascribes his success to his 'awesome and a frightening blend of brilliance, drive, competitiveness and personal intensity'. Born of a socially adept and confident mother and a lawyer father, the urge for success was learned from an early age. Even family pastimes as cards and quiz games became serious events, where winning counted a great deal. Despite his awesome success, the reported reality behind the facade is of Bill Gates as an unfussed man, who could easily do without worldly goods, as long as he was able to maintain health and the resolve always to move forwards. His driven nature within the workplace is seemingly matched by a quiet fortitude at home, where his wife, similar to his mother, displays a socially comfortable manner and an instinct for engendering comfortable social relationships.

Gates's style, manner and sharp intellect would place him in the constructive narcissist category. His cool calculation and striving for success is matched by a constructive perspective towards others and life. His £12 million research grant to Cambridge University, highlights a man whose enormous impact on the world is balanced by a concern for humanity and a social conscience. Qualities of risk taking and reflection are also commonplace in the political as well as the business domain, typified by such figures as the UK's Prime Minister, Tony Blair and the United States' likely next Presidential candidate, Al Gore. Both are in their own ways resourceful, yet pragmatic, coupled with a humanitarian concern for the communities under their stewardship. Blair, in particular, conscious of the need to be internationally competitive, is balancing business drive with promoting social and health care programmes for the benefit of the British public. Although such leaders are not beyond the occasional act of opportunism, they maintain open relationships with most that they come across, including subordinates.

Overall, narcissistic leaders take responsibility for their actions and are ready to help others when events do not proceed as planned. The constructive narcissistic leader, as Bill Gates, has a positive impact, as he/she radiates a contagious self-confidence and purposefulness. They balance being flexible with being focused. Their social adeptness helps them promote strong, workable relationships. Their weak point is that they can react badly to critical comment on the basis that they can see little wrong in themselves and find it distressing that others do not view them as one of the 'good guys'. Constructive narcissistic leaders are equivalent to Lowen's soft 'hold-up' personalities.

Reactive narcissists

Leaders with strong narcissistic tendencies, termed 'reactive narcissists', tend to have poorly integrated feelings of reassurance and confidence, as much from having been set unrealistic expectations from their parental figures. As a result, they are often unable to distinguish their desires from reality. Leaders with a reactive narcissistic orientation frequently distort outside events in their favour, in an attempt to prevent loss and disappointment. Although examples of reactive narcissistic leaders can be found in private and public sector organizations, they stand out in the political sphere, with figures such as Serbia's Slobodan Milosovic and Croatia's Franjo Tujdman, falling into that mould. Besides their tendency to be ruthless, grandiose and exhibitionist, reactive narcissistic leaders also tend to attract and be attracted by followers who display psychopathic tendencies. Reactive narcisissists display a desire to dominate, control, and are transformationalists in that they are likely to use their followers to further their more grandiose needs. Such people comply more with Lowen's harsher 'hold-up' personalities – with Iran's Ayatollah Khomeni, Libya's Gadhafi, and the Bosnian Serb leader Radovan Karadjic, dramatically illustrating the transformational and damaging narcissistic elements of leadership. The case of Karadjic provides an interesting example of reactive narcissism, as he, a trained psychiatrist, practised his craft in the Yugoslavian health sector, until he seized the opportunity for leadership in that crisis ridden society, which he has taken from bad to worse. His rival and President of Republika Srpska, Liljana Plaisic, even with Bill Clinton's support, is still unable to bring Karadjic to heel and send him to the Hague to stand trial as a war criminal.

Self-deceptive narcissists

The third category, of self-deceptive narcissists, hold self-delusory, and unrealistic beliefs, primarily created by their primary carers. A self-deceptive narcissist leader is likely to suffer from deficiencies in bonding in relationships, due to the unrealistic ideals given to them by their parental figures. As a result, on the one hand, self-deceptive narcissist leaders tend to look to others to provide structure to their lives, a result of not being given the opportunity to face up to criticism and take control of their lives during their development. On the other, they like to be liked. Although self-deceptive narcissistic leaders have many similarities with reactive leaders, they tend to be less exploitative, more tolerant of dissenting opinion, and more approachable. Further, they are more transactionally grounded, at times, over-focused on making small advances at the expense of the big picture, the reason being that they are reluctant to disrupt unduly present relationships and be tarnished with the critical comments that follow unpopularity. They are somewhere in the middle between healthy and pathological narcissism. Although some would place Benjamin Netanyahu, Israel's Prime Minister in the reactive narcissist camp, including some of his own Jewish supporters in the USA, he has withdrawn from pursuing a course of action on a number of occasions, after first confirming his commitment. A recent example, reported in *Foreign Report*, 6 November 1997 concerns his chief of staff Amnon Shahak, who angered his boss by contradicting his intent to use American Apache combat helicopters to quell Palestinian civil disturbance. Netanyahu's anti-riot ideas were reversed in cabinet and although seemingly contemplating the sacking of Shahak, Netanyahu is unlikely to do so for fear of upsetting the army. Netanyahu seems to fall into the odd mixture of Lowen's 'hold-together' and 'hold-up' personalities. In addition to his supposed desire for acceptance, his actions denote an individual driven by tactical success, but devoid of its strategic implications.

Overviewing narcissism

The constructive narcissistic or soft 'hold-up' leader's ability to radiate self-confidence and thus excite followers, is particularly effective for organizations in crisis. They offer purpose, create excitement and provide a cohesion which binds all to a common goal. They help others become alert to internal and external dangers. The word charisma is often used to acclaim the constructive narcissist.

An excess of such behaviour, however, can be counter-productive. At what point *constructive* becomes *destructive* depends on the situation and context, as exemplified by Radovan Karadjic and thus, determining the turning point between these two polar ends is not always an easy task. History provides ample examples of charismatic leaders who have not fallen into the pathological mode of charisma, such as Ghandi and Churchill, as well as those who went in the opposite direction, namely, Saddam Hussein and Stalin, as well as certain of Stalin's vicious henchmen, typified by Beria.

Enigmatic nature of charisma

Is charisma simply an attribution, a term used in the adoration of leaders whose positive display of constructive narcissism has won the day? 'Could be', is the answer, but equally, it could be more than that!

Charisma is the term commonly adopted to highlight the dominating and yet inspiring relationship between leader and follower. Circumstances of dramatic change attract individuals who inspire and project charismatic-like qualities. The cultural heroes of history and the great law givers as Moses, Caesar, Napoleon, Lenin, de Gaulle, Kennedy are often noted as the examples. Within such a framework, charisma is made to be a force inseparable from the Kantian great man/great woman, rather than a condition of a social organization.

Max Weber, the German philosopher and sociologist, examined the topic of charisma and concluded that it is a particular quality of personality by virtue of which certain individuals 'stand above' ordinary people and are treated as endowed with exceptional, almost superhuman qualities. In primitive cultures, this kind of deference is given to prophets and great warriors. In more civilized society, charisma is attributed to those who display outstanding qualities, as well as occupants who hold particular prominence. What is clear, is that the decisive element in the recognition of charisma is the extent and depth of its acceptance by those who follow. Although, according to Weber, the truly charismatic individual is not dependent upon followers for their acclamation as their charisma survives irrespective of the opinions of others, the attraction of the followers, according to the majority of social psychologists and anthropologists in this field, is crucial.

Weber further identified an additional element of charisma, namely, the routinization of charisma and its impact on society. The routinization of charisma refers to heredity and its incorporation into families, offices, races and even communities and countries. As the process of routinization extends itself through the generations, it cannot help but become traditionalized. Hence, charisma becomes hereditary and recognition is no longer paid to the supernatural qualities of the individual, but to the legitimacy of the position the individual has acquired by hereditary succession. Weber cites castes in India as a classical case of hereditary charisma, characterized by the house of Nehru, from Nehru senior, to his daughter Indira Ghandi and to his grandson Rajiv Ghandi. In turn, many British still proclaim that their country is 'class ridden', some with pride, others with disdain.

Thus, 'charisma', has an enticing attractiveness, an ability to obtain compliance from others, which enables the leader to motivate followers to achieve outstanding performance. The leader's ability to exercise an intense influence over the beliefs, values, behaviours and performance of others, through his or her own behaviour, beliefs and personal example, underpins the born-to-be-great leader. The born-to-greatness leader's dominance, self-confidence and strong conviction in the moral righteousness of his/her beliefs, is reflected in his/her personal vision and in communicating this vision in a manner that relates a compelling, empowering image of ultimate goals and positive self-regard.

The adjectives describing the born-to-greatness leader are, classical, masterful, dominant, heroic, visionary, agile, alert, resilient, dramatic, charming, in fact all embracing terms which cover the mind, the body and the affections. Simply, every part of their human form is so great, for, as with the late Princess Diana, who could resist the privilege of her followership?

The US researcher into leadership, Bob House, has pursued the study of the psychological characteristics of charismatic leaders, arguing that such factors can be identified and measured. In his more recent work, House has focused on studying the leadership qualities of US presidents. His research yielded results that differentiate effective from ineffective national leaders, judged by panels of historians, on the basis of the imagery of power generated in public speeches and writings that are charismatic and transformational, rather than transactional.

Other researchers have taken different positions, but overall four major traits in contemporary writings appear to characterize charismatic leaders and are defined as, having vision (a goal, agenda, results and expectations around which stakeholders can converge); an ability to communicate their vision (verbal, non-verbal or symbolic); trust-building skills (being constant, reliable, and persistent); and having a positive self-regard (recognizing personal strength in others, and nurturing and developing talent).

Several individuals, such as John F. Kennedy and Martin Luther King, are recognized as having had these qualities, which helped them project a powerful image. John F. Kennedy's line, 'Ask not what your country can do for you; ask what you can do for your country', was powerful, enthusing American people into being active participants in public life. Similarly, when Martin Luther King said, 'I have a dream', he drew to the surface the repressed traumas of all oppressed people.

Ronald Reagan, with contrastingly Republican values, generated a similar kind of excitement through clever use of metaphors to describe his vision, so that others could visualize it and feel it. One of Reagan's many metaphors was in describing one billion dollars as one dollar on top of another piled to the height of the Empire State Building. Reagan was trying to motivate Americans to be more pro-active in achieving results. His skill was in helping others visualize what he meant, as in the metaphor of what one billion dollars would look like piled high. Like Kennedy, Reagan was able to create a platform for action and to inspire others. In the words of Jack Welch, the CEO of General Electric, 'Leaders need an overarching message, something big but understandable . . . every idea you present must be something you could get across easily at a cocktail party with strangers. If only aficionados of your industry can understand what you're saying, you've blown it'.[8]

Despite its obvious attraction charisma has to be approached with caution. It is a vague concept. Empirical studies which have examined charismatic leaders have not produced a universally accepted set of behaviours and attributes. Moreover, charisma has several potential dark-sides which are frequently glossed over in the more popular management literature. Even Weber provides a balanced view, for in addition to the great and good figures of history, charisma includes an enticing but perverse kind of magician with a powerful but dark nature. This magician is often prophetic, attracting those who desire prophecy, but leading them in to dark corners as a result of their own demagogic blinkers. Erring on the side of caution, Peter Drucker, claims that charisma becomes the undoing of leaders, and he seems to have a point when taking into account one of the latest cult mass suicides, under the direction of Heaven's Gate leader, Marshall Applewhite, whose intent seems to have been that through death, contact would be made with UFOs. All those that followed Applewhite into death highlight the notion of a charismatic leader not being able to distinguish between moral, immoral and amoral intentions, a theme that has been pursued through history. For example, while Lee Iaccoca of Chrysler is often cited as a charismatic leader with integrity, other leaders are not always seen as favourably, as exemplified by the many fallen tycoons in the late 1980s, such as the Australian Alan Bond, who recently appealed against his latest prison sentence, only to succeed in having it doubled by the appeal judges! Similar analysis can be applied to the arrests of Italian corporate leaders.

However, what is emerging from research is that there exist common characteristics necessary for charismatic leadership. An analysis of exceptional transformational leaders, for example Henry Ford, who masterminded mass-produced automobiles, and Jan Carlzon, who turned Scandinavian Airlines from an $8 million loss into a $71 million profit in a little over a year, reveals that all had acted in crisis, and turned loss into gain. Manfred Kets de Vries supports the view that charismatic leaders arise in time of crisis, due to the leader's own superego, the group's sense of helplessness and dependency, and a shared desire to reduce life's complexities. Even Max Weber noted that charismatic leaders seem to emerge particularly when uncertainty and unpredictability exists, thus setting the scene for transformational application.

Charisma and the needs of followers

The contrasting view is that charisma is a relationship and not a characteristic of a leader's personality. Charisma exists only because followers desire to be led and to be given direction concerning how to behave. Fundamental to such a desire is the belief that followers will perform exceptionally under a leader's influence. The willingness on the part of followers to sacrifice their personal interests for the sake of being led to a collective goal, is the distinguishing feature of the attribution element of charisma.

The social researcher, Wilfred Bion, has shown that groups regress to immature patterns of behaviour to protect themselves from discomfort and those experiences they find unpalatable. He suggests that groups tend to revert to one of three styles of operation, 'dependency', 'pairing' and 'fight-flight', as their defence against threat and pain.

In a dependency mode of operation, it is assumed that the group needs some form of leadership to resolve its concerns and release it from its traumatic experiences. The group is given hope, and hence turns its attention to the leader and away from its anxiety provoking circumstances. Leaders are idealized, while group members readily accept their inadequacies. For reasons of dependency and anxiety, leaders tend to have more influence during crisis than non-crisis periods. Should, however, the leader fail to live up to expectations, the group is likely to react by first, denial, then anger 'how could we have been so fooled?', leading to, at times virtual character assassination, followed by searching for a substitute.

The second pattern of response groups adopt to deal with their problems, is through 'pairing'. A fantasy grows, whereby the members of the group believe that a 'saviour' figure will emerge to deliver the group from its terror. The expectation that the Messiah is about to arrive, inhibits, and in extreme cases paralyses a group from confronting its own problems.

A third pattern of response is described as 'fight-flight', namely projecting a fear on a supposedly hostile enemy, which may take the form of a competitor, a government regulator, the attitude of the public, or a particular person or organization. While the fight-flight process unites the group, it also tends to destroy the group's appreciation of reality and hence, its ability to cope. Effort and energy is 'soaked up' in fighting or defending the group from the so-called predatory force, rather than coolly contemplating and assessing the problems at hand. One of the accusations made against Margaret Thatcher is that she used the conflict over the Falklands to turn British people's attention away from her unpopular restructuring policies, and used, what some called an unnecessary war, as the opportunity to win popularity with the electorate.

All three dysfunctional group dynamics can trap leaders into what Irving Janis terms 'groupthink', popularly exemplified by Kennedy's negative influence on his advisory group, during the Cuban crisis, concerning the abortive invasion of Cuba, at the Bay of Pigs, by 1200 US-sponsored anti-Castro Cuban refugee forces on 17 April 1961. The President's charisma, profound in promoting the myth of the openness of King Arthur's Camelot, in reality inhibited dialogue at policy level, which, in turn, bred conformity among key decision makers and advisors. An unhealthy, but assumed consensus emerged, that in turn discouraged the expression of doubts. Similarly, policy failure, as a result of further 'groupthink', was seen in the case of Pearl Harbour, in the escalation of US involvement in the Korean and Vietnam Wars, in the Iran rescue mission, and in the Iran-Contra affairs.

Many researchers and writers are critical of Kennedy. However, does not the Bay of Pigs event typify so many experiences in today's business world concerning mergers, takovers, divestments and entering or not entering into new markets? A common feature of consultancy is to be at the receiving end of the comment, 'I know it won't work! Why doesn't somebody tell them?' only to later discover that they (top management), as individuals, had already reached the same conclusion, but experienced their surroundings as unsupportive of forthright and honest comment. Captured in Chapter 8, but in many ways, a fundamental essence of this book, is that one distinguishing feature between an outstanding leader and one of moderate capability, is the maturity and discipline to *action insight*, namely the resilience to discuss and fully examine what is already known. As inhibition is an outright enemy of all positively minded executives, it is amazing how many repeatedly have their own Kennedy/Bay of Pigs experiences.

As shown in Chapter 1, even without the presence of a powerful leader, a group can become closed minded to suggestions or comments which highlight different ways of thinking about situations or alternative ways of behaving. It should be noted that closed mindedness should not be confused with people sharing similarities. If time has shown nothing else, it has highlighted that individuals develop relations with individuals similar to themselves, thus forming a community of kindred spirits who share similar tastes, interests, values, ethnic or personal backround, attitudes and even idealogies. Such similarities are re-inforced by certain daily routines that bind people together. What is unhealthy is the forming of such strong ties, which, inhibit alternative views being expressed, which in turn, leads to dysfunctional ways of thinking.

Groupthink actively discourages what the group would perceive as critical or negative input. The group's reaction could be aggressive, dogmatic, and rejecting of comments made. What suffers is the quality of discussion and decision making. Such groups are often termed as close minded. Some members of the group may recognize what is happening and leave the group. Others, as aware, may feel themselves as unable to reverse the situation and hence, flow with the stream.

Groupthink circumstances induced or not induced by charismatic leaders are likely to require a charismatic leader to break the mould. However, that is not always successful, for research from the USA suggests that the average reformist police chief lasts two years before the former corrupt network secures his/her removal and achieves a replacement with their nominee. Hence, more direct action may need to be taken, as was witnessed in Canada (the example below is also referred to in Chapter 10).

The Canadian Federal Department of External Affairs and International Trade (EAITC) with its 5150 employees, of which approximately 3711 were internationally job mobile, had for years experienced the darker-side of group-driven reality. Under Foreign Service Directives (FSD), diplomats and their families abroad were entitled to a certain number of trips home as an employee benefit. Over the years, members of the close-knit diplomatic network, posted in Europe, Africa, Latin America, Asia and Australia, were booking the full-fare airline tickets to which they were entitled, cancelling them and then travelling on reduced-fares. The full-fare ticket stubs were submitted as expense claims, and the difference pocketed. An internal investigation found that programme staff, desk-bound support personnel and ambassadors were participating in the scam. The travel scam arrangements were 'open knowledge' among the network members for some years. Further, the information regarding various deals with travel agencies was readily passed on to new members, and frequent use was made of the EAITC's IT infrastructure, such as secured communication lines, to make arrangements from the country with the best travel deal. The scam was not reported until August 1988, when a promotion-seeking employee in the Paris embassy reported it to the internal auditors; and certain relevant information was subsequently leaked to the press. Although the department had a long reputation for weak administration, it always enjoyed a high-flying status, both at home and abroad. The fraud allegations dealt a serious blow to the image of Canada's Diplomatic Corps and the Department as a whole.

Hence, if an externally appointed leader cannot change current practice, a particularly drastic measure to disrupt groupthink is external investigation. Further, at the time of succession, a strong countervailing force that can be used to bring greater reality to a top team, is the board of directors. This is also the time when other key stakeholders, such as shareholders and trustees can have a significant influence on the board, as it is the board that has to approve the choice of successor. As the board, potentially, has extraordinary influence on the shape and future of the organization through its influence on succession, the transition process can be considerably enabled by the non-executive members of the board who can act as personal counsellors to the outgoing and incoming leaders.

Such assistance may well be needed, for the obstacles facing a newcomer leader to an organization can be formidable. In addition to confronting certain bad practices that exist in the organization, Manfred Kets De Vries highlights that the newly appointed leader may also face others' tendency to idealize past leaders, and refers to the work of the industrial psychologist, Alvin Goldner, who terms the phenomenon of idealizing the past as the 'Rebecca Myth', in reference to the Daphne Du Maurier's novel concerning a young woman's marriage to a widower. The newly wed lady had to endure others' recollections of the saintly, but distorted memories of the widower's first wife. Dealing with the supposed virtues of the past, as if they are in the present is undoubtedly taxing, even for the more resilient. Any fantasy can be conjured up, especially as only the substitute (the new leader) is exposed to the discomfort of reality testing. One of the implications of the Rebecca myth is that the senior executives of an organization and the non-executive members of the board may underplay or just ignore the actions of previous leaders and promote the myth of, 'a better world gone by', to which the present hardly measures. Not only does the successor face ghosts from the past, but may equally succumb to the guilt of adhering to such beliefs. 'What is it about me that is not good enough', is the greatest trap in which to fall.

Leaders understanding leadership

What is the value of understanding how the early years of development have influenced an individual in later life? What is the benefit of knowing how one's emotions, mind and body have grown and been moulded by a series of significant early childhood experiences? What is the purpose of analysing the early developmental experiences of leaders? The purpose is for leaders to better understand leadership.

Leaders, understandably, make a powerful impact on others, their organization and their surrounding world. As leaders can form agendas and set trends, so they can also distort agendas and break with existing trends. As leaders can form and forge relationships with others, so they can also break relationships and undermine the relationships others share. Leaders can as much break as they can make. Leaders can mend and nurture, as much as they can damage whatever they touch. For leaders to understand themselves is a crucial step towards the positive development of organizations and even nations. Leaders not under-standing how their early influences imprint on their leadership style, their orientation, and personal values, are people who can go down the road of being compulsive, over-dominant, narcissistic, and consider themselves as indispensable. Hence, one reason for such learning is that leaders appreciate to guard against the destructive impact of uncomfor-table or distorted experiences in early childhood.

Equally, a lack of awareness of feelings, and a reliance on formal logic can also be ruinous, especially with regard to decisions about people and life, such as creating, or changing the culture of an organization and the values people deeply hold which give meaning to their working existence. If a leader can understand and consequently express his/her feelings and convictions with courage, balanced with consideration for the feelings and convictions of other persons, he/she shows that he/she has reached a balance in life whereby, in order to define meanings for others, leaders first need to define meanings for themselves, and understand their own philosophy on which their values are based. Knowing one's own emotions (self-awareness/mindfulness, recognizing a feeling as it happens), managing emotions (handling one's own feelings in an appropriate manner), driving oneself (marshalling emotions towards a goal), recognizing emotions in others (empathy), and appropriately handling relationships (managing emotions of others) are indicative of an executive who understands the nature of the forces within him/herself, and can direct his/her energy to promote a shared sense of high quality performance and openness of communication between the top and the bottom of the corporate structure. It is postulated that only through self-understanding can a leader inculcate a positive philosophy into the organization.

Key points summary

■ Attention is given to exploring possible unique characteristics of leadership that make particular individuals stand out as leaders.
■ Desire and will, mind and body, and their relationship and impact on leadership aspirations and behaviour are the focal points of the chapter.

Freudian thinking

■ Freud hypothesized that the childhood experiences of reconciling the demands of sexuality and the forces of external control and constraint are deeply influential in determining the characteristic traits of adult life. Freud's analysis of libidinal desires, their gratification or frustration, led to his postulating that five stages of development are crucial to consider in adult-forming experiences in childhood, namely, the oral, the anal, the pre-genital, the phallic and the genital phases.
■ The oral phase addresses the experiences of the baby in the first year of life, in terms of meeting or not gratifying the child's need for security. A child that feels secure becomes more psychologically confident. The baby who feels that a sense of trust has not been established with his/her primary carer, can become withdrawn and clingy, leading to narcissism and a drive to satisfy personal needs, in later life.
■ The anal phase, which occurs towards the end of the first year of the baby's life, addresses the experiences of the child in separating emotionally from its primary carer in order to develop a unique sense of self. If the child is given the chance to detach him/herself, but feels the security of the primary carers nearby, the child's confidence continues to grow. If the primary carers are over-controlling, the child can suffer a deep lack of confidence which continues throughout his/her life.
■ The pre-genital stage, relevant more in the third year of life, is the stage when the dependence needs of the child are healthily or

negatively addressed. If the experiences are negative, the later adult may habitually enter into dependent relationships.

■ The phallic phase, emerging at the end of the third year of life, addresses how the child experiences his/her sense of identity through play, imagination and his/her attraction to the primary carer of the opposite sex. If not supported to explore, or if frustrated, the child can become wilful or withdrawn, which in later years may emerge as aggrieved, individualistic, winner-take-all type of behaviour.

■ The genital phase, occurring between the ages of five and ten years, examines the experiences of the child in discovering his/her personal power in the outside world. A child deprived of praise and reassurance can feel resentment, which in later life can emerge as the drive behind workaholism.

Bioenergetics

■ Based on the thoughts of Freud and post-Freudians, Alexander Lowen developed the concept of bioenergetics, which examines the relationship between early experiences and their impact on a person's mind and body. It is emphasized that during the formative years, there exist five stages of development which influence the growth and development of the person. If during these five stages the child is distressed, the mind and body respond defensively to the pain experienced. These five stages or mind-body types, known as holding patterns, are known as the hold-together, hold-on, hold-up, hold-in and hold-back types of personality.

■ The hold-together personality is formed in response to damaging experiences from birth onwards, such as staying in hospital longer due to premature birth, or illness, or due to hostile and abusive behaviour from the primary carer. As a result, the child tries to hold him/herself together against such a hostile environment, which leads in later life to an adult who is unreachable, difficult to understand and a perfectionist.

■ Hold-on personalities are formed from being deprived of attention and touch early in life, which causes one in later life, to hold onto others in dependent relationships.

■ Hold-up personalities developed in children who, from about the age of three, were not given the opportunity or support by the primary carer to develop their own identity. Hence they hold themselves up against diversity, which in later life emerges as behaviour in which the adult accepts enormous challenge and displays substantial intuition and an ability to make for changes of direction. Hold-up personalities can couple charm with utter ruthlessness.

■ Hold-in personalities are formed from being over-disciplined and consequently hold-in their feelings so as not to upset their primary carers. In later life they are likely to display a lack of assertiveness and find feedback a traumatic experience.

- Hold-back personalities are formed from the experience of not being given the chance to come to terms with their own sexuality, emerging as individuals holding back their tender feelings and compensating by striving for excellence.

Narcissism

- Freud and post-Freudian thinkers concluded that frustrations in early life could also lead to an individual exhibiting narcissism, identified as constructive, reactive and self-deceptive.
- Constructive narcissists are leaders who project self-confidence, purpose, get on well with others, but are sensitive to criticism.
- Reactive narcissists are poorly integrated personalities who attempt to manage their anxieties by distorting outside events in their favour. They can be ruthless, controlling and unable to accept information that runs counter to what they believe.
- Self-deceptive narcissists are people who hold a low sense of self-esteem due to the desire to live up to their illusion of parental self-worth. As they are insecure, they are more likely to be conservative and analytical, and probably more effective in transactional rather than transformational circumstances.

Charisma

- Charisma has been viewed as those extraordinary qualities exhibited by particularly gifted personalities.
- Charisma has equally been seen as the result of the inadequacy needs of followers who attribute to the leader the extraordinary qualities which the followers themselves lack.
- Charisma is also viewed from a routinized, hereditary point of view, whereby through the generations, charismatic qualities are not attributed to individuals, but to position and status in life.
- Whether charisma is an aspect of an individual's character structure, or the manifestation of the dependency needs of followers, dysfunctionality occurs when 'groupthink' arises, and an inhibiting climate of consensus becomes part of a group's way of operating.

Notes

1 Kets de Vries (1989) coined the phrase 'inner world of leaders', which we have adopted. We acknowledge the work of Manfred Kets De Vries as probably one of the finest analyses that currently exists, penetrating the psyche of leaders.
2 Quote from Brown (1964:25).

3 Quote from Cotter (1996:4).
4 The section on bioenergetics is adapted from the readable and insightful text by Cotter (1996).
5 Quote from Cotter (1996:27).
6 Quoted from Freud (1922:123–4).
7 Reported by Walter Isaacson (1997).
8 Quote from Tichy and Sherman (1993:246).

Further reading

For further reading on Sigmund Freud, see Freud (1922, 1936, 1974) and Brown (1964).

For further information on post-Freudians, see Klein (1959, 1981), Pierrakos (1990), Reich (1949) and Alexander Lowen (1975). For an insightful view of how bioenergetics can be applied to management and leadership, see Cotter (1996).

For analysis of narcissism, read Kets de Vries (1989) and for further information on Bill Gates, read Issacson (1997) and on Benjamin Netanyahu, see Anonymous (1997).

For an analysis of the existence of charisma and whether leaders are born or self made, read Weber (1968), who falls more into the 'born-with' end of the spectrum and researchers such as House (1977), House et al. (1991), perceiving charisma as the result of the relationship between the leader and led. In contrast, Drucker (1990) considers charisma as exuding more negative qualities, while others highlight the moral righteousness of charisma (Pauchant 1991).

For an analysis of the impact charismatic leaders have on groups, read Bion (1968) and Janis (1982), on how groups influence leaders (Manz and Sims 1991), how the darker side of organization influences the manner in which groups operate (Gouldner 1954, 1974) and on the ever increasing influence of IT on people and groups (Korac-Boisvert and Kouzmin, 1994).

For those interested in how leaders can become more self-understanding, read Goleman (1986), and how leaders can more effectively communicate, read Gardener (1993).

For those who wish to pursue a psychoanalytic approach to understanding an organization and its leaders, read Berry (1996) and Unger (1987).

CHAPTER 6

Power of Demographics

Case analysis

The one big room

Lola Okazaki-Ward a Cranfield colleague and I (Andrew), were interviewing a number of main board members and other senior managers of the Honda organization at their head office, Tokyo. 'Every major market, Japan, US, Europe, is facing over capacity problems', commented one of the directors. Another director continued:

> What we are facing are rapid, lifestyle changes. In a situation of an appreciating yen . . . , one of our strategies is to shift production overseas . . . out of 1.5 million product sales worldwide, about half a million are produced overseas . . . we are increasing the ratio of overseas production to domestic production.

The conversation continued by exploring the impact of shifting a greater volume of production overseas. Shortly, the discussion focused on the orientation and attitude being adopted at Honda main board level to addressing the enterprise's interesting strategic challenges.

> From a purely financial point of view, it is better to shift production overseas . . . but board members here are insisting employment is more important.

The conversation turned towards how effectively the board members communicated with each other, and whether the differences of view of each of the members of the board led to tensions and difficulties. The response was interesting.

> . . . one of the unique systems, at home that is, is that all these members of the board are in one big room – no individual rooms!

> Really, they don't have their own offices?

Actually, the President sits less than ten feet from me. Communication is very good. And that is deliberately done, for communication purposes.

I had to ask, 'Do people find it comfortable to work in a room like that?'

Yes, communication is very thorough. Messages get to the important people very quickly. It is a long established tradition in Honda. It has existed in Honda for over twenty years – just one big room.

The respondent paused.

When I call somebody or somebody calls their contact, we all hear what is going on. This way we all know what is happening. It is so successful, that we have now expanded this to the global operation whereby senior managers share one big room. In America, they found it unusual, perhaps uncomfortable, but it seems to work.

Another director stated, 'Mr Honda was one of the greatest engineers. In the case of Honda, our traditions are quite different from other large companies.'

As the Honda director indicated, the corporation has an unusual way of structuring the office accommodation of the top management – and all in the pursuit of improved communications. In their opinion, through sharing one room, communications are far better as a result. In effect, the demographics of the situation has enhanced top management communications in Honda. What are demographics?

Demographics is the study and analysis of populations and society, or particular subsets of society. The reason governments periodically conduct a census is to identify trends in society in terms of births, deaths, marriages, age and gender distribution. Such information is used to determine where to locate schools, hospitals and other community facilities, as the appropriate location of a social service requires an understanding of population needs and movements. Equally, a decision by government to invest or not invest in any one region will attract various companies, or force the exit and bankruptcy of certain enterprises, affecting employment and possibly the rise or fall in the incidence of crime and other social repercussions. Hence, demographics is the study of social forces that influence or determine patterns of life, behaviour and attitude.

The Honda practice of sitting together in a large room promotes a level of communication desired by the corporation, irrespective of whether it is desired by the individuals. The people, through sitting in close proximity to each other, will naturally hear the phone conversations of their colleagues. It would take extreme self-discipline to resist becoming part of certain conversations and interactions. Circumstances have been created whereby each person listens, becomes involved, interacts and communicates, or just leaves.

As powerful as demographics are in moulding and shaping sectors of society, demographics are equally influential in shaping the behaviour, attitudes and philosophy of individuals at the enterprise level. Many business leaders refer to particular demographics such as the size of the organization, company location, the length of time in the job, the length of time in a department or in the organization, gender, age, ethnicity as powerful drivers of opinions and actions, whether positive or negative, in their enterprise. The views of the UK managing director of the famous Japanese trading corporation, Marubeni, highlights the importance of significant demographic influences on the corporation.

> I don't know much about European and American companies, because I haven't worked in one, but looking at their operation, they, the management, have very strong authority and they are authorized to do many things. The boss directly orders or tells his staff to do something. But in Japanese companies, the bottom-up system is very common, as you know, so for the boss and the staff, communication takes a different form and is a very important matter. The difference in the style of management, from the Japanese point of view, of European or American management is that the CEO can do whatever he likes so long as he is successful. If his policy is not good and results are poor, he can be easily dismissed. But in the Japanese case – I don't know if this is a merit or a demerit – we are always sharing information, as a kind of common bond. If you have something that needs to be discussed, formally or informally, a discussion is held. So when the boss takes a decision, the staff usually know it very well, because they already have been involved in the decision making process (H. Taida, Managing Director, Marubeni (UK) plc).

The above comments highlight perceived differences of two demographic factors, ethnicity, i.e. the differences between Japanese, European and US management and leadership styles, and the use of authority. The perception portrayed is that European and US management rely more on the use of authority in order to achieve objectives, due to their perceived short-term results orientation, but at the expense of internal communication, upon which, in contrast, Japanese companies heavily depend. Effective communication for Japanese organizations provides the essence of co-operation and positive relationship-building.

Despite the array of demographical factors that can possibly make an impact on contexts, ten key demographic factors are considered to influence significantly the attitudes, behaviours and philosophies of individuals and groups. Following the discussion of the ten demographic factors, studies of world leaders whose approach and style are purported to be driven by particular demographic influences are examined. An overview of the most powerful demographic drivers, and their influence on the philosophies of leaders and their impact on their organization and external stakeholders, is presented. The chapter is concluded by discussing the need for continuous learning and development, as the view portrayed is that despite early childhood influences, or being blessed with particular faculties through accident of birth, socialization and life's influences are never-ending.

The ten demographics[1]

Sociologists popularized the topic of demographics by arguing that particular experiences in life provide the fundamental influences which shape communities, people's expectations, cultural values and norms. The argument is that the more demographics influence social structures, the more that influence is reflected in people's social relations and interactions, the more these assignations influence personal and group dynamics and people's behaviour, which in turn, influence organizational outcomes. Ten significantly influential demographic factors have been identified from research.

Tenure

Tenure refers to time; how long individuals have spent in the organization, and how long they have spent on the job. The assumption is that a shared way of thinking, feeling and talking emerges between people who have experienced substantial periods of tenure within the same organization, department or unit. In effect, staff and management begin to talk 'the same language'. They evolve a common frame of reference which guides their behaviour and reactions. Evolving a commonality of understanding engenders both positive and negative aspects. The positive aspects are, that,

- people in the organization are more likely to understand each other,
- people who understand each other are more likely to trust each other,
- people who trust each other are more likely to want to communicate with each other,
- people who communicate with each other are more likely to want to co-operate with each other,
- through such experiences is generated a common platform of understanding, which provides people with the confidence to speak their minds and take calculated risks in their comments to each other,
- people who share a sense of belonging tend to feel good about themselves and the organization.

The negative aspects are that,

- people wish to preserve the status quo,
- people who wish to preserve the status quo resent change, even when it is obvious that change is in their best interests,
- people who do not change can become too comfortable and lose the habit of learning,
- people who are too comfortable find it more difficult to sense the emergence of external threat,
- people who become too embedded in their ways can scapegoat others new into the organization, who may be different and hold different attitudes and values,
- people whose life becomes too comfortable also become too routinized, because they have learnt that is the way they keep the established culture going,
- people who become driven by routine may find challenges threatening and find those who disagree, irritating.

Research highlights organizational tenure as one of the most powerful influences on people's growth, development or inhibition.

Location

Location can refer to both organizational and geographic placement. Organizational location identifies where the person is placed in the organization, at the centre, or in one of the large or small subsidiaries in the enterprise. Although located in one of the subsidiaries, the person may be geographically in the same building as the Group Chief Executive and the headquarters staff. Alternatively, the person may be located in an outlying office. Location is likely to influence feelings of identity. Do the managers in the organization identify with the policies that emerge from group headquarters? The likelihood is that the nearer a person is physically or functionally located to group headquarters, the more the individual is exposed to the ideas and issues of the day that emanate from the centre, the more the person will identify and work with centre-driven initiatives. The more isolated people are from the centre, the less they are likely to perceive as relevant the policies the headquarters staff identify as necessary to pursue for the development of the organization. In more distant locations, people are more likely to be influenced by their immediate markets and communities. Hence, when people more distant from the centre resist new ideas or innovations, that does necessarily mean that they are resistant to change and innovation. They may be, but they could equally fail to appreciate the value of the changes driven by the centre, for in their eyes, the changes proposed may hold little or no relevance to them in their context. On this basis, resistance to change can as much reflect the centre's lack of under-standing of the far reaches of the organization, or poor communication practices, or the downright resistance of staff and management to new ideas and practices.

In a corporate organization whose business portfolio extends to a wide range of interests, it could well be that the agendas and intentions of any one subsidiary may not fit well with the rest of the organization. Companies that are an amalgamation of businesses may not survive together for long, as the portfolio of businesses concept has, in practice, shown limited term viability on the basis that the investment required for future growth and profitability could well be beyond the means of the group. Vickers, the group of companies that holds interests in land defence systems (tanks), marine propulsion, Rolls Royce cars and Cosworth engines, faces an interesting challenge. What are the synergies between these business interests that lead to positive, long-term investment? Whatever the synergies may or may not be, location is likely to drive the attitudes, values and vision of particular managers. Will the senior managers within the businesses identify with the group, with the centre, or with just their operation? Interestingly, Rolls Royce cars have been put up for sale, thereby providing greater focus for the company in terms of engineering excellence. Under the leadership of Sir Colin Chandler, the Vickers future looks positive, with growth and innovation as the likely outcomes. Chandler has been extolling the virtues of shared synergies, especially those of in-house expertise. Other companies face less rosy prospects. Within loosely linked portfolio companies, location is likely to promote a mix of vision at top management levels.

Size of organization

Size of organization introduces additional complexities. The bigger the organization, the more difficult is, and hence the greater the attention that needs to be paid to, communication. The smaller the organization, the more likely are people to get to know each other and communicate naturally. In larger organizations, communication does not simply refer to projecting a message clearly, but equally taking into account, context. As indicated in both Chapters 2 and 3, context is a powerful determinant of the attitudes and behaviours of the people in the organization. The larger the organization, the more varied and numerous the differing contexts to be found in an enterprise, the more the leadership needs to consider how to pitch a message so that it is both heard and meaningful to the different parts of the organization. The smaller the organization, the more likely are the leaders to be familiar with individuals and their key contextual drivers, and hence the more likely communication will be both heard and acknowledged.

Configuration

Configuration refers to structure of organization. Is the organization more decentralized or centralized? – Do the senior managers in the organization pay greater attention to the issues and concerns of the wider enterprise or, are they in reality driven by the issues prevailing within their function? Hence, do the directors of the company think enterprise-wide, or more as functional managers? The answer to these questions can be determined by an examination of the impact of configuration on the behaviour and attitudes exhibited in the organization. The structural design of the organization influences the deeply held perceptions of individuals. (See Chapter 1 for an analysis of structures, in the Era of the Ideal section.)

A functional structure, for example, is considered as having a myopic impact on the leaders of the organization. People see, think and act function, and not total business. In contrast, a divisionalized structure requires that its top managers adopt a broader view of the organization and the external environment, so that they can reasonably debate broad policy and strategy. For example, if top management does not fully appreciate the needs of different divisions in the organization, it is then almost impossible to decide on the R&D investment patterns to pursue for the medium term. However, the potential drawback to divisionalized structures is that mistrust between the leaders of the organization may be more rampant. The agendas pursued by each of the top directors, sensible as far as his/her own organization is concerned, may not fit comfortably, if at all, with the demands and needs of colleagues who run the different parts of the organization. Hence, in each attempting to pursue his/her own agenda and yet accommodate the views of colleagues, the circumstances give rise to temporary alliances and cabals. The changing nature of debate, and allegiances in a divisionalized structure can substantially undermine long-term collegiate-based relationships, but extend individuals to sharpen their negotiation skills.

Specialization

Specialization is one form of functionality, which may relate to organizational position, or to client orientation, or to background and training, such as nuclear physicist, and or to being a member of a profession. Holding specialist status or qualifications influences people's attitudes and actions. Equally, special training and or professional membership may also provide for the specialist identity that distinguishes one person or group from the rest of the organization. A director of a company may continue to behave and display the attitudes of a professional specialist, even though he may not occupy a specialist role, but is a qualified professional specialist, who attends the meetings of his/

her professional association and is strongly influenced by that association. Certain researchers argue that configuration and specialization are
elements of the same demographic factor, whilst others support the view
that specialization is a particularly potent influence and should be
treated as a separate demographic characteristic.

Background

Background, or the history of individuals, groups and organizations can
be influential in moulding people's identities and views on life.
Background can refer to income levels, which can strongly influence
expectations and perceptions towards society, namely the working class/
upper class debate. Long after individuals have moved out of any one
income group, they may still consider themselves to be members of their
original grouping. The classic example is that of the person who has
originated from a working-class, lower-income group background, who
has achieved substantial wealth and status, yet still speaks with his/her
original regional accent, is proud of that fact, but has no contact with his/
her former friends and family, as he/she lives a much richer lifestyle.
Similarly, with organizations, the background and history of the
enterprise can substantially influence its dominant values and culture.
One not so well-known story is that of the 'matchbox toy cars', which,
apparently, began life as the hobby of one of the owners of a foundry/
engineering works in London. Even when the predominant business of
the company became the design and manufacture of matchbox toy cars
and vehicles, the owners still saw themselves as foundry engineers,
dabbling with their hobby, miniature toy cars. Old habits and traditions
die hard, especially those whose roots lie in established communities
with pronounced identities and principles. Background is a powerful
influence on the behaviour, principles and philosophies of people long
after individuals and organizations have departed from their roots.

Age

Age is a particularly pertinent issue, especially with the controversy
surrounding ageism. Principally, two arguments prevail. Older managers
and employees are more set in their ways, are less likely and willing to
learn, are likely to find change difficult, are likely to resist innovation
and new ways of working and hence are likely to become a burden to the
organization.

The alternative argument is that older individuals have evolved a
wisdom that helps them find pathways through complex and demanding
circumstances, have matured, are less concerned about promoting
themselves and hence more interested in developing others. Their years
in the organization, or industry, have imbued them with a corporate

memory which enables them to be effective networkers. The older and more mature staff and managers have 'seen it all before' and hence do not become anxious or inhibited in terms of their words and actions. From their experience of the organization, they more calmly find ways through demanding circumstances. Hence, a direct relationship between age and learning, age and motivation to learn, and age and problem solving, is assumed to exist. Whether such relationships exist or not, the research examining age and effectiveness of overall performance, is inconclusive.

One reason for not being able to identify a link between age and performance capability is that it is difficult to distinguish between the effects of ageing, and the impact of time spent in an unstimulating environment on work performance. A 33-year-old, who has spent 11 years in a dull job, in an uninspiring organization, may well exhibit similar characteristics to a 56-year-old, who has experienced a similar work environment. Despite all the current assumptions concerning ageism, age as a determinant of performance, is still, in practice, assumed to be as powerful a determinant of attitudes and behaviour as other demographics, such as tenure, background and size of organization. Overall, the assumption that older employees are not worthy of further investment and attention, is anything but proven.

Gender

Gender is currently one of the more emotive of the demographic topics. Since the introduction of women, on a mass scale, to the labour force during the First World War, gender has been a controversial subject for two reasons. The first is that women are considered to face the 'glass ceiling' phenomenon, that of being held back or prevented from appointment to senior and challenging positions despite having the ability for such jobs. The second is that women are assumed to have substantially different styles, philosophy and approach to management and leadership, than do men. Both issues are fully examined in Chapter 7. However, the overall conclusion reached is that ample evidence supports the case that a glass ceiling, an invisible block to further progress, exists for women who are upwardly mobile. The belief that women are substantially different to men in their approach and values is, however, not substantiated. In fact, evidence exists to confirm that once in a senior position, gender is one of the least distinguishing factors determining effectiveness of performance. Whatever the evidence, the debate continues to rage.

Ethnicity

Ethnicity is almost, if not equally, as controversial a topic as gender. Periodically, in the 1960s and 1970s, the results of studies appeared in the press indicating that 'coloured people' were inferior, in particular ways, to whites, findings which have been discarded as much due to poorly structured research, as to not clearly thinking through the nature and impact of cultural differences on people. The emphasis of the late 1980s and the 1990s has focused more on exploration of the impact of people's varying ethnic backgrounds, on personal, team and organizational performance (see Chapter 2). However, the results of these studies are equally not clear. Virtually all researchers acknowledge that social differences, and differences of background and upbringing exist between one country/region and another, but the relevance of such differences to workplace performance, is questionable. It is clear that substantial regional differences exist within any one country, for example, the differences between urban and rural dwellers; New Yorkers may well have more in common with the inhabitants of Tokyo, than with their fellow Americans in rural Nebraska. Hence, regional differences in any one country could be a more powerful influence than ethnic differences between countries. Second, people, especially those who have undergone formal education and/or vocational training, have been developed to discern – they can think and make decisions for themselves! They can see what is required to keep their company afloat, to improve performance, to sell more products and to respond to the demands of their markets and influential stakeholders. On this basis, people are just as, if not more, likely to focus on the challenges facing their organization, recognizing that ethnic differences may be of secondary importance. To support this argument are the findings to have emerged in the areas of power and culture pursued in Chapters 2 and 3, whereby organizational level is identified as a more critical issue than country or ethnicity in terms of workplace effectiveness. In contrast, researchers, such as Geert Hofstede, argue from an opposite perspective. There is no denial of ethnicity in terms of its existence, but its relevance as a determinant of workplace efficiency is another matter.

Communication

Communication has traditionally been viewed as an outcome of the impact of other demographic forces. However, as downsizing, decentralization, responsiveness to customers, the adoption of a service orientation, and the need for a continuous reassessment of costs have become a daily reality in both private and public sector organizations, communication is increasingly being treated as a demographic influence in its own right. The question that has remained is, what is meant by communication? The clear projection of a view or policy, either spoken or published? The behaviour of the leaders of the organization, in terms of how the leaders symbolize what they say or proclaim (see Chapter 8, Providing direction, and Providing example)? or the varying interpretations or understandings of any key message by the recipients? Various studies, in exploring any one or more of these aspects of communication, have treated communication both as the result of a number of other demographic factors, and also as a driver of demographic influences, especially in studies of top teams. Numerous researchers have identified that effective use of communication between the senior managers of an organization is a primary influence in generating cohesion, interdependency and helpful relationships at senior and more junior levels in the organization. Considerations of communication at a team level go beyond speech and the written word and extend to that of understanding and empathy. The point being made is that where understanding and empathy exist, relationships improve, which improvement in turn, allows for more in-depth dialogue. Through deeper understanding and openness of conversation, issues are more effectively addressed. An enhanced quality of relationships at the top team level, substantially influences the adoption of particular values and behaviours by others in the organization.

Power of demographics: the results of research

The still to be answered question of history is, are leaders born (or are distinguishing characteristics shaped at a very early age), or do people, in general, and leaders in particular, continually develop themselves and are, in turn, developed by their surroundings? The developmental viewpoint assumes choice, in that if people better understand what is influencing them they can choose to 're-engineer' themselves, and draw the best out of themselves and those around them.

Having explored the thinking and assumptions underlying Kets de Vries's 'the inner world of leaders', attention is next given to an examination of the social forces that may mould leadership approaches and philosophies. Separate studies conducted at the International Management Development Centre at Cranfield School of Management, explored the impact of demographics on leadership thinking, philosophy and behaviour, and focused on three groups, 750 top civil servants in the Australian Federal Government, 550 top managers of National Health Service (NHS) Trusts in the UK, and 5500 top private sector leaders (Chairmen, CEOs, MDs, directors, general managers), spanning 12 countries, namely, the UK, Japan, USA, China, Germany, France, Sweden, Spain, Hong Kong, Finland, Ireland and Austria. These studies outline the influence of demographics on the philosophy and behaviour of leaders, and in turn of the leaders' varying impact on the organization and on the external world.

Two distinct clusters of demographic factors emerged as significantly and powerfully shaping the more deeply held philosophies and behaviours of top management. These are termed, the power of accountability and the power of time.

Power of accountability

In the Cranfield NHS Trusts survey (UK), those jobs with a high level of executive accountability, as opposed to jobs of other and substantial responsibilities, differentiate two fundamentally different philosophies, attitudes and behaviour among senior health service managers (see Table 6.1).[2]

CEOs, finance and human resource directors, medical directors (i.e. clinicians holding senior executive positions) and a small number of CEOs who are medically qualified, fall into one category known as the 'Executive'. Clinical directors (doctors holding management roles but are not members of the top team of the Trust), chairmen and non-executive directors fall into a second grouping, termed the 'stakeholders'. The executive group are responsible and accountable for both the operational and strategic development of the Trust. In contrast, there exists an imbalance of responsibilities and accountabilities in the roles of the stakeholder group. Chairmen and non-executive directors are responsible for the strategic progress of their Trust, but may not be accountable for the initiation, and are certainly not accountable for the implementation, of certain strategic initiatives. Equally, they are neither responsible nor accountable for broader operational activities concerned with Trust-wide performance. Clinical directors are responsible and accountable for operational activities within their sphere of influence. Equally, they may input opinions and put pressure on the top executive team on strategic matters, but as a body, are not accountable for their endeavours in promoting the long-term development of their Trust.

Table 6.1 Demographic distribution of two leader groups (NHS)

Function	Executive directors(%)	Stakeholders: clinical directors/non-executive directors(%)
Chief executives	19	
Medical directors	20	
Finance directors	24	
HR directors	9	
Clinical directors		14
Non-executives		9
Chairmen		5
% Total	72%	28%

Note: % refers to percentage of total sample
Source: Adapted from a Cranfield internal working paper by Kakabadse and Myers (1997).

Leadership attributes: the executive

Positive	Negative
Team oriented	Trust strategy
Job satisfied	Trust mission
Communicative	Leadership
Disciplined	Internal systems
Committed	
Dependable	
Clinicians viewed positively	

Those falling into the executive category are identified as team oriented, and as sincerely wishing to enhance positively their relationships with their colleagues. Such a positive attitude is carried over to the job, in that those in the Executive group indicate that they are satisfied with their role, enjoying the challenge of contributing to the short- and long-term development of the Trust. They feel themselves to be stretched positively and similarly attempt to stretch and develop their colleagues and subordinates. These senior managers see themselves as effective communicators, attempting to make known clearly the objectives of the Trust to all in the organization. They attempt to establish positive relationships with other managers in the Trust and in so doing, gain benefit from their endeavours by being regularly informed about how new developments and initiatives are progressing. These senior managers are well disciplined, and attempt to introduce an equally structured and disciplined way of managing the Trust. Their level of commitment to the Trust, its objectives, the enhancement of patient care and the development of its staff and management, is high. The directors who fall into the Executive grouping equally display a positive attitude towards clinicians. They consider that clinicians relate well to each other, as well as to the directors on the Trust Management Team.

In terms of internal systems, the directors consider that the budgeting processes and other internal practices in the Trust adversely affect the quality of service provided, hence undermine, in particular, patient care. However, the greatest degree of attention that the directors consider needs to be given is to the development of the leadership and the strategy of the Trust. Further work in terms of clarifying the Trust's mission is seen as requiring to be undertaken. Equally, the objectives and strategy of the Trust are seen as unclear and require further focusing and clarification. One reason for the lack of clarity is that the senior managers feel that the Trust top team does not provide sufficiently clear direction, partly because the quality of decision-making at senior levels within the Trust is viewed as also requiring attention. The view held is that improvements in the areas of mission and strategy will take place only if investment in the development of the leadership of the Trust occurs, which involves senior management needing to become better listeners, thereby minimizing the accusation that they are too distant from what happens on a daily basis. Further, it is seen that attention needs to be given to enhancing understanding as to which areas require improvement in terms of patient care. The view that emerges is that through improving the performance of individual top managers and equally the Trust team, progress in the areas of mission, strategy and service provision (in particular patient care) will equally occur.

Leadership attributes: the stakeholders

Positive	Negative
Job satisfied	Pressured
Disciplined	Negative internal culture
Details oriented	Leadership poor
Committed	Trust strategy
Team oriented	Independent
Dependable	Systems are hindrance
Independent	Top team poor

The stakeholder group indicate that they value their independence and further, find the systems and controls in the organization a hindrance. They feel that too many constraints are placed on them. They also feel themselves to be pressured at work, an experience which not only undermines their performance, but which they say equally impacts negatively on their home life. A number comment that the pressures of the job are at times too much to handle. It should be noted that these comments are driven home more by the clinical directors, than by the chairmen or non-executive directors.

However, as far as their job is concerned, high levels of job satisfaction are reported. Chairmen, clinical directors and non-executive directors report that they enjoy the challenge of their role in the Trust, and are motivated by their work. As such, they consider themselves to be disciplined at follow-through, ensuring that projects and activities are effectively completed. They are, however, concerned that other members of the Trust Executive team do not display a similar discipline in their management of the Trust.

In addition to being disciplined, clinical and non-executive directors insist on being regularly briefed concerning new developments. They state that they expect to be kept informed of progress on agreed initiatives, and consider that they should be regularly updated on how new developments and initiatives are progressing. With such attention to briefing and discipline, it is not surprising that the stakeholders indicate that they respect people who stick to the rules. They also encourage that the traditions of the Trust be respected.

Overall, clinical directors, chairmen and non-executive directors highlight their commitment to the Trust. They indicate that they feel themselves to be part of the Trust, and accept the responsibility for projecting a positive image on behalf of their organization. They consider the staff and management of the Trust to be of high quality and dedicated to its success. Staff development is taken seriously as the means to improve performance and promote a more positive attitude by the staff to their employing organization.

The views of the stakeholders concerning health care management issues are that team-work, in particular, is a positive experience. Clinicians are seen to work well with the directors on the Trust management team.

In contrast to the executive group, however, the stakeholders are more critical of the strategic management of the Trust. Similar to the executive group, they consider that the way the Trust is managed means that attention is diverted away from patient care. The reasons given for diminished levels of quality of service are that too much time is spent on management related issues, and that the current budgeting practices do not support enhancing standards of service. In addition, they consider that the standards laid down by the government, are not being fully met.

Further, clinical directors, chairmen and non-executive directors view that the long-term objectives of the Trust are not clear, and that executive management are losing sight of their objectives. Hence, the Trust top team are seen as not providing clear strategic direction, as they, as top managers of the organization, have been misguided about many of the changes they have sponsored. The reason given for the poor strategic development of the Trust, is that of political in-fighting in the Trust. As a result, decisions are seen to be made behind closed doors, inconsistently applied and also to change from one day to the next. For these reasons, the culture of Trusts and their leadership are viewed as problematic.

The current leadership is additionally seen as 'out of touch'. Top management are viewed as too distant from what happens on a daily basis. Both the Trust top executive team and the board (on which the chairman and non-executive directors sit) are seen to have little impact on the daily running of the Trust. Isolation, as well as dysfunctional internal politics, are considered by the stakeholders to be the reasons that the needs of patients are not well understood by those in senior management positions. Another reason is that senior management are considered as inattentive to the needs of lower level staff and management. Overall, the senior management of Trusts are viewed by the stakeholders as not performing sufficiently effectively, and in need of development. However, as individuals, the executive directors are viewed as highly motivated, trustworthy people with every intention of promoting the best interests of the Trust. For this latter reason, the stakeholders declare their support for senior management.

Demographic impact of accountability

The attitudes towards governance, namely the requirement to lead or steer the organization, are identified as being substantially influenced by the degree of exposure to accountability by senior managers (see Figure 6.1). The Cranfield NHS Trust survey identifies that those in roles of executive authority (the executive group), irrespective of their professional

Figure 6.1   Power of accountability

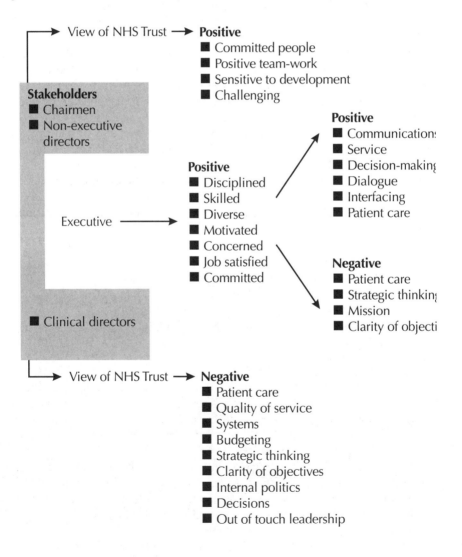

background, hold strongly similar views concerning the organization, its strengths, weaknesses and future requirements.

Those clearly interested parties, with responsibilities for the development of the Trust but in roles with little or no strategic executive authority (the stakeholders), display a more negative view of the Trust organization. Their role in the hierarchy, be it chairman, non-executive director or clinical director, or difference of functional and professional expertise, makes little difference to the strength of their views.

Being held accountable for driving the organization forward requires that the senior manager adopts a detailed but integrated view of how effectively the enterprise is proceeding. The significance of any singular event or action is placed in perspective, when compared with where the organization was, where it is now and where it is intended to be. Through being the person accountable, the individual senior manager is required to ask, 'How does what is happening now really influence where we are trying to get to, and as a result, should I do anything different?' The person is required to adopt a detailed, step-by-step, longer term perspective in order to assess the quality of his/her actions and decisions at any one point.

However, through being a stakeholder, and thereby not being held directly accountable for strategic, or even operational initiatives, but feeling responsible for the development of the organization, the individual senior manager is likely to adopt a shorter-term perspective. Any single event may appear more damaging or more glamorous; any one act or decision may appear more incompetently or brilliantly managed than it is; why?, because the individual is not exposed on a daily basis to transactionally and transformationally lead the organization. Because interested onlookers are not required, through daily managerial transactions, to push towards transformational outcomes, they can adopt a 'distorted' view of events as they arise, seeing them better or worse than they are in reality. The Cranfield NHS survey, highlights the internal stakeholders as adopting a more negative view than their executive colleagues. For other organizations, external stakeholders, such as shareholders or the press, may also adopt a distorted, and on many occasions, a far more favourable or unfavourable view of the CEO, or the executive team, due to the reflected glory or shame of a single activity or event. That single activity or event may be flattering or damaging, but is definitely deceptive as to the reality within the organization.

The principle is that through being held to account, effective governance improves, as senior managers are likely to adopt a far more balanced perspective as to the true nature of the challenges and constraints they face. Interested onlookers can afford to be more reactive as they are not required to stand by their comments.

Power of time

The results of two other Cranfield studies emphasize that time can be powerful in shaping the philosophies, attitudes and behaviours of leaders. The time-related dimensions are time in the job, time in the organization (job and organization related tenure), experience of senior management positions and responsibility, and age.

Global leader survey

The chairmen, Presidents, CEOs, executive and non-executive directors, and general managers, spanning 12 countries, form the sample of the private sector top executive leadership capabilities survey. The two senior tiers of the Australian Commonwealth (federal) government, SESs (Senior Executive Service), and SOSs (Senior Officers) form the government sample (see Table 6.2).[3]

Leadership attributes: radicals

Positives	Negatives
Open style	Hypercritical
Enjoy challenge	Dislike controls
Committed	Dislike interference
Encourage dialogue	Need to be in charge
Service driven	Dissatisfied
Outward focused	Negative view of company
Follow through oriented	Naive

Radicals have a background of employment in more medium-sized organizations, have spent a shorter time in the organization and in their

Table 6.2   Global leader survey profile

Leader philosophy	Sector	Size of organization (persons)	Years in organization	Years in job	No. of senior management appointments	Age
Radicals	Private	1,000–5,000	6mths–1.5yrs	6mths–1yr	1.85	26–35
	Government	500–2,000	1–4 years	1–2 years	2.6	26–35
Politicians	Private	6,000–20,000	4–7 years	1–2 years	2.1	36–46
	Government	5,000–10,000	10–15 years	2–3 years	3.4	46–55
Strategists	Private	6,000–20,000	4–7 years	4–7 years	1.7	46–55
	Government	2,500–5,000	16–25 years	5–10 years	2.8	46–55

current job, are the youngest of the three leader groups, and have held, on average, few senior management appointments (see Table 6.2).

Radicals project a swashbuckling image, being independently minded, disliking controls, but enjoying challenge and that of motivating people. Radicals focus on customers and the community, are market driven and do whatever they consider it takes to be more competitive. Although they are focused, they also adopt an overview of their organization and its external impact. They are quick to spot internal tensions and constraints and attempt to eradicate such problems in order to improve performance. Similar energy and flexibility are applied to people. In order to help staff and managers become flexible and focused towards customers and clients, radicals adopt an open style, and encourage feedback throughout the organization.

The radicals' people orientation is balanced by their discipline, consistency and independence. They are disciplined in terms of effectively promoting follow-through and demanding attendance at meetings. They insist on being regularly briefed and attempt to promote consistency in their own and in their direct reports' work.

However, despite their respect for discipline, they are equally strong-minded people who display a need to be in charge. Their desire to have their own way, motivated by wishing to excel in the marketplace, or community, can push them to being hypercritical of the organization and their colleagues. Systems and internal controls are viewed as a hindrance, or just ineffective. They feel resources are wasted, and that the morale and motivation of staff and managers is poor. Middle and lower level managers are viewed as not being given a chance to manage, as they are inhibited by the more traditional styles and philosophies of their bosses. With so many internal, work, morale and structural problems being identified, the company is seen as ineffectual at managing change.

When irritated or dissatisfied, radicals can become over-demanding. Their need to attain high performance, and their lack of patience can make them cynical and punitive. Their criticisms and comments can inhibit others from offering suggestions on how to improve current circumstances. The irony with radicals is that their drive and enthusiasm can be undermined by their intolerance and lack of patience with others who they view as being unwilling or unable to face their problems and challenges.

Leadership attributes: politicians

Positive	*Negative*
Committed	Structured
Respect communication	Intolerant
Impartial	Critical of company

Rules oriented	Negative impact
Disciplined	Need to be boss
Details driven	Dislike being controlled
Service conscious	Driven by protocol

Politicians are identified as being employed principally by large organizations, have been in the organization for some time, but have been in the job for only over two years. They have, however, held more senior management appointments than the other two leader profiles (see Table 6.2).

Politicians are the natural communicators. They enjoy being with people, and project the feeling that people are important to them. Their people management skills are equally well applied to customers, members of the community and other external stakeholders with whom they effectively communicate and clearly display their commitment to the organization and the client. Overall, politicians display their enjoyment of working as senior general managers.

As with radicals, politicians, too, display a capacity for discipline. They are attentive to detail and can be rigid in following established work procedures. They insist on being regularly briefed and dislike surprises. They are especially disciplined at attending meetings. Their orientation to detail and routine is partly driven by their need to be in control, and partly by their deeper need for structure and systematic ways of working. Their discipline orientation is projected onto others by their insisting that their direct reports are equally attentive to detail and follow established channels in terms of work procedures. Further, their orientation to being disciplined is likely to have arisen from their specialist background, which they indicate they still find fulfilling.

Despite their organizational orientation, politicians dislike being controlled. They exhibit strong control needs in desiring to be 'the boss'. Their capability to interact sensitively with other people is used in more manipulative ways, especially in support of the push for command. They are also likely to use protocol to their advantage, particularly in resisting others' attempts to intervene in what the politicians see as their affairs.

In a similar way as radicals, politicians display frustration with the organization. Criticism is of the organization, not their job. They consider that poor leadership and inadequacy of systems make the organization inefficient and disjointed. Communications, in terms of briefings, are poor and the situation is exacerbated by poor discipline in attendance at meetings. Further, they consider that meetings are changed with little or no notice given. Because of the perceived complexity of the organization, and the preoccupation politicians have with their own part of the organization, little attempt is made by them to appreciate how the totality functions, which in turn leads to a lack of tolerance, on their part, for the problems and challenges others face. Add to that a significant communication frustration. In feeling that they are not regularly and effectively briefed, politicians display their negativity, but covertly. Even when changes are introduced, politicians exhibit little trust in the organization's ability to manage the change process. However, it should also be noted that politicans seldom 'stay around' long enough in the job to see through changes that they or others have initiated. Overall, the organization is viewed as having a poor history of change and is misguided by the changes it pursues.

Leadership attributes: strategists

Positive	Negative
Performance/people oriented	Can appear conservative
Communicative	Poor history of change
Committed	Open to criticism
Encourage checking out	
Team driven	
Mature/Tolerant	
Encourage dialogue	
Encourage discipline	
Realistic about colleagues/organization	
Eclectic approach	

Strategists have worked for a considerable period in the organization and have spent up to ten years (on average) in their current job. They are older than the other two leader profiles, but have held only a few senior management appointments (see Table 6.2).

Strategists are strongly people-oriented leaders. Their orientation is to grow a performance-oriented culture, whereby staff and managers feel they are not only making a contribution, but equally have the opportunity to develop both their skills, and themselves as people. Strategists adopt an open style of management whereby inviting feedback and openness of communication are seen as natural ways of operating in the company. People are encouraged to speak their minds, and to check out their understanding of issues and debates in the enterprise. The watchword is 'encouragement'. People are encouraged to discuss their work problems. They are equally encouraged to pay attention to details and be disciplined in the ways they go about their work. Further, staff and middle level managers are supported in expressing their views on issues and, if they feel it necessary, in trying to persuade senior management to alter their views.

An equally supportive attitude is adopted towards the organization. The internal systems and controls are viewed positively, although certain concerns are acknowledged to exist in the organization. Meetings can be changed too often, and initiatives and projects may not be followed through sufficiently well, so that momentum is lost. As with radicals and politicians, so, too, strategists recognize that the organization has faced problems with change, but they are less critical of the errors, failures and inadequacies of the past and present.

What strategists display are maturity, tolerance, discipline and a broad skill base. They recognize that managing a large organization is in itself problematic. The problems and issues that arise are never ending. On this basis, a prime capability is to hold a positive attitude towards managing diversity. Strategists recognize that encouraging people and being disciplined go hand in hand. Strategists would make statements such as, 'a disciplined organization is fundamental to success', but would equally feel it important to be attentive to having staff and management adopt a shared sense of responsibility. Strategists insist on being regularly briefed, require that commitment and discipline become performance values in the organization, and yet display a sensitivity to individual and team needs. However, their more structured approach can make them appear more conservative in their actions and decisions. Strategists are likely to take longer to act, as they will genuinely attempt to confer with others, in order to gain the necessary support and ownership for the policies and tactics to be pursued.

Overall, strategists are concerned with improving internal performance, and meeting customer needs. Their strength comes from the fact that they know the organization and have remained in their senior position for a substantial period of time. They have had to live with their mistakes. Strategists have evolved a maturity of knowing what it means to manage people and systems in their organization over the longer term. Seeing challenges and initiatives through to fruition, and working to gain the respect of colleagues and subordinates, crucially differentiate strategists from radicals and politicians. Interestingly, all three leader profiles indicate their satisfaction in being involved in specialist activities. The strategists, however, seem to have better integrated their specialist work with their general management duties, and express that they enjoy both aspects of their workload.

Age and development: the additional factors

Distinction is drawn between younger and older senior managers, and between those older senior managers who have experienced job-related development and those who have not (see Table 6.3). Development may consist of having been given the opportunity of a challenging role, having been exposed to feedback that induced a positive outcome, or having attended relevant and well-run training programmes.

As already stated, the younger senior managers (26–35), namely the radicals, emerge as results driven and positively minded, but critical of their organization, and as people, impatient. Their attitude towards the

Table 6.3   Age and development

Younger (26–35) Radicals	Older without development (46–55) Politicians	Older with development (46–55) Strategists
Impatient	Structural	Performance-oriented
Critical	Sensitive (for self)	Team-oriented
Results driven	Cynical	Dialogue oriented
Positive	Results driven	Results driven
People oriented	Demotivating	Supportive
Daunting		Vulnerable

organization, its staff and management, and towards their own role, is partly driven by the fact that they are new to the organization and have not fully integrated, and partly because they are immature, as typified by displays of impatience if actions and activities are not proceeding to plan and time schedule. Experiencing similar developmental opportunities to those of many of their older colleagues, did little to change their perspective. If anything, provided with more tools, their criticisms and impatience increased.

Those older senior managers (46–55), namely politicians, who see themselves as having had little or no exposure to development, or have not determined their own development, consider themselves to be disadvantaged and hence emerge as more cynical and intolerant. The impact of such managers is that they demotivate others in the organization just as negatively as the younger age group, who are perceived by others as inhibiting dialogue and promoting anxiety.

The older age group who have been held to account for their successes and errors and who have turned numerous experiences into developmental opportunities, namely the strategists, embrace a broad and positive attitude to performance and are seen as supportive of colleagues, bosses and subordinates. However, their positive orientation leaves them vulnerable to the more negative interactions that can take place in dysfunctional senior management groups.

Further, age is identified, in the Cranfield NHS Trust's survey, as being influential in shaping the attitudes and behaviours of top managers in NHS Trusts.

Table 6.4 highlights that older senior managers emerge as more disciplined, exhibit more situationally effective leadership behaviours, are more able to take a balanced view on issues before reaching a decision, and are more likely to evolve positive relationships with colleagues, subordinates and people from other departments internally, and agencies externally, than their younger colleagues.

Table 6.4   NHS Trusts: comparison by age and other demographics

Transactional	Age	Time in hospital	Time in med.prof
Job satisfaction	Older	Less	Less
Working relations	Older		
Patient care	Older	Longer	Longer
Communication		Less	Less
Discipline	Older		
Decision-making	Older		Longer
Leadership behaviour	Older		
Culture of trust			
Transformational			
Top relationships	Older		
Strategic decision-taking	Older	Longer	
Top team sensitivities better handled	Older		

Source: Adapted from Korac-Kakabadse and Korac-Kakabadse (1997) (originally researched by Andrew Myers).

In particular, relationships within the top team are likely to be positive, the older the top team members (both male and female). The effectiveness of transformational leadership and the implementation of policy are likely to be enhanced by the presence of older senior managers in the top team. By taking a balanced view of the issues at hand and by entering into full and open debate with colleagues, the likelihood is that a greater sense of cabinet responsibility will grow among the top team members, which will immeasurably assist in consistently pursuing the application of strategies that have already been decided in the top team. On this basis, the opportunity costs that may arise from poor strategic decision-taking and inconsistency of application of strategy, are minimized by the presence of older senior managers.

The survey respondents also emphasize that patient care is better provided for by medical practitioners and managers that are older, more experienced and have spent longer in a particular hospital. Experience of the practice of medicine, coupled with a deeper understanding of the culture, values and attitudes within the health care establishment, provides for improved quality of care. In fact, time spent in the hospital as a practising physician and time spent in the medical profession, are identified as having a positive significant impact on strategic decision-making at Trust level.

Although with experience, decision-making improves, the same does not apply to job satisfaction and communication skills. The pressures of the job, the frustration of dealing with communication and interfacing issues within the hospital, the boredom factor of experiencing and applying similar routines on a daily basis, become more pronounced the longer the senior person stays in the job and in the hospital. However, what the individual learns to do is come to terms with the negative emotions that arise from the 'daily grind' of transactional leadership, by taking a more balanced view of his/her life, more maturely allocating time to work, to non-work, and to personal pursuits.

Demographic impact of time

The Cranfield studies highlight the length of tenure, the age of the individual and the opportunity for personal development, as crucial influences in the shaping of the philosophy, attitudes and behaviours of organizational leaders (see Figure 6.2).

Limited job and organizational tenure especially, when experienced by younger managers, promote a 'get it done' perspective, emphasizing a short-term and task-driven orientation. The short-term nature of the manager's time horizon is likely to engender a too critical view of him/herself and of others towards achievement and effectiveness. If events do not proceed as planned, and if too many mistakes are seen to be made, the manager is likely to both experience and express frustration, even more so the younger his/her age. Naturally, the manager's view of the organization, of colleagues, superiors and subordinates, will be coloured by the volume of errors or 'blockages' he/she encounters. The greater the number, the more critical and damning the shorter-term-oriented manager can be. Although the manager may achieve the targets set, the ease with which he/she finds fault can inhibit people from offering their views as to how to improve present ways of working. Hence, although the organization may gain operationally, opportunity costs are likely to arise in terms of improvement in quality of service and delivery over the longer term, as people are not naturally encouraged to participate in the continuous improvement of the organization.

In contrast, extended tenure of both job and organization, coupled with being older and also having been exposed to development, have a considerably different but equally profound impact. The Cranfield results highlight that a longer term perspective is adopted by just such a senior manager, in that the person has had to learn to live with his/her decisions and accordingly re-balance relationships with others. People adopt a longer-term time frame once they emotionally recognize their effect on others. A more sensitive consciousness of how a person impacts on others is adopted, especially if the individual is aware of his/her own development needs and is motivated to address those needs. The results emphasize that the demographic impact of 'long time' is that leaders are more likely to adopt a 'work it through' perspective, which helps consolidate the infrastructure of the organization by developing people so

Figure 6.2 Power of time

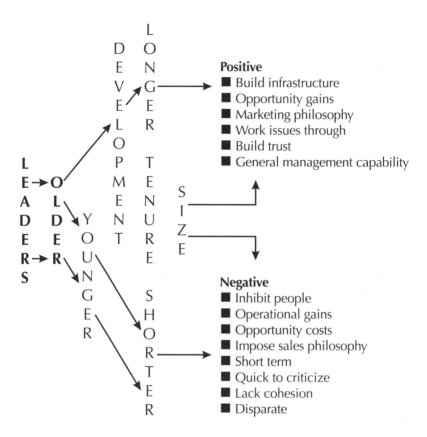

that they drive projects and policies to successful fruition. 'Long-term time frames' (long-term in the job and organization), generate situations of opportunity gain, even though operational costs may be experienced in patiently building up the morale and capabilities of staff and management. Extended organizational and, in particular, job related tenure at senior management levels, is likely to inculcate in its senior managers a deeply held marketing philosophy.

The size of the organization, did not emerge as a powerful predictor of leadership philosophy. In medium or larger-sized organizations, a shorter-term sales, or longer-term marketing, philosophy can equally well emerge. A great deal depends on whether people live through and face up to their mistakes and decisions with those around them. Having nowhere else to run to does marvels for promoting a more mature outlook on life.

Case for continuous development

A recently published book by Frank Sulloway (1996), a researcher at MIT (Massachusetts Institute of Technology), USA, offered the proposition that Charles Darwin was no more intelligent than his contemporaries, but the reason for his ability to rewrite evolutionary history was that he was in his family, the fifth of six children. Sulloway's thesis is that it is not the first born who manages to break out of moulds, but the offspring that follow, as they are the ones who have to strive more for parental care and attention, an experience which strengthens their character and which, as a discipline, carries through to later life.

An alternative view exists, and that is that Darwin simply did not relate well to conventions and had a stronger inclination to break out of existing moulds than others of his generation. Darwin simply did not wish to fit into the parameters of the day. In effect, he chose to stand apart.

Although the arguments presented in Chapter 5 – that people are shaped from an early age – are powerful, equally substantive is the argument that people continue to develop throughout their lives. They are likely to be moulded by their dominant experiences, but will also have the opportunity to choose the direction they wish to take, and quality they wish to experience. In the three distinctly different, Cranfield private and public sector survey groups, the length of time in the job, length of time in the organization, work-related accountability, and the age of the individual, are identified as the dominant forces of socialization. The more people stay in one situation, the more they become influenced by that environment. The less people stay in any one situation, the less likely are they to accept the issues and prevalent attitudes that face them. However, the choice factor is emphasized by the findings concerning personal development, whereby people of similar demographic background can choose their own pathways to pursue, and as the studies indicate, for the betterment of themselves and those around them.

There is no need to accept the status quo. As the Cranfield studies imply, change any one or more of the demographic factors and people's view of reality can equally be altered. Once armed with such insight, demographics can also be controlled, for example, by letting managers know that remaining longer in key jobs can enhance their maturity levels, and that it is ultimately their choice as to how to develop the particular leadership qualities desired by the organization. Through choice, people become inextricably in charge of their own destinies and development. On the premise that development is totally within one's own grasp, the alternative view to the 'born to lead' thesis of leadership, is that leaders are made through a willingness to examine the circumstances and then choose their own destiny, always nurturing their potential for learning so that they can, after due consideration, alter course if they so desire. The ultimate question is one of belief, namely, does the individual believe that he/she is born with something extra and will progress to great heights, or in contrast, is lacking in certain qualities and chooses to develop him/herself to heights that he/she may have initially considered improbable? The emerging evidence strongly suggests that people can make themselves into leaders, if their desire to do so is sufficiently powerful!

Key points summary

- The topic of demographics has emerged from anthropological and sociological research in examining those forces that mould the movements, needs and structure of populations.
- At the organizational level, it is considered that demographics are distinctly influential in determining the behaviour, attitudes and philosophy of staff and managers in organizations.
- The ten key demographics of tenure, location, size of organization, configuration, specialization, background, age, gender, ethnicity and communication are postulated as being potentially powerful in determining people's perspectives and actions in organizations.

Cranfield studies

- The results of the Cranfield studies are used as examples of the impact of demographics on the functioning of the organization.
- Two distinct clusters of demographics emerge as distinctly shaping the more deeply held philosophies, views and behaviour of managers, namely that of the power of accountability, and that of the power of time.
- The Cranfield NHS Trusts survey highlights that the different levels of accountability in the jobs of senior managers strongly influence their view of the organization, so that those with greater executive accountability in their role adopt a longer term view to the challenges they face, placing current concerns within a perspective of working towards improvement. Those with less executive accountability in their role adopt a more criticial view of the same issues, seeing these as problems of a far worse and deeper nature, than the group whose jobs held greater accountability.
- The surveys of top managers in the private sector, and of senior civil servants in the Australian Commonwealth government, emphasize that time, in the form of organizational and job tenure, and age, have a significant impact on the forming of people's views, attitudes and behaviours. Those younger and with less organizational and job-related tenure, are more likely to be forthcoming with critical

comment, are less likely to have thought through the impact of their comments, and are more likely to raise the anxiety levels in others, to the point where others are unwilling to offer new ideas or innovative practice for fear of being seen to have made an error. Those who are older and with greater job and organizational tenure, are less likely to react negatively, or make comments that could dampen people's enthusiasm, and are more likely to accept the longer-term perspective, in terms of nurturing a performance-oriented culture where people feel comfortable to explore and try out new ideas.

■ Exposing managers to both on and off-the-job opportunities for development is considered to have a positive impact, especially if any one or more of the following factors is present; the individual has been in the organization and/or their job for a 'period of time' (relevant period of time varies by context) and/or is older.

■ It is postulated that if people recognize the impact of demographics on the individual, they are more likely to exhibit greater confidence in pursuing experiences that will personally develop them, enhance their performance, and make them less dependent on other individuals or the organization.

Notes

1 For further discussion of demographics related to the Cranfield studies, see Korac-Kakabadse and Korac-Kakabadse (1998).
2 The NHS research programme has been conducted by Andrew Myers and is briefly mentioned in Korac-Kakabadse and Korac-Kakabadse (1997).
3 In the research texts published or shortly to be published, different titles for the leadership categories highlighted above have been used. The reason different terms are adopted in this chapter is to simplify and abbreviate in order to focus on the key findings emerging from the overall Cranfield studies.

Further reading

The demographics given greatest attention in the literature are:

■ *organizational tenure*, from the point of view of the shared frames of language, reference and values that emanate from people who have been together for a long time (Katz, 1982) and from the perspective of resisting change (Michel and Hambrick, 1992),
■ *top team tenure*, namely the degree of cohesion and shared logic that emerges when people have worked together for some time (Prahalad and Bettis, 1986),
■ *size*, namely increases in size, which induce greater complexity (Quinn and Cameron, 1983), induce greater resistance to change (Tushman and Romanelli, 1985), but equally can induce greater heterogeneity (Dearborn and Simon, 1985).

For further information on the Cranfield studies outlined in the chapter, read Kakabadse *et al.* (1996), Kakabadse and Myers (1997) and Korac-Kakabadse and Korac-Kakabadse (1997); Korac-Kakabadse and Korac-Kakabadse (1998).

CHAPTER 7

Women As Leaders

Case analysis

Helen

Helen Shift is a fast tracker, a 'high flier', a Senior Executive Service officer (SES) in the Australian Public Service (APS), and has been for the last five years. She is in her late thirties, with two young children. She considers she has a supportive partner, who is a self-employed IT consultant. She is intelligent, energetic, confident, and works hard. She comes over as aware, insightful and astute, and somewhat philosophical about the 'maleness' of her surrounding workplace. Although Helen's career rise appears to have been rapid and won with ease, she has had to work hard to earn credibility and respect from her colleagues. In her opinion, being a woman means it is much harder to be heard. From her current position, she feels she is able to accommodate gender and other differences, and exploit those differences if necessary, but expects accommodation to be both ways. She feels that she is now in control and has the confidence and courage to take risks. She provides a good role model, and is admired by many of her colleagues. However, her actions may be difficult to emulate, because she displays much energy, a high level of focus, and her image is that of being 'one of the boys'.

Helen feels that she has been fully included in the 'SES club', whose members' shared self-perception is that they are intelligent, hard working, achievement-oriented, socially conscious, and wanting to make a contribution. The SES officers agree that they would use positional power to attain that purpose. The 'club' motto is 'all in it together', without breaking the 'club rules'. Betrayal of the 'club' is not about divulging 'tribal' information. Betrayal is poor performance and self-indulgence. However, talking frankly about people issues and persisting with a different style of leadership, can be seen as being a bit deviant, but not necessarily negative. 'Club' language is based on a common knowledge and understanding of the hardships and problems in the SES. Helen feels that acceptance into the 'club' is not gender based, but is due to the displays of drive, commitment, and to effectiveness of performance. Nevertheless, she feels that there exists some gender-based support.

Helen came from a family where the dominant mother was a key influence in the household. Her mother was well educated, and insisted that the girls in the family should be educated on the basis that they would then make better mothers, while the boys were educated for prospective careers. Helen was an outstanding student, a senior prefect at school, and thrust early into a leadership role, requiring that her presentation skills be developed, although public speaking and presentations did not, and still do not, sit comfortably with her. It was expected that she would go to university. Three weeks into the start of an Arts degree, Helen realized that life experience was essential, and she abandoned her degree programme. After many casual jobs, which included laboratory technician, she was prompted to pursue a degree in medicine. After four years of the medical degree, she chose to pursue part time medical research, which provided a career path and prospects, while concurrently completing an additional Arts degree with units in psychology and international politics. In turn, she left medicine. She refers to her single days as the experimental days of her life, until she met her partner. She followed her partner to the Australian capital, Canberra, and joined the APS as there was little other work available at the time. At Canberra, she started her honours degree in clinical psychology. The idea of a career in the APS became more of a genuine prospect and she chose to move to a policy-oriented department to gain experience in policy work. The workload of the honours degree became too much when coupled with a demanding job which she enjoyed, so she reluctantly left study.

A decision to move to the management arena prompted Helen to apply for the Executive Development Scheme (EDS) programme, provided by the APS, and after completing, she was promoted to an SES position. Helen was the youngest woman and least experienced person ever to be promoted to SES level. As policy and management had been tackled, the next choice for her further development and experience was as State Director (state capital city) in a large department. After a year's maternity leave, she transferred from the State to a central policy division of the Commonwealth (federal) government.

Helen is pragmatic. She has sorted out her values and needs and has developed good strategic judgement. She is self-aware, willing to take measured risks, confident in her abilities and flexible enough to learn from her male role models. In her opinion, there are too few women who have made it to senior positions, and even so, they made it alone. She is now confident enough to say what she is not willing to undertake activities which conflict with her values. She says a broad range of interests help her to keep balance and perspective.

The case of Helen Shift is true. Helen is one of the more senior and well-respected female leaders in the Australian Public Service. The question is how usual or unusual is Helen Shift in terms of career background, career success, personal style, and as a person typical of her gender? One point can be made and that is, Helen is far more successful in her working life than most of her counterparts, male and female. She has also experienced a more colourful career background than most, having being trained in medicine, psychology, politics and clinical psychology. According to some, whose views are examined later in this chapter, she is additionally unusual in being career successful and, in her terms, equally having a satisfactory and supportive home life and partner. Career success and success in personal relationships, especially for women, have not always sat well together. She would again be seen as unusual by some, in declaring that gender differences are not a significant issue for managers at her level.

There is little doubt that gender issues are hot topics in the organizational management and leadership fields. Considerable research has been undertaken in order to appreciate the differences between men and women in terms of their career progress or the lack of it, the varying demands made on them, the social pressures placed on them and the manner in which both respond to their varying pressures and circumstances.

In this chapter, attention is given to a brief historical examination of how women have been viewed and treated in society. Further, attention is given to an analysis of the current issues women face in the workplace and in the home environment. Distinction will be made between getting there and got there, namely the challenges, opportunities and constraints women face in terms of career progress, and their capability to perform effectively in roles of responsibility, once appointed. Finally, recommendations of how to harness better the potential of women as managers and leaders in the workplace, will be made.

Historical overview

Male and female roles in the workforce have been, and are, undergoing a revolution. The emerging view is that rather than share their best features, men and women executives have, too often, been unwilling to accept their natural gender traits and work together as co-equals. Some men see their female counterparts as persons obsessed with form and the subtleties of expression and appearances. Other men see women using sexism as a crutch, sometimes misconstruing genuinely innocent behaviour and even common courtesies as a form of sexual harassment. Many males say they are afraid to criticize women executives because they tend to over-react and become too emotional.

Many women executives, on the other hand, say of their male counterparts that they treat women differently, for some patronizingly, even if the intention is to protect. Irrespective of intent, a current strongly held view is that men do not help women who want to grow into managerial and leadership roles. The emerging view is that men lack the basic confidence in a woman's natural ability as a leader. The result is that men and women executives, at times, do not relate to each other supportively in the work environment.

The strongly shared view is that discrimination exists, whether direct, indirect, or institutionalized. Certainly, observation and analysis would support the institutionalized discrimination viewpoint. Organizations and executives are often encouraged to be rational, analytical, strategic, decision oriented, tough and competitive. These values, promote discriminatory stereotypes, build barriers and are a major impediment to the mobility of talented women into executive positions. Such barriers are variously defined in the literature as the 'glass ceiling', 'greasy pole', 'protective shield', 'concrete ceiling' and 'barrier at the top'. The present predominant assumption is that women's under-representation at senior levels in organizations is not a matter of choice, or failure on the part of women (and in particular of ethnic women), but is a consequence of structural barriers that have a strong flavour of a 'man only perspective'.

The embodiment of a male managerial culture may be partly ascribed to the fact that when today's management were first being formed, only males were in the workforce, and partly because of that historical fact, for many years men were able to hold power at all levels, because they were free of child-rearing duties and thus were available to participate in all forms of community and organizational life. Add the command and control nature of business organizations, not only driven by a male-centred ethos, but also by the need financially to control costs and place substantial emphasis on focusing on revenue, then the emerging result is a conservatism that precludes women, as well as other new entrants into the labour force, from executive positions. For example, in Britain, the TMS Management Consultants' 1992 report, *Without Prejudice? Sex Equality at the Bar and in the Judiciary*, reveals that women's career progress in the British judiciary system relies on the opinion of their majority male colleagues, through a system of 'secret sounding'. Civil servants solicit views on candidates from judges and senior practitioners. The disadvantage to women operating within such institutions is obvious, but their plight is further compounded as the report revealed that patronage, being noticed through being known, are commonplace practices. The point is, that if one is not in such a system to begin with, it is going to be difficult to break through. Unfortunately, trying to break through is going to make such a fortress defend itself with greater proclivity.

Interestingly, the theme of the dominance of men over women has not been consistently pursued through history, for sexual behaviour, as much as women's position and role in society and life, has dominated attention. A historical analysis of social groups up to the Middle Ages, shows that few distinctions were drawn between public and private life, in that open displays of sexual behaviour were quite common. The social historian, Gipson Burell, has identified writings which indicate that even in medieval monasteries, convents and churches, outrageous sexual behaviour presented a major problem. Manuscripts from the seventh and eight centuries reveal varying punishments for different classes of sexual misconduct, such as:

- for extreme offences, castration or extensive penitence,
- for guilt of simple fornication with unmarried persons punishments of a year on bread and water for monks, three to seven years of fasting for nuns, and twelve years fasting for bishops, would be applied,
- for masturbation in church, the punishment was forty days' fasting,
- for a bishop caught fornicating with cattle, eight years' fasting for a first offence and ten years' fasting for each subsequent offence.

For a considerable period, rules and regulations paid close attention to the control of sexuality, even up to the nineteenth century, where, for example, the British Factory Act of 1833 gave much attention to the problem of controlling sexual behaviour at work. Even the early industrial masters espoused the virtues of abstinence, restraint and clean living.

From a historical perspective, repressing sexuality is one fundamental influence that has shaped the nature of organizations. However, more recently, attention has switched from institutionalizing control to the question of disbarring certain members of society from holding any position of substantial influence. One such group is women who, although in the twentieth century were released into the workforce through the onset of the two world wars, could make little progress towards gaining leadership positions due to perceptions of their inferiority. Such perceptions were not based on women's inexperience or lack of exposure to education, training and the opportunity for development, but simply on the assumption that an overall deficiency of sorts exists due to differences of body shape, functioning, and being of lesser physical strength (the latter statement being scientifically supported).

For example, even Freud in his work on personality development, describes female development as more complex than that of males and by implication, more inadequate, than that of males. Freud postulates that as the girl's genital organs appear inferior to those of the male, the girl develops an envious desire to be like the boy, a state of mind which Freud termed 'penis envy'. Freudian interpretation, assumes that girls think 'I have been punished', while the boys fear 'I may be punished', and is believed, by Freudians, to have important consequences for later development. It is against this historical backdrop, that women have entered into the workplace.

Whether one identifies with the Freudian view of the inferiority of women; or a control view of organizations, namely that once one group is in the driving seat, a natural conservatism overtakes decision-making; or something new becoming something threatening; or the fact that sexuality, in whichever form it shows itself, needs to be controlled; or the simple conclusion that insufficient time has elapsed to assimilate an economic equality between the sexes as change has taken place on an unprecedented historical scale, the plain fact of the matter is that society is dependent on women staying in the workforce. Dr Susan Vinnicombe, Dean of the Cranfield School of Management, highlights a few interesting statistics supporting the view that women in the workforce are here to stay.

■ According to Warwick University's Institute for Employment Research (IRE), one million new jobs will be created by the year 2000, with most of these being part-time jobs for women.
■ The IRE prediction is that unemployment in the UK will be experienced by males who have been in full time employment.
■ According to the Hudson Institute, by the year 2010, the total American labour force will be represented by less than 40 per cent white males, with women and people of various ethnic backgrounds occupying the greater proportion of the 20 million jobs that are expected to be created.
■ In Europe by the year 2025, it is expected that more than 20 per cent of the population will be above the age of 65 years, and the greatest proportion of new entrants into the labour market will be women.

With the globalization of capital and its impact on the mobility of labour, the least likely occurrence is that women will simply accept lower paid jobs and positions of diminished responsibility. The demand for equal reward and open and just competition for senior positions is an already visible and inevitable fact.

Getting there

The US Department of Labour's initial 'Glass Ceiling Review', in 1988, found that barriers to women's managerial progression existed at a much lower level than was initially anticipated. Further, the US General

Accounting Office's research concluded that the percentage of women and minorities in the Senior Executive Service of Government, was unacceptable. Overall, in the USA, women represented 45.5 per cent of the total civilian workforce in 1992, according to the US Bureau of the Census (1992a). However, women fill 46 per cent of federal white collar jobs, but they hold only 18 per cent of senior management positions. At the top of the federal government hierarchy, women hold only 12 per cent of the available positions, according to the US Merit Systems Protection Board (1992). In contrast to the private sector, 'less than 0.5 per cent of the highest paid officers and directors in America's larger public companies are women'.[1]

In Canada, women comprised 45.4 per cent of the workforce in 1993, a steady increase from 41.9 per cent in 1983. During the same period, and unlike the USA, the distribution of women in managerial and administrative positions had increased from 29.2 per cent in 1982 to 42.2 per cent in 1993 (Statistics Canada, 1993). In 1994, women occupied 18.3 per cent of 3875 Senior Management Executive (SME) category positions in the Federal Government, according to the Treasury Board of Canada (1994).

Women comprise a majority of the Australian population (51 per cent) and an increasing proportion of the workforce. Women make up 42 per cent of the workforce according to the Australian Bureau of Statistics (1993). Unlike Canada, but similar to the USA, only 3 per cent of senior management positions are occupied by women. A survey of 500 companies and over 70,000 employees in Australia found that men, on average, held 95 per cent of all senior management positions within companies, including that of CEO and principal executives in the legal, finance, human resources and marketing departments. Furthermore, when a woman attained a senior executive role, she was paid less than her male counterpart. The inevitable conclusion is that highly qualified women in Australia are discriminated against at entry level and throughout their career.

Sexual discrimination has equally been identified in the information systems industry. Gender bias was identified in a study reported in the 24 June 1996 issue of *Computerworld*, in that women's salaries, on average ranging from $10,000–$20,000 per annum in the USA, are considerably less than their male counterparts' salaries. Equally, other studies have identified that women have fewer advancement opportunities, and receive lower job ratings than men. Kim Clancy of the US Department of the Treasury's Bureau of Public Debts, considers that women information systems (IS) managers should confront the issue of discrimination with supporting documents and details. In her opinion, women should not give way, and if necessary should seriously consider lodging complaints with the Equal Employment Opportunity Commission (EEOC).

Another study of trends in the accountancy profession reported in the journal *Selections*, in the winter of 1996, considered that the foreseeable scenario would be one of accounting emerging as a two-tiered, or multi-tiered profession, with women concentrated at the lower levels. This conclusion emerged from an examination of trends of turnover rates of female accountants, the predominance of women in para-accountant professions and in linked degree programmes, and the present number of female partners in professional practices.

In 1992, women accounted for just over half the population, and 46 per cent of the labour force in the UK, of which 85 per cent have jobs in service industries, according to a report from the UK Foreign and Commonwealth Office (1993). However, despite the established equal employment opportunity infrastructure in place since 1975, for example the Equal Pay Act 1970, which came into force in 1975 and was widened in 1984, women remain under-represented in senior management jobs. Only 25 per cent of managers and only 3 per cent of senior executives were women in 1993, an increase from a 0.5 per cent female component of Senior Executives in 1983 (UK Foreign and Commonwealth Office, 1993:12). Women represent only 0.5 per cent of main board executive director positions, and 3.9 per cent of non-executive directors, according to the Hansard Society for Parliamentary Government (1990). As already suggested, gender inequality is perhaps most prominent in the judiciary system. Of the ten Law Lords, there is no woman in that position; there exists one woman out of 36 Lords Justice of Appeal, and there exist seven women out of the 96 High Court judges. Hewson, the social researcher highlights that in 1985, there were three women at the Bar of the Family Division, and 11 years later, in 1996, there are still only three women at the Bar, although there is a plentiful supply of women barristers in the lower family courts, from whom to choose.

It appears that the 'ceiling at the top' for women in executive positions, has become a statistical normality in private and public organizations in Anglo-Saxon societies. Contemporary women can be viewed as 'caged eagles', as they are able and willing to play larger roles in organizations and in society at large, but are often thwarted by restrictions. As a result, an increasing number of women leave their organization, deciding that the best way of achieving their ambition is to start their own businesses, a growing phenomenon that has now become a major trend. In Britain, women account for one in four of the self-employed, or approximately 7 per cent of all working women (UK Foreign and Commonwealth Office, 1993:14). Similarly in Australia, ambitious women are setting up their own businesses in order to achieve their full potential. In the USA, 4.1 million women in 1987 owned 30 per cent of all businesses (US Department of Commerce, 1992b), which grew to an estimated 6 million women business owners in 1992 (US Department of Commerce, 1992a).

The debate as to the nature and substance of such restrictions has identified five possible sources of causation: the obvious discrimination that takes place in organizations, the downside of women operating differently to men; the influence of certain demographic factors; the different response and communication patterns of women to men; and the difficulty of progressing beyond the status quo.

Sex, harassment and discrimination

Many writers argue that in Western society, especially in Anglo-American organizations, the most obvious and visible forms of sexual and racial harassment have been outlawed, but with the effect that, in certain situations, less visible but equally insidious forms of discrimination have arisen. The idea of women gaining advancement in return for them offering favours, has probably diminished, although observation of press reports would indicate that the problem of heavy-handed discrimination still sits uncomfortably with us, and may even be on the rise. Astra, the Swedish drug makers, are somewhat unusual in that they made no attempt to hide cases of scandal in their organization. *Business Week* (a more up-market management magazine) reporters confronted the organization with allegations of widespread sexual harassment and other abuses at its Astra USA Inc subsidary (13 May 1996). The company responded promptly by suspending three of its top executives, and dismissing the Astra USA President and CEO, Lars Bildman. The internal investigation found that Bildman had purportedly, inappropriately administered certain company functions, and that the former CEO had used company funds to pay for about $2 million worth of expenses. In fact, the company is also facing a number of lawsuits from former and current employees, claiming sexual harassment and other grievances. The reason is the alleged, recent discovery of a 15-year pattern of sexual harassment, emanating from the President's office and working its way down the organization.

A report by the *Far Eastern Economic Review* 1996, highlighted that sexual harassment, diminished equal opportunity, and 'glass ceilings' for women, are commonplace across a whole variety of business organizations in the region.

Another example of sexual harassment stemming from the top is that from an investigation by *Business Week* in 1996, namely of Milan Panić, Chairman of ICN Pharmaceuticals Inc.[2] He is being investigated for insider-trading and is also being hit by Debra Levy, a former secretary, in a paternity suit, and on the allegation of sexual harassment.

An ongoing case is that of Mitsubishi Motors USA, where the Equal Employment Opportunity Commission (EEOC) has filed a lawsuit on behalf of a large number of female employees who are employed at Illinois car manufacturing plant, alleging that the women have been sexually harassed over several years. One of the underlying causes seems to have been the poor integration of USA and Japanese top managers, leaving the USA managers with little authority to address sensitive but pertinent issues.

A federal court in Tampa, Florida, USA ruled that Domino's Pizza must pay almost one quarter of a million dollars to a former employee who was found to have been sexually harassed by his then female boss.

A survey by the law firm, David, Haguer, Kuney & Krupin, reported in *Lodging Hospitality*, conducted in the Washington DC area, concluded that sexual harassment lawsuits are likely to cost more than other workplace related issues in 1996. In fact, in 1995, the EEOC counted a record 15,549 complaints of sexual harassment in the USA, more than double the number in 1990. Likewise, in New York, they have nearly doubled, while in California they have more than trebled.

The USA army has also recently received considerable attention in this area. A *Time* magazine article (25 November 1996) highlighted a deeply perturbing picture of sexual harassment in the military. A hotline set up in Maryland's Aberdeen office, in one week logged 3930 calls of which only 10 would be described as crank calls. Of the calls, 50 per cent were considered sufficiently serious to be referred to the Criminal Investigation Command for further examination. Currently, a number of officers and enlisted men have been suspended pending investigation.

The situation has now become so serious in the USA, that in the private sector, as reported by David Katz, employment practices liability insurance is being offered by a number of different insurers, such as Chubb and Lexington. A new XL policy spearheaded by March and McLennon and reinsured by Zurich American Insurance and ACE Insurance Co, offer limits of $100 million with a minimum retainer of $5 million.

The situation can, at best, be described as pronounced and dramatic. Sexual discrimination, principally against women, is still a significant concern.

Women-as-men discrimination

Since the mid-1980s, a considerable legislative infrastructure, designed to reduce the segmentation and segregation of women in the workforce, has been established in most developed societies. Sex Discrimination Acts, Affirmative Action, Equal Employment Opportunity (EEO) for Women Acts, Equal Employment Opportunity (Commonwealth Authorities) Acts have become commonplace features of social legislation. Although EEO policies are important initiatives in opening the workplace to diversity, they alone cannot, and do not, create conditions that capitalize on the full potential of heterogeneity.

The problem of inequality of opportunity appears to be a more complex phenomenon that requires a cultural change, instead of merely changing women to meet the 'man-as-standard' norm, as coined by Warren Bennis. Thus, there is a need for a qualitative shift from the current EEO policy infrastructure and culture that operationally translates into 'let us give them a chance', to a culture whereby every person within an organization is enabled to perform to the utmost of his/her abilities. However, a positive response to the call for an intellectual and moral leap forward, as seemingly was the case with Helen Shift of the Australian Public Service, has not been the experience of many women in executive positions.

A considerable number of writers argue that women have been masculinized by attempting to adopt the so-called 'normal' managerial and leadership styles appropriate for running an organization. What has been adopted are the masculine traits of aggressiveness, toughness, independence, control and masterfulness, as opposed to the more feminine characteristics of caretaker and peacemaker associated with communal or expressive behaviours. In organizations with an entrenched male culture, ways of behaving may even be reinforced by dress codes of dark grey and dark blue suits, tough talk, and no-nonsense approaches to managing people and to the taking of decisions.

Such behaviour is reinforced through selection and assessment processes which can exhibit an inherent bias towards particular cultures or more male stereotypic behaviours. Certain of the biases that can creep into the selection process are as follows.[3]

The forming of early impressions in selection interviews

Although interviews are most commonly used in selection and assessment situations, the effectiveness of the event in terms of forming clear and accurate views in the minds of the interviewers, leaves a great deal to be desired. Bias may creep in due to dress, looks, posture, colour, eye contact or the lack of it, physical attraction, and poorly thought-through and untested assumptions over the suitability of women for so-called male jobs. Despite attempts to reduce bias, studies have shown that male rather than female applicants are still preferred for certain jobs. A recent study reported in the *Human Resources Magazine*, 1996, identified that interviewers are more likely to ask questions requiring 'yes' or 'no' responses during interviews where the interviewee is of a different race, gender or national origin. In contrast, interviewers talking to applicants with whom they feel comfortable, are more likely to pursue open-ended questions and hence hold a dialogue. As a consequence, the interviewer is likely to learn more from the latter candidates and at the same time have their assumptions reinforced concerning the appropriateness or inappropriateness of people for jobs, or even their capability to fit into the organization.

The manner in which psychological tests are interpreted

An additional mechanism to interviews, for the purpose of selection, is psychometric testing, examining for elements of both personality and ability. The advantage of tests is that the bias that can creep into interviews, can be minimized. The downside to tests is that persons hired to administer and interpret the test(s) are test experts and may have little insight into organizational context, or the dynamics of particular roles among professional groupings. For example, would giving feedback on the results of a Myers Briggs Personality Inventory, the questionnaire that provides information on individual personality preferences, be conducted in similar fashion if one audience were boardroom directors, and another audience, nursing managers of health service organizations? Would the person administering the Myers-Briggs, expert in the test, its structure and intellectual complexities, be aware of the dynamics of boardrooms and the behaviours of boardroom directors as opposed to the hustle and bustle of nurses in health care enterprises? A person with limited experience of one context, but experienced in handling people, could reasonably quickly ascertain a certain understanding of particular situations, for example, the likely experience of being a boardroom director. However, as most company boards are staffed by white males, the role model of boardroom behaviour adapted by the tester may be inappropriate to use as a guide to giving feedback to a senior female manager. Although experienced in the administration of a psychological test, the person providing feedback may be inexperienced in offering feedback with particular contexts in mind, and thereby undermine the testees' morale, self-confidence and their drive to achieve. This point is aptly made by Beverly Alimo-Metcalfe, whose examination of scoring patterns between male and female samples on tests of achievement motivation, highlights that women's scoring pattern responses are interpreted as showing women to be less motivated than men. One reason was that the tests were developed on almost exclusive samples of males. Another reason is that research seems to indicate clearly that achievement motivation is defined and valued differently by females and males. Further, subsequent research has established that under relaxed conditions women scored higher than men, but the researchers on the project did not consider that to be of significance.

Similar bias could just as easily creep into giving feedback to males, of whatever ethnic background, but in different contextual circumstances, such as attending a management course for senior nurses. Still today, it is likely that most of the course members would be female, with the men being in the minority grouping. The motivation of the males, as well as the dynamics of nursing contexts, and nurse/director professional relationships, may not be appreciated, introducing a bias into the feedback process, which could be equally as damaging to the morale and confidence of the male course participants.

The latent criteria used at assessment centres

Assessment centres, a now commonly used mechanism for assessing managerial potential, are equally prone to unintended bias and discrimination. Many companies outsource this activity, which means consultants are used not only to design the assessment centre tests and exercises, but also to run the events. An assessment centre is often run off-the-job, more than likely in a hotel, with the company paying for the full expenses of the event, as well as inviting senior managers from the organization to participate in the process as principally assessors, but also mentors. Although on a task related basis, the assessment centre process may accurately decide the weaker from the stronger candidates, in examining far more complex senior managerial roles, assumptions need to be made determining model profiles of candidates. The danger is that the more expensive the assessment centre, the more the assessors may stick to their assumptions, and the less they may reflect on their predispositions if particular candidates, directly or indirectly, challenge their views. The pressure is on to get it right, with the selection of 'appropriate' candidates. The bias that can creep in to the assessment process could involve:

■ Inadequate behavioural frameworks. The behavioural benchmarks that are used for the assessment centre may reflect the context of the organization, which in turn may reflect the predominantly white male managerial population in the organization.
■ Assumptions that do not adequately distinguish the different ways in which men and women communicate. Numerous studies conclude that females have more accomplished verbal skills, as they are more likely to be polite, ask questions, use expressions such as, 'I know that I am not qualified to offer an opinion, but . . .', and use more supportive and caring words and phrases. Women are more likely to listen and wait until the other person has ceased speaking, whereas men are more likely to interrupt. However, studies equally indicate that being assertive, being clear, and appearing decisive, are behaviours that assessment centre assessors are more likely to respect. Such behaviours, valued as benchmarks for assessing managerial potential, highlight a strong masculine emphasis, with the result that feminine-oriented behaviours may be considered as inappropriate, weak, ineffective or insufficient for the demands of managerial work. Hence, women are more likely to be ignored or rejected by the assessment centre process of selection.
■ Inappropriate group assessment exercises. Certain of the assessment centre exercises involve activities conducted in groups. A group exercise may involve examining problem solving aptitude and skills, leadership skills, coaching skills, team-work skills; the list is almost

endless. Often participants are given roles to play. In other exercises, especially some of the outdoor exercises, such as rescuing people who are supposedly stranded, or have had an accident, leadership skills are expected to emerge, but studies have shown that this may not be the case. Where no specific roles are allocated, women may be less likely to take a command role, as women have been identified as finding mixed-sex conversations difficult, and often ending up being the listeners, whereas the men were the drivers of conversations. In an assessment process, probably dominated by males, such behaviour could be interpreted as inappropriate or insufficient for management.

Impact of demographics

Cranfield School of Management has attracted a reasonably balanced proportion of women and men to the faculty. However, on the MBA programme, there still exists a disproportionate number of men to women, a trend that Cranfield has been seriously trying to reverse for a number of years, but with little shift in the number of women who enter the programme year by year, except for a period a few years ago. The current Cranfield Dean, Dr Susan Vinnicombe, successfully negotiated a bursary for female applicants from the now defunct original journal, *Working Woman*, then edited by Audrey Slaughter. While the bursary was operational, more women sought entrance to the Cranfield MBA programme. Once the bursary was terminated (due to the collapse of the journal), the number of women who chose to join the programme dropped down to its previous position. Adjusting for minor fluctuations, year on year, approximately 14–25 per cent of the full time MBA programme is occupied by women, but when supported by Working Woman, the number increased to almost 33 per cent. Other MBA programmes have attracted more women onto their courses. The question is, why such differences? For Cranfield has tried hard to increase the number of females onto the programme. Two factors seem to be influential, location and sector.

The Cranfield programme, somewhat unusual to the majority of the MBA programmes in the UK, is deliberately positioned to attract people who already have substantial working experience (the average age of participants on both the full-time and part-time programmes is 32–34 years), who hold a degree and/or professional qualification, and who for many on the full-time programme especially, are experiencing a transition. The candidates may have been engineers or accountants who wish to change and become managers. Alternatively, the candidates may have held positions abroad (Middle East) and now wish to return to their home country, but to a position of greater status and salary than their present role offers. Most certainly, none wishes to fall behind in a labour market that he/she left a few years previously.

Most other full-time MBA programmes attract a younger age group, who may not even have started their careers, but are entering the programme, freshly graduated. Inevitably, more women attend these programmes.

One reason as to why such differences exist is not due to a lack of trying on Cranfield's part to attract female candidates, but location. Cranfield is situated in the middle of the countryside, approximately 50 miles north of London and an equal distance south of Birmingham. Consequently, the part-time MBA programme cannot be run on an evening basis, but is organized to run over weekends (Friday/Saturday), for a set number of weekends per year. Those MBA programmes, part-time or full-time, that attract more females than does Cranfield, are usually located in, or near to, urban areas and have a programme structure of evening classes. The more favourable location allows women to continue with their jobs, not unduly disrupt the family, but also attend to their intellectual development through evening classes. Cranfield, simply due to reasons of geographic location, has to adopt an alternative programme structure, disruptive to both men and women, but one which has women more disadvantaged. The bursary from Working Woman helped provide an alternative source of finance, so that women could give up their jobs and thereby minimize the disruptive impact of location.

A similar point is also made by Susan Linz, who in the 1996 issue of the *Journal of Economic Issues*, highlighted gender differences in the Russian labour market. Despite a history of equality, constituted by both Lenin and Stalin, gender differences in Russia are clearly shown in employment patterns. Susan Linz highlights that educational standards between men and women are comparable, but differences are due more to job choice. Russian women report that they have little or no choice of job. For various reasons, such as family circumstances, children's education, husband's job, women take the job most available to them. Again, location has driven their job choice, and employment pattern behaviour in many ways parallels the Cranfield experience. The Helen shift case at the beginning of this chapter highlights a somewhat unusual circumstance, in that Helen was not driven by location, she determined the location, but as she mentioned, this was principally due to opportunity, a supportive partner, and positive family circumstances!

Location is one powerful demographic factor. For women in particular, sector also plays an important role in influencing choices concerning employment. Far more women in senior positions are employed in the service sector, in publishing and government, than in manufacturing and the chemical industries. Sector is also equally important in attracting candidates to the Cranfield MBA. As mentioned, most other MBA programmes are positioned to attract a younger age group. The Cranfield MBA in attempting to attract a different age sector, is less likely to attract a large number of women. Many women in their late twenties and early thirties are rearing a young family, which would make attending an MBA too challenging than at other times in their life. The demographic influence of sector is highlighted in a recent 1996 article on women managers in the public service by Gayle Lawn-Day and Steven Ballard, who emphasize that although men and women are being disincentivized to continue in the public sector, through being made redundant, women still feel that these conditions are, overall, not sufficiently significant barriers to advancement. The study highlights that although the number of incidents of discrimination are unacceptably high, the advantages of the public sector, such as the opportunity to make a contribution to society, job security, health and retirement benefits, have made the public sector more attractive than the private sector. In the opinion of Susan Vinnicombe, such behaviour typifies certain women's attitudes concerning career, in that such women are less likely to invest time or money on what they would consider to be more risky ventures.

Different response and communication patterns

As discussed, research highlights different patterns of communication between men and women which, in turn, is considered to be partly responsible for the differing patterns of response to various situations and contexts. For example, women are considered to be more sensitive to non-verbal communication. In contrast, male behaviour is exhibited by a tendency to take controlling and leading roles during social interactions, such as meetings. Further, women's expressive behaviour is exhibited by their inclination to adopt the role of facilitator, thus commanding less airtime at meetings. Men tend to express an authoritative opinion or make a factual statement, while women tend to ask questions or express a personal point of view. Perhaps because of the different social roles played, men's voices are generally more forceful and confident, while women's voices are reassuring and placatory; hence, a woman's voice can become culturally devalued.

Differences in communication are often exhibited during informal, and sometimes formal, references to male and female managers. Comments such as she 'looks after' the branch's operation, which may employ 120 people, and he 'oversees' the smooth operation of a large branch (which may employ only 90 people), are often heard. Similarly, distinct gender differences in networking practices and preferences for like-minded member contacts, further disadvantage women's access to discuss key issues with influential individuals in the organization. Men's socialization attunes them to understand more from 'subtle messages' expressed by being 'in the know', or 'reading between the lines', than do women. Thus, women may not fully comprehend cultural messages that are often symbolic, as women tend to communicate more by clear, verbal and prominent messages that give meaning to 'how' something is done, rather than 'what' is done.[4] Women, for example, are considered to have 'little sympathy for office politics', as such sensitivity stems from an interest of the office environment.[5]

Further, women's 'feminine attributes' are seen as sources of creativity, that give a sense of purpose and worth in the workplace. Contemporary literature suggests that excellent organizations need to be more female oriented, as competent organizational leaders are probably more likely to be found among those individuals who are sensitive to different individuals, but who speak openly and directly when facing issues that need to be addressed. The emerging literature suggests that women are more suited to the flatter organizations of the 1990s, as shown by the case of Frances Hesselbein, discussed later in this chapter, where the leader is at the centre and not at the top, as is the case in hierarchies. Another reason why women are considered to be in tune with flatter structures, is because women are more 'natural' disseminators of information, while men 'keep' information. It is also suggested that women are much more likely to use personal power, such as charisma, track record and contacts, as opposed to men, who are more likely to use structural power, such as organizational position, title and the ability to reward and punish.

The result of such differences of behaviour is that women can be seen as both unable to take charge, as well as being culturally and politically inappropriate, because of their supposed inability to read circumstances. Their comments and views can be seen as causing crises, and as being disruptive to present circumstances. Hence, the view of being too gentle, coupled with the possible perception of being politically inept, are considered to be influences which disbar many women from being taken seriously as suitable candidates for senior positions.

Power of the status quo

Whether or not any of the biases outlined are recognized, or even true, custom and practice become strong organizational realities, whereby certain discriminatory activities are enacted and sustained on a daily basis and hence become wedged into the culture of the organization. The more particular behaviours and attitudes become part of the organization, the more a pattern of socialization is naturally, and at times inadvertently, reinforced. The prejudice and discrimination that accompany such patterns and biases could well be subtle, as men may genuinely feel they have done the best they can to remove any impediments to women's progress. Women, too, can become victims of current norms, by all too readily accepting their position, and not pursuing their careers any further. Equally, some may become overly aggressive and dominant, in order to break any real or perceived career ceilings. As a consequence, women can be stereotyped as mother, seductress, pet, or iron-maiden, the polarity of such extremes reinforcing present-day stereotypes. If a woman chooses acceptance of the status quo, she will, more often than not, attract protection. By trying to resist, she will become especially threatening to men, because she will be perceived as wanting to change the dominant culture, whether or not that is the case. Learning to adapt to the prevailing organizational culture by steering along the narrow path between 'protection' and 'abandonment' is unlikely to change the status quo. Cultures that propound strong, deep-seated views about one or more particular social characteristics (gender, race, age) are unlikely to be sufficiently flexible to change such beliefs quickly. Indeed, these perceptions are likely to be controlled by the beliefs that it is mal-adaptive and potentially dangerous to change. The strong sense of shared 'reality' increases the realization of common values and experiences.

Got there

The dominant view to have emerged from researchers, commentators, and social theorists is that women have faced and are facing considerable 'road blocks' to attaining senior positions. Do comparable dynamics and hurdles exist for those women who have attained positions of responsibility? In answering the question, attention now switches to examining the behaviour and circumstances of women who have successfully achieved senior office. An overview of the findings from research of the the attributes of female and male leaders, is provided in Table 7.1.

Overview of research

In terms of working style, women are viewed as more participative, team oriented, and supportive of their colleagues, bosses and subordinates (see Table 7.1) Men, in contrast, are seen as forceful, disciplined and focused, displaying considerable drive and energy. As a consequence, men are more likely to present themselves as confident, and command centred, rather than be consultative.

In terms of priorities, as leaders, women are likely to hold people-oriented values, paying attention to the provision of service and to the team of which they are a member. Men are more likely to be entrepreneurial, displaying a strong vision, valuing success and the achievement of goals. The feminine 'us' orientation is counter-balanced by the 'me' self-concern of men.

Again differences emerge in terms of the management of relationships. Women leaders are more likely to be responsive to feelings and to the

Table 7.1 Female/male comparison of leadership attributes and performance: overview of research

	Female	Male
Working style	■ Participative ■ Works with others ■ Accessible ■ Supportive/strong ■ Team oriented ■ Service driven ■ Care/love sensitive ■ Creative use of others ■ Consultative	■ Forceful ■ Confident ■ Sells self ■ Clear direction ■ Career oriented ■ More self-driven ■ Disciplined ■ Organized ■ Tell oriented
Priorities	■ Team ■ Service ■ Care ■ Sensitivity ■ People values ■ Us	■ Vision ■ Entrepreneurial ■ Results ■ Goals ■ Success values ■ Me
Relationships	■ Understanding ■ Sensitive towards others ■ Attention to feelings ■ People count ■ Empathetic ■ Response to different needs ■ Approachable ■ Fun oriented	■ Supports team ■ Defends subordinates/ colleagues ■ Protects interests of team/ colleagues ■ Manipulates relationships ■ Uses pressure ■ Enjoys influencing others ■ Can communicate with many ■ Likes to be on stage ■ Uses power to influence
Communication	■ Polite but direct ■ Soft voiced ■ Tag question ■ Uses qualifiers ■ Softer words ■ Averts gaze ■ Ladylike posture ■ Uses feelings ■ Democratic ■ Support of others' viewpoints	■ Direct and blunt ■ Lower pitch ■ Makes statement ■ Is brief ■ Statements ■ Stares direct ■ Takes up talk time ■ Focuses on objectives ■ Task driven ■ Qualifies one's view
Decision-making	■ Considered ■ Not dramatic ■ Familiarization with people/ details ■ Issues and details	■ Quick ■ Event driven ■ Analytical (detailed, disciplined)

Table 7.1 Female/male comparison of leadership attributes and performance: overview of research (*continued*)

	Female	Male
Values/philosophy	■ Supportive ■ Mentoring ■ Input oriented ■ Status free	■ Achievement ■ Mentoring as potential coalition ■ Output concerned ■ Status conscious
Work/home interface	■ Balance responsibilities ■ Unhappiness most damaging ■ Dual demands not most damaging	■ More work sided ■ Failure as most damaging ■ Can balance home/work demands

different needs of their colleagues and subordinates. Women are more likely to be approachable, treat others around them as equals and be considerably aware of the impact of self on others. The empathetic orientation of women is viewed as their influencing others through the effective handling of relationships.

In one sense, men also share a similarity with women leaders and that is in their team orientation. Male leaders are likely to be highly supportive of their team, defend their subordinates and colleagues, as well as protect their own interests. However, as far as relating outside their immediate environment is concerned, men are likely to use pressure, and openly enjoy influencing others.

Men are seen as effective at communicating with many people simultaneously. Women are considered to have a softer approach to forming and maintaining relationships. Women's style of communication is likely to be more listening oriented in conversation, making extensive use of softer words, with the likelihood that fewer pronounced statements are made. Male leaders on the other hand are considered to be more likely to offer clear views, make statements, take up far greater task time, while being brief, direct and blunt. Women can also be direct, but are likely to be more polite.

Decision-making practices also emerge to highlight considerable differences of behaviour. Female leaders are identified as being more considered in their approach, taking a balanced view in debate, by familiarizing themselves with the issues and with detail, before reaching a conclusion. Their overall decision-making style is viewed as one of not being dramatic. Male leaders are likely to be more event driven, being substantially influenced by the circumstances of the situation they face, valuing as a positive attribute, speedy decision-making. In the process of making a decision, they are likely to be equally as attentive to detail as women, but more analytical and personally disciplined.

In terms of personal values, the caring theme is maintained for women leaders. Women are identified as valuing being supportive and making time to discuss and 'mentor' through issues. Mentoring is considered to be the more natural way of operating for women. Women are identified as being more concerned with what they can offer (input oriented), while paying less attention to status in relationships. Male leaders are recognized as valuing achievement, and are driven by what they can attain (output oriented). The processes of discussion and facilitation are in themselves valued, but are seen more as a necessary part of forming coalitions and making contacts. Men are considered to be more conscious of status, and value the same as a reward.

Certain similarities and differences emerge over the topic of the work–home interface. Women are seen as being able to balance their home–work responsibilities. The emerging picture is that the dual demands are not the most damaging, whereas living with personal unhappiness is a destructively negative experience. Although the strain of meeting home and work demands is extensive, it is possible to strike a balance by strength of will and a positive attitude. Men are considered to be far more work oriented, and their greatest fear is failure at work. Although a considerable number of studies have shown that men, in dual and single career families, do less housework, shopping and looking after the children, they are nevertheless viewed as more able to balance home and worklife, even though doing so has been experienced as a more difficult and demanding process.

Cranfield studies

A somewhat different picture emerges from the Cranfield surveys examining the demographic impact on leadership behaviour in government and the health services (see Chapter 6 for an in-depth explanation of demographics). A comparison of the responses from male and female top managers in the Australian Commonwealth (federal) Government public service, and in national health service (NHS) Trusts in the UK, display none of the contrasts highlighted in Table 7.1.

Australian Public Service (APS) Survey

The Australian survey identified certain prominent attitudes and values held by the senior managers of the APS. However, of the key attitudes and values identified (see Table 7.2), no significant difference emerges in terms of work satisfaction, performance orientation, being a specialist, being independently minded, being sensitive to people, the provision of service, being loyal to the organization, workplace democracy and the

Table 7.2   Leadership behaviour: gender differences – Australian Public Service Survey

Attitudes and values	Gender	Organization level
Work-related attitudes		
Being performance oriented	NS	NS
Work satisfaction	NS	NS
Being disciplined	NS	SOs less
Being specialist	NS	NS
Being independently minded	NS	NS
Being service oriented	NS	SES more
Being people development driven	NS	NS
Values		
Performance-oriented values	NS	NS
Organization-oriented values	NS	NS
Effectiveness of service values	NS	NS
Rights and duties values	NS	NS
Workplace democracy values	NS	NS
Personal values	NS	NS
Use of information technology		
Response to IT training	NS	SOs less
Effectiveness of IT application	NS	NS
Using IT to meet organizational needs	NS	NS
Adept in IT skills	NS	SOs more

Note:
Org – Organization level
NS – Not significant
SES – Senior Executive Service (top-level managers)
SO – Senior Officer (subordinate to SESs)

exercising of rights and the duties of people at work. Similarly, in the use of information technology (IT), no significant difference was found in terms of responsiveness to IT training, the use of IT in the organization, adapting IT skills to meet different needs, and using IT to meet different organizational demands.

In similar fashion, on issues of transformational and transactional behaviours (see Table 7.3), no significant difference was found between the genders. Both male and female leaders could be as effective, or as ineffective, at interfacing within the top team, interfacing across the organization, and in holding a clear or distorted strategic view of the direction the organization should pursue. Further, entering into dialogue on sensitive issues could be just as positively or inappropriately addressed by both men and women. On the key issue of visioning, male

Table 7.3   Leadership behaviour: gender differences – Australian Public Service Survey

Transformational behaviour	Gender
Top team interfacing	NS
Organizational interfacing	NS
Clarity of view of strategic direction	NS
Quality of top team dialogue	NS
Cohesion/splits on visioning	NS
Transactional style	
Sensitive to people	NS
Power oriented	NS
Rules and regulations oriented	NS
Valuing performance and professionalism	NS

Note: NS – not significant

and female leaders alike could just as effectively discuss and emerge with a shared and cohesive view of the future of the organization, or fall into conflict and dispute with colleagues and other key stakeholders, and be divisive and split on key issues.

Further, very few differences are identified even by level in organizations (see Table 7.2). The SOs are identified as less disciplined than the SESs, and the SESs emerge as more service oriented. On the issue of workplace values, no significant differences are indicated. On the issue of IT applications, the SOs hold a more negative attitude towards IT training, presumably because they are more likely to be required to update their skills, but equally they are identified as more flexible in using their IT skills to meet different situational needs.

The most significant demographics to have emerged from the Cranfield studies which significantly determine leadership behaviour and attitude (described in Chapter 6), are job tenure, organization tenure, and the number of senior management appointments held.

NHS Trusts Survey

A similar picture emerges from the NHS Trusts Survey, whereby demographics other than gender surface as more significant influences on the attitudes, values and behaviours of medical and managerial leaders, and on the performance of the organization. Table 7.4 highlights only two key differences between males and females in senior positions. Men are identified as more disciplined in their day-to-day activities, and in terms of follow-through, and women as more able to manage sensitive relationships within the top team. Otherwise, similar results emerge for

Table 7.4 Leadership and NHS Trusts: comparison by gender

Transactional orientation	Gender
■ Job satisfaction	NS
■ Working relations	NS
■ Patient care	NS
■ Communication	NS
■ Discipline	Males
■ Decision-making (personal)	NS
■ Leadership behaviour	NS
■ Culture of trust	NS
Transformational orientation	
■ Top relationships	Females
■ Strategic decision-taking	NS
■ Top team sensitivities	NS
■ Opportunity costs	NS

Note: NS – not significant

NHS Trusts as for the APS (see Chapter 6), where tenure, in terms of time in the medical profession, and the length of time employed in the hospital, are significant influences on transactional and transformational performance.

Implications for women leaders

The emerging evidence is contradictory. The results of the Cranfield surveys of the Australian government and the NHS Trusts, highlight that gender, except for certain significant differences, and when compared with the results in Chapter 6, is the least influential predictor of behaviour and attitudes at senior management levels. This contrasts sharply with the results of research outlined in Table 7.1.

The reason for such differences is that the research captured in Table 7.1 has interpreted gender as a male/female comparison, whereas the Cranfield studies have examined the impact of a number of demographic factors, of which gender is only one. The Cranfield studies indicate that the blockages, unsupportive attitudes, bias and discrimination experienced by women, in terms of their career progress, are not necessarily replicated, once women have achieved appointment to senior office. The circumstances facing the individual, the nature and culture of the organization, the approaches used by the female leader to address the challenges she faces, her motivation, morale and capabilities at that period, are likely to determine her success or failure. The message to have emerged, is that there are many differences between women, as there are between men and women. Further, substantial differences exist across organizations, where some would be discriminatory and others not so. Also, there is no reason to assume that morale and determination are constant for men and women. Both may display high drive at one point in their lives, and feel demoralized and lacking in confidence at other times. In fact, the degree of morale experienced at particular points in time, is more likely to determine success or failure in terms of performance as a leader, than differences between men and women.

In further examining the experience of women as leaders, a random number of case studies of successful women are identified in order to examine more deeply the theme of what makes a successful woman.

Pin-pointing women leaders

Initially, three case studies are scrutinized, those of Frances Hesselbein, Gro Harlem Brundtland and Hilary Clinton.

Frances Hesselbein

Frances Hesselbein, started from the bottom. From being a voluntary leader she was appointed to the post of executive director of the Talus Rock Girl Scout Council, and then was awarded the job of national executive director of the National Girl Scout organization. She has been named by *Savvy* magazine as one of the top non-profit executives in the USA, receiving in 1984, the first Entrepreneurial Woman Award for excellence for non-profit management. She attends numerous boards and advisory committees, including that of the board of visitors to the Peter Drucker Graduate Management Center, Claremont Graduate School.[6]

Reflecting on everything she had learned on her way up the leadership ladder, she says that one of her first tasks was, 'to develop a corporate planning system in which planning and management become synonymous'.[7] She and her team evolved a corporate plan to harness the contribution of 600,000 adult volunteers and 335 local councils in order that they nurture and help grow young girls to women of considerable potential. She feels that she and her team have achieved substantial unity and cohesion in the organization.

Hesselbein's perspective is that there was 'a compelling need to have a clear planning system that defines roles, differentiating between volunteers, operational staff and policy planners' (Bennis 1989:207–8). The planning system permitted her senior managers to know what was going on, from, in the smallest troop, to appreciating the long-term needs and trends of the organization. With an organization of three million members, the process of listening to the girls and their parents has been greatly enhanced through the system devised.

Hesselbein has created a web organization, where she is in the centre of a circle and around her are seven bubbles, the group directors, and around them are additional circles, the team directors, and so on. Her concern is less with communication moving up or down, but more laterally, across the organization. She believes that the best aspect of her organization is that, 'every girl in America can look at the program and see herself'.[8]

Gro Harlem Brundtland

Gro Harlem Brundtland was three times elected Prime Minister of Norway, from February to October 1981, from 1986 to 1989, and again from November 1990 until November 1992. In Norway, she was the first woman and the youngest Prime Minister to be elected.

Gro Harlem Brundtland studied medicine and was educated in Oslo and Harvard. She was a consultant at the Ministry of Health and Social Affairs from 1965–67. Then from 1968 until 1969, she held the position of Medical Officer in Oslo's City Health Department. In 1969 she became Deputy Director of School Health Services in Oslo. From 1974 until 1979 she was Minister of the Environment.

Apart from holding senior positions, she also wrote numerous articles on preventive medicine, and conducted school health and growth studies. Brundtland became Deputy Leader of the Labour Party, from 1975 until 1981, and from 1981 until 1992 she became Leader of the Labour Parliamentary Group. Brundtland has consistently supported women's rights and concerns. For her political work, she was awarded the Third World Prize for Work on Environmental Issues in 1989; the Indira Gandhi Prize in 1990; and the Onassis Foundation Award in 1992. She promoted many women politicians and included eight (women) in her 19-member cabinet. Women hold 36 per cent of the parliamentary seats in Norway. According to Brundtland 'the participation of women at the highest level of Norwegian politics has transformed the country, with the emphasis now on the environment, employment, children and youth'.[9]

Hilary Clinton

Although most voters knew little about Hilary Clinton at the start of the 1992 campaign, when she first came to widespread public attention defending her husband against allegations of womanizing, opinions quickly polarized. Although attracting criticism for her non-traditional approach in the 1992 election, Hilary Clinton in no small measure has boosted her husband's popularity. Like her husband, she is a lawyer and a strong-willed articulate leader. The couple made much of her taking a 'partnership' role with her husband when they took up residency in the White House in January 1993.

On assuming the Presidency, Bill Clinton appointed Hilary, against howls of criticism, and defending his wife's intelligence and qualifications, to head a vast overhaul of the US health care system, one of the key promises of his campaign. During Clinton's first term, Hilary led a panel that designed the unwieldy omnibus health care reform. The 1992 health care platform had declared that all Americans should have universal access to quality, affordable health care. Hilary endorsed a series of incremental steps that would be the pathway towards achieving the reform goals. Further, she tackled head-on, the Republicans' charge that her book, *It Takes a Village*, endorsed obsolete big-government intervention. Hilary argued that it takes family, teachers, clergy, business people, 'all of us', to raise a healthy child. Furthermore, it takes a village and a President who not only hold these beliefs, but act on them.

However, the 1996 platform changed and merely stated that Democrats were committed to ensuring that Americans have access to affordable, high-quality health care. The President in 1994 had been dealt one of his biggest political defeats when efforts to pass a massive health-care reform plan, failed in Congress. Instead of firmly supporting affirmative action, as the 1992 platform had done, the 1996 document promised reform. A comparison between the 1992 and 1996 Democratic platforms offered evidence of the party's turn towards the political centre.

Even though Hilary's official role has diminished, she continues to exert considerable, sometimes decisive, influence over administration policy and political strategy. Although she linked herself increasingly, over the past year, to issues concerning women and children, a traditional concern of First Ladies, at the same time, she is a woman who has been a political activist for as long as her husband, dating back to the early 1970s. She remained the most requested stand-in for Bill Clinton on the 1996 campaign trail. Notwithstanding that she was upset at the rejection of her health care plan by both Congress and the public, and uncertain of the reasons why, she agreed with the advice of some of the administration's political advisers that it was no longer wise for her to be wielding authority in a public way. Despite being constrained, she has influenced policies to: guarantee new mothers at least two days in the hospital after the birth of their child; expand family leave for doctors; create more flexible rules on overtime work, and also to broaden health care coverage. Besides her involvement in the health care reform, Hilary openly participated in, and influenced, other major issues, including the budget, during the President's/her husband's first two years in office.

Hilary Clinton has changed the traditional behind-the-scenes, power clout that many first ladies have wielded, and experimented in exercising formal power as a presidential spouse.

Although polls have shown the controversial Hilary to be one of the least popular First Ladies in US history, many Democrats support Hilary, some because she fought for health care, others because she is a professional woman, and still others because they see her as a liberal influence on her husband. Many suggest that the health care failure stemmed from her stubbornness, which in turn was the result of bad advice, as well as the impact of various lobby groups and interests, and the huge Republican opposition. Some suggest that there was a built-in problem with putting the First Lady in charge, especially one who was such a strong personality. As there seems to have been a reluctance to tell the spouse of the president that she had a bad idea, bad ideas live longer than they otherwise would.

The view that Hilary Clinton did not get what she bargained for in Washington, is driven by the perception that she did not live up to her end of the bargain, which is ascribed to her strength, and uncompromising determination of character. From the earliest days of the Clinton partnership in Arkansas, she supposedly was the one who provided for those areas he lacked. She is apparently orderly, disciplined, cool to the point of being cold, but most of all, clear. Ironically, Clinton himself supposedly shows more, so-called feminine characteristics of being exuberant and chaotic. According to numerous journalists, the history of the first three years of the Clinton administration shows that a considerable number of the most spectacular misjudgements have Hilary's stamp. A current and common theme is of her extreme mistrust by those outside her circle of loyal supporters and friends, a situation which she may have reversed with her clear and forthright denunciation in late January 1998, of the 'sex scandals' surrounding her husband. Like or dislike Hilary, consider her effective or ineffective, the will and resolve of the First Lady has consistently stood out.

Looking at women leaders

Hesselbein's systematic planning, her caring, her political adeptness at reading situations, contrast sharply with Hilary Clinton's image of being allegedly cold and focused to the point of political incompetence. Against this picture is the contrast of Brundtland, as a highly educated and intelligent woman, who is clear, decisive, in charge, but sensitive and concerned. Do these short biographies say more about these women, or more about their circumstances? Could Hilary Clinton have been a more sharing, caring and non-centralist CEO if she had been appointed to run the Girl Scout movement? Would Hesselbein have behaved in much the same way as Hilary Clinton, had she found herself in similar political circumstances?

An initial scan of women leaders provides a mixed view. It was a developing society, Sri Lanka, that produced the first elected woman to the executive head of state position, Prime Minister, some three and a half decades ago, namely Sirimavo Bandaranaike, in 1960, followed by

India's Indira Gandhi in 1966, Israel's Golda Meir in 1970 and Argentina's Isabel Peron in 1974. In western society, this was achieved nearly two decades after Bandaranaike, when Margaret Thatcher, in 1979, became the first woman Prime Minister of the UK, followed by Iceland's Vigidis Finnbögadottir in 1980; Norway's Gro Harlem Brundtland's brief experience in 1981, with further re-elections in 1986 and 1990; Netherlands, Antilles' Maria Liberia-Peters in 1984; Ireland's Mary Robinson in 1990, followed by Mary McAleese in 1997; and Kim Campbell's brief 1993 experience of leading Canada. In 1995, Ruth Dreyfus was elected as State Councillor in Switzerland, the highest leadership position in the country held by a woman. While former eastern bloc societies took thirty years to achieve similar results, Lithuania's Kzaimiera-Danute Prunskiena in 1990 was followed by Poland's Hanna Suckcka in 1992.[10]

Surprisingly, women leaders have come into prominence in the most unlikely areas, namely developing countries, including those of the Muslim background. Six major world religions, Buddhism, Catholicism, Hinduism, Islam, Judaism and Protestantism have women leaders as heads of state, including the Islamic countries of Bangladesh, Pakistan and Turkey, challenging the belief that Islam and other religions, are prejudiced against women rising to power. The reality is that the privileged, wealthy and well-connected have the opportunity to reach the top political office, whereas the poor are deeply down-trodden and have no chance of progressing anywhere. In, so-called, developing societies, Eugenia Charles, became Prime Minister in the Dominican Republic in 1981; the Philippines' Corri Aquino was elected in 1986; Pakistan's Benazir Bhutto was elected in 1988 at the age of 35, the first woman to head a modern Muslim state. In 1990, Nicaragua's Violeta de Barros Chamorro, and Haiti's Ertha Pascal-Trouillot, assumed leading roles. Turkey's Tansu Ciller was elected head of state in 1993; and for the second time in Sri Lanka, in 1994, Chandraka Bandaranaike Kumaratunge, daughter of the first female Prime Minister, became the second female Prime Minister of the country.

The differences between these women are substantial. The supposedly iron maiden view of Margaret Thatcher as not nice but necessary for the time, contrasts exceptionally sharply with the pleasant Mary Robinson of Ireland, who has contributed greatly to social care issues and to raising social consciousness as well as highlighting the positive profile of Ireland abroad. Again a different view emerges when examining the undemocratic activities of Tansu Ciller of Turkey, with the extremes in behaviour of Pakistan's Benazir Bhutto, who was sacked by the President of Pakistan for corruption. While Ciller and Bhutto were both accused in the press of corruption, only Bhutto has purportedly, been associated with her brother's assassination.

Two trends are identified in the studies and case analyses of women leaders. The first is that successful women take pride in their accomplishments and enjoy their autonomy, independence and freedom. However, and second, these very same women express mixed feelings about the pleasure, on the one hand, of being in charge of their own lives, but also that they may have, or have had, to sacrifice a deeper relationship with a partner with whom they could exchange intimate feelings and pursue a committed and durable relationship. A Canadian study of executive women shows that 70 per cent are single or divorced, of whom some have children. Similarly in Australia, a review of women in parliament shows that 80 per cent of women parliamentarians are single or divorced. However, the divorce rate of male counterparts, although above the national average, is not as disproportionately high as with women (Australian Department of the Prime Minister and Cabinet, 1994).

In Britain, a considerable number of female leaders are to be found in the single women category. For example, Esther Rantzen became a prominent female broadcaster (later married); Eve Pollard rose through the ranks of journalism and left the powerful position as editor of the *Sunday Express* to explore writing novels; Anna Ford, the former Open University Researcher, after the loss of her husband, Mark Boxer, has continued as a highly rated news presenter. Similarly in the USA, Susan Crosland, after the loss of her husband Anthony, UK Foreign Secretary, became an accomplished writer.

However, there exist exceptions to the rule, with Steve Shirley's (founder of the FI Group) long and successful marriage, and Anita Roddick's highly successful, personal and business partnership with her husband.

A recent *Fortune* magazine article (5 August 1996), added to the list of exceptions and reported that a number of highly successful female top executives, most of whom are married, do not try to hide their femininity, and are as different from each other in terms of leadership philosophy and approach, as they are to their male counterparts. Women such as Rebecca Mark, CEO of Enron Development, the international ventures business of the Enron Corporation; Jill Barad, identified as Matel's next likely CEO; Charlotte Beers, CEO of the advertising agency, Ogilvy and Mather (part of the WPP group); and Diana Brooks of Sotheby's were highlighted in the *Fortune* article, as was the variety of reasons for their success, such as (according to some of these women) use of their sexuality, the fact they did not plan their careers, the fact that they do not always blend into the organization, the fact that they do not favour women, but they do have a remarkable appetite for hard work and can absorb considerable pressure. The emerging picture is one of individualists who know the direction they wish to pursue, do not conform to norms, and are not afraid to go against the stream and make unpleasant decisions, yet in no way try to hide their gender, their feelings and what they value in life.

Again in contradiction to the single, divorced-woman image of highly successful women, the Rosener Study surveyed International Women's Forum foundation members and reported that 67 per cent of women respondents were married. The Rosener Study concluded that both married men and married women experience moderate levels of conflict between the work and family domains. When the children are at home, women experience higher levels of conflict than men. The Rosener Study equally contradicted current wisdoms on the issue of pay in revealing that certain women leaders earned slightly more than their male counterparts, but both male and female leaders paid their female subordinates some $12,000 less than their male subordinates. An alternative study of British women graduates, concluded that women top earners had fewer career breaks, had fewer children, and these mostly later in life, and that they were solicitors, academics, were in medicine or in business.

Reviewing the family life experiences of women in political leadership positions Nancy Adler adds to the view of the single leader. Of the 23 above-mentioned political female leaders, 12 entered power as single women, but only four of them achieved high office entirely on their own political platform. Israel's Golda Meir, with two children and long separated from her husband, came to power at the age of 72 as one of the oldest leaders. Iceland's Finnbögadottir, adopted a child after her divorce, but her rise to high office followed. Canada's Kim Campbell, similarly came to power after her divorce, while Dominican Republic's Eugenia Charles was elected as a single woman.

Seven top women leaders shouldered the responsibilities of top office after the assassination of their husbands. Sri Lanka's Sirimavo Bandaranaike, Argentina's infamous Isabel Peron, Philippines' Corazone Aquino (who narrowly missed assassination herself). Nicaragua's Violeta de Barros Chamorro, Bangladesh's Khaleda Zia and to close the loop, we return to Sri Lanka, where Chandriaka Bandanaraike Kumaratunge (Bandanaraike's daughter) was elected after the assassination of her politically active husband.

Chandriaka Kumaratunge provides an interesting link with two more prominent women leaders whose rise to power was, directly or indirectly, associated with their fathers'. India's Indira Ghandi, long separated from her husband who lived with her two children at her father's home, benefited from the exposure to a politically vibrant household, as well as having access to privileged connections. Benazir Bhutto, elected the youngest ever woman Prime Minister at the age of 39, followed her assassinated father. Ghandi and Bhutto had privileged societal access to the levers of power, greatly benefiting from the limelight that shadowed their fathers' glory trail.

To date, Pakistan's Benazir Bhutto, is the only Prime Minister who has given birth during her term in office. Furthermore, although almost all political women leaders have children, most of these had grown into adulthood before their mothers assumed office, such as Margaret Thatcher, Indira Ghandi and Corazone Aquino. However, a minority, like Margaret Thatcher, the former Irish President, Mary Robinson and the newly elected Irish President, Mary McAleese, have experienced consistent support from their husbands during their years of leadership or struggle to gain senior office.

In contrast, only a handful of men, out of all the male political leaders, ascended to power while single; for example, Canada's eccentric bachelor and longest serving Prime Minister, William Mackenzie King, from 1921–30 and 1935–48; Pierre Elliott Trudeau, who came to power in 1968 as a single man and then married in 1971, only to be separated towards the end of his second term in office 1980–84, and finally divorced in 1984; as well as Britain's committed bachelor, Sir Edward Heath. The ratio of single women assuming leader positions appears to be out of proportion to that of single men.

Avenues for development

The distinction drawn between career path (getting there) and performance in role (got there) seems particularly pertinent. The striving for recognition and respect, requires a particular set of actions and attributes. The performance of leaders once in role, brings out an additional set of challenges to address. This point is nowhere more clearly highlighted than in the case of Ireland's Mary Robinson. She visited more constituencies than any other Irish politician, before her candidacy for the Presidency was taken seriously by the opposition. Although she had to work harder than her counterparts to achieve credibility as a candidate for President of Ireland, once having realized her leadership position, she displayed a similar balance of strengths and misjudgements as her contemporaries and predecessors.

Bearing in mind the distinction between getting there and got there, the question to address is what are the appropriate pathways that women should take to enhance their development? Other than the more obvious circumstances of deliberate sexual harassment, is the issue one of gender, focusing on women's development, or a much broader question? Certainly, evidence exists that gender is an issue, but it is only one of many demographic forces that impact on individuals and the organization. The two emerging views from gender studies are that, on the one hand, it is important to concentrate on improving the lot of women in the workplace, and on the other, emphasize generating an internal organizational culture of diversity capability, whereby both staff and management have the maturity to confront challenges and concerns as they arise, of which gender is but one. The latter view of managing for diversity is the perspective adopted in this chapter. The premise adopted is that not all circumstances can be pre-accounted for and that the lot of women in the workplace is probably best served within a diversity framework, whereby they are treated on an equal footing with all of their colleagues. Five separate strategies for enhancing diversity capability in general, and for the development of women and other minorities in the workplace in particular, are explored.

Promote diversity capability

Diversity thinking assumes that numerous differences exist in the workplace, which may be due to gender, colour, ethnicity, disablement, etc., but need to be addressed, with full account taken of the context in which they have arisen. Such an obvious statement, however, holds considerable implications. The most obvious is to be flexible to create programmes for improvement that meet the needs of different circumstances. For example, while solely promoting a programme of development for women throughout the organization may be recognized as important at headquarters, the same issue may hold only marginal importance in one or more of the operating businesses/divisions. Hence, a corporate-wide programme for the enhancement of women may be restricted by certain sections of the organization due to their intransigence, and in other parts of the organization because it is simply not pushed hard enough due to its perceived relative unimportance. Enforcement of a programme promoting the development of women may well alienate those would-be supporters who are driven by what they see as other more pressing issues, such as trying to overcome a revenue shortfall, keeping the business alive, and keeping people in jobs.

The alternative would be to adopt a diversity management perspective to discrimination, and in so doing, senior management would need to consider and debate three issues: equality, legitimacy, and learning.

The most popular approach to addressing discrimination positively has been the fairness/equality track, often captured in affirmative action initiatives. Pursuing this line of thinking requires companies to push through the organization, programmes intended to evaluate discrimination, improve cultural understanding, train people to respect cultural, racial, or gender differences and, by implication, treat everyone the same. Such programmes are often codified, require a top-down push, and also continuous monitoring to ensure consistency of application. Affirmative action programmes can provide considerable benefit to organizations, in that, if top management are sincere and provide their support, inequalities can be rooted out.

However, the 'fairness-for-all' approach has its limitations. Based on the premise that 'we are all equal', taken to extreme, the same assumption could be one of 'we are all the same', when patently that is not the case. Especially with international organizations, different regions of the world have different traditions with which people identify, to varying degrees. Pushing through one policy could ironically lead management to being culturally and ethnically blind. Where genuine disputes arise, for example over working hours, workloads, or work definition, debate could be misconstrued as being difficult, politically incorrect, or promoting in the organization undesired attitudes, in the blind belief that 'we are all the same'. The danger is the retaliation that any person could attract who questions the fundamental assumptions of a fairness-for-all policy, which could result in even more discrimination. 'Fairness for all' programmes tend to be useful for more structured organizations, such as military establishments, which easily lend themselves to codified practices. Those organizations that are more customer/community responsive, suffer considerably under the strain of equality programmes, due to the fact that they strive to be flexible, but have to address a policy which may not allow for diversity. Single discriminatory programmes, for example gender training, fall into the danger of becoming oblivious to other developments and at the extreme, punitive towards those who wish to debate or disagree with the presumptions behind the policy.

An alternative approach is that of legitimacy, namely to legitimize local differences, and thereby display sensitivity to contexts by giving people a chance to improve their standing in their local communities. The attempt is to depart from a position of blind conformity to one of contextual responsiveness. For example, many Japanese companies, in their endeavour to be socially acceptable, go out of their way to appoint and promote senior management in their operating businesses who are the locals of that country in which the company has set up its operation. Companies that have products that are marketed on a gender or ethnic ticket, may well appoint individuals of that background to champion the product and give it 'credibility', irrespective of whether the appointees are, or are not, the most professionally suitable for the job. In effect, a policy of segmentation is matched by a human resources policy of appropriateness to context. Such a policy has considerable advantages.

Opportunities of both a professional and managerial kind arise for women and others of different ethnic backgrounds, by being driven by contextual considerations. Equally, the sensitivity shown to the segmentation process is appreciated by the customers or recipients. They see the organization as being sensitive to local communities, sympathetic, and listening oriented towards local issues. However, the legitimacy policy of, let us respect local concerns, too, has its problems. The outstandingly difficult issue to address is one of integrating the various pockets of development that have taken place in the organization. From a policy of fairness and equality, the pendulum has now swung to the other extreme of, whatever is right for you, do it! If the primary reason for local legitimization is one of branding, and the company sincerely attempts to live its brand, and implement what it proclaims, then the policy may well be appropriate. However, should centralization of costs or more corporate branding be required, the challenge that still remains is that of integrating different localized institutions, or even just understanding the capabilities required to manage across multiple boundaries. The legitimacy approach can considerably weaken the centre and also leave the organization open to a form of indirect blackmail – 'If the local team do not get their own way, they walk! – So who else can do the job?' The legitimizing of localities requires an excessive attention to communication and relationship building, in order to stem the potential for a damaging corporate memory loss, by having the best of the local people leave.

A third approach is the learning option, whereby diversity is, and is shown to be, respected, through people promoting their views, defining activities, offering feedback on strategy, undertaking initiatives, but most of all, through being held accountable for their actions in terms of how their contribution fits into the overall organization. The learning approach perspective makes the most of diversity. Through well-applied learning programmes which examine the broad nature of social, organization, gender, ethnic and business diversity, how to address known concerns, how to respect people and their traditions, and most importantly the degree to which each individual needs to improve his/her own level of maturity in order to address effectively diverse circumstances, the staff and management of the organization become more responsive to new ideas, and are helped to evolve a philosophy of consistently pursuing affirmative employment practices. In order to encourage contributions from all, and the continuous maturing of the organization's employees, top management need to truly live up to the expectations of their staff in terms of applying the 'best practice' behaviours that have been identified. Further, nurturing an internal culture of openness and of feeling valued, is important in encouraging contribution, and promoting identity with policies, emerging from the top.

Whichever of the three approaches the organization adopts, at least pursuing the elimination of discrimination in the workplace, through improving the capability of the management to handle diversity, does allow for a debate as to which appropriate strategy to pursue.

Codes of conduct

It may seem contradictory to recommend managing diversity by introducing code(s) of conduct, as by nature codes are restrictive and can lead to punitive behaviour. However, in cases of obvious sexual harassment and discrimination, not only does the organization need to protect itself, it also is required to prevent further incidents from arising.

A code of conduct can clearly spell out desired behaviours and practices, thereby establishing a common benchmark for the employment of best practice. With an appropriately and unambiguously drafted code of conduct, people are given clear dividing lines between what they can and cannot do, without endangering themselves and their company with a lawsuit.

Secondly, those who face being disciplined, but are genuinely unaware that their conduct is viewed as offensive, at least are given guidance. The recent case of a Dr John E. Smith, reported by Abraham Laurie in the *Journal of Medical Economics* in February 1996, highlighted the case of a practitioner who was acquitted of unreasonable behaviour, on the grounds that he was out of step with new standards of care. Those who knew Smith have described him as an inept communicator.

Third, the organization is given some way of addressing an almost impossible situation between sexual harassment and wrongful dismissal. The recent case driven by the Equal Employment Opportunities Commission (EEOC) of suing Mitsubishi Motors USA on behalf of approximately 700 female workers, who allegedly suffered sexual harassment by, among other things, having their bottoms pinched, could involve the company in paying damages in excess of $210 million. The problem for a company is that if an organization dismisses someone for telling an offensive joke in front of a female operative, he/she in turn, can sue for wrongful dismissal. As government may not provide sufficiently clear pathways forward, it is necessary for an enterprise to show that it has taken charge of the situation by providing a clear code of conduct for its employees to follow. As highlighted in the May 1996 issue of *Risk Management*, a leading insurer for 'not-for-profit' organizations, Nonprofits Mutual of Concord, New Hampshire, USA, emphasized that the way to protect the organization against the rising number of sexual harassment, improper termination of employment contract, and discrimination suits, is to constitute clear employment practices. One of the most effective is an unambiguous code of conduct, which not only spells out the policy and behavioural guidelines, but also the education and training that staff and management will need to experience on how investigations, once allegations are made, will be conducted.

Management education and training

The overwhelming evidence that female managers are still less likely to be promoted than men, does mean that women should be paying particular attention to improving their technical, professional and managerial capabilities. The goal is to develop a mosaic of leadership capabilities and talents, where the achievements and merits of the individual stand out in their own right. The acquisition of technical skills and expertise are identified as being critical pre-determinants of appointment to a senior position. Biographies of women leaders in politics reveal that most of the leaders were highly educated, with only a very few, such as Argentina's Isabel Peron, never having formally attended university; nevertheless she graduated from the 'university of life' as Vice-President, serving under her husband prior to his demise. Perhaps the best educated women politician is Tansu Ciller, with a PhD from Harvard and appointed as one of the youngest professors in her country. The one with the broadest education is likely to be Iceland's Finnbögadottir who, after leaving high school, studied French, theatre, French philosophy and, finally, English literature and education. Although broad in spread, Finnbögadottir who studied in France, Denmark, Sweden and Iceland is similar to other top women leaders who supplemented their education, internationally, such as Ghandi in UK, Ciller in the USA and similarly Brundtland in the USA. Others display a variety of academic backgrounds, with the majority having a degree in law (Margaret Thatcher, Kim Campbell, Mary Robinson, Mary McAleese, Corazone Aquino and Hanna Suckocka), economics (Edith Cressen, Kazimiera-Danute Prunskience, Chandrika Bandaranaike, Kumaratunge and Tansu Ciller) and political science (Kumaratunge and Bhutto). These women's educational background in law, economics and political science is equally the experience of their male counterparts. However, some studied a much broader range of fields including medicine (Brundtland), chemistry (Thatcher), and history (Indira Ghandi), while Mary McAleese had been a practising academic up to her election as Irish President.

From an organization's perspective, how then to provide management education and training is an interesting question. Should training be gender specific and/or mixed, and/or focused on particular issues? The more functional the training, the less likely is the need for gender specific training, as managers are being trained in specific skills, which require general application. However, where role related issues, eloquence, motivation, self-confidence and emotional robustness are the key issues, different organizations have pursued different avenues.

Under the able stewardship of Dr Susan Vinnicombe at Cranfield School of Management, British Telecom have run a highly successful gender-specific programme for women managers, for over a decade. The client thinks so highly of the programme, that they want more!

In contrast, McDonald's UK, have opted not to go for gender-specific training but to run mixed programmes. McDonald's who serve fast foods ranging from soup to burgers, to nuts, in 18,380 restaurants in 91 countries, have evolved a recipe for global success which is to translate its winning people and employment practices into many different cultures. The company pays special attention to local cultures. For example, McDonald's opened a restaurant in 1996 in India with no beef products, although it has vegeburgers and burgers made from mutton or lamb. In Saudi Arabia, McDonald's will open up a restaurant with two dining areas, one for men and the other for women and children. McDonald's careful practice in the restaurant is replicated in its training programmes, where at the Hamburger University at Oak Brook Illinois, it can provide training in 22 different languages, and even teach two languages at the same time, as well as support training in other countries to suit local conditions.

A different version of training for leadership is provided at the Bradley Hospital in Cleveland, USA, inspired by its CEO, Jim Whitlock. He sponsors mixed programmes which not only include leadership, but also the hospital's history, management philosophy, time management, communication skills, ethics, labour laws, sexual harassment and its prevention, budgeting, and performance review, all in one extensive 18-course programme.

The variety of approaches to leadership development is considerable. Certain of the pundits support segregation in training, while others baulk angrily against any single gender/single ethnic programme, on the basis that people are not assisted to cope with their workplace environment. The guiding line to pursue is context. Address what is needed in the company at that moment in time.

Mobilizing women in organizations

Numerical strength lends credibility to an argument, both to the waverers on the protagonists' side and to the more sympathetic outsiders, such as senior executives. Isolated women or minority representatives do not have the social resources, or power, to re-socialize groups in the organization to accept or conform to different norms. Hence, lobbying activity is needed if any group is to challenge successfully established norms of behaviour. Lobbying can be undertaken on an individual basis, or driven by the issues at hand, or through networks. The value of a woman's network group is that it can help develop a new culture consisting of shared assumptions in the areas of equality, competence and adaptability, and can provide an impetus for changing organizational culture and for further eroding the presence of 'glass or concrete ceilings'.

Successfully mobilized women, through women's networks or alliances, can strategically exercise their influence and achieve equity and trust, and further, nurture a willingness to be responsive to change. Such positive attitudes can propagate changes that lead to a culture of excellence. Furthermore, a women's network increases the circle of contacts, and negates the social isolation that is often felt by high-profile female pioneers.

Focal network groups can also lobby for political support from outside the organization. The successful implementation of non-discriminatory policies that are initiated by governments, or corporate policy matters, such as Equal Employment Opportunity (EEO) or Affirmative Action (AA), may depend on the pressure of group support within the organization. An organizational culture that facilitates, or otherwise supports, sex discrimination, can render useless, equal employment opportunity policies established by legislation. Women's networks should encourage unions, AA and EEO officers to educate key organizational personnel about the need for change. The exchange of information across women's networks within the organization and across the industry can also save time by not reinventing the wheel, and gaining the momentum for change.

A study of British anti-discrimination policies suggests that even after twenty years of implementation, the political alliance between professional EEO officers, personnel management professionals, and trade unionists is necessary for a grievance brought under the Act to be successfully addressed.

However, it is worth noting that being a woman, and having concern for traditional women's issues, are not synonymous. Support for both women and for their concerns varies among women political leaders. Both Norway's Brundtland, who appointed eight women in her 19-member cabinet, and Ireland's Mary Robinson, who was elected on a social consciousness platform, have consistently supported women's concerns. In contrast, Britain's Margaret Thatcher was accused by female MPs of being unsympathetic to women's progress. Not that political affiliation has anything to do with it, for the *Mail on Sunday* (30 November 1997) catalogues similar accusations against Labour's Social Security Secretary, Harriet Harman, planning to cut benefits to single mothers, 'Harriet has built her reputation on the back of women. It makes me want to spit', are the quoted words of one senior woman MP.[11] Bangladesh's Khaleda Zia has been described in the press as 'similarly hostile', and Dominican Republic's Eugenia Charles, Israel's Golda Meir and India's Indira Ghandi are equally considered as showing little interest in feminist issues.

Similarly, in the corporate world, there are endless examples of successful female executives who seemingly do not promote the advancement of other women. The *Fortune* 17 December 1990 article about Marion Sandler, who with her husband Herb, runs Golden West Financial in Oakland, California, says that she is less likely to compromise than her husband, when people do not perform to their standards.[12] While her husband describes himself as 'soft', both describe themselves as 'organized' and 'results-oriented', and 'call the notion of males and females having or displaying separate management styles, nonsense'.[13]

Use of diversity audits

In addition to the various developmental strategies outlined, additional attention may need to be given to how attitudes are shaping and changing in the organization, particularly in the area of discrimination. On this basis, it may be necessary to audit the cultural assumptions prevalent in the organization, in order to gauge the success of programmes and policies instituted to combat discrimination. An audit provides information on the degree to which patterns of behaviour have become institutionalized into the fabric of the organization. Equally, an audit can highlight the degree to which certain assumptions concerning appropriate behaviour are ingrained in key people in the organization. An additional benefit of audits is that they can pinpoint self-selection in recruitment practices, whereby senior management make key appointments of people who replicate senior management's values and behaviours in the organization.

Inevitably, a diveristy audit needs to include an appraisal of organizational leadership. Studies have shown that organization processes and structures are simply little more than extensions of the self-construct of the leaders in the organization. Their influence pervades the enterprise, setting a tone which, if it requires changing, is most effectively changed, top down.

On this basis, the diversity audit can provide the information necessary to debate change. Diversity audits can promote greater self-awareness that permits a redefinition of behaviours and accepted assumptions in the organization. Senior management may find the audit threatening, as inevitably they will come under the spotlight. What is worth bearing in mind is that an audit really examines whether the capacities of all individuals are being fully tapped or held back by inherent practices in the organization. Through the use of diversity audits, organizations can considerably increase their awareness of the cultural limitations inhibiting and discriminating against their potential effectiveness. Such is the case with NCR (previously National Cash Registers), now a subsidiary of AT&T, who are conducting a diversity audit under the able stewardship of Darryl Strickler. NCR's intention is to take a broad-brush view, examining social issues, gender and ethnicity, as well as business issues. NCR have recognized that if the discomfort of being challenged can be accommodated, the impact of an audit can be resounding and positive.

Key points summary

■ Gender is a much discussed and researched topic in the leadership and management field.
■ Historically, the theme of the dominance of men over women has not been consistently pursued, as has that of appropriate and inappropriate sexual behaviour in the workplace.

■ In contrast, the strongly held twentieth-century view is that discrimination against women exists, promoting the perspective that male executives are unwilling to accept as co-equals their female colleagues.
■ However, due to demographic shifts, the role and importance of women in the workforce in particular, and as a determined force in society in general, is going to become ever-more important.
■ Two key concerns have faced women in employment, the reality of being considered for and attaining promotion to a senior position, (getting there) and the performance challenges and impediments faced once a woman has been appointed to a senior role (got there).

Glass ceiling issues

■ Statistics show that women occupy a small proportion of senior jobs in both private and public sector organizations, and also are paid less than their male counterparts in comparable jobs.
■ The ever-present discrimination against women is identified as having five sources: obvious discrimination, women being different to men, demographic influence, different response patterns to different contexts, and being driven by the status quo.
■ Obvious discrimination refers to visible forms of harassment, often sexual in nature, which seem to be on the increase. The problem is reaching such proportions that insurance companies are offering guidelines to client organizations on the human resources practices to introduce into their company, in order to limit potential liability, in addition to offering insurance cover.
■ 'Women-different-from-men' discrimination is identified as potentially occurring in the selection process for jobs, in the interpretation of psychological tests, in the giving of feedback, and in the interpretation of 'relevant' behaviours within assessment centre settings.
■ In terms of context, two demographics, location and sector, seem to be influential in women's choice of employer, and of type of work (part-time/full-time/temporary). Taking into account family circumstances, husband's job, and quality of life considerations, women have been more constrained in their choice of job or personal development (education, evening classes) by these factors.
■ The different patterns of communication between women and men, such as being facilitative as opposed to authoritative, being reassuring as opposed to forceful, not understanding politics, are considered to be more supportive of women in flatter, devolved organizations, as opposed to centrarchies, which supposedly suit men more.
■ Discrimination is also considered to exist in organizations that have developed a 'strong' culture, i.e. one that can be resistant to change.

Performance as leaders

■ One school of thought equates 'getting there' with 'got there', in that women are seen as being disadvantaged in terms of career progress, and equally prejudiced against once in a senior role, due to differences of values, attitude and behaviour. The results of particular studies emphasize this point, in that women, once in senior positions, are identified as being more supportive, service driven, team oriented, soft spoken, democratic, using feelings more than men, which causes them to be disadvantaged in the 'tougher' world of male senior executives.

■ In contrast, the Cranfield studies identify very few differences between males and females who hold senior roles. Chapter 7 highlights significant demographic differences, other than gender, that influence personal and organizational performance.

■ Case studies of female business, public sector and political leaders, highlight substantial differences of attitude, behaviour and sympathy between women and their attitude towards women's issues.

■ The case studies discussed in the chapter highlight that most women leaders are well educated. Equally, the case studies emphasize that a far higher proportion of women are single, divorced or widowed, than men in comparable positions.

Developing women leaders

■ Five avenues for the development of women, so that they may successfully command positions of responsibility, are identified: promoting diversity capability in the organization, introducing codes of conduct, management education and training, mobilizing women in organizations, and using diversity audits.

■ Promoting a diversity capability in organizations to address and overcome issues of gender, ethnicity, minority or other discrimination, can be pursued through a corporate-wide programme, championed by the centre, through the pursuit of equality programmes (such as affirmative action), through the legitimizing of local differences, and through a continuous learning strategy. Each of these approaches has its own advantages and disadvantages and needs to be balanced against the overall demands of the organization, and the particular contexts in which reform is being driven.

■ Codes of conduct establish benchmarks for best practice, and especially highlight the behaviours and attitudes that are undesired and will not be tolerated in the place of work. Codes of conduct display that organizations are addressing their work-related problems by providing guidelines for people as to appropriate behaviour.

■ Management education and training can be applied as gender specific, mixed, or focused towards addressing particular issues, or towards enhancing particular skills and capabilities. The choice of which strategy to pursue is dependent on the views of the key decision makers in the organization, in response to the training and development requirements of the organization.

■ Mobilizing women in the organization is considered an additional strategy to improving the position of women. Lobbying, and promoting women's issues through networks and alliances are often-used mechanisms that can propagate change.

■ Similar to internal organizational surveys, diversity audits are recommended as information gathering exercises and data feedback mechanisms, which identify the changes that need to be made, encourage debate and promulgate an internal climate of wishing to improve the present circumstances.

Notes

1   Fireman (1990:115)
2   Maremont, M. and Saseen, J.A. (1996) 'Abuse of Power', *Business Week*, 13 May, pp. 86–98.
3   The following three sections are adapted from the work of Beverley Alimo-Metcalfe (1994).
4   The questions of 'how' and 'what' are attributed to Marshall and McLean (1985).
5   Quote from Marshall (1993:317).
6   Adapted from Bennis (1989:207–8).
7   Quoted from Bennis (1989:136).
8   Quoted from Bennis (1989:137).
9   Quoted from Benn (1995:A4).
10 Adapted from Korac-Kakabadse and Kouzmin (1997).
11 Quote from Duckworth (1997:6).
12 Quote from Fireman (1990:116).
13 Ibid.

Further reading

For further information on 'career ceilings', see Marshall (1993) and Gutek (1989), glass ceiling (Hede and Ralston, 1994), protective shield (Burton, 1992), the greasy pole (Carmody, 1992) and the concept of the concrete ceiling, see Korac-Boisvert and Kouzmin (1995). In terms of the what and how of 'getting there', see Marshall and McLean (1985). For an analysis of why women are unlikely to accept the status quo, read Vinnicombe and Colwill (1995).

For further information on the discrimination and the holding back of women, see Fireman (1990), in the areas of pay (Howard, 1994) and managerial positions (US General Accounting Office, 1991; UK Foreign and Commonwealth Office, 1993; Australian Bureau of Statistics (ABS), 1993), and for examples of the computer industry (Didio, 1996, which refers to the Kim Clancy statement). For further information on the demographic position of women in the workplace, read US Department of Commerce, Bureau of the Census (1992a; 1992b), US Merit Systems Protection Board (1992), Burrell (1984), Sinclair (1994), Still *et al.* (1994), Statistics Canada (1993), Treasury Board of Canada (1994) and The Hansard Society for Parliamentary Government (1990).

For perspectives on fighting conscious discrimination read Lawn-Day and Ballard (1996); and for the ICN Pharmaceuticals case, read Byrnes (1996), Mitsubishi Motors USA (Elstrom and Brull, 1996); Pizza Hut (Alger and Flanagan, 1996b); for Astra, read Maremont (1996) and Maremont and Saseen (1996); for increases in sexual harassment suits, see Anonymous (1996a); for sexual harassment in the US armed forces, see Gleick (1996) and the fact that codes of practice are necessary for employers to insure themselves against sexual harassment cases, see Anonymous (1996b), Anonymous (1996c) Anonymous (1996d) and Anonymous 1996e). For an overview of sexual harassment cases, read Updike and Holstein (1996) and Laurie (1996).

For further information on unintended discrimination against women, such as selection processes, see Alimo-Metcalfe (1994), for psychological testing, see Rizzo and Mendez (1990) and on the influence of demographics, see (Linz, 1996).

For other forms of discrimination, such as sensitivity to non-verbal communication, especially over assessment centres, see (Tannen, 1992), the fact women are more suited to flatter organizations, see Rosener (1990), and the fact that women are at a disadvantage in political environments, see Marshall and McLean (1985). For further information on the human resources study of tone of voice, questions asked and interviewer expectations mentioned in the chapter, see Martinez (1996).

For views concerning the performance of women, once they reach positions of responsibility, see Ehrenreich, *et al.* (1986), and Korac-Kakabadse and Korac-Kakabadse (1998) and Kakabadse and Myers (1996). For case studies of particular women leaders, see World Almanac (1994), the *Europa World Year Book* (1994), International Who's Who (1997–98), Australian Department of the Parliamentary Library (1994), Benn (1995), Bennis (1989), Washington Post Service (1996). For further information on the Harriet Harman case, read Duckworth (1997), and for the case analyses of seven women at the top of business organizations, see Sellers (1996). For women in politics see Finaly (1994), Adler (1995) and *The Europa World Year Book*, 35th edition (Europa, 1994).

For references to pursue in the area of segregation, see Davidson and Cooper (1992).

For an examination of how to develop management skills, see Thomas and Ely (1996) and on how to prevent the organization from being caught between sexual harassment lawsuits and wrongful dismissal law suits, see Alger and Flanagan (1996a, 1996c).

For further reading on the management education and training, see Bullard and Wright (1993). For further information on networking, see Genovese (1993); and on political activity in terms of lobbying and learning to wield greater power and influence, see Dickey (1994).

An interesting text to pursue on conducting diversity audits and feedback exercises is Korac-Boisvert and Kouzmin (1995).

CHAPTER 8

Seven Sides to Great Leaders

Case analysis

Patricia Vaz

Patricia Vaz was appointed to the position of British Telecom's (BT) Director of Supply Management in January 1996. Her responsibilities cover procurement for BT, and logistics, warehousing and distribution. The job is enormous in its scope and powerful in terms of its impact on the organization. Her budget is very close to £5 billion per annum. Further, she is accountable for two and a half thousand people. Patricia Vaz oversees a spending programme that is larger than any other civil organization in the UK, as she manages purchasing for the whole BT group, including overseas activities. She is equally responsible for one of the biggest distribution fleets (vans, cars) in the country, as well as seven warehouses. She is the only female director in the BT top team, and as a woman, is held up as a role model of success for other women. She is courted by the press, as shown recently by the more popular journals, such as *Fastrack*, who exclusively featured her in their winter 1996 issue. Her dazzling achievements hide an interesting tale, rooted in humble beginnings.

Leaving school with one 'A' level, she shortly married and by the age of 19 was living in a one-bedroom flat with a husband and a new-born baby:

> After a couple of years, when my baby was very young, I went back to work and worked for six years with the printing unions [Federation of Printing Unions] in an administrative capacity – I enjoyed the job tremendously.

Unfortunately, her career in the trade union movement was short lived, as the amalgamation and nationalization of the unions meant that the Federation was no longer required:

So they disbanded the Federation and I was made redundant, which was rather a shock because I had just started to get used to the money. So I had to quickly find another job and I decided I would join BT, as a clerical officer. Because they (BT) were so big, I had a clear idea they were right for me, as I did not wish to become redundant again.

In her opinion, she, 'joined a tremendous organization. I needed a big organization that would give me the opportunity to work my way into a career. And that, for the last 22 years, is what she has been doing, working her way across and up the BT organization. She has experience of numerous functions in BT, network design, marketing, managing a sales team, and engineering. A particular feature of Patricia Vaz is that she learns quickly. In order to become a sales manager, she needed a driving licence, but did not know how to drive. With the help of her colleagues, she learned to drive in a yellow van, in three days, passed her driving test, but admits that two days later, the van had to be brought in for repair, as she had not been taught how to park. Patricia applied the same principles of determination to succeed, to engineering and computers, and through part-time education and correspondence courses, she was able to obtain her professional qualifications in these areas. From a secretary, to a £5-a-week network planner, to an area manager overseeing 4000 engineers, and having to cope with a national strike, and a hurricane that hit the Tunbridge Wells area, where she was put in charge of BT payphones, to now a main board director.

Her turn around of BT payphones is impressive. Defined as part of BT's social obligation, and with a privatized BT putting enormous effort into focusing on core business performance, Patricia Vaz not only had to do something about a neglected service, but also to change the mindset of her colleagues. For her, payphones held the significance of being the 'shop window' of the company. UK and foreign customers use payphones daily, and instinctively judge the company accordingly. With only 77,000 payphones servicing a population of 56 million, and with only 72 per cent of these in working order on any one day, Patricia Vaz set about improving profitability and quality.

Payphones' track record (%)

	1987	1990	1995
Faults per box	32	15	11
Serviceability	72	95	96
Customer dissatisfaction	33	9	negligible
Population	77,000	97,000	130,000
Profit	Unheard of	(£70m)	£60m

they [payphones] got to a point in 1988 where they were really an image of disaster for the company and all the good work we were doing everywhere was being destroyed by the media attention on the state of payphones.

Patricia Vaz initially focused on the fault rate. At the time, this was 32 per mechanism. She contracted for considerable improvements from the equipment suppliers and equally, through good teamwork, substantially improved her engineers' track record of time to detect and respond to faults. She extended the concept of team-work to the whole of the BT corporation, when she urged everyone in the company, from the Chairman down, to check their local payphones on their way to work, and report faults immediately. She mobilized 240,000 people overnight to act as the faults 'eyes and ears' of BT. From there, Patricia Vaz introduced further modernization with the introduction of new payphone units and new, cleaner, easier to enter, all-round visibility kiosks. On top of additional innovations, she established a security enhancement team, which worked closely with BT's Investigation Branch, police forces and magistrates, in an effort to curb criminal acts on payphones. With improved detection and a comprehensive educational programme for police, schools and magistrates, a 60 per cent fall in the level of crime against payphones and a 400 per cent rise in arrests, was the end result. She left the payphones business £60 million in the black, increased the number of payphones to 130,000, improved serviceability so that 90 per cent of payphones were operational on any one day, and reduced costs by slimming down a workforce of just under 4000, to 2780. She and her team were awarded the Chairman's Quality award for 1994.

In her current role, she is rationalizing the warehousing and distribution facilities, whereby she expects to reduce a 2500 workforce to 1000 people. She is currently pondering how to manage procurement with the proposed MCI merger with BT (subsequently not realized).

From secretary to main board director, over a period of 22 years, in one of the world's largest and most innovative telecommunications companies, her capabilities and achievements were recognized when she was selected the UK's Business Woman of the Year for 1994.

There is little doubt that Patricia Vaz is a remarkable individual. Quickly apparent is her determination, clarity of view and long-term focus. She is clear and precise in her analysis of circumstances, and focused and unambivalent in her vision. She learns quickly and is not fearful of asking for help. She exerts similar fortitude in dialogue. For her, effective team-work is not just co-operation, but openness, trustworthiness, and high quality dialogue. She is quite clear that respect for others is not to speak in platitudes, as people are capable of thinking for themselves, and hence, being honest and courageous makes for positive collegiate relationships. In conjunction with viewing the broader scene, Patricia Vaz emphasizes that an additional aspect of sound leadership is 'keeping a finger on the pulse'. Attention to detail on activities and projects is matched by equal care with relationships, and knowledge of the people around her. Patricia Vaz exhibits sound visioning, a robustness towards surfacing issues, a flair to engage others in dialogue and communication, an attention to detail, an infectious passion and enthusiasm for success, a willingness and belief in team-work, and an insightful perspective of context, as she has seen and lived the numerous parts of BT for the last 22 years. Patricia Vaz displays the fundamental capabilities of a high-performing discretionary leader, clear as to what she wants, determined to achieve, sensitive in her approach, and mindful and knowledgeable of circumstances.

Makings of leaders

Three particular avenues of enquiry, searching for what great leaders do and why, have dominated thinking for the last 70 years. The search has been on first to identify, the desired leadership attributes that make for outstanding performance (partly drawing from the 'leaders are born' camp); second, clarify the key leadership tasks, so that from that understanding will emerge those qualities that will successfully fulfil the requirements of leadership; third, understand the demands of the leadership role, so that the leader can better appreciate what attributes and qualities are desired in order to perform effectively.

The 'key leadership attributes' concept has dominated thinking and research in the quest for those mystical qualities. However, the results of such endeavour portray a scatter of skills, attributes and qualities presumed to project effective leadership, some of which range from supposedly deeper, ingrained factors over which an individual has little control (born-with characteristics) to qualities which the individual can nurture, as the person is presumed to be in charge of his/her own destiny (see Table 8.1).

For example, certain authors identify leaders who seem to display a flair for vision and passion to communicate that vision, as attributes that can be traced to childhood (see Chapter 5). Others provide supporting evidence of leaders who do not display any particular strengths in their early life, but through a mindset of continuous learning, as much from mistakes, exhibit an enviable competence as clear- minded leaders with a passion that can inspire people to pursue crucial goals. A case example is Richard Branson, who has been identified as possessing attributes that fall into the 'born with' but also 'totally developed' camps. The Insead

Table 8.1   Leadership attributes

Leaders' attributes	Leaders' attributes
Possess wisdom ■ Life's experiences ■ Deep ■ Background of hardship	Sensitive ■ Sensitive to others before self
Mature ■ Feedback driven ■ Not judgemental ■ Life/not success oriented ■ Strong ethics ■ Always developing	Persistent ■ Disciplined ■ Learned ■ At times needs to be insensitive
Visionary focus ■ Clear ■ Uses judgement ■ Success driven ■ Superhuman ■ Stands out	Consistent ■ Developed ■ Learned on-the-job
Communicator of vision ■ Natural flair ■ Learnt	Reliable/dependable ■ Developed ■ Made into a value
Insightful of 'emotional intelligence' ■ Sensitivity ■ Values non-rational attributes	Positive self-regard ■ Confidence ■ Good news ■ Comes from success ■ Comes from within
Creative ■ Intuitive ■ Spontaneous ■ From childhood ■ Due to knowledge of business/market	Knowledgeable ■ Makes time to learn ■ Enquiring mind
Trust ■ Developed ■ Worked hard to attain	Practical ■ Ability to make things happen

professor, Manfred Kets de Vries, takes a clinical life history analysis of Branson, highlighting qualities that have been present in Branson since childhood. Others emphasize the manner in which Branson developed, that his learning was predominantly on-the-job, in his pursuit of being a life-long entrepreneur.

A similar contrasting view is adopted over the topic of creativity. Certain authors emphasize the need for creative leadership by highlighting those creative leaders who seemed to display intuition and spontaneity from childhood. Others emphasize particular creative acts or contributions from individuals who may not in their early lives, have displayed creative tendencies, but who because of their knowledge of their organization, or the markets with which they are familiar, possess insights into how to tackle particular challenges and improve current ways of operating.

A similar mix of concepts emerges when differentiating leadership tasks from leadership attributes (see Table 8.2). Certain tasks are clearly identified, such as goal setting. Others not so, as the requirement to apply certain leadership attributes in order to achieve particular tasks has become confused with the tasks to be done. In effect, a myriad of overlapping views have emerged as to what leaders need to do, are required to do, how they should go about doing what they have to do, and the qualities necessary for so doing.

One fundamental reason for the overlap of concepts between tasks and attributes, is due to context. In different contexts, different requirements

Table 8.2 Leadership tasks

Creates a vision.	Pioneers' behaviour that reflects key organizational values.
Articulates a vision that empowers and builds. Motivates by communicating and living the vision.	Understands 'formative contexts'.
Exhibits personal commitment to the vision.	Exchanges sensitive information with group, listens to them and communicates clearly with them.
Sets up tough goals in partnership with employees.	Exhibits a passion to be involved in enterprise achievements for their own sake, rather than being reward driven.
Helps people become winners.	Empowers others.
Leads by example.	Responsible for what is being created without the control of compliance.
Creates environment which encourages innovation, new ideas, risk-taking and generates intellectual capital.	Encourages feedback.
Ensures that followers have necessary resources and training to achieve the vision of the organization.	Invests in people.
Influences employees to act in a particular manner and to focus on particular outcomes.	Projects empathy. Understand one's limitations, takes feedback and learns.

exist as to the attributes desired of leaders and the tasks they are required to fulfil. In fact, the never-ending debate is that between concept and context. The concept could be vision, or strategic planning or marketing, but the question is how does that concept fit into the context of a particular organization? The alternative to leadership attributes and tasks in attempting to understand what effective leaders do and how they do it, is that of discretionary leadership.

An underlying assumption of discretionary leadership is that irrespective of the nature and qualities of each person, leaders are only leaders when occupying a leadership role. On this basis, different leaders occupying different roles, each with their distinctly different elements of character, exhibit leadership qualities particular to their circumstances.

From the insightful work originally conducted by Elliot Jacques in his analysis of the Glacier Metal Company, managerial work is categorized as 'prescribed', namely, structured, leaving the individual little room to exercise judgement, and discretionary, whereby considerable judgement is necessary in order for the individual to function effectively in the role. A 'prescribed' role is one in which 51 per cent or more of that management role requires the occupant to pursue and complete tasks and objectives that have already been pre-set. A 'discretionary' role is one where, theoretically, 51 per cent or more of that role is determined by the role occupant. By this distinction, a prescribed role is more of a structured, middle-management job whereas a discretionary role is the leadership role.

The degree of discretion may be planned for in the role and/or driven by the role incumbant's capability to influence and determine the boundaries, responsibilities and accountabilities of his/her role and/or allowed for by the person's boss. Different bosses set different boundaries and responsibility levels according to contextual pressures, their trust in their subordinate, and each individual boss's wishes and desires. On this basis, any one organization may possess a considerable number of discretionary roles within the structure of the organization (see Figure 8.1).

All those individuals who occupy a discretionary leader role, by its nature, need to set boundaries around that role, in order for the leader and those with whom he/she works, to make sense of the role and what is desired to be achieved. The boundary-setting process highlights how the person encompasses within the role, their vision for their function/ department, and their view of the purpose of the organization. For example, a director of human resources (HR) needs to decide the shape of his/her job, the configuration of the function, its overall place and value to the organization, and its contribution to the organization. In making sense of the present nature and the future direction of the job, the individual is also displaying his/her familiarity with the function, its professional HR aspects, and how and whether to integrate with the

Figure 8.1   Discretionary role analysis

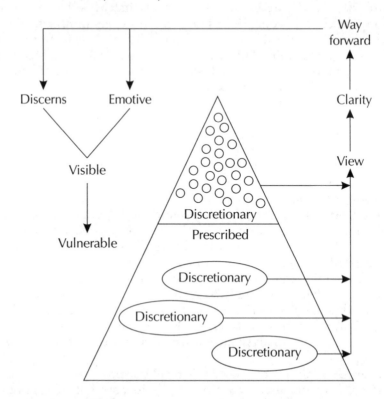

Source: Adapted from Kakabadse (1982)

other support and line functions in the organization. A poor HR director clearly stands out. His/her ability to discern a view on how to move forward, and provide role and functional clarity, is driven by being personnel systems oriented. The person wants, for example, to draft the 'best' appraisal system for the organization. In effect, the individual wants to be an HR manager, but in a director's job.

An alternative would be to take a broader business view of the world, examining the various market and economic forces at play, and from that perspective design an HR department that will provide an added-value service to the company. With the latter interpretation, the individual adopts a business perspective as opposed to the more limited functional view. How long does it take for colleagues to recognize that an individual discerns in a more myopic, middle-management manner, as opposed to a broader strategic way? Probably little more than a few minutes. In a situation where clarity is needed, others quickly recognize the limited or enriched capacity of the person by the way the individual naturally discusses, analyses and projects his/her views as to the way forward.

An R&D (research and development) director, for example, may naturally discern on a broader basis, but equally display that he/she finds pressure difficult to tolerate. For him/her, coping with conflict and antagonism can be a damagingly stressful experience. At meetings, rather than face unpleasantness and indulge in robust debate, he/she gives way on issues. He/she allows him/herself to be browbeaten into adopting a view that he/she instinctively would not have accepted. In effect, the individual, although business broad-minded, displays emotional vulnerability. Another director may display emotional rigidity, while a third shows an openness of approach, a non-hierarchical view of the world, and a non-jealous nature. Hence, those occupying discretionary leader roles not only show their rational side, in terms of how they think, decide and discern between alternatives, but also display their emotive nature – are they robust, weak, pleasant, nasty? As Chapter 6 strongly highlights, people change; they advance, they regress, they learn – although some may even be unaware of the learning that they are experiencing. However, what they are like, at any one point in time, once occupying a discretionary role, shows, especially their emotive and interactive side. Others immediately around, within seconds recognize the person in front of them as, warm and smiling, cold and serious, or a bully. A key feature of occupying a discretionary leader role is that the person is visible. No role protection is provided. Individuals who are so continuously visible, are equally potentially, permanently vulnerable. They are open to comment, criticism, and praise. They exist in a 'goldfish bowl', an experience which can become wearisome and, in extreme circumstances, can lead to a condition of emotional depletion, known as 'burn out' (see Chapter 9).

The number of discretionary roles that exist in an organization theoretically determines the number of visions and ways of operating that can shape, positively or negatively, the future of the organization. The number of discretionary roles that exist varies from one organization to the next, and not all discretionary leader roles need be congregated at the top. Those executives who hold general management positions, namely chairmen, CEOs, directors, managing directors and general managers, are likely to occupy discretionary leader roles, the leadership responsibility difference between them being one of degree. However, lower down the organization, younger, key-client account managers may well occupy discretionary leader roles, shaping the future of the company, not because of their involvement in strategic debate, but because if any one or more key-client account is damaged, the loss in revenue and the damage to external credibility, could severely undermine the image of the corporation. Discretionary leaders from lower down the organization influence strategic direction more by the mistakes they make (losing clients), or by their leaving and taking key-client accounts to a competitor (see Figure 8.1). They impact strategy, but more from a negative perspective.

By adopting a discretionary role analysis to leadership, identifying best practice involves examining the interactions among the leaders of the organization. How different leaders work and relate together in order to progress fruitfully and advance their organization, can determine the success or failure of the organization. Hence, in providing best practice recommendations for the effective leadership of private and public sector organizations requires that attention be given to individual and group-related behaviour. Towards this end, seven areas of capability for enhancing the performance of discretionary leaders are identified. The seven sides to great leaders are:

1 conviction to craft the future
2 strength to surface sentiments
3 wisdom for pathways through paradox
4 flair to engage through dialogue
5 discipline to communicate
6 passion for results
7 staying power

The seven areas of capability are neither exclusive nor sequential. Leaders are likely to call upon their seven sides in any number and combination in order to address the challenges they face. In so doing, leaders will spring from being transformational to being transactional, and to being transformational once more, with each of the seven sides displaying elements of both the transactional and transformational. How the combinations are brought together, for what purpose, and then how one or more of the seven sides is exercised, distinguishes the outstanding leader from the mediocre.

Conviction to craft the future

Well, broadly speaking, the job of the CEO of a major corporation is primarily to give strategic direction to the company, not short term fire-fighting, it is a long term directional responsibility. Obviously, it breaks down into a series of sub-components which include a lot of short termism in the context of achieving goals within given time frames – the discipline of American finance, the responsibility of reporting on a quarterly basis, which introduces a certain short termism in the way a lot of American corporations operate . . . we are all concerned about our stockmarket rating and the value of our shares . . . so you study the strategy for your corporation and then sustain it in highly volatile capital markets with a vigilant press and an extremely inquisitive investment community (Dr Tony O'Reilly, Chairman of the Board, H. J. Heinz Co.).

I think the number 1 issue for us is to update our vision of what we want to do. We are in the UK, a group of regional businesses that need to become much more of a UK business and the initial factor is getting everybody to understand what it is that we are trying to achieve. Now, I think we are a long way down that track. What we have done now is to encapsulate the idea in a phrase we call 'creating the advisory firm', and what that means is essentially, we should be setting out the parameters . . . We have got to get a lot more focused than we have in the past and go for greater depth of quality in our business and our services! (Colin Sharman, UK Senior Partner, KPMG).

Tony O'Reilly and Colin Sharman highlight determining future direction as a prime requirement for them, as leaders, to apply and pursue in their role. Once in a position of strategic responsibility, leaders are required to form a view as to the current and future shape of the organization. Certain top managers foresee, and desire, considerable changes; others, not so. The views formed would be an expression of the desired shape and texture of the organization, taking into account the degree of vulnerability of the corporation and its operating businesses, and also how to address the oncoming challenges. Not all of the leaders may agree with each other in terms of what to do and how to do it. Often only in retrospect, do they recognize who was more right or more wrong in their pursuit. Equally, different leaders use different terms to describe their crafting and forging of the future. Top managers' views may be expressed under the banner of terms such as vision, mission, strategic direction. Certain writers and leaders sharply distinguish between 'vision' and 'mission', the former emphasizing direction and the latter highlighting identity, namely what the organization stands for. Some use the terms of vision and mission the other way round, while others scoff at the idea of even trying to distinguish between the two. However, virtually all would agree with Tony O'Reilly and Colin Sharman, that promoting a shared view concerning clarity of direction and purpose is of paramount importance for the leader to establish. For the purposes of brevity, the term 'vision' is used in this chapter to denote longer-term, future direction.

The Cranfield surveys identify that generating and promoting a cohesive and shared view of the future among the leadership of the organization, is difficult to achieve (see Chapter 6 for further details of the Cranfield survey).

One of the key questions asked in the private sector, National Health Service (NHS) and Australian Public Service (APS) surveys was, 'Do the members of the Senior Executive (President/Chairman/CEOs/MDs/EDs/Directors/GMs/SESs/SOs)[1] hold different views as to the future direction of the organization?' (see Table 8.3).

The greatest discrepancy occurs among top Australian civil servants, who consider that the members of the senior management group hold

Table 8.3 Fundamentally different views concerning the direction of the organization (%)

	Japan	UK	France	Ireland	Germany	Sweden
Yes %	23	30	39	48	32	20

	Spain	Austria	Finland	USA	China	Hong Kong	NHS Top Team	Board	APS
Yes %	40	31	25	39	33	42	20	21	56

Source: Adapted from Kakabadse *et al.*, (1996) and also Korac-Kakabadse *et al.*, (1998); Korac-Kakabadse and Korac-Kakabadse (1997); Korac-Kakabadse and Korac-Kakabadse (1998).

fundamentally different views as to the shape and nature of the APS in general, of their departments, and in particular the future pathways that should be pursued. Of the NHS Trust organizations, 20 per cent of the executive team members and 21 per cent of the majority non-executive Board members highlight that fundamentally different views on the vision, future direction and shape of the organization are held by members of their respective groups. Of the private sector respondents, the Irish, Spanish and French top managers compare with such a diversity of view. The Swedish and Japanese respondents highlight the least difference of view concerning strategic direction at senior management level.

Yet the downside to not pursuing a coherent and shared vision is equally clear to leaders and managers. From both the surveys and from separate consultancy assignments conducted by the team members of the Cranfield International Management Development Centre, managers were able to relate to the problems awaiting a company that did not clarify its mission, vision and longer-term ways forward. The following concerns are highlighted as likely to emerge in an organization that lacks any clear or specific vision:[2]

■ *Organizational chaos.* In the view of numerous senior managers, staff and lower level management expect their bosses to provide a definitive view of the organization's future. In the absence of such clarity, direction is provided by each individual senior manager guessing top management's vision, or promoting his/her own view of the future, and leading his/her own department or division to achieve specific goals which fit with the manager's particular vision. Such circumstances lead to splits, dissension and chaos. From an organizational point of view, splits of vision lead to the pursuit of poorly, or at least contradictory, thought-through goals, and limited application of resources for the attainment of results.

■ *Short-term orientation*. Within such a context, the only common denominator shared among the leaders of the organization is the achievement of results, making the sustainment of competitive advantage problematic, as most of the top management have become short-term oriented.

■ *Paradoxical empowerment*. For those in middle management roles, the communication of contradictory messages by upper management leads to confusion and a lack of willingness freely to apply themselves to motivation and challenge. After all, why bother doing what senior management wants, when the expectation is that a different view will be communicated with a different line to pursue in the very near future? The feeling of middle management could be, 'whatever I do is meaningless'. Not surprisingly, the attitude that middle management can adopt is 'tomorrow it will all go away and something new will take its place'. At the same time, certain middle managers will use such contradictions as an opportunity to manipulate the circumstances, or their own bosses, to their own advantage. The more proactive of such managers are likely to pursue their own line of argument and try to establish an identity for their unit which suits them.

■ *In-fighting*. Eventually, the leadership of the organization will have to choose between the competing logics being pursued. As a result, strongly promoting one's view may lead to substantial 'in-fighting', resulting in the departure of one or more key managers. The morale of the rest of staff and management in the organization could deteriorate even further, leading to the departure of key staff, and damaging the capacity of the organization to do business.

To generate a shared vision is recognized as vital, just as the damage of not doing so is obvious. Despite such insight, poor visioning and a lack of shared vision are identified in the survey as commonplace weaknesses in organizational life, with half of the sample of the Australian federal level civil service reporting that it is deeply split. Understandably, managers, due to uncertainty and instability having become key factors of everyday life, may say that visioning, as a concept of the long term, is unrealistic and a luxury. However, that is different from the senior managers of the organization reporting that they are pursuing a different line to their colleagues. Such perspectives place organizations in a dangerous loop, for the reasons presented above. In order to prevent short-termism, in-fighting and an inability to sustain advantage for any length of time, the need for negotiating a meaningful shared vision has become ever more crucial.

Steps to quality visioning

The following four steps towards effectively generating a meaningful vision have been identified from research: conviction; involve all of the 'top team'; nurture a feedback environment; establish a platform for visioning.

Conviction

A: What we are finding difficult is, surprisingly, some of the intellectual arguments about fit into the 'advisory firm' – does audit fit in? . . . So there are one or two intellectual gymnastics going around. There is confusion, at this stage, as to what the 'advisory firm' means – is it an advertising strap line or a description of the firm? People get hung up on that and we have got to work our way through the process. We will have more difficulty with the developing parts of the KPMG practice, than we will with the mature ones. Those of us who are in the mature markets, where we are sitting on market shares of 20+%, are well aware of the need to differentiate and the need to improve our margins . . . If you are out in the Pacific Rim or in India, and are in a developing practice, the tendency would be to grab anything you can to build the base quickly and that is where we will have to be very careful . . .'

Q: And was that a difficult process, namely clarifying fit and focus?

A: Very difficult, yes . . . Basically, a year ago I went to the Executive Committee and said, 'you have got to bite the bullet', which is to decide what sort of consulting practice we want worldwide, rather than worry about transferring technology and bits and pieces. Let's sit down and say what we want as a consultancy practice, and then figure out how to build it, and the only way we can do that is on a global basis.

(Colin Sharman, KPMG, 1994.)

Colin Sharman is clear. He knows what he wants; he recognizes the reality of the external market and the internal dynamics of KPMG, and confronts these issues. What clearly emerges from conversation with him, is his strength of conviction.

Visioning involves projecting into the future, but a future of uncertainty. Strong conviction is necessary from the leadership in terms of their expectations, bearing in mind the variety of imponderables facing the organization. Hence, one element of visioning is to have an underlying conviction that one's views concerning the future and best requirements for the organization, are the most appropriate views to hold under the current circumstances. Therefore, vision becomes a kind of organizational ambition, namely a strength of purpose that is beyond personal ambition.

Involve all of the 'top team'

Unlike a middle management team, which is fundamentally a unit for the achievement of particular tasks or objectives, a senior management team is a group of individuals brought together for the purpose of clarifying direction, as much through debate, whereby exploration, planning, offering recommendations, and decision-making are essential processes requiring participation. As already stated, the number of individuals in the organization occupying roles with a high discretionary content could vary from 15, 20, 60 or even 120 persons, making the 'top team' people who occupy discretionary leader roles and who, in turn, may be members of multiple groups or committees. Hence, who is and is not in the overall 'top team' is a crucial question to answer.[3]

In order to involve all of the top team, consideration needs to be given to the array of discretionary roles, and the mode and quality of communication that would bind together a potentially disparate group. The top team may consist solely of the official senior executive group (executive/management committee) of the corporation. However, the top team may also include the senior executive group and a number of interlinking committees, on which sit certain of the heads of the operating businesses, corporate centre directors, and certain of the operating businesses' functional directors. A top team could involve all of the above mentioned plus those executive and non-executive directors sitting on subsidiary boards. If the corporate centre top team treats the senior managers of the subsidiaries or operating businesses as middle managers, then these senior managers are going to respond negatively to the centre's direction and requirements. On this basis, one crucial aspect of visioning is to be clear as to who are and who are not members of the 'top team', and treat them with the respect that their position merits. Treating people with respect helps individuals differentiate organizational ambition from personal ambition. Because senior managers feel a part of a greater whole, they are more able to differentiate between what they desire and what is best for the organization, a phenomenon which 20–50 per cent of the enterprises reported in Table 8.3 found impossible to achieve!

Nurture a feedback environment[4]

Having recognized those who are involved in top team work, promoting appropriate channels of communication and involvement, in order to accommodate the expression of the views driving the varied agendas of each of the senior managers within the structure, is the vital next step.

Allowing for a continuous flow of opinions upwards, downwards and across the organization is tantamount to valuing openness of comment as a way of life. Hence, in order to minimize the degree of dysfunctionality in the organization, management's ability to invite feedback is crucial to the effective running of the enterprise. The skill is to invite and receive well, both positive and negative feedback. Positive feedback is easy to handle. Inviting and appropriately responding to more critical/negative feedback, is far more difficult, as what may be offered, may be personally hurtful to any one or more senior managers. However, if managers unduly display their discomfort or displeasure upon receiving feedback, then it is unlikely to be given, and hence concerns remain unspoken.

In order to promote a more effective feedback climate, particular consideration needs to be given to the degree of openness and robustness of relationships among the managers in the organization. Openness is achieved through a consistency of behaviour which promotes effective communication, such as walking the floor, making oneself available to be with others in order to receive comment from these others, or even attending social events, lunches, dinners, or out-of-work activities. It is the consistency and the discipline applied to adopting behaviour that promotes more open relationships that are crucial to the generation of a robustness of relationship.

To promote consistency, it is first necessary to recognize the need for a feedback relationship. Recognizing and then actioning such a need provides the opportunity to grow the relationship, which allows for views and opinions to be given more freely. By enhancing the capability of people to comment as they desire, and by promoting a pattern of behaviour that supports such processes, differences between people are teased out and are used positively. In this way, diversity contributes to a team's development. Obviously, functional and operational differences are easier to surface than longer term strategic issues, as the solutions to problems are more readily identified. However, through a consistent promotion of feedback, greater commonality of vision may emerge.

Promoting a commonality of vision by highlighting differences between each of the key managers, and then working through the differences by themselves or with the assistance of a third party, naturally takes longer, and is a more sensitive process to manage.

Establish a platform for visioning

Having worked on the processes for enhancing conversation about, and contribution to the process of direction setting, senior management are more prepared for participation in the process of generating a workable vision. However, top teams do not have to first establish a positive dialogue before starting. The process of learning to talk to each other can be the 'kick off' for more positive dialogue, as then the active involvement of the members of the top team is required. Working on the processes as well as the vision, places senior management in a multi-level learning process, learning to give positive feedback within a team, learning to make something out of that feedback, learning to pursue collective visioning, learning to make collective strategic decisions, and learning to change and adapt their influencing behaviour to become consistent with the emerging shared vision. Ironically, the visioning process itself is potentially a way to enhance the quality of interaction between team members, irrespective of whether or not a shared view for the future emerges.

Hence, through sound dialogue on visioning, a supportive context is generated. However, if a supportive context is not forthcoming, or if working relationships become too inconsistent, or if opposite or contradictory values are displayed, then teams have no real, positive, shared experience of change. In such an environment people will lack trust in each other, and no sustainable or effective vision is likely to emerge. Attempting to generate a meaningful, shared vision under such circumstances is likely to lead to gamesmanship, which in turn is likely to generate instability and a more chaotic situation. Hence, part of growing a sound basis (platform) for visioning, is to nurture and maintain a supportive context.

The second element to building a common platform, is to create a common experience of change and thereby establish, or re-establish, satisfactory milestones concerning progress during phases of change. Once a common and positive experience of change has been achieved, people are more likely and willing to look together to the future.

The third part to creating a sound platform, is to establish a common language. The logic of this step is to provide a positive experience of changing elements of the present, before starting to influence the future! Focusing and acting on the potential in the here-and-now will generate new energy, new beliefs and a new motivation to address the future and thereby enhance the desire to change. Today's positive experiences contribute to influencing the future, and to enter into such a mindset senior managers need to find ways to change some elements of the present. The past, as the future, is in the present. Instinctively, every leader knows that. However, most decision makers seem to act according to a linear concept of time – 'we have to carry the past with us into the future!' What is unfortunate is that in so many cases, the past is experienced as an unpleasant burden, limiting the exploration of new possibilities. The visioning process gives the broader top team the chance to find a new balance by creating a process whereby a non-linear view of time can be adopted – 'We have found new ways to behave through deciding now what we want to be tomorrow!'

From thereon in, many ways exist for a platform to emerge. It is possible to create a global platform for the whole organization, or to build first an experimental or local platform in a department, as a test site for the rest of the organization. Whichever alternative is pursued, it is the CEO's and senior management's responsibility to display and to act in the way they have pronounced. Growing a supportive environment, a common language at the top, and a common experience of change, a positive communication of the vision is enhanced throughout the organization. The basis for visioning needs then to be consistently applied in order to avoid a 'one shot exercise'. The platform must be stabilized so that all those involved in the organization can learn from their new experiences.

Strength to surface sentiments

Unfortunately, a considerable number of top teams have started a visioning process only to discover they have no reliable starting point in their current context. Their context may be too unstable and not ready to support the process. The end result may be that no meaningful vision emerges. Alternatively, through probing and more significant conversation, deep splits appear in the top team on issues of vision. On a less negative note, the team may emerge with new ways of working which go towards creating a workable platform, for example, the creation of a management charter, yet despite some headway, no shared vision emerges.

Such was the case with a certain UK retailer. A new CEO was appointed who, upon examination of the company's portfolio, decided to divest the more unprofitable businesses, soon after his entrance into the organization. The surviving functional and operating business directors reacted by being defensive at meetings, arguing on behalf of their part of the business and seemingly ignoring the CEO's initiatives to integrate the remaining businesses, and provide the organization with a much improved corporate profile. Over a period of a few months, the tension at Board meetings worsened, with the CEO increasingly pronouncing his dissatisfaction with the meetings and the lack of progress on corporate initiatives. The situation came to a head shortly after the appointment of a Group Marketing Director, a new role to the organization, which the CEO had pushed through the Board. Previously, marketing had been the responsibility of each of the business heads, but according to the CEO, no progress had been made in properly identifying and jointly pursuing a strategy for group marketing. Shortly after the appointment of the Group Marketing Director, one of the business heads stated at one of the monthly board meetings:

> We weren't really on board with this role! We don't know what group marketing is all about. We are all separate businesses and marketing has always been best done within the businesses.

The conversation became strained and tense. The CEO decided to confront the situation:

> Look, not just about group marketing, but about anything – whenever we turn up to meetings I feel as if I am the only one who is taking on a corporate view and yet we are all corporate directors. We are a

corporate Board. You seem to treat me as the enemy! I get the feeling I am dealing with a bunch of Scottish shop stewards – a bunch of convenors, out to screw management. Is this true or am I off the wall?

After a few silent moments, the various Board members expressed their feelings of negativity towards the changes in the group, their own feelings of insecurity as to whether they would survive, and the ever-increasing centralization seriously impinging on their discretion. What equally emerged was their admiration for the CEO, for his courage in taking the tough decisions, and for redirecting the Group to the path of profitability. Aside from their own futures, they highlighted their displeasure as to what was happening to the organization in terms of the undermining of a positive culture, and the discarding of good people. This airing of views led to a far more fruitful debate over a period of two months, whereby the confidence of each of the directors to speak his/her mind increased, and the group felt more able to set the basis of a corporate mission statement, and to identify the parameters of the group's corporate strategy.

The case underpins, especially in change circumstances, the need to surface the deeply held philosophies of the top managers of a corporation (see Figure 8.2). The directors of this UK retailer discovered the degree of difference in the deeply held philosophies and sentiments that each held, and how substantially that influenced their views about each other, the strategic process upon which they had embarked, their view of the future of their organization, and their current manner of interaction.

The experience of the directors of the UK retailer is commonplace. In determining a way forward for that part of the organization for which the discretionary leader is accountable, the individual will display his/her deeper-seated sentiments, in essence, his/her philosophy concerning life, and the way life should be conducted in the enterprise. In identifying what the individual considers an appropriate way forward for his/her part of the organization, or for the organization as a whole, how people on a daily basis should live that mission, is equally exhibited. Certain of the deeply held sentiments contrast with each other and when expressed, generate tension, as their life and work style implications appear to be incompatible. From observation and experience, six dichotomous sentiments, have been identified.

Citizen versus mercenary

Senior managers who hold 'citizen' sentiments display a concern for nurturing a spirit of community within the organization. They promote deeply held, shared values concerning how to behave towards one another, how to care for and support each other, and how to promote long-term employment and security for the organization's employees.

Figure 8.2 Dichotomy of sentiments

Citizen		Mercenary
	vs	
■ Community		■ Get rich
■ Shared values		■ Short term

Convenor		Executive
	vs	
■ My patch		■ Shared accountability
■ Defend/attack		■ Corporate loyalty

Achiever		Listener
	vs	
■ Out there		■ In here
■ Drive for success		■ Supportive

Prescriber		Mentor
	vs	
■ Work for		■ Work with
■ Command		■ Patience

Rationalist		Contextualist
	vs	
■ Context resistent		■ Context driven
■ Logical		■ Harmony

Forgiveness seeker		Permission seeker
	vs	
■ Do, then see		■ See, then do
■ Distaste for protocol		■ Driven by protocol

'Citizens' assume trust, in the sense of expecting colleagues and subordinates also to express similar needs of trust in the conduct of their relationships. Trust is shared, as the values that predominate within a given context provide the unspoken parameters within which people operate. The 'citizens'' primary concerns are with people, in preference to revenues, costs and infrastructures.

In contrast, 'mercenaries' hold strong inclinations to 'get rich'. The orientation of the mercenary is short term. Increase the share price, promote the company brand, and move up and out of the organization having achieved one's objectives, paying little attention to the repercussions of one's actions on others. The mercenaries' tactics are, sell more and reduce overheads. One key overhead is people, which the 'mercenary' sees as a cost needing to justify its existence, and not necessarily as a prime part of the organization.

Convenor versus executive

The trade union shop steward orientation of *'this is my patch for which I will get all I can'*, captures the philosophy of the 'convenors', sometimes accompanied by the sentiment of *'and damn all of you'*. A director, vice president, or general manager exhibiting convenor sentiments is someone who may be intellectually diverse, but is also emotionally myopic. As a person, he/she may find it easy to discuss, but difficult to identify with and reconcile, contrasting opinions and philosophies. Location, namely, division/operating business or the corporate centre, is likely to influence substantially the values, mission and direction the individual wishes to pursue. 'Convenors' are likely to promote the interests of their part of the organization, irrespective of overall corporate needs. Such sentiments are not driven by negativity, but more by an inability to position oneself in a world of continuous paradox. On this basis, 'convenors' are primarily tactical, in that their orientation is defend/attack. Rather than attempt to view the broader scene, they are likely to see the parties with whom they negotiate as the enemy.

In contrast, a director who holds an 'executive' perspective clearly dons a broader business mantle. Fundamental to holding a broader view, is shared accountability. A senior manager with 'executive' sentiments firmly believes that loyalty to the overall organization, and not just to certain sections, is a primary requirement to behaving as a responsible director. On this basis, sharing accountability for decisions reached is matched by a sense of sharing views on the problems and challenges each director faces. Only when all issues are on the table, can meaningful decisions be reached. Deeply held, shared accountability sentiments desire robustness of relationships and openness of dialogue among the members of the top team. Robustness and openness are considered by the shared accountability 'executive', as the two prime elements of maturity, which in turn, are viewed as the basis for being able to adopt an overall perspective of the organization.

Achiever versus listener

'Achievers' strive for success, so that targets are reached, or preferably surpassed, and the competition has been, 'truly whipped'. 'Achievers' focus their energies and problem-solving capabilities on addressing challenges in the external world, the market. Their focus is constantly out there! Internal organizational processes, such as meetings, shared decision-making, checking-out, conducting appraisals, are seen as necessary evils or irritants which inhibit initiative and flair being displayed in the challenging and demanding world of competitive markets. 'Achievers' not only become easily bored with internal organizational interactions, but also see themselves as being held back, unable to respond appropriately to the speed of activity in the marketplace. 'Achievers' are likely to display little corporate loyalty once they feel no further challenge exists within their current organization. They move on to another organization or site which better suits their temperament.

Those aspects of organizational life which 'achievers' find tedious, are the areas which 'listeners' consider vital to address. 'Listeners' are responsive to internal organizational processes, and the interactions between people. They are supportive of their colleagues and concerned that the development of their subordinates is given due care and attention. 'Listeners' genuinely believe that a powerful avenue for the development of potential in people is on-the-job experience, supported by counselling. Hence, their concern is to delegate, and to help others learn to accept responsibility, which contrasts sharply with 'achievers', who can become impatient with others and end up undertaking most of the key tasks. 'Listeners' would make the time to evaluate the situation and identify appropriate ways forward through others, whereas achievers are likely to pursue tasks and goals, and in retrospect, evaluate others' contribution and errors.

Prescriber versus mentor

'Prescribers' are hierarchical in orientation. Others do not work with prescribers, as the emphasis is – others work for me! 'Prescribers' use command! They give directives and set the deadlines by which completion is required. To not achieve targets, or to not achieve targets by the deadlines set, is likely to induce punitive behaviour. 'Prescribers' are likely to react to poor performance by asking, 'What's wrong with these people?', and *'How should poor performers and wrongdoers be punished?'* Inevitably, 'prescribers' are considerably judgemental. Their need for dialogue and exchange of views and ideas, is low. Their orientation is to establish clear goals and parameters, and to highlight the punitive repercussions for displays of incompetence or non-achievement of targets.

'Prescribers' are not necessarily nasty, but can come over as such. Their prime emphasis is clarity. They need well-established boundaries between themselves and others and, by nature, the clearest of all are in hierarchical relationships. 'Prescribers' find it difficult to appreciate that these exist others who have less need for boundaries and for whom relationships and issues are negotiated and re-negotiated, namely 'mentors'. Senior managers with deeply-held mentor convictions firmly believe that for people to commit themselves, they need to feel ownership for what they are being asked to do. Ownership is gained through talking. Similar to 'listeners', 'mentors' display considerable patience with people. They give their time to developing and nurturing relationships. The parallels between 'listeners' and 'mentors' in terms of on-the-job development, delegating and learning from mistakes, are strong. Where the differences lie, is in the boundaries (or the lack of them) within relationships. 'Listeners' instinctively assume equality in relationships. Subordinates are treated as colleagues. Even children are treated as adults. Although the maturity to so do may be admirable, 'listeners' too easily disregard the fact that the maturity of others may not be sufficient to cope with relationships that are so open, where all is discussed and decided. 'Listeners' do not easily appreciate that others require boundaries in order for them to function. 'Mentors' are more likely to be sensitive to boundary creation and maintenance, according to the needs of each individual.

Rationalists versus contextualists

Senior managers with a 'rationalist' orientation, critically examine business challenges in a logical and clear-minded manner. Their focus is on the challenge at hand, whether it be a market-driven or an organizationally centred issue. The 'rationalist' will attempt to understand clearly and to delineate the elements of the concerns they face, in order to find a solution. The solutions reached will be entirely the result of their logical analysis, irrespective of the influence of context. 'Rationalists' are likely to pursue a course of action which denotes what is logically best to do, irrespective of the sentiments of others in the situation. 'Rationalists' may, in fact, be surprised to find negative reactions to their recommendations and actions because, for them, it is obvious what needs to be done.

'Contextualists' are not only context-sensitive, but are also context-driven. For them, the views and feelings of others in the situation are of paramount concern. Whatever may be the logical way forward, 'contextualists' will be influenced by the views of others in their immediate environment. 'Contextualists' value harmony, and strive to attain a sense of balance between individuals by accommodating their interests. Hence, someone who proposes a logical solution to a problem, but one which disrupts context, is viewed as undesirable and threatening. Driven by the sentiments of others, 'contextualists' need to ensure that they understand how others feel, and whether these relevant others have 'bought in' to the ways forward, before 'contextualists' advance.

Forgiveness seeker versus permission seeker

Certain people are likely to pursue a course of action prior to seeking approval, and then communicate what they have done. In so doing, protocol is placed as secondary to their desires, a fact which can irritate others, or be taken by them as a sign of disrespect. People who make it a practice to behave as they see fit, hold a strong independence orientation. However, in order to repair any relationships damaged by the individualistic action of any one person, action needs to be followed up with checking out the opinions of others in order to re-establish relationships on a positive footing. Unfortunately, the individual's distaste for protocol, means they seldom check out others' opinions, as to do so is experienced as inhibitory.

In contrast, other senior managers may be particularly sensitive to protocol. For them, informing others of what is happening is important in order to prevent distortion of communication and also to maintain relationships. Individuals who ask for permission have evolved strong sentiments to see what others think, then do. Their orientation is organizational and their practice is respect for customs and established ways of behaving. For them, those who act and then ask for forgiveness have a damaging influence, for in pursuing their own course of action, even with the best of intentions, confusion arises from unexpected actions and also from poor, after-the-fact communication, which can be experienced as distressing for others, and time-consuming to put right. In response to those who ask for forgiveness, those who need permission, find it exceptionally difficult to forgive.

Strength to surface sentiments

Having established the mission, and/or vision of the organization, as was the case of the UK retailer, or having embarked on such a journey, the next challenge is to confront the sentiments held by the other discretionary leaders. Realizing the desired shape and nature of the organization is only possible when people know how they are to be treated, and what key values, in practice, will prevail in the organization. What importance will be given to concepts of care, equity, success, democracy and professionalism? Inevitably, sentiments will be expressed, overtly or covertly, as the leaders of the organization, in determining the nature of the organization, will undoubtedly express their feelings concerning the meaning and purpose of work, organizational activities, and the value of people.

However, whether overtly stated, or covertly discussed, surfacing deeply held sentiments requires harnessing considerable personal strength and robustness to see through the experience meaningfully. The process is uncomfortable. Not only do colleagues try to establish the nature of the organization they desire, they equally attempt to attract the 'right sort of people' for the future, which may involve their divesting the organization of those senior managers whose values they disrespect or disregard. The *Sunday Times* (15 December 1996) reported, on the front page of its business section, the changes in top management at Cable and Wireless (C&W) under the new leadership of Dick Brown. Out were Jonathan Solomon (Strategy and Business Development Director) and Edward Astle (International Services Director), with more departures expected to follow. The reason implied in the article and supported by views expressed by Cable and Wireless managers was that Dick Brown wanted to clear out those directors associated with Lord Young (former Chairman) and James Ross (former CEO), both of whom had departed earlier in 1996 (the Cable and Wireless managers did not wish to be named). The Young/Ross period had been characterized by conflict, poor relationships and unwelcome splits at senior levels. A leader who is pushing through change and reform needs to display considerable robustness to enter into such an affray and to work through tense emotions. The individual pushing through reform could even lose out in the process and end up departing him/herself. Although absolutely vital to surface, few people look forward to entering into a forum where others' deeply held views and feelings are to be released, with no guarantee that the ensuing debate will be successful or even constructive.

The consultancy group, Bains,[5] identified in one of its studies that of all the strategic management tools being used, visioning was voted number one. However, it was voted only fourth in terms of the measure of satisfaction linked to its usage. The reason given is the frustration, once having embarked on a visionary process, of modifying one's aspirations, and having to contend with the perspectives of others. Some top directors, in the Bains study, reported disillusionment and scepticism about the relevance of visioning as a strategic management tool. However, in order to stretch individuals, redesign roles and structures, and build a different logic among the leaders of the organization, bringing sentiments to the surface, confronting negative emotions, and emerging with a sense of common purpose are vital elements to growing a disciplined and successful enterprise.

A year later, the effectiveness of the process can be tested. Ask any one of the senior management of the organization to relate the formal vision statement and he/she may, or may not, be able to do so. Ask the senior managers to talk about the spirit of the vision and they are likely to intermingle statements about the core of the vision with revelations of the experiences of how it was built, put together in the form of stories, incidents and high and low points of experience. What is likely to remain the same as the year before, when the vision was being formalized, is the expression of passion, the passion that emerged on having broken through the sentiments of the past.

Having surfaced and worked through deep sentiments is also that point in time when long-term visions can be meaningfully debated. Using words such as 'vision' and 'mission' can distort the time frames that particular individuals may hold. Some people may hold a 3-to-5-year perspective. Others may hold a 30-year dream. In a recent and an interesting 1996 *Harvard Business Review* article by James Collins and Jerry Porras, the authors focus on visioning, but from a long term standpoint. Phrases such as 'core ideology', 'core values', 'core purpose' are used and defined as separate entities. The Cranfield surveys highlight a growing usage of these terms, but with top managers understanding different meanings to each of these phrases. Hence, effectively surfacing sentiments displays not only how the leaders of an organization feel about their present circumstances and the future, but also their perception of time, and for how long they are likely to continue to feel strongly about a particular mission and direction, if their sentiments could be appropriately channelled.

The longer term the time perspective of the vision being pursued, the more are the future core purpose and identity of the organization likely to reflect the desires of a single individual, more often than not those of the chairman, president or CEO. This is not necessarily problematic, for the process of surfacing sentiments should unearth how people feel about the principal leader, the chairman, president or CEO, for example, and where he/she is taking the company. However, in order to make the longer term vision acceptable and part of the fabric of the organization, the CEO would need to coach each member of the senior team in order to help him/her envision his/her role in the new order. Hence, the value in surfacing sentiments not only highlights how people feel about the future, and how they can be brought close together to channel their energies, but also how they view the person(s) who is pushing for change, and the nature of that person's contribution in the 'new world'. Research, observation and experience dictate that only from such openness and honesty can people effectively proceed forward.

Not the dark side of politics

The surfacing of sentiments to then provide the momentum to move forward to a clearer future is not about the politics of influence or manoeuvre. For some of those involved in the process, however, the experience can feel political. If the process of raising and discussing fundamental issues falters or fails, the experience and its instigator(s) can be labelled as political. However, the process of visioning, and by implication the surfacing of sentiments, requires each of the senior managers to declare his/her fundamental values, intent and feelings towards the others. No level of accomplishment at political manoeuvre can help at this fundamental stage of re-thinking the organization and revitalizing the top team. In fact, displaying political aptitude at a time of surfacing sentiments can be counter-productive. Robustness and sincerity are the two prime requirements to help the top team and the organization move forward.

Wisdom for pathways through paradox

Shaping a future and teasing and focusing senior management's deep-seated emotions to drive forward towards that future, surfaces a third challenge, operationalizing the vision. Making vision(s) work, draws into question the strategic and tactical skills of the leadership of the organization.

> what we sought to do in the 80s is we wrote the company's low cost operator drive very vigorously and improved our gross margins . . . the story of the 90s has been that the tide of inflation has ebbed. It became impossible to put prices up . . . so you have to drive your margin enhancement by even more vigorous cost cutting at a time when there was actually price eflation on the top line. That has proved very difficult for all food companies . . . the environment in which all of us are trading is a much tougher one. (Dr Tony O'Reilly, Chairman of the Board, H. J. Heinz Co.).

Tony O'Reilly is describing the changed economic conditions of the 1990s in comparison with the 1980s, and the impact these had on the Heinz Corporation. He is equally reflecting on an additional challenge so many business leaders have had to confront, namely a paradox: be as good as you were before, but with less. The question is, how?

A paradox, namely being caught between at least two contrasting forces, pulling in different directions, while at the same time not being able simply to opt for one or the other, but having to reconcile both, when both are contradictory, is a position many top managers have described themselves as being in at certain points in their careers. Effectively working one's way through contradictory pulls and pushes, has been crucial to the survival and future success of the company. However, to be able to address competently those forces that are fundamentally incompatible, it is important to recognize the nature of the paradox(es) being faced. Two paradoxes of leadership, in particular, are identified as likely to confront private and public sector organization leaders today, namely the paradox of strategy and the paradox of feedback.

Paradox of strategy[6]

What is the purpose of strategy? One prime purpose is to identify and sustain competitive advantage for the organization in the communities and markets it serves. In order to gain advantage, particular strategies have to be pursued which take account of current challenges, and where the organization should ideally position itself now and for the future, in order to enhance its value. Within such a scenario, considerable differences of view are likely to emerge concerning current circumstances, the present 'strengths' and future developments of the organization, irrespective of the attention given to vision and mission. It should be no surprise to report that strategy holds different meanings for different people. Such differences are captured and examined in an analysis of *vertical* and *horizontal* synergies. The particular combination of vertical and horizontal synergies that gives strategy meaning, and can additionally surface differences between leaders.

Vertical synergies are concerned with economics, costs, structures of organizations, overheads, namely those aspects of organization that need constant attention and adjustment in order that the organization can operate efficiently. A vertically integrated organization is one that is economically well structured and efficient in order to meet its key objectives. Clarity and cohesion of view emerge, on issues of vertical integration, through reliance on data. Is this organization too expensive? Does the organization have the cost/overhead base needed to respond effectively to current and future demands? Does the organization have too many people? Such questions require information in order to support their resolution. If nothing else, top management can make unilateral decisions and then apply financial and organizational levers to ensure that the organization remains on course. On issues of vertical synergy, command-oriented decision-making works. The value of such an approach, is to restrict excessive debate and reconsideration, as not clearly focusing on costs and, hence, not maximizing on the investment made, can be disastrous. Why pursue a vertical synergy strategy? Because the organization is primarily sustaining competitive advantage on price and/or margin.

In contrast, horizontal synergies are concerned with issues of quality, being responsive to market needs, providing a service, and being sympathetic to the requirements of clients and other agencies externally, and to staff and management internally. In effect, horizontal synergies require a consultative management style, namely effective team-work, open dialogue, and an attitude of sharing and co-operation, in order to be responsive to shifting external demands. Why pursue a horizontal synergy strategy? Because the organization is attempting to sustain competitive advantage on the basis of service and quality, despite considerations of cost and price. Horizontal synergy promotion needs devolution of structures, the empowerment of people, and reliance on informality rather than formality, and clarity of jobs and roles.

Therein lies the paradox (see Figure 8.3).[7] How can the leadership of an organization control costs and prune expenses, and at the same time promote an internal environment of openness, trust and co-operation? How can one, as a senior manager, say to a subordinate or colleague, 'Give me feedback on what our clients need, even if it is critical of me', and expect that person to respond freely, when he/she feels that the very

Figure 8.3   1990s leadership: a paradox

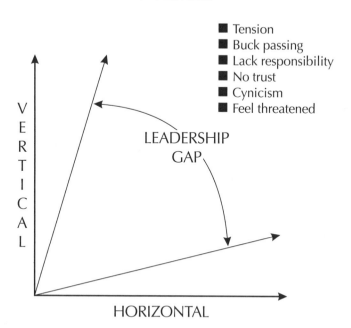

same senior manager who is asking the question may remove his/her job within the next financial year?

It is possible to lead effectively, but separately, for vertical and for horizontal synergy strategies. However, the alternate joint pursuit of vertical and horizontal synergy strategies can rapidly promote a gap in leadership, a gap that may be filled by strife, division, tension, fundamental differences of view concerning the future, buck passing upwards, and feeling no sense of responsibility for one's leadership role. Left unaddressed, the gap in leadership widens.

The phenomenon of a leadership gap is a common experience for top managers of private and public sector organizations, largely because, in order to gain advantage in desired markets or communities requires the pursuit of both! The point that needs to be made is that being caught in the paradox of strategy is not a one-off event. It is a continuous experience whereby, in any one financial year, it may be necessary to pursue a vertical synergy strategy, then switch to team-building and service provision, and again, within a few months, review costs and enter into further cost reduction, outsourcing and outplacement.

> The environment in which all of us are trading is a much tougher one. So the role of the CEO in all of that is to recognize that the 'US cavalry' are not going to come over the hill and say, we are here to rescue you, chaps . . . you have to do it yourselves . . . We have simply got to set our own home to rights. (Dr Tony O'Reilly, Chairman of the Board, H. J. Heinz Co.)

As stated, O'Reilly clearly recognized that the 1980s' Heinz could no longer continue. Yet such realization did not minimize the vertical and horizontal pressures and the tension that was being generated in the company. Heinz was operating on three fronts – focusing more on food service, promoting baby foods across the world, despite not having a major presence for baby foods in America (Heinz is comparable in size to Gerber through its extensive market share in baby foods outside the USA), and being geographically focused in terms of retailers and access to markets.

> We have the capacity to take our factories and our skills and our recipes for manufacturing capability to any country in the world – plan our flight and say 'Heinz is here' – this is what we are going to do! (Dr Tony O'Reilly, Chairman of the Board, H. J. Heinz Co.)

Tony O'Reilly's clarity of thought concerning manufacturing, sales and marketing, falls more at the unique end of the spectrum. The Cranfield surveys highlight that irrespective of ethnicity, background and other demographic factors, one particular outcome of jointly pursuing vertical and horizontal synergies is that senior managers can end up holding widely varying interpretations of the terms 'sales' and 'marketing' (see Table 8.4). A considerable number of managers identified 'sales' concepts in the 'marketing' category, and vice versa. Certain concepts such as 'price', 'quality', 'service', 'brand' fell into both categories.

In reality, 'sales' and 'marketing' are whatever the individual wants them to mean, according to how he/she interprets his/her context and the economic and strategic forces shaping the organization. Such a broad range of meanings can make the strategic debate confusing, irritating and unwieldy, because clarity concerning certain terms is non-existent. Whatever effective team building may have been achieved through the visioning process and the surfacing of sentiments, could now be undermined through not being able to operationalize the vision. Being buffeted between contrasting business forces, unable even to establish a language of how to trade, namely, how to sell and market, can both demotivate and generate strife within a basically cohesive team. One way forward is to request feedback from colleagues on the nature of sales and marketing, and the capability of the team to clarify the direction to be pursued. On receiving feedback, the steps to clarify direction and promote greater commitment to the agreed way forward, are discussed in the section, Wisdom, paradox and ownership below.

Table 8.4 Mix of meanings: sales and marketing – results of research

Marketing	Sales
■ Product range/Service quality	■ Quality of technical service
■ Price	■ High quality products/service
■ Direct mail	■ Competent, trained staff
■ Efficient distribution	■ Direct mail
■ Reputation	■ Reputation
■ Financial facilities	■ Price
■ Promotional aids/literature	■ Building relationships/clients/suppliers/ distributors
■ Effective client contact	■ Marketing/Research
■ Good public relations	■ Knowing client requirements
■ Professional sales staff	■ Working long, unsocial hours
■ Value for money	■ Regular customer contact
■ Cold calling	■ Marketing product skills
■ Sales intelligence	■ Product knowledge
■ Word of mouth reputation	■ Training
■ Reputations for selling to best	■ Being innovative in marketing
■ Customers	■ Free samples, good demonstrations
■ Television promotions	■ Brand building
■ Location of retail outlets	■ Value for money
■ Mail shots	■ Cold calling
■ Efficient sales teams	■ Targeting key potential clients
■ Track record	■ Good literature
■ Sound IT back-up	■ Understanding the sales cycles
■ Delivery on time	■ Face-to-face contacts
■ Low interest rates	■ Long-term commitment
■ Skilled sales force	
■ Training	

Paradox of feedback

One common reaction by staff and management in response to the tensions of working between the extremities of vertical and horizontal synergies, is to blame top management. The discomfort and distrust experienced through, on the one hand, cutting costs, and on the other, building relationships and teams, is often viewed as an incapability of the top team to lead and manage. Such is the case with Australia's top civil servants whose views, captured in the Australian Commonwealth government survey, referred to a need for stronger, more decisive leadership, which were then contrasted by comments outlining a desire for greater integration and sharing among key personalities. The need expressed for top management in government to display greater honesty, more openness, greater tolerance and more and better consultation, was contrasted by comments that emphasized that the very same top management should be providing clearer direction in terms of goals and strategy, and that they should be more decisive.

The results of the Australian survey parallel the paradoxical nature of the feedback continuously received by top managers in many private and public sector organizations (see Table 8.5).

How can such contrasting messages be utilized? They cannot be. Senior management cannot simultaneously take charge and be strong, display a no-nonsense attitude, and yet be flexible, delegate, and make the time to listen more. At any point in time, senior management will act more in one way than the other. As a result, it is virtually inevitable that staff and middle level managers will feel aggrieved that their recommendations are apparently rejected. Negativity such as this cannot be eradicated; the issue is more one of reducing the level of discontent to a workable level. Just as a pathway through strategic paradox needs to be routed, so too does a way through the contrasting messages from feedback.

In order to find ways through a paradox, it is necessary to identify the degree of ownership people hold towards realizing their responsibilities.

Wisdom, paradox and ownership

Teams that are not experienced in honesty of debate concerning the organization, its future, the styles and personalities of colleagues, or do not recognize that their market and economic circumstances are changing more fundamentally and not just experiencing a downside, are likely to be teams that find it difficult to accept the responsibility for confronting the strategic challenges facing them and their organization. Worse still are those teams that recognize the nature of the strategic problem they face, but have leaders who possess neither the wisdom nor the will to move forward.

Through a series of case studies conducted by Cliff Bowman and Andrew Kakabadse of Cranfield School of Management, it became clear that to improve team performance it is necessary for team members

Table 8.5   Feedback paradox

■ Be strong	■ Listen more
■ Take charge	■ Delegate
■ Drive down through the organization	■ Work through issues
■ No nonsense	■ Be flexible
■ Be decisive	■ Be a team player

to recognize the context in which they find themselves. Once the team members appreciate the impact of context on them, they can then identify how to enhance their sense of responsibility and ownership in order to improve their circumstances. Team context, therefore, is defined along two dimensions, 'internalization' and 'inclusion'. 'Internalization' examines the degree to which team members have, or have not, accepted the responsibility for setting and implementing strategy. 'Inclusion' explores whether team members feel themselves to be involved or excluded from the strategy-setting process. The studies highlight four possible ownership postures that the members of top teams may take (see Figure 8.4).[8]

Those senior managers who feel themselves detached from the strategic process are not necessarily discontented. Left alone, they are quite comfortable with their position, as their focus is to concentrate on operational agendas. The *detached* leader wishes to be left alone to run his/her department in his/her own way. The detached executive does not necessarily undermine any process of strategy generation, he/she simply does not show willing to become involved in devising the future of the organization, or even to gain more of a strategic overview.

Figure 8.4   Four ownership postures

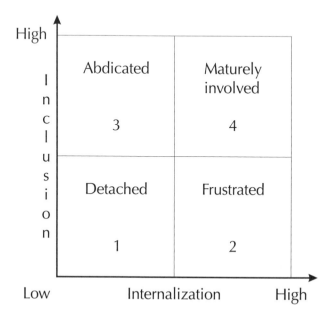

Source: Bowman and Kakabadse (1997)

In contrast, the *frustrated* executive is one who wishes for ownership but feels excluded from the real debate. The frustration experienced through not taking part, whether that perception is real or imagined, may be manifested through displays of anger, experiences of disillusionment or regression to cell 1 in Figure 8.3 as a result of dejected resignation. However, since few regress but rather live out their anger, they are consequently perceived as a threat by others. The tension generated by the expression of anger could further inhibit dialogue concerning strategy.

The senior manager who *abdicates* is not barred from being involved in the strategy debate, but shuns the responsibility for inclusion in the strategic process and hence stands aside, often critiquing from a distance. A possible reason why the person voluntarily 'steps aside' from the strategic process is that he/she may feel anxious and threatened by the sense of the enormity and complexity of the strategic process, and hence, may feel inadequate to contribute. Feelings of inadequacy may be camouflaged by nit-picking and complaining outside the formal meetings.

Senior managers who feel *involved* in the strategic debate are likely to experience a strong sense of responsibility for their contribution. Such positive sentiments are the result of having experienced strategic meetings as satisfactory events, and having concluded that the 'right people' are attending. As a result, the senior manager is prepared to engage in honest and robust debate. Mature involvement requires that colleagues respect each other's contribution and are equally prepared to accept the outcome of a debate on the understanding that not all of the participants' desires are going to be accepted.

If a team has been able to satisfactorily surface sentiments, each of its members is likely to have grown in maturity. If not, or if strife in a team has disrupted its members' confidence in each other, five steps for promoting greater ownership and involvement are identified. The wisdom in so doing, is to recognize why ownership is lacking, and to appreciate the manner in which the five steps should be applied. The five steps are: away days; on-the-job coaching; broadening strategic involvement; off-the-job training; set clear objectives.

Away days

On the basis that different individuals hold different views of strategy and the strategic process, one commonly practised way to help individuals grow greater ownership for the strategic debate and its outcomes, is to take people away from the workplace to discuss the strategy and the manner in which it is being addressed. Away days can be useful in highlighting the paradoxical challenges facing the top team, and how to establish clear ways through. However, away days can also result in artificially contrived conclusions, whereby little is achieved and people walk away from such events apparently polite and friendly, but covertly, more defensive and critical than before. The setting and preparation for discussion were either inadequate, or the various members of the group did not feel sufficiently prepared to speak their minds. Individuals who have an already set track record for entering into challenging and emotionally demanding debate through the visioning process, may simply require to be reminded of their established skills. Alternatively, for those team members who have not experienced the intensity of debate, as their experience may be that of incremental change, attention through training and development may be necessary, to enhance in each individual a greater robustness for open conversation.

On-the-job coaching

An additional approach to nurturing a greater sense of ownership for the strategic process among the members of the senior executive, is to coach them on a one-to-one basis. Those individuals who are detached probably provide the greatest hurdle, as they can become symbols of passive resistance – the debate is irrelevant, so why waste time? – could be the attitude that is projected. Individuals who feel negative about the strategic process may be attracted to the detached executive, as he/she is the one who displays being non-threatening but distant from the process. To overcome passive resistance, the detached executive may need to be removed from the group, or from the organization, to display symbolically that isolationism from strategy is not to be tolerated. An alternative is sharp feedback, making the point that deliberately not accepting responsibility for enhancing the process of strategic debate and its outcomes is one of the worst possible behaviours from a senior manager. No senior manager should promote the message that it is OK to walk away from responsibility. Through coaching, the way forward can be clarified, either the person changes his/her attitude, or he/she leaves.

Broadening strategic involvement

Of the four ownership postures (see Figure 8.4), the frustrated executive is the easiest to deal with, as he/she desires involvement and hence is satisfied when allowed to enter into the 'inner circle' of debate. The question is, is this executive's contribution valid and organizationally acceptable? In certain cases, his/her involvement may not be organizationally appropriate, as being elevated to membership of the strategic inner circle could lead to further discontent at senior levels, in that others may feel that they have an equal right to participate. An additional consideration is that to widen the circle of membership might dilute the quality of discussion, as too many people, some of whom may be too junior, could then be involved in the strategic debate.

An alternative idea promoted by Sir Ian Prosser, Chairman and CEO of the Bass Group (the brewers, pubs, restaurants, betting, and worldwide franchise for the Holiday Inn Hotel business group), has been to involve the top 100 executives below main Board, Corporate Director, and even subsidiary Board levels, in the strategic process, through various projects and activities (see the case analysis in Chapter 11, for further information on Bass's programme of development). Known as the Chairman's list, this has been added to by Ian Prosser successfully involving the more junior, but highly capable, of the senior managers, in the strategic process. From the debate and project results the whole corporation benefits, and with on-the-job development experience, individuals equally benefit. The next generation of top level directors for the Bass Group, are being grown.

On/off-the-job training

A change of tactic is required for those individuals who have absented themselves from the process of strategic dialogue, as much due to their lack of confidence. As individuals, they may be over-promoted, or have been promoted too early, or been so over-loaded with operational tasks that a combination of 'burn out' and an over-concentration of day-to-day concerns are the reasons for feelings of inadequacy in strategic forums. However, the CEO/President may consider such persons to be worthy of investment. The confidence of these people can be raised by meeting their needs through training and development. Sending a senior manager to attend a leadership or high-status strategy training programme can provide the tools for better appreciating strategic processes, and through liaising with other managers on the programme, the person's confidence is likely to grow, as he/she recognizes that the problems and challenges experienced are common to managers at that level of seniority. The best results are gained if off-the-job training is combined with an on-the-job development programme, whereby the person is given the message that greater responsibility, status and promotion can be achieved by visibly exhibiting progress.

Set clear objectives

Making strategy work requires paying attention to setting, and committing to pursuing, in detail, clear objectives. Operationalizing strategy, is likely to involve a number of people. Committees, working parties, teams, or simply single individuals, by their involvement in setting targets and in providing feedback on what is realistic to achieve within particular time frames, will influence how actively the targets set will be pursued. People's 'buy-in' to the targets and objectives set, provides a strong indication of how realistic are the aspirations captured in the vision, and of what is the depth of trust among senior managers, and of how robust are the relationships that exists between them.

Commitment to the pursuit of objectives emerges after successfully surfacing and deeply examining the motivation and ownership of the organization's strategy by the members of the top team. Objectives are likely to be consistently pursued once the members of the top management of the organization display a respect for, and commitment to, each other. Displays of respect and commitment provide the strength and versatility that the rest of the organization needs from its leaders. Also, respect and commitment are necessary prerequisites to utilizing feedback. If feedback from the rest of the organization indicates that the objectives set are unrealistic, the leadership can respond by listening, debating and implementing their conclusions in a cohesive manner, which actively displays the leaders' confidence in each other and in what they are asking the rest of the organization to pursue. The leaders can show that they are strong enough to change their minds, if it is shown that they are unrealistic in their pursuit of particular tactics and targets. Equally, through respect and commitment, senior management display strength to strive for taxing and demanding goals and, through exhibiting extraordinary behaviour, they act as a role model which requires extraordinary behaviour from others.

Wisdom: its necessity and limitations

Away days, workshops, training and development opportunities, and cleverly designed strategic project teams assist in nurturing wisdom, but do not singly, or in combination, provide for wisdom. Wisdom is self-grown and has to emerge from each individual, if he/she so desires.

Wisdom is defined as, 'a capability to identify pertinent pathways forward when direction is obscure(d)'; in effect, the weaving of a way through complex and subtle challenges. Direction may be obscure because of the nature of the markets in which the organization trades, as possibly typified by the variety and mix of terms used to describe the processes of sales and marketing (see Table 8.4). Direction, equally, may be obscured by colleagues who adopt different viewpoints, are distrustful of, and disrespect, those for whom they work, those who work for them, and those with whom they continuously interact. Finding pathways through may not be easy.

In the enhancement of wisdom, and the pursuit of workable ways through obstacles, the following considerations assist. First, and as repeatedly stated, identifying the nature of each context, and displaying respect through treating each circumstance as unique, are important. No evidence has been found that highlights how to navigate through the contrasting forces of vertical and horizontal synergies – there is no 'north-east' (see Figure 8.5)! No explicit ways that are transferable from one company's experience to another's, have been found to help senior managers through the quagmire of attending to costs and, by implication, treating people as a cost and then treating them as a unique and vital entity, and still expect them to trust their leaders. Each organization and each senior manager has to examine the circumstances for each to find its/his/her own pathways through their situation. In order to do so, each senior manager needs to respect context more than the desire to promote solely his/her own course of action. In today's world, positive responsiveness to context counts substantially.

Second, through life's experiences, through training, and through work-related development, individuals need to build on the maturity they have evolved, in order to be comfortable with feedback. The ability to invite, receive, and handle well the comments and views of others is crucial to maintaining constantly open channels of communication with all stakeholders inside and outside the organization, and thereby extract from those views which ways to take to reach settlement. Helping people to feel sufficiently comfortable to offer their views and sentiments concerning present and past activities and experiences, is the food of wisdom.

Third, taking a non-judgemental view to balancing interests, is the means by which pathways are formed. Should attention be given to business issues – for example, clarifying the meaning of sales and

---

Figure 8.5 No North-East

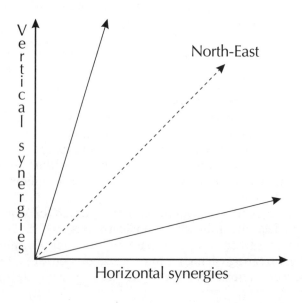

marketing for the organization through robust discussion of current, as well as future-desired, sales and marketing practices? Should attention be given to process? Irrespective of the issues, greater attention should be given to how people talk to each other, as the inability to surface true sentiments means little ownership exists for the outcomes of discussion. Knowledge of the people and the circumstances helps to decide whether process, or business and organizational issues, or both, should be addressed. Equally, where to start, and with whom, requires sober, balanced reflection. The combination of knowledge of context, openness to feedback, and making time to be available for feedback, allow for a positive attitude to develop for a growing of confidence in one's own abilities. Every new challenge is viewed as a chance to learn, which adds to the individual's repertoire of appropriate pathways through context. Not that such high quality perspectives can be continually replicated. Fatigue, being over-loaded with demands and tasks, and personal problems which emotionally drain the individual, can induce erratic, inappropriate and judgemental comments and responses which the person may later regret. Irrespective of the reactions of any one day, the positive attitude of wishing to learn continuously of information and of contexts, is the bedrock of wisdom.

Everyone has 'off days'. Off days are when the senior manager, as much due to strain and overload, behaves in an unwise manner. However, off days, or the making of mistakes are not limitations to wisdom. Off days and mistakes are as much about the development of wisdom as are other learning experiences. 'Mistakes are the next step of learning on the road to high accomplishment!'

In contrast, the limitations to wisdom are when considerations of context become immaterial, namely when discipline needs to be applied in the singular pursuit of a particular goal or principle. Pursuing a principle, such as equal rights or a 10 per cent cost cut right across the organization, requires focus, discipline and consistency. Once it has been decided that a principle needs to be pursued, irrespective of outcomes, to attempt wisdom in circumstances where discipline and consistency are required, can be damagingly counter-productive, as the process of patiently working through various interests, being flexible and by implication responsive, is perceived as weak and indecisive leadership. Wisdom is synonymous with context, and when appropriately applied can be immensely valuable in both transactional and transformational circumstances. Directness, a non-contextual concept, can be severely blunted by a sincere, but inappropriate exposure to wisdom.

Flair to engage through dialogue

Emphasized throughout this book is the view that fundamental to effective leadership, is high quality dialogue. The exploration of issues, the pronouncing of views, the expressing of sentiments, the asking of questions and the declaring of intent, involve entering into deep debate, which can reach a depth of discomfort, in order to re-emerge with a shared truth and a cohesive view as to how to proceed beneficially as the senior management leading the organization. On the basis that dialogue, as opposed to casual conversation, is a capability to address and/or resolve issues of sensitivity at senior management level, the following question was asked in the Cranfield surveys (see Table 8.6): 'Are there issues or sensitivities that merit attention but do not receive attention, at senior management levels?'

The Chinese and Japanese top executives highlight the greatest number of concerns, indicating that important but disregarded issues predominate among senior management. The Australian civil servants follow the Irish and Austrians in their concern about issues not attended to, while the British, Finnish and French senior managers identify the smallest numbers of sensitive issues impacting on the quality of dialogue at senior levels. The NHS executive directors also report inhibited dialogue at senior levels.

The vast majority of business and public service leaders report outstanding issues remaining unaddressed at senior levels, but which need to be addressed in order to progress the organization. To leave important issues unaddressed is likely to stimulate a latent crisis, in effect ever-growing opportunity costs. No company immediately goes bankrupt because of poor quality dialogue, but quality is progressively minimized. Hence, the survey results highlight that positive leadership is dependent on effective teamwork, which in turn, is dependent on openness and quality of dialogue. It is all too easy to discuss particular points when certain people are not present. However, penetrating dialogue can only really take place in their presence, even if the discussions are sensitive, and resentment may be generated, as these key people's 'buy in' to what is being debated is crucial, if for no other reason

Table 8.6 Sensitivity of dialogue (%)

	Japan	UK	France	Ireland	Germany	Sweden
YES	77	47	36	68	61	50

	Spain	Austria	Finland	USA	China	Hong Kong	NHS Top Team	Board	APS
YES	63	67	49	62	80	58	70	66	66

Source: Adapted from Kakabadse et al. (1996); Korac-Kakabadse and Korac-Kakabadse (1997); (1998).

than to prevent possible sabotage later on. It takes considerable flair and wisdom to steer between key stakeholders in order to encourage them to speak in forums that count. Having already examined, in the previous sections, how to encourage dialogue at the individual level, promoting high quality top team dialogue is substantially assisted by taking into account who is, or is not, in the overall top team, which forums are key for debate, and what it takes to engage those parties.

Broadening the forum

As identified in the earlier section, 'Steps to quality visioning' (p. 297), the number of discretionary leader roles in the organization may well be in excess of the number of members of the current perceived top team (i.e. Board or Senior Executive Committee meeting). Hence, the challenge is to involve the 'broadened' top team in the strategic process.

Case example: helping bankers participate

The top management of a major UK bank reportedly faced the criticism from its staff and management that internal communications were problematic. Although acknowledging that concern, top management did little to understand more clearly the nature of the disaffection. After a time, top management began to realize that while pursuing vertical synergy strategies, operational and strategic objectives were met. However, with horizontal synergy strategies, that involved looser targets through addressing issues of quality and service, a considerable variation of performance was displayed across the bank. One strategy in particular, to grow market share in the small business sector, showed the greatest variation of performance throughout the regions of the retail bank.

An internal survey identified that the area directors, some of whom individually held a responsibility for over 95 branch outlets, were people-oriented managers, concerned with the promotion of service and quality, but who were feeling considerably demotivated, feeling neglected, and were unclear as to the value and purpose of themselves and their roles. Role analysis also highlighted that they occupied discretionary leader roles. However, area directors considered themselves to be being treated as if they were holding more middle-management jobs. In the opinion of some, they were treated worse than 'office boys'. It was concluded that although area directors held considerable sway in the bank, it was less so on vertical synergy strategy issues, and more on horizontal synergy concerns, such as the transfer of personnel, interfacing with key local clients and suppliers, issues of service, quality and morale, and most of all, on the promotion of the small businesses strategy.

The CEO's reaction on receiving the results of the leadership and attitude survey was to express his indignation:

What? Now you want me to be nice to a bunch of pissed off area directors, when they are the ones who seem to have not being pulling their weight behind some of the key initiatives upon which this bank relies! Is that what you are saying?

The surveys had identified the area directors as discretionary leaders and, by implication, members of the extended top team. However, their isolation from the strategic debate led to inconsistency in their promoting horizontal synergy strategies. The CEO's original view was that he had 87 key leaders in the bank. The task was to persuade him that he, in fact, had 123 leaders (including the area directors) with whom he had to communicate constantly and motivate. The CEO did not take much persuading once he recognized the damaging impact that demotivated discretionary leaders could have on horizontal synergy initiatives, and shortly changed the structure of his meetings, so that he would communicate directly with his 123 key top managers. Within six months, improvements were noticed in service and quality, and especially in the better response from the markets in the small business arena.

The above example highlights that not knowing who is in the top team has an impact on the doing of business in the organization. By having certain senior managers feel neglected in terms of participation in the strategic dialogue – as typified by the UK retail bank example – is likely to have little impact on vertical synergy strategies – hitting the 'hard' targets. The danger with feeling neglected is in the possible undermining of quality and service initiatives. If certain discretionary leaders feel detached from the strategic process, which they consider to be part of their job-related responsibilities, the result is likely to be a diminished sense of ownership towards achieving the 'softer' horizontal synergy targets. By nature, horizontal synergies are the easier to undermine, for they are so very dependent on senior management's sense of ownership. If the crucial layer of management at the discretionary/prescriptive boundary does not display 'full support', staff and management below will take their lead and will similarly neglect service and quality initiatives. Getting rid of an 'awkward' layer of management equally does not help. The problem is simply shifted to another level of management that has survived the downsizing. Including those senior managers on the discretionary/prescriptive boundary in the strategic dialogue, is an important requirement to making horizontal synergy strategies work.

Flair to engage

Having drafted a more representative meetings structure, the task is now to engage those attending the meetings in the strategic debate. First, the purpose of the meetings would need to be clarified. Are certain meetings called to ascertain views? Are certain meetings for probing and brainstorming? Are decisions made at still other meetings?

Having ascertained both a structure which equitably represents issues and clarifies the purpose of meetings, the flair of the leader is now in balancing personalities, quality of dialogue, and realizing the objectives of the meeting. How far can the attendees of the meeting be taken down the pathway of an in-depth examination and openness of expression of views without entering the damaging zone of uncomfortable debate? Is it important to manoeuvre the debate into areas which colleagues are likely to find uncomfortable in order fully to unearth underlying issues? Depending on the purpose of the meeting and the leader's view of his/her colleagues' capability for clear minded expression of views and discourse, the meeting's leader may further open up the discussion, or may be more personally attentive to individuals, coaching and counselling them to build their confidence to engage positively in the debate. The balance lies in ensuring that on the one hand people do not retreat, or, alternatively, do not gain a false sense of security, which in turn may lead to their disregarding the purpose of the meeting.

Whichever style is adopted, whether nice or nasty, the flair is in reading the circumstances and in engaging appropriately. Effective engaging is denoted by the continuation of dialogue irrespective of the topic, because due respect is shown to the subject at hand, to the people present at the meeting, and to the process of conversation. Those leaders exhibiting the flair to engage continuously, open doors, as opposed to having them shut in their faces!

Discipline to communicate

Communicating effectively at a meeting is fine, but how do senior managers effectively communicate with the different parts of an organization? The answer is in many different ways, including memos, e-mail, presentations, company information sheets, meetings, cascade processes – the list is almost endless. Frank Flynn, during his period of office as Communications Officer for the Bank of Ireland, Dublin, identified an extensive number of different avenues of communication that the Bank pursued or nurtured. However, as Frank pointed out, attending to various communication routes does not necessarily provide for improved communications within an organization. Communication is two-sided: that communication which provides direction and that which provides example.[9] Frank's point is that organizations pay undue attention to providing direction, whereas the key communication challenge is in the latter category.

Providing direction

In the Cranfield studies, four key levers for communicating direction were identified – the mission of the organization, key corporate and operating business objectives, and key areas of job-related responsibility – in a select number of companies from different countries (see Table 8.7). Senior, middle and lower-level management were asked whether they knew, understood, and could relate (in their own words) the essence of their organization's mission, objectives, and primary areas of responsibility of the key managers in the organization. In terms of key managerial responsibilities, the chairman of the company, for example, may make the statement that a prime task for the chairman during the next year would be to promote growth through merger and acquisition, or alternatively, the statement made might be that the CEO would make it his/her responsibility to drive through the organization an initiative of cost containment and quality improvement.

Swedish companies, Hong Kong-expatriate and Chinese-based companies, and USA companies highlight that senior, middle and more-junior management display a high degree of understanding of the mission of the organization (see Table 8.7). Managers of British companies display the lowest level of shared understanding of the content and purpose of the mission statement.

German, and Hong Kong-based companies indicate that management have a high level of understanding of the corporate objectives that the organization is pursuing. Spanish and USA enterprises declare the least-shared knowledge of corporate objectives, with scores of 62 per cent and

Table 8.7   Providing direction: communication

Country	Shared understanding %			
	Mission	Corporate objectives	Functional/operating business objectives	Key areas of responsibility
Sweden	93	78	74	81
Austria	75	75	68	87
Spain	75	62	67	77
Germany	67	81	70	88
France	66	72	64	89
Britain	62	76	78	91
China	72	73	68	85
Hong Kong	84	81	86	91
USA	86	66	67	83

Table 8.8 Providing example: communicating behaviours – comparative response by seniority (%)

	Japan		UK		France		Ireland		Germany		Sweden		Spain		Austria		Hong Kong		US		APS	
	TOP	GM	TOP	GM	TOP	GM	TOP	GM	TOP	GM	TOP	GM	TOP	GM	TOP	GM	TOP	GM	TOP	GM	TOP	SOs
Easy to talk to	✔	✔	✔	✔	✔	✔	✔	✔	✔	✔	✔	✔	✔	✔	✔	✔	✔	✔	✔	✔	✔	✔
Not easy to talk to										×								×				×
Discuss sensitive issues	✔		✔		✔		✔		✔	✔	✔		✔		✔		✔		✔		✔	
Address safe issues	✔		✔	×	✔	×	✔	×	✔		✔		✔	×	✔	×	✔	×	✔	×	✔	×
Understanding	✔	✔	✔		✔		✔		✔		✔		✔		✔		✔		✔		✔	
Not understanding				×		×		×		×		×		×		×		×		×		×
Trust each other	✔		✔		✔		✔		✔		✔		✔		✔		✔		✔		✔	
Not trust each other				×		×				×				×		×		×		×		×
Implement decisions made in top team	✔	✔	✔	✔	✔	✔	✔		✔	✔	✔	✔	✔		✔	✔	✔	✔	✔	✔	✔	✔
Implement decisions that personally suit				×		×		×								×		×		×		×
Address long- and short-term issues	✔	✔	✔		✔		✔		✔		✔		✔		✔		✔	✔	✔	✔	✔	✔
Address short-term issues				×		×		×		×		×		×		×		×		×		×

Note:
TOP Presidents/CEOs/Chairmen/MDs
SES Senior Executive Service
✔ – Positive perception of Top Team
× – Negative perception
APS Australian Public Service
SOs Senior Officers
GM General Managers

Source: Adapted from Kakabadse et al. (1996), also in Korac-Kakabadse and Korac-Kakabadse (1998).

66 per cent respectively. A more subdued set of scores emerges for overall knowledge of operating business and functional objectives.

However, the highest range of scores emerges for those key tasks the senior manager has declared will be his/her prime area of responsibility. British and Hong Kong-based companies highlight 91 per cent respectively of top, middle and junior management declaring that they clearly appreciate the aims and objectives of the leader(s) of the organization. Overall, the more personal the message, the greater attention people pay, particularly so highlighted when communicating through providing example.

Providing example

George Vasiliou, current Chairman and former CEO of MEMRB (Middle East Management Research Bureau) – the extensive Cypriot business consultancy organization spread across the Middle East, Asia Pacific and USA – and former President of the Republic of Cyprus, agrees with the view that key messages need to be personalized, as it was he who stated that:

> 25 per cent of communication problems can be 'designed' for [meaning, cascaded through the organization], but no matter what you do, 75 per cent of communication problems are down to people. What the leader does, communicates far more than what is said, written or presented.

On the basis of the 25/75 per cent ruling, a select number of CEOs, directors and general managers who took part in the Cranfield surveys were asked to identify core leader behaviours that communicate important messages to the rest of the organization. Six key communicating behaviours emerged, namely approachability, openly addressing sensitivities, being understanding, being trustworthy, displaying commitment to decision implementation, and possessing the long-term/ short-term orientation of top managers. Top managers (CEOs, presidents, chairmen, SESs) rated how effectively they applied themselves to the six core communicating behaviours. Their subordinates, general managers and SOs, were asked to rate how effectively their bosses adopted the six behaviours in their day-to-day work. The aim was to identify whether compatibility of view existed between top level managers and the general managers/SOs below them, concerning the effectiveness of the communicating behaviour of the top team, and if not, to identify the divergence of view between these levels which distorted internal communications (see Table 8.8).

The Irish, Germans and Australian civil servants consider that the members of their top team are 'not easy to talk to'.

In contrast, in response to the question 'Do the members of the Top Team openly discuss sensitive issues?', only German top managers and their direct reports consider they openly address sensitive issues. For all other countries, top management and general management admit to considerable inhibition on this topic.

Regarding the issue of understanding, Japan is the only country to indicate that the views of both the top managers and GMs are positive and supportive. In contrast, a large percentage of private sector GMs and senior officers in the APS consider that their top management make little attempt to understand the challenges and concerns of each other, or of their subordinates. On the issue of trust, the Japanese responses highlight similar levels of compatibility to those of the Swedes. The top managers of both countries indicate that the levels of trust among the members of the top team are high, an opinion that is shared by their GMs. For all others, the GMs consider that the behaviour of their bosses is indicative of low levels of trust among the top leaders of the organization.

The Japanese, French, Germans, Swedes, Spanish and Americans display compatability of view in response to the issue of cabinet responsibility, emphasizing high levels of cohesion at senior management levels. The British, Irish, Austrians and Hong Kong expatriate and Chinese executives and the Australians paint a different picture. The view to emerge from general management is that top managers implement only those decisions that personally suit the individual, irrespective of whatever was jointly agreed.

In response to the question, 'Do the members of the Top Team address long and short term issues?', the Japanese respondents, Hong Kong expatriot and Chinese executives and Americans provide the most comparable, positively oriented responses. In contrast, the remainder of the GMs consider that the top team addresses only short term issues.

Overall, British, Irish and Australian business and public sector leaders, followed by French, American, Hong Kong, Chinese and expatriot business leaders indicate greatest tension at the top manager/general manager interface points, the repercussions of which are that top management are seen by the rest of the organization as not meaning what they say and hence, should not be trusted. Why? Because their own general managers do not trust them! The results highlight a substantial contrast between what is said, and what is done, emphasizing how easily messages can become distorted following strategic debate and decision-making. The conclusion is that interfacing is viewed in a large number of organizations as disruptive, making working in flattened structures problematic. In order to improve communication through positive example by the leaders of the organization, four best practice disciplines are identified.

Think issue, not territory[10]

Today's reality is that top managers are attending meetings, hearing agreement on key issues, walking out of meetings recognizing that commitment is not likely to be forthcoming because they believe their colleagues do not mean what they have said, and thereby knowing that the agreements reached are worthless. Most have an insight into what is happening around them, but find it difficult to action such insight because of the personal discomfort experienced in addressing such problems. The first step to overcoming tension and low trust is to concentrate on organization-wide issues and not be driven by territorial concerns:

> people who can learn . . . have a broader perspective which they bring to bear on the analysis and contemplation of a problem. They can actually think about a range of options . . . you can see the richness of their ideas (SES, APS Survey).

If the example provided by top management is that of being able to take an overview of a situation, such a perspective is more likely to emerge from staff and management lower down the organization. However, if the example from the top is the preservation of one's territory, that pattern of behaviour is equally likely to be replicated lower down.

Be disciplined at key interfaces

The fundamental thesis is that effective interfacing is crucial to positive communications, but if not valued, then distortion of strategy during implementation occurs. It is crucial, then, to portray a consistency of message, so that in a disciplined way, important initiatives can be effectively cascaded down the organization. Quality interfacing needs to be recognized as an important area of senior management responsibility. Engendering a feeling of responsibility is substantially assisted if the senior managers feel themselves to be respected and integrated members of the executive. Having clarified who is and is not in the broader executive, such feelings of responsibility are then inculcated by the establishment of ground rules concerning best practice leader behaviour, namely:

■ *Respect meetings.* Executive work is conducted at meetings. Meetings are the forum where current issues and ways forward are aired and clarified, namely processes that are effective precursors to positive decision-making and implementation. To make the best use of meetings requires respecting the meeting's forum. Learning to conduct oneself effectively at meetings demands a degree of flexibility. What issues should be raised, and when? How should those issues be raised? Do colleagues need to be informally forewarned and prepared so that they find it easy to enter into the debate? The flexibility to think 'issue' and 'process' assists considerably in reaching resolution, and ownership of that resolution, by all involved.

- *Behave the message.* As already shown, lower level staff hearing one thing but then witnessing quite different behaviour from the manager who uttered the words, does little for trust, drive and motivation. Winning the trust and commitment of staff and management relies heavily on top management's behaving in a manner that is conducive to promoting the best practice they require others to display. Senior management, irrespective of the size and complexity of their extended top team, have to maintain a discipline to ensure that full participation in best practice behaviour occurs.
- *Promote a networking culture.* In addition to the good example from the top, promoting sound strategic and operational relationships, is effective networking. Building a network of relationships is an essential aspect of strategic management. The process takes time, requires patience, and is achieved by displaying discipline, consistency and honesty at meetings, and showing humanity and concern outside meetings. Effective dialogue is conducted within trusting relationships which evolve over time. The real question is, how do senior managers see their jobs? As a series of tasks, as meeting particular leadership requirements, as hanging on to their job, or as leader of an organization to whom the fabric of the organization and the morale of its employees are as important as meeting targets? The practice of promoting a networking culture is an active display of leadership.

Promote cabinet responsibility

Cabinet responsibility is displayed through good example on a daily basis in the organization. Having identified the membership of the extended top team and agreed upon a discipline for behaviour, the basis to cabinet responsibility is set. Its continuation is dependent on the strength of the feedback culture established at senior levels. Could one, for example, face a colleague and say, 'You said you were going to do that, and you have done the opposite!'? Only when a quality of dialogue which allows for such comments to be made and is seen as positive, does full cabinet responsibility exist. Otherwise, one is playing with words. Attaining and maintaining cabinet responsibility is a process fraught with difficulties/ challenges, but it does have its rewards. Full acceptance of cabinet responsibility provides the 'grit' which stimulates positive debate as opposed to inhibitory and backroom conversation.

Structure to communicate

It was said of Sir Ralph Halpern that upon accepting the job of leading the Burton Group, he structured his job as CEO to promote effective communications in the organization. According to one of his senior managers – who did not wish to be named – Halpern spent the first few months of his appointment driving to various stores within the regions, listening to the regional managers' and store directors' concerns, and overall, winning the trust and respect of the management. Halpern wanted acceptance of his view that the buying function should be centralized and not the responsibility of regional managers. Listening to their concerns, offering his own views, but most of all having made the time and effort to go to them, displayed a powerful message – Halpern cares about what we think!

Whether the story is true or not, Halpern's initiative is, in itself, nothing new. The common parlance is 'walk the talk', get out and about with the other people in the organization. However, such activity is demanding, and what is underestimated is the amount of time necessary to devote to communication. Halpern needed to restructure his role in order to communicate effectively and consistently. Structuring in order to communicate requires consideration of:

- the reason for communicating,
- the time required to focus on the communication of key messages,
- the demands of the exercise, in terms of detracting one's attention from other duties,
- the capability and willingness of colleagues and subordinates to have key tasks delegated to them in order that the leader can fully exercise communication.

Exercises in effective communication are necessary but demanding, and require more than willingness and energy. Focusing people's attention and resources in a structured manner also needs to be considered.

Passion for success

What breathes life into an organization is passion, enthusiasm and a will to achieve and succeed. Passion is two-sided, emotional zest, and attention to daily life and detail.

Zest

Most people in a leadership role would find it difficult to pursue a course of action for any length of time without considering whether what they were doing was worthwhile and provided value. The more a leader displays his/her belief in his/her actions and policies, the more other people are enthused. Leadership holds strong symbolic connotations, in that people need to have displayed by their leader, those signals which highlight the appropriate behaviour to apply, and the beliefs to hold. An infectious belief in success, in itself, promotes greater enthusiasm. In order to project passion, and as highlighted in Chapter 1, the importance of building winning teams is crucial. In so doing, attention should be given to becoming acquainted with individuals. Displaying personal interest can make people feel special. The more enthusiastic the boss, and the more he/she shows that he/she knows his/her people, the greater the enthusiasm for success will others display.

Eye for detail

However, passion also has an element of sobriety. In order to turn passion into an operational reality, particular attention needs to be given to detail, highlighting the transactional nature of leadership emphasized in Chapter 1. Nothing is more impressive than seeing a boss who is clearly involved in the lives of individuals and teams, displaying not only personal knowledge of them as people, but also of their day-to-day contribution and performance. An eye for detail confirms concern and involvement. An eye for detail, together with discipline and application, further promotes effectiveness at follow-through. Setting achievable short-term targets as stepping stones to achieving objectives, helps keep people on track, and the boss informed as to what progress is being made.

Displaying a passion for success is an operational concept. The emphasis is on how people can influence success from one day to the next. Success is achieved by attendance to the concerns of the day-to-day, but with enthusiasm. The combination of passion and detail is a potent mixture.

Staying power

For how long should discretionary leaders stay in post before they fully appreciate the nature of the challenges they face in their role and before becoming stale, lacking in innovation and finding it difficult to respond positively to demanding suggestions for improvements? The transition experience evidence highlighted in Chapter 11 suggests not less than 30 months, that being the minimum period for any individual to begin to appreciate the sales, marketing, and organizational ramifications of different contexts. Further, the impact of the two key demographics, organizational and job tenure, as highlighted in Chapter 6, strongly suggest that in order to promote added value, a more substantial length of time is required, not only to understand the nature of contextual intricacies, but equally to be around to remedy and live through mistakes made. Respect is gained by being seen to be around to bring to fruition the policies and objectives one initiated, and to make adjustments according to the needs that have arisen (see Table 8.9).

A particularly challenging aspect of general management work is interfacing across the organization. Effectiveness at interfacing is not simply a question of building up a network of contacts, but equally

Table 8.9   Impact of staying power

Issue	Impact
Interfacing internally	5+ years in the job
Building trust	5+ years in the job
Renegotiating budgets	More effectively done, 5+ years in the job
Differentiating sales/marketing	5+ years in the job
Understanding/responding to customer/ market needs	5+ years in the job
Building respect to address paradox	5 to 7 years in the job
Addressing shareholder/stakeholder paradox	More effectively done, 5 to 7 years in the job

Source: adapted from Kakabadse (1991)

involves understanding the challenges and constraints faced by colleagues. Gaining a realistic perspective of the circumstances of colleagues in different parts of the organization leads to a greater appreciation of both the nature and purpose of interfacing. Armed with insight into context, it is possible to differentiate between a colleague who is personally awkward and difficult, and one who makes uncomfortable suggestions, but is honourably driven to enhance people's development and improve organizational performance. The Cranfield research highlights that gaining more penetrating and essential insight into people and their particular circumstances requires approximately five years in the job, as that is the timespan reported as necessary in which to build and grow relationships, work through disagreements and differences and gain trust and respect. As reported in Chapter 6, the top managers of the Honda organization do not have their own offices but share the same large office at the Tokyo headquarters. In so doing, they report that they more freely discuss issues, through being present during each other's telephone calls and other conversations, which helps to promote a climate of open and useful debate. The senior managers involved are proud of the legacy Honda, the founder, left them. They do, however, admit that it takes a little time to adjust to sharing an office, when they have spent a considerable part of their managerial career in the privacy of their own office.

Apart from improving the quality of interfacing and internal communications, the building of trust and respect holds particular business implications for the setting and attaining of cost and revenue budgets and targets. Are cost and revenue targets set according to the aspirations of corporate centre directors, or according to an accurate appreciation of the revenue potential of particular markets? Alan Saunders, the ex-Managing Director of Pitman Moore, the animal health business, and a subsidiary of the USA corporation Imcera, in discussing the negotiations of financial targets and budgets that took place between his operating business and the corporate centre in the USA, described the process as one fraught with frustrations/contradictions. However, his solution was one of promoting co-operation and trust.

> But one thing I would say is that, if the Centre is making the demand, the operating businesses should work closely together – I wouldn't keep them separate. I wouldn't sit in Group and say, 'we have got to have $100 million [revenue]' and then go out to a GM and say – 'you have got to get $20 million' – I wouldn't have the GM work merrily away, present a fabulous plan and say 'I can give you $6 million' – to which the response is 'rubbish!' You have got to do it together. Each operating business has got to understand where the others are coming from . . . Each has got to know that the total is $100 million and the GMs need to know the Centre is comfortable with $75 million . . . you have got to do it together (Alan Saunders).

The respect required to interface appropriately across and upwards, emerges with time. On the one hand, the centre has to trust that the operating business heads have a clear view of the sales and marketing potential of their markets. On the other, the operating business heads need time to grow a relationship with the centre before offering the feedback as to what added-value benefit the centre could provide, rather than the centre pushing for unrealistic targets. Rethinking and renegotiating budgets, clearly differentiating sales and marketing, and understanding and appropriately responding to customer needs, have been identified as skill areas the mastery of which requires approximately five years' experience in the job.

Attention to detail, and staying power in combination with a sense of purpose and mission, make visions work. Trust and respect, the two sides of the same capability coin, are at their peak when a leader displays strength of character by staying to be held to account for his/her own mistakes. Mistakes will always be made. Their correction, however, commands purposeful attention.

Key points summary

- Three contrasting approaches to analysing the capability of leaders are identified, namely the desired attributes of leaders, the tasks leaders have to address, and the reactions of individuals when placed in a discretionary leader role.
- A considerable array of desired leader attributes have been identified, but the question remains, from the array of conflicting and overlapping qualities, as to which of these are more 'born with' characteristics, as opposed to 'learned and developed' through personal growth and experience.

■ A similar mix of concepts arises when examining leader skill and capability, from the point of view of what is necessary to fulfil the key tasks of leadership.

■ Due to the mix of assumptions underlying the fields of leadership attributes and tasks, a third route is explored and forms the basis of the chapter, namely that of discretionary leadership.

■ Discretionary leadership is determined by the degree of will and capability to exercise choice as is exhibited by a senior manager, assuming the exercise of discretion is required of the person in his/her role. A varied and considerable number of discretionary leader roles can exist in any one organization, at any one point in time.

■ Discretionary leadership emphasizes that each person will discern and respond differently, according to the challenges he/she faces in the role, his/her view as to how current and future challenges should be addressed and the manner in which the individual's feelings (robustness, inhibitions) influence his/her thoughts and actions. According to the concept of discretionary leadership, attaining cohesion and shared views on key issues across the organization, can be a difficult and trying/frustrating process, as each of the discretionary leaders may hold a contrastingly different agenda and further, the total number of discretionary roles may not be fully represented in the organization's meetings structure, generating resentment and resistance from those not appropriately involved in determining the future of the organization.

Best practice leadership

■ Seven areas of best practice discretionary leadership are identified, conviction to craft the future, strength to surface sentiments, wisdom for pathways through paradox, flair to engage through dialogue, discipline to communicate, passion for results, and staying power.

■ Conviction to craft the future highlights the need for discretionary leaders to promote a clear and cohesive view of how to proceed into the future (vision). Negotiating towards a shared perspective of the future requires strength of character (conviction) from the key leaders, in order for each individual to have the confidence to pursue what is considered best for the organization, and to then involve all of the top team in the vision debate, in the nurture of an internal environment where feedback can be readily offered, and in jointly establishing a common base (platform) from which to pursue a meaningful, shared view (vision, mission) of the future.

■ The strength to surface sentiments requires at least one top manager initiating a dialogue in which the other leaders in the organization can state their views of the organization as it is now, and where they consider it should be in the future. In debating the nature, shape, size and future of the organization, it is likely that the philosophies and deeply held convictions of the discretionary leaders will, in part, or whole, emerge. Sooner or later, these sentiments need to be fully surfaced, irrespective of the discomfort in so doing, in order to work towards senior management holding a shared philosophy as to the nature of the organization they desire.

■ The wisdom for pathways through paradox, involves addressing challenging issues in operationalizing the vision, when contradictory pressures are the commonplace experience. Discretionary leaders need to find ways through two paradoxes, the paradox of strategy and the paradox of feedback. The paradox of strategy involves reconciling the requirements of efficiency, cost management and curtailment (vertical synergies) with investing in people and internal organizational procedures in order to promote quality of service, flexibility, and team work (horizontal synergies). Discretionary leader teams that have not evolved a shared vision and philosophy, when required to reconcile vertical and horizontal synergy pressures, are likely to display symptoms of buck passing, cynicism, not wishing to be held to account, and being unable to agree on the interpretation of 'sales' and 'marketing', thus making it difficult to determine quality, service provision and branding. In order to improve the situation, senior management may request feedback in order to surface people's views concerning the current circumstances, and how to improve the situation. Feedback can be equally paradoxical, providing contrasting perspectives on how to proceed, placing senior management in the position of rejecting some or all of the feedback they receive. The wisdom needed to find ways through contrasting demands involves recognizing the degree or lack of ownership in addressing strategic challenges at senior management levels, why ownership is not forthcoming, the means by which ownership could be enhanced through on and off-the-job development experiences, the value of setting clear objectives which positively focus people's attention, and realizing that no easy-way-through exists. Wisdom is a context-related concept in that the finding of ways through difficulties is determined by the unique nature of each context. On the basis that a different approach is required to suit the circumstances of each context, a fundamental element of wisdom is respect for context, for without such respect being visibly displayed, the credibility of the leader and his/her strategies, is unlikely to be realized.

■ The flair to engage through dialogue highlights the inhibitions that need to be overcome in promoting penetrating, high quality debate about prevalent issues. Improving dialogue may require re-configuring the structure of meetings, so that a broader range of opinions is voiced and represented. The skill of engaging others in dialogue, involves balancing the comfort level of those attending the meetings with the need to examine pertinent issues, which may be perceived as too sensitive to discuss, so that a full debate takes place.

■ In order to communicate effectively key messages throughout the organization, two avenues are identified, the one providing direction and the other providing example. Providing direction involves clearly and unambiguously, through various channels, stating the nature of the mission of the organization, the corporate and operating business objectives, the key areas of the job-related responsibility of top managers, as well as other key messages. However, the more powerful form of communication is that of top management providing example, through consistently matching words with actions. Research highlights a substantial distortion of communication through the medium of providing example. In order to ensure the provision of positive communication by example, senior management are recommended to address issues, and not defend organizational territory, to display disciplined behaviour at key interfaces, promote a shared sense of cabinet responsibility and, if necessary, to restructure their jobs, even temporarily, to allow for more effective communication.

■ In order to 'inject' passion into others actively to pursue success, leaders need to display their own enthusiasm, and pay particular attention to detail, especially detail concerning people's daily experiences.

■ Staying power emphasizes that effective senior managers are those who have remained in post for a sufficient period of time and have become accustomed to the broader and more intricate issues that need to be addressed, have learnt from their mistakes, and have reconciled their relationships with superiors, colleagues and subordinates.

Notes

1   CEO   Chief Executive Officer
   MD   Managing Director
   ED   Executive Director
   GM   General Manager
   SES   Senior Executive Service
   SO   Senior Officer
2   Adapted from Korac-Kakabadse *et al.* (1998).
3   Adapted from Korac-Kakabadse and Korac-Kakabadse (1997).
4   The following sections are adapted from Korac-Kakabadse *et al.* (1998).
5   See Korac-Kakabadse *et al.* (1998).
6   Adapted from Korac-Kakabadse and Korac-Kakabadse (1998); also (1997) and (1996).
7   The Leadership Paradox model appears Korac-Kakabadse and Korac-Kakabadse (1998); and also (1977) and (1996).

8 From Bowman and Kakabadse (1977).
9 The distinction between providing direction and providing example is made in the *Wealth Creators* by Andrew Kakabadse. Since then, the database supporting this distinction has been extended and is reported forthwith.
10 Certain of the best practice disciplines discussed above are adapted from Korac-Kakabadse and Korac-Kakabadse (1998).

Further reading

For information on discretionary leadership, see Jaques (1951) and for the application of discretion and cognitive complexity, see Jaques (1979). For further examination of key leader attributes, see:

■ For wisdom (Kaplan, 1994),
■ For maturity (Warburton, 1993),
■ For visionary focus (Kouzes and Posner, 1987; Bennis, 1993),
■ For being an effective communicator of Vision (Senge, 1992),
■ For being committed to the vision (Manz and Sims, 1991),
■ For positive self-regard (Bass, *et al.* 1987),
■ For clear judgement (Castonguay, 1993),
■ For spiritual leadership (De Pree, 1993),
■ For integrity (Thomasma, 1993),
■ For leaders with intellectual energy (Conger, 1993).

On the tasks of leadership, see:

■ For articulation of a vision that empowers (Tichy and Sherman, 1993),
■ For leading by example (Conger, 1993),
■ For creating an environment which empowers, and generates intellectual capital (Bennis, 1993),
■ For champions that reflect the key organizational values (Nadler and Tushman, 1990),
■ For exhibiting passion to be involved in enterprise achievements for their own sake, rather than being reward driven (Senge, 1992).

For additional reading of boardroom behaviour, read Olins (1996) report on Cable and Wireless in *The Sunday Times*, and also Collins and Porras (1996) and Bowman and Kakabadse (1997).

CHAPTER 9

Burn Out

Case analysis

Sandy Wilson

Sandy Wilson exclaimed

> My God! Am I getting frustrated with Carter and his mob at the MOD [Ministry of Defence, UK]. Every time we get close to agreement, the chairs move round again and everything changes – so we start from the beginning, new job specification, costings, different consultants – collect their CVs, fax them through to the client, and more of 'yes, I like that person; no I don't'. We will soon be running out of bodies.

Claire Jenkins, one of the senior consultants on the MOD project, commented

> I know, Sandy, but when have the MOD been different? In fact, when ever have any of our larger clients been different? This backwards/forwards before a major project starts is just a natural part of the process.

There was little doubt that the MOD project was complex. The rationalization of jobs and the delayering of the organization had generated considerable resistance and hostility from MOD personnel. The obvious target was the consultant team, who had experienced resentment, a lack of co-operation, and continuous changes to the terms of reference of the project. The current concerns focused on the personnel function's contribution to the organization. The team were simply attempting to establish clarity concerning the purpose and value of certain of the roles in the personnel structure. The senior civil servant leading the personnel side of the organization study seemed to be changing his mind as to the requirements and terms of reference of certain roles.

The brief given at one point would be to examine the tasks, accountabilities and responsibilities of particular jobs. If the duties of these roles could be allocated to other jobs, which in turn would lead to a head-count reduction, then that line of enquiry would be the one to be pursued. The problem, in Sandy Wilson's eyes, was that once a lead was given, and recommendations made, the civil servant concerned would contradict his previous statements and declare that the consulting team had got it wrong. One of the client's responses would be to state that the roles under scrutiny would not be the ones in question that were needy of attention. For Sandy Wilson, the charade would start again, altered terms of reference, and requests for new consultants to substitute certain of the members of the existing team who had lost credibility. The consultants on the team were as frustrated as Sandy. However, a number considered that Sandy Wilson was substantially to blame for the present fluctuations. Most had come to the realization that Sandy, as the Lead Partner on the project, had not positioned himself to be close enough to key clients, such as Carter, in order to influence them and thereby reduce their counter-productive impact on the project. As one of the consultants put it, 'What . . . is up with Sandy? He is having no impact on Carter! Why the hell is he not taking him out to dinner, looking after him; doing bloody something to relieve the situation?'

Not that doing something to influence Carter would have been easy. One of the consultants described the MOD as a *mafiosi* array of tribes. Each had its own tribal chief who would fight the others for territory or other small gains, but under threat, the lot would get together to ensure a 'no way through policy' for outsiders.

> 'Someone needs to prise that lot open. Whoever it is, needs energy, brains and bags of street cunning to form the right linkages and stop those bastards choking us and driving us crazy by changing the brief every bloody day', commented the same consultant. Sandy Wilson had the street cunning, the experience, the political as well as the professional ability, but just at this moment, was a little low on energy.

Sandy Wilson, aged 49, was a partner and consultant with the well-established audit/consultancy practice of Murray-Matlock. The firm, structured on a regional basis in the UK, and with offices or joint venture locations throughout Europe, USA, Africa and Australasia, offered the customary range of audit services, tax as well as consultancy and, recently, executive search. In order to penetrate particular industry sectors, functionally mixed groups of industry specialists, under a lead partner, were tasked with providing a comprehensive, 'one-stop-shop' service to clients, whereby any intervention could provide an opening for other specialists into the client organization.

That, however, was not the basis of Sandy Wilson's intervention. The organizational change programme at the MOD had been separately negotiated with Sandy Wilson, being the lead partner of the human resources team. Apart from rationalizing the Personnel Unit at the MOD, Sandy was equally required to introduce an appraisal system, appraisal training, and team development to an organization that, in the eyes of the senior civil servants, was considered besieged and beleaguered.

In keeping with most other days, Sandy arrived home shortly after 8.30 pm. June Wilson, Sandy's wife, an IT manager with one of the retail banks, had long since been home, and greeted him with her normal, 'Hi! How was your day?', to which the response was, 'Oh, fine, thanks; much the same'.

Sandy, an accountant by training, had successfully switched over to consultancy and, latterly, carved a reputation for himself in HR consulting. He had been married for 23 years, had two sons, Adam, aged 15, preparing himself for his intermediate grade exams (GCSEs), and Stephen, a successful first year university entrant. Sandy's view of his home life was, on reflection, quite good. There was little doubt that he and his wife cared deeply for each other. Both worked hard to communicate with each other, spending between three to four evenings per week talking. However, Sandy's relationship with Stephen had been strained for quite a while. Sandy blamed himself for this poor standing with his son, highlighting his excessive workload, and the fact of not having built a sufficiently strong relationship with the boy at an earlier age, which would have helped to sustain a young man, tense during the exploring and flexing of his identity.

'All over your face is written "not a good day". I'll clear the dishes and we can sit together.'

'Have you heard from Stephen?', shouted Sandy after her.

'No, but he seemed okay when I spoke to him last week; although reading between the lines, he is overdoing the socializing bit', Jane responded. 'Oh, Sandy', she continued, 'I hope you're not going to disappoint Adam this Saturday. You promised you'd take him to the rugby. You know he likes being with you, and especially at rugby matches.'

Sandy knew it only too well. He also knew how many times he had disappointed Adam, through feeling obliged to turn up at the office, or to be with clients, over weekends. The way things were progressing with Carter, this weekend had the makings of disappointing Adam once more. He did not wish to say anything to his wife just yet.

'So, what's been happening to you?', asked Sandy, as his wife sat down.

She replied:

Oh much the same; problems with the branches. Constantly been receiving complaints of getting it wrong; customers upset. The IT Delivery Working Party have still not sorted out terms of reference acceptable to the branches. It's just a hassle, made worse with Mike Jasper constantly upsetting the team. He looks for faults. Usually he's right, and that makes things worse. What about you?'

Sandy said: 'Ditto to terms of reference; ditto to clients; ditto to all the Mike Jaspers on my team as well – like you, just hassle.'

The two just looked at each other.

'Sandy, what's really wrong? Both of us have had this sort of hassle before, but I've noticed with you recently, there is something more. It's not just the hassle any more, something else is affecting you', said Jane.

He just looked at her, then said:

It's eh . . . it's just that the fight in me is gone. I was in the loo and I overheard one of the guys commenting that the problems with Carter are the result of my not managing him. I wanted to rush and just hit that guy. If only they knew how difficult Carter is. Having sat back, however, I'm afraid he's right. I am a bit low on the energy side at the moment.

Sandy did not look happy. He swished the wine around his glass, stared at it for a few minutes and said,

I'm bored, I'm tired and I'm going nowhere. There are no more promotions. The work does not get easier. Yet what's pushed hard in the firm? More commitment! More drive! More time for work. Get the client! Keep the client! Maximize the chargeable hours. To think I have 11 more years of this, minimum; that is if I do not lose my job in the meantime. Sometimes it can seem just so pointless; not that it is like this always. Some days are better than others.

His wife looked on sympathetically. She knew he was overworked. He had been a partner now for 12 years, with little prospect of his gaining anything more senior. She knew him to be a good family man, but was slowly becoming less mentally and emotionally available to the family. Basically, he was coming home tired, very tired. At home, he would try and take part in the activities of the family, but recently less so. Perhaps he drank slightly more than before, but worst of all was his losing his enthusiasm for exercise. He regularly used to go to the gym three times a week. Now his attendance was more sporadic.

Jane continued:

I know; I've noticed you're losing your enthusiasm. Is there anyone you can talk to about this? You know I would always listen, but is there someone specifically that you could confide in, perhaps to even discuss changing your job, or bits of it, to take the pressure off you?

Sandy responded:

I don't know who to approach; certainly no one in the firm, and what good would that do? I'd be seen as copping out, burnt out, incapable. I may not know where the hell I'm going from here, but wherever it is, if I started talking about the way I feel, I'd kill my chances for certain.

Then Jane said:

How are you going to find a way through this one, Sandy? You're working hard, but you're also burning yourself out. There seems to be no one to talk to, and the boys, not so much me, are suffering. Adam is a little disappointed with your having to cancel on Saturdays. You need to spend time to get closer to Stephen. The tensions between the two of you are simply not good.

'I know', responded Sandy.

What is wrong with Sandy Wilson? His symptoms of feeling bored, tired, fed up, going nowhere, and facing problems at work and home are, in one sense, relatively commonplace, and possibly nothing deeper than described.

On the other hand, symptoms such as erratic behaviour at both home and in the workplace, loss of temper, excessive drinking, and a slow insidious decline in the performance of the person, for no obvious reason could be the start of something else. Such is the case with Sandy Wilson who, apart from currently experiencing further frustration with his MOD client, recently lost his temper with his boss, whom he felt was being unreasonable in his criticism of Sandy's mismanagement of the MOD situation. The boss, equally perplexed as to what to do, but mindful of the fact that to lose the MOD contract could severely damage the revenue forecasts for the year, blamed Sandy for not being sufficiently close to the client to shield the consultant team and Murray-Matlock from the excesses of the troublesome senior civil servant, Carter.

Under excessive pressures, certain individuals resort to extreme measures. As reported by Manfred Kets de Vries, Eli Black, an ordained rabbi, businessman, Chairman, President and CEO of United Brands (a $2 billion multi-national food company), on 3 February 1975, leaped to his death from the forty-fourth floor of Manhattan's Pan Am building. The exact reasons for Black's tragic act are not known. What is reported of Black is that he seemed reserved, controlled, but seemingly from a stable background, being a descendant of ten generations of rabbis.[1]

Eli Black and Sandy Wilson, although different personalities, one who did not show his feelings, and the other who did, are, however, seemingly victims of a difficult to pinpoint phenomenon, but one which is becoming an ever more common experience, *executive burn out*. The distress of burn out is apparent. People's lives deteriorate, for some, ruined, and for a minority, even ended, but the question is, is it a condition at all? Is burn out just a more excessive form of stress, or an ailment in its own right?

The fact that a considerable number of senior managers seem to be increasingly prone to this debilitating experience suggests that serious attention should be given to the topic, irrespective of whether it be treated as a unique condition. A phenomenon remarkably similar to burn out is now recognized by the medical profession, known more generally as chronic fatigue syndrome, more particularly as ME. In fact, in a study reported in the 1995 issue of Hospitals and Health Networks of middle and senior managers (including CEOs), conducted by Opinion Research Corp, 73 per cent of the survey respondents believed that the threat of burn out was greater then than 20 years earlier. The factors cited for their opinion were increases in stress, job pressure, increased competition, higher and more intense work-related complexity, faster pace of life, and the greater likelihood of redundancy.

As the subject matter is increasingly becoming a concern and a seemingly more prominent phenomenon in the lives of leaders of organizations, it is included in this book as an important element of leadership.

In this chapter, attention is given to understanding how burn out emerges as an experience of so many managers and their leaders. Further, ways of coping and negating the phenomenon are discussed and explored.

Nature of burn out

Managers use different expressions to describe their experiences of burn out; can't cope; have lost energy; have lost interest; the routine and daily grind is getting me down; just could not face what I could previously handle; just too much for me; emotionally choked up. Hence, as already stated, one interpretation is that burn out is another way of describing stress. There is little doubt that burn out involves experiences of stress, as the energy needed for working under pressure is greater, and as constant demands are made on the person to contribute. Under such circumstances, the energy level needed for coping with pressure, means that less is available for productive work. We know that the central nervous system and the immune system influence the mind, the emotions and the body. The result is that constant emotional strain demonstrates itself physically as well. This field of study is known as psychoneuroimmunology (PNI), now leading edge medical science, which has shown that the emotions have a powerful effect on the nervous system. The nervous system is an essential influence on the proper functioning of the immune system as it powerfully influences a number of functions, such as blood pressure levels. However, the link between emotions and the immune system is also influenced by certain chemicals such as adrenalin, released under stress. Despite the biochemical complexity, the fundamental outcome is that these hormones in their race through the body, hamper the functions of the immune cells. In effect, stress suppresses immune resistance, so as to prioritize the defences of the body to deal with the threat that is endangering survival. However, if stress is intense and continues, then such suppression may become lasting.

An alternative interpretation to the medical view of stress, is the presumption that certain personalities are more prone to it than others. Type A personalities, characterized by being individualistic, competitive, ambitious, success driven, and almost obsessive in their attempts to control their work environment, have been thought to be prime candidates for stress-related problems. In contrast, type B individuals, considered more as people and consensus sensitive, and not so driven to achieve, are viewed as being less prone to stress, due to a more relaxed approach to life.

However, numerous studies have shown that working with type A people induces such tensions in the workplace that the resulting tensions and poor relationships can place others emotionally, at risk. Thus, type B individuals are as vulnerable to strain, as their need for collaborative and caring work environments may be disregarded in the hard nosed, profit driven organization. Further, experience also indicates that individuals may drift in and out of being type A or type B oriented people, depending on the demands of the circumstances they face. As circumstances are often dictated by particular demographics, it is easy to conclude that the impact of demographics can be profound! (see Chapter 6).

Whatever the temperament of the individual, a considerable number of people experience substantial strain over prolonged periods of time. In order to get ahead, managers often feel that they need to identify fully with the organization, and hence tend to relate to organizational norms that demand rushed, missed or over-indulgent meals, and long hours of work, six or seven days a week. In effect, they become workaholics, whereby work becomes an addiction and even a crutch, and leads to unbalanced personal development, consequently creating many problems and challenges in family life. Even those that cannot be described as workaholics, but lead a workaholic lifestyle, under pressure they have little spare time for their spouse and children and are frequently absent from home. Further, progression up the organization's career ladder requires frequent changes of job, and may involve moving from one city, or country, to another.

The negative impact of such sustained pressure on home life, and the incidence of marital and family breakdown, is enormous. In the case of dual-career families, the strains and tensions are equally amplified. While the individuals involved ultimately make the choices that shape these events, they are in many cases driven by a wish to comply with the norms and values of the corporate world, where they desire to make their mark, or simply survive.

For so many executives and professionals, it is often difficult to find the balance in work life that many experts and family counsellors suggest is desirable. Corporate life requires that deadlines are met. Corporate life is also unfair, especially over workloads, which so often are unevenly spread. In this sense, many organizations generate their share of workaholics, irrespective of the wishes and inclinations of individuals. Most organizations implicitly demand that their executives be corporate persons, living and dreaming about attaining success in organizational life.

Many studies confirm that continuous exposure to disturbing and damaging emotions is bad for one's health. People who experience chronic anxiety, continuous sadness, prolonged pessimism, incessant exposure to hostility, and undeserved criticism, have been found to be more at risk to a number of ailments and diseases, including asthma, arthritis, headaches, peptic ulcers and heart diseases. The fact that sustained, emotionally damaging pressure is a major threat to health, differentiates stress from the prolonged nature of burn out.

It is important to recognize that burn out and stress can considerably overlap, especially in the areas of displaying the emotional and physical symptoms of anxiety, such as imagining that certain situations are worse than they really are, experiencing ulceration, colds, 'flu, and even cardio-vascular diseases.

However, in the pursuit of clarity, burn out is distinguished from stress in the following ways:

- Burn out is not just person related, but is consistently situationally driven; that is to say that no one person or type may be particularly prone to stressful circumstances, but he/she like anyone else, over time, can experience burn out related symptoms.
- Time is crucial, in that anyone exposed to strain over a prolonged period of time is likely to experience some sort of trauma, which may emerge as symptoms of burn out.
- Equally, over time, the experience of and response to pressure may change. The individual may previously have found a particular situation challenging and enthralling, but over time, found the same circumstances to be slowly debilitating. Hence, a fundamental distinguishing feature is that a situation now viewed as a negative experience, would formerly have been seen as stretching and developmental.

■ As much as the result of relentless and sustained pressure, burn out can also be an outcome of boredom, which, in turn, can arise from having little to do, or just being on 'auto pilot', doing what one knows well, but without experiencing any development or personal improvement, at times to the point of despising that activity or experience.

The consistent repetition of tasks, activities and demands that may previously have been experienced as positive, but have become routine, dull and demotivating to the point of the individual becoming pathological, is a prime element of burn out. Examining the track record of individuals who are considered to be burnt out is likely to show that previously they were on top of the demands that they now view as the prime source of complaint. Thereby, burn out is defined as, *an emotional deterioration arising from prolonged exposure to perceived debilitating circumstances, resulting in not being able to continue doing that in which the person was previously accomplished.* On this basis, burn out is an insidious, slowly emerging phenomenon, which only in retrospect may be recognized to have been damaging, as the person may have appeared to have been coping well with his/her circumstances for considerable periods.

Six reasons for burn out are identified, repetition, over-exposure, living in downsized environments, loss of will, feeling trapped, and becoming expert at coping with dysfunction.

Reasons for burn out

Repetition

Owing to the advances in information technology, to globalization, and to the need to cut costs, many organizations have been forced to reinvent themselves through strategies of restructuring, downsizing, right-sizing, re-engineering, re-focusing, all of which imply taking the middle layers of management from the organization, thus achieving flatter structures that are more responsive to clients and to market forces. Although these strategies for organizational renewal are championed by senior managers, they impose even more demands on top management. The elimination of middle managers leaves senior managers with the requirement to perform more routine tasks previously carried out by the now redundant management strata (see Chapter 2 for an analysis of the changing nature of the power and role culture relationship). In addition to the repetition of routine transactional tasks, executives are adding these tasks to their already wide repertoire. Furthermore, considering that flatter organizations are created in order to be more responsive to clients, this implies that the time given to the performance of tasks is shorter, as external stakeholders are likely to desire a quick response to their demands. The scenario is one of more tasks to be completed even more quickly, while still nurturing relationships, attending meetings, and communicating internally and externally, all of which then seem more demanding than before.

Over-exposure

An additional reality of a downsized and re-engineered organization, without the buffering comfort zone of an extended middle level management, is that the organization is more prone to crisis. The syndrome of ever more tasks, accompanied by the other duties of stakeholder management, corporate leadership, and the need for communication, increases, for each manager the likelihood that he/she will spend much time fighting fires. Instead of fully dealing with the real causes of problems, the time is used in overcoming only the symptoms. Further, fighting fires increases for each executive his/her exposure to transactional activities of a non-routine nature. Non-routine challenges are demanding, especially so in large organizations, as not only are people learning how to address the demands they face, but they may have to co-ordinate more with each other than previously was the case. Pursuing inappropriate pathways, or simply making mistakes, increase fire fighting circumstances. Making the time to meet and fully explore the challenges at hand, is unlikely to occur, due to the other demands the senior manager has to face.

Unfortunately, as fewer managers are available to share the load, the need for clearer accountability is likely to be accompanied by responding to short term, but demanding requirements. Clarifying accountabilities in itself is desirable. However, being overloaded with accountability does not allow for the satisfactory completion of any one task or activity. In addition, the co-operation necessary from colleagues and others in the organization may not readily be forthcoming, as they are busy pursuing their own areas of accountability. Under such circumstances, people at meetings may verbally commit themselves to an action, but then find it difficult to follow through on that commitment. For the executive held accountable for the actions identified, they still need the active participation of colleagues, when the enthusiasm and willingness of others may be waning or dissipated. Lean organizations, needing to be novel and imaginative in volatile and uncertain conditions, can place their executives in circumstances where individuals may wish to resist or deflect their accountabilities. As a result, people may feel let down by each other, and as a consequence, behave in a hostile way towards each other.

Understandably, leading, managing and working with people can be experienced as negative. The exposure to too many demands and requirements to face, too many individual agendas to respond to, can go hand in hand with people not considering themselves to be responsible for the accountabilities in their job, not because they are negative, but because they are finding it difficult to cope. Work becomes a daily hassle. The constant lack of job satisfaction can promote feelings of loss of direction. The reason for doing the job in the first place, is lost. The job may be experienced as one of dealing with only negative people, some of whom may be colleagues, subordinates, but equally may be clients, customers, suppliers and/or other stakeholders. Flatter organizations, by nature, expose their management to more praise and complaints, although experience highlights an inordinately greater volume of complaints than praise.

Over-exposure to such phenomena leads to a deterioration in performance and morale. What a person could previously handle, is currently experienced as an inability.

Living in downsized organizations

Downsizing and de-layering produce the 'survivor syndrome', namely low morale, lack of trust, and a decline in the commitment to the organization displayed by its 'survivors'. These outcomes have multiple and ripple effects on virtually every aspect of business, as survivors find themselves in new, and not necessarily friendly environments.

One outcome is that the terms of the 'psychological contract' between employees, middle and senior managers and the now 'lean' organization have fundamentally altered. Worried executives, concerned about their future, direct their motivation to keeping their jobs, not to achieving organizational goals, which, in today's climate are likely to be constantly changing and are often perceived as ambiguous. If over-exposure to high levels of uncertainty continues for a prolonged period of time, managers, including the leaders of the enterprise, are likely to adopt a cynical view of their circumstances, manifesting mistrust, conservatism, an aversion to risk taking and the diminution of drive. Overall the attitude is, 'do what you can but look after yourself first!' Deeper and longer-term organizational problems are simply left untouched. Managers recognize the deterioration effect of not addressing deeper organizational challenges, but feel themselves unwilling or unable to respond.

Attempts to improve circumstances through the publication and communication of positively worded mission statements are simply met with resentment, and in extreme cases, sabotage. In the absence of other alternative remedies, such organizations require their managers and leaders to be willing to contribute even more than usual. After a while, people resent being in a job that is, in reality, treated as a 'cash cow' revenue stream. People will ask themselves, 'Is it worth making money for others? What am I getting out of all this?', in essence, emotionally difficult questions to respond to satisfactorily, when downsizing has reduced career prospects. Without the goal of career progress, experience and research suggest that people become stale and saturated with both the routine and non-routine sides of their jobs. The ultimate irony is that the organization may be facing new and ever more challenging goals, but such diversity is not reflected in the personal goals of staff and managers.

Research has shown that re-engineering has involved white-collar staff cuts ranging from 10 to 80 per cent of total management and administrative positions. Research has also shown that up to 80 per cent of re-engineered organizations observe, to varying degrees, decreased employee morale. For example, 80 per cent of US respondents to a Conference Board survey of organizations employing more than 10,000 people, reported substantial drops in motivation among staff and management.

The human costs of organizational restructuring are exemplified in the emotional costs employees pay, through suffering stress related injuries, and through other factors such as corporate 'memory loss', loss of external contacts, loss of knowing how the organization really works, absenteeism, and productivity loss, as well as other organizational risks, which offset the potential initial cost savings. For example, the *Canberra Times*, in 1993, reported that the Australian Department of Employment, Education and Training (DEET), in 1992–93 (the year of re-engineering) paid a 61 per cent increase in workers' compensation premiums (Comcare) from the previous year, resulting in a total claim of AUD$5.7 million. Although the stress-related cases in DEET officially accounted for only 25 per cent of the compensation pay out, it was reported likely that the other injuries were also due to some form of stress, such as lack of concentration on work, because of the fear of imminent job loss. An additional example is that of one of the largest Australian re-engineering exercises involving counter staff at the Australian Post, which transformed the traditional post office into retail postal outlets. Australia Post adopted IT as its lever for change in promoting improved service delivery, and as a vital tool in attracting additional retail services, such as payment collection (using bar-coding) for other agencies. Although considerable staff training had been undertaken, there was a significant human cost in the process, a large part of which was considered to have been stress related injuries.

Loss of will

Over-exposure to continuous strain is likely to lead to emotional deterioration. The individual may not have sufficient will or the ability to face challenges, or to confront others, in order to arrest an actual or perceived decline in performance. Facing up to others may feel beyond the individual's capacity at that moment in time. Challenging others at meetings, giving feedback on a one-to-one basis, inviting feedback, and entering into robust but honest dialogue, can be felt to be overwhelming.

The decline in emotional stamina can also be accompanied by increasing dependency on others, who may be allowed to get their own way, at times knowingly, and against the better judgement of the senior manager. Individuals who enter into a dependency/inability-to-confront cycle, may try to justify their actions by convincing themselves that they are being democratic; that they are empowering others. When confronted with their inabilities, the person would be tempted to deny absolving him/herself from his/her responsibilities.

Low morale at work could spiral into damaging the home interface. The inability to face up to the demanding emotional requirements of leadership in the workforce is displayed on the home front by the individual not becoming fully involved with his/her family. Failing to take part in home life, allowing issues that require attention to slide, and simply not listening, are commonplace symptoms, as shown in the case of Sandy Wilson. The feeling of being saturated, of not having the personal resources to interact further and to be an active member of the family, are powerful symptoms of burn out.

For the 'burning out' manager, such experiences can be viewed as 'those at home/the family/my spouse does not understand me'. Over time, the support the person may then need from the home environment may be found to have progressively dwindled.

Feeling trapped

Following, or even accompanying, the experience of loss of will and resilience, is the feeling of being trapped.

The manager can feel trapped by age. To continue to strive to perform, even to pretend to perform and enjoy the job, may be important actions to portray publicly as the person may realistically recognize that he/she could otherwise be made redundant. With the current attitudes towards ageism, what other employment opportunities are available? For many, their conclusion is, few to none. It is either, do the best in this job, despite its perceived overwhelming negativity, or become unemployed.

Even if the prospects of finding alternative employment are viewed as realistic, the question is, will it be possible to maintain a comparable level of earnings? Family demands and needs, status, physical comforts and expectations, earning power, and lifestyle at particular periods in a person's life, can substantially influence decisions concerning lifestyle and work style. Leaving a current unsatisfying job and accepting a drop in income in order to work on less strenuous but more interesting activities, may require considerable adjustments to one's lifestyle. The two most common questions are, 'How could we as a family, cope?', and 'Why, after having worked so hard, should I take a drop in my standard of living?' Feeling that he/she is unable to escape, the person tries to do as well as he/she can in a job that has come to be disliked or even despised.

Not that the individual is unrealistic in his/her assessment of the situation. The expense of children's education at secondary and tertiary levels keeps a large number of people in jobs and organizations that they would otherwise have left. Once such demands have lessened or ceased, a considerable number of even substantially senior managers resign, and attempt to pursue personal interests, at a reduced level of income. For those who do not change because they feel that their lifestyle would be substantially damaged by a reduction in income level, in reality are earning money in jobs that are probably emotionally and even physically damaging to them, in order to pay for luxury properties, for large quantities of food and alcohol for the entertainment of friends at dinner parties. The emotional quandary of 'How could we cope if earning less?', is in reality a shallow question. To choose to continue paying a large mortgage on a property that probably looks splendid, and to maintain an extravagent social lifestyle, means that the individual is no longer earning (money) to enjoy simply a comfortable life, but to over indulge self and others who, in reality, may be of little or no real consequence or significance in the person's life.

The feeling of being trapped at work can be accompanied by feelings of being trapped at home. Personal and professional relationships stagnate. The emotional decline of the person leaves little energy for challenge or change. Despite a growing dissatisfaction with one's life, a common reaction is to stay with what is familiar and safe. Hence, partners continue living together, wanting to change, not knowing how to alter and improve their personal and professional circumstances, gradually coming to despise each other, but needing to pretend satisfaction with each other in order to continue to function in the status quo, but why? Because change is viewed as a worse alternative!

Taking pride in coping dysfunctionally

The literature on stress is abundant with studies indicating that prolonged exposure to stressful circumstances, feeling trapped for too long, with fewer resources to call upon to combat such circumstances, leaves a considerable number of people emotionally and physically damaged, with some individuals never fully recovering. Relationships may also be irreparably damaged. However, the Cranfield studies and experience strongly suggest that for many people, over-exposure to feeling trapped, and losing emotional drive, can have an opposite effect, that of being more determined, and of attempting to improve oneself. In fact, the person may feel that he/she had gone through the worst stages of a motivational down cycle and is now emerging positively. He/she may be, but equally the individual may be simply learning to cope, and unfortunately to cope dysfunctionally. In attempting to improve one's situation, it may be difficult to distinguish between genuinely having learned how to accept and make the best of one's circumstances, and stubbornly not wishing to be perceived as a person whose performance is diminishing.

Coping dysfunctionally does not involve attempting personally to re-adjust, but is more learning how to display an even greater discipline than before in a situation of emotional stagnation. Making the extra effort results in a display of greater professionalism in performance and of pride in oneself. The regimented individual has learned to resist strain and promote an image of being in control and doing well. The renewed effort may reassure the person that his/her values and old style of life are worthwhile. However, for a large number of people, such is not the case, as the renewed effort is a short-term phenomenon. Greater discipline and pride in oneself is likely to promote even greater dysfunctionality in the medium to long term. The doubts and the self-questioning return, as do the feelings of saturation. The professionalism and greater discipline are not equally accompanied by sustained enthusiasm, an improved sense of self-worth, and enhanced flexibility.

Gender response to burn out

A number of studies have shown that female executives are more susceptible to burn out owing to the multiple role demands inherent in running a career, home and family. The time demands impose a tighter schedule on the personal lives of executive women, than on those of men, with the result that women are less able to relax at the end of the day. Further evidence indicates that women in the upper levels of the organization tend to experience significantly greater amounts of 'internal strain', because of conflicting role demands on their time and energy. The stress research team at UMIST (Manchester University Institute of Science and Technology) under the leadership of Professor Cary Cooper together with Marilyn Davidson, in their study of 60 male and female executives from private and public sector organizations, found that 92 per cent of women experience moderate-to-high stress and strain at work. Many felt they were subjected to work overload due to the pressure to work harder, in order to prove themselves. Some women claimed that they had to be better at their jobs than their male colleagues, in order to succeed. Another study of senior educational administrators researched at a time of organizational restructuring, found that slightly more female than male executives perceived time management to be the greatest stressor.

Numerous case examples have been cited in the literature which support the view that women suffer more from burn out than men. Linda Kesley, aged 42, mother of an 8-year-old child, resigned in 1995 as editor of *She* magazine, after suffering 12 months of stress, panic attacks and palpitations. Her road to recovery, as reported in *Health*, in 1996, included drug therapy, hypnotherapy, tactics for dealing with hyperventilation, cognitive behaviour therapy, relaxation therapy and acupuncture.

Equally reported in *Health*, are the cases of Jackie Cooper and Jenni Russell. Jackie Cooper, at the age of 24, started her own public relations company. After five years of working non-stop over weekends and evenings, she became sick with the Epstein-Barr virus just three weeks after taking the company into profit. According to Jackie Cooper, she could not even lift herself up off a chair. For a year she stayed at home with post-viral fatigue syndrome. In her words, it was all she could do to get out of bed and get dressed. She lost the power of concentration, could not even read, and felt afraid and depressed. Similarly, Jenni Russell, a high-flyer journalist for the BBC, in her mid-30s, ignored burn out signals until she was struck by a virulent bacterial infection which triggered such a reaction, whereby she reported her body was attacking its own digestive system. She never thought of her life as stressful, as she felt positive about her job, her family and her friends. After two hospital admissions and a slow recovery, she realized that squeezing more activities into every day does not make for a more fulfilling life or for more fun.

In complete contrast, another study which investigated the effect of occupational gender desegregation on men, found that men in mixed work settings reported significantly lower job-related satisfaction and self-esteem and more job-related depression, than men in either male- or female-dominated work settings. The conclusion of the study was that men need a more homogeneous work setting in order to function more effectively. Being exposed to greater heterogeneity and demographic tensions, supposedly renders men more vulnerable to burn out.

Combating burn out

A fundamental conclusion to reach is that potentially all people can become victims of burn out. Through no fault of the individual, anyone can find his/her performance deteriorating under the burden of pressure and debilitating strain. Appreciating the nature of burn out, the problem to address is how to redress the person's circumstances. Ten strategies for improvement are identified, four falling within the remit of the person experiencing burn out, and six for the manager of the person under pressure, to pursue.

Self strategies

Understanding self

Recent work by the emotional intelligence guru, Daniel Goleman, suggests that people fall into distinctive styles in terms of recognizing and dealing with their emotions. There are those who are:

- self-aware, namely, people who are aware of their moods and their impact on them. Such people have become accomplished at balancing tensions and strains and have learnt to manage emotional challenges. They display a sure-footed self-confidence and hold a positive perspective concerning life. As such, they are able to emerge out of negative moods more quickly.
- engulfed, namely, people who often feel overwhelmed by negative emotions. They present an image of hot and cold; loving and angry, as they live out their emotional upswings and downturns. Climbing out of such damaging moods can feel impossible and, as such, the level of distress experienced can be prodigious.
- accepting, namely, people who are insightful as to the impact their emotions have on them but are also 'accepting of their moods' and so do not try to change the experience of their emotions.[2] Such individuals may fall into two categories, those who are positively emotionally inclined and those who recognize the damaging nature of their emotional downturns. As far as the first group is concerned, why change? Despite the insights of the second group, no will to change is forthcoming, and as a result, aware individuals knowingly enter into phases of emotional decline and in extreme cases, depression.

Appreciating the nature of one's response to sustained experience of strain is an important first step to responding positively to problems. Understanding one's self highlights the significance one will place on the symptoms of burn out. The more the individual attempts to be self-aware, the greater the respect he/she is likely to show towards the signs of burn out they are experiencing. The less they attempt to be self-aware, the more they are likely to be dismissive of or unresponsive to the growing signs of emotional distress, the more they are likely to allow a deteriorating situation to continue.

Recognizing and respecting deterioration

As stated, recognizing one's reactions to emotionally demanding challenges, indicates the respect the person displays towards self and towards the desire to improve. The next step is to recognize the symptoms of burn out as they arise. Symptoms such as ever increasing fatigue, not listening effectively, feeling saturated, a sense of being incapable of entering into conversation with others, feeling unable to fully partake in and concentrate on meaningful, but nevertheless routine and more operational conversations, are particular symptoms to observe. Equally, an ever decreasing morale and feelings of vulnerability that possibly inhibit the individual from confronting others and circumstances, are additional symptoms, but they may be more difficult to recognize and respect as signs of burn out. Most people in burn-out inducing circumstances do not suddenly feel vulnerable. Such damaging and negative emotions are likely to emerge slowly and insidiously and hence, recognition of these emotions as problems may not occur until something goes particularly wrong. People can become accustomed to a situation of slight but progressive deterioration, as that does not challenge their bounds of normality.

Until a crisis occurs, the person could justify to him/herself that that is how he/she is and always has been – 'that's just me!' That sentiment may well be true, as the person may never have really recognized his/her emotional vulnerability, and may have always found addressing uncomfortable situations difficult. With sustained and increasing pressure, such inabilities become more pathological, which may lead to additional symptoms, such as deterioration in social and home-based relationships, when the lack of communication and tensions at home are not down to simply the individuals involved, but are due also to their inability or lack of interest to discuss and address the home issues.

Recognizing that these symptoms are the consequences of burn out is necessary in order to appreciate what approaches to adopt to improve the situation. It is equally important to conclude that being 'macho', combined with denial, although possibly effective in the short term, is simply postponing facing up to a problem.

Tackle manageable problems

Having recognized the nature of the circumstances that have beleaguered the person allows him/her to categorize the emotionally damaging experiences as burn out, which equally frees the person to relegate the existing ways of coping to the wastebin. However, through so doing, greater insecurity may then be experienced. The person may feel, 'What I did up to now at least allowed me to function, but if that is no use, what do I do?'

In order to address the situation effectively, it is important to focus, and not try to tackle all issues at once. The need to build confidence and skill in improving one's situation, is the key priority. Hence, individuals should tackle those issues that are immediate, and feel manageable. It matters little where the person begins, so long as he/she begins to address even the symptoms of burn out. For some people, it may be easier to begin in the home environment. Talking through with one's partner/

spouse the emotions and experiences that the person has undergone, can be a positive start. If both share an understanding of what has been happening, that can act as a platform, in effect, the jumping off point, from which jointly they can face up to making some of the changes that need to be made.

For others, entering into discussion on how to address particular issues in the workplace may be the start of their pathway forward. However, many managers, especially those of more senior status, may feel, and accurately so, that confidentiality is unlikely to be maintained, as the necessary levels of trust and understanding are not present in the workplace. Hence, it may be necessary to talk to a third party from outside.

Talking sometimes helps, but sometimes does not. For certain individuals, talking with others may be a more uncomfortable experience than their present circumstances. Through talking, certain people may consider they are losing face. Others can view talking as time-wasting as they are already aware of the nature of their concerns. Still others may feel that 'talking things through' is not valuable as what they feel they need to do is 'steel' themselves to face up to their predicament. If the discomfort of discussing and sharing is debilitating, then it would be wrong to pursue the route of talking. At this early stage, all that is required is to do something different in order to break the previous negative cycle.

Some people take short breaks/holidays. Others seek professional assistance through counselling or stress reduction techniques. Alternatively, relaxation through day-dreaming is another approach that can help the busy executive cope with burn out.

The day-dreaming technique of relaxation assists in emotionally escaping from pressure and stress, and provides for greater defence against stress induced diseases. A number of different relaxation approaches have gained in popularity over the last few years, for example, a 'fast track' relaxation technique called 'freeze-frames', developed by the Institute of HeartMath, a non-profit making organization, is claiming to reduce the stress effect of high blood pressure by 26 per cent, and have a reduction rate of 36 per cent on the six common stress symptoms: headaches, heartburn, indigestion, sleeplessness, palpitations and trembling.[3] The technique comprises a twofold approach. The first step is to recognize the stressful situation, and the second step is to focus on the feelings from happy memories. The approach focuses on positive feelings rather than positive thoughts, and as a result, apparently dampens down the negative emotions which send messages from the brain to the heart.

Other approaches are equally available. Significant gains can result from small beginnings. Sometimes, a timely visit to the family doctor or specialist in general medicine, can prevent the development of burn out related ailments. However, the majority of men (more than women), seem to not visit the doctor until they have experienced more damaging problems, such as difficulties in breathing, pains in the chest or pains in the stomach. Our (the authors) local family doctor related to us his experiences with an internationally well-known company that retains his services as the organization's physician. He is firmly convinced that burn out 'explains over 90 per cent of his consultations', whereby extreme fatigue, blood pressure problems, distress and irritability, depression and disturbed family relations are the result of overwork and too much international travel.

Furthermore, psycho-related therapies are available, and would be valuable in addressing long-standing emotional problems, stemming from early childhood.[4] The purpose of psychotheraphy would be to bring these disturbances back into consciousness in order that their cause be understood and with such insights overcome these concerns. Psychotherapy, the talking cure, is helpful in seeking to dig out the root of deep-seated emotive traumas and also overcome problems stemming from maladjusted social behaviour. Through effective psychotherapy, the cause would be attacked, and not just the behaviour that is exhibited.

Some complementary therapies and medicines have also been found useful for the treatment of various symptoms associated with stress and burn out. These are acupuncture, herbalism, homeopathy, naturopathy and the physical manipulative therapies, namely chiropractice and osteopathy. Acupuncture, a therapy used in China for more than 2000 years, works by mobilizing one's own self-regenerative and self-healing mechanisms in the body in order to counteract the experience of stress in terms of tension, migraine, sinusitis, asthma and stomach or bowel disorders.

Another remedy is herbalism, which has been around since time immemorial. Different combinations of herbs, usually administered orally, are purported to hold remedial qualities. Whether that assertion is valid, at least no particular side effects have been identified, as there have been with drugs.

Further, there exists the homeopathy discipline, introduced by the German doctor, Samuel Hahnemann in 1810. Hahnemann, concluded that in certain circumstances, people mistake feelings that are the result of a reaction of the person's immune and defence system, in their effort to combat disease as symptoms of illnesses. Hahnemann's contribution was to devise a system of medicine based on enhancing the healing process whereby the homeopath finds a remedy which, when administered, stimulates the person's immune system to energize their own defence system. Homeopathy has become a respected means for combating burn out, as well as helping in reversing illnesses as diabetes, bronchial asthma, arthritis, skin disorders, as well as a variety of affective disorders.

An alternative therapy is naturopathy, one of the oldest and simplest forms of complementary medicine. Naturopathy is really a philosophy concerned with enhancing the natural way of life, in simple terms becoming of pure mind and healthy body. In many ways, naturopathy is based on an 'everyday, commonsense' belief, such as, do not over-consume rich food, alcoholic and other less healthy liquids such as coffee and tea and ensure you get enough exercise, fresh air, rest and sleep.

The physically dominant therapies are chiropractice and osteopathy, which originated in the USA in the second half of the nineteenth century. Osteopaths use more massage techniques, as they work to relieve tension in muscle groups and the soft tissues, as well as improve the movements of joints. Chiropractitioners believe that they positively affect the nervous system by the manipulation of the spine, because the branches of the autonomic nervous system are carried through the spinal column. The fundamental difference between the two approaches is that osteopaths believe that greatest benefit is attained in improving the circulation as a whole, in contrast to principally working on the spinal cord. Chiropractice and osteopathy have been found to be most effective for relieving lower back pain, painful joints and migraine, all of which can be triggered off, or intensified, by burn out.

Reinventing oneself

Improving one's confidence and ability to face up to and address particular issues, learning to become more relaxed, and accepting help from others, leaves the person with a choice; he/she can continue to build up the capabilities to cope with strains and demands, and find a new level of functioning, probably not as demanding as previously was the case, but at least workable, or to attempt to reinvent him/herself.

Reinventing oneself involves exploring what are the key values to pursue in life. Reinventing oneself equally requires fully recognizing and accepting that the responsibility for improving one's life lies totally with oneself. Only from such recognition can one move to the next step, which is to determine a quality of life that has so far been missing in one's existence.

Part of attempting to find new pathways, may require exploring, together with one's partner/spouse, ways around the earnings trap. Restructuring one's life is likely to involve changes, perhaps change of job, of organization, and/or career and/or professional direction. The greater the change, for example that of career direction, the more likely is it that the restart is going to involve a drop in income. It is important that both partners accept and recognize the implications of such a move on their lifestyle.

Whatever direction the person decides to pursue, it is important that he/she is clear as to the values he/she desires in life. What quality of working life does he/she wish for? What importance will work hold in his/her life? How valuable will be the home and family experience?

These are just some of the questions that require consideration. Whatever emerges from an examination of these questions, the individual is likely eventually to question why he/she experienced burn out in the first place. Through probing and self-examination, the person is likely to realize that a mismatch existed between his/her deeply held values and personal beliefs, and his/her attempts to bend or compromise these sentiments, to fit with the organization. Had the individual been discerning about choice of work style and organization, the excessive symptoms of burn out may not have arisen.

The process of deeply examining lifestyle, values and context, equally can extend into home life. Not only may the person conclude that his/ her current organization does not provide for the satisfaction desired, he/ she may come to a similar conclusion concerning personal relationships. In order to proceed, the person may attempt to talk through with his/her partner/children that the nature of their quality of life should change, thereby creating a richer and deeper understanding between them. Alternatively, the person may decide to call a halt on the relationship with their partner and start afresh.

Reinventing oneself can be as exciting as it can be anxiety provoking. Becoming more aware of what one needs in terms of quality of life, and becoming more inventive in pursuing alternative ways of living, is accompanied by experiencing vulnerability. The maxim of 'no gain without pain', applies considerably to such a fundamental rethink.

Bosses' strategies

Clarify the psychological contract[5]

The psychological contract is the deeply felt contractual relationship that binds the person to the organization, and vice versa, and covers such issues as social support, promotion prospects, job satisfaction, in return for effort, commitment and work results. Just what binds the organization and its people in a relationship that can induce high levels of contribution, is dependent on the context in which people find themselves, the issues they face and how they feel as individuals.

In today's downsized, cost-conscious world promotion prospects have diminished, but not workload. For many people, job security is out! For many organizations, loyalty has also gone 'out of the window'. In effect, the psychological contract between employer and employee, is in a state of flux. In today's world, neither the individual nor the organization should assume that a clear understanding of the nature of their psychological contract exists. That does not mean to say that the concept of a psychological contract is worthless. Far from it; for all parties involved in a contractual relationship need to appreciate their own level of contribution and how they, in turn, are going to benefit. Hence, establishing a contractual understanding is crucial. Two contractual perspectives are identified, either of which, bosses could pursue.

Entering into the bargaining process with the perspective of a contract of employment, emphasizes a bilateral view of 'tit for tat', namely effort for security, hard work and endeavour for promotion prospects, and loyalty for respect, especially of seniority. If the individual is emotionally driven by such terms, he/she may emerge from the employment experience dissatisfied. In today's world, a psychological contract that offers loyalty and commitment for job security and the opportunity of promotion prospects, is likely to be difficult to realize. Whatever organizations may intend, the need to re-allocate and/or reduce costs is a reality of responding rapidly to changing external conditions. The modern day term of human resources, substituting the original term of personnel management, does mean that people are viewed as a resource, and in many organizations just one more resource, that is to say people adopt a commodity status. People are considered a cost, which like all other costs, needs to be respositioned, reinvested or discarded according to circumstances. Even the Japanese, who strongly profess care and attention for their employees, are identified, through the Cranfield studies, as facing one outstanding problem, that is, what to do with a considerable over-capacity of white-collar workers.

The alternative is to focus on employability, whereby the individual is offered the tools, the environment and the opportunity for assessing and developing his/her skills and capabilities. In return, the employee is desired to work effectively on behalf of the organization, but equally to accept responsibility for his/her own career by offering the organization an adaptable and responsible skill base, and commitment to the organization's success. However, the transition to greater self-sufficiency may be a psychologically painful process. One aspect of the new psychological contract is an acceptance by both employee and employer that their employment relationship will terminate when a 'win-win' relationship is no longer possible. The traditional expectations of loyalty and security are absent from the employability psychological contract. The concept of employability involves far less emphasis on benevolence, and highlights the pecuniary aspects of the job.

Employability may initially be considered as the more attractive philosophy of employment to promote, for both employer and employee. However, emerging evidence does not suggest such a clear picture. In Japan, despite the fact that business organizations are facing substantial cost related challenges concerned with white collar productivity, the reluctance to venture from employment to employability, is distinct. The staff and management of the corporation are seen as the prime stakeholders to be nurtured. The view of top executives, such as Goto of Family Mart, Kume of Nissan Motors, Niimi of Showa, Shell, and Suzuki of the Mercian Corporation, is that positively responding to the needs of employees not only improves the prospects of good business in the future, it is a value in its own right. Although the counter argument is that the Japanese live in a more protected market, where such sentiments are possible, the evidence to have emerged from the Cranfield surveys, and outlined in Chapter 3, is that a key element of supportive cultures is the emphasis on long term relationships and positive employment prospects for people. For example, Tony O'Reilly, Chairman of Heinz, emphasizes the long-term nature of contractual relationships. Loyalty and endeavour are central to the success of the Heinz corporation, irrespective of the upturns and downturns of the organization.

The concepts of providing employment, or promoting employability, are reflections of more deep seated philosophies concerned with market growth, market share, enhancing sales, acquisition based growth, and the role of people in promoting these ends. Neither is right, wrong or inappropriate from the bosses' perspective. However, in order to promote clarity and consistency in an organization, the issue is, to be clear as to which of the two is being pursued.

Prepare the scene

From the bosses' points of view, the symptoms of burn out likely to be displayed by colleagues and/or subordinates are:

- the inability to face up to or confront people whose behaviour requires attention,
- defensiveness in being given feedback, or as a result of exploring particular issues and concerns,
- slow deterioration in morale and performance,
- touchy and over-sensitive, to even jokes which most others would not find offensive or negative.

The boss of the person who is displaying burn out, has two choices, ignore the symptoms and behave as if no problem exists, or do something. For many, the temptation is to ignore the signs. Entering into dialogue with someone experiencing emotional deterioration requires sensitive handling and making the time to explore and build an open-as-possible relationship with the other person. No single conversation or meeting is likely to achieve much. Time needs to be invested in working with the person, for improvements to take place. On this basis, the boss must feel that the person is worthy of such investment. If not, the boss should be prepared to refer the person on for counselling. The worst option is to watch a colleague or subordinate deteriorate, not talk about it, nor to attempt to halt the slide.

Give time off

Providing individuals with the opportunity to take time off from daily pressures in order to overcome feelings of exhaustion and of being overwhelmed, and to re-think their position, is extremely valuable. Some people use the time to sleep well into the day, in order to combat extreme fatigue. The value of undisturbed sleep was discovered after the First World War, when it was found to be an effective measure for combating shell shock, in many ways, an extreme form of burn out.

Alternatively, organizations such as McDonald's provide sabbaticals, in the form of two months' paid leave, for executives who have worked for the company for over 10 years. Currently, more businesses are providing the opportunity for sabbaticals as ways of trying to combat the exhaustion, cynicism, chronic fatigue, and helplessness that many managers come to feel. A similar programme was begun in late 1996, by the consultant group, Frank Russel Co, whereby an eight-week paid leave is offered to eligible employees every ten years, which does not require involvement with educational or professional development. People can take time off and decide for themselves what they wish to do with it.

Redress the task balance

One way of reducing the negative experiences of burn out is to lighten the workload of the sufferer. In so doing, it helps if the person is provided with clear parameters and clear goals, thereby reducing the level of ambiguity that may otherwise be experienced. In this way, the person knows what he/she has to do, and by when, without having to accommodate different people's needs, and having to negotiate outcomes that may involve compromises between the parties. In the more clearly structured job, the opportunity may be used to re-think goals and priorities. The individual can be given more easily attained job-related goals, which can help in the building-up of the person's confidence to achieve. Further, as part of the process of job restructuring, the boss may wish to remove some of the more mundane tasks in the person's job that may have been partly responsible for the onset of burn out, and substitute these with activities which are within the remit of the person to achieve.

Counselling and training

As the person's confidence to undertake the task grows, so too will his/her confidence improve to explore and develop him/herself. One avenue to pursue is that through counselling and facilitation. An alternative route is through training, which should be seen as an investment. Training helps the person to rebuild his/her skills and enhances the emotional strength to accept responsibility. While a person is reinventing him/herself, the desire to improve is likely to be at its utmost. In-house training and off-the-job programmes equally are likely to pay the greatest dividends for the person and the organization. The training could vary from a personal development programme, to strategic or functional skills training. Which avenue is pursued matters little. What counts is that the person feels the benefit from his/her developmental experience.

Recognize the limitations

There is only so much a boss can do. The prime imperative is that the person experiencing burn out must accept the personal responsibility for his/her own life. What both parties need to acknowledge is that the boss can only build around what the person can tolerate or accept in terms of his/her own improvement and development. Hence, if the person experiencing burn out is considered worthy of attention and facilitation, the boss should offer breathing space and recovery time. The individual may need time away from the workplace, possibly on a sick leave basis, for a suitable period.

Alternatively, it may be necessary to accept that the person can no longer cope, nor wishes to pursue employment in the organization. Under such circumstances, the person needs to be helped to leave the job and or the organization. From the organization's viewpoint, severing links may be the only realistic way forward. A workable rule of thumb is, if the boss considers the individual who is experiencing strain and burn out to be worthy of support and development, and is given permission, even tacit permission, to broach the subject by the person, then by all means, he should pursue a developmental strategy in partnership with the person. If the person is deemed (by the boss) to be not worth investment, or is unapproachable, for the benefit of both parties, leaving the organization may be the only way forward.

Key points summary

- An increasingly commonly reported phenomenon of the executive experience, is burn out.
- The phenomenon of burn out, a parallel experience to those experiences of stress, is viewed as different in the sense that no particular triggers induce, or personality type is prone to, burn out. Burn out is identified as an experience of slow deterioration, due to a combination of personal and circumstantial factors, whereby the individual becomes emotionally and even physically disabled, so that he/she finds it difficult to cope with the very same circumstances previously addressed effectively. Burn out can be as much the result of continuous pressure, or the profound impact of sustained boredom.

Reasons

- Six reasons for burn out are identified, namely, repetition, over-exposure, living in downsized environments, loss of will, feeling trapped and becoming expert at dysfunctional coping.
- *Repetition.* As a result of the removal of middle management tiers in organizations, a greater number of senior managers are being required to undertake a greater volume of repetitive, detailed, often tedious tasks and activities. Further, due to downsizing, more limited career prospects mean that individuals are more exposed to involvement in the same type of work for far longer periods. The greater exposure to repetition is considered to contribute to the experience of burn out.
- *Over-exposure.* A further outcome of a reduced middle-tier management, is that the survivors of downsizing are more exposed to comment, criticism, or a greater number of tasks, often of a non-routine nature, and are still required to respond appropriately. Hence, the incidence of crisis is higher, and with greater demands on managers, many end up responding to the symptoms of problems, rather than their causes, leaving individuals increasingly dissatisfied and strained.
- *Impact of downsizing.* Working in downsized, ever-more-demanding organizations can make managers defensive, mistrustful, inward-looking and unwilling to address longer-term issues, due to responding to too many demands and being watchful of not making too many mistakes. With reduced prospects of satisfactory career progression, the motivation to wish to continue addressing challenges diminishes.
- *Loss of will.* The result of being exposed to circumstances of prolonged demotivation, emerges as an emotional deterioration.
- *Job trapped.* A feeling of being trapped can arise when a manager recognizes that despite a reasonable level of remuneration, he/she needs to remain in his/her current job, due to not being able realistically to find suitable alternative employment because of age (too old), rewards (unlikely to negotiate the same terms elsewhere), and family needs (to pay for children's education, meet lifestyle requirements).
- *Dysfunctionality due to discipline.* Feeling deeply dissatisfied, but equally feeling unable to leave their job, individuals may take pride in being personally disciplined to perform effectively in the current circumstances, resist the emotions of ever-mounting strain, strategies which can be effective in the short term, but lead to greater dysfunctionality in the longer term.

Combating burn out

■ The results of research suggest that, overall, women are more prone to burn out due to the multitude of role demands inherent in managing a career, home, social and family life.

■ Irrespective of gender, four strategies for addressing burn out are identified for the individual experiencing burn out, and six strategies for the boss to pursue in assisting the individual under threat. The self-help strategies are, improving understanding of one's self, recognizing the symptoms of burn out, tackling manageable problems, and reinventing oneself. The strategies the boss can pursue are, clarify the psychological contract between employer and employee, prepare the scene, give time off, redress the task balance, offer counselling and mentoring, and recognize the limitations of the situation.

■ Those individuals who are self-aware and are proactive in managing their emotional lives, as opposed to feeling engulfed or being self-aware but too accepting of their own moods, are the ones who are more likely to find ways of effectively minimizing burn out experiences.

■ From a better understanding of oneself, the next step to combating burn out is to recognize and respect the symptoms of emotional decline and strain. It is only when a problem is seen as a problem, that people commit to doing something to overcome their predicament.

■ It is considered that addressing problems of burn out on an incremental basis is a more appropriate way to proceed, for as the person succeeds in overcoming particular manageable challenges, so his/her confidence increases. To take on too much change too quickly, may lead to a feeling of not being able to cope, or to failure once again. To address manageable challenges, stress reduction techniques could also be adopted, which range from taking more holidays/breaks, to undergoing various therapies such as relaxation and exercise therapies, psycho-related therapies, and more natural therapies.

■ Re-orienting oneself, involves facing up to the need to change one's attitudes, workstyle and lifestyle expectations, and restructuring one's life, realistically recognizing that a drop in income and status may result.

■ From the boss's perspective, recognizing that the nature of the psychological contract between employer and employee has changed, is the first step to projecting clearly a working relationship based on employment with loyalty, endeavour and security expectations, or one of employability based on limited-term tenure, flexibility and self-reliance. For senior managers to project one form but mean the other, is likely to add to the mistrust and dissatisfaction that already exists.

■ In order for the boss to assist the person displaying symptoms of burn out, it is important that the individual has been prepared/helped to enter into conversation about his/her personal and professional decline. To not do so could induce greater defensiveness in the person experiencing burn out.

■ Giving time off, offering sabbatical leave, or even just sufficient time to relieve the strain on the person, can be beneficial in tackling the more distressing symptoms of burn out, as well as giving the person time to consider his/her future.

■ Equally, reducing the number of tasks and the more ambiguous challenges the person may be facing, can help reduce the strain that he/she is likely to be experiencing, which, in turn, can provide the opportunity for the person to gain greater control over his/her personal and work lives.

■ Offering the facilities of coaching and counselling helps individuals to reconsider their present circumstances, to talk through on a professional basis the pathways that the individual could pursue to improve him/herself and also to learn new skills to help them expand their portfolio of capabilities.

■ Ultimately, the boss needs also to recognize the limitations of what can be done, and whether further investment in terms of time and effort will induce improvement. If the perception is, 'not much that I can do will help', then it may be best for all if the person suffering from burn out be helped to leave the organization.

Notes

1 The Eli Black case is adapted from Kets de Vries (1989).
2 Goleman (1986:48).
3 Adapted from Rowlands (1996).
4 Adapted from Livingston-Booth 1988).
5 It was Rousseau (1989) who related the employment contract to the psychological contract.

Further reading

For further information on burn out, namely being increasingly 'ground down' by circumstances that were previously managed effectively, read Levinson (1996). For further information on how particular circumstances can induce burn out, such as organizational restructuring and workforce cuts, read Coleman (1993), on strategic re-engineering, read Cascio (1993), on time pressures, read Agor (1986), on being a survivor of downsizing, read Brockner et al. (1993).

For references of a more medical nature, see Wilkinson (1996), and in particular Rowlands (1996) on freeze frames techniques. In addition, a useful area to explore is that of the changing nature of the psychological contract (Rousseau, 1989).

Similarly, burn out has been examined from the standpoint of burn out due to differences of gender (*Health*, 1996).

For reading on how to cope with burn out, some of the following texts may be of interest; managing stress (Coleman, 1988), medical and more natural therapies approaches to burn out (Livingston-Booth, 1988), managing burn out as a successful top executive (Quick, *et al.*, 1990), personal approaches to releasing tension (Bing, 1996), coping with dysfunctional relationships (Kogan, 1996), and the building up of a resilient workforce (Waterman, *et al.*, 1994).

CHAPTER 10

Working Through Ethical Dilemmas

Case analysis

I fear her disfavour more than anything else

A senior, well-known, popular and well-respected manager of a federal US public agency agreed to be interviewed to discuss the ethical dilemmas he had experienced when employed as a top manager with a tobacco company. He held particular responsibilities for the Middle East and a considerable number of other developing countries. The interview began with his being asked to describe the dilemmas thrown at him by the nature of the role he occupied.

Q. So what were the issues?

A. Number one issue was the kind of company I worked for. I was employed by a tobacco company . . . it became an issue for me, my family . . . and it became a social issue. It even became an issue for my children at school when they were doing anti-smoking . . . The second type of issue was that of bribery and corruption. An awful lot of money floats around big international branded groups' business, where, in fact, you can transfer a bottle of whisky or packet of cigarettes, or a container-load of these, into money, and they float around the world. Obviously, some very interesting people get involved . . . in, parallel exporting and parallel movement businesses, a euphemism for product smuggling . . . How much does the individual take, and how much does the individual disperse as a member of the organization? . . . How do you work with partner organizations, particularly in joint ventures? How do you actually deal with your partner when sometimes being fair and reasonable to your partner, you miss an opportunity to enhance the business of your own company? . . . I think perhaps the fourth issue . . . do you actually want to belong to a company which has quick and dirty barrow-boys, crooks, hard, ruthless, bribing, and a nasty kind of culture?

Q. One view is, that everybody ultimately has the choice! People can choose to be out of the dilemmas if they so wish . . . What is your view on choice?

A. I think choice is a little bit of an illusion. Yes, ultimately, one can pack his bags and go, but there are huge pressures on you not to do that, particularly in a company that pays extremely well, is extremely exciting, with an enormous corporate hype to go and fix a problem – you come back dusting your hands saying, 'Fixed that one; I've done another great job'. The other factor that confuses the choice issue . . . is being offered the job of my dreams; to become CEO of a company – easy to turn around and fix. So how much choice one really has, especially when one does not have any personal capital, is open to debate.

There are also specific situations where choice is limited. If you are sitting in front of the Minister of Supply of country X and he explains to you how you are really going to win the order, then you are considering your options . . . and then you realize what you have done . . . First of all, you are employed by the tobacco company and have obligations to the people who are paying your salary – if you get it wrong, you will end up eating mice in the local prison, because bribery is always totally forbidden and you might be having the conversation taped – or you get it wrong and don't get the business . . . you are not held accountable for every individual order, but it is quite visible in orders when one single order does not arrive – it is visible in bottom line terms. So your choices are constrained and progressively more so the longer you are in the organization, especially in a senior position.

Q. Interesting – what is the dilemma part of all this?

A. Well, the dilemma part is when the phone rings and the individual at the other end says they may become Minister of Finance, but they really cannot afford to be that and need x, y, z, and they know your situation and drive for profitability, very well indeed. So that is the dilemma, when you actually face taking a specific big decision, as opposed to having accommodated progressively in particular circumstances. The two are related to each other, because if you come to a dilemma, you are much more likely to say, 'No, I'm not going to do it'. However, if you become accustomed to a situation over time, you reduce and blunt your own conscience. The first time I did not go to church was when I was a student in France. I felt terrible, but it wasn't so bad the next day. After that, I didn't go to church and it got easier. Accommodation is the process whereby you blunt your conscience. A dilemma is when you really sit up and think about it, but it is important to recognize that companies very rarely give you an open terrible moral dilemma, because nobody actually talks about it. You find in the tobacco industry, young people can get into deep trouble. When writing a marketing plan, you are not allowed to write, 'We wish to attract young new smokers', because the industry has very callously said, 'We are only competing for share in the established market'. That may or may not be true, but a continuous accommodation takes place in the organization, which is OK for old hands like me, but what about the younger people? What about your responsibility to them? Do you slowly corrupt them, but because it's slow, you blunt your own and their conscience?

Q. What if a friend or subordinate were caught, but genuinely working on behalf of the company – what would you do?

A. There was a group coming from a particular Middle Eastern country and the senior man was a mega person in his own country – a real king maker – a Mr Fix-it, and he would be accompanied by one of our younger men, well-educated, cultured, lovely wife, and we said to him, 'There is nothing you have to do other than just stay with this man – if you don't want to get laid, you don't have to get laid'. Nevertheless, it all happened – a big night out, a big dinner, too much drink and all went back to his mega house and Mr Fix-it phoned up some ladies and my colleague got a 'dose of the pot'. What on earth do you do? I had said to him, 'You are not forced to do anything', but he was in the situation. As it turned out, my colleague found that Mr Fix-it had strong links back to the owner of our company, so he was more influential than all of us initially imagined. So what did my colleague hear? 'Treat him extremely well, pay the bills'. I said to him, ' . . . nothing you have to do'. Was I not forceful enough, or was he too weak, or is there some sort of disintegration and degradation of people's values in situations as that? . . . I think it is very difficult to have a very rigid conscience. Those people who care and are sensitive are the most vulnerable, and it is unfortunate that their lines between what is right and wrong are being more and more pushed . . . as there is a great pressure on people to deliver bottom line. The only real safeguard is that it is important to know where you stand, and the point beyond which you will not go. In West Africa, bribery and corruption are endemic. You can't get anything done unless you facilitate a bit, but is it really that bad to pay somebody some money in circumstances of abject poverty and of an inadequate government? We in the West do not have that, but what do you think we would be like if we did?

Q. Who would you fear most in an unethical situation?

A. Fear most? – My wife. I find her clarity helpful. Some say the ultimate test is 'what would your mother think of you?' In this case, it's my wife. She is close to me. She understands me! I have never taken money for personal gain. I have never got laid outside my marital bed. I would say I am quite a weak person seeking approval, but that is what makes me good with people. I really do care about them and I try to do the best I can for my people. But the one thing I fear is, I fear her disfavour more than anything else in the world! As a result, I am really on a track where I can take some pride in my actions.

The individual in this case talked openly about his experiences as a top manager of a tobacco company, the manner in which business was conducted, the corruption, the bribery, the temptations and the need to survive in such circumstances. In so talking, he made a number of interesting points. He drew a sharp distinction between an ethical 'dilemma', a circumstance of glaring contrasts, and 'accommodation', the art of becoming slowly accepting of circumstances. Dilemmas he placed more in the category of distinct personal choice, whereas accommodation is related more to socialization processes, particularly those in the company. The subject remarked on a number of occasions how powerful is the impact of company culture, especially as the level of denial in organizations to being an influence in wrongdoing is high.

A further point being made is that few people can rigidly withstand the pressure to adjust and compromise. In fact, how could any organization function if its management and employees become contextually resistant? Being sensitive to the needs of others and wanting to do a good job nudge a person continuously to be contextually sensitive. What value then, questioned the subject, in giving guidance and strongly worded advice to people, when the company has placed its own employees in a potentially compromising situation? Asking people to change dramatically from being contextually sensitive in one circumstance to then be contextually resistant in another situation, is an almost impossible task. The point being made is that the exercise of ultimate choice is not easy. The senior manager stated:

It's all too easy for people in the comfort of their own country, never having been really exposed to getting deals, loving the excitement, fearing the failure of not getting the deal, feeling frightened at being caught bribing and knowing the risks one exposed colleagues and subordinates to, to know what they would do in these circumstances.

The manager is drawing attention to hypocrisy. It is all too easy to hold different standards for others than for oneself, especially so in cases of ethical dilemma.

Understanding ethics

Ethics is a philosophical term, derived from the Greek word *ethikos* and *ethos*, meaning custom or usage. As employed by Aristotle, the term includes the idea of character and disposition. Ethics reflects the character of an individual and in contemporary usage, it also denotes the disposition of an organization, conveying a meaning of moral integrity and consistent application of values of service to the public. More formally defined, *ethical behaviour* represents that which is morally accepted as 'good' and 'right' as opposed to 'bad' and 'wrong', in particular contexts.[1] The challenge of what constitutes ethical behaviour lies in a 'grey zone', where clear-cut right-versus-wrong and good-versus-bad dichotomies do not always exist.

In terms of present-day interpretation, ethics is not only concerned with distinguishing between good/bad dichotomies, but also with the commitment to do what is right and what is good. As such, the concept of ethics is inextricably linked to that of values; enduring beliefs that influence the choices leaders make from available means and ends. While some values (wealth, success) have relatively little direct connection with ethics, others (fairness, honesty) are in essence concerned with what is right and good and as such, can be described as ethical values.[2] The critical link between ethics and values is that ethical standards and principles can be, and are being, applied to the resolution of value conflicts and dilemmas.

One commonplace interpretation of ethics is the adoption of a moralist perspective, namely the use of guidelines for resolving dilemmas, through acting rightly or wrongly. Such an interpretation of ethics is judgemental by nature. Scant attention is given to this view in this chapter.

A less popular, but more powerful view of ethics is to be found in an exploration of the various philosophies of ethics, which highlight the varying interpretations of morality that people can adopt. This latter view provides for the basis of this chapter, through an in-depth examination of the philosophy of ethics. It is considered that a philosophical appreciation of ethics and their history provides a platform of understanding, from which a person can be guided to help him/herself address the ethical dilemmas he/she may face. One outcome of the detailed examination of the philosophy of ethics, is that three key strategies for tackling ethical dilemmas are identified The strengths, weaknesses and likely impact of each of the three strategies for working through ethical conflicts, are discussed. The chapter concludes by emphasizing the ever growing need to give attention to corporate governance, which is viewed as the basis for promoting a philosophy of positive values and ethics in the corporation, rather than just the establishment of a code of practice. A point strongly emphasized is that only when leaders champion and personally and consistently apply ethical standards and behaviour, does corporate governance hold real meaning in an organization.

Moralities and philosophies

Moralities

From one perspective, ethics and morality are viewed as broadly synonymous, whereby standards, appropriateness of conduct and rules which govern behaviour hold ethical connotations and outcomes.[3] Standards and rules of conduct can be determined at a personal level, whereby individuals base their personal moral philosophy on their concept of what is right and wrong, make judgements and act accordingly. Equally, standards and conduct can be determined at a much broader level, such as group, societal, or a movement transcending societies, the moralities of which are many and varied, are contextually driven and have evolved through history. There exist a multitude of ethical moralities; Christian, Jewish, Islamic, Buddhist, Hindi, Confucian and so on. Each ethical standpoint has something distinctive to convey, although some/all may share certain elements. One example of significant similarity is between the Confucian rule of reciprocity, 'do unto others as they should do unto us' and the Jewish golden rule: 'what is hateful to you do not do to your neighbour'.

Equally, certain components are common, but have different values attached to them. For example, although many culturally different milieus hold common understanding over a given period of time, such as, mornings, midday, evening, night, they contrastingly view time differently. Most Judo-Christian cultures have a preoccupation with time. To be late for an appointment is regarded by some, as rude, and by others, unethical. Setting a deadline is quite acceptable in many western societies, as at is indicative of the commitment to act and achieve, and thereby is considered ethical behaviour. However, in other parts of the world, time takes on different meanings. In many parts of Africa and the Pacific Islands, time is viewed as flexible, not rigid or segmented, as people and friendship matter more than time. It was the social researcher, Hawkins who quoted, 'if an individual is pressed for time and hurries throughout a meeting, agenda or negotiation, he/she will generally be suspected of cheating and thus may be accused of displaying unethical behaviour.'[4]

Above and beyond socially shared moralities is the individual's sense of morality and moral worth, mediated by his/her circumstances and by sense of duty and obligation. The challenge is in pulling together the two forces of social expectation and personal sense of ethic, to a more integrated sense of acceptable virtue (that is, acceptable to the individual). In the western world in particular, concepts of egoism, which emphasize maximizing self-interest, involve each person realizing his/her unique feelings and experience and using such emotions as a guiding force to action. Such an ethical perspective leaves people in a quandary. Should individuals pursue their own moral intent, independent of others around them, or reflect more the shared views of right and wrong that prevail within that context? The great philosopher Emmanuel Kant was clear about his belief for he accused the western world of not assisting people to nurture a more positive morality through adhering to duty and obligation. Kant's view was that personally-driven motives undermine morality, as individuals are driven to the betterment of their self-interest and through this, 'calculation, remain indifferent to the separation of virtue from vice'.[5]

As Kant rightly recognized, people's choices are influenced by a motivation that is dualistic in nature, their own individual sense and sensibility and the shared norms and views in each context. Hence, to take instinctively a moral view of ethics, forces opinion into one of two camps, the individual's or the organization's, thereby polarizing views and raising the level of dissent and destructive influence in the organization.

Although ethics is a valuable tool for thinking through rights and wrongs, applying the principle of polarization can be counter-productive, due to the danger of emerging with inappropriate, shallow or prejudiced views of right or wrong. An alternative to the morality perspective, is to enter into an examination of the philosophy of ethics.

Philosophy of ethics

Despite the number of ethical viewpoints that have been developed to date (utilitarianism, justice, rights, cultural relativism), all have their roots in one or other of two fundamental philosophies, theology and deontology. These two philosophies have been pivotal influences in the development of numerous theories, all of which have given rise to countless interpretations of ethics.

Theological philosophy

Theological philosophy has its origins in ancient Greece, and centres on the impact of human action or behaviour. A theological perspective addresses the question of good or bad from the perspective of behavioural consequences. Hence, a theological philosophy of ethics links the moral worth of human actions with their consequences, thus giving rise to consequentialism. The moral worth of any behaviour is assessed afterwards, by analysing the person's impact on a situation, i.e. through examining consequences. On this basis, behaviour itself has no moral status, as worthiness, or the lack of it, is attached to outcomes. Reaching a theologically-based ethical decision is based on an assessment of projected 'pros' and 'cons'. Although the theological perspective contains a controversial branch that defines ethics in terms of personal gain (egoism), usually theological decisions and actions are assessed in terms of the utility of outcomes, utilitarianism, namely, *the greatest good for the greatest number*.[6]

Deontological philosophy

Conversely, deontological-based theories focus on the inherent righteousness of behaviour. In contrast to theological philosophy, deontology highlights the non-consequential outcomes of ethics. Deontological philosophy maintains that the concept of duty is logically independent of the concept of good, and that actions should not be justified by their consequences to individuals. Of importance are the motives and characters of people, rather than the impact of their behaviour. Therefore, the deontological perspective focuses on the preservation of individual rights, the intentions associated with a particular behaviour, and conformity to moral principles. Deontologists proclaim that individuals have certain undeniable rights, which include freedom of conscience, freedom of consent, freedom for privacy, freedom of speech and due process. Standards to defend personal ethics are often developed from a deontological philosophy platform. Similar to theology, deontological philosophy has a rich, intellectual history, again dating back to the ancient Greeks.

Adopting a deontological and a theological assessment of circumstances in order to emerge with an acceptable ethical decision, can be illustrated by an executive decision regarding the prevention of threat to human life. If a loss of life occurs on a building site as a result of poor safety standards, an executive with a deontological philosophy would decide that safety must be improved, irrespective of the cost. He/she may carry out this decision, even to the extent of financially damaging the firm or by putting many employees out of work, on the basis that it is felt as, 'the right thing to do'. An executive with a theological philosophy, would analyse all the costs and benefits in relation to improving safety or maintaining the status quo, and may even come to the same decision, namely to promote better quality safety. However, the decision to enhance safety standards will be 'because that will provide the best projected consequences for all concerned'. The balance could be between making people unemployed or employees suffering further injury or possible loss of life.

Driven by consequences

The two most influential consequential theories born out of the theological perspective, examine whether consequences focus on outcomes central to the individual or to the community – egoism and utilitarianism.

Egoism focuses on the individual's long-term interests. Philosophers supporting the notion of theological egoism contend that acting against one's own interests is contrary to reason. Egoism, as a means to the common good, is a view propounded by the great economist, Adam Smith, who maintains that, under certain conditions, the best way of promoting the common good, is to promote individual good and well-being. Hence, egoism centres around the idea that it is both rational and right to aim to improve one's own interests. Ethical egoism, derived from accepting the premise that what is ethical must also be rational, and that since acting out of self-interest is rational, then it is also ethical, holds that conventional morality is tinged with irrational sentiments and indefensible constraints on the individual, a thesis strongly supported by the philosopher Hobbes. However, such arguments have a downside. Egoism has no way of solving conflicts between egoistic interests, and thus does not satisfy one of the prime goals of ethical philosophy, the development and maintenance of conditions that allow people in a society to pursue a stable and contented life. Ethical egoism is criticized on the basis that, as a philosophy, it ignores what most people would agree are blatant wrongs for the majority, even though the individual may emerge as satisfied.

Utilitarianism, like egoism, is theological in nature, with the main difference between the two schools of thought being the subject of the decision. Utilitarianism focuses on community and/or society's wider interests, as its thrust is a concern with the consequences of individual or corporate decisions on society at large. Not only is an action right if it leads to the greatest good for the greatest number, but it is also acceptable to consider the least possible balance of negative consequences. Utilitarian theory proposes that a leader should evaluate all of the outcomes of actions or inactions and weigh these against the alternatives, to determine what is best for the community's broader interests. The senior manager in the case presented at the beginning of this chapter, displayed himself as a utilitarian by his reference to limited choice and the need to adapt to context. In its purest form, the utilitarian standpoint argues that a leader should calculate the amount of both good and bad in an action, and from that perspective, reach a conclusion as to what direction to pursue.

Utilitarianism is further branched into two sections, 'act' and 'rule'. 'Act' utilitarianism deals with each and every action a person takes, with the assumption that no one act is, in itself, wrong. Act utilitarianism focuses on how right an act is, in terms of producing the greatest ratio of good to evil, for all concerned. Act utilitarianism holds that in every situation, the individual should consider acting to maximize the total good, even if that means rules are violated.

Pursuing a 'rule' utilitarian philosophy requires developing rules that are believed to be in the public's interest. Rule utilitarianism advocates that the rules denoting ethical conduct should be evaluated according to the ratio of good versus evil, but also according to whether the rules are obeyed. Having identified the most appropriate set of rules, utilitarianism requires a leader to act consistently in different situations, in line with the prescribed rules.

The utilitarian standpoint is associated with the two most famous philosophers, Jeremy Bentham and John Stewart Mill, who argue that enterprises operating in their own self-interest produce the greatest economic good for society, through an 'invisible hand'. Fascination with utilitarianism is prominent among economic rationalists and those interested in cost/benefit analysis, which in many ways underpins the current philosophy driving business organizations.

Many of the criticisms levelled at utilitarianism come from deontologists, whose primary argument is that some actions are inherently wrong and should never be justified as a means to happiness or to maximize wealth and opportunity. Equally, deontologists argue that utilitarianism provides inadequate guidelines for addressing choice between actions which provide much good for a few, or a little good for many. The weakness lies in determining how the individual can know what is, in fact, the greatest good for the greatest number. Hence, the deontological criticism stands, in that utilitarianism ignores actions that are wrong in themselves, so long as the end justifies the means. It could be argued that the utilitarian's preoccupation with maximizing good, is overly focused on efficiency and is indifferent to considerations involving merit and need, which in some instances favour the adoption of actions which violate community or more broadly, society's basic sense of justice.

Impervious to consequences

Deontology focuses on universal statements of right and wrong, thereby not needing to justify duties by showing that they are productive or good. The deontological moral argument is that particular actions and behaviours are intrinsically ethical or unethical, defined by being within or outside the rights and justice principles. For example, cheating is dishonest and hence unethical. The behaviour or action being wrong, is not mitigated by how good are either the motives behind it, or the ensuing consequences. According to the German philosopher, Emmanuel Kant, deontological assertions are not found in observable phenomena, but in *a priori* 'laws and reasons', or according to St Augustine, 'divine law'. Kant was one of the first to develop an unambiguous formulation of a deontological theory of ethics. He considered that both contextual considerations and human behaviour have to be formed, organized and dominated by a single rationality. The Kantian 'categorical imperative', or the establishment of moral rights, is a leading example of deontological ethics, portraying a universal approach, where 'reason' is interlocked with notions of truth, and both pay homage to morality, which in reality means obedience to established principles.

Deontological ethics have been criticized for being over-reliant on overriding moral principles, dictated by a single reason. What then happens in circumstances of conflicting duties and loyalties? Accordingly, the Kantian 'fundamental moral rule' has limited capacity for dealing with clashes of duties and rights, or for providing assistance in situations where neither the fundamental rules that are in conflict, nor the rights of two different groups, or individuals, can be met by any of the actions or rules which might apply. The rights of both parties may be legitimate according to deontological ethics, but deontological philosophy does not aid the resolution of the conflict that exists. For example, increasing the rights of people to have access to information held by government agencies, through a Freedom of Information Act, may decrease the rights to privacy of other individuals, groups and corporations. Further, the consequentialists contend that if consequences are disregarded, individuals blindly accept duty without questioning the direction they have been set, or who set it. Thus, individuals are vulnerable to being manipulated to commit unlawful acts, simply because of their acceptance of a single logic.

From a more positive view, the deontological approach to ethics, aspires, at the very least, towards promoting justice in society, where 'justice' is a cover-all term to describe the end state of attempts to perform universal good. The ethics of justice have been developed from the writings of Aristotle, who held that *'just' means, 'that which is lawful and that which is equal and fair', and that 'unjust' means, 'that which is illegal and that which is unequal or unfair'.*[7] Hence, a justly treated person is given what he/she is due or owed, or what the person deserves or can legitimately claim. That which is deserved, however, may be of advantage or simply burdensome. Justice in our contemporary world is concerned with the fair distribution of benefits and burdens, where the basis of equity may be needs, rights, effort, contribution, merit or the equal distribution of effort. Hence, from the justice ethic perspective emerge a series of rights, such as, to each person an equal share, to each according to individual need, to each according to his/her rights, to each according to individual effort, and to each according to merit.

The burden element of justice occurs when calls for the prevention of harm, or protecting the rights of others affected by the actions of individuals, groups, or businesses, require that limitation to action involves penalties being imposed on society for having allowed particular actions to occur. For example, not all individuals pollute rivers and waterways, but in order to prevent pollution by 'anti-social' businesses, legislation provides restrictions and penalties to all.

The fundamental criticism of justice ethics has been the over-focus on the rights of the individual, whereby the basic needs and rights of people as individuals are more important than the maximization of overall good for the community. Right theory rests on the assumption that every person has basic rights, which include the right to free consent, the right of privacy, the right of freedom of conscience, the right of freedom of speech and the right to due process, come what may. The rigid application of rights may be damaging to the silent majority, on whose goodwill society depends. In addition to individual rights, rights can be granted to certain entities. The state, for example, has the right to enforce the law if someone breaks it. The paradox is that although rights imply that people have power all the time, this power can be taken away when 'bad' choices are made, such as the removal of the right to vote on being found criminally guilty, or in certain societies, being confined as insane.

Relativism

Both the theological and deontological perspectives have been accused, each in its own way, of 'ethical absolutism', in that both promote the view that there exists only one true ethical code or guide to behaviour.[8] On this basis, philosophers have stated that neither is relatively applicable and what only will work is a synthesis of the two, whereby there exist certain duties and obligations, but then people have to balance their options, determining their courses of action. Such thinking has spurred the concept of ethical relativism, which maintains that decisions concerning what is ethical are a function of culture and individualism and hence no universal rules exist that apply to everyone. In addition to theology and deontology, the relativist perspective also has its roots in the great thinkers of ancient Greece. Protagoras, in the fifth century BC, held that moral principles cannot be shown to be valid for everyone and that people ought to follow the conventions of their own grouping. On this basis, moral standards cannot be universally valid, because of value differences in culture. Hence, moral norms are culture specific, and morality is a matter of conforming to the acceptable standards and rules of one's culture. Moral views are based on how a person feels, and on how a culture accommodates the desires of its communities when driven by some deeper set of objectively justifiable principles. From a relativist perspective, moral standards are the result of history, endorsed by custom.

The relativist weakness is the view that, deep down, there is no real difference between moral beliefs. In effect, if people are given sufficient chance to explore and develop their own ethical standpoint, sooner or later they will reach a similar conclusion.

Business ethics

The topic of business ethics has reflected the fundamental dichotomy of the philosophy of ethics, namely that of responsiveness to context through being aware of the consequences of one's actions, contrasted by embracing a universal set of principles, irrespective of contextual influence.

The world of business ethics, prior to the 1960s, was primarily driven by moralist, religiously-oriented philosophies. The emerging interest in social issues in the 1960s, corresponding with the anti-business, anti-military movement among the youth of the USA, saw the rise of business ethics as a topic in its own right. The anti-business perspective continued in that, disenchanted with the limitations of control by means of economic or bureaucratic sanctions, management theory widely promulgated, throughout the 1980s, the development of a supportive and moralist corporate culture as a means of enhancing managerial influence. Thus the view emerged that, 'ethical business practice stems from an ethical corporate culture'.[9] Throughout this period, numerous recommendations were made as to how the culture of the organization should be cultivated towards the ethical highground. Practitioners and theorists, attempting to convert flawed organizational ethics, asserted that it was the culture that needed to be 'put right'.

A minority did not agree, on the basis that linking 'business ethics' to culture absolved individuals of their personal responsibilities – as long as the culture was 'right', individuals could do what they wanted, within the framework of that culture, hence making a 'ruthless, bottom line perspective' a desired way of functioning. Peter Drucker, argues that separating business ethics from other spheres of activity is to create an artificial distinction between business and the rest of life. The contrasting viewpoint, therefore, is that the application of business ethics requires a set of rules, standards, codes and principles that provide guidelines for morally right behaviours for all people, all of the time. Hence, people are not driven by their immediate environment, but have standards and guidelines which can be applied across situations.

The corporate culture view, essentially theological in nature, pursues the argument that people have a remarkable capacity to be flexible, despite the impact of longstanding relationships and powerful experience. Hence, people can set aside their previous standards and learning, and adapt to their new context. Thus, the application of ethics standards needs to be synergized with the broader context within which relationships evolve. If interactions and relationships can be established on a more ethically dominant footing, then people will more naturally evolve a sense of ethical consciousness through their socialization experiences.

In contrast, professional ethics centred on particular professions – law, medicine, journalism, engineering, accountancy – have adopted a deontological approach. Most professions have drafted a code of ethics that provides rulings concerning the profession's ethical conduct in terms of behaviour, irrespective of context and culture. Unlike corporate cultural codes of ethics, professional codes in western societies are often legally enforceable. Entry into professional life is usually much more uniform and regulated than is entry into a career in business.

The medical profession, for example was the first to develop a modern code of ethics in 1803, based on the work of the physician, Thomas Percival. In the USA, in an attempt to abate the decline of the status of the medical profession, at the first meeting of the American Medical Association (AMA) in 1846, a committee was appointed to report on a code of ethics for the organization. Some 60 years later, in 1908, the legal profession, through the American Bar Association (ABA), adopted its first code of professional ethics, Canons of Ethics, based on the work of Judge George Sharswood. The accountant's desire for professional prestige led to the development of a code of professional ethics in 1907.

Contrary to the view of some, the 1990s have not witnessed a consolidation between the theological culturalists and the deontological, code-driven purists. In fact, to expect consolidation between the two contrasting philosophies is considered to be unrealistic. The net result of no emerging clarity implies that leaders are more likely publicly to face ethical dilemmas in the making of business decisions in a world of downsized, openly accountable organizations. In fact, the argument being pursued is that further clarification of ethical positions would amount to wasted effort, as no compromise is likely to emerge from the theologists and deontologists. What, however, would be of value, would be to clarify the ethical dilemmas that are likely to confront public and private sector leaders, in order to guide them through the pitfalls they are likely to face. The theme of guidance through ethical traumas, dominates the remainder of this chapter.

Ethical dilemmas

In attempting to understand the nature of an ethical dilemma, a distinction is drawn between an ethical dilemma and an assessment of risk, the latter being equally mentally and emotionally taxing because of the exposure factor. Risk involves delineating the consequences of a policy and assessing the likelihood of various possibilities occurring. If a poor assessment of a policy's consequences is made, the policy may backfire, causing financial embarrassment to the decision-maker and the company. Risk assessment involves answering the question, 'What could go wrong?'

In contrast, an ethical dilemma involves answering the question, 'Is this right to do in the first place?' An ethical dilemma involves coming to terms with one's own sense of moral purpose and worth, namely one's conscience, while being exposed to the risk of criticism, blame and punishment, should others consider the wrong decision to have been made.

Instead of balancing externalities, ethical dilemmas force an internal debate in a person concerning what he/she views as right and moral and equally how he/she should act, which may or may not be in line with what key stakeholders view as right. Hence, leaders experiencing an ethical dilemma may also be confronted with the question, 'What could go wrong?', which addresses risk exposure, but in terms of ethical importance, is a question of secondary status, resulting from pursuing a line of action which the individual feels is morally unworthy.

Table 10.1 highlights four key ethical dilemmas that are likely to confront leaders:

1 contractual obligation versus moral determination,
2 inducement (bribery) versus self-determination (honesty),
3 privacy versus freedom of information,
4 universalistic versus particularistic treatment of individuals.

The nature of the philosophical juxtapositions is identified, as well as considerations as to the pathways through such dilemmas.

Table 10.1 Ethical dilemmas: their juxtaposition and pathways through

Dilemmas	Juxtaposition	Ways through
Contractual obligation versus Moral determination	Rule utilitarianism versus deontology	Address/confront avoidance/ defensiveness
Bribery versus honesty	Theological egoism versus deontology	Accept, confront or leave
Privacy (or secrecy) versus Freedom of information	Deontology (or theological egoism) versus deontology	Case by case Powerplay: battle of wills
Universalistic versus Particularistic norms	Deontology versus act utilitarianism	Political influencing skills

Contractual obligation versus moral determination

The contractual obligations of a senior manager, to shareholders for example, may place the person in a moral dilemma if what they are asked or required to do is viewed as immoral. The dilemma is often portrayed in the media, as that between profitability and public safety.

One view of a corporation is as a 'nexus' for a set of contractual relationships between individuals and several interest groups.[10] The question is, how can a senior executive ethically negotiate that nexus? Explicit contractual relationships exist between various stakeholders, including shareholders, creditors, managers, employees, customers and suppliers. However, the principal and most influential relationship is that between the shareholders and the management of the corporation. The former supply the capital and the latter accept the responsibility for tactical and strategic decision-making necessary to operate the corporation. The manager (agent) is under a contractual obligation to shareholders (the principal) to operate the organization in the latter's best interests. The objective of the firm, therefore, is to maximize the shareholders' wealth, which explicitly means maximizing the company's stock price. As a consequence, the dilemma that exists is between the person's contractual responsibility to shareholders, and his/her own ethical beliefs.

A case in point is that of the Ford Pinto. The Pinto car was so designed (unintentionally) that the petrol tank took a direct impact on collision, resulting in the increased probability of the fuel igniting. Ford evaluated the necessity for engineering against the number of lives that might be lost. Using essentially a utilitarian perspective, by, basically, assigning a likely value to those lives, Ford manufactured the car without changes, resulting in consequential loss of life.

Similarly, the *Challenger* disaster, which claimed seven lives, destroyed two billion dollars' worth of hardware and punctured NASA's and America's aura 'of high-technology invincibility',[11] provides another example of the dilemma between public safety versus organizational image and, ultimately, profitability. On 28 January 1986, the space shuttle flew for 72.163 seconds before disintegrating into flames. The Solid Rocket Booster's (SRB) O-ring failure was identified by the *Presidential Commission* on the Space Shuttle Challenger Accident, 1986, as the primary cause of the explosion and the Morton Thiokol Corporation was held legally responsible for the disaster.

The inquiry into that disaster revealed that engineers at Morton Thiokol, which manufactured the solid rocket booster, had repeatedly expressed concern, verbally and in written memos, about the possible failure of O-ring seals in cold weather launches. These concerns received a 'wait and see' response from the launch decision making management at NASA who, until the Space Transformation System's *Challenger* explosion, had achieved 24 consecutive shuttle flights without human mishap.

Furthermore, US Congressional pressure on NASA to utilize more shuttle operational capacity, emerged as a result of the Strategic Defence Initiative (SDI or 'Star Wars'), as well as the impetus for a renewal of the mid-1970s' Apollo–Soyuz successes, which were founded on novel research and development activities. The research and development activities were welcomed by NASA's scientific and other professional networks which, otherwise, were reduced to servicing an increasingly military-dominated space programme, particularly so by 1984, when the US Air Force sought to obtain a greater influence over the shuttle's operational role. Dysfunctional inter-agency 'turf-battles', entrenched opinions and institutional myopias, all contributed to NASA's ineffi-ciencies. Although the *Challenger* disaster cannot be attributed solely to economic rationalism, the Commission's findings revealed that all of these factors were related to the cause of the shuttle explosion.

The two cases highlight that under continuous strain, senior and responsible managers develop defences that result in collective patterns of avoidance. These defences include under-evaluating, or not wishing to acknowledge, relevant warnings; inventing new arguments to support a chosen policy; failing to explore ominous implications, and misperceiving signs indicating the onset of actual danger. Under stress, people can quickly engage in 'group think', when their striving for unanimity can override their motivation to appraise realistically alternative courses of action. Through so doing, individuals choose to engage in acts they would otherwise have considered unethical, especially when the culture of an organization and its prevailing reward structure overwhelm personal beliefs.

However, the stark, polarized simplicity of 'yes we should, no we should not' do something, captured in the Ford Pinto and Challenger cases, hides a more challenging complicity which has taxed numerous executives. The World Bank, for example, has been criticized as insensitive to the needs of developing countries through using an 'orthodox' economic model to determine the terms and conditions of aid to the developing world. Through so doing, the World Bank has been accused of undermining the long standing and valued social intricacies of local communities, in the quest for economic discipline. What would the World Bank say in its defence? Perhaps certain of the arguments they would advocate are:

■ loans that are uncontrolled lead to a spiral of disaster for all, and in that argument they would be well supported, for 1996 UNDP figures show debt to the developing world standing in, 1970, at US$100 billion to a recent US$15,000 billion in 1992;

■ at the end of the day, it is your (i.e. western society's) money that is in our charge. Through your governments, we administer resources where they will most benefit, while also being watchful of your interests;

■ we have helped a great deal, look at the dams that have been built, the infrastructure programmes in place, the land that has been reclaimed and all of these projects are now supporting thousands and thousands of people.

The World Bank has a point. Most executives experience of contractual obligations versus moral rights do not fall into simple either/or categories. The underlying philosophical juxtaposition or tension being highlighted in the Ford Pinto and Challenger cases is that between rule utilitarianism and deontology, namely that between universal principles and guidelines generated to satisfy the greatest number of people in a situation (see Table 10.1). For most, however, choices are not that clear. It is so often considered that organizations engaged in free market trade, are naturally likely to promote strategies based on creativity, flexibility and focus, but have one inequity, they are based on one economic rationalism, which by implication, can favour only those who end up on the plus side of the balance sheet. Yet, in order to trade, what is the alternative? Possibly a bottom line mentality, which favours quite a number but cannot favour all, makes economic rationalism and free market thinking, in philosophical terms, rule utilitarianism. Although rules, codes or guidelines have to be established, outlining what is ethical and unethical in terms of trading, equally the freedom to trade and to respond effectively to different contexts and circumstances has also to be allowed for, in order to favour those involved in business activity. As the World Bank case shows, multiple stakeholder interests exist, and those responding to contrasting demands need flexibility to respond to what they deem as appropriate. This is a case of rule utilitarianism requiring deontological compromise, the ultimate anathema.

It is possible to work through such a dilemma, as both rule utilitarianism and deontology share one common feature, the need for rules and order. The intention would be to work through the reactions of avoidance, defensiveness and reluctance to face up to discomfort, in order to reach a point of openly addressing the ethical implications of particular decisions or actions. The requirement would be to build a sufficient level of trust and confidence in order to allow for a high quality dialogue to emerge among those senior managers facing the dilemma, of how to proceed with their contractual obligations. The aim would be to help managers recognize where they stand as individuals, the degree of cohesion in the team, who are their true constituents and whether their emerging views help or hinder servicing that broader community. However, dilemmas such as this will not be revealed unless they are openly acknowledged as problematic and unless time is invested in their discussion and resolution. Despite the rules and codes drafted to minimize the recurrence of contractual obligation versus moral principles dilemmas, their resolution lies in management's willingness to face up to these predicaments. Despite its attraction, the application of deontological rules has its limitations.

Bribery versus honesty

Classical Greek and Roman writers recorded that 'sharp' business practices existed in ancient times, when business persons were just as keen to make a fast 'drachma', as some are to make a 'buck' today. Fortunately, in both ancient and contemporary societies, there exist members who take a firm stand against the minority who infringe. Plutarch cites Aristides (520–486 BC) who describes Themistocles as a 'clever fellow, but apt to be light fingered'.[12] In another extract, Plutarch cites Thucydides and members of his party, who denounce Percicles (495–429 BC) for 'squandering public money and letting the national revenue run to waste'.[13]

Bribery holds connotations of personal gain. In the late 1980s, a succession of business scandals drew escalating criticism about the apparent lack of controls of business conduct in Anglo-American corporations. The very essence of business self-regulation came under fire and scrutiny. At one end of the spectrum were cases of simple fraud, as with the investment firms Barlow Clowes and Brent Walker in the UK, where savers' funds were identified as 'stolen' by the founding chief executives of the firms. At the other end of the spectrum lies Polly Peck, where corporate funds were supposedly siphoned off into offshore companies owned by the CEO and founder, Asil Nadir. Similarly, a theft of over £1 billion in employee pension funds, purportedly carried out by the business mogul Robert Maxwell, was used to support his ailing business empire. Other scandals have involved stock manipulation. In Britain's largest ever takeover of the time, namely the bid by Guinness, a number of eminent business leaders were jailed for their part in a conspiracy to 'inflate' the value of Guinness shares, during the controversial battle for Distillers.

While cases of actual or supposed inducement abound in the private sector, so too does scandal emerge in the public sector. One such case is that of the Canadian Federal Justice Department's investigation of the ex-Prime Minister, Brian Mulroney (later cleared) regarding allegations that he was party to a scheme in which the European aircraft manufacturer Airbus Industries paid US$20 million in kickbacks to win a US$1.2 billion order from Air Canada, with Mulroney supposedly gaining a direct benefit of US$5 million. Another case is that of the British government in the 'cash for questions' row. A number of members of Parliament (MPs) and in particular two Ministers, Tim Smith and Neil Hamilton, in the John Major government, were accused of accepting money for asking questions in Parliament. Tim Smith admitted that he had so done. However, the whole affair dragged in the

UK's ex-Prime Minister, as the *Guardian* newspaper (Friday, 21 March 1997) published the charge that John Major knew of the 'sleaze' and allowed Tim Smith to remain as Northern Ireland Minister. John Major strongly rebutted the accusation. The Labour opposition accused the conservatives of a 'cover up' just before a general election. The Parliamentary Commissioner, Sir Gordon Downey, declared the *Guardian* newspaper as having betrayed national justice by publishing evidence that the newspaper had submitted to his investigating commission before he had the opportunity to publish his report on standards in public life among MPs in Parliament.

Official and unofficial accounts of corruption in developing economies and economies in transition (from planned market to free market), emerge with remarkable regularity. In the former Soviet Socialist Republic, evidence suggests that corruption was not organized, but bribes were taken independently, making corruption more discretionary. In post Soviet Russia, corruption is supposedly taking place on such a large scale that it has now become not only organized, but is a feature of everyday life. The scale of bribery in economies in transition is so great, that it risks causing political unrest to the point of a backlash against free-market reforms. In Venezuela, in 1993, it was discovered that the Central Bank had made a payment of US$17 million to the then President Perez's 'discretionary' fund. The US$100,000 Ferrari Testarossa given to Argentinian President, Carlos Menem from an Italian company bidding for government business, raised a few 'eyebrows'. Furthermore, western bribery of foreign governments contributes to this unrest. For example, it is estimated that 500 to 600 million Deutschmarks are deducted from German corporate tax returns as an allowance against supposed foreign corruption, passed off as 'necessary expenditure'. In response, the US has adopted anti-bribery codes of ethics (American Foreign Corrupt Practice Act), which a number of social commentators consider do not work well, as the business world and government have not made it a priority to promote such laws. However, the US is not giving up! According to the *Intelligence Newsletter* (29 May 1997), the US Department of Commerce's Advisory Network claims that between mid-1994 and the end of 1996, foreign companies had offered 'kickbacks' of approximately 64 billion US dollars across 13 per cent of international contracts. Through the OECD structure, the US is pressuring other countries to tighten up on audits and to stop 'external commercial expenses' (bribes) as being deductible from corporate tax (permitted in Germany and accepted in France).

Further bribery-like circumstances have occurred, even though the individuals involved did not stand to gain directly from any transaction. In the case of County Natwest, the senior executives of the investment bank were accused (and subsequently acquitted) of inflating the success of the rights issue of one of their clients, Blue Arrow, by selling shares in non-arm's length transactions. Although the charge was of felony, the case examined the nature of distortion that can occur when individuals are considered to favour their own circumstances. Interestingly, in the case of the senior manager whose interview was presented at the start of this chapter, he drew the line between personal gain, direct bribery and inducement almost as a form of moral defence – not personally gaining is akin to being OK!

However, irrespective of the distinction between direct bribery or inducement to favour one's own circumstances (but without personal gain), nothing attracts the headlines as does the accusation of bribery. The reason is that personalities are involved and highlighted. Onlookers can identify with those in the limelight and 'love them or hate them'. Passions run high, as the key players are presented in a black and white fashion.

Deeper analysis of the philosophical juxtaposition does support the polarization taken by society and the press. The personalized nature of bribery is evident, placing direct or indirect inducement in the category of theological egoism. The emphasis is, 'I am going to go for what is good for me'. The alternative position of, 'I will not be involved because I know it is wrong', forces to the surface a deontological position (see Table 10.1). No halfway house exists, as to accept direct or indirect inducement sucks the person into a web of conspiracy. The choices are simple – accept the circumstances, or confront what is happening, recognizing the possible ensuing consequences for refusal to be bribed, or for whistle-blowing. In plain terms, the choice is 'Do you or do you not wish to be part of a corrupted, inducement-driven context?' The choices may be simple, but exercising them is not, because of the powerful passions and fears lurking underneath the surface.

As the socially conscious senior manager highlighted at the beginning of this chapter, exclaims, being involved in a situation of providing inducements to others is exciting. The exhilaration of 'getting the deal', the competitive dynamic of winning bigger deals than colleagues, is seductive. It is all too easy to become entwined in a fast-moving world of hype and stimulation, while facing the sobering prospect of redundancy if one does not become involved in an inducement-based culture. Some can lose all sense of proportion and become 'corrupt'. Others will go only so far, having established their own standards, beyond which they will not proceed. The senior manager in this chapter benchmarked his behaviour by his wife's opinion of him and his actions.

The deep emotive undertones to bribery emphasize the non-rational nature of the dilemma between being bribable and being honest. Until an individual is truly tested, he/she may not appreciate his/her response to being enticed into bribery or other comparable unethical contexts. Such was the case of the spouse of a Canadian Civil Servant involved in an expenses sharp-practice. Canada's reputation for having a decent, reliable and neutral public service had been steadily eroded by episodes such as the travel scam in the External Affairs and Trade department (see Chapter 5). A number of executive level officers flew on excursion air-fares, but submitted full-fare ticket stubs as expense claims, and pocketed the difference. In addition to fraudulent travel claims, the investigation turned up evidence of further illicit activities by a dozen other employees, such as 'falsification of exchange-rate receipts, failure to report salary over-payments, contravention of conflict-of-interest guidelines, and visa fraud and harassment'. One senior civil servant was caught submitting over-inflated travel claims, but like so many others was given the opportunity to pay back the difference that had mounted over the years, on the understanding that no further investigation would ensue. The individual, not in possession of the sizeable sum required, turned for assistance to his spouse who had accumulated substantial savings from her own independent, but honestly acquired earnings. The spouse had long supported a deontological ethical philosophy. She truly believed in universal rights and universal ethical standards. However, confronted with her husband's plight, she handed over the sum, even though it offended her ethical position. Her decision was driven by the emotive nature of their relationship, which ultimately enticed her.

Those most at risk to explicit or implicit involvement in bribery are those who have not experienced the powerful emotions involved. They are in danger of falling into the trap of being deontological with everyone else, but theological about themselves. The possible lack of awareness of such a dichotomy in themselves leaves them vulnerable to becoming embroiled in the bribery versus honesty dilemma, and only discover that fact after they are committed. The way through, is to recognize that the choices are stark, the passions are distortingly powerful, and that choices need to be made or the person, however inadvertently, will be sucked in.

Privacy versus freedom of information

The proliferation of IT and its associated ease of information-sharing poses additional difficulties for the traditional concept of confidentiality, but equally emphasizes an underlying tension, namely a person's belief about his/her right to relevant information may conflict with another person's belief about his/her right to withhold information from circulation. Information that is considered to be relevant to one person, may be viewed as private by another. Thus the ethical concern is that of privacy, namely what information about one's self or one's associations must a person reveal to others, under what conditions and within what safeguards, versus accessibility, or what information does a person or an organization have a right or a privilege to obtain, under what conditions and with what safeguards?

Developments in information technology highlight a number of potential threats to individual privacy. These include the use of non-intrusive methods of data collection, the use of department store scanners to record sales, permitting detailed recordings to be made of all financial transactions, facilitating database files established for one purpose (e.g. credit cards) to be joined with files established for another purpose (e.g. medical history) to create a detailed dossier on individuals, which could be utilized for a variety of purposes through remote access and fast dissemination of information, without a person's permission or even knowledge. However, information technology also has the potential to empower individuals by giving them greater access to information that is relevant to their lives. An information highway founded on database and telecommunications technology makes possible, amongst other things, a news retrieval service on a wide range of topics, bulletin boards that allow individuals to share information with other like-minded individuals on a global basis, and information regarding goods and services for sale. Privacy advocates, however, warn that firms collecting information regarding individuals' lifestyles make this information available to anyone willing to pay.

Social, political and technological issues influencing policy require the development of conditions for highly complex and interdependent decision-making. The integration of different inputs often requires participation from private sector organizations, various government and semi-government agencies, as well as the active participation by members of target groups and their representatives in the decision-taking and decision-implementation process. The development of cross-sectional and global links, exemplified by a common database of clients, pose challenges to the traditional values of privacy and stability, through shifts to policy openness and public information. For example, the rise of the institutional investor and the move to extended share ownership, has seen the increase in demand for information on companies and on their activities.

The situation can be further complicated by the fact that many executives may be subject not only to their organizational code of ethics or the government's code of ethics, but also to codes developed for their professions (law, medicine, engineering), and codes developed by professional associations (e.g. Accounting Code of Practice; Institute of Public Administration of Canada; American Society of Public Administration), none of which comfortably integrates, leaving individuals more exposed to accusations of malpractice. The IT move to openness, considerably exposes the senior manager at the centre to such a paradox.

In the private sector, Coopers & Lybrand and Deloitte & Touche, two of the world's big six auditing firms, were purported as ready to make a bid for the business intelligence organization Kroll Associates (at the time of writing, *Intelligence Newsletter*, January 1997). Business intelligence organizations, Kroll Associates being one of the largest and most renowned, but also others such as Parvus and Kirk Tyson

International, are organizations that gather intelligence on business organizations, their activities and their management. Some in the industry feel positive about the possibility of having a powerful business intelligence network with access to the highest management levels in the corporate world. Others, however, express considerable disquiet at the prospect of business intelligence organizations being merged with accounting practices who audit corporate accounts. A detailed analysis of a company's books by an auditor whose organization has a business intelligence division, which would, in turn, be of advantage to competitors, is a scenario possibility that cannot be discounted. Even if that possibility were never to be realized, there would still remain the issue of conflict of interests, which may tarnish the trust clients have in the audit practice.

Equally, the British government, through Parliament's Public Accounts Committee (PAC) raised a similar disquiet (mid-December 1996) over the activities and increasing influence of electronic data systems (EDS), the company founded by Ross Perot, the American Presidential contender. EDS holds a dominant position in the UK's public sector outsourced information technology market, with contracts with the Inland Revenue, Ministry of Defence, Home Office and Department of Social Security. EDS's position is that its share of public sector contracts is less than 10 per cent. The concern of legislators, however, is that the government's Information Technology Service Agency (ITSA) could not provide satisfactory information on the amount of work EDS has undertaken, nor could specify whether a contractor like EDS, could sell information after removing personal details. Although all EDS contract staff have signed Britain's Official Secrets Act, PAC chairman, Robert Sheldon described EDS as being 'almost in a science fiction type situation in that it has enormous access to confidential government information' (*Intelligence Newsletter*, 2 January 1997).

Similar disquiet over EDS has been expressed in Spain, where EDS's sub-contractor in Madrid, Servico, responsible for collecting and processing traffic fines, has been accused of alleged irregularities and is under investigation by the fraud division of Spain's Justice Ministry. Although EDS claims it has stopped using Servico, concern exists in both Spain and the UK, over the practice of sharply 'undercutting rivals'. It is purported that EDS's recently secured contract to computerize 250 national and regional courts in England and Wales, was won on the basis of price.

In the privacy versus freedom of information issue both elements are of the deontological philosophy, in that both are universal rights (see Table 10.1). On this basis, what is and is not philosophically ethical, can only be determined by an in-depth, case-by-case examination. However, what can distort the picture is the issue of secrecy. Attempting to determine an appropriate ethical position between two conflicting, but nevertheless universal rights, is one matter, but keeping particular information from the public, does blur boundaries.

At the individual level, shareholders may require greater details in the form of published information on the remuneration received by directors. In response, directors may be reluctant to disclose such information on the grounds of privacy, especially as directors are employees, like others in the organization and these others do not have to disclose publicly their level of salary. Thus far, the debate falls squarely into the deontology versus deontology conundrum. However, if directors' salaries are published as the total sum paid to directors, but within that are hidden particular payments to directors, such as fringe benefits of which shareholders might disapprove, the debate has changed and become one of secrecy versus freedom of information, or theological egoism (gain for the few) versus deontology.

The same applies at the organizational and government level of analysis. Take for example the case of the FISA, established under the Foreign Intelligence Security Act (FISA). The FISA organization apparently authorized a record number of wiretaps (697 is the recorded number) in the USA, outside normal constitutional procedures. The FISA, originally created under the Carter Administration, as a mechanism for counteracting hostile foreign governments and international terrorist organizations in the USA, was discovered in 1993 to have inadequately reviewed wiretap applications. The FBI applied to a little known part of the Justice Department, the Office of Intelligence Policy and Review (OIPR) for wiretap authorization. However, on the unexpected death of the head of the OIPR, Mary Lawton, it was discovered, in 1995, that the FBI had not requested a single court-authorized wiretap for the surveillance of terrorists. Further, the *Intelligence Newsletter* (28 November 1996) reported that FISA was then additionally being used for economic espionage, particularly against the French. In response, government could well propose the public interest argument, that certain activities should be undisclosed.

However, secrecy is no longer privacy, thereby departing from the deontological position of a universal right and entering into theological egoism, whereby one person or small group decides to hold something back for his/her own ends and desires, as with the FBI actions on FISA cases. The original reason for FISA involvement, namely as a measure for counter espionage, seems to have been substituted by that for economic espionage. The circumstance of theological egoism masquerading as deontology encourages 'whistle-blowing', namely leaking documents or confidences to the press or media. Apart from all other ethical considerations, the officers of any organization, driven by their own beliefs and consciences as to what is ethical and proper, may make public, certain developments. Where the boundary lies between exposing information which undermines certain people's right to privacy, damaging confidence in the institution, and exposing improper conflict of interests, is again difficult to determine. As stated, a case-by-case analysis, being guided by precedence, is recognized as the only practical way forward.

Universalistic versus particularistic norms

Universalistic norms are deontological by nature and hence are displayed as abstract codes or rules which are not contextually determined. Deontologists are likely to display a strong tendency to resist suggestions for change, or the making of exceptions which may weaken the rule. The fear is that once one starts to make expectations to unique conduct, the system may be corrupted and ultimately collapse.

Particularistic behaviour, on the other hand, focuses on the exceptional nature of current circumstances. For example, if a person is not just a 'citizen' but also a friend, relative or a neighbour, and as such has a unique importance, the decision-maker may protect or discount this person, no matter the rules (see Table 10.1).

In today's world, managers are expected to serve their clients well, and in order to do so, they must know their clients' needs. In order to appreciate client needs, managers must develop close relations with them. Business leaders and managers who build alliances through interactions with clients and suppliers, based on particularist ties, also help their organization realize its targets, since only through facilitating relationships can business objectives be achieved. Thus business leaders and managers are placed in the paradoxical situation, through their membership to various networks, of simultaneously being required to display particularistic and universalistic behaviours. Considering that business activity occurs through transactions driven by positive personal relationships, the underlying philosophy of business is that of act utilitarianism. Universalistic norms, on the other hand, require that one treats people without favour and as they deserve. It is obvious that prolonged universalistic norms practice would simply lead to business and economic ruin. If long-standing clients of a consultancy or accounting practice were treated as strangers walking in off the street, or dedicated users of IT services were treated as casual users, all would probably forego their loyalty and choose another supplier. Corporate leaders are thus required to navigate between an ethic of care and being sensitive to circumstances, and one of respecting the rights of all.

An extreme universalist will hold that particularists cannot be trusted because they are tempted to help their friends, irrespective of the circumstances. An extreme particularist will perceive universalists as cold, devoid of sentiment, and inflexible, unwilling to help even a friend. Those from the one end of the spectrum of ethical philosophy will tend to think of those at the other, as ethically incapable.

A commonly expressed dilemma highlighting the universalistic/ particularistic dichotomy is shown in the way organizations handle job vacancies and applications. A job that is advertised as open for all to apply, may in fact be earmarked for an already known and favoured candidate, often an already existing member of the organization. The reason for the double standard is 'fit': 'we [in the organization] know the person; we know what they can and cannot do, but most of all we know they will fit in and contribute'. The fear is that anyone new may turn out to be problematic and, even if not so, will have to go through an extended learning curve. Reality indicates that most executives are apt to use both philosophies, bouncing from one to the other when it personally or organizationally suits.

At the organizational level, cost-cutting exercises can raise universalistic and particularistic dilemmas. The CEO may decide to introduce a 10 per cent cut in overheads across the organization. Certain directors may, in theory, agree with the policy, but also may resist it on the grounds that they consider themselves and their part of the organization to be a special case (and they may be). The same applies in rationalization exercises, whereby the most cost effective sites would be expected to be maintained, while others would be sold off or closed down after cost-based criteria have been universally applied across the company. However, the closure of certain sites could cause substantial damage to the local economy, in terms of the consequences of mass redundancy. Hence, certain sites may be kept operating, even though their economic viability is below standard, while those slightly more efficient may be closed down, putting people out of work, but overall those latter local economies may be more robust and better able to take the blow. However, that is of little compensation to those who have lost their jobs.

A further example is provided by a USA based multi-national company (which did not wish to be identified) which, through its human resources department, has been trying to introduce the discipline of 360 degree feedback to its line management, worldwide. Certain of the regional directors and vice presidents, line of business executives and support service directors have accepted the initiative. Others have resisted, on the basis that 360 degree feedback procedures could be more damaging than beneficial to a management that is emotionally not ready for such an intensive experience. Headquarters management are currently in a quandary as to how best to proceed. A universal application of 360 degree feedback could be genuinely damaging to certain of the subsidiary management teams. To not apply 360 degree feedback throughout the organization, could damage the credibility of top management in their not displaying the determination to pursue reform and improvement in performance.

Thus, the two moral positions of 'treat others fairly' and 'pay particular attention to someone in need', capture the executive ethical paradox, and the need for a balance between justice and care in the organization. Overall, people-centred, responsible behaviour is seen as providing for different options under different circumstances, through collecting enough information to know what other parties need and from that, knowing what one is obliged to supply. Inevitably, responding positively to one person's welfare needs will vary according to context and need. On this basis, people will be treated differently, but with the honest intent of applying humanity and fairness. In keeping with such a philosophy, many contracts are written so that what exactly is required for different people varies according to circumstance. The prevailing wisdom is that outcomes cannot effectively be achieved in organizations without relationships being governed by an ethic of care, which denotes the creation of a web of obligations. A network tied together by an ethic of care, proclaims particularist norms.

The universalistic/particularistic ethical contrast is philosophically a deontological/act utilitarianism juxtaposition. However, unlike the contrast between contractual obligation and moral determination, whereby it is possible to nudge towards a position of settlement due to the ordered and structured nature of deontology and rule utilitarianism, the contextual and sentimental nature of act utilitarianism places the potential clash on a different dimension. The understood way of doing things, so prevalent in act utilitarianism, switching at times from what is best for the overall community to what is best for certain individuals, both of which would be acceptable in particular contexts, would be seen as unethical by deontologists, not just from the point of view of any single act, but also because of the perceived inconsistency. A deontologist would say, 'what you are doing I would not agree with, but the fact that you are sometimes favouring your friends as well, is just too much'. The greater degree of consistency of action between deontology and rule utilitarianism, makes negotiation more possible. In contrast, the likely outcome of interaction between deontologists and act utilitarians would be a political battle of wills, a power play between key figures in the organization. Dependent upon who gains the upper hand or who is appointed to a dominant position, such as chairman, president or CEO, will be the nature of the philosophy of the organization for the future. The losing party would probably leave, or even be required to leave, in order to return the organization to a position of stability. The clash between deontologists and act utilitarians is tantamount to a long and dirty little war.

Special case of the public sector

For a considerable period, the Japanese have kept faith in the honesty and efficiency of their public servants. Although the public became disillusioned with the corruption scandals surrounding politicians, the overall opinion towards public servants has been that of being beyond reproach. However, such beliefs are now being called into question. The Prime Minister, Ryutoro Hashimoto has made it his mandate to reform government structure, with deregulation being at the top of his agenda. Further, the public want change, as a number of scandals have surfaced. The Kobe earthquake in 1995, surfaced flaws in the process of approving building licences; the Finance Ministry failed to monitor irregularities in banking and securities; and civil servants in the Health and Welfare Ministry were linked to a cover-up in HIV-tainted blood supplies.

The cause for concern in Japan is symptomatic of a worldwide movement of deregulation, decentralization, and the enhancement of discretionary influence to the lower levels of government organizations. Consequently, lower level employees are given greater scope to decide on resource issues on behalf of the public. Hence, the ethics of the individual have become more prominent in the provision of service. Such developments introduce the question of 'gifts, freebies, doing favours for mates' and generally, 'a bit of nepotism here and there',[14] in the business of building relationships. For example, during the launch of the new software product, Natural New Dimension, a system for PCs, the software corporation SPL Worldgroup (Australia) presented each attendant with a free software package. Of the 210 attendants, 180 were public sector employees who attended the two-hour presentation during working hours, as part of a government initiative to keep abreast of IT developments (SPL Worldgroup Australia, 1995). Considering that software licences were issued under individuals' names, not the organizations', and that the individuals were IT professionals, each individual took home a package worth AUS$2100.

The dilemma is that public servants in the new context of commercialization are still required to play a role in public trust through having to maintain independence, calling into question the distinction of private benefit from their public role.

The shift from the more traditional, paternalistic control culture to the newer decentralized structure poses a dilemma for executives (see Table 10.2).

In essence, a network of more informally-based social relations will be needed to support the newly defined service-driven structures.

In Australia, for example, government officers, most at executive levels, on overseas postings on behalf of the Australian Department of Foreign Affairs and Trade, 'have made a healthy second income on the duty-free luxury car market'.[15] How widely fraud and consequent disorder spreads, depends substantially on how the network of social relations is structured. Sometimes the most elaborate and blatant schemes of political corruption take on the solidity of the established institution, so that those public officials finally brought to account for their actions, invariably defend themselves by explaining that they only participated in the system as they found it.

Table 10.2 Public sector dilemma

Paternalistic cultures	Decentralized structures
■ Low risk-taking	■ Innovation
■ 'Red tape'	■ Responsiveness
■ Management versus employee	■ Manager/employee partnership
■ Traditional 'power' structure	■ Empowered employees
■ Rules, procedures, guidelines	■ Self-control with rules/guidelines
■ Multiple-level management	■ Decentralized/interfacing structures
■ Autocratic style (mandarins)	■ Participative
■ 'Top-down' directives	■ Towards team consensus
■ Skills in one function	■ Skills in multiple functions
■ Controlled/limited information	■ Open communication/shared
■ 'Pay cheque' mentality	information
■ Reward according to level/grade	■ Commitment and involvement
■ 'Status quo'	■ Achievement-based rewards
■ Precedence-driven	■ Continuous improvement
■ Service determined by bureaucrat	■ Client driven
	■ Competitive service and quality

Again in Australia, in addition to federal government incidents of unethical acts, each state has been plagued with Royal Commission Inquiries, ranging from an investigation into the activities of the public officers of Queensland, after which the Minister for Health and the Deputy Speaker of the House had to resign because the officers had been identified by the Criminal Justice Commissioner as misusing their parliamentary travel allowances, through to the New South Wales Inquiry into the activities of the police service, alleged to have been involved in bribery and corruption scandals, to Western Australia, where corruption occurred on a large scale, concerning a number of commercial deals in which the government, its ministers and associates were involved. In 1992–93, for example, the New South Wales Independent Commission Against Corruption (ICAC) received 3951 complaints of potentially unethical and corrupt practices in the New South Wales public sector.

In response to media attacks and increasing incidents of political corruption in the 1980s, many governments have put ethics on the agenda, during their transition to a market discipline. The manner in which ethics are being applied varies as do their form and context, as exemplified by the United States' ten-part *Code of Ethics for Government Service* adopted in 1958, typified as the 'ten commandments approach', in which a small number of general precepts are expressed in broad terms. Australia's *Guidelines on Official Conduct* provide a comprehensive coverage of ethical rules, with guidelines for their implementation. Somewhat different is Canada's *Conflict of Interest Code* (1985) (revised by the Armstrong Memorandum in 1987), which is near the middle of the continuum, ranging from commandments to guidelines. Whether ethical rules in general, or codes in particular, take the form of legislative or administrative measures and guidelines, varies from country to country. The United States, for example, relies more on legislation to regulate public service ethics, than do Australia, Britain and Canada.

In order to understand more completely the views of senior management towards consideration of ethics and values in workplace behaviour, we, the two authors of this book, in part of the Cranfield study of the Australian Public Service (see Chapter 9), required the two ranks of senior executive service (SESs) and senior officers (SOs) to identify the five key values that they considered to be significant in the effective performance of their job. Repeatedly, in private conversation, in interview and to open-ended questions in a questionnaire, 'quality advice to ministers' and 'support for ministers', were quoted as the most highly rated and practised values. However, when asked to rank the most significant values, considerable variance emerged (see Table 10.3) below.

Out of 53 separately identified values and attributes, quality advice to Ministers was marked 14th by SESs, while support for Ministers was 42nd. For SOs, quality advice to Ministers was ranked 32nd, while support for Ministers was ranked 43rd. Otherwise, there emerged a considerable degree of overlap on key job-related values and attributes between the two groups. The discernible differences are that SOs value opportunity and recognition, while SESs reflect more on career, position and ambition.

Table 10.3   Kakabadse/APS study: key job-related values and attributes

Rank SESs	Rank SOs
1 Effectiveness	1 Communication
2 Communication	2 Team-work
3 Integrity	3 Professionalism
4 Professionalism	4 Integrity
5 Competence	5 Probity
6 Accountability for powers/privileges	6 Respect
7 Team-work	7 Quality
8 Quality	8 Opportunity
9 Probity	9 Excellence
10 Respect	10 Responsibility
11 Commitment	11 Recognition
12 Honesty	12 Competence

As highlighted in Chapter 8, the leadership of an organization should live its espoused values, otherwise ethical progress will not be made and cynicism in the organization will arise. As the office of the Auditor General (UK) proclaimed in 1990, 'Value statements can be strong positive tools, but management must be consistent and act accordingly. Announcing them, and then not living by them, is deadly.'

Pathways to ethical application

The comment of the UK's Auditor General highlights a fundamental challenge for working through ethical dilemmas: how should it be done? Various views prevail:

■ A study of retired middle managers of Fortune 500 companies revealed that corporate crime was strongly determined by top managers who pushed their subordinates so hard that illegal practices were tacitly necessary in order to survive in the corporation. The study concluded that corporate culture norms need attention, as prevailing norms are the reason people are socialized into patterns of unethical behaviour.[16]
■ An alternative view is that codes of ethics are the only fertile means of minimizing the dark side of networks and in-group thinking.
■ Expunging unethical behaviour is an impossible task, leaving minimizing negative practices as the only viable way forward.
■ Winning the hearts and minds of leaders and middle level managers is fundamental, as leaders are the locus of ethical responsibility.

Incorporating the above views, with the contrasting demands made through the application of the theological/deontological perspectives, three distinct pathways to ethical application in organizations are identified (see Figure 10.1), namely, the North-East passage, the South-West trail and the issuing of decrees.

North-East passage

Leaders who pursue the route of the North-East passage hold utilitarianism as the cornerstone of their philosophy, and in so doing are sensitive to context, emphasizing the greatest good for the greatest number of people. The prime aim of pursuing the North-East passage is for top management to communicate a philosophy of ethics that captures people's imaginations, helps adapt the way people work, but preserves present 'good practice', and overall, becomes a way of living and working in the organization. By adopting a North-East passage perspective to ethical change in the organization, the process of how improvement and change in the organization are applied is as important as the final goals. A measure of successful ethical change is the degree to which the change agents are sensitive to context. Either through internal attitude and

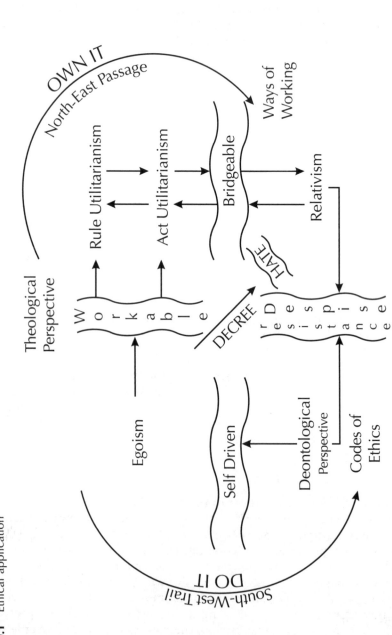

Figure 10.1 Ethical application

culture surveys, or through workshops, or through executive dinners and briefings where senior management meet an invited number of staff and middle level managers, senior managers become intimately acquainted with the views, feelings and ethical core of the greater number of people in the enterprise.

Recognizing the nature of sentiment and reality in the organization, the leadership appropriately positions and then promote the values it aspires the organization to adopt through example, in terms of its members' own behaviour and morals. In so doing, individual senior managers will have been required to make the transition from theological egoism to theological utilitarianism, either by personal choice or through facilitation and planned debate. Each senior manager would need genuinely to discard what is good for him/her, his/her function or department, and pursue an ethic of what is the best for the greater whole, the organization. The discussion that brings the members of a senior management together, could focus on related business topics, or directly on issues of ethics and values. Debates as to the nature and wording of the mission of the organization, as described in Chapter 8, can achieve the necessary level of cohesion to push forward on the ethical front. Then again, senior management may require facilitation and coaching to adopt more community and executive-based values, emphasizing a strong sense of shared accountability. Whatever approach works to help senior management bridge the gap between egoism and utilitarianism, should be used, as ethical change is being driven at the individual level of behaviour through the leadership's display of shared values and consistency of behaviour. As leaders have the capacity to insulate, reinforce and change the values and ethics contained in the organization's philosophy, one fundamental aspect of North-East passage way forward is that behaviour speaks louder than words.

In attempting to communicate fundamental change, especially that of an ethical nature, the Cranfield studies highlight six key behaviours that it is imperative consistently to maintain (see Chapter 8 on the various approaches to communication).

- *Approachability*; senior managers need to display concern and respect for others, as they make themselves available for the purposes of feedback.
- *Robustness to address known sensitivities*; whereby senior managers confront known but difficult-to-discuss issues in the organization, thereby highlighting their strength of character to promote an ethical organization.
- *Being understanding*; senior managers should be attentive and responsive to the views and emotions expressed by others in the organization.

- *Being trustworthy*; senior managers, by their actions, demonstrate that others in the organization can place in them their trust.
- *Cabinet responsibility*; whereby senior managers jointly and consistently follow through on decisions made, by matching words with actions.
- *Addressing both long and short term issues*; whereby senior managers display their long-term interest in the organization, indicating that they will see through reform and innovation.

Depending on whether the organizational norms are more 'rule' or 'act' utilitarian driven, is likely to influence whether or not the desired ethical standards are written down and internally published. However, 'real' ownership for applying ethical ways of working is negotiated day by day. The more utilitarian the organization and the leadership, the more ethical norms need to be incorporated into the daily ways of working in the organization, rather than the publication and enforcement of mission and value statements.

South-West trail

Alternatively, taking the South-West trail involves codification, and the establishment of universal rules. For reasons of benchmarking standards, or displaying a break with the past, or responding to media attacks over issues of corruption, or because of personal beliefs, one or a small number of leaders may promote their ethics in a deontological manner. In Australia, the federal government and the state parliaments supported the Public Sector Ethics Acts as the basis for declaring their intent to promote the moral high ground for 'good' public administration. In addition, a number of federal departments supplemented this initiative by their own departmental codes of ethics, and ethics manuals. Furthermore, following reports by the Electoral and Administrative Review Commission (EARC, 1992) and its Parliamentary Committee (PCEAR, 1993), in December 1994, a national network of public sector ethics was formed, in order to promote and increase public sector ethical awareness.

For those in the organization who identify with the ethical standards in the codes and, equally, agree with deontological ethical promotion, they are likely to fully support and push for the universal application of codes. For those who disagree with certain of the ethical standards being pursued, but agree with the deontological approach, they are likely to have to learn to live with the new regime, but overall still offer their support. In contrast, those of a non-deontological orientation, irrespective of the ethical points being made, are likely to resist the application of a common code. For those who hold 'act utilitarian' especially, or relativist values, their resistance is likely to be driven by a despise of codes and their deontological supporters. The ways adopted by deontologists would be seen as authoritarian, even brutal. 'Act' utilitarians and relativists hold process of ethical application and ethical content in identical order of priority. People need to be wooed and won over. Discretion has to be applied in order to make allowances for the pursuit and application of local contexts. The greater the pressure that is exerted for the application of codes, the deeper the resistance, and the greater the antipathy displayed by utilitarians and relativists.

Decree

Either due to stiff resistance to the implementation of a code of ethics, or simply due to the self-driven nature of one or a small number of theological egoists – 'I know what's best for you and the organization' – the CEO and/or chairman may resort to the issuing of decrees, 'These are the ethics to be portrayed. Why? Because I say so!'

For those who believe that ethical standards need to be fairly applied throughout the organization (deontologists), they may find the issuing of decrees distasteful. However, if the issues that need addressing have been captured in the decree, support is likely to be forthcoming. In contrast, the issuing of decrees is likely to arouse volatile and negative passions in act utilitarians and relativists. The perceived heavy-handed approach of one person dictating ethical standards is likely to generate emotions more deep and powerful than those emotions which determined resistance to codes. Deep resentment, on the verge of hate, is likely to emerge. Utilitarians would perceive the issuing of decrees as there being no attempt made to appreciate the unique nature of the various contexts in the organization and thereby, the positive, but different ethical standards that exist. Whereas resistance to codes of ethics may be overt, leading to dialogue, possibly thereafter reaching a position of tolerable settlement, the negative reaction to decrees are likely to generate covert, undermining behaviours, 'whatever can be done to upset the application of a decree should be done'. The chairman or CEO, in turn, would need to be particularly stringent in the application of the decree throughout the organization, reverting to 'sacking' people, not because of any unethical action on people's part, but because of their refusal to apply the decree, and their determination to oust the offending executive. However, it should be noted that reliance on decrees emphasizes the shift from deontology to theological egoism, hence the backlash of passions!

Paradox of corporate governance

A topic of current and popular interest in the field of ethical improvements and which is profound in its display of the deontogical/ theological dilemma in organizations, is that of corporate governance.

The term governance comes from the Greek 'Kybernan' and 'Kybernetes', meaning to steer and pilot, or helmsman; cybernetics has the same root base. Under this meaning, governance is viewed as a process whereby an organization, or even a whole society, steers its way through challenges and blockages, with effective communication being the central platform.

Under the corporate governance banner, the Canadian government has drawn up a round-table of senior Canadian government officials, private sector executives and researchers who have examined, for the last six years, the impact of information technology on society, and its implications for the process of governance.[17] The emerging conclusions of the round-table are that in a world of rapid change, epitomized by eroding social boundaries, ever-growing numbers of special interest groups, and the fragmenting of institutions and belief systems, a 'more distributed system of governance and more learning-based approach to how we organize and govern ourselves', is crucial. The attitude of the Canadians towards governance is displayed as much in the manner in which they explored the subject, as in their conclusions. In clarifying the governance implications for Canadian society, various interest groups were brought together in a round-table forum to represent their views.

The Canadians seemingly recognize corporate governance as a concept of utilitarianism, whereby various interests are brought together, people learn and then forge a cohesive set of values and ethics which need to then be owned by the rest of the organization or society. The leaders of the organizations would need to be exemplary of the governance codes they generated, in order for others lower down to desire to pursue and practise the ethical guidance that had been provided.

Peter Drucker, a prolific writer in the area of corporate governance, highlights the 'institutional investor paradox', as a condition plaguing Anglo-American driven organizations. The paradox is that investors cannot act as 'owners', involving themselves in the management of the business, as their holdings are so big that they cannot simply sell their holdings to the ordinary investor, but only to other institutional funds (pension, insurance).

Sir Adrian Cadbury, Chairman of the Cadbury Report on corporate governance in the UK is less critical, in that he argues that because of the proportion of shares owned by institutional investors and their potential influence in company affairs, they have a 'compelling incentive to improve the governance of the companies in which they invest, rather than selling out, given that they broadly only effectively sell to each other'.[18]

In contrast, and on the basis that, in Cadbury's view, the non-Anglo-American corporation, such as the Japanese or Continental European, is really a coalition of interests serving a wider purpose than providing a return to shareholders, corporate governance holds a different interpretation. For the Anglo-American corporation, governance essentially refers to the rights and responsibilities of shareholders. In order to allow for flexibility of investment, self-regulation is desired.

The Continental European places great store on the relationship between management, employees and other parties, allowing statutory control to regulate board representation and behaviour. The increasing influence of stakeholders, such as employees, suppliers and constituents who have a broader remit, for example politicians, the media, and the professions, is making a significant difference in their clamour for increasing the sense of social responsibility of organizations. Their demand for harmonizing the structure and standards of corporate governance on an international basis, is likely to clash sharply with the Anglo-American economic-based goals and desire for self-regulation.

The 1990s' Anglo-American corporation would argue that progress has been made since the 1980s and that there is no need for the continental, deontological perspective to be applied. The poor performance of certain major corporations in the 1980s, due to hostile takeovers, leverage buyouts, and what Drucker calls, 'bubble-economy scandals' that led to financial collapse, drew attention to the fact that self-interested directors could manipulate operations at the expense of shareholders and other fiscal stakeholders. The reaction to such occurrences was that irresponsible corporate behaviour was widespread, and not just confined to company boards, but also to non-profit organizations. As a result of scandals, in the UK for example, the Cadbury Committee was established in May 1991 by the Financial Reporting Council of the London Stock Exchange. The ensuing report emphasized voluntary choice, through reliance on independent, external directors, to provide a check on internal management, through the main board and through the audit and remuneration committees. However, problems still remain as outlined in the *Business Week* article (15 September, 1997) identifying Tony O'Reilly as being under the corporate governance spotlight. Despite Heinz's business performance, O'Reilly is being criticized for being too lavish in terms of corporate entertainment. Further, *The Economist* (6 December, 1997:7) adds the comment that O'Reilly packed the Heinz Board with his chums! As O'Reilly is finding out, self-regulation has a drawback, namely having to cope with the changing nature of guidelines oscillating between acceptable and unacceptable practice.

Many commentators agree that the Cadbury recommendations have made a substantial impact in the UK, as the external directors had previously been regarded as insignificant to the governance process, described by the press as 'decorations on a Christmas Tree' (*Sunday Times* 1993). Cadbury has strengthened the role and position of the non-executive director, and although the situation, in governance terms, has improved, there still remains a conflict of interest, the non-executive director's professional fees. Unless non-executives are independently wealthy, there still exists the danger of being reluctant to turn on the host that supports them.

Hence, the paradox remains. The Anglo-American corporation desires self-regulation, as typified by the Cadbury recommendations, for reasons of flexibility, in order to be responsive to the demands and requirements of the marketplace. The European-constituted organization supports statutory intervention, in order to ensure adequate representation of stakeholders in the boardroom. In effect, there exists no common philosophical definition of corporate governance. Today's world of corporate governance reflects the societal values in which governance is being applied, and the likely resistance that would be stimulated should one interpretation of governance attempt to swing the other.

Questioning the ethical self

Despite the contrasting philosophical arguments being pursued and resisted at the organizational and societal levels, what provides for the effective application of governance, is leadership. Leaders still have to identify, promote and/or enforce, intentionally or inadvertently, ethical ways forward. However, the questions that leaders have to face, vary. To what extent do the leaders of an organization consistently apply universalistic principles, such as respect for the person, or integrity? To what extent do the leaders promote Socratic virtues, such as a willingness to talk, and listen to others, and as a result, weigh up the consequences of their own actions on others? The locus of ethical responsibility lies with the leaders of an organization, whose passions, actions and concern for voluntary acceptance or reinforcement of particular standards, determine the nature of the norms of a multiplicity of contexts in the organization. Actioning ethical responsibility requires insight into the nature of one's personal convictions, and understanding as to the depth of resilience required to face up to the dilemmas and paradoxes that will be experienced in pursuing ethical reform.

In moving towards a greater appreciation of one's ethical self, forming a view in response to the following questions, can greatly assist.

■ Do I really apply the same principles to all, or try to achieve the greatest good for the greatest number in the organization?

The question asks whether a person believes him/herself to be more of a deontologist or theologist?

■ Do I consider myself first, before I act/proceed?

This question asks whether a person's ethical philosophy is that of a theological egoist and hence concern for self is what really drives behaviour. A similarly-worded question asked of others who are close to the person concerned, in order to provide for feedback, helps confirm the degree to which the person holds egoist theological values.

■ If I am really honest, have I regularly acted in ways which are good for me and at times, my immediate circle (team, group, department), but applied universalistic principles to everyone else?

The above question highlights whether a person is egoist, or even utilitarian, as far as he/she is concerned, but deontological towards others. The greatest inconsistency, probably perceived as hypocrisy by others, is that between declaring a deontological philosophy, but then behaving in an egoist or utilitarian manner to satisfy one's own needs.

■ Do I believe it is better to win 'hearts and minds', or publish words and documents in order to communicate clearly key values and standards of behaviour?

The question explores the degree to which a person is act utilitarianist or deontologist in behaviour. Appreciating one's attitude to making change happen, helps minimize projecting mixed messages and double standards.

■ Do I feel I need the approval of others, on most occasions, before I act?

This question again probes the degree of act utilitarianism held by a person, but also highlights the emotional vulnerability of the individual in applying ethical standards in a deontological manner, when required to do. Certain leaders and managers may find themselves in a position of no choice – a situation may require a deontological push in order to improve circumstances. Whether the person has the will to sustain a comprehensive drive, before being seen to be 'corrupted', i.e. become part of the local culture, is a question that needs exploring.

■ Do I overtly define for others (i.e. colleagues, subordinates) the ethical boundaries of the organization, emphasizing that they should not act in an unethical way, but covertly allow them to enter into a dilemma situation, because that is the way business is really done, and then feel guilty afterwards?

Although this question explores the degree to which a person is deontological towards others but not to him/herself, it also explores the degree to which insight about the unethical nature of a situation is, in reality, denied, or ignored, or measured by the guilt that is felt.

■ Am I influenced by the size or volume of the unethical event or act? – meaning that if I turn a blind eye to some minor unethical occurrences, e.g. small bribes, it makes it OK?

Again the above question reflects the degree of act utilitarianism sentiments held by a person, but also the degree to which he/she can succumb to the creeping nature (inducement) of unethical growth. Any single action may be genuinely intended to influence for positive reasons. On reflection, however, a number of more minor unethical acts may lead to the person being found in an unethical and compromising situation. However, the individual may have felt him/herself to be ethically correct when examining any one act or event. The answer to the above question may assist the emergence of a wisdom that is proactive and that guides a person through paradox, as opposed to the person gaining wisdom retrospectively through pain and retribution.

Each individual's response to the above questions will help the individual to determine his/her ethical nature, and his/her maturity, robustness and strength of will to face up to, and work through, the circumstances that confront him/her. In fact, people's answers to the above questions will highlight their preparedness to enter into paradoxical circumstances. Recognizing the conflicting views and alternatives that exist in any situation, and once having decided what to do, and having done it, a new challenge arises, as people take different positions according to their views and feelings at that moment in time. Hence, any leader is continuously working through dilemmas and conflicts, as highlighted by the senior manager interviewed at the beginning of this chapter. The most vulnerable person is the one who holds misleading assumptions about him/herself and his/her circumstances. As mentioned, it is all too easy to be deontological about others but not about one's self. There is no point in taking the South-West trail and ending up like John Wayne – 'when under attack from them injuns, ya git yur wagons in a circle an' shoot them thar, pesky redskins!' – in other words, start with a deontological outlook and end up with a siege mentality.

Leaders exercise social power and in so doing, apply social responsibility. Their true sense of social responsibility is important for them to recognize, as their potential influence on others is profound. Some have argued that the pursuit of profitability corrupts. It does not, but the denial of hypocrisy does!

Key points summary

■ Dilemmas of an ethical nature are likely to be experienced by those in leadership positions in an organization, as providing direction in a discretionary role involves displaying how an individual will or will not make choices in circumstances where moral dichotomies prevail.

The concepts

■ Three philosophical positions are identified, theological, deontological and relativist.
■ Theologically based concepts of ethics, focus on the impact or outcomes of people's behaviour in particular circumstances. In effect, the moral merits of human actions are linked to the value of their consequences.

Theological ethics are further subdivided into three branches, theological egoism, rule utilitarianism, and act utilitarianism.

■ Theological egoism is primarily concerned with the morality of maximizing the greatest good for the greatest number by aiming to improve one's own interests. Only through satisfying individual self-interest can broader communal best interests emerge.

■ Rule utilitarian philosophy requires drafting rules highlighting ethical conduct, which are believed to support the interests of the majority of the community.

■ Act utilitarianism focuses on the value and benefit of individual and communal action, in terms of producing the greatest benefit for all concerned. Essentially, the utilitarian philosophy of the greatest good for the greatest number is subdivided into assessing the consequences of actions, or establishing rules more to focus and control actions (rule utilitarian) in order to attain the greatest benefit for all.

■ Deontological ethics emphasize the non-consequential aspects of ethics, in that particular principles, such as justice, freedom of speech, and freedom of privacy are, in themselves, the ethical duties to pursue. Deontology emphasizes a mindset of universal statements of right and wrong, which should be applied irrespective of the outcomes of such application.

■ Relativism takes a 'middle position' between the theological and deontological absolutes, which pursues the notion that no universal rules exist but that people's values are driven, and ought to be driven, by the moral norms and conventions of their own grouping or context.

Ethics in application

■ Historically, the application of ethics has adopted a moralist/religious flavour, or a deontological perspective, as exemplified by professional codes and guides of practice.

■ It is postulated that the effective application of ethics in organizations requires an understanding of the ethical dilemmas that are likely to confront managers. Four ethical dilemmas are identified, namely, contractual obligation versus moral determination, bribery versus self-determination, privacy versus freedom of information, universalistic versus particularistic treatment of people.

■ The contractual obligation versus moral determination dilemma involves working through the paradox of rule utilitarianism versus deontology, whereby a senior manager is torn between feeling obliged to meet his/her contractual obligations, but which he/she may be reluctant to pursue, feeling them to be immoral.

■ The bribery versus self-determination dilemma involves working through the paradox of theological egoism versus deontology, and is more commonly placed under the banner of bribery versus honesty.

- The privacy versus freedom of information dilemma involves working through the contradiction of a deontological versus deontological circumstance, whereby two universal rights conflict with each other, and by one being given greater providence, it follows that the other is negated.
- The universalistic versus particularistic norms dilemma involves working through the paradox of act utilitarianism versus deontology, whereby the universal application of certain codes of practice is contradicted by managers making exceptional circumstances for certain people, such as friends, clients, and others with whom they have a personal relationship.
- The public sector is considered as a particular case in point, as the downsizing and dramatic changes that have taken place over the 1980s and 1990s are postulated as having shifted prime values from those of a broad-ranging, deontological nature, to those of a particularistic, utilitarian, economic-rationalist perspective. The challenge for public sector managers to adjust to such changes, is considered as daunting.
- Three distinctly different pathways to ethical application are identified, termed the North-East passage, the South-West trail and decrees.
- The North-East passage route involves ethical change and growth by adopting a utilitarian philosophy, through being sensitivite to context.
- The South-West trail involves introducing change of an ethical nature in a deontological manner, through a consistent and disciplined application of codes and universal rules.
- The third alternative, driven more by the particular perspective of the theological egoist, is to issue a 'decree' as to how change or progress is to be made in the company. Decrees, more often than not, are issued by one person, or small group, are paternalistic in nature, and may be inconsistently applied. Decrees are likely to be most heavily resisted by relativists and utilitarians, not simply because of the content of the decree, but also because of the manner in which it is promulgated.
- Corporate governance displays the paradoxical contrasts of the desire for self-regulation (theological) as displayed by the Anglo-American corporation, and state intervention in order uniformly to address the stakeholder needs of sharing a similar degree of influence (deontological) in the corporation, as displayed by the Japanese/European organization. In effect, corporate governance reflects the societal values in which governance is applied.

Notes

1   Quoted from Simms (1992:506).
2   Adapted from Kernaghan and Langford (1990).
3   Particularly influential on our thinking concerning morals, behaviour and outcomes are Hunt and Vitell (1986).

4   Quote from Hawkins (1983:50–1).
5   Quote from Kant (1909:15–16).
6   For the phrase *'the greatest good for the greatest number'*, see Shaw and Post (1993).
7   Quoted from Aristotle (1986:257).
8   The term 'ethical absolutism' was coined by Tsalikis and Fritzsche (1989).
9   Quoted from Murphy (1989:8),
10 The phrase 'nexus for a set of contractual relationships' can be found in Jensen and Meckling (1976:310).
11 Quoted in *Life* (1988:17).
12 Plutarch (1981:113).
13 Ibid., p 181.
14 Quoted from Gaze (1995:3).
15 Quoted from Walsh (1993:34).
16 The study was conducted by Clinard, (1983).
17 Input from discussions held at ICL's Hedsor House, debating the future of IT in present day society 13/14 January, 1997.
18 Quote from Cadbury (1992:184).

Further reading

For further information on the virtue-based approach, see Kernaghan and Langford (1990). For further reading on contextual philosophy, read Reidenbach and Robin (1991). In examining the virtue/context debate, read Hawkins (1983). For more information on the justice perspective of deontology, read Granovetter (1985), and for an examination of equity, read Frederick et al. (1988). For an overview of deontology and professional codes, see McDonald (1992). For further reading on theological philosophy, see Pettit (1993); for theological egoism read Adam Smith (1776) and Thomas Hobbes (1651), for utilitarianism, see Jeremy Bentham (1989) and John Stewart Mill (1969), and for an overview, see Wiley (1995). Rawls (1971) provides for an interesting analysis of role and act utilitarianism.

For further reading of Protagoras, read Kerford (1981).

For further information into the Ford Pinto car case, see Velasquez (1992). For the *Challenger* disaster, see NASA (1987), *Life* (1988) and the *Report of the Presidential Commission on the Space Shuttle Challenger Accident* (1986). For further insights into the World Bank and the subject of development economics, read Turner and Hulme (1997) and UNDP (1996).

For further reading on the issues of bribery vs honesty, see Plutarch (1981) and Cowell (1956). For the cases of Barlow Clowes and Brent Walker, see Boyd (1996); on Polly Peck, read Brummer (1993); on the Canadian Federal Justice department's investigation of Brian Mulroony, read Serrell (1995); on the corruption taking place in the transition from planned market to free-market economies, particularly Venezuela, Argentina and also German corporate tax returns, see Elliott (1994); on the travel scam of the Canadian External Affairs and Trade department, read Allen, *et al.*, (1992). For further insights into sleaze and the UK's former Conservative Government, see the *Guardian* (1997) and *The Economist* (1997).

For further reading on the rights and privileges of individuals and organizations to privacy, or freedom of information, see Masson (1986) and on issues of developments in IT and privacy, see Lally (1996). On the case example of Kroll Associates, read the *Intelligence Newsletter*, (1997a); on EDS read the *Intelligence Newsletter* (1996b; 1997a); on the FBI and the FISA, see the *Intelligence Newsletter* (1996a); on large-scale kickbacks, read the *Intelligence Newsletter* (1997b).

For further reading on universalistic and particularistic norms, see Heimer (1992).

As far as ethics in the public sector is concerned, over developments in Japan, see Foreign Report (1996), for the various scandals in Australia, read Gaze (1995) and Walsh (1993), concerning the USA, see ASPA (1984) and for Canada, see Canada Treasury Board (1985).

On incorporating ethical standards in the organization, including initiatives in the area of corporate governance, see Clinard (1983) and the American Society for Public Administration (1984), Drucker (1993), *The Sunday Times* (1993), *The Economist* (1992), and in particular, the Cadbury Report, see Park (1992).

CHAPTER 11

Developing Leaders

Case analysis

The Bass Organization: linking business strategy to executive development[1]

The Bass Group, the pub retailing, leisure, hotel, brewing and soft drinks organization, with a turnover in 1994 of £4452 million, employing 76,000 people worldwide, is an example of an organization that directly links the development of its managers to the business strategy pursued by the organization.

Following the intervention of the Monopolies and Mergers Commission into the UK brewing industry, which resulted in a fundamental re-configuration of the industry, and Bass's decision to acquire the Holiday Inn hotel chain, the identity and self-image of the Bass organization, by 1991, had changed. Gone was the traditional brewer's profile, to be replaced by autonomous business divisions, with the Holiday Inn part of the business being truly international in nature. The divisions faced fierce competitive challenges, with each needing to display proficiency in the areas of customer focus, customer service and delivery, quality, cost effectiveness and purchasing. One distinct element of Bass Group headquarters' strategy to meet these business challenges, was to link directly management development with business development. The initiative turned out to be a remarkable innovation and break with tradition for Bass, as previously little or no investment had gone into business education, strategic leadership or general management skills training.

The strategy of management development encompassed:

■ the drafting of a management competencies model tailored to meet the needs of the Bass Group,

- the launching of a group-wide, organization and management review analysis,
- the launching of a selection of management training and development programmes, targeted to meet the needs of specific managers and high flyers exhibiting management potential.

The competencies framework emerged out of each of the division strategy reviews, which highlighted the business competencies required for each business to attain realistically market leadership in its field. The competencies, termed 'behavioural imperatives', initially reflecting the way each business defined its critical success factors, were integrated into statements of 'core competence', including those of the group centre and the CEO downwards. The competency concept was then related to a key jobs and organization level of analysis, whereby through taking account of the discretionary differences, common and unique characteristics of desired performance were identified. The most critical success factors to emerge were:

- processing information,
- making decisions,
- managing relationships,
- encouraging initiative, innovation and accountability,
- exercising power and influence.

From the same base, the desired competencies of a Bass main board, or subsidiary board, director down to a management trainee, had been identified and linked together through establishing criteria for assessing individual capability and through identifying the 'route-ways' for moving laterally and horizontally. In Bass's view, three key benefits have emerged from applying the core competencies model,

- considerable improvments in self-development and career planning, through providing a 'template' against which any manager can assess his/her current competence level and seek both on and off-the-job development in preparation for a chosen career path,
- establishing a psychological construct, whereby through pursuing the competencies approach, it has become clear to the organization that a new psychological construct (new desired attitudes) is now in place, emphasizing accepting responsibility for enhancing one's own employability, and,
- improving the success of external recruitment, whereby people are being brought in with specific skills and experience, and equally people are leaving the organization to promote positively their careers in their chosen fields.

In parallel to the competency model, Bass introduced, in 1992, the organization and management review, which requires senior management to examine annually the viability of their business plans, future organization requirements, and capability of their managerial talent, to realize and achieve their plans. Together with the competencies model, it is possible for senior management at divisional and group centre level to identify their current skills base and future potential management development needs, and to move towards bridging the gap between the two. Hence, the review process, in addition to clarifying the level of potential in the organization, also provides a mechanism for regularly monitoring individuals as they develop, and as job opportunities occur.

As a result of the competencies and review innovations, management development programmes have become more streamlined, in that they are designed as vehicles of both people development and change enhancement. From a decision made by the Bass Executive Committee in 1991, to fund centrally educational programmes, three specific groups of Bass managers were targeted, namely those who would:

- realize short-term benefit, through increasing the competence of most of the senior managers (divisional board level, or just below) to drive the business forward and introduce change. The programme involved individual coaching and 360 degree feedback exercises, as well as management conferences, attended not only by the targeted population, but also by the top executive managers of Bass,
- realize medium-term benefit, namely high potential managers (late 20s/early 30s) for whom development is accelerated through a three year modular business education programme, known as the Bass Programme. Entry depends on meeting certain standards derived from the competencies model, and progress on the programme is equally measured in similar fashion,
- realize long-term benefit, through the corporate graduate recruitment and development programme (the UK Bass Management Scheme), whereby newly recruited young people are introduced into the Bass development streams with the intent that those successful will, in due course, qualify for the Bass Programme.

The Bass organization provides an interesting case example of an enterprise keenly interested in inculcating a deep seated culture of success in its managers.

Bass deliberately entwined business direction and strategy with the development of people, so that leadership is now elevated to being one of the prime levers for attaining competitive advantage. Such a scheme was not 'dreamed up' overnight, but rather dedicated teams of professionals devoted considerable time and effort to drafting conceptually tight models and then examining and logging the progress of Bass managers against these models on implementation. The competencies model, for example, drew on the work of Douglas Bray, whose approach substantially influenced the development of assessment-centre thinking in the USA and Europe, as well as on the work of Gillian Stamp of Brunel University, who has further developed the ideas of Elliott Jaques. Through professionalism, in both design and application, and through realistically linking business issues with leadership development, Bass have been able to:

- promote a consistent language of performance and success throughout the group,
- provide clear operational definitions of management behaviour,
- promote common methods and applications for on and off-the-job development,
- promote a consistency of standards of performance,
- provide for shared values of fairness and openness.

Bass would be the first to admit that the system has its flaws. However, the enviable, consistent, focused and 'all round' development of their current and future leaders makes them a corporate role model for the effective development of leaders.

Very few today would challenge the value of effectively developing the organization's managers and leaders. That was not so clearly the case two decades or more ago. A manager keen to realize his/her potential may have faced unhelpful and dispiriting comments and questions such as, 'Why go on courses?', 'What value is training?', 'Hope you enjoy your holiday!' The incidence of such comments, less so today, is substituted by a senior management far more eager to harness the people potential in the organization, having recognized that development, as the Bass case highlights, can be directly related to enhancing revenue, growth, profitability and success. The reason that executive development, as a concept, seems to have progressed from the 'nice to have' to 'vital to ensure' category, is that organizations are essentially hybrids. As highlighted in Chapters 1 and 2, downsizing, the increased need for customer responsiveness, ever greater competition, and the pull/push impact of IT, have generated a greater reliance on people, rather than on structures, to hold the organization together. The willingness, maturity and actions of individuals have substituted the steadying, and at times, nullifying, impact of formal role and authority relationships.

Recognizing that the development of managers and leaders is now an important reason for the success of an organization, in this chapter, the recommendations for leadership development are driven by the results of a number of Cranfield surveys, which highlight particular ways for developing the actual and latent capacity in individuals, for them ultimately to attain and effectively hold high office. Particular emphasis is given to on-the-job development, highlighting the career track exposure beneficial to enhancing leadership qualities. Discussion also focuses on the opportunity costs at the organizational, team and individual levels of not providing opportunities for development. Off-the-job development focuses on an exploration of how individuals can be assisted to develop and effectively apply transformational capabilities and transactional skills. Throughout, examples of different company approaches to development are provided to support the points being made.

Career track development

Four areas of career development are identified, adopting a wider perspective, enhancing relationship management, early leadership exposure and building confidence through challenge.

Adopting a wider perspective

A particularly powerful and positive experience for prospective leaders is to gain a broader view of their organization. Damaging comments and decisions may arise when individuals in positions of responsibility do not appreciate the potential of other functions, and departments, or the constraints and hurdles to be overcome by other functions, in addressing particular challenges. To overcome organizational myopia, a breadth of functional experience can best be gained at an early age, through deliberate career placement. Numerous mid to large-sized corporate organizations second younger managers to two or more functions, for limited periods, in order to provide for that overview.

Apart from understanding more clearly the strengths and weaknesses of the organization, and how to harness the potential of other departments, gaining a broader functional experience establishes the groundwork of awareness necessary for adopting a general management perspective. Research shows that having direct experience of two or three separate functions prior to the age of 35, well prepares high flyers for senior responsibility. If placement proves to be difficult, managers displaying high potential can be allocated to project groups, working parties, or task forces, in order to enable them to evolve a wider view of the business and its manner of operation.

Relationship management

Breadth of experience, coupled with exposure to different stakeholders, satisfies one of the prime development requirements identified by top executives (in a study by Charles Margerison and Andrew Kakabadse) – that of an ability to work with a wide variety of people, supported by an ability to do deals and negotiate. Strong emphasis is placed by the senior managers in the surveys on developing people skills through job-related experiences. Particularly highlighted are the people skills of communication, delegation, and patience to work through difficult-to-resolve issues.

Early leadership exposure

The third area of practical experience for prospective leaders is that of early responsibility for a team, and for delivering to a budget. Unless a manager can learn how to allocate work, resolve differences of opinion, chair meetings, encourage and motivate colleagues and subordinates, confront tensions and conflicts, and be held accountable for decisions made, the person is less likely to grow the confidence to manage the pressures of high office. In the Margerison and Kakabadse comparative study of USA and UK, CEOs, the respondents indicated that leadership responsibility should come before the age of 30 years. Over 66 per cent of the study respondents reported that they had received their first leadership post prior to the age of 30, with 41 per cent of the respondents stating they had gained leadership responsibility by the age of 25 years.

Building confidence through challenge

Early leadership experience and breadth of job responsibility provide the challenge that will push people not only to make decisions, but also to learn to live by their consequences. Living with and remedying one's own mistakes is primary to nurturing maturity and confidence-building. However, for those from more specialist backgrounds, whose professional training is lengthy, it may be necessary to pay particular attention when placing them in demanding leader roles, as they are entering the career hierarchy at a later stage and their earlier formative work experience may have precluded the 'rough and tumble' of management.

Similar attention may need to be given to high flyers in more centralized organizations, where less opportunity is available for managing profit and loss accounts. If nothing else, young managers should be given the opportunity to lead teams, so that they experience the challenging emotions of knowing 'the buck stops with them', not only for their performance, but for the overall performance of their subordinates.

Whether individuals are selected and supported in challenging roles, or are simply exposed to the strain of demanding accountabilities, building confidence is assisted considerably if the manager receives regular feedback on his/her performance. Through senior managers making time for feedback, the individual can receive the guidance and constructive criticism necessary for improvement.

On-the-job development

As a result of the Cranfield studies, four approaches to on-the-job development are offered, determining individual and team impact, recognizing and managing the dynamics of transactional change, creating developmental opportunities through survey enquiry, and maintaining discipline over appraisals.

Determining impact

In determining the approach to take to on-the-job development, the senior managers (General Managers, Directors, MDs, CEOs, Chairmen) in the Cranfield surveys were asked, 'If an unlimited budget for your development was available to you, how would that be spent?' The most favoured response is highlighted in Table 11.1.

From 42 per cent of the Japanese respondents to 80 per cent of the German respondents, the single strongest view is that the most productive form of development is in addressing issues that all face, but together as a team. Off site, team discussions are considered as far more valuable than attending training programmes, counselling or other forms of personal and strategic development. Off-site meetings allow for policy, strategy and operational issues to be discussed by the team and implemented with the approval of the team. Hence, a particularly potent and powerful experience for senior manager development, is working through issues, in teams. As highlighted in Chapter 8, most senior managers are aware of the issues they face. Insight is not their primary concern, but more how to utilize their insights within the context of the organization. The Cranfield research highlights one area of team

Table 11.1   Development as a team (% of top executive respondents)

Country	Percentage
Japan	42
Sweden	52
Finland	56
France	56
Austria	57
Britain	57
Ireland	67
Spain	68
Germany	80

development that has been particularly penetrating in assisting individuals and teams to reconsider their perceptions and approaches, and that is to feed back to the members of senior teams how the quality of interactions among them enhances or damages the approach to visioning and the implementation of strategy.

Team visioning

In order to capture the views, perspectives and approaches to discussing and then pursuing a vision, the Cranfield team designed a 'visioning map', an instrument for capturing the dynamics of discussing and then implementing an agreed vision by senior teams. From the original breakthrough by four Cranfield researchers (Charles Margerison, Jacquie Drake, Ralph Lewis and Chel Hibbert) but then developed by us, the authors, the visioning map was developed to assist individuals in understanding the different approaches adopted in the team, for visioning. Four dimensions are identified (see Figure 11.1).

Centredness, refers to how a person leads his/her life in the outer world, preferring to spend more time interacting with other people, or in an inner world, preferring to spend more time alone in his/her own company.

Action orientation, refers to how individuals are likely to act in different circumstances by adopting a more controlling stance, attempting to have people, others' actions, events and situations more under their personal control through the use of authority and command styles, or by being more participative, inviting comment and views on how to address challenges, and facilitating a more team-based approach to decision implementation.

Interfacing practice, examines how individuals co-operate and interrelate across the organization. Certain people adopt a more rational approach, concentrating on the shared task and challenges at hand, but pay little attention to the nature of the context(s) of their colleagues and superiors with whom they interface. In contrast, pursuing a more personalized approach to interfacing across the organization involves taking account of people's situation, their preparedness to act, the constraints and challenges they experience, which may only indirectly impact on the immediate issues that require attention. Hence, certain senior managers interface to address current challenges, while others naturally interface in order to build relationships so as to address more effectively problems whenever they arise.

Challenge focus identifies the manner in which individuals address challenges, exhibiting either an intuitive approach, namely utilizing imagination, insight and a restlessness to pursue possibilities and new avenues, or by being practical, relying on experience, tangible information and a step by step, steady approach to solving problems.

Figure 11.1   Visioning map

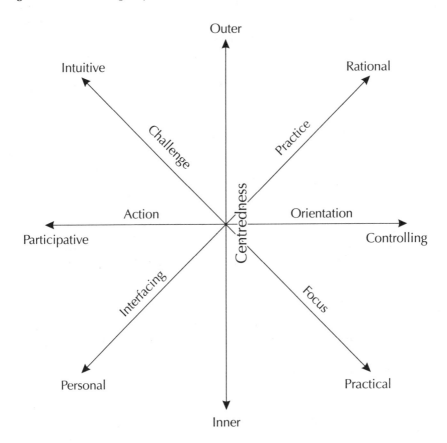

Through completion of a questionnaire which plots out each individual's response on the above dimensions, the data is transferred on to single sheet maps. Each team member's completed map is placed alongside the others' (maps) and feedback is given to the team on how the various approaches to conceptualizing and implementing vision are likely to impact on the organization, how the quality of relationships within the team enhances or constrains bonding and communications, and each team member's impact on his/her colleagues, subordinates and those with whom he/she has closely to interface.

Case example: the banking top team

The top team of an international investment bank, headquartered in London, faced considerable unrest at senior management level. The investment bank was a subsidiary of an established retail bank, which held the ambition of becoming a global force. The CEO of the investment bank was a young, aggressive merchant banker, whose meteoric rise had become legend in the City. The chairman of the investment bank, who also sat on the main board of the retail bank, was an older man, less exciting, more steady and far less willing to take risks. The two men and their eight investment bank director colleagues shared similar aspirations, to become an established global investment house – to be a household name – to be at the forefront of some of the largest, dramatic and awe-inspiring deals. That is where the sharing ended. From there on in, most observers commented that chaos reigned. Endless meetings were followed by more endless meetings. Meetings to discuss current client contracts, meetings to discuss client portfolios, meetings on new products or ventures, co-ordination meetings, meetings to discuss meetings and protocols become the norm. Further, decisions reached in the meetings were inconsistently followed through. If any one of the directors did not agree with a point of view or decision made, he/she would see the CEO or chairman privately, after the meeting. In fact, the CEO and chairman had become accustomed to making time for private meetings after the team meetings. Although the energy drive and entrepreneurial flair of the management of the bank was admired by the City of London financial pundits, the inconsistencies, changes of direction, hard-nosed and uncompromising stances taken by individual directors, led to an obvious, noticeable wastage of resources, and to the considerable demotivation of staff and middle management, and an uncomfortably high turnover of personnel.

The greatest degree of wastage was in the IT area. The money intended for investment in upgrading technology and new systems was either deliberately ignored, rejected or under utilized. The inconsistent application of IT across the organization led to damaging communication and co-ordination concerns.

The internal splits and tensions were considered by the chairman and the CEO to be unacceptable, and as a result of consultation with the Cranfield team, the directors agreed to complete the questionnaires and to receive feedback using the visioning mapping approach.

The results highlighted considerable splits of perspective among the members of the top team. Three key directors, whose responsibilities required paying greatest attention to developments in the marketplace and not to internal organizational processes, held a 'let's go do it' attitude (see Figure 11.2). As individuals, they were identified as focused, clear minded, logical, extrovert, in control of their functional area, and charming, but also as insensitive and cold despite an outward appearance of social ease. To varying degrees, the three directors were as intuitive, quick to spot and pursue opportunities, as they were down-to-earth and practical. These three were rarely wrong about the potential of the

Figure 11.2 Go do it

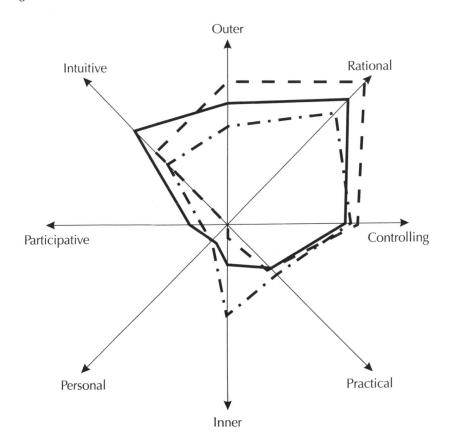

market opportunities they pursued. However, they were seen by their colleagues as arrogant, unapproachable and caring little about the rest of the organization.

For two other directors, life was fun (see Figure 11.3). Extrovert, logical and extremely intuitive, these two individuals considered most problems as challenges, and the bigger and better the challenge, the greater the excitement. Their need for stimulation was high. Even the most challenging task, once having become routine, was experienced as boring. When bored, the two men lost interest, put little effort behind pursuing further activity, and made mistakes over details. Ironically, if an assignment were perceived as interesting, the capacity of these directors to manage even the most intricate details, was impressive. Once bored, their inability to manage routine led to damaging errors being made. Not

Figure 11.3 Life's fun

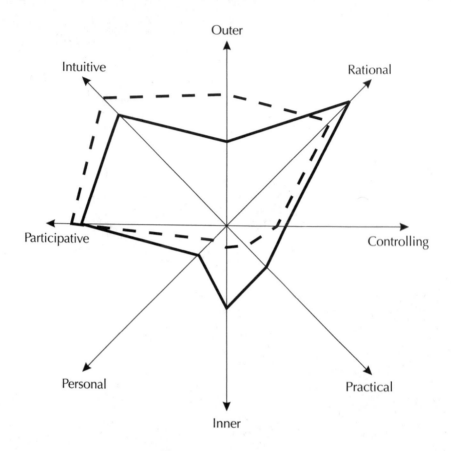

unexpectedly, they found most meetings uninspiring, and although effective in dealing with clients, they were inconsistent in honouring commitments made at meetings.

In complete contrast, one other director, although considerably intuitive and driven to succeed, also displayed a capacity for sensitivity towards others (see Figure 11.4). He was deeply disturbed by the lack of care and attention shown to staff and management internally, and by certain of the sharp practices entered into with clients. This director also held the additional role of Compliances Officer. In effect, he monitored the ethical/unethical practices within the organization and at times found himself in an extremely uncomfortable position. He enjoyed the stimulating 'nothing is a problem environment', but was concerned by what he perceived as daily examples of unethical behaviour.

Figure 11.4 Sensitive and concerned

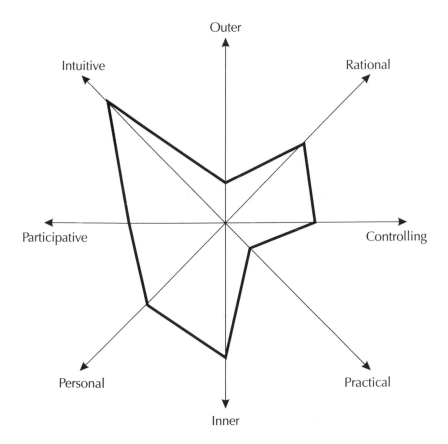

Perhaps the two most surprising results, as far as the other team members were concerned, were those of the CEO (see Figure 11.5) and of the Chairman (see Figure 11.6). The 'all rounder' in the team was identified as the CEO. His capability to appreciate the differing perspectives of his colleagues, to be disciplined and yet invite comment and encourage participation, to be focused, rational and clear in his ability to spot flaws in arguments, was balanced by a sensitivity towards individuals and the issues they faced in their jobs or in their part of the organization. The CEO emerged as interested in people and their circumstances, but not overbearing; opportunity driven, but also disciplined at administration, dealing with details and follow through; analytical yet concerned. In fact, the CEO displayed the characteristics of a chairman.

Figure 11.5 CEO as chairman

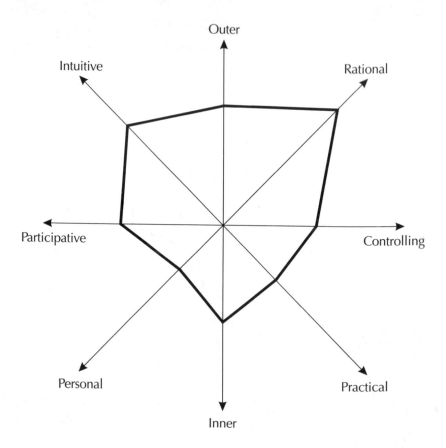

Perhaps the greatest surprise to all in the group was the Chairman's map. The chairman displayed the instincts and drives of a chief operating officer. The attention to detail, the high focus on achieving targets, the strong control needs, the extremely logical approach to finding solutions and managing the organization, emerged as his key, deeply held, characteristics. Despite a charming and affable front, the Chairman was identified as the most introverted in the team and admitted he found interacting with others strenuous and tiresome. Although a highly practical person, he did display some capability for intuition, and flair for problem solving, but had little wish to share and work with colleagues as a team.

The feedback was given to the team, with each person listening to the overall team and to individual feedback. In addition, the facilitator made the following comments:

Figure 11.6 Chairman as chief operating officer

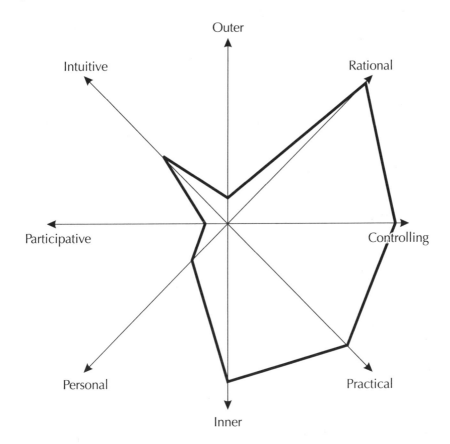

- you as a group, are probably surprised to discover that the CEO displays considerable chairman qualities,
- most of you probably interact more effectively with the chairman, but not with the CEO, because the chairman provides the additional support of paying considerable attention to detail, which many of you find boring and tiresome to exercise,
- your experience of the CEO is of his being interfering and dominant, but he has emerged from this analysis as neither. However, he does seem to be able to 'read' what you as people are like and recognizes when he has to be assertive with some, in order to curb their behaviour and activities, something which at least three of you despise,

- socially, you are likely to have a fondness for each other, even respect for each other. Professionally, you probably do the best you can to 'trip each other up'. For at least four of you, in reality, team-work and co-operation likely means others' adherence to your point of view,
- managerially, most of you do not understand, or do not want to understand, or make little or no attempt to develop, the qualities and attributes of a director of a company. You still behave as dealers, running after glamorous deals, displaying a level of ego which must, by now, be inhibiting others, who are not directly in your part of the organization, from offering you even the mildest of comment or critical feedback,
- the person who is holding the show together is the CEO, who must feel, at times, despair that on the one hand, professionally talented people, capable of bringing in the business, are equally damaging the infrastructure of the organization, setting a bad example to others lower down, which will soon be visible to clients as bad leadership. However, he probably recognizes your immense talents in the marketplace and must be wondering what to do next!

The group remained silent. One of the directors eventually said:

> You mean, apart from everything else, you are telling us that Crosbie [the CEO] is the good guy, whom we've always thought was the bad guy, but in reality, we are the bad guys.

'Something like that', commented the facilitator.

Following a further brief silence, certain members of the team requested additional information and insights concerning their individual maps. As further comments were made, others in the group offered their views and insights in addition to the feedback given by the facilitator. The additional comments provided the catalyst for the flood that followed.

The Chairman confirmed what all others knew, he had found the interface between the investment bank and the parent organization difficult to manage. In fact, the task was so onerous, he had become ill, which was officially explained as, 'the chairman is taking a break'. In the interim periods, Crosbie, the CEO, had taken on the responsibility of chairman, and had made sure that the news of the illness went no further. What equally emerged in the ensuing discussions was that the reporting relationships relating to the overseas offices, were in disarray. Three of the directors, through their functional responsibilities, had both straight and dotted-line relationships with New York, Sydney, Singapore, Tokyo and Hong Kong. A considerable number of the overseas general managers had been vocal in their criticisms of the quality of relationship between them and their corporate centre directors. Whenever problems arose, or whenever any general manager was seen to be difficult, the directors and the general managers colluded to switch the reporting relationship to Crosbie. At least Crosbie listened and attempted to do something about the overseas managers' circumstances. In most cases, the CEO (Crosbie) accepted the responsibility, ending up with 19 and at times more, direct reporting relationships.

Further, most of the team admitted that most of the concerns they faced as an executive team were of their own making and that the situation could not continue. The Chairman revealed to the facilitator, privately after the team workshop, that even he had plotted to undermine the CEO with some of the other directors. All felt threatened by Crosbie's growing influence and presence in the investment bank and parent bank. However, although Crosbie was accused of being a bully and pushing for his own way, the chairman and certain of the directors did, later, admit that they would have behaved in a similar fashion to Crosbie if they had strived to grow and improve the organization. After further meetings, the group agreed to pursue the following actions:

- the reporting relationship between the headquarters' directors and the country general managers were to be allocated on functional lines and kept that way,
- leadership development and management training should be organized for directors and assistant directors. The team concluded that whatever problems they were responsible for initiating, people and organizational concerns were substantially exacerbated by the poor management skills displayed at these two levels,
- the further and continued growth of the organization should be conducted on a planned and disciplined basis, with each of the directors paying greater attention to the forward planning and development of people in his/her department,
- that a greater sense of cabinet responsibility should be displayed over key issues in order to present a unified front to the rest of the organization, and externally to the marketplace,
- that reporting relationships should be streamlined, with further modifications to the executive committee and to the structure of the organization being introduced,
- that the directors and the deputies of each of the major functions adopt a procedure, drafted by Crosbie, for presenting plans, objectives and forecasted performance in line with the parent bank's corporate policy,
- that each of the top team directors commit to undertake the visioning map feedback exercise with each of his/her own team, in order to integrate the existing entrepreneurial drive in the organization with a more mature sense of corporateness and cross-functional co-operation,
- that a management conference for the top 100 managers in the investment bank be organized, where the above commitments could be presented and discussed, in order to display to the other managers in the bank that new ways of working were being introduced.

It is unrealistic to expect people facing difficulties to be motivated and capable of accepting, and immediately working through, feedback data. In the case of the investment bank, subsequent discussion days had to be organized in order to revisit the data and enter into further exploration with each of the directors.

In certain circumstances, the feedback and discussion process may well extend to over a year. In extreme cases, feedback about how individuals are impacting on each other, their colleagues, their function and organization, would be impossible to undertake, as the relationships may have become so dysfunctional. The management would find the experience damaging, exceptionally threatening, and would probably refuse to participate. In order to accomplish on-the-job development through team feedback effectively, individuals need to be guided through the following six stages.

Assess the resilience levels

Receiving feedback about one's self can be a daunting experience. Being told a few 'home truths' in front of others is an even greater ordeal. Before offering feedback, the facilitator needs to assess whether the clients who request feedback are sufficiently emotionally robust to benefit from the experience. If not, and the team proceeds with the feedback exercise, the event could be so traumatic that the individuals will not only reject the data offered, but also are likely to decline from entering into such an experience in the future. To offer feedback prematurely can make the situation worse. The facilitator may need to spend time with the team, individually preparing each one for the feedback experience, while also making him/her aware of the benefits of feedback. Through so doing, the facilitator is helping to build up each team member's emotional resilience to withstand the process. Strengthening the members of the team to cope with the feedback process may require more time and effort than the actual offering of the feedback, and the working through of issues.

Jolting out the past

No matter how well prepared individuals are to receive feedback concerning their views, attitudes and behaviour, when feedback is offered, they are still likely to be startled. The members of the investment banking team in the case above were shocked and initially stunned into silence. Through offering feedback, the identity of the individuals and of the team has been challenged. The senior managers are being told that the view they hold of themselves, is not that held by others. However, most people are aware, to some degree, of the real persona beneath the facade presented to the outside world. However, to have that spelt out to a substantial degree of accuracy is disturbing. Even more disturbing, is having the tensions that exist between colleagues clearly stated, so that the repercussions of poor behaviour are equally obvious. In the investment banking case, the three 'let's go do it' directors were startled to be told how dysfunctional were their attitude and behaviour in the organization, even though the very same attributes were desirable in the marketplace. In a sense, the facilitator was telling them to 'grow up'. Even more amazing was the feedback about Crosbie, the CEO. The degree to which the team, and by implication the organization, had been held together by Crosbie, was a revelation, for most were comfortable with the belief that Crosbie was the 'bad guy'. Even Crosbie had lost sense of his own self-worth, through facing, as he did, continuous critical comment. Crosbie, considerably later, privately admitted to the facilitator that the feedback could not have come at a better time, for he had reached the point of beginning to lose confidence in himself. The jolt from receiving feedback, especially in a more public domain, is disorientating. However, the shock experience also provides an opportunity to abandon outdated assumptions, that one instinctively knows are damaging, and begin to work towards growing more helpful perspectives, behaviours and views.

Anger and denial

Feedback exercises do not manufacture new data. Effectively conducted feedback, utilizing reliable and valid instruments (questionnaires, exercises), can only capture what exists. Unfortunately, anger, denial, and rejection of the information provided is a common reaction. The identity the manager or team wishes to portray, has been challenged, and publicly at that. Individual or team members feeling threatened, can respond in one of three ways:

- try and accept the information they are given, through exploring and working through its implications,
- reject the facilitator,
- reject the data, and possibly also, the facilitator.

If the facilitator is rejected, he/she could be accused of:

- being insensitive to the group and its needs,
- having misread the situation,
- being dramatic and seeing problems where they do not exist; not being what the organization needs at this moment in time, thereby tacitly acknowledging that the facilitator's comments are accurate, but inappropriate,
- just having 'got it wrong' and so should get out.

Concurrently, or alternatively, the instruments and data could be at the receiving end of people's negative dispositions. The comments made could range from:

- the data is wrong, inaccurate and of no use,
- there is some truth in what is said, but the instruments have missed all the good points about this team,
- the real story has been missed, because all the questionnaires have done is concentrate on negatives,
- the reliability and validity of the instruments is poor and hence the results cannot be trusted.

Anger, rejection, denial and deflation are the 'to be expected responses' in feedback exercises. However, not all people will respond in such ways. Accurately capturing the real picture, for some, can act as a positive release. Someone has helped a senior management team shed an outworn image that many of the team members wished to discard, but were unable to, until they capitalized on the opportunity offered through feedback. For others, their desired self-image can be so tarnished that they react disturbingly emotionally. Overall, the range of reactions of any senior management group is difficult to predict. For the facilitator, this stage of the feedback process is likely to be the most uncomfortable experience. The credibility of the facilitator and of the data is being questioned, and if mishandled, the intervention could come to an abrupt end. The facilitator needs now to enter into the phase of 'catharsis', helping people talk through their anger and mixed emotions.

Catharsis

Rather than shying away from further criticism, the facilitator should encourage discussion of the data and of the comments made, so that the team members can talk through and talk out, their negative sentiments. Through so doing, negative feelings can be placed to one side, so that the senior managers are more prepared to consider the implications of the data.

In order to assist the process of discussion, and depending on the size of the team, sub-groups can be created, each examining a particular issue and then presenting its findings to the others. If the team members still feel too negative towards the data, the sub-groups could be asked to prepare a SWOT (strengths, weaknesses, opportunities, threats) analysis of either their team, their organization, them as people, or of all of these topics. The feedback data and any other data or consultancy reports, can be viewed as one more input into their SWOT debate. Once the sub-group discussions and presentations have been completed, the team could then isolate the key messages they wish to pursue, in terms of remedial action.

For some people, a limited number of team development events suffice as mechanisms for working through the negative emotions that can emerge post-feedback. For others, the uncomfortable stage of rejection and denial needs more time and constant revisiting. Individuals may need to talk through time and again, the content of the feedback data, the relevance of that data, the personal implications for them, and what is required of them to adjust and improve. Hence, arranging for meetings on a regular basis, helps individuals come to terms with themselves, and the reality of their situation. The extended process of discussion helps each person re-build and re-learn. Uncertainty, lack of confidence, a need to think through in detail new and alternative approaches, testing out new ideas, being rebuffed and going back and re-thinking, are common experiences of development through feedback.

Whatever process is adopted, the interactions, discussions and checking out with the facilitator and colleagues on the team, positively contribute to building up a robustness of relationship within the group. As the resilience of the team is enhanced, so is each individual member's capability to offer feedback to the other. Building a robustness in the team ensures that the team more comfortably facilitates its own development in the future.

Towards ownership

The patient building up of a robustness of relationship within the team has an ultimate purpose and that is for the managers involved in the exercise to own, and identify with, the emerging strategies for improvement. No matter who originally conceived of, or initiated the way forward, top managers need to be committed to the changes they are about to introduce. A sense of owning and being committed to change is as dependent on the perceived value, clarity and logic of the feedback data, as on the manner in which the feedback process is managed. A team that is respectful of data, is likely to be one that displays a higher quality of relationship among its members and a greater degree of resilience to challenges. The more data-driven the team, the more likely it is to adopt an all-embracing approach to change and hence is more likely to address the issues it faces, despite the discomfort of being exposed to robust dialogue. Effectively handling data suggests a considerable level of maturity among the team members, in that the individuals are already accustomed to focusing on issues, once they have been provided with information.

However, others may not be as capable of quickly focusing on concerns. For them, greater attention needs to be given to process, the manner in which data is handled, and not primarily on the data itself. For those individuals and teams who are more process than data focused, they are likely to wish to pursue what they feel are the most comfortable, as opposed to the ideal, strategies for change. For them, ownership of the steps to take to improve, depends on what the team members feel they can openly discuss. Where generating comfortable relationships is the prime concern of a team, the time required for owning the desired strategies for change is likely to take longer. An incremental approach to introducing change needs to be adopted.

However, certain individuals and teams could resist all attempts at development, often because the dialogue is experienced as damagingly uncomfortable. The team members may not wish to enter into that 'zone of uncomfortable debate'.[2]

At this point, it may be necessary for the facilitator to back off. Recognizing when to 'back off' to prevent the whole intervention from collapsing, is important. When hostility reaches the point of rejection of the facilitator, and possibly of the feedback data, it is important not to destroy the chances of team development in the future by unduly persisting with an experience that may be becoming destructive.

Post-feedback support

Continued facilitation may be desired by the client to provide support during strategy implementation. The trust established between the facilitator and the client during the cartharsis and gaining-ownership stages, allows for confidential discussions to take place, exploring how to overcome resistance to change in the organization, and how to assist in changing attitudes lower down the hierarchy. The insight that the facilitator has already gained about the organization and its leadership, can be particularly helpful if further team feedback, and development programmes and events are to be provided for middle and junior management. Using the same facilitator and approaches to management development, for the rest of management, as was used for the top team, provides for a consistency of language and philosophy underlying the whole exercise.

Personal coaching

Throughout the stages of team development, providing the facility of personal and confidential coaching can be immensely helpful, especially at the initial stage of assessing the team members' levels of resilience, and in the catharsis and follow-up stages, as individuals may wish to talk through their individual experience of the exercise and their intent for the future.

However, one-to-one coaching is valuable as an on-the-job lever in its own right. Similar to team feedback, comparable stages of learning are experienced, from preparing the ground for people to receive feedback, providing the support and counselling to help individuals through the stages of anger and denial, and providing the challenge and care to help people re-examine how they are going to restructure their roles, approach to work, and to their life, in the follow-up and assimilation stages.

Although the process of development between personal coaching and team feedback is paralleled, the individual attention of personalized coaching provides for the following advantages:

- exploration conducted on a one-to-one basis provides for a greater sense of comfort, in that the individual is not exposed to the reactions of others,
- greater openness of dialogue is more possible between the senior manager and the coach, as the purpose of coaching is to explore the needs and concerns of the client, in privacy,
- the individual has the confidence of knowing that his/her likes for the future, and personal ambitions can be freely expressed, without the anxiety that such comments might damage his/her prospects in the organization,
- the individual, together with the coach, can explore how to restructure his/her job, examining the implications of each of the potentially different directions, without any fear that those who may directly or indirectly be involved would react negatively to such considerations, even though such options may never be actioned,
- the opportunity to discuss and explore can be treated as part of a process of confidence building. The supportive nature of coaching, protected by the boundaries of confidentiality, helps individuals build a robustness to explore issues, allow themselves the freedom to be seen from different angles, and make appropriate or even inappropriate comments without feeling that they are making a fool of themselves.

To address the challenges of discretionary leadership effectively, both personal coaching and team feedback are powerful pathways to building capability. In many circumstances, both options are required, or should be made available. However, depending on the context, on the individuals involved, and on the issues that need to be addressed, preference may have to be given to coaching, or team-based feedback. Ideally, coaches should be equally versatile in either arena, although, in reality, most facilitators tend to favour one more than the other.

Dynamics of personal change[3]

When people change jobs, change location and undertake a new challenge, they are likely to experience a period of having to learn how to function effectively in their new circumstances. In effect, people experience a transition of letting go of old habits, and re-learning new skills and ways of working.

The concept of the transition curve, originally championed by Elizabeth Kübler Ross in helping patients confront and come to terms with the trauma of terminal illness, is now a popular developmental concept in executive development. The transition, or executive change curve, is used as a tool to help managers realize the time required for re-learning, and to come to terms with the experiences of re-learning. Observation and research highlight that, depending on the nature of the change, different individuals display a variety of, at times, contrasting behaviours when deeply immersed in the change experience, particularly so for those holding senior management positions.

For those in senior roles, who are changing their role and organization, and for those entering, for the first time, into a role of substantial general management responsibility, particular experiences related to the change process have been identified through the Cranfield studies. The time taken for newly appointed senior managers successfully to negotiate their learning curve and to emerge as confident and effective as their 'first day of appointment', can vary between 9–35 months, and in exceptional cases up to 40 months. The individual may be operationally competent. However, errors of judgement are likely to be made in terms of managing relationships, interfacing, and in understanding and appropriately responding to the politics in the organization. Eventually, an inability to adapt may induce operational errors, which makes it more obvious that the person is in the midst of a transitional experience. It can take up to 35 months before an individual fully appreciates the nature, values and deeply held attitudes of the organization, and negotiates sufficient credibility with the key opinion formers in the enterprise, to be able to perform at the level of 'added-value'.

Additionally, each time a person changes his/her job in the organiza-tion, the person is likely to enter into a learning curve, which is likely to be shallower or deeper, according to how accustomed he/she is to the different contexts in the organization and to the various individuals he/she will encounter. The way the learning experience is managed, substantially influences the level of confidence of the person over the longer term. If the transition experience is too daunting and the person leaves, or moves on to another job at a negative point in the learning cycle, he/she is unlikely to mature sufficiently into a position of command. The lacking in confidence and maturity is likely to show in the next appointment. Yet to stay and negotiate a job change in circumstances damaging to the individual, is equally unwelcome. Hence, appreciating the dynamics of the executive change curve is important, in order to minimize the impact of damaging experiences and to maximize the learning from change.

The original and fascinating study by Chris Parker and Ralph Lewis, outlining the experiences and stages of learning that middle managers undergo through job change, has been developed and applied to leaders who experience change. Five phases of change have been identified (see Figure 11.7).

Figure 11.7 The executive change curve

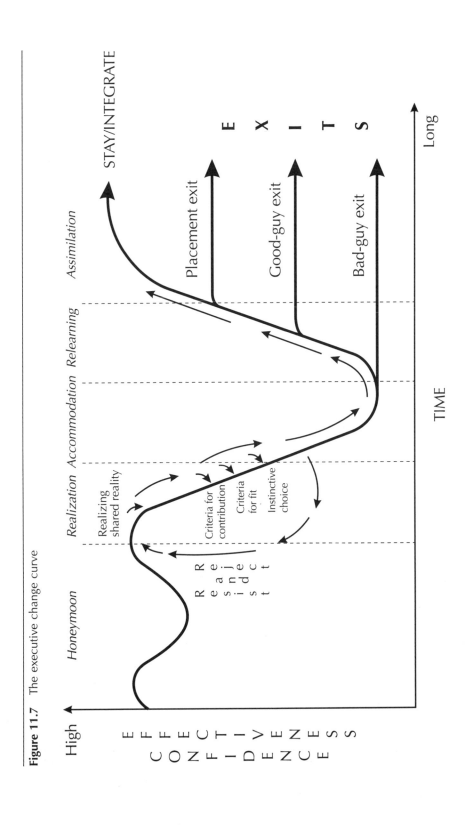

Phase 1: honeymoon period

A person newly appointed to a general management role, or already in general management and offered a position of greater responsibility in another organization, is likely to have been promoted because the person was seen to be effective, confident and capable of accepting the responsibilities of his/her new role. On starting the new job, effectiveness and confidence initially drop. The surroundings are new, the way people do things in the organization is unlikely to be similar to the way they were done in the previous organization or job, the issues to face may be difficult to appreciate, and the range of tasks to address may feel overwhelming. Especially for someone newly appointed to a senior role, he/she may feel inhibited and reticent about relating to other top managers, particularly if they are critical of the new organization.

Within a matter of a few weeks, the greater majority of new appointees become accustomed to the immediate demands of the new role. They become accustomed to 'the ways' in which contributions are made at meetings. They have developed the confidence to challenge and discuss issues with senior colleagues. The initial experiences of inhibition, shock and reluctance to interact openly with senior colleagues, are likely to have subsided. The individual may see him/herself as having successfully emerged from the learning curve and now operating effectively within the new context. Having broken down the barriers between self and colleagues, bosses and subordinates, the individual may now find it easier to enter into dialogue with these others. Further, having become accustomed to the initial demands of the job, the person naturally feels ready to accept full responsibility. At this point, the person is drawing upon established skills and experience from his/her last job. The person has entered into the honeymoon phase, the phase of false hope, in the belief that the skills and experiences of the past, with a certain amount of adaptation, can be applied to the new role.

Phase 2: realization

The person, during the honeymoon phase, may have behaved either passively, in order to build up his/her confidence to learn how to interact with others in the new surroundings, or more assertively, in trying to make an immediate impact on the new organization. However, most people quickly learn that the honeymoon phase is one of false glamour. Once others in the organization have become accustomed to the newly appointed person being around, they treat him/her the same as anyone else. At this point, the realization dawns that calling upon established skills and experiences that had worked in the past, is inappropriate. The person begins to realize what others require from him/her as a team member, as a person who has to meet targets, and as a person who needs to take command in a way acceptable to the newly entered organization. The individual begins to realize the substantial nature of the changes he/she needs to make in order to perform effectively in his/her new role.

For the person newly appointed to general management, coming to terms with the considerably greater discretion, is crucial. It is a challenging experience to be required to form a personally unique view as to the shape, size and direction to pursue for the function/department for which one is accountable, to convince colleagues of the validity of one's view and then be held to account for the vision presented, especially if it is one's first experience of responsibility at senior level. Hence, considering deeply what one needs to do, and not arguing on behalf of hastily formed views concerning strategy and objectives, has to be coupled with building up the confidence to nurture relationships with other key senior managers.

For the person already experienced in general management, relearning involves coming to terms with the 'true meaning' of effectiveness in the new job, the immediate context and the broader organization. The questions a newly appointed senior manager may wish to ask are:

- To what extent are the accountabilities, authority and responsibilities in the role well-aligned?
- To what extent am I (the appointee) being held to account for activities for which I am not responsible?
- What does 'effectiveness of performance' really mean in this job and in this organization?
- What is it that I really need to learn to gain credibility in this situation?
- To what extent am I being pushed into a situation of adopting a participative or dictatorial style with my subordinates or others around me, when I am not comfortable to do so, especially when I feel a different and more fruitful approach is required?

When considering questions of accountability, authority and responsibility, the senior manager is probing as to what criteria are practised in the organization to assess each person's effort. In certain organizations, accountability, authority and responsibility are well-aligned. The individual is provided with the authority and the 'tools' to do the job required of them. Other organizations may display a more dysfunctional mode of operating and managers may find themselves being held accountable for activities over which they have little or no authority. In even more negative circumstances, the contextual reality of the organization is that feelings of threat, anxiety, insecurity, and the lack of confidence which undermines the judgement of managers, are normal. In more dysfunctional organizations, what is learnt is the skill to deflect being held accountable and, in effect, to place the blame on someone else. If the true criterion for contribution in the organization is 'buck passing', that is a reality that the person needs to consider.

Essentially, the newly appointed person needs to review what 'fitting into the organization' means, in effect, what is appropriate conduct and behaviour. The person needs to question:

- What are the shared, but also unshared, attitudes of the members of the top team?
- To what extent are positive and enabling, or undermining and disabling, relationships and behaviours exhibited at senior management levels in the organization?
- To what extent is it important to pay special attention to particularly powerful individuals at senior management levels?

Learning how to interact with new colleagues, bosses and subordinates in a manner that is sufficiently comfortable for them, is crucial. Teams, departments and units have a particular identity, a contextual reality, each with its own norms and behaviour patterns. Learning how to become a credible member of a group, and how to gain respect from other groups, requires consciously attempting to integrate oneself with key opinion makers in the organization.

At the realization stage of the transition experience, the individual is recognizing the true nature of what it means to fit into an organization. In every organization, there exist assumptions concerning the manner in which relationships are conducted, and the processes that people enter into in order to be able to work together. The more unfamiliar the individual is with the organization, and the newer the person is to general management, the deeper and longer the realization part of the learning curve, as people are coming to terms with what effectiveness means in these circumstances. They are learning what are the sensitive issues that need tact, timing and consideration in order for them to be addressed meaningfully. The newcomers are learning to what extent issues of ego and personality pervade considerations of business and strategy.

The more the individual examines the true criteria for contribution, and the unspoken requirements in order to be accepted and to fit, the more the person is reaching a point where he/she has to make a choice. The basis of choice is more instinctive than conscious; more emotive than rationally thought through, and involves coming to terms with who has to change – me (the individual) or them (the others in the organization)? Anxiety, depression and even a loss of confidence are commonly reported during the realization phase, as the individual recognizes the true nature of his/her circumstances. What worked in the past may not necessarily work in the new job, or new organization.

Certain people resent learning. Others are more dramatic in their response. Such people display their distaste for the way relationships are conducted, the way decisions are made, and the manner in which work is allocated in the organization. They do not wish to, or will not change, to integrate better into the organization. Their instinctive response is, 'I'm not going to change; others will just have to get used to me'. The person regresses and climbs back up to the top of the realization slope, only to find him/herself reliving the experience of frustration, not adjusting, blaming others and the organization, and convincing him/herself that others have the problem, not him/her. Depending on the demands made on the person, the nature of his/her immediate context, and the culture of the organization, the person can go up and down the realization slope for months, each time finding his/her frustration more difficult to control.

Phase 3: accommodation

At the depth of the learning curve, possibly having experienced going down and up the realization slope on a number of occasions, the individual recognizes that his/her behaviours and attitudes carried over from the past, and his/her continuous resistance to change, cannot continue. Adjustments need to be made. Those persons who feel that they have no desire to change are likely to decide to leave the organization. It is likely that people's reluctance to make adjustments to their new surroundings may have made them unpopular and cast them in the mould of being uncompromising and difficult. They wish to leave, and others are glad to see them depart. Their exit is likely to be acrimonious, with both sides blaming the other for the current problems being experienced. The departure is one of a 'bad-guy exit', with both sides relieved that the painful period is over.

Phase 4: relearning

The alternative response is to let go of past attitudes, past behaviours and expectations, and to try to promote new ways of working and interacting, more suited to the new job and the organization. The person becomes more pro-active, as he/she is now positive about the transition, and is more accepting of the new reality and challenge. Having recognized the underlying norms, behaviours, protocols and organization values, the person is now motivated to try out new work practices, new approaches and different styles to forming and maintaining relationships. The person is relearning, testing, and discarding what does not work. However, the experiences of frustration at the relearning stage can be as awesome as those experienced at the realization stage. Particular behaviours adopted may be ineffective, mistakes may be made, and the individual can become irritable with self and others. There is no easy way round these negative feelings, as they are natural to the learning experience. However, persistence prevails and through the application of styles more appropriate to the situation, the individual is establishing him/herself in a new world, where he/she is progressively negotiating ever greater credibility with important internal stakeholders.

Even though a certain degree of accomplishment may have been attained, some persons still do not successfully negotiate their transition. Despite their progress in the organization, the commitment and energy to continue enhancing their profile is not sustained. Either the person went through the 'resist and reject loop' too many times that he/she emerged as unduly de-motivated, or, although he/she has made the effort to adjust, the will to continue is not forthcoming. Others in the organization recognize the effort that the person has made, but also see that the person's staying power is expended. As a consequence, the person decides to leave. However, unlike the 'bad-guy exit' – where the question will always remain, did the person jump or was he/she pushed? – no such negativity exists, as the person leaves voluntarily and on good terms. The feelings of the parties concerned are mutually positive, tinged with a note of remorse, 'pity things did not work out'. The farewell handshake of 'good luck' denotes a 'good-guy exit'.

Working through the relearning stage and by implication becoming accustomed to the new responsibilities, realistically thinking through what direction to provide for one's now-established role, and learning to re-negotiate the status quo, so as to introduce new philosophies, attitudes and behaviours, all bring the person to the point of internalization. New philosophies, perspectives, attitudes and behaviours are all adopted, and integrated with valuable elements of previous attitudes and behaviours. The individual is consolidating his/her learning, and with new confidence, is working towards operating at a higher rate of effectiveness than he/she has over the past few months.

It is at this stage that the person more clearly appreciates the nature of the markets in which the company operates, the need to maintain positive relationships with different key stakeholders such as suppliers, distributors, pressure groups, and displays greater respect towards the internal functioning of the organization. This is the point at which credible strategies for change and improvement are likely to be identified and promoted by the person, accepted by the members of the top team, and then championed throughout the organization.

This is also the point when managers on secondment or, especially expatriate managers, are all too often relocated to a new assignment. For expatriate managers in particular, who may be adapting to a different ethnic culture, who are perhaps also coming to terms with a new language, reorientating their style in order to form linkages effectively with ethnically different, but nevertheless powerful, stakeholders, and who are coming to terms with new market conditions, their transition experience is likely to be deeper and more extended. Unfortunately, at the point when their new learning is being truly assimilated, they are moved on! Their assignment, of possibly 24–30 months, has come to an end, just at the point when their true worth is about to emerge. The net result is an opportunity loss, in that the senior manager is able realistically to appreciate market circumstances and the capacity of the organization to pursue particular targets, is able meaningfully to set budgets for others and realistically to accept or re-negotiate budgets set from even more senior management, but is not given the time to utilize such skills and insights. Just at a time when the senior manager in transition is able to differentiate accurate forecasting from guesswork, he/she is moved on, leaving colleagues and subordinates with the uncomfortable task of needing to 'train in' a new boss. Too many rotations of key senior manager roles leave subordinates demotivated and feeling that trying to convince senior management of what is realistic in the circumstances, is wasted energy.

Phase 5: assimilation

For those who complete the transition experience, their intimacy of appreciation of the true nature of the organization will have reached a deeper, instinctive level of understanding. The research conducted at the Cranfield International Management Development Centre suggests that once into the job and the organization, a five to nine year tenure in a senior and responsible role allows for full use of a senior manager's potential (see Chapter 8). After that, and especially after ten years in the same role, certain individuals are in danger of exhibiting signs of saturation. The energy and will to pursue new challenges are likely to diminish, as the person has been so absorbed into the culture that he/she is unable to maintain the necessary level of grit in dialogue with colleagues. The time has come to move on. However, a surprising number of exceptions are identified, as, within vibrant, positively oriented cultures, senior managers can be as effective, challenging and positive after 15 or more years in the same role, and 25 or more years in the same organization.

Cascading through organizational change

The Executive Change Curve can also be applied to aid understanding of how to manage change at an organizational level (see Figure 11.8).

Level 1 of the organization, namely senior management or the top team, agrees to pursue a particular programme of change. As individuals and as a team, they explore, commit errors, re-adjust, but eventually learn how to pursue effectively the changes they desire. The top team members undergo their transition curve and when they have genuinely emerged from the relearning experience, are likely, in a consistent and

Figure 11.8   Cascading change

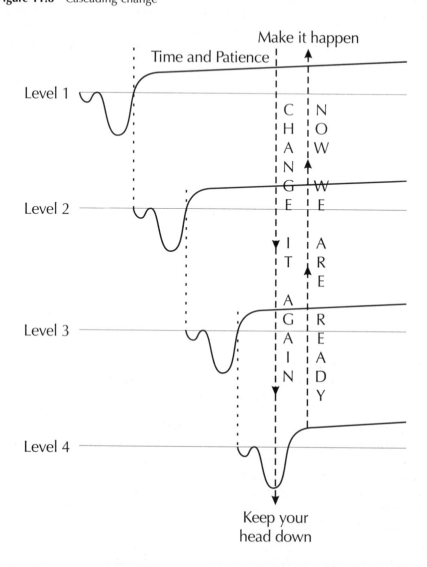

Make it happen

Time and Patience

Level 1

Level 2

Level 3

Level 4

CHANGE
IT
AGAIN

NOW
WE
ARE
READY

Keep your
head down

disciplined manner, to push level 2 in the organization to promote change.

Up to this point, level 2 have recognized that change is imminent, but are likely to have experienced inconsistencies and contradictions from their bosses (level 1), as the top team has been learning how to manage effectively the change process. Now level 2 managers recognize the seriousness of level 1's intentions, and also see that they cannot resist the change demands of their superiors. It is at this point that they, too, enter into their learning curve, exploring how to apply change to themselves and their subordinates. If they successfully negotiate their transition, they too will emerge from the experience, determined in their pursuit of change.

Similarly, levels 3 and 4 have recognized that changes are taking place, but have been able to resist the initiatives from their superiors, due to the inconsistent nature of the ways/manner in which change has been pursued, as levels 1 and 2 have been learning how to promote change. Although staggered in interval, levels 3 and 4 enter into their learning curve examining how to interpret the initiatives of their superiors, how change will affect them, how they can positively benefit from the changes being pursued, and how the changes can be tactically applied. Meanwhile, level 1 awaiting the results and benefits of change may interpret these debates, the apparent resistance to change, and the re-examination of issues from the levels below, as symptoms of change failure. Just at the point when level 4 are recognizing how realistically to apply change and how they as managers can benefit, level 1 introduces further change in order to bolster what it perceives as an issue that is losing ground.

The learning for level 1 is, change takes time. As a top manager, be realistic about the time needed for change to be understood, assimilated and applied in the organization. Each programme of change is likely to require a different time horizon in order for the desired changes to be successfully negotiated. Level 1 needs to learn to appraise time realistically and become sufficiently tolerant for the rest of the organization to say, 'Now we are ready!'

Should level 1 not learn the lessons of time and patience, level 4 learn something else, 'if you keep your head down and do nothing, they [top management] will forget it'. On this basis, level 4 learns that through doing nothing, nothing changes. The executive change curve applied to the context of organizational change, helps leaders appreciate the force of the most powerful change blocker of all, passive resistance.

Organizational surveys

Conducting surveys is now commonplace in organizations. Survey results may be used for the purposes of providing attitudinal and behavioural feedback to different groups in the organization, or utilized as a benchmark, highlighting the position of the organization when compared with industry or sector norms. Equally, surveys are used as market intelligence tools for gathering facts and opinions on current market trends, future trends, opinions on perceptions of customer satisfaction, and overall perceptions of the well-being of the organization.

However, interviewing people, editing their views into a meaningful model, drafting and validating questionnaires, gathering data through questionnaires, writing a report and using that report as a vehicle of feedback, are lengthy processes. Senior managers may be the subjects of a number of surveys in any one year, and as a result may experience frustration through survey fatigue. An emerging view is that something more has to arise from the process than simply a report, or series of interim presentations and a report. The demand is that the survey enquiry process needs to be positioned as a developmental experience. The feeling of 'we want something more in order to get our money's worth', is likely to pervade survey enquiries, as data-gathering and data feedback have reached the point of client saturation – too many requests for information and too many surveys mean that people do not have the patience to wait for the final results. The desire is for an experience of development during the process of enquiry. Turning interviews and discussions into a more interesting, learning experience, requires attention to three issues, negotiating trust, negotiating credibility, and being more than passive, through prompting.

Negotiating trust[4]

Negotiating the necessary trust, so that senior managers wish to invest their time in dialogue and enquiry, is strongly influenced by the interviewer's sensitivity to executive exposure.

As emphasized in Chapter 8, senior managers, such as chairmen, chief executives and managing directors who are either at subsidiary, divisional or corporate centre level, by the nature of their discretionary roles, are required to exercise choice in order to provide and promote vision and identity to their role. Whether the choices made are conscious, in terms of clarity of detail and consistency of argument, or are more emotive, in terms of what the person passionately feels is right, or are more assumed, namely on a taken-for-granted basis, choice is nevertheless exercised. Clarity of strategic thinking by a senior manager should not be assumed. The person may not appreciate the full extent of the issues and concerns he/she faces. The person may be ignorant of the tools available for addressing complex challenges. The person may not be emotionally or intellectually capable of exercising choice, or may be faced with substantially conflicting evidence concerning options, whereby choice may seem like guesswork. However, after a period of time, the quality (or lack of quality) of the choices made become clear. Hence, one feature of occupying a role in which discretion predominates, is the likelihood of being judged in retrospect, as the impact of the choices made is felt and is visible. As one chief executive commented in interview:

> who was to know what was the right thing to do at the time with our particular problem, but with the ensuing shareholder neglect and the subsequent panic response, it became very clear two years on.

The CEO was referring to the shared perception of most of the directors of the organization. At the time in question, their problems did not feel as requiring urgent attention. However, sometime later, the perceived muted response to the so-called crisis was viewed as inadequate and incompetent by key internal and external stakeholders. It was only later, and in retrospect, that the senior managers of the organization were judged as incompetent.

Coming to terms with one's own emotions of anxiety, sensitivity and defensiveness to potentially permanent exposure and critical comment, is necessary simply in order to function at the senior level. Accommodating feelings of vulnerability while occupying a strategic role, is a likely experience for top level managers. Hence, in order to establish trust with a view to accessing in interview the more deeply held and meaningful viewpoints and attitudes of top managers, it is important that the interviewer exhibits an understanding of the experience of being potentially, permanently exposed and vulnerable. Such understanding is displayed through focusing on questions which show an awareness of the potential pitfalls senior managers may encounter, such as:

- How do you feel about working/interacting/co-operating with colleagues who seem to be committed to a different point of view to you, but talk as if they are not?
- How do you feel about colleagues/bosses who say one thing, but then seem to behave in a manner that is different/contradictory to what was said?

According to the response of the interviewee, switching the line of questioning from an examination of issues to an exploration of underlying strategic processes, portrays empathy with the person who is faced with the difficult-to-resolve tensions of high office.

Negotiating credibility

The greater the level of trust between the interviewer and interviewee the more is the senior manager likely to be encouraged towards greater disclosure. However, greater disclosure is likely to expose the interviewer to more open and intense dialogue, which in turn, exposes the interviewer to the senior managers being interviewed, who question what does this person know about business and organization? If the interviewer exhibits interesting insights into strategic processes, the interview can become a valuable developmental experience for the senior manager, because as his/her views are being challenged, he/she is learning and is, as a result, motivated to probe more deeply into pertinent issues. Deeper probing tends to take place if two themes are pursued, the surfacing of opportunity costs, and distinguishing between people problems and structure problems.

Surfacing opportunity costs

As highlighted in Chapter 8, should any manager make a mistake or should something go wrong, the effects are likely to surface as an error. In contrast, a lack of concern for nurturing key interfaces, or neglecting certain stakeholders, or putting off pressing concerns, will still crystallize in some shape or other, but only after time has elapsed. Problems that emerge after some time, or are only indirectly related to their source, are issues of opportunity costs, which at the time of making are experienced as 'maybe problems' – maybe there exists a problem, maybe not – time will tell! Opportunity costs issues which remain unaddressed can, in the medium to longer term, be damaging to the organization. An additional feature of opportunity cost challenges is the acceptance by senior managers of 'accommodating present circumstances', in effect, 'not quite' addressing key concerns and allowing issues which require resolution, to linger. In effect, senior managers become accustomed to poor performance being the norm. Entering into conversation over opportunity cost issues is no easy task. People are naturally reluctant to admit their weaknesses to someone else. However, to unearth opportunity cost concerns and experiences can turn an interview into a meaningful discussion of the performance blockages to both the senior manager and to others within the organization. Apart from the insights the manager may gain from the discourse, the cathartic relief of being able to unearth deep-seated tensions can prove to be positively unburdening. The development gained through intense conversation can prove to be immensely valuable. The manager has found someone who understands, who is willing to listen, and who can steer him/her person towards avenues for improvement.

People versus structure problems

In complex organization structures, whereby senior managers need to respond to multiple interfaces, differences of view may emerge as to whether the structure of the organization is working effectively. In so doing, it may be necessary to explore the distinction each person draws between the challenges of communicating across a structure, and the irritation of dealing with difficult people. Portrayals of tensions and difficult-to-resolve concerns may be attributed to the structure of the organization, which is seen by some people to encourage dysfunctional behaviour among the key managers of the organization. Equally, others could interpret identical symptoms as arising due to the unco-operative attitude of those individuals occupying important interfacing roles. Hence, substantial differences of view can arise in attributing cause and effect to the same events. Sensitive examination of interfacing behaviour and an exploration of whether tensions are due more to people and their behaviour, or due to the strain of their working in a poorly structured organization, can generate interesting and fruitful discussion. At least, through conversation, feeling that cause and effect can be clearly differentiated promotes a sense of having learnt something, a sense of having worked through an important issue. The interviewee is left with a feeling of having spent time well.

Prompting: being more than passive

In addition to identifying which issues to pursue in order to increase the level of credibility of survey interviewers, and in order to promote a learning experience for the senior managers taking part in a survey, the question of how the process of interviews should be managed requires examination. Current and proclaimed best practice is to ask open-ended questions, listen, and feed back the comments of the interviewee, all of which highlights a substantial degree of passivity on the interviewer's part. Being non-judgemental and non-reactive, however, may not create the vibrancy required to make interviews a positive learning experience. The interviewer may need to be more proactive and prompt the participants to reflect more intensely on past and current experiences. Effective prompting is identified as constituting two elements: providing mental linkages and feeding from other respondents.

Providing mental linkages

Questions are identified by the interviewer which may or may not be considered by the interviewee to be immediately relevant, but at least start a line of enquiry which might otherwise have been neglected. In effect, the questions being pursued by the interviewer allow for linkages to be made between two or more initially unconnected areas of interest. One case example is that of a Chairman/Chief Executive who held both of these roles as head of a large multi-national concern, whose preoccupation was with examining external market/competitor circumstances, but who devoted little time to addressing the internal interfaces, except when perceived hindrances emerged and blocked the implementation of strategy. The interviewer asked why one particular group of senior managers had repeatedly been omitted from the strategic dialogue. In the interviewer's opinion, the senior managers in question could have strongly influenced the effectiveness of strategy implementation. The Chairman's response was to ask why the interviewer had posed such a question. The interviewer's response, in turn, led to a lengthy discourse on the reasons for the current circumstances of the organization and the nature of the organization's internal blockages. The Chairman acceded that the conversation had brought new light to his thinking which influenced his analysis of subsequent organizational issues. From the interviewer's point of view, attention has been drawn to what seemed to have been an area of neglect, as well as having substantially raised the credibility of the interviewer.

Feeding from other respondents

In order to stimulate further discussion, relevant issues and/or perceptions gathered from other respondents can be fed into the discussion with any one interviewee. Challenging a respondent in interview about events or processes that have been highlighted in other interviews or group meetings, allows for a more penetrating analysis. The danger is that offering data that contrasts with the participant's viewpoint may lead the individual down an avenue of enquiry which he/she would not otherwise have pursued, and which could, unnecessarily, deflect the individual from his/her original line of thought. However, the advantage is that the interviewee has a chance to reflect, reconsider and explore more deeply, particular lines of enquiry. The immediacy of the challenge may stimulate deeper probing and re-thinking, whereas the waiting for a report to be submitted, and only then thinking through the implications, is unlikely to spark off a similar level of response. Too much time may have elapsed between the interview and the feedback of data – people have simply lost interest. The message is, 'strike while the iron is hot!'

Helping senior managers to feel that they have gained benefit from internal surveys and data-gathering exercises, involves a straddle process, straddling between enquiry and understanding, involvement and intervention. Adjusting the boundary between data-gathering and executive counselling through exploration, is likely to be ongoing, due to the ever-changing demands of different respondents in different contexts. To resist becoming immersed in, and responsive to, the fuzzy nature of the straddle between surveys, data-gathering and executive development, is, in today's market, likely to marginalize the consultant or the survey analyst. Senior management is likely to demand a more immediate response, and may lose interest in the exercise if there is a lengthy period of time before data is formally fed back. With the demands made on the members of top management, they in turn are more demanding of consultants, trainers and those in the field of executive development. Senior managers want to know now how they are going to benefit from investing their time in any developmental activity.

Off-the-job development[5]

Impactful off-the-job development should endeavour to capture the nature of strategic and leadership work and equally help individuals be challenged and stretched, in order to prepare them for leadership. If off-the-job development is to be considered as meaningful, the manner of interaction among senior managers needs to be replicated in a programme of training, so that the capabilities required for effective leadership can be understood, appreciated and practised. Such paradoxes as having to be participative and yet strong, of having to take charge but still listen, require to be accommodated and will have meaning only when purposefully enacted.

Off-the-job leadership development provides an opportunity for those already in a leader role, or for high quality middle level managers, or individuals leading particular project groups, or those displaying the potential for responsibility and senior office to explore and develop their leadership capabilities within a controlled and structured setting.

A programme of strategic leadership should expose its participants to the following inputs.

Resolving conflicting agendas

As stated, discretionary leaders need to provide an identity as to the nature and purpose of their role. They need to promote a vision. The clarification and pursuit of agendas which take into account current and future circumstances, is a necessary process in the establishment of sense and meaning to leadership roles. What complicates the situation is that the number of agendas being pursued could potentially be as many as the number of discretionary roles in the organization, and as varied as the personalities who occupy them. Hence, in any one strategic forum, it is likely that a number of strategic agendas may be promoted. Recognizing how key senior managers relate to each other, and how they communicate mixed messages to the rest of the organization while pursuing alternative visions and direction, is a reality that needs to be accommodated. Living in a world of conflicting realities while still having to manage an organization is a prospect that most leaders are likely to face in a role of leadership. Once such a reality is acknowledged, the confidence to begin to realign strategic options, can emerge.

Conceptualizing restructuring

Structuring work groups and departments, integrating and merging with other work groups or departments internally or with other agencies externally, are challenges of how to re-configure effectively organization structures. The ability to visualize the form and shape of the desired organization, and to promote the appropriate quality of interfacing in a newly designed structure, are conceptual challenges. Being knowledge-able as to the different blueprints of organization structure, their strengths and weaknesses, and how to configure an organization to achieve its purpose, are skills which can be developed. The questions to pursue on a programme of leadership development are:

- What is the purpose of the present structure of the organization, and do the key managers share compatible purposes?
- What are the design needs of a command structure?
- What are the attributes and people-based requirements of a more interfacing structure?
- Under what circumstances should strong consideration be given to a top-down, as opposed to, a bottom-, or middle-up programme of change?
- Under what circumstances does structural change planning need to consider the morale of people and their trust in senior management, to the same degree as the details of the structure and roles?

These considerations need to be addressed as vital components of strategic leadership development.

Rituals, routine and culture

Introducing change, especially of structures, impacts on the culture of an organization, which in turn affects the rituals and routines that have become a part of most people's work experience. The meaning and symbolism of everyday, recurring habits and routines in people's lives, and the power of such to inhibit or enhance change, are additional considerations in structural reform. How to introduce new ways of doing, which will then consolidate as positive symbols of progress through enacted daily rituals, are leadership considerations. Effective follow through on key initiatives, the nurture of individuals and work teams, and the consolidation of change through new ways of working, enhance the prospects of a new forward-looking, positively-oriented culture being established in the organization. Leaders will need to introduce new habits and rituals into their daily routine, so that through example, new ways of working become part of the fabric of the organization. Although a positively-oriented culture enhances the development of people, any programme of leadership needs to emphasize that positive leadership promotes high performance-related cultures and not vice-versa, a point that is often intellectually appreciated, but emotionally disregarded.

Enhancing vision capability

The Cranfield surveys highlight visioning as a key element of corporate leadership. In order to help people appreciate the nature of visioning, the following questions are offered for deeper consideration of this topic:

- What is the shape and configuration of key client/supplier/stakeholder groups?

- What is required now, and likely to be required in the future, to service these groups?
- What does the individual understand to be the needs of important suppliers/distributors and how can such understanding be used to nurture further the relationship between suppliers/distributors and the organization?
- How prepared are various departments/functions/project groups to improve performance?
- How prepared are the various departments/functions/project groups to co-operate and more effectively interface than is presently the case, in each programme participant's organization?
- What levels of expenditure are required to provide effectively for high quality levels of service in each programme participant's organization now and in the future?

As emphasized in Chapter 8, the answer to these questions requires an understanding of, and access to, details concerning the management of departments and units. It is through a detailed understanding of the expectations and requirements of stakeholder groups, the behaviours of suppliers, the needs and likely demands of external agencies, the likely life cycle of any service or product, the level and speed of responsiveness required by different client/co-unit groupings, and the degree to which other agencies require supervision, that meaningful conclusions can be formed as to the level of expenditure required, and as to the cost of service which needs to be taken into account. To form a view as to the size of the cost base to be accounted for, how departments and units need to be structured, and how to position new and current services for them to be utilized by clients, requires a detailed intimacy with the organization and equally an ability to extrapolate from this detailed view, appropriate ways forward. Hence, a senior manager's ability to be concerned with detail and with the broader debate, with intimate day-to-day understanding of the functioning of the organization, and yet the broader but realistic picture as to how to proceed, are the distinguishing features of visioning. The Cranfield studies highlight that it is from relevant details that meaningful visions/missions are formed. In essence, effective visioning involves a capability for broad conceptualization, while having a discipline for, and an interest in, detail.

The Cranfield surveys equally emphasize that the capabilities required for discretionary leadership are developable. These capabilities are not genetic 'born with', phenomena. Helping individuals recognize their current ability towards managing both detail and broader extrapolation, can be achieved through feedback from questionnaire-based exploration, and personal coaching. This feedback can then be used as a basis for helping each person develop his/her visioning capability in terms of exhibiting greater discipline to address effectively day-to-day details and/ or to enter into debate over broader issues.

Balancing transactional and transformational approaches

The processes of visioning, conceptualizing, restructuring, thinking through and analysing strategy and policy, while nurturing interfaces, resolving or settling conflicts, building and maintaining relationships, and drafting budgets, require that each individual determines a balance between the transformational and transactional elements of leadership. The transformational, and certainly the more glamourous aspect of leadership is more attractive than the day-to-day grind of routine, transactional, maintenance-type activities. However, Chapter 1 emphasized that a fundamental requirement of good leadership is attention to detail. Heinz's Tony O'Reilly states that one reason for his success is this focus on detail. As one chief executive suggests, 'providing good leadership is mostly day-to-day grind, and some inspiration – make sure you know what is happening around you, and make sure that you get it right!' Examination of what makes for a balanced leadership work portfolio is an area worthy of debate on a leadership programme.

Ways towards reconciliation

The respondents in the Australian Government survey (see Chapter 6) were asked: 'If the members of the Top Team hold different views as to the future direction of the organization, are such differences reconcilable?'

Of the 'yes' responses (i.e. differences are reconcilable), which account for 73 per cent of responses to the question, the majority of respondents indicate that improvements can be achieved by the way people are managed and by being flexible about which leadership style to adopt. In effect, the respondents highlight that most leadership tensions within the organization are not the result of deeply held, fixed views, but due more to the incumbents' inability to address effectively the processes of negotiating towards an acceptable shared perspective. The Australian results tally with the views of numerous senior managers, that the resolution of differences, or just their settlement, is possible in most circumstances.

Five steps to enhancing people's abilities to work effectively towards the resolution of differences and tensions, or at least the reaching of a workable settlement, are identified below.

1 Strengthening

Strengthening individuals to partake fully in a process of reconciliation or reaching settlement, is crucial to performing to a high standard as a senior manager. Coaching individuals to greater robustness enhances their ability to enter into and maintain dialogue. However, part of that process involves clarifying the issues dividing people. Equally, part of the process also involves venting feelings about how others in the organization have behaved. Both elements of the process are a necessary catharsis, so that all involved can appreciate how deeply individuals have experienced the frustration of interacting with each other. However, the force of comments made could cause offence. At the receiving end, some individuals may emotionally retreat, troubled by the comments made, and as a result lose confidence. Others may retaliate aggressively, inflaming already tense relationships. Strengthening individuals to embark on a journey of reconciliation or settlement requires their appreciating the dynamics of reconciliation and the impact that the process is likely to have on them. It is equally important to evolve a robustness in order to work effectively through aggressive feedback. The more focused and pertinent the feedback can be on a programme of development, the more prepared is the individual likely to be for negotiating the reconciliation of conflicting visions, improving tense relationships, or reaching the best possible settlement.

2 Impact awareness

In addition to helping individuals become more robust, focused feedback also helps a person to appreciate his/her own impact on others. Whatever the intention of the person, an appreciation of how he/she is seen and why, helps the individual to adjust to being more able to work through issues with others. Part of the process of helping individuals to assess accurately their impact on others, is to help the person become more sensitive towards others. However, that equally involves challenging assumptions. For example, what one person means by robustness may be taken by others to mean aggression. The value in challenging assumptions is to assist people to be more responsive to the different meanings that others in different contexts attach to the same words. Being sensitive, responsive and understanding of the dynamics of contexts helps each person to recognize how far, and at what pace, he/she can realistically introduce change. Most certainly, understanding context does not mean accepting current circumstances. Understanding how meanings vary by context simply provides each individual with more information which can equip him/her to cope with the challenges he/she faces.

3 Ego or vision?

What is the basis for the vision being pursued once a person occupies a leader role, to satisfy one's ego, or a belief in the vision being proclaimed? What really motivates the individual? A belief in the vision, or the fact that it is his/her vision, his/her ideal, him/herself as the key driving force? Basically, what motivates for leadership, vision or ego?

Anyone in a role of command needs the confidence to clarify and pursue particular courses of action. However, to what extent does the person need to clarify and pursue his/her own direction as opposed to accommodating alternative viewpoints, win the commitment of others and still maintain his/her particular course of action? Accommodating others' viewpoints essentially requires a capability to work with contradiction. Understanding the agenda of others, the reasons as to why they hold their particular perspective, and the degree to which they can realistically manoeuvre from their original position, requires a capability beyond an interpersonal skill of communicating effectively, and being seen as accessible. What is required is the capacity to recognize the spread of strategic agendas within a senior management forum, why people are committed to any one or more strategies or visions, and the possible pathways towards a shared platform. Undoubtedly, the personal skills of winning confidence and working with others are important in the process of negotiating and reconciling differences, but so also are the conceptual skills of finding ways through contrasting logics.

On a programme of leader development, exploration should be undertaken of an individual's current capability to work with contradiction. The person can begin to recognize the degree to which he/she needs his/her view to predominate, as opposed to working with the discomfort of having to accommodate other viewpoints. The person's current capabilities to address multiple meanings, can then, through counselling and facilitation, be related to the perceived requirements of his/her context. Through helping the individual appreciate his/her present ways of discerning, the person can then emotionally experience the gap of learning that needs to be bridged in order to adopt a multi-perspective on life. The more that exercises of feedback, analysis and simulation can be related to the complexity of workplace circumstances, the more the individual is likely to be committed to pursue learning, on-the-job, post the programme.

If nothing else, the person can recognize whether he/she just 'wants his/her own way', or whether the direction being pursued realistically needs a clear, singular and disciplined approach in order to attain success.

Feedback, through exercises, case analyses, questionnaires and observation, is a vital lever for development, whether for enhancing robustness in the person, making him/her more aware of how he/she impacts and influences people, or for helping the individual to recognize his/her capability to live with, and work through, paradox. However, feedback needs to be 'grounded', i.e. made practical and relevant, in order to be accommodated more effectively. Feedback can be grounded in 'context', that is to say that the relevance of feedback is to appreciate how to gain greater credibility in any one situation. Equally, feedback can be grounded in 'purpose', that is, what purpose is served in providing feedback, for example, to help an individual to appreciate his/her impact on others, or to help grow to greater robustness and maturity. The more grounded the feedback, the more the individual can discern how to use the data, and pursue meaningful ways forward.

Discerning feedback data accurately is an especially important requirement when faced with substantially contradictory data. An experienced regularly quoted by managers is that of being 'wrongly' criticized or accused of satisfying their aspirations at the expense of others – 'he/she only wants things his/her way!' Exploration and analysis on a leadership development programme may confirm a perception the individual has of him/herself, that he/she is a broad minded person who genuinely tries to do the best for the organization. However, in his/her place of work the individual may be seen as single minded, not listening, and caring only that his/her objectives are achieved. Through an exploration of the impact of self, the individual may well recognize that he/she does have a capacity to discern broadly, perhaps also recognize that he/she can 'get on well' with people, but that work related circumstances require of him/her a forcefulness of leadership, in order to establish a clear strategy for the future. What is to be learned? As far as the person on the leader programme is concerned, 'there is nothing wrong with you, you get on fine with others, just grit your teeth and push through with what you are doing'. Through grounding feedback in reality, the learning process is enhanced, as the person is more able to work through the information that he/she has been offered and identify what is of relevance to him/her.

It is especially important that leaders emotionally appreciate that different people hold different perceptions, leaving the person receiving feedback with a query, 'Of the feedback I receive, which is of value?' Making sense of conflicting data involves an appreciation of the dynamics of situations, what the individual is trying to achieve within particular contexts, which key opinion leader(s) is the person attempting to influence, and perhaps most important, of the feedback given, which is the person willing to accept and utilize. Discussing such questions helps the person become more accustomed to living with paradox. If nothing else, the person is, at least, more prepared for the emotive nature of strategic change processes.

4 Emotive nature of strategic change

In the process of developing leaders, one point needs to be emphasized, namely that outcomes and processes are totally intertwined. What any one individual or group of senior managers wishes to achieve is intimately linked with how they go about attaining their goals. The reason is that on broader-based issues of a longer time perspective, a 'leap of faith' is required. People need to believe that the goals, objectives, mission and targets that are being pursued are worthwhile, can be achieved, and are the best goals, objectives, mission and targets to aim for in the present circumstances. On more operational matters, it is far easier to highlight, in a logical, linear manner, that what one wishes to achieve and how one goes about achieving it, are related. Why? As far as operational matters are concerned, time frames are shorter and far more distinct parameters surround tasks and activities. On broader-based issues, time frames are much longer, making it far more difficult to predict when an outcome will be attained, or if an outcome will even be of similar shape to that originally conceived.

Second, the parameters providing shape to strategic issues are the result of dialogue at discretionary leadership levels. Over time, people's views alter as circumstances change, with the likelihood that agendas will shift and, hence, the parameters defining strategy equally will alter. Therein lies the need for belief. People need to have faith that the journey upon which they have embarked is desired and of value to them. The journey begun may not end up being the same as that started by the individual, but at least the journey is more likely to be completed because the individual believed it to be a worthwhile exercise.

No matter how appropriate and right are the goals and targets set by senior management, their reinforcement is as crucial as their appropriateness. As Chapter 8 highlights, a lack of shared perspective between top management and general management, leads to dysfunctionality and unsatisfactory communication between the managerial levels. Of the six key behaviours which, if well practised, lead to positive communication in the organization (see Chapter 8), the British, Irish, USA and Australian samples of managers, when benchmarked against the others, are identified as the most problematic on issues of trust, cohesion and openness of communication. Hence, how can lower-level staff and management identify with and believe the mission and policies that are presented, if what they visualize is ill-feeling among the senior managers?

Whatever strategic choices are made, who presents them, how they are presented and how communications are managed, are as important considerations as the choices themselves. Certain individuals can become identified with certain of the strategies being pursued. If strategic change is required, it may be important to signal such change by selecting different people to be involved. The reality of rethinking options as well as the people, makes the situation volatile, emotive and tense. Recognizing that strategic choice is unlikely to be divorced from choices about the people involved in the strategic process, then the seemingly irrational, not-easy-to-handle nature of strategy needs to be appreciated on a programme of leadership development.

5 Learning displays of unity

In developing leaders, one fundamental precept is important to grasp, namely that the medium is as important as the message. Hence, unity over issues and clarity of communication are vital if leaders are going to be believed. Therefore, on any leader development programme, debate and analysis of the terms cohesion, consistency and cabinet responsibility are vital.

Attendees of a leadership programme, again through questionnaire feedback, and/or through case analysis, or workshop discussion, have the opportunity to explore their loyalty to the mission of their organization and to the strategies being pursued. Further, in-depth examination could also highlight the degree to which each programme participant's true feelings concerning the shape and future direction of the organization are visible and obvious to his/her colleagues and to lower level staff and management.

Attention to cohesion and sense of cabinet responsibility at senior levels in the organization not only surfaces the degree of agreement and identity with the shape of the organization, but equally highlights the best practice behaviours those senior managers need to display when operationalizing strategy. Chapter 8 highlights that the Cranfield surveys identified a substantial number of non-behavioural, formal and informal channels of internal communication, such as presentations, e-mails, newsletters, cascade processes, etc., which are presumed, at best, to service 25 per cent of communication concerns in an organization. The remaining 75 per cent of communication challenges improve only if the behaviour of senior management changes. Messages through written or spoken words highlight intentions. As consistently argued throughout this book, effective leadership is communicated through good example, namely through the behaviours of the leaders of the organization.

Hence, examination of the behaviour of senior managers needs to be more focused, so that each individual can compare his/her perception of self with the perception others hold of the individual. The more workplace-related feedback can be an input in a leader development programme, the greater the likelihood that each individual will concentrate on improving his/her effectiveness as a leader with behaviours that are contextually relevant. In so doing, an additional paradox of leadership is highlighted, namely that in order to attain the necessary cohesion required for achieving strategic intent, senior managers may exhibit considerable inconsistency of behaviour. Why? Because in order to achieve more-long-term objectives, individuals may need to adjust to changing circumstances over the shorter term and, hence, appear to be inconsistent. Incremental change takes time. Leading incremental change is likely to require responding, over time, to different agendas. In order to respond appropriately to different agendas, even the most effective leaders are likely to be accused of being inconsistent (see Figure 11.9).

Identity with the vision and mission provides for guideline parameters to decision-making and behaviour. Cabinet responsibility then provides

Figure 11.9   Discretionary leader behaviour

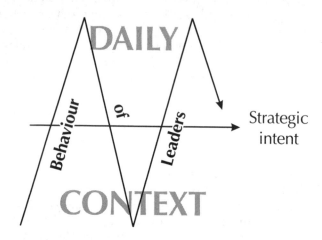

for the necessary discipline for the effective implementation of strategy. Through cabinet responsibility the way forward is clear, but at the same time each senior manager may have to make adjustments to suit his/her context. The complexity of relationship between cohesion, consistency and context requires stressing during programmes of leader development.

The confidential leadership consultation

The experience of the inputs described above, no matter how well delivered, highlights two key learning points, namely utilizing already known insights, and the power of context. Individuals who have held senior management positions are unlikely to be surprised by the learning they have gained. They are likely to have experienced the challenges, dilemmas, behaviours and circumstances outlined in the programme. The question is, to what extent are they prepared to action the insights that they already hold of their work context? Developing the will and robustness to address known challenges in the workplace involves tying together the learning gained during the programme, through reflection. A programme of leadership needs to allow the participants the opportunity for exploration, whereby through reflection, contextually relevant ways forward, and the courage to apply oneself to address known concerns, can be talked through with a third party, but in confidence. The confidential leadership consultation is the bridge between knowing and applying; between broadening mental and emotional parameters and developing the wisdom and maturity to operationalize learning without having to fear what others may think or how they will react. Through personal consultation, confidence is more firmly grounded. Whatever may be included in or omitted from a programme of leadership development, the opportunity to discuss how to apply learning, is a vital component.

Key points summary

- Effective leader development needs to be linked to the business and organizational challenges facing the enterprise.
- Three key areas of leader development are identified, namely enhancing career development, promoting relevant on-the-job development experiences, and tailoring off-the-job development to meet the needs of individuals, and, if necessary, the context of their organization.

Career development

Developing leaders through career track experience is considered to require helping individuals adopt a wider perspective of their organization, and thereby promote a positive attitude to relationship management. Further, it is identified that individuals should be given early exposure to leadership, so that they come to appreciate the nature of the challenges of leadership, grow in confidence, and from that experience realistically accept the responsibility for their own development and that of other people. Through so doing, individuals become accustomed, from an early age, to being held accountable for their own performance.

On-the-job development

- Research highlights that senior managers perceive on-the-job development as a powerful experience in learning to improve as leaders.
- On-the-job development can be conducted through exercises of team feedback, personal coaching, appreciating how the dynamics of change impact on individuals, and through the use of data feedback, using organizational surveys.
- Team development is exercised through providing feedback to the team on how the current modes of discerning and pursuing action, by each member of the team, impact on how visions are formed and then actioned.
- Coaching the team through the difficult and possibly daunting stages of receiving and working through feedback, through anger and denial, helps individuals and the group to accept the nature of the current circumstances and to work towards improving themselves and the organization.
- Personal coaching allows for one-to-one exploration of what each executive needs to do to improve his/her performance. The confidential

nature of the discussions allows for more in-depth exploration without the fear of losing face, and considerably assists in building confidence to confront previously damaging inhibitions.

■ The Executive Change Curve highlights the challenges individuals need to address in learning how to manage change at a personal level. Changes could be the result of a change of job and/or organization, but could also apply to changes of a more personal nature, such as marriage or divorce. Five stages of change learning are identified, the honeymoon period, the realization of the impact of change on one's self, accommodating and coming to terms with the changes that need to be made, relearning and assimilating new skills and attitudes. Four change outcomes are identified, the 'bad guy exit', the 'good-guy exit', the placement exit, and staying in post and effectively performing.

■ Organizational surveys are recognized as long-established tools for the on-the-job development of managers, and for initiating change into the organization.

■ It is postulated that a survey can be a more powerful learning experience for senior managers if they are more intimately involved in the survey process.

■ In making the survey a more developmental experience for managers, attention needs to be given as to how trust and credibility are negotiated between respondents and the survey consultant, and to how to prompt individuals in interview to explore issues more fully, thereby enhancing their own learning from the exercise.

Off-the-job development

■ Off-the-job development, through structured leadership programmes, is most effective when replicating the dynamics of strategic and leadership work in practice and thereby realistically preparing individuals for the leadership challenge. Seven elements for impactful off-the-job development are identified. These are:

1 learning how to accommodate conflicting agendas in the organization,

2 being able to conceptualize organizational structures to meet the challenge of particular circumstances,

3 working within, influencing, and changing the dominant rituals, routines and overall culture of the organization,

4 enhancing the visioning capability of individuals,

5 balancing the transactional and transformational approaches to suit current circumstances and forthcoming challenges,

6 developing individuals, in terms of maturity and robustness, to work towards reconciling differences and/or reaching settlement on difficult-to-resolve issues,

7 providing for personal and confidential consultation, so that each programme participant can talk through his/her relevant experiences on the programme in order to prepare him/herself to address his/her on-the-job challenges and career ambitions.

Notes

1 The authors are grateful to Tony Buley for allowing us access to his paper entitled, 'Using Behavioural Competency to Link Management Development to Business Strategy', presented at the International Quality and Productivity Centre Conference, June 1995.
2 The term 'zone of uncomfortable debate', was coined in their lectures and seminars by two Cranfield colleagues, Gerry Johnson and Cliff Bowman.
3 Adapted from Kakabadse (1991: Ch.1.).
4 The following sections on data feedback are adapted from the internal Cranfield Working Paper entitled, Ethnography, Discretion and Executive Behaviour: Lessons from Research, by Kakabadse et al. (1996).
5 Adapted from Korac-Kakabadse and Korac Kakabadse (1998).

Further reading

For further information on the comparative study of USA and UK CEOs, see Margerison and Kakabadse (1984), on the study of UK and Irish top teams (Kakabadse, 1991), the Australian Government survey (Korac-Kakabadse and Korac-Kakabadse, 1998). For an examination of the private sector European top teams (Kakabadse and Myers, 1996) and on the study of Japanese top managers (Kakabadse et al., 1996).

A particularly attractive work to pursue which neatly couples management development practice with strategic management, is that of Hall et al. (1995).

For more information on personal change and the transition curve, see Parker and Lewis (1980) Kübler Ross (1969).

For further reading on making the process of data-gathering a developmental experience, see Kakabadse et al. (1997). For more information in ethnomethodology and grounded theory see Ackroyd and Hughes (1981) and Eden and Huxham (1993).

References

(ASPA) American Society for Public Administration (1984) *Code of Ethics and Implementation Guidelines*, American Society for Public Administration, Washington, DC.

Ackroyd, S. and Hughes, J. A. (1981) *Data Collection in Context*, London, Longman.

Adler, N. J. (1995) 'Twenty-first Century Leadership: Global Women Leaders', Paper presented at The European Group for Organisational Studies Conference, 6 July, Istanbul.

Agor, W. H. (1986) 'The Logic of Intuition: How Top Executives Make Important Decisions', *Organisational Dynamics*, 14, 3:3–18.

Alger, A. and Flanagan, W. G. (1996a) 'A Field Day for Lawyers', *Forbes*, 157, 9:109.

Alger, W. H. (1986) 'The Logic of Intuition: How Top Executives Make Important Decisions', *Organisational Dynamics*, 14, 3:3–18.

Alger, A. and Flanagan, W. G. (1996c) 'Sexual Politics', *Forbes*, 157, 9:106–10.

Alimo-Metcalfe, B. (1994) 'An Investigation of Female and Male Constructs of Leadership and Empowerment.' Paper presented at the twenty-third International Congress of Applied Psychology, Madrid, 17–22 July.

Allen, A., Fisher, L. and Fulton, E. K. (1992) 'Issues of Trust', *Maclean's*, 23 November: 16–18.

Anonymous (1996a) 'Non Profits Cut Legal Risks with Better Personnel Policies', *Risk Management*, 43, 5:7.

Anonymous (1996b) 'Harassment from the Outside', *H P Focus*, 7, 3:14.

Anonymous (1996c) 'Sexual Harassment Suits Most Feared, Employers Say', *Lodging Hospitality*, 52, 3:20.

Anonymous (1996d) 'Nonprofits Cut Legal Risks with Better Personnel Policies', *Risk Management*, 43, 5:7.

Anonymous (1996e) 'ASEAN Executives Poll', *Far Eastern Economic Review*, 159, 27:34.

Anonymous (1997) 'Sharon's Scheme', *Foreign Report*, 6 November, 2471:1–2.

Argyris, C. (1994) 'Good Communication That Blocks Learning', *Harvard Business Review*, 72, 4:77–85.

Aristotle (1946) *The Politics*, Oxford, Clarendon.

Aristotle (1986) *Nichomachean Ethics*, Irwin, J. (trans), Indianapolis Hacket Publishing Company.

Australian Bureau of Statistics (ABS) (1993) *The Labour Force – Australia*, Catalogue No 6203, ABS, Canberra.

Australian Department of the Parliamentary Library (1994) *Current List of*

Women Members of Federal and State Parliaments, Department of the Parliamentary Library, Information Services, Canberra, pp. 1–23.

Australian Department of the Prime Minister and Cabinet (1994) *Women and Parliament in Australia and New Zealand*, Department of the Prime Minister and Cabinet: Office of the Status of Women, Canberra, July.

Australian Electoral and Administrative Review Commission (EARC) (1992) *Report*, AGPS, Canberra.

Australian Parliamentary Committee Electoral and Administrative Review Commission (PCEAR) (1993) *Report*, AGPS, Canberra.

Australian, New South Wales Independent Commission Against Corruption (ICAC) (1995) 'Morals and Mores in the Workplace', *Direction in Government*, February: 14–15.

Bachrach, S. B. and Lawler, E. J. (1986) 'Power Dependence and Power Paradoxes in Bargaining', *Negotiation Journal*, 2, 2:167–74.

Baddeley, S. and James, K. (1987) 'Owl, Fox, Donkey or Sheep: Political Skills for Managers', *Management Education and Development*, 18, 1:3–19.

Bandura, A. (1977) *Social Learning Theory*, London, Prentice-Hall.

Barnard, I. Chester (1938) *The Functions of the Executive*, Boston, Harvard University Press.

Barnard, I. Chester (1948) *Organisation and Management*, Boston, Harvard University Press.

Barry, D. (1991) 'Managing the Bossless Team: Lessons in Distributed Leadership', *Organisational Dynamics*, 20, 1:31–47.

Bass, B. M., Avolio, B. and Goodheim, L. (1987) 'Biography and the Assessment of Transformational Leadership at the World Class Level', *Journal of Management*, 13, 1:7–20.

Benn, M. (1995) 'The Women who Rule the World', *Cosmopolitan*, February: A1–A10.

Bennis, W. (1974) 'Conversation . . . with Warren Bennis', *Organisational Dynamics*, 2, 2:51–66.

Bennis, W. (1984) 'Where Have all the Leaders Gone', in Rosenbasck, W. E. and Taylor, R. L. (eds) *Contemporary Issues in Leadership*, Boulder, Westview Press, pp. 42–65.

Bennis, W. (1989) *On Becoming a Leader*, New York, Addison Wesley.

Bennis, W. (1993) *An Invented Life: Reflections on Leadership and Change*, Reading, Addison-Wesley.

Bentham, J. (1989) *Introduction to the Principle of Morals and Legislation*, New York, Hafner.

Berry, T. J. (ed.) (1996) 'Psychoanalytic Contributors to Leadership and Organisational Development', *Leadership and Organisational Development Journal*, 17, 6:1–56.

Bhagat, R. S., Keeha, B. C., Crawford, S. E. and Kaplan, M. R. (1990) 'Cross Cultural Issues in Organisational Psychology: Emergent Trends and Directions for Research in the 1990s', in Cooper, C. L. and Robertson I. T. (eds) *International Review of Industrial and Organisational Psychology*, 5, New York, John Wiley, pp. 59–99.

Bing, S. (1996) 'Stress Busters for Busy Execs', *Fortune*, 134, 1:37–8.

Bion, W. R. (1968) *Experiences in Groups*, London, Tavistock.

Boettinger, H. M. (1989) 'And That Was the Future Telecommunications: From Future-Determined to Future-Determining', *Futures*, 21, 3:277–93.

Bolweg, J. (1976) *Job Design and Industrial Democracy*, Leiden, Martinus Nijhoff.

Bowman, C. and Kakabadse, A. P. (1997) 'Top Management Ownership of the Strategy Problem', *Long Range Planning*, 30, 2:197–208.

Boyd, C. (1996) 'Ethics and Corporate Governance: The Issues Raised by the Cadbury Report in the United Kingdom', *Journal of Business Ethics*, 15, 2:167–82.

Brockner, J., Grover, S., O'Malley, M. N., Reed, T. F. and Glynn, M. A. (1993) 'Threat of Future Layoffs, Self-esteem and Survivors' Reactions: Evidence from the Laboratory and the Field', *Strategic Management Journal*, Summer, 14, Special Issue: 153–66.

Brown, J. A. C. (1964) *Freud and the Post-Freudians*, London, Penguin Books.

Brown, W. (1960) *Exploration in Management*, London, Heinemann.

Brummer, A. (1993) 'The Boardroom Watchdogs Who Failed to Bark', *The Guardian*, 30 October:38.

Bullard, A. M. and Wright, D. S. (1993) 'Circumventing the Glass Ceiling: Women Executives in American State Governments', *Public Administrative Review*, 53, 3:189–202.

Burke Warner, W. (1976) 'Organisation Development in Transition', *Journal of Applied Behavioural Science*, 12, 1:22–43.

Burns, J. M. (1978) *Leadership*, New York, Harper and Row.

Burrell, G. (1984) 'Sex and Organisational Analysis', *Organisation Studies*, 5, 1:97–118.

Burt, R. S. (1990) 'Kinds of Relations in American Discussion Networks', in Calhoun, C., Meyer, M. W. and Scott, W. R. (eds), *Structures of Power and Constraint*, New York, Cambridge University Press, pp. 411–51.

Burton, C. (1992) 'Finding the Words: Glass Ceiling or Protective Shield?' *Women in Leadership Public Lecture Series*, Edith Cowan University, Perth, Western Australia, November.

Byrnes, N. (1996) 'Milan Panic May be Starting to Sweat', *Business Week*, 1 July: 88–9.

Cadbury Report (1992) *The Financial Aspects of Corporate Governance*, London, Gee and Co. Ltd.

Canada Treasury Board (1985) *Conflict of Interest and Post-Employment Code for the Public Service*, Ottawa, Supply and Services.

Carlson, S. (1951) *Executive Behaviour: A Study of the Workload and Working Methods of Managing Directors*, Stockholm, Stromberg.

Carmody, H. (1992) 'No Job for a Woman', *ABC Four Corners*, 12 November.

Carnevale, A. P. and Stone, S. C. (1994) 'Diversity: Beyond the Golden Rule', *Training and Development*, 48, 10:22–39.

Cascio, W. F. (1993) 'Downsizing: What Do We Know? What Have We Learned?', *Academy of Management Executive*, 7, 1:95–104.

Castonguay, C. (1993) 'A Personal View of Leadership', *Business Quarterly*, 58, 2, Winter, 16–20.

Clinard, M. (1983) *Corporate Ethics and Crime*, Beverly Hills, Sage.

Coleman, S. (1993) 'Tightening the Belt', *Pacific Computer Weekly*, 905:8.

Coleman, V. (1988) *Stress Management Techniques: Managing People for Healthy Profits*, London, Mercury Business Books.

Collins, J. and Porras, J. (1996) 'Building Your Company's Vision', *Harvard Business Review*, 74, 5:65–77.

Commonwealth of Australia (1982) *Guidelines on Official Conduct of Commonwealth Public Servants*, Canberra, AGPC.

Conger, J. A. (1993) 'The Brave New World of Leadership Training', *Organisational Dynamics*, 21, 3:46–58.

Cotter, S. (1996) 'Using Bioenergetics to Develop Managers: Ten Years of Practical Application of Body-mind Psychology with Over a Thousand Managers at Cranfield University', *The Journal of Management Development*, 15, 3:2–76.

Covey, S. R., Merrill, A. R. and Merrill, R. R. (1994) *First Things First*, New York, Simon and Schuster.

Cowell, F. R. (1956) *Cicero and the Roman Republic*, New York, Pelican Books.

Davidson, M. J. and Cooper, C. L. (1983) *Stress and the Woman Manager*, Oxford, Martin Robertson.

Davidson, M. J. and Cooper, C. L. (1992) *Shattering the Glass Ceiling: The Woman Manager*, London, Paul Chapman.

De Pree, M. (1993) *Leadership Jazz*, New York, Dell.

Deal, T. E. and Kennedy, A. A. (1982) *Corporate Culture: The Rites and Rituals of Corporate Life*, Reading, Addison-Wesley.

Dearborn, D. C. and Simon, H. A. (1985) 'Selective Perception: A Note on the Department Identification of Executives', *Sociometry*, 21, 2:144.

Dickey, C. (1994) 'Bride, Slave or Warrior', *The Bulletin*, 13 September:61–4.

Didio, L. (1996) 'Sexism in IS: Not Gone, Not Forgotten', *Computerworld*, 30, 6:84.

Doherty, N. (1995) 'Helping Survivors to Stay on Board', *People Management*, 1 January:26–31.

Drucker, P. (1990) *The New Realities*, New York, Harper and Row.

Drucker, P. (1993) *Post-Capitalist Society*, New York, Harper Business.

Duckworth, L. (1997) 'Labour MPs Threaten Mass Rebellion Over Hermon Cuts', *Mail on Sunday*, 30 November, p. 6.

Economist, The (1992) 'Editorial: In Search of Better Boardrooms; Corporate Governance', 30 May:70.

Economist, The (1997) 'Parliamentary Sleaze: Too Many Smells', 22 March:42.

Eden, C. and Huxham, C. (1993) 'Distinguishing Action Research: Theory, Method and Practice.' Paper 93/18, September; paper presented to the British Academy of Management Conference, Milton Keynes.

Ehrenreich, B., Hess, E. and Jacobs, G. (1986) *Remaking Love: The Feminisation of Sex*, New York: Anchor Press.

Elliott, M. (1994) 'Money Talks', *The Bulletin*, 116, 5950:46–55.

Elstrom, P. and Brull, S. V. (1996) 'Mitsubishi's Morass', *Business Week*, 3 June:35.

Europa (1994) *The Europa World Year Book*, Vols I–II, (35th edn), Rochester, Staples Printers.

Fairholm, G. W. (1993) *Organisational Power Politics: Tactics in Organisational Leadership*, London, Praeger.

Fayol, H. G. (1916) 'Administration Industrielle et Generale – Prevoyance, Organisation, Commodidement, Coordination, Controle', *Bulletin de la Société de l'Industrie Minérale*.

Finaly, F. (1994) *Mary Robinson: A President with a Purpose*, Dublin, O'Brian Press.

Fireman, J. (1990) 'Do Women Manage Differently?', *Fortune*, 17 December: 115–18.

Flax, J. (1990) 'Postmodernism and Gender Relations in Feminist Theory', in Nicholson, L. J. (ed.), *Feminism-Postmodernism*, New York, Routledge, pp. 39–62.

Follett, M. P. (1920) *The New State*, Boston, Longman.

Follett, M. P. (1924) *Creative Experience*, Boston, Longman.

Foreign Report (1996) *The Battle of Tokyo*, 5 December:5–6.

Frederick, W. C., Davis, C. K. and Post, J. E. (1988) *Business and Society*, 6th edn, New York, McGraw-Hill.

French, J. R. and Raven, B. (1959) 'The Bases of Social Power', in Darwin, Cartwright (ed.) *Studies of Social Power*, Ann Arbor, Institute of Social Research, The University of Michigan.

Freud, S. (1922) *Group Psychology and the Analysis of the Ego*, London, International Psychoanalytic Press.

Freud, S. (1936) *The Ego and the Mechanisms of Defence*, revised edn, New York, International University Press.

Freud, S. (1974) *Introductory Lectures on Psychoanalysis*, Harmondsworth, Penguin Books.

Gardener, H. (1993) *Multiple Intelligence: The Theory in Practice*, New York, Basic Books.

Gaze, A. (1995) 'How Ethical Are You?' *DEET Times*, 8, 1:2–3.

Genovese, M. A. (ed.) (1993) *Women as National Leaders*, Newbury Park, Sage.

Gleick, E. (1996) 'Scandal in the Military', *Time*, 25 November:20–23.

Goleman, D. (1986) *Emotional Intelligence: Why it Can Matter More Than IQ*, London, Bloomsbury.

Gouldner, A. W. (1954) *Studies in Leadership*, New York, Harper.

Gouldner, A. W. (1974) 'Attitudes of "Progressive" Trade-union Leaders', *American Journal of Sociology*, 52:389–92.

Granovetter, M. (1985) 'Economic Action and Social Structure: The Problem of Embededness', *American Journal of Sociology*, 91, 3:481–510.

Guardian (1997) 'Sleaze', 21 March 21:1.

Gutek, B. (1989) 'Sexuality in the Workplace: Key Issues in Social Research and Organisational Practice', in Hearn, J., Sheppard, D., Tancred-Sheriff, P. and Burrell, G. (eds) *The Sexuality of Organisation*, London, Sage, pp. 56–70.

Hall, P. D., Norris, P. W. and Stuart, R. (1995) *Making Management Development Strategically Effective*. Wadenhoe, Wadenhoe Centre/Silver Link Publishing Text.

Handy, C. (1978) *Gods of Management*, London, Penguin Business Series.

Harrison, R. (1972) 'Understanding Your Organisation's Character', *Harvard Business Review*, 15, 3, May/June:119–28.

Hawkins, S. (1983) 'How to Understand Your Partners Cultural Baggage', *International Management, European Edition*, September:48–51.

Health (1996) 'When Your Body Decides to Lay Down the Law', 10 November: 29.

Heimer, C. A. (1992) 'Doing Your Job and Helping Your Friends: Universalistic Norms about Obligations to Particular Others in a Network', in Nohria, N. and Eccles, R. G. (eds) *Networks and Organisations: Structure, Form and Action*, Boston, Harvard Business School Press, pp. 143–64.

Hede, A. and Ralston, D. (1994) 'Managerial Career Progression and Aspiration: Evidence of a "Glass Ceiling"?' *International Journal of Employment Strategies*, 1, 2:253–82.

Hersey, P. and Blanchard, K. (1988) *Management of Organisational Behaviour*, Englewood Cliffs, NJ, Prentice-Hall.

Hesse, H. C. (1985) *The Journey to the East*, London, Picador.

Hobbes, T. (1651) *Leviathan* (Plamenatz, J. P., ed.), London, Collins.

Hofstede, G. (1980) *Culture's Consequences: International Differences in Work Related Values*, Beverly Hills, Sage.

House, R. J. (1997) 'A 1976 Theory of Charismatic Leadership', in Hunt, J. G. and Larson, L. L. I. (eds) *Leadership: The Cutting Edge*, Carbondale, Southern Illinois University Press, pp. 76–94.

House, R. J., Spangler, W. D. and Woycke, J. (1991) 'Personality and Charisma in the US Presidency: A Psychological Theory of Leader Effectiveness', *Administrative Science Quarterly*, 35, 3:364–96.

Howard, P. (1994) 'Seniority No Guarantee of Equal Pay', *The Canberra Times*, 6 October:13.

Huber, G. P. (1990) 'A Theory of the Effects of Advanced Information Technologies on Organisational Design, Intelligence and Decision Making', *Academy of Management Review*, 15, 1:47–71.

Hunt, S. P. and Vitell, S. (1986) 'A General Theory of Marketing Ethics', *Journal of Macro-Marketing*, Spring, 6, 5:5–16.

Intelligence Newsletter (1996a) United States: How a Top Secret Court Operates, 28 November:4.

Intelligence Newsletter (1996b) Corruption: Questions over EDS in Spain, 12 December:6.

Intelligence Newsletter (1997a) Spotlight: Business Intelligence Takeover by Big Six?, 2 January:1.

Intelligence Newsletter (1997b) Spotlight: New Crusade against Corruption, 29 May:1.

Isaacson, W. (1997) 'In Search of the Real Bill Gates', *Time*, 149,2, 13 January: 34–55.

Janis, I. L. (1982) *Groupthink* (2nd edn), Boston, Houghton Mifflin.

Jaques, E. (1951) *The Changing Culture of the Factory*, London, Tavistock.

Jacques, E. (1979) 'Taking Time Seriously in Evaluating Jobs', *Harvard Business Review*, 57, 5:124–32.

Jensen, M. C. and Meckling, W. (1976) 'Theory of the Firms', *Journal of Financial Economics*, 3, 3:305–60.

Kakabadse, A. P. (1982) *Culture of the Social Services*, Aldershot, Gower.

Kakabadse, A. P. (1991) *The Wealth Creators: Top People, Top Teams and Executive Best Practice*, London, Kogan Page.

Kakabadse, A. P. and Myers, A. (1996) 'Boardroom Skills for Europe', *European Management Journal*, 14, 2:189–200.

Kakabadse, A. P. and Myers, A. (1997) *Leadership for the NHS: Requirements for Best Practice*, Bedford, Internal Cranfield School of Management Paper, Cranfield University.

Kakabadse, A. P. and Parker, C. (1984) 'Towards a Theory of Political Behaviour in Organisations', in Kakabadse, A. P. and Parker, C. (eds) *Power, Politics and Organisations: A Behavioural Science View*, London, John Wiley.

Kakabadse, A. P., Ludlow, R. and Vinnicombe, S. (1988) *Working in Organisations*, Penguin Business Books, London.

Kakabadse, A. P., Myers, A., McMahon, T. and Spony, G. (1995) 'Top Management Styles in Europe: Implications for Business and Cross-National Teams', *European Business Journal*, 7, 1:17–27.

Kakabadse, A. P., Myers, A., Alderson, S. and Okazaki-Ward, L. (1997) *Ethnography, Discretion and Executive Behaviour: Lessons from Research*, Bedford, Occasional Paper, Cranfield School of Management.

Kakabadse, A. P., Nortier, F. and Abramovici, N. B. (1998) *Success in Sight: Visioning*, Aldershot, International Thomson.

Kakabadse, A. P., Okazaki-Ward, L. and Myers, A. (1996) *Japanese Business Leaders*, Aldershot, International Thomson.

Kant, I. (1909) 'Preface to the Metaphysical Elements of Ethics', in Abbott, T. K. (trans), *Kant's Critique of Practical Reason and Other Works on the Theory of Ethics*, 6th edn, London, Longmans, Green, pp. 45–80.

Kaplan, D. I. (1994) 'Small Gains Everyday: An Atmosphere of Trust, Make for Effective Leadership in a Service Function', *Plant Engineering*, 48, 6:126–8.

Katz, R. (1982) 'The Effects of Group Longevity on Project Communication and Performance', *Administrative Science Quarterly*, 27, 1:81–104.

Kerford, G. B. (1981) *The Sophistic Movement*, Cambridge, Cambridge University Press.

Kernaghan, K. and Langford, J. (1990) *The Responsible Public Servant*, Toronto, Institute of Public Administration of Canada and Halifax, Institute for Research of Public Policy.

Kets de Vries, M. F. R. (1989) *Prisoners of Leadership*, New York, John Wiley.

Ketchum, L. D. (1992) 'How Redesign Plants Really Work', *National Productivity Review*, 3, 2:246–54.

Kilman, R. H., Saxton, M. J. and Serpa, R. (1986) 'Introduction: Five Key Issues in Underacting and Changing Culture', in Kilman, R. H., Saxton, M. J., Serpa, R. and Associates (eds) *Gaining Control of the Corporate Culture*, San Francisco, Calif.: Jossey Bass.

Klein, M. (1959) 'Our Adult World and its Roots in Infancy', *Human Relations*, 12:291–303.

Klein, M. (1981) *Love, Guilt and Reparation and Other Works*, London, Hogarth Press.

Kogan, M. (1996) 'Like Parent, Like Boss', *Government Executive*, 28, 7:40–45, July.

Korac-Boisvert, N. and Kouzmin, A. (1994) 'The Dark Side of the Info-age Social Networks in Public Organisations and Creeping Crisis', *Administrative Theory and Praxis*, 16, 1:57–83.

Korac-Boisvert, N. and Kouzmin, A. (1995) 'Biting the Bullett: from Glass and Concrete Ceilings', and 'Metaphorical Sex Changes to Psychological Audits and Renegotiating Organisational Scripts.' Papers presented at The Royal Institute of Public Administration, Australian Conference, 30 November, Brisbane.

Korac-Kakabadse, A. P. and Korac-Kakabadse, N. (1997a) 'Information Technology's Impact on Quality of Democracy: A Philosophical and Administrative Framework.' Paper presented to The International Conference on Public Sector Management for the Next Century, 29 June–2 July, Manchester University.

Korac-Kakabadse, A. P. and Korac-Kakabadse, N. (1997b) 'Best Practice in the Australian Public Service (APS): An Examination of Discretionary Leadership', *Journal of Managerial Psychology*, 1, 7:431–91.

Korac-Kakabadse, A. P. and Korac-Kakabadse, N. (1998) *Leadership in Government: Study of the Australian Public Service*, Aldershot, Ashgate.

Korac-Kakabadse, A. P., Korac-Kakabadse, N. and Myers A. (1996) 'Leadership in the Public Sector: An Internationally Comparative Benchmarking Analysis', *Journal of Public Administration*, 16, 4:377–98.

Korac-Kakabadse, N. (1997) 'Leadership Philosophies and Organisational Adoption of New Information Technology.' PhD thesis, University of Western Sydney – Nepean.

Kouzes, J. M. and Posner, B. Z. (1987) *The Leadership Challenge: How To Get Extraordinary Things Done in Organizations*, Jossey-Bass, San Francisco.

Kübler Ross, E. (1969) *On Death and Dying*, London, Macmillan.

Lally, L. (1996) 'Privacy Versus Accessibility: The Impact of Situationally Conditioned Belief', *Journal of Business Ethics*, 15, 11:121–6.

Laurent, A. (1996) 'The Great Divide', *Government Executive*, 28, 4:12–14.

Laurie, A. (1996) 'Dr Smith Goes to Sexual-Rehab School', *Medical Economics*, 17, 3:175–200.

Lawn-Day, G. and Ballard, S. (1996) 'Speaking Out: Perceptions of Managers in the Public Service', *Review of Public Personnel Administration*, 16, 1:41–58.

Levinson, H. (1996) 'When Executives Burn Out', *Harvard Business Review*, 74, 4:152–63.

Life (1988) 'Whistleblower', March:17.

Linz, S. (1996) 'Gender Differences in the Russian Labour Market', *Journal of Economic Issues*, 30, 1:161–85.

Livingston-Booth, A. (1988) *Stressmanship*, London, Severn House.

Lowen, A. (1975) *Bioenergetics*, New York, Penguin.

Machiavelli, N. (1958) *The Prince* (Marriott, W. K., trans), London: J. M. Dent and Sons.

Mair, V. N. (1990) *Tao Te Ching Leo Tzu: The Classic Book of Integrity and the Way*, New York, Boutain.

Manz, C. C. and Sims, H. P. Jr (1991) 'Superleadership: Beyond the Myth of Heroic Leadership', *Organisational Dynamics*, 19, Summer, 318–65.

Maremont, M. (1996) 'Day of Reckoning at Astra', *Business Week*, 8 July: 36.

Maremont, M. and Sasseen, J. A. (1996) 'Abuses of Power', *Business Week*, May 13:36.

Margerison, C. J. and Kakabadse, A. P. (1984) *How American Chief Executives Succeed: Implications for Developing High Potential Employees*, AMA Survey Report, New York.

Marshall, J. (1993) 'Organisational Culture and Women Managers: Exploring the Dynamics of Resilience', *Applied Psychology: An International Review*, 42, 4:313–22.

Marshall, J. and McLean, A. J. (1985) 'Exploring Organisational Culture as a Route to Organisational Change', in Hammond, V. (ed.) *Current Research in Management*, London, Frances Pinter, pp. 2–20.

Martinez, M. N. (1996) 'Looking for Young Talent? Inroads Helps Diversity Effects', *H R Magazine*, 41, 3:73–6.

Masson, R. O. (1986) 'Four Ethical Issues of the Information Age', *MIS Quarterly*, 10, 1:46–55.

McCall, M. W. (1992) 'Executive Development as Business Strategy', *Journal of Business Strategy*, 13, 1:25–31.

McClelland, D. C. (1975) *Power: The Inner Experience*, New York, Irvington.

McDonald, M. (1992) 'The Canadian Research Strategy for Applied Ethics: A New Opportunity for Research in Business and Professional Ethics', *Journal of Business Ethics*, 11, 8:569–83.

Michel, J. and Hambrick, D. (1992) 'Diversification Posture and Top Team Characteristics', *Academy of Management Journal*, 35, 1:9–37.

Mill, J. S. (1969) 'Utilitarianism', in Robson, J. M., Priestley, F. E. L. and Droter, D. P. (eds) *Essays on Ethics, Religion and Society*, Toronto, University of Toronto Press.

Mintzberg, H. (1973) *Nature of Managerial Work*, New York, Harper and Row.

Mischel, W. (1977) 'Self-Centred and the Self', in Mischel, T. (ed.) *The Self: Psychological and Philosophical Issues*, New Jersey, Bowman and Littlefield.

Murphy, P. (1989) 'Creating Ethical Corporate Structures', *Sloan Management Review*, 30, 2:81–7.

Nadler, D. A. and Tushman, M. L. (1990) 'Beyond the Charismatic Leader: Leadership and Organisational Change', *California Management Review*, 32, 2:77–97.

NASA (1987) *Leadership and America's Future in Space*, National Report to the Administration, Washington, DC, NASA.

Nietzsche, F. (1969) *The Will to Power*, New York, Vintage.

Olins, R. (1996) 'C&W's New Broom Sweeps Away Old-guard Directors', *Sunday Times*, 15 December, front page, section 2.

Park, M. (1992) 'Cadbury Committee – A Code to put Firms to Shame', *Sunday Times*, May 31, front page.

Parker, C. and Lewis, R. (1980) 'Moving up: How to Handle Transitions to Senior Levels, Successfully.' Occasional Paper, Cranfield, Bedford, Cranfield School of Management.

Pauchant, T. C. (1991) 'Transformational Leadership: Towards a More Complex Understanding of Charisma in Organisations', *Organisational Studies*, 12, 4:507–27.

Pettigrew, A. M. (1977) 'Strategy Formulation as a Political Process', *International Studies of Management and Organisation*, 7:78–87.

Pettit, P. (1993) 'Consequentialism', in Singer, P. (ed.) *A Companion to Ethics*, Oxford, Blackwell.

Pfeffer, J. (1983) 'Organisational Demography', in Cummings, L. L. and Staw, B. M. (eds) *Research in Organisational Behaviour, Vol. 5*, Greenwich, JAI Press, pp. 299–357.

Pfeffer, J. (1992) *Managing with Power: Politics and Influence in Organisations*, Boston, Harvard Business School Press.

Pierrakos, J. C. (1990) *Core Energetics: Developing the Capacity to Love and Heal*, New York, Liferhythmn.

Plato (1956) *Republic*, Jarret, B., trans in Edman, E. (ed.) *The Works of Plato*, New York, Random House.

Plutarch (1981) *The Rise and Fall of Athens* (Scott-Kilvert, I. trans), New York, Penguin.

Prahalad, C. K. and Bettis, R. A. (1986) 'The Dominant Logic: A New Linkage between Diversity and Performance', *Strategic Management Journal*, 7, 4:485–501.

Pugh, D. S. and Hickson, D. J. (1993) *Great Writers on Organisations*, Dartmouth, Omnibus.

Pugh, D. S., Hickson, D. J. and Hinings, C. R. (1973) *Writers on Organisations*, 2nd edn, London, Penguin.

Quick, J. C., Nelson, D. C. and Quick, J. D. (1990) *Stress and Challenge at the Top: The Paradox of the Successful Executive*, Chichester, John Wiley.

Quinn, R. E. and Cameron, K. (1983) 'Organisational Life Cycles and Shifting Criteria of Effectiveness: Some Preliminary Evidence', *Management Science*, 29, 1:35–50.

Rawls, J. (1971) *A Theory of Justice*, Cambridge, Harvard University Press.

Rawnsley, J. (1996) *Going for Broke: Nick Leeson and the Collapse of Barings Bank*, London, HarperCollins.

Reich, W. (1949) *Character Analysis*, New York, Farrar, Straus and Girous.

Reidenbach, R. and Robin, D. (1991) 'A Conceptual Model of Corporate Moral Development', *Journal of Business Ethics*, 10, 4:273–84.

Report of the Presidential Commission on the Space Shuttle Challenger Accident (1986) Washington, DC.

Rizzo, A. and Mendez, C. (1990) *The Integration of Women into Management*, Westport, Quorum.

Rosener, J. B. (1990) 'Ways Women Lead', *Harvard Business Review*, November–December, 68, 4:119–25.

Ross, N. W. (1980) *Buddhism: A Way of Life and Thought*, New York, Knopf.

Rousseau, D. M. (1989) 'Psychological and Implied Contracts in Organisations', *Employee Responsibilities and Rights Journal*, 12, 1:34–78.

Rowlands, B. (1996) 'Stressed Out? Let Your Feelings Flow', The *Independent*, section two, 1 October:8.

Scott-Lennon, F. (1996) 'A Case Analysis of Forms of Contextual Issues and Outcomes of Empowerment Approaches, with Particular Emphasis on Leadership Roles in Effecting Major Change,' Paper presented for Second Doctoral Review, Cranfield School of Management, 2 October.

Sellers, P. (1996) 'Women, Sex and Power', *Fortune*, 5 August:30–45.

Selznick, P. (1957) *Leadership in Administration: A Sociological Interpretation*. New York, Harper and Row.

Semler, R. C. (1993) *Maverick*, London, Arrow.

Senge, P. (1992) *The Fifth Discipline: The Art and Practice of the Learning Organisation*, Sydney, Random House.

Serrell, M. S. (1995) 'Unfinished Business', *Time International*, 146, 23:42.

Servaes, J. (1989) 'Cultural Identity and Modes of Communication', in Anderson, J. A. (ed.) *Communication Yearbook*, Newbury Park, Calif., Sage, pp. 383–416.

Shaw, B. and Post, F. R. (1993) 'Amoral Basis for Corporate Philanthropy', *Journal of Business Ethics*, 12, 10:745–51.

Simms, R. R. (1992) 'The Challenge of Ethical Behaviour in Organisation', *Journal of Business Ethics*, 11, 7:505–13.

Sinclair, A. (1994) 'Life Matters', interview, 5 December, ABC Radio National, Melbourne University Business School.

Smith, A. (1776) *An Inquiry into the Nature and Causes of the Wealth of a Nation*, 6th edn, London, Methuen.

SPL Worldgroup Australia (1995) *Natural New Dimension*, Launch at Park Royal, 19 May, Canberra.

Statistics Canada (1993) *Employment Statistics, Catalogues 71–001, 71–220 and 71–529*, Ottawa.

Stewart, R. (1982) *Choices for the Manager: A Guide to Managerial Work*, New York, McGraw-Hill.

Still, L. V., Guerin, D. and Chia, W. (1994) 'Women in Management Revisited: Progress Regresion or Status Quo?' in Kouzmin, A, Still, L. V. and Clark, P. (eds), *New Directions in Management*, Sydney, McGraw-Hill, pp. 44–64.

Storrs, C. (1949) *General and Industrial Management*, London, Pitman.

Sulloway, F. (1996) *Born to Rebel*, New York, Little Brown.

Sunday Times (1993) 'Business Comment – Non Executives Fail Queens Moat', 31 October, front page.

Sundstrom, E., De Meuse, K. P. and Futrell, D. (1990) 'Work Teams: Applications and Effectiveness, *American Psychologist*, 45, 1:120–33.

Tannen, D. (1992) *You Just Don't Understand: Women and Men in Conversation*, London, Virago.

The Hansard Society for Parliamentary Government (1990) *The Report of The Hansard Society Commission on Women at the Top*, London, A. L. Publishing Services.

The International Who's Who (1997–98) 61st edn, London, Europa.

Thomas, D. A. and Ely, R. J. (1996) 'Making Differences Matter: A New Paradigm for Managing Diversity', *Harvard Business Review*, 74, 5:79–90.

Thomasma, D. C. (1993) 'Moral Integrity and Healthcare Leadership', *Healthcare Executive*, 8, 1:29.

Tichy, N. M. and Sherman, S. (1993) *Control Your Destiny or Someone Else Will: How Jack Welch is Making General Electric the World's Most Competitive Corporation*, Doubleday, New York.

TMS Management Consultants (1992) *Without Prejudice? Sex and Equality at the Bar and in the Judiciary*, London, TMS Management Consultants Report.

Treasury Board of Canada (1994) *Employment Statistics for the Federal Public Service, 1993–94*, 30 April:5.

Trist, E. L., Higgin, G. W., Murray, H. and Pollock, A. B. (1963) *Organisational Choice*, London, Tavistock.

Trompenaars, F. (1993) *Riding the Waves of Culture: Understanding Cultural Diversity in Business*, London, The Economist Books.

Tsalikis, J. and Fritzsche, D. J. (1989) 'Business Ethics: A Literature Review with a Focus on Marketing Ethics', *Journal of Business Ethics*, 8, 5:695–743.

Tucker, R. C. (1981) *Politics as Leadership*, Columbia, University of Missouri Press.

Turner, M. and Hulme, D. (1997) *Governance, Administration and Development. Making the State Work*, Basingstoke, Macmillan.

Tushman, M. and Romanelli, E. (1985) 'Organisational Evaluation: A Metamorphosis Model of Convergence and Reorientation', in Cummings, L. L. and Staw, B. M. (eds) *Research in Organisational Behaviour*, 7:171–222.

UNDP (United Nations Development Programme) (1996) *Human Development Report 1996*, New York, Oxford University Press.

Unger, R. M. (1987) *False Necessity*, Cambridge, Cambridge University Press.

United States of America (1958) *The Code of Ethics of Government Services*, 85th Congress, 2nd Session, Concurrent Resolution 175.

Updike, E. H. and Holstein, W. J. (1996) Commentary: Mitsubishi and the Cement Ceiling, *Business Week*, 13 May:62.

Urwick, L. F. (1947) *The Elements of Administration*, London, Pitman.

Vaughan, G. (1992) *Sex Differences in Occupational Attainment*, Australian Bureau of Statistics, Cat. No. 6283.0, Canberra.

Velasquez, M. G. (1992) *Business Ethics: Concepts and Cases*, 2nd edn, Englewood Cliffs, Prentice-Hall.

Vickers, Sir G. (1983) *Human Systems are different*, London, Harper and Row.

Vinnicombe, S. and Colwill, N. L. (eds) (1995) *The Essence of Women in Management*, London, Prentice-Hall.

Vroom, V. and Yetton, P. (1973) *Leadership and Decision Making*, Pittsburgh, University of Pittsburgh Press.

Walsh, K. A. (1993) 'Public Servants are Political Slaves', *The Bulletin*, 15, 5896:30–6.

Warburton, F. E. (1993) 'Enhancing Competencies Through Leadership in Management', *Business Council Bulletin*, October:28–30.

Washington Post Service (1996), 'How Hilary Clinton Misled Washington: A Climate of Secrecy, 12 February p. 34.

Waterman, H. R., Waterman, J. A. and Collard, B. A. (1994) 'Towards a Career Resilient Workforce', *Harvard Business Review*, 72, 4, July–August:87–95.

Weber, M. (1968) *On Charisma and Institution Building*, Chicago: University of Chicago Press.

Weick, K. E. (1979) *The Social Psychology of Organising*, 2nd edn, Reading, MA, Addison-Wesley.

White, H. (1992) 'Agency as Control in Formal Networks', in Nohria, N. and Eccles, R. G. (eds) *Networks and Organisations: Structure, Form and Action*, Boston, Harvard Business School Press, pp. 92–117.

Wierzbicka, A. (1991) *Cross-cultural Pragmatics: The Semantics of Human Interaction*, New York, Mouton De Gruyter.

Wiley, C. (1995) 'The ABCs of Business Ethics: Definitions, Philosophies and Implementation', *IM*, January–February:22–32.

Wilkinson, G. (1996) 'My Health Lifestyle Nearly Killed Me', *Health*, 10 November:26–30.

Williamson, C. (1995) 'Frank Russel Co offers Employees Cure for Burn Out', *Pensions and Investments* 23, 16:8.

World Almanac (1994) '10 Facts About Women Workers', *The World Almanac and Book of Facts 1994*, World Almanac p. 132.

UK Foreign and Commonwealth Office (1993) *Women in Britain*, Foreign and Commonwealth Office, November, IB/2273, London.

US Department of Commerce, Bureau of the Census (1992a) *Statistical Abstract of the United States* (112th edn), US Government Publishing Office, Washington, DC.

US Department of Commerce, Bureau of the Census (1992b) *1987 Economic*

Consensus Characteristics of Business Owners, US Government Publishing Office, Washington, DC.

US Department of Labour (1988) *Glass Ceiling Review Report*, US Dept of Labour, Washington, DC.

US General Accounting Office (1991) 'Federal Workforce: Continuing Need for Federal Affirmative Employment', *Report GAO/GGD-92-27BR, GAO/GGD*, November, Washington, DC.

US Merit Systems Protection Board (1992) *A Question of Equity: Women and the Glass Ceiling in the Federal Government*, US Government Printing Office, Washington, DC.

Index